1850 Mortality Schedule *of* Tennessee

By:
Helen C. and Timothy R. Marsh

Southern Historical Press, Inc.
Greenville, South Carolina

This volume was reproduced
from a personal copy located in
the Publishers private library

Please direct all correspondence and book orders to:
SOUTHERN HISTORICAL PRESS, Inc.
1071 Park West Blvd.
Greenville, SC   29611

Copyright 1982 by:
    Marsh Historical Publications
Copyright Transfered 2003 to:
    Southern Historical Press, Inc.
        ISBN #978-1-63914-677-2
Printed in the United Sattes of America

SEVENTH CENSUS
OF
THE UNITED STATES

ORIGINAL RETURNS OF THE ASSISTANT MARSHALLS OF TENNESSEE
THIRD SERIES
PERSONS WHO DIED DURING THE YEAR ENDING JUNE 30, 1850
VOL.
CONTAINING THE COUNT OF JUNE 30, 1850

COUNTIES INCLUDED ON ROLL 26, 1850

ANDERSON	HANCOCK	MORGAN
BEDFORD	HARDEMAN	OBION
BENTON	HARDIN	OVERTON
BLEDSOE	HAWKINS	PERRY
BLOUNT	HAYWOOD	POLK
BRADLEY	HENDERSON	RHEA
CAMPBELL	HENRY	ROANE
CANNON	HICKMAN	ROBERTSON
CARROLL	HUMPHREYS	RUTHERFORD
CARTER	JACKSON	SCOTT
CLAIBORNE	JEFFERSON	SEVIER
COCKE	JOHNSON	SHELBY
COFFEE	KNOX	SMITH
DAVIDSON	LAUDERDALE	STEWART
DECATUR	LAWRENCE	SULLIVAN
DEKALB	LEWIS	SUMNER
DICKSON	LINCOLN	TIPTON
DYER	McMINN	VAN BUREN
FAYETTE	McNAIRY	WARREN
FENTRESS	MACON	WASHINGTON
FRANKLIN	MADISON	WAYNE
GIBSON	MARION	WEAKLEY
GILES	MARSHALL	WHITE
GRAINGER	MAURY	WILLIAMSON
GREENE	MEIGS	WILSON
GRUNDY	MONROE	
HAMILTON	MONTGOMERY	

COUNTIES ARRANGED IN ALPHABETICAL ORDER IN THIS BOOK

INDEXED BY CENSUS PAGE NUMBER

COUNTY OF ANDERSON, STATE OF TENNESSEE.

PAGE NO. 1 PERSONS WHO DIED DURING THE YEAR ENDING 1st JUNE, 1850. (30th)

No. of Visit	Name	Age	Sex	Color	Free or Slave	Married/Widowed	Place of Birth	Month Died	Occupation	Disease or Cause of Death	No. Days Ill
1	William R. Laudy	84	M			W	N.C.	April	Farmer	Dropsy of heart	4 weeks
2	William R. Butler	50	M			M	Va	May	Farmer	Infection of brain	C(100 da)
3	Mary Katharine	11m	F				Tenn	May		Bold hives	4 weeks
4	Robert Risdon	84	M			M	N.C.	March	Blk-smith	Old age	2 weeks
5	Daniel Buts	60	M			M	unknown	June	Farmer	Cholera	1 day
6	Ransom M. Moore	26	M				Tenn	Jan	M.preacher	Typhoid fever	2 weeks
7	Jacob Gwinn	4	M				Tenn	Oct		Burn	2 weeks
8	William Warrick	48	M			M	Tenn	May	Farmer	Bleeding at the nose	4 weeks
9	Stephen M. Evans	1m	M				Tenn	Oct		unknown	7 days
10	Mary Ann Dale	11m	F				Tenn	Jan		Whooping cough	7 weeks
11	Katharine Hutchinson	9m	F				Tenn	Jan		Whooping cough	5 weeks
12	Thursy O. Weaver	1	F				Tenn	March		unknown	4 months
13	Peeny Snoderly	6	F				Tenn	July		Flux	17 days
14	Elie Cooper	12	M				Tenn	Dec		Brain Dropsy	4 days
15	Franky B. Masham	6m	F				Tenn	Aug		Flux	7 days
16	Mary A. McCoy	6m	F				Tenn	Oct		Bold hives	10 days
17	James McKoy	23	M				Tenn	Nov		Consumption	C(100 da)
18	Augusta Wilson	100	M			M	Maryland	Feb	none	Old age	6 years
19	Parly Stuksberry	18	F				Tenn	Sept		Palsy	C(100 da)
20	Mary Bray	11m	F				Tenn	Jan		Whooping cough	3 weeks
21	Fanny Jarnagin	16	F	B	S		Tenn	Sept		Cold	7 days
22	Milly Jarnagin	21	F	B	S		Tenn	Oct		Fever	3 weeks
23	Clark Ashlock	7m	M				Tenn	Jan		abscess on the lungs	4 weeks
24	William Weaver	52	M			M	Tenn	Dec	Farmer	fall from horse	3 months
25	Samuel Gilbert	1	M				Tenn	April		Diarrhea	5 days
26	..(not named)..	1m	F				Tenn	March		unknown	4 weeks
27	Harriet Elliott	39	F			M	Va	July		Female disorder	C(100 da)
28	Delany Rhea	11m	F				Tenn	Sept		Cholera	3 days
29	Sarah A. Taylor	5m	F				Tenn	June		Flux	2 weeks
30	Emily J. Taylor	7	F				Tenn	Dec		Flux	3 weeks
31	Rowlin Chiles	33	M			M	Tenn	May		kick of horse	5 days
	Page 4										
1	Katharine Black	65	F			M	unknown	July		Fever	9 weeks
2	Handy Black	28	M	B	S		Tenn	May		Liver complications	13 weeks
3	William P. Foy	4m	M				Tenn	Feb		Whooping cough	4 weeks
4	Rebecca Young	70	F			M	N.C.	April		Dropsy	6 weeks
5	Sarah K. Frost	6	F				Tenn	Nov		Whooping cough	6 weeks
6	Matilda Aultum	50	F			M	Tenn	June		Flux	2 weeks
7	Emeline Tucker	10	F				Tenn	June		Flux	7 days
8	Sarah J. Herington	12	F				Tenn	Aug		Breast complaint	4 weeks
9	Pleasant H. Kerby	4	M				Tenn	Feb		Worms	2 days
10	Peter S. Mounger	25	M				Tenn	Aug	Farmer	Rheumatic	C(100 da)
11	James T. Underwood	15	M				Va	March	Farmer	Fall	3 days
12	John E. Underwood	8	M				Va	April		Worms	9 weeks
13	William Right	22	M			M	Tenn	Sept	Farmer	Fever	9 days
14	William Norton	7	M				Tenn	March		Worms	2 weeks
15	Louise Katharine	4	F				Tenn	May		Whooping cough	3 weeks
16	Sarah Gamble	68	F			M	Va	Jan		Dropsy	C(100 da)
17	John Armstrong	18	M	B	S		Tenn	Nov		Fever	2 weeks
18	Sarah Freels	6	F				Tenn	May		C. Pox	18 days
19	Tabitha Watkins	25	F			M	N.C.	Feb		Brain Dropsy	sudden
20	Richard Right	2	M				Tenn	Nov		Bold hives	9 days
21	Poliecy A. Cross	6m	F	B	S		Tenn	Feb		Whooping cough	2 weeks
22	George Haskins	71	M			M	N.C.	May		Rheumatism	C(100 da)
23	Caroline McKamy	7	F	B	S		Tenn	April		Whooping cough	7 weeks
24	Martha J. Johnson	6m	F				Tenn	July		Cholera infantum	2 days
25	Rachael Walker	19	F	M	S	M	Tenn	Feb		Consumption	7 months
26	Katharine	4m	F	B	S		Tenn	Nov		Whooping cough	2 months
27	Henry Whitson	4	M	B	S		Tenn	Aug		Fever	4 months
28	Mary Trigg	34	F			M	Va	July		Consumption	C(100 da)
29	Lucinda M. Brock	4m	F				Tenn	Feb		Bold hives	9 days

COUNTY OF ANDERSON, STATE OF TENNESSEE.

PAGE NO. 4 PERSONS WHO DIED DURING THE YEAR ENDING 1st JUNE, 1850.

No. of Visit	Name	Age	Sex	Color	Free or Slave	Married/Widowed	Place of Birth	Month Died	Occupation	Disease or Cause of Death	No. Days Ill
30	James White	49	M			M	Tenn	Oct	Farmer	Breast complaint	13 days
31	James Braden	52	M			M	Va	March	Farmer	Dropsy	C(100 da)
32	Hannah Kirkpatrick	70	F	B	S		Va	June		Diphtheria	8 months
33	Michael Keeny	54	M			M	unknown	Nov		Dropsy	C(100 da)
34	Elizabeth Queener	17	F				Tenn	July		Cold	9 weeks
35	Sarah Jane	9	F				Va	June		Dropsy	C(100 da)

COUNTY OF BEDFORD, STATE OF TENNESSEE.

PAGE NO. 5 PERSONS WHO DIED DURING THE YEAR ENDING 1st JUNE, 1850.

Civil District No. 20, 21, 22, 23, 24 & 25

No. of Visit	Name	Age	Sex	Color	Free or Slave	Married/Widowed	Place of Birth	Month Died	Occupation	Disease or Cause of Death	No. Days Ill
1	John Miller	85	M			W	Va	June	none	Old age	3 days
2	___ ___	28	M	B	S		___	Dec	___	unknown	10 days
3	John H. Floyd	28	M			M	Tenn	Jan	Farmer	Consumption	3 months
4	___ ___	6m	M	B	S		___	Jan		unknown	1 day
5	Susan M. Anthony	3	F				Tenn	Oct		Worms	3 weeks
6	___ ___	21	F	B	S		___	Nov		S. Fever	3 weeks
7	Louis U. Pollock	26	M				Tenn	Nov	none	Phistula	2 years
8	William Frost	18m	M				Tenn	Aug		Fever	2 months
9	___ ___	2	F	B	S		___	July		unknown	6 hours
10	William Pearson	25	M				Tenn	Aug	Farmer	Fever	3 weeks
11	___ ___	18	M	B	S		___	April		unknown	10 days
12	___ ___	18m	M	B	S		___	April		unknown	2 weeks
13	Hannah Stewart	25	F			M	Tenn	March		Fever	2 weeks
14	John Arnold	3	M				Tenn	Oct		Conj. fever	1 day
15	Jasper N. Anthony	11m	M				Tenn	Dec		Burned	
16	Amanda J. Shoftner	2	F				Tenn	Feb		Croup	7 days
17	Ely S. Euless	4	M				Tenn	Oct		Croup	4 days
18	___ ___	17	M	B	S		___	Jan		Consumption	1 year
19	Harriet Hoosier	12	F				Tenn	June		unknown	1 week
20	James K. Williams	2m	M				Tenn	Feb		Croup	10 hours
21	Infant of B. Koonce	6da	F				Tenn	March		unknown	
22	Infant Koonce	1da	F				Tenn	March		unknown	
23	George W. Stone	1m	M				Tenn	Aug		Croup	3 days
24	William Montgomery	40	M			M	Tenn	March	Farmer	Pleurisy	9 weeks
25	George Hufman	13	M				Tenn	Sept		Conj. fever	11 days
26	Joshua Yates	73	M			M	N.C.	Sept	Minister	Conj. fever	9 days
27	___ ___	42	F	B	S		___	Sept		Conj. fever	9 days

Remarks: Being no prevailing disease which may be seen by reference to the return of deaths during the Census year, the whole District interspersed with limestone rock.

John Castleman, Ass't Marshal

COUNTY OF BEDFORD, STATE OF TENNESSEE.

PAGE NO. 8   PERSONS WHO DIED DURING THE YEAR ENDING 1st JUNE, 1850.

No. of Visit	Name	Age	Sex	Color	Free or Slave	Married/Widowed	Place of Birth	Month Died	Occupation	Disease or Cause of Death	No. Days Ill
1	Elizabeth Casteel	25	F			M	Tenn	March		labor	
2	Warren Kingry	20m	M				Tenn	March		R. fever	5 days
3	John Castleman	2m	M				Tenn	July		unknown	10 days
4	Agnes Dwiggins	34	F			S	Tenn	April		Consumption	10 years
5	Milton Warren	8	M				Tenn	Feb		Pleurisy	9 days
6	Alsa Wilhoit	19m	F				Tenn	Jan		Croup	3 days
7	____ ____	60	F	B	S		____	May		fever	12 days
8	Willis Rodgers	15	M				Tenn	Dec		Dropsy	2 years
9	F. B. Norman	1m	M				Tenn	March		unknown	4 days
10	Isaac N. Hix	2	M				Tenn	Jan		S. fever	2 weeks
11	Jane Hastings	22	F			M	Tenn	April		Fits	5 weeks
12	Elizabeth Casteel	52	F			M	Tenn	Feb		Ch. Rheumatism	1 year
13	Margaret E. Blakemore	18	F			M	Tenn	Aug		fever	2 weeks
14	Thos. F. A. Blakemore	2m	M				Tenn	Sept		Pneumonia	2 days
15	William B. Pearson	27	M			S	Tenn	Sept	Clerk	Inflamation	4 weeks
16		1	F	B	S		____	April		unknown	1 day
17	William W. Phillips	31	M			W	N.C.	Dec	Farmer	Consumption	1 year
18	Mary E. Hester	2	F				Tenn	Jan		S. fever	5 days
19	Jane Russell	37	F			W	Tenn	Feb		Consumption	1 year
20	David Greer	24	M			M	Tenn	Sept	Farmer	accident	
21	Dianah Greer	23	F			M	Tenn	Sept		fever	2 weeks
22	Margaret Newsom	30	F			M	Tenn	March		Child birth	2 weeks
23	Richard Ivy	11	M				N.C.	June		Liver Condition	1 year
24	James H. Thompson	6	M				Tenn	Dec		S. fever	3 weeks
25	Infant	1m	M				Tenn	May		unknown	
26	Abner Colier	16	M				Tenn	Nov	none	In Bowels	9 days
27	Cynthia Haysting	35	F			M	Tenn	Nov		Consumption	1 year
28	Samuel Haysting	7m	M				Tenn	Sept		Consumption	2 weeks
29	Jane Suford	30	F			M	N.C.	July		Cholera	1 day
30	Infant Suford	1m	M				Tenn	March			
31	James Hudd	40	M			M	England	June	Miner	unknown	2 months
32	James H. Hix	3m	M				Tenn	Feb		Croup	10 hours
33	____ ____	63	M	B	S			Sept		Cramp C.	2 days
34	Nancy Evans	25	F				Tenn	July		Consumption	2 years

Remarks: The Division of which these papers is the return embraces 6 Civil Districts, containing about 25 square miles each and is bounded on the South by a high ridge, dividing the waters of Elk from those of the Duck River, and on the North by Duck River. The whole being rather hilly than undulating. Well watered by a great number of springs of excellent and pure water, which make the District very healthy. (cont'd)

COUNTY OF BEDFORD, STATE OF TENNESSEE.

PAGE NO. 9   PERSONS WHO DIED DURING THE YEAR ENDING 1st JUNE, 1850.

No. of Visit	Name	Age	Sex	Color	Free or Slave	Married/Widowed	Place of Birth	Month Died	Occupation	Disease or Cause of Death	No. Days Ill
1	William S. Wade	41	M			M	Tenn	June	Wagon-mkr	Cholera	3 days
2	Jesse	37	M	B	S		Tenn	June		T. fever	14 days
3	W. C. Ray	27	M				Tenn	May	none	drowned	sudden
4	James T. King	29	M			M	Tenn	April	Farmer	Consumption	C(100 da)
5	Neil	1	M	B	S		Tenn	Feb		unknown	C(100 da)
6	Eli Hugh Hopkins	37	M			M	N.C.	July	Farmer	T. fever	12 days

COUNTY OF BEDFORD, STATE OF TENNESSEE.

PAGE NO. 9   PERSONS WHO DIED DURING THE YEAR ENDING 1st JUNE, 1850.

No. of Visit	Name	Age	Sex	Color	Free or Slave	Married/Widowed	Place of Birth	Month Died	Occupation	Disease or Cause of Death	No. Days Ill
7	Richard H. Rogers	23	M				Tenn	Feb	Laborer	T. fever	9 days
8	Martha A. Wheeler	9	F				Tenn	Oct		drowned	sudden
9	Mary Spence	17	F				Tenn	Nov		T. fever	21 days
10	James	3	M	B	S		Va	July		Flux	12 days
11	Henry H. Foster	19	M				Tenn	Dec	Laborer	T. fever	9 days
12	William W. Foster	17	M				Tenn	Dec	Laborer	T. fever	28 days
13	Hartwell J. Foster	9	M				Tenn	Dec		T. fever	28 days
14	James Anderson	30	M			M	Tenn	June	Farmer	Dropsy	C(100 da)
15	William Thomas	1	M				Tenn	July		unknown	C(100 da)
16	Mary E. Atkinson	2	F				Tenn	June		Flux	15 days
17	John Capley	37	M			M	N.C.	Jan	Cabinet-mkr	T. fever	8 days
18	John	3m	M	B	S		Tenn	Oct		unknown	C(100 da)
19	Charles Orr	1	M				Tenn	Oct		teething	
20	Elisha	10	M	B	S		Tenn	Nov		T. fever	16 days
21	Henry	21	M	B	S		Tenn	March		T. fever	20 days

Remarks: Typhoid Fever. The face of this District is remarkably rough, then being extensive ledges of lime stone rock with intermediate spaces of good land. Duck River washes the southern border of this District. Cedar timber prevails.

COUNTY OF BEDFORD, STATE OF TENNESSEE.

PAGE NO. 11   PERSONS WHO DIED DURING THE YEAR ENDING 1st JUNE, 1850.

District No. 1

No. of Visit	Name	Age	Sex	Color	Free or Slave	Married/Widowed	Place of Birth	Month Died	Occupation	Disease or Cause of Death	No. Days Ill
1	Sarah Jane Martin	31	F			M	Tenn	April		Gastritis	24 days
2	Peter	85	M	B	S		Va	July		Old age	
3	Mary	22	F	B	S		Tenn	Oct		Consumption	C(100 da)
4	William Brooksher	16	M				Tenn	Jan		T. Fever	7 days
5	Charlot Robertson	1	F				Tenn	Dec		Dropsy	C(100 da)
6	Nancy	25	F	B	S		Tenn	June		Kick of horse	sudden
7	Rebecca	30	F	B	S		Va	April		unknown	
8	Malinda	45	F	B	S		Ky	Sept		Child bed	8 days

Remarks: This Civil District is exceedingly fertile 99/100, at least is _____ of cultivation. Well watered by excellent springs of pure limestone water. Farms growth: Poplar, Beech, Sugar maple, Linn, Box elder, Buckeye, Walnut, Black Locust. There is not a _____ spot in the State of Tennessee.

COUNTY OF BEDFORD, STATE OF TENNESSEE.

PAGE NO. 13 PERSONS WHO DIED DURING THE YEAR ENDING 1st JUNE, 1850.

District No. 3

No. of Visit	Name	Age	Sex	Color	Free or Slave	Married/Widowed	Place of Birth	Month Died	Occupation	Disease or Cause of Death	No. Days Ill
1	James	12	M	B	S		Tenn	May		Inflamation of Brain	7 days
2	Amelia Shofner	55	F				N.C.	Aug		Cancer	C(100 da)
3	William J. Miller	17	M				Tenn	Aug		Typhoid fever	28 days
4	Rima	7	M	B	S		Tenn	Oct		T. fever	14 days
5	Pleasant	5	M	B	S		Tenn	Oct		T. fever	10 days
6	Franciss	23	F	B	S		Tenn	March		T. fever	14 days
7	Able Nelson	53	M				N.C.	April	Farmer	fall from a horse	sudden
8	Ailcy	27	F		S		Tenn	May		unknown	C(100 da)
9	Houston	17	M	B	S		Tenn	Dec		T. fever	7 days
10	Susan	57	F	B	S		Va	Oct		Dropsy	C(100 da)
11	Salona	2	F	B	S		Tenn	Nov		Croup	1 day
12	Ebenexer N. McGee	26	M			M	Tenn	Jan	Cabinet-mkr	Consumption	C(100 da)
13	Elvira Coffey	56	F				N.C.	July		Hemorrhage of lung	C(100 da)
14	Easter	8m	F	B	S		Tenn	March		Scrofula	C(100 da)

Remarks: This Civil District is partly broken and partly ___, the broken portion is rock, the ____ _____ and caves with extensive forest of red cedar and a vast ledges of lime stone rock. The N & C Rail Road passes through a portion of the District. The broken part has many springs. The ____ part is _____ of water above ground.

COUNTY OF BEDFORD, STATE OF TENNESSEE.

PAGE NO. 15 PERSONS WHO DIED DURING THE YEAR ENDING 1st JUNE, 1850.

District No. 4

No. of Visit	Name	Age	Sex	Color	Free or Slave	Married/Widowed	Place of Birth	Month Died	Occupation	Disease or Cause of Death	No. Days Ill
1	Susanah Lynch	25	F			M	Tenn	Sept		T. fever	13 days
2	Nancy H. Lynch	7	F				Tenn	Sept		T. fever	13 days
3	Mary F. Lynch	3m	F				Tenn	Jan		Diarrhea	4 days
4	Susan J. Lynch	4m	F				Tenn	Jan		Croup	3 days
5	Mary Hoover	26	F			M	N.C.	July		T. fever	12 days
6	Susan	1	F	M	S		Miss	Jan		Cholera	C(100 da)
7	William B. Newsom	4	M				Tenn	July		..(illegible)..	C(100 da)
8	Mary	11m	F	B	S		Tenn	Nov		Inflamation of brain	17 days
9	Edward	7m	M	B	S		Tenn	Aug		Croup	3 days

Remarks: The same description given of District No. 1 will apply to this being adjoining district. The face of the country broken rock and well watered, growth: popular, beech, sugar maple, linn, buckeye, etc.

COUNTY OF BEDFORD, STATE OF TENNESSEE.

PAGE NO. 17 PERSONS WHO DIED DURING THE YEAR ENDING 1st JUNE, 1850.

District No. 5

No. of Visit	Name	Age	Sex	Color	Free or Slave	Married/Widowed	Place of Birth	Month Died	Occupation	Disease or Cause of Death	No. Days Ill
1	Warner Deason	29	M			M	Tenn	May	Laborer	Consumption	C(100 da)
2	Sarah Sikes	87	F			W	Va	Feb		Old age	
3	William R. Hicks	16	M				Tenn	Nov	Laborer	T. fever	30 days
4	Josiah S. Hicks	11	M				Tenn	Nov		T. fever	40 days
5	Isabella	37	F	B	S		Miss	Aug		Consumption	C(100 da)
6	W. D. Blankenship	23	M				Tenn	Oct		B. fever	25 days
7	Lucy	35	F	M	S		Va	March		Female obstructus	C(100 da)
8	Lewis	18	M	B	S		Tenn	Dec		freezing	
9	Ely	70	M	B	S		Tenn	May		unknown	sudden
10	Nancy Threat	27	F			W	Tenn	Jan		Consumption	C(100 da)
11	Matilda	50	F	B	S		Maryland	Dec		T. fever	30 days
12	Willie	1	M	B	S		Tenn	Jan		Croup	7 days
13	Mina Wilks	65	M			M	Tenn	Nov	Farmer	Pneumonia	5 days
14	Sarah Ann Hoover	34	F			M	Va	Sept		Cancer	C(100 da)
15	Sarah Jones	87	F			W	Va	July		Old age	
16	Anderson	38	M	B	S		N.C.	Feb		unknown	C(100 da)
17	Roda Jane	2	F	B	S		Tenn	July		Cholera morbus	3 days

Remarks: About one half this District is rich, broken and well watered. The other being the next half is lime and not so good or well watered. The broken portion is timbered with beech, popular, sugar maple, linn, ash and the best part principally timbered with red cedar, oak and etc...

COUNTY OF BEDFORD, STATE OF TENNESSEE.

PAGE NO. 19 PERSONS WHO DIED DURING THE YEAR ENDING 1st JUNE, 1850.

District No. 6

No. of Visit	Name	Age	Sex	Color	Free or Slave	Married/Widowed	Place of Birth	Month Died	Occupation	Disease or Cause of Death	No. Days Ill
1	John Eakin, Esq.	53	M			M	Ireland	Sept	Merchant	Paralysis	8 days
2	Lucretia E. Gregory	8m	F				Tenn	Sept		Scarlet fever	6 days
3	Sophiah	2	F	B	S		Tenn	May		unknown	14 days
4	Nathaniel M. Norton	7	M				Tenn	Nov		Broken limb	7 days
5	Adalin	9	F				Tenn	March		Typhoid fever	30 days
6	Charles L. Wagster	2m	M				Tenn	Dec		Croup	7 days
7	Cintha P. McCutchins	2	F				Tenn	Sept		Scrofula	C(100 da)
8	Lorenzo Hookes	32	M			M	Tenn	May	Laborer	Consumption	C(100 da)
9	May Rolin	60	F			M	N.C.	May		Dropsy	C(100 da)
10	James Holland	55	M			M	N.C.	May	Stone-mason	Cholera morbus	3 days

Remarks: About one half of this Civil District is susceptible of cultivation, generally level and quite stoney, has two or more excellent Sulphur Springs which are much watered among the summer months.

COUNTY OF BEDFORD, STATE OF TENNESSEE.

PAGE NO. 21 PERSONS WHO DIED DURING THE YEAR ENDING 1st JUNE, 1850.

District No. 7

No. of Visit	Name	Age	Sex	Color	Free or Slave	Married/Widowed	Place of Birth	Month Died	Occupation	Disease or Cause of Death	No. Days Ill
1	Paralissa	5	F	B	S		Tenn	Feb		Scrofula	C(100 da)
2	Rebecca Sims	70	F			W	Penn	Nov		Paralysis	9 days
3	Ann	12	F	B	S		Tenn	July		Dropsy	C(100 da)
4	Kenneth Hamlin	1m	M				Tenn	Oct		Croup	1 day
5	Mary Jane Hamlin	24	F			M	Tenn	Sept		Child bed	10 days
6	Jane Fuller	20	F			M	Tenn	July		Child bed	13 days
7	Jane	7	F	B	S		Tenn	Oct		Cholera infantum	31 days
8	C. D. Martin	6	M				Va	April		unknown	4 days
9	Rebecca Story	80	F				Va	April		Old age	C(100 da)
10	George W. Fogleman	1	M				Tenn	May		Scarlet fever	3 days
11	Samuel Fogleman	2	M				Tenn	May		Scarlet fever	15 days
12	J. A. Evans	1	M				Tenn	Aug		Cholera infantum	C(100 da)
13	Alexander Howard	33	M			M	N.C.	Jan	Wheel-wright	Dropsy	C(100 da)
14	Elizabeth Easters	9	F				Tenn	Jan		T. fever	13 days
15	J. R. Loyd	1	M				Tenn	March		Croup	3 days
16	Mary Wardlow	60	F				Ireland	Oct		Fever	14 days
17	Squire Thompson	70	M	B			N.C.	Jan	Baker	Dropsy	C(100 da)
18	Charity	30	F	B	S		Tenn	June		Cholera morbus	3 days
19	Elinor	29	F	B	S		N.C.	June		Cholera morbus	1 day
20	E. J. Frierson	47	M			M	S.C.	Dec	Lawyer	Paralysis	3 days
21	E. W. McGee	2	M				Tenn	Jan		Croup	3 days
22	Henry	13	M	B	S		Tenn	April		killed by horse	sudden
23	Susan	12	F	B	S		____	Dec		killed by horse	13 days
24	Joseph	50	M	B	S		____	March		Cold	20 days

Remarks: This Civil District is situated on both sides of Duck River and embraces the Town of Shelbyville. The land on the River bottoms is excellent and quite extence. The upland is farm and civil with excellent water, plenty and good, etc..... same being lime stone.

COUNTY OF BEDFORD, STATE OF TENNESSEE.

PAGE NO. 23 PERSONS WHO DIED DURING THE YEAR ENDING 1st JUNE, 1850.

District No. 17

No. of Visit	Name	Age	Sex	Color	Free or Slave	Married/Widowed	Place of Birth	Month Died	Occupation	Disease or Cause of Death	No. Days Ill
1	Sarah A. Forman	1	F				Tenn	July		Summer Consumption	20 days
2	Matt	4	M	B	S		Tenn	July		Teething	14 days
3	Martha Brantley	57	F			M	S.C.	April		unknown	6 days
4	Hannah	50	F	B	S	S	Tenn	Jan		Paralysis	5 days
5	Sarah Cortner	19	F			M	Tenn	Feb		Typhoid fever	15 days
6	James Blackwell	36	M			M	Tenn	Feb	Farmer	Pneumonia	7 days
7	Eliza	17	F	B	S		Tenn	Jan		Fever	14 days
8	Charlott	6	F	B	S		Tenn	Aug		Neuralgia	21 days
9	Archibald Adams	40	M			M	____	Feb		Consumption	C(100 da)

Remarks: This Civil District is rich and broken. Well watered by excellent springs. Forest good, beech, popular, linn, walnut, etc....

COUNTY OF BEDFORD, STATE OF TENNESSEE.

PAGE NO. 25   PERSONS WHO DIED DURING THE YEAR ENDING 1st JUNE, 1850.

District No. 2

No. of Visit	Name	Age	Sex	Color	Free or Slave	Married/Widowed	Place of Birth	Month Died	Occupation	Disease or Cause of Death	No. Days Ill
1	Francis Burks	8	M				Tenn	Sept		Diarrhea	20 days
2	Harriet P. Thompson	30	F			M	Tenn	April		Consumption	C(100 da)
3	Nica	17	F	M	S		Tenn	April		Child bed	7 days
4	Allen Knight	59	M			M	N.C.	Sept	Farmer	Carbuncle	10 days
5	Elija H. Cully	1	M				Tenn	Aug		Croup	4 days
6	Luther R. Jonson	25	M			M	Tenn	Sept	Carpenter	Gun shot	sudden
7	Nancy E. Keller	27	F			M	Ga.	July		T. fever	14 days
8	Emily	3m	F	B	S		Tenn	March		Croup	3 days
9	Mary	35	F	B	S		S.C.	March		Child bed	10 days
10	Richard	2	M	B	S		Tenn	Feb		Inflamation of bowels	25 days
11	William	1m	M	B	S		Tenn	March		Cold	9 days
12	Bartly Gordon	11m	M				Tenn	May		Dropsy of head	C(100 da)
13	Lena	3	F	B	S		Tenn	Feb		unknown	20 days

Remarks: This Civil District is a rich broken country. Well watered by many springs of pure lime stone water. Forest growth: yellow popular, walnut, black locust, oak and chestnut, cherry, buckeye, etc.

J. T. Wortham

COUNTY OF BEDFORD, STATE OF TENNESSEE.

PAGE NO. 27   PERSONS WHO DIED DURING THE YEAR ENDING 1st JUNE, 1850.

District No. 18

No. of Visit	Name	Age	Sex	Color	Free or Slave	Married/Widowed	Place of Birth	Month Died	Occupation	Disease or Cause of Death	No. Days Ill
1	Sarah	2	F	B	S		Tenn	Aug		Flux	10 days
2	George Earnhart	83	M			W	Penn	March	Farmer	Old age	C(100 da)
3	Susannah Earnhart	1m	F				Tenn	June		unknown	2 days
4	B. F. Nicholas	1	M				Tenn	Jan		unknown	2 days
5	W. H. H. Cook	6	M				Tenn	Oct		Disease of the head	C(100 da)
6	N. C. Cook	2	M				Tenn	Oct		S. fever	13 days
7	Mary Lawwell	1	F				Tenn	July		Cholera	C(100 da)
8	Elizabeth	2	F	B	S		Tenn	July		Cold	C(100 da)
9	Manerva	15	F	B	S		Tenn	Aug		Disease of worms	C(100 da)
10	Manah	40	F	B	S		Tenn	April		Consumption	C(100 da)
11	Rachael	9	F	B	S		Tenn	May		Consumption	C(100 da)
12	Nancy	4	F	B	S		Tenn	May		Consumption	C(100 da)
13	Nancy Dean	27	F			M	Tenn	March		Child bed	9 days
14	Charlotta	30	F	B	S		Tenn	May		Consumption	C(100 da)
15	William	18	M	B	S		Tenn	May		Consumption	C(100 da)
16	Presley Thorn	23	M				N.C.	Jan	Laborer	Cholera	3 days
17	B. F. Pennington	25	M				N.C.	Oct	Sch-teacher	Fever	21 days
18	Richard Musgrave	35	M				N.C.	Dec	Farmer	Cholera	3 days
19	America S. Watkins	1	F				Tenn	July		S. fever	16 days
20	William G. O'Neil	12	M				Tenn	April		T. fever	17 days

COUNTY OF BEDFORD, STATE OF TENNESSEE.

PAGE NO. 29   PERSONS WHO DIED DURING THE YEAR ENDING 1st JUNE, 1850.

District No. 9

No. of Visit	Name	Age	Sex	Color	Free or Slave	Married/Widowed	Place of Birth	Month Died	Occupation	Disease or Cause of Death	No. Days Ill
1	Moses Guest	67	M			W	S.C.	Nov	Farmer	Bronchitis	23 days
2	Nancy Harrison	96	F			W	N.C.	March		Old age	
3	Sarah M. Webb	28	F			M	Va	Jan		Consumption	C(100 da)
4	Logan	13	M	B	S		Tenn	March		T. fever	C(100 da)
5	Moses Jones	69	M			M	N.C.	Dec	Blk-smith	White swelling	C(100 da)
6	Harriet	3m	F	B	S		Tenn	Dec		Cold	7 days
7	Mary Rucker	20	F			M	Tenn	Oct		T. fever	21 days
8	Elizabeth Atkinson	67	F			M	Va	Oct		Consumption	C(100 da)
9	Ruth Pinkerton	40	F				N.C.	April		T. fever	35 days

Remarks: Typhoid Fever. This Civil District is all most ____ ____ so much so that at least 1/3 its surface is covered in water. ____ the _____ and _____. The soil is ____ rate ____ __ ____ in form of grass. Cedar timber prevails.

COUNTY OF BENTON, STATE OF TENNESSEE.

PAGE NO. 31   PERSONS WHO DIED DURING THE YEAR ENDING 1st JUNE, 1850.

No. of Visit	Name	Age	Sex	Color	Free or Slave	Married/Widowed	Place of Birth	Month Died	Occupation	Disease or Cause of Death	No. Days Ill
1	Babe	8da	M				Tenn	Sept		Croup	3 days
2	Nancy Massey	26	F			M	Tenn	Oct		Conj. chills	3 days
3	Marja	15	F	B	S		Tenn	Jan		T. fever	19 days
4	Rasmus Wagoner	7	M				Tenn	March		Fits	3 days
5	Catharine Nowell	21	F			M	Tenn	July		Scurvy	91 days
6	Charles	7m	M	M			Tenn	Nov		unknown	sudden
7	Babe	4da	F				Tenn	Oct		unknown	3 days
8	William Smith	48	M			M	N.C.	March	Farmer	T. fever	21 days
9	Jeremiah Roswell	21	M				Tenn	Aug	Farmer	T. fever	18 days
10	John Oatwall	6	M				Tenn	Feb		Inflamation of brain	4 days
11	Narcissa Combs	78	F				Tenn	Sept		White Swelling	4 months
12	Babe	3da	F				Tenn	Aug		unknown	1 day
13	Nancy Davidson	51	F			M	N.C.	Jan		Consumption	lingered
14	Rachael Bridges	21	F			M	Tenn	May		Consumption	lingered
15	Parlee Saunders	4	F				Tenn	April		unknown	14 days
16	Riley Saunders	2m	M				Tenn	Jan		Croup	sudden
17	Elizabeth Aulston	16	F				Tenn	Feb		Cold	2 days
18	Drucilla Presson	4m	F				Tenn	Jan		Croup	3 days
19	Albert Niceler	35	M			M	N.C.	March	Farmer	Consumption	8 months
20	Mary Ann Dorris	1	F				Tenn	March		Croup	4 days
21	Levin Rushing	2m	M				Tenn	Jan		Croup	1 day
22	William Dardan	23	M				N.C.	Aug	Farmer	unknown	sudden
23	Kiziah Davidson	56	F			M	S.C.	May		T. fever	42 days
24	William Lindsey	20	M				Tenn	March	Farmer	Cholera	5 days
25	Sarah Davis	36	F			M	unknown	April		Child birth	1 day
26	Babe	1wk	M				Tenn	Oct		unknown	4 days
27	Babe	6hr	M				Tenn	June		unknown	sudden
28	Jefferson C. Alsup	6	M				Tenn	Dec		Inf. of bowels	9 days
29	Sarah Cottingham	62	F			M	N.C.	June		Dropsy	6 months
30	Agnes Lightner	49	F			M	N.C.	Jan		Change of life	sudden
31	Margaret Wynns	2	F				Tenn	March		Dropsy	sudden
32	Elizabeth Mizell	30	F			M	Tenn	Oct		Conj. chills	3 days
33	Babe	8da	M				Tenn	Aug		Lock-jaw	3 days

COUNTY OF BLEDSOE, STATE OF TENNESSEE.

PAGE NO. 33 PERSONS WHO DIED DURING THE YEAR ENDING 1st JUNE, 1850.

Eastern District

No. of Visit	Name	Age	Sex	Color	Free or Slave	Married/Widowed	Place of Birth	Month Died	Occupation	Disease or Cause of Death	No. Days Ill
1	Thomas Crawford	1	M				Tenn	April	none	Measles	3 weeks
2	William O. Hail	9	M				Tenn	Feb	none	fever	8 days
3	Jane Cartright	18	F				Tenn	May	Female domestic	Dropsy	Chronic
4	Sarah Swafford	1m	F				Tenn	Dec	none	unknown	1 day
5	Catharine Hamilton	1	F				Tenn	Aug	none	Flux	7 days
6	Nancy McClarrin	63	F			W	S.C.	July	Female domestic	Chronic	
7	Gemima Sebby	9m	F				Tenn	June	none	Flux	15 days
8	Mary E. Green	16	F				Tenn	Sept	____	Inflamation of the head	3 weeks
9	Eliza J. Moore	3	F				Tenn	June	none	burnt	3 days
10	John Keeton	3	M				Tenn	June	none	Fits	sudden
11	Hyram Godsey	32	M			M	Tenn	April	Laborer	Executed	sudden
12	Francis M. Holaway	7	M				Tenn	March	none	unknown	sudden
13	Henry Houston	11	M				Tenn	June	none	eating dirt	2 years
14	James P. Myres	26	M				Tenn	Sept	Sch-teacher	Disease of the lungs	2 weeks
15	Myra A. Coleman	8	F				Tenn	Feb	none	Rheumatism	3 years
16	David Skiles	35	M			M	Tenn	Feb	Laborer	Consumption	2 years
17	Samuel A. Gentry	1	M				Tenn	April	none	Pneumonia	7 days
18	Benjamin	24	M	B	S		Tenn	Feb	Laborer	Bleeding at the lungs	2 months
19	William	18	M	B	S		Tenn	Feb	Laborer	Fever	3 weeks
20	Susan J. Mathis	20	F				Tenn	March	Female domestic	Bold hives	4 weeks
21	Alfred Sutherland	12	M				Tenn	May	none	Dropsy	2 years
22	Virginia Boutin	8	F				Tenn	Feb	none	Dropsy	5 years
23	William L. Briant	1m	M				Tenn	Sept	none	fever	10 days
24	John	42	M	B	S		N.C.	March	Laborer	Cold	3 months
25	Martha Hisaw	9	F				Tenn	April	none	Croup	3 weeks
26	James B. Morgan	5	M				Tenn	June	none	Croup	2 days

Remarks: The remainder of the County lies upon the mountain. It being a sort of table land, very level covered mostly with oak. The soil is light and sandy. The water is mostly free stone interspersed with various chalybeate springs. The rocks are mostly sand. Stone pool is abundant upon the mountain. The surface of the mountain is covered with grass and affords good summer range.

COUNTY OF BLEDSOE, STATE OF TENNESSEE.

PAGE NO. 36 PERSONS WHO DIED DURING THE YEAR ENDING 1st JUNE, 1850.

Eastern District

No. of Visit	Name	Age	Sex	Color	Free or Slave	Married/Widowed	Place of Birth	Month Died	Occupation	Disease or Cause of Death	No. Days Ill
1	Eliza L. Galbraith	40	F			M	Tenn	Nov	Female domestic	Pneumonia	12 days
2	Benjamin Griffy	75	M			M	Ga	March	Miller	Diarrhea	60 days
3	Rebecca Heard	16	F				Tenn	March	Female domestic	Cold	60 days
4	John	1m	M	B	S		Tenn	Feb	none	Cold	3 days
5	Ephraim Hunter	11	M				Tenn	Feb	none	unknown	60 days
6	James Hixon	1m	M				Tenn	May	none	unknown	3 days
7	____ Bowan	1m	F				Tenn	Sept	none	Disease of the head	6 days
8	Julia	1m	F	B	S		Tenn	July	none	____	sudden
9	____ Smith	1m	F				Tenn	Sept	none	unknown	6 days
10	David Smith	3	M				Tenn	Jan	none	Burned	sudden
11	____ Clark	1m	M	M	F		Tenn	Sept	none	unknown	sudden
12	Sarah Clark	2m	F	M	F		Tenn	Oct	none	unknown	sudden
13	Joseph Clifton	7m	M				Tenn	June	none	Hives	3 days
14	Mary Oxsher	2	F				Tenn	July	none	Croup	1 day
15	Mary Sky	50	F	M	F		Va	Feb	F. Domestic	Dropsy	Chronic

COUNTY OF BLEDSOE, STATE OF TENNESSEE.

PAGE NO. 36   PERSONS WHO DIED DURING THE YEAR ENDING 1st JUNE, 1850.

Eastern District

No. of Visit	Name	Age	Sex	Color	Free or Slave	Married/Widowed	Place of Birth	Month Died	Occupation	Disease or Cause of Death	No. Days Ill
16	Mahaly	3	F	B	S		Tenn	Aug	none	Drowned	sudden
17	Charles	9m	M	B	S		Tenn	Nov	none	Disease of the head	40 days
18	Rebecca	4	F	B	S		Tenn	Oct	none	Dropsy	Chronic
19	Franklin Boyd	6	M				Tenn	March	none	kick of horse	3 days
20	Delia	44	F	B	S		unknown	Feb		Consumption	2 years
21	Richard Faine	1m	M				Tenn	May		unknown	2 days
22	Robert F. Barnett	91	M			W	Va	April	Farmer	Dropsy	Chronic
23	Adaline	1m	F	B	S		Tenn	Feb	none	Croup	8 days
24	Aquilla Johnson	80	M			W	S.C.	Feb	Farmer	Gravel	86 days
25	Jonas	1	M	B	S		Tenn	Oct	none	unknown	sudden
26	Elizabeth Beaty	24	F				Tenn	June	F. Domestic	Dead Palsy	sudden
27	Nancy Swafford	60	F			M	Tenn	April	F. Domestic	Pneumonia	12 days
28	Nancy Gentry	33	F				Tenn	Sept	F. Domestic	Bilious fever	11 days
29	William R. Barger	2	M				Tenn	Sept	none	Hives	2 days
30	____ Snodgrass	1m	F				Tenn	March	none	unknown	3 days
31	Teresa A. Swafford	10m	F				Tenn	Aug	none	Worms	12 days
32	George	23	M	B	S		Tenn	May	Laborer	Dropsy	Chronic
33	Larkin Smith	8	M				Tenn	Jan	none	Measles	28 days
34	Nancy Gentry	32	F				Tenn	Sept	F. Domestic	Fever	11 days
35	Mary Hall	65	F			M	Va	March	F. Domestic	Cold	15 weeks

Remarks: The best portion of the County of Bledsoe is situated in a cove of the Cumberland Mountains. The valley being of an average width of four miles, extending in length some seventy five miles. The soil is clay and highly fertile. Well watered with lime stone springs and riverlets. The natural growth is oak, popular, hickory, walnut and maple. Lime could be manufactured in great abundance.

COUNTY OF BLOUNT, STATE OF TENNESSEE.

PAGE NO. 37   PERSONS WHO DIED DURING THE YEAR ENDING 1st JUNE, 1850.

No. of Visit	Name	Age	Sex	Color	Free or Slave	Married/Widowed	Place of Birth	Month Died	Occupation	Disease or Cause of Death	No. Days Ill
1	James Cochran	8m	M				Tenn	June		Fever	21 days
2	Sarah Aiken	50	F				Penn	May		Dropsy	9 months
3	Eliza Orr	82	F				Penn	Nov		Old age	3 months
4	Jane Shanks	84	F				Va	Jan		Old age	4 days
5	Elim Taylor	30	F				Tenn	June		Consumption	1 year
6	Chas. Black	10m	M	B	S		____	Sept		Croup	2 days
7	George W. Barker	11m	M				N.C.	July		Diarrhea	3 weeks
8	Hannah Hamontree	27	F				Tenn	June		Consumption	3 months
9	Elvira McGhee	4	F				____	March		Fits	6 days
10	Sarah Bayless	38	F				____	Dec		Dropsy	5 years
11	David Greenway	55	M				____	June		Fever	7 days
12	Samuel McCaslin	20	M				____	April	Farmer	Inflamation of bowels	2 days
13	Alex Humphreys	55	M				____	June		Pneumonia	4 days
14	John Humphreys	5	M				____	May		Croup	3 days
15	Robert Humphreys	8m	M				____	May		Liver complaint	2 months
16	Ruth Goodman	60	F				Va	Sept		Apoplexy	sudden
17	Joel Williams	7m	M	B	S		Tenn	March		unknown	1 day
18	Lavonia Jones	37	F				____	Jan		Fits	9 days
19	Delilah Jones	26	F				____	Aug		Fever	14 days
20	Henry Hicks	26	M				____	July		Cong. fever	12 days
21	Mary Malcom	26	F				____	May		Cold	2 months

COUNTY OF BLOUNT, STATE OF TENNESSEE.

PAGE NO. 37 — PERSONS WHO DIED DURING THE YEAR ENDING 1st JUNE, 1850.

No. of Visit	Name	Age	Sex	Color	Free or Slave	Married/Widowed	Place of Birth	Month Died	Occupation	Disease or Cause of Death	No. Days Ill
22	Chaney Skate	44	F	B	S		____	July		Fever	10 days
23	Jacob Kegley	?	M				Va	June		T. fever	4 weeks
24	Kathr. Kegley	17	F				____	June		T. fever	5 days
25	William Pugh	77	M				Tenn	Jan		Fever	3 weeks
26	Mary Hackney	1	F				____	Aug	M-----	Flux	7 days
27	Malima Sterling	43	F	B	F	M	____	June	Farmer	Consumption	3 months
28	Albert Robinson	22	M				____	Oct		T. fever	7 weeks
29	Samuel Saffell	72	M				____	Sept		Poison	5 days
30	Thomas Aikman	26	M				Ala	July	Sch-teacher	Consumption	3 months
31	Moses Hooper	55	M				N.C.	July		Inf. of brain	2 days
32	John McCall	44	M				Tenn	Aug		Dropsy	3 months
33	Claiborn Stone	19	M	B	S		____	July		Cong. fever	8 days
34	Tailor Stone	1	M	B	S		____	March		Inf. of bowels	12 days

COUNTY OF BRADLEY, STATE OF TENNESSEE.

PAGE NO. 39 — PERSONS WHO DIED DURING THE YEAR ENDING 1st JUNE, 1850.

26th Subdivision

No. of Visit	Name	Age	Sex	Color	Free or Slave	Married/Widowed	Place of Birth	Month Died	Occupation	Disease or Cause of Death	No. Days Ill
1	Marinda	10	F	M	S		Tenn	Aug		Fever	30 days
2	Charles	8	M	B	S		Tenn	July		Fever	30 days
3	Infant	1m	M	M	S		Tenn	Sept		unknown	1 day
4	Clemant Huskison	70	M			W	Va	Feb		Old age	3 days
5	David A. Humphries	3	M				Tenn	Jan		Dropsy of the brain	14 days
6	Henry Homewood	12	M				Tenn	July		Accident	4 days
7	John Tare	1	M				Tenn	June		Diarrhea	10 days
8	James Cate	1m	M				Tenn	June		unknown	1 day
9	Charles Cate	1m	M				Tenn	Dec		unknown	2 days
10	Mary Rose	7	F				Tenn	Nov		Worms	18 days
11	Mary Broomfield	82	F				Va	Sept		Old age	5 days
12	John W. Seagle	3	M				Tenn	Dec		Fever	7 days
13	Elizabeth H. Harris	30	F				Tenn	July		Fever	21 days
14	Rachael Ruble	16	F				Tenn	March		Fever	18 days
15	Mary Hicks	35	F				Tenn	June		Fever	1 day
16	Penelope Blizzard	30	F				Tenn	Dec		Diarrhea	3 months
17	John Roberts	3m	M				Tenn	Sept		Croup	11 days
18	Calvin	19	M	B	S		Tenn	Jan		Fever	30 days
19	Martha E. Willis	7m	F				Tenn	July		Whooping cough	30 days
20	Alexander Ramsey	1	M				Tenn	Sept		Croup	35 days
21	Anna	1	F	B	S		Tenn	April		Weakness	18 days
22	Seratha Gold	2	F				Tenn	June		Fever	7 days
23	Martha E. Fox	1	F				Tenn	Jan		Fever	5 days
24	Andrew Johnson	8	M				Tenn	May		Chicken pox	3 days
25	Elizabeth Goins	28	F				Tenn	June		Child bed	1 day
26	Sarah E. Goins	1m	F				Tenn	July		Croup	4 days
27	Robert J. Williams	2m	M				Tenn	Aug		Hives	5 days
28	Rhuben D. Sexton	28	M				New York	Sept	Clerk	Consumption	1 year
29	William Shelton	25	M				New York	Dec		Accident	1 day
30	Malinda Thornbury	21	F				N.C.	Oct		Consumption	2 years
31	William Hall	82	M				Va	July	Farmer	Old age	30 days
32	John Brantley	4m	M				Tenn	April		unknown	1 day
33	John Manice	42	M				Tenn	June	Farmer	Sore leg	2 years
34	Jasper Allison	3m	M				Tenn	July		Diarrhea	5 days
35	Catharine M. Henson	6	F				Tenn	May		Dropsy	90 days

COUNTY OF BRADLEY, STATE OF TENNESSEE.

PAGE NO. 42 PERSONS WHO DIED DURING THE YEAR ENDING 1st JUNE, 1850.

The 26th Subdivision
East Tennessee

No. of Visit	Name	Age	Sex	Color	Free or Slave	Married/Widowed	Place of Birth	Month Died	Occupation	Disease or Cause of Death	No. Days Ill
1	Daniel Hunter	63	M				Tenn	Aug	Farmer	Dropsy	7 months
2	Zachariah Murphy	36	M				Tenn	Jan	Farmer	Disease of heart	3 days
3	George Parson	89	M				Va	Aug	Farmer	Old age	2 days
4	Hugh Hanner	43	M				Tenn	May	Farmer	Fever	21 days
5	Lucinda Rogers	95	F				S.C.	Nov		Old age	25 days
6	John White	38	M				Tenn	Sept	Farmer	Liquor	
7	Arnon C. Davis	1	M				Tenn	June		Whooping cough	26 days
8	Tennessee Davis	4m	F				Tenn	May		Croup	2 days
9	Alexander Barger	21	M				Tenn	June	none	Fits	
10	Catharine Loftes	37	F				Tenn	April		Child birth	1 day
11	Benjamin F. Hill	1	M				Tenn	July		Fever	12 days
12	Nancy Armstrong	70	F				Tenn	Dec		Breast complaint	2 years
13	James P. Randolph	1m	M				Tenn	May		Hives	1 day
14	Elkin Gad	55	M				Tenn	July		Fever	36 days
15	Ann I. Sisk	3m	F				Tenn	Oct		Croup	3 days
16	William Blankenship	1m	M				Tenn	July		Croup	4 days
17	Letta Chilcut	19	F				Tenn	Dec		Child birth	9 days
18	Sinathe L. Gold	2	F				Tenn	May		Diarrhea	12 days
19	Infant	1	M	B	S		Tenn	Sept		unknown	
20	Infant	—	M	B	S		Tenn	Oct		unknown	
21	Infant		F				Tenn	June		unknown	
22	Malvina Pack	1	F				Tenn	Oct		Diarrhea	18 days
23	Elizabeth Phelps	70	F				Tenn	Dec		Old age	4 days
24	Robert Steel	22	M				Va	Aug		Diarrhea	1 year
25	Mary J. Eldridge	6	F				Tenn	Sept		Fever	6 weeks
26	Hannah Eldridge	1	F				Tenn	Sept		Fever	6 weeks
27	William Cates	19	M				Tenn	Nov	Farmer	Consumption	4 weeks
28	Jane S. Swan	79	F				Va	May		Old age	6 weeks
29	Manerva	29	F	B	S		N.C.	May		Measles	3 months
30	Jack	3	M	B	S		Tenn	May		unknown	2 days
31	Jane	1m	F	B	S		Tenn	June		Croup	1 day
32	Elizabeth Nealy	38	F				Tenn	Feb		Child birth	1 day
33	Nancy Rinkle	18	F				Tenn	April		Consumption	6 months
34	Thomas Ruins	23	M				Tenn	March		Fever	5 days
35	Jason ____	20	F?				Tenn	Nov		Fever	27 days

COUNTY OF BRADLEY, STATE OF TENNESSEE.

PAGE NO. 43 PERSONS WHO DIED DURING THE YEAR ENDING 1st JUNE, 1850.

The 26th Subdivision
Eastern Division

No. of Visit	Name	Age	Sex	Color	Free or Slave	Married/Widowed	Place of Birth	Month Died	Occupation	Disease or Cause of Death	No. Days Ill
1	Hester Johnston	1	F				Tenn	Feb		Fever	6 weeks
2	Anna More	50	F				Tenn	May		Dropsy	6 months
3	Frances Alexander	72	F				Va	April		Old age	8 months
4	Jamima Weare	2	F				Tenn	Sept		Whooping cough	1 month
5	Nancy Branum	12	F				Tenn	March		Sore throat	3 months
6	Sarah Branum	5	F				Tenn	March		Sore throat	2 months
7	Martha Wilson	9m	F				Tenn	July		unknown	6 days
8	William Reeling	3	M				Tenn	Feb		Worms	6 days
9	David Pulum	40	M				Tenn	March	Farmer	Accident	1 day
10	David Humphrey	1	M				Tenn	Aug		Fever	30 days
11	George Turner	25	M				Tenn	Feb	Farmer	Fever	18 days
12	Elizabeth Easley	23	F				Tenn	Feb		Fever	25 days

COUNTY OF BRADLEY, STATE OF TENNESSEE.

PAGE NO. 43 PERSONS WHO DIED DURING THE YEAR ENDING 1st JUNE, 1850.

The 26th Subdivision
Eastern Division

No. of Visit	Name	Age	Sex	Color	Free or Slave	Married/Widowed	Place of Birth	Month Died	Occupation	Disease or Cause of Death	No. Days Ill
13	Samuel Bradwell	35	M				Tenn	Jan	Farmer	Fever	50 days
14	David Wilson	35	M				Tenn	June	Farmer	Fever	10 days
15	William L. Adams	1	M				Tenn	Aug		Swine-pox	6 days
16	John Myer	100	M				Penn	July	Farmer	Old age	2 days

COUNTY OF CAMPBELL, STATE OF TENNESSEE.

PAGE NO. 45 PERSONS WHO DIED DURING THE YEAR ENDING 1st JUNE, 1850.

The 17th Subdivision

No. of Visit	Name	Age	Sex	Color	Free or Slave	Married/Widowed	Place of Birth	Month Died	Occupation	Disease or Cause of Death	No. Days Ill
1	Ellis Right	5	M				Tenn	Feb		Scarlet fever	sudden
2	Oliver Huff	9m	M				Tenn	April		Burnt	4 days
3	Minerva Adkins	1	F				Tenn	Nov		Whooping cough	14 days
4	Chesley Adkins	7	M				Tenn	Dec		Whooping cough	10 days
5	Ransom Adkins	1m	M				Tenn	Nov		unknown	28 days
6	Robert Stoublefield	82	M			W	N.C.	Oct	none	unknown	39 days
7	David Hudleston	13	M				Tenn	May		Fever	23 days
8	Milly Keller	23	F			M	Tenn	March		Fever	13 days
9	George Davis	78	M			M	unknown	April	Farmer	unknown	39 days
10	James Douglass	7	M				Tenn	Sept		unknown	2 days
11	Samuel Douglass	5	M				Tenn	Sept		unknown	4 days
12	Jesse Lay	84	M			W	unknown	March	none	Old age	9 days

Remarks: And great permanency in dry weather, particularly a stream called Cedar Creek which for the number of its falls and its durability is, I think not excelled anywhere. It is fed by hundreds of fine springs breaking out of the emmence hills into its course. There are many chalybeate and sulphur springs, some having valuable medicinal virtue soil. In the valleys (about one sixth of the County) the soil is stiff clayey and rich. In the rest of the County, the soil is gravelly or sandy and on the creeks and rivers very rich. The Cumberland Mountains occupies about one half the County. It has much rich table land and other lands that are cultivated.

Rocks: In the valleys, the rock is lime stone. In the mountains, sandstone and slate. Timber: is tolerably large, of fine quality and abundant of forest trees, oak is most abundant, then pine, hickory, beech, popular(poplar), walnut, cedar, sugar maple (from which a considerable quanity of sugar is made), elm. sycamore, birch, linns, also wild cherry, magnolia, persimmon, locust, red bud, cercis sorrel tree, etc... Fertilizer: Lime is obtained by burning the limestone of the valleys. The plasterers, who have used it say it is the best they have ever seen made from limestone. Ores: There are considerable quantities of lead ore which however is not worked. The iron ore is of superior quality and vastly abundant. One vein particularly runs across the County (20 miles) where the mountain and Powell Valley joins just at the base of the mountains. This ore is only worked in a small way though it yields a large per cent of the best ore. Coal: There are many vast beds of coal. Mostly of good quality though some contains sulphur. It is only used by blacksmiths. Charcoal being used in iron making.   John Phillips

COUNTY OF CAMPBELL, STATE OF TENNESSEE.

PAGE NO. 48 PERSONS WHO DIED DURING THE YEAR ENDING 1st JUNE, 1850.

The 17th Subdivision

No. of Visit	Name	Age	Sex	Color	Free or Slave	Married/Widowed	Place of Birth	Month Died	Occupation	Disease or Cause of Death	No. Days Ill
1	Henry Queener	77	M			M	Maryland	June	Farmer	Breast Complaint	15 days
2	Daniel Queener	84	M			M	Penn	Dec	Farmer	Gravel	8 days
3	Mary J. White	1	F				Tenn	July		Cholera morbus	11 days
4	Leannah Lovet	5	F				Tenn	June		Whooping cough	35 days
5	Mary E. H. Wheeler	10	F				Tenn	Nov		Inflamation of the brain	5 days
6	Cumfret Baker	10m	F				Tenn	March		Hives	15 days
7	Mary Hutson	25	F			M	Tenn	March		unknown	6 days
8	Cristian Brock	90	M			M	N.C.	March	none	Dropsy	20 days
9	Eli Jarmon	1m	M				Tenn	March		Hives	3 days
10	Mary Gray	11	F				Tenn	May		Drowned	
11	John Richardson	61	M			M	Va	March	none	unknown	6 days
12	Henry Malicoat	1	M				Tenn	Oct		unknown	30 days
13	John Reed	20	M				Tenn	March	Farmer	Dropsy	60 days
14	Ann E. Agee	1m	F				Tenn	Nov		Hives	4 days
15	Febee Cox	20	F				Tenn	Aug		Fever	11 days
16	Susan Nelson	75	F			W	Va	June		Old age	30 days
17	Sarah Witt	8	F				Missouri	Jan		Burned	10 days
18	Frances Phillips	79	F			W	Va	July		Old age	15 days
19	John Flatford	24	M			M	Tenn	Aug	Farmer	Consumption	120 days
20	Lucy Miller	48	F			W	Va	Aug		unknown	6 days
21	James Smith	2m	M				Tenn	Sept		Hives	4 days
22	James Cannon	8m	M				Tenn	July		Whooping cough	10 days
23	Oliver Collins	22	M	M		M?	N.C.	Aug	Farmer	Consumption	180 days
24	Parlena Heatherly	1	F				Tenn	Jan		Croup	8 days
25	Martha Smith	23	F				Tenn	Feb		unknown	13 days
26	Euricus Smith	67	M			M	Va	Feb	Farmer	Cancer	150 days
27	John H. Muringo	1m	M				Tenn	Sept		unknown	2 days
28	John Herrin	1	M				Tenn	Feb		unknown	30 days
29	Elijah Braden	26	M			M	Tenn	March	Farmer	Fever	14 days
30	Dicy M. Turner	1	F				Tenn	May		unknown	6 days
31	Napoleon Futts	3	M				Tenn	May		unknown	14 days
32	Anna Lay	15	F				Tenn	Jan		Fever	9 days
33	Sarah Sharp	83	F			W	N.C.	June		unknown	40 days
34	Morris Bridges	49	M			M	N.C.	June	Farmer	Fever	20 days
35	Elizabeth Bridges	6	F				Tenn	July		Fever	35 days

Remarks: Disease in this County is of a very diversified character, mostly chronic fevers are mostly Typhoid though some intermittents on the creeks and Rivers. Scrofula and Pulmonary disease are prevailent. Some cases of Goiter. Water: This County is finely watered. In the Valleys, the water is a strong limestone, in the balance of the County, it is called free stone water. Perhaps no country has finer water power for machinery. The streams have many falls.

COUNTY OF CANNON **, STATE OF TENNESSEE.**

PAGE NO. 49 **PERSONS WHO DIED DURING THE YEAR ENDING 1st JUNE, 1850.**

Alexander's 2nd & Brady's Rock 4 District

No. of Visit	Name	Age	Sex	Color	Free or Slave	Married/Widowed	Place of Birth	Month Died	Occupation	Disease or Cause of Death	No. Days Ill
1	Anna Cooper	1	F				Tenn	Aug		Flux	30 days
2	Sally	4	F	M	S		Tenn	July		Bowel complaint	15 days
3	Nancy J. Parkes	5m	F				Tenn	Nov		Fever	15 days
4	Archabald Finley	5	M				Tenn	Aug		Flux	15 days
5	Mary J. Lush	9m	F				Tenn	Aug		Flux	12 days
6	Elizabeth Cooper	6	F				Tenn	Aug		Flux	9 days
7	Andrew Cooper	1	M				Tenn	Aug		Flux	11 days
8	Thomas Byford	5	M				Tenn	Aug		Flux	16 days
9	William S. Bowen	10m	M				Tenn	Oct		Flux	9 days
10	Jasper N. Patton	10m	M				Tenn	July		Cholera morbus	10 days
11	Matilda Hill	4m	F				Tenn	May		Bold hives	1 day
12	Fanny R. Whitfield	38	F			M	Tenn	April		Dropsy of heart	185 ?
13	Joseph Safeley	55	M			M	Tenn	Jan	Farmer	Accident	sudden
14	William J. Arnold	20	M			M	Tenn	Oct	Farmer	T. fever	30 days
15	Infant of A. H. Stacy	1hr	F				Tenn	May		unknown	1 hour
16	William I. McElroy	5m	M				Tenn	Aug		Cholera morbus	10 days
17	Susan L. Thompson	6m	F				Tenn	July		Flux	4 days
18	Rebecca Conely	45	F			M	Va	Oct		unknown	365 days
19	Elizabeth Hollis	86	F			W	N.C.	June		Old age	8 days
20	Infant, Peter Mahey	1m	M				Tenn	Sept		Croup	5 days
21	Jane Burnett	65	F			W	Tenn	Sept		Dropsy	182 days
22	Margaret A. Hays	1	F				Tenn	July		Flux	15 days
23	Rebecca Hays	25	F			M	Tenn	Aug		Flux	28 days
24	Anna Campbell	27	F			M	N.C.	Nov		Flux	21 days
25	Buson Campbell	10m	M				Tenn	Nov		Flux	8 days
26	George Wesley	21	M	B	S		Tenn	June		Flux	21 days
27	Zachariah Y. Smith	1	M				Tenn	Dec		Flux	8 days
28	James A. Justice	2	M				Tenn	July		Flux	8 days
29	Jackson Cornatzer	19	M				Tenn	March	Sch-teacher	sudden	sudden
30	Eli Nichols	52	M			M	Kentucky	Dec	Stone-mason	Flux	21 days
31	Mary P. Reed	47	F			M	Va	Aug		Flux	15 days
32	Infant of D.L.Warin) twins	1hr	M				Tenn	Oct		unknown	1 hour
33	Infant of D.L.Warin)	1hr	M				Tenn	Oct		unknown	1 hour
34	Martha A. Wood	12	F				Tenn	Oct		Spasms	
35	Washington	21	M	B	S		Tenn	___		Cold	45 days

Remarks: Martha A. Wood was sick from childhood till her death.

COUNTY OF CANNON **, STATE OF TENNESSEE.**

PAGE NO. 52 **PERSONS WHO DIED DURING THE YEAR ENDING 1st JUNE, 1850.**

5th & Brydyville 12th District

No. of Visit	Name	Age	Sex	Color	Free or Slave	Married/Widowed	Place of Birth	Month Died	Occupation	Disease or Cause of Death	No. Days Ill
1	Infant of J. R. Brooks	1m	M				Tenn	Dec		unknown	1 day
2	Mariah	50	F	B	S		Va	Jan			10 days
3	John Varner	55	M			W	unknown	Dec	Sch-teacher	Cold	7 days
4	Alexander Banks	7	M				Tenn	Jan		S. fever	150 days
5	Infant of S. Alexander	1m	F				Tenn	Dec		unknown	1 day
6	Lucresa Jones	20	F				Tenn	Nov		T. fever	38 days
7	Easter J. Curtis	19	F			M	Tenn	March		Consumption	365 days
8	William J. Campbell	14	M				Tenn	Jan		T. fever	21 days
9	Aaron M. Brooks	1m	M				Tenn	July		Cholera morbus	3 days

COUNTY OF CANNON, STATE OF TENNESSEE.

PAGE NO. 52 PERSONS WHO DIED DURING THE YEAR ENDING 1st JUNE, 1850.

5th & Brydyville 12th District

No. of Visit	Name	Age	Sex	Color	Free or Slave	Married/Widowed	Place of Birth	Month Died	Occupation	Disease or Cause of Death	No. Days Ill
10	Tennessee L. Sain	5m	F				Tenn	Sept		unknown	1 day
11	Nelly C. Jones	23	F				Tenn	Sept		Consumption	365 days
12	Infant of D.M. Patton	1da	F				Tenn	Dec		Hives	1 day
13	Jane Parkes	28	F			M	Tenn	Feb		Consumption	900 days
14	James D. Jones	2	M				Tenn	Oct		T. fever	23 days
15	Nancy A. Jones	100	F			W	Scotland	March		Old age	sudden
16	Infant of S. Hollis) twins	—	M				Tenn	April		Still born	
17	Infant of S. Hollis)	—	M				Tenn	April		Still born	
18	Isaac H. Finley	1	M				Tenn	March		Cholera morbus	2 days
19	Mary M. A. Bowin	4m	F				Tenn	Sept		Inf. of the brain	5 days
20	Jude	8	F	M	S		Tenn	Aug		Flux	10 days
21	Wyatt A. Brown	48	M				S.C.	Dec	none	Dropsy	35 days
22	Peter Simpson, Sr.	80	M			M	N.C.	May	Farmer	Old age	11 days
23	Easter Hollis	45	F			M	Tenn	July		Cong. chill	15 days
24	Eliza Harris	26	F			W	Tenn	July		Flux	9 days
25	Loucinda C. Faulkenberry	6m	F				Tenn	July		Flux	21 days
26	George C. Brandon	11	M				Tenn	Dec		Carbuncle	30 days
27	Ruth B. Brandon	28	F			M	Tenn	Sept		unknown	60 days
28	Frances Brandon	1da	F				Tenn	Sept		unknown	1 day
29	John A. Perry	11m	M				Tenn	June		Flux	11 days
30	Martha Carroll	76	F			W	Va	April		Old age	15 days
31	Elizabeth Thurston	57	F			M	Va	April		Consumption	730 days
32	James D. Rucker	1	M				Tenn	Sept		Flux	54 days
33	Susannah	60	F	B	S		Va	June		unknown	90 days
34	Nancy Sullivan	90	F			W	N.C.	June		Palsey	9 days
35	Emily Owen	27	F			M	N.C.	May		Consumption	730 days

COUNTY OF CANNON, STATE OF TENNESSEE.

PAGE NO. 53 PERSONS WHO DIED DURING THE YEAR ENDING 1st JUNE, 1850.

Nichol's 1st & Sanderson ?th District

No. of Visit	Name	Age	Sex	Color	Free or Slave	Married/Widowed	Place of Birth	Month Died	Occupation	Disease or Cause of Death	No. Days Ill
1	Caroline	18	F	M	S		Tenn	Aug		unknown	35 days
2	Jane Coulter	55	F			W	N.C.	March		Dropsy	365 days
3	Margaret C. Travis	1	F				Tenn	May		Inflamation of brain	
4	Mary Carrethers	84	F			W	N.C.	Jan		Dropsy	150 days
5	Easter S. Rogers	26	F			M	Tenn	Sept		Consumption	365 days
6	Infant of D. Travis	1m	M				Tenn	Nov		unknown	1 hour
7	Moses McKnight	58	M			W	N.C.	Nov	Farmer	Cancer	400 days
8	Virginia A. Smith	2m	F				Tenn	June		Croup	2 hours
9	Lucy Smith	40	F				Va	April		Consumption	730 days
10	Infant of John C. Luch	1m	F				Tenn	Nov		unknown	1 day
11	James Duggin	11m	M				Tenn	Nov		Croup	2 days
12	Emily C. Bond	32	F			M	Tenn	Aug		Consumption	182 days
13	Drury M. Thomas	1	M				Tenn	Sept		Worms	7 days
14	Hiram T. Bogle	5	M				Tenn	Aug		Worms	31 days
15	Nicy Davenport	1	F				Tenn	Aug		Cholera morbus	15 days
16	Samuel Reed	24	M				Tenn	June	Farmer	Cold	365 days
17	Enos S. Wetherspoon	40	M				Tenn	May	Farmer	Consumption	182 days
18	Harriet Mathews	15	F				Tenn	Jan		Consumption	61 days
19	Margaret A. Jones	16	F				Tenn	Nov		Consumption	730 days
20	Abner Luch	8m	M				Tenn	June		Croup	3 days
21	Elizabeth Francis	28	F				Tenn	March		unknown	2 hours

COUNTY OF CANNON, STATE OF TENNESSEE.

PAGE NO. 53   PERSONS WHO DIED DURING THE YEAR ENDING 1st JUNE, 1850.

Nichol's 1st & Sanderson __th District

No. of Visit	Name	Age	Sex	Color	Free or Slave	Married/Widowed	Place of Birth	Month Died	Occupation	Disease or Cause of Death	No. Days Ill
22	Infant of M. Francis	1m	M				Tenn	April		Croup	7 days
23	Louisa Rackley	12	F				Tenn	Dec		Dropsy	365 days
24	Sarah J. Odom	7m	F				Tenn	Aug		S. fever	10 days
25	Mary E. Milligan	3m	F				Tenn	June		unknown	4 days
26	Lockey J. Willson	3	F				Tenn	April		Croup	3 days

COUNTY OF CANNON, STATE OF TENNESSEE.

PAGE NO. 55   PERSONS WHO DIED DURING THE YEAR ENDING 1st JUNE, 1850.

No. of Visit	Name	Age	Sex	Color	Free or Slave	Married/Widowed	Place of Birth	Month Died	Occupation	Disease or Cause of Death	No. Days Ill
1	Tom Thumb	8m	M	M	S		Woodbury, TN.	Feb		Premature	7 days
2	Mary E. George	21	F	W	F	M	Tenn	Jan		Consumption	60 days
3	James M. George	15	M	W	F		Tenn	Dec		Fits	
4	Sam	13	M	B	S		Tenn	June		T. fever	20 days
5	Jessee Brewer	38	M	W	F	M	Va	April	Farmer	Drowned	
6	Benjamin Brewer	36	M	W	F		Va	April	Farmer	Drowned	
7	William Peyton	1	M	W	F		Tenn	Aug		Flux	9 days
8	John Tenpenny	3	M	W	F		Tenn	Oct		Flux	9 days
9	James Sandridge	2	M	M	F		Tenn	April		Flux	40 days
10	Henderson Hayse	8	M	W	F		Tenn	Feb		Spasms	2 days
11	Tomesia Vinson	1	F	W	F		Tenn	April		Flux	8 days
12	Hardy	4	M	B	S		Tenn	Feb		Scrofula	150 days
13	Horace Bates	16	M	W	F		Tenn	Dec	Farmer	Killed	
14	Martin B. Wale	48	M	W	F		Va	May	Farmer	Cholera	1 day
15	Malissa McAdoo	7	F	W	F		Tenn	Aug-'49		Cholera infantum	5 days
16	Josephine McAdoo	7m	F	W	F		Tenn	Sept		Cholera infantum	20 days
17	Rebecca Preston	60	F	W	F	M	Va	Aug		Flux	5 days
18	Maret. J. King	13	F	W	F		Tenn	Dec		unknown	2 days
19	John Hollinsworth	5m	M	W	F		Tenn	Sept		Croup	10 days
20	Hyram Morrison	9m	M	W	F		Tenn	Oct		Scalded	8 days
21	Emily C. Smithson	1	F	W	F		Tenn	Aug		Croup	8 days
22	James A. Pendleton	6m	M	W	F		Tenn	May		Bold hives	7 days
23	Narsissa M. Newbey	24	F	W	F		Tenn	July		Pneumonia	20 days
24	Charles P. Crane	11m	M	W	F		Tenn	July		Cholera morbus	10 days
25	Easter Merritt	30	F	W	F	M	Tenn	July		Pregnancy	8 days
26	Mary Ann Perry	28	F	W	F	M	Tenn	Jan		unknown	7 days
27	Elizabeth Gilly	11	F	W	F		Tenn	Feb		Ulcer	120 days
28	William F. Elige	36	M	W	F	M	Tenn	Dec	Farmer	Palpitation	35 days
29	John Blanton	38	M	W	F	M	Tenn	Dec	Farmer	Consumption	730 days

COUNTY OF CARROLL, STATE OF TENNESSEE.

PAGE NO. 57   PERSONS WHO DIED DURING THE YEAR ENDING 1st JUNE, 1850.

The 11th Civil District

No. of Visit	Name	Age	Sex	Color	Free or Slave	Married/Widowed	Place of Birth	Month Died	Occupation	Disease or Cause of Death	No. Days Ill
1	James A. Carver	8	M				Tenn	April		S. fever	1 week
2	Julia A. Reden	6	F				Tenn	April		S. fever	6 days
3	Mary Ann	23	F	B	S	M	Tenn	April		Poison	2 weeks
4	Crawford	6m	M	B	S		Tenn	Feb		Cold	4 days
5	Mary Traywick	21	F			M	Tenn	Jan		Consumption	6 months
6	Elizabeth Peoples	18m	F				Tenn	July		Pneumonia	4 weeks
7	Elizabeth J. Howard	15	F				Arkansas	Oct		S. fever	15 days
8	Susan E. Colwell	10	F				Tenn	Nov		S. fever	1 day
9	Robert A. Colwell	10m	M				Tenn	April		S. fever	10 days
10	Stephen	2	M	M	S		Tenn	March		Pneumonia	1 month
11	Robert M. Grizzard	4	M				Tenn	May		S. fever	3 weeks
12	Daniel M. Bibb	8m	M				Tenn	July		Dropsy	7 weeks
13	Mary J. Weathers	27	F			M	Va	Feb		Child birth	2 weeks
14	S. B. Holaday	5	M				Tenn	Jan		Diarrhea	1 month
15	Neely T. Bibb	8	M				Tenn	March		Pneumonia	3 weeks
16	Thomas Springer	23	M			M	Tenn	Nov	Farmer	Cholera	4 days
17	Jerry	22	M	B	S	M	Tenn	Aug		Dropsy	7 months
18	William H. Scott	10	M				Tenn	Feb		Accident	sudden
19	Benjamin F. Tosh	11m	M				Tenn	Sept		Thrash	2 weeks
20	Martha Falkner	14	F				Tenn	March		Consumption	19 days
21	Sarah Parker	10	F				Tenn	July		T. fever	3 weeks
22	William Philips	31	M			M	Tenn	Aug	Farmer	Intemperance	sudden
23	William P. Hampton	10	M				Tenn	Jan		T. fever	3 weeks
24	Robert Bradford	51	M			M	S.C.	Dec	Farmer	Inflamation of lungs	3 weeks
25	Clorina Quillin	33	F			M	Va	Dec		Consumption	3 months
26	Arnold Thomason	76	M			M	N.C.	July	Farmer	Dropsy	1 year
27	Lavina Wray	3	F				Tenn	April		S. fever	2 days
28	Mary A. Traywick	22	F			M	Tenn	Jan		Pneumonia	6 weeks
29	J. Angeline Jordan	25	F			M	Tenn	Sept		Consumption	1 year
30	Burrell	2	M	B	S		Tenn	Jan		Worms	4 days
31	Jacob Martin	41	M			M	Tenn	Aug	Farmer	unknown	sudden
32	Agness	38	F	B	S	M	N.C.	April		Consumption	3 months
33	Lydia Forest	59	F			M	N.C.	Oct		unknown	sudden
34	James Monroe	24	M				Va	June	Farmer	Pleurisy	2 weeks
35	James Brown	38	M			M	N.C.	Oct	Farmer	Pneumonia	3 months

COUNTY OF CARROLL, STATE OF TENNESSEE.

PAGE NO. 60   PERSONS WHO DIED DURING THE YEAR ENDING 1st JUNE, 1850.

18th Civil District

No. of Visit	Name	Age	Sex	Color	Free or Slave	Married/Widowed	Place of Birth	Month Died	Occupation	Disease or Cause of Death	No. Days Ill
1	Ralph	1	M	B	S		Tenn	Sept		Chills	3 weeks
2	Treacy Eason	18	F				N.C.	July		B. fever	2 months
3	Colier	6m	M	B	S		Tenn	Sept		Hives	2 weeks
4	John	70	M	B	S		Va	Jan		Old age	———
5	William	80	M	B	S		N.C.	May		Old age	———

COUNTY OF CARROLL, STATE OF TENNESSEE.

PAGE NO. 61   PERSONS WHO DIED DURING THE YEAR ENDING 1st JUNE, 1850.

The 1st Civil District

No. of Visit	Name	Age	Sex	Color	Free or Slave	Married/Widowed	Place of Birth	Month Died	Occupation	Disease or Cause of Death	No. Days Ill
1	John Stewart	34	M			M	Tenn	April	Blk-smith	Dropsy	4 years
2	Nancy M. Boyd	23	F			M	Tenn	Nov		Child birth	1 day
3	John Putman	29	M			M	S.C.	May	Farmer	unknown	sudden
4	Augustus P. Holmes	4	M				Tenn	June		Bronchitus	4 days
5	David S. Holmes	2	M				Tenn	June		Bronchitis	11 days
6	Jordan Shuffle	33	M			M	Kentucky	July	Farmer	Measles	4 weeks
7	Young T. McLemore	16m	M				Tenn	Nov		Croup	sudden
8	Rosetta	1m	F	B	S		Tenn	Sept		unknown	sudden
9	Frances A. Cannon	5m	F				Tenn	July		Croup	sudden
10	Mary B. Jones	6m	F				Tenn	Aug		Diarrhea	5 days
11	Thomas Clark	14	M				Tenn	Feb		Nervous disease	7 weeks
12	John R. Hall	78	M			W	Va	Dec	Farmer	Old age, Pneumonia	
13	Joannah	6m	F	M	S		Tenn	Jan		Pneumonia	3 weeks
14	Richard Byrn	76	M			M	Va	April	Farmer	Old age	
15	Joseph D. Leech	2	M				Tenn	July		Croup	sudden
16	John W. Hannah	23	M				Alabama	March	Farmer	Diarrhea	5 weeks
17	Catharine	6	F	B	S		S.C.	Aug		B. fever	12 days
18	Martha	2	F	B	S		Tenn	Sept		B. fever	10 days
19	Nancy Moore	6m	F				Tenn	Nov		Accident	sudden
20	David Hurt	10m	M				Tenn	Sept		Gravel	2 weeks
21	Robert	73	M	B	S	M	Va	Jan		Old age	sudden
22	Alice	1m	F	B	S		Tenn	Nov		unknown	sudden
23	Amanda A. Berry	7	F				Tenn	June		Cong. fever	2 days
24	R. A. F. Huffman	18	F				N.C.	July		S. fever	11 days
25	John W. Smith	16m	M				Tenn	Jan		Diarrhea	3 weeks
26	Lewis C. Smith	8m	M				Tenn	June		S. fever	11 days
27	Luta	6m	F	B	S		Tenn	May		Diarrhea	1 week
28	Hannah S. Cole	2	F				Tenn	Nov		S. fever	1 week
29	Wiley	2	M	B	S		Tenn	Nov		S. fever	5 weeks
30	David W. Jackson	7m	M				Tenn	April		unknown	3 weeks
31	Samuel Bowen	10	M				N.C.	Aug		T. fever	5 weeks
32	Ruphus	8m	M	B	S		Tenn	Aug		Diarrhea	2 months
33	Frank	40	M	B	S	M	Kentucky	Feb		Pneumonia	3 weeks
34	Robert Griffin	45	M			M	S.C.	Aug		Cholera	5 days
35	Gilbert	5m	M	B	S		Tenn	Nov		Epileptic Fits	2 days

Remarks: The general health of the four Districts above have been very good during this year.

COUNTY OF CARROLL, STATE OF TENNESSEE.

PAGE NO. 64   PERSONS WHO DIED DURING THE YEAR ENDING 1st JUNE, 1850.

The 5th Civil District

No. of Visit	Name	Age	Sex	Color	Free or Slave	Married/Widowed	Place of Birth	Month Died	Occupation	Disease or Cause of Death	No. Days Ill
1	Sarah Ann	1	F	M	S		Tenn	Dec		Cold	3 weeks
2	Ezekiel Thomas	57	M			M	N.C.	Jan	Farmer	Intemperance	4 days
3	Martha	6m	F	B	S		Tenn	March		Croup	sudden
4	Thomas Harrell	26	M				N.C.	March	Farmer	Dropsy	6 months
5	Adley Alexander	85	M			W	N.C.	Sept		Old age	
6	Benjamin Harrell	13m	M				Tenn	March		Inflamation of stomach	1 day
7	Gray	45	M	B	S	M	N.C.	Sept		Poisoned	10 days
8	G. W. F. Boswell	28	M			M	N.C.	June	M.D.	T. fever	4 weeks
9	Mary E. Carlton	6m	F				Tenn	June		Diarrhea	2 weeks

COUNTY OF CARROLL, STATE OF TENNESSEE.

PAGE NO. 64 PERSONS WHO DIED DURING THE YEAR ENDING 1st JUNE, 1850.

The 5th Civil District

No. of Visit	Name	Age	Sex	Color	Free or Slave	Married/Widowed	Place of Birth	Month Died	Occupation	Disease or Cause of Death	No. Days Ill
10	David Marshall	42	M			M	Tenn	Sept		Intemperance	1 year
11	Samuel	2	M	M	S		Tenn	Dec		Worms	2 months
12	John Harvey	66	M			M	Va	April	Farmer	unknown	sudden
13	George	8m	M	B	S		Tenn	May		Rickets	2 months
14	E. J. Adams	28	M				S.C.	Feb	Farmer	Accident	sudden
15	Mary L. Blow	11m	F				Tenn	Dec		Inflamation of stomach	4 days
16	John W. Parker	16	M				Tenn	Sept	Farmer	Cholic	3 days
17	Elizabeth Whiteside	58	F			M	Kentucky	April		Pneumonia	2 weeks
18	James W. Kelly	52	M			M	S.C.	July	Farmer	Consumption	2 years
19	Martha	11	F	B	S		Tenn	Jan		Pneumonia	2 weeks
20	Thomas	13	M	B	S		Tenn	Feb		Dropsy	18 months
21	Euin Randle	32	M				Tenn	March	Farmer	Pneumonia	20 days
22	Porter	5m	M	B	S		Tenn	Feb		Cold	3 days
23	Nancy Roach	11m	F				Tenn	June		Cholera infantum	2 weeks
24	Rosannah J. Bryant	4	F				Tenn	Sept		S. fever	3 days
25	Jerryline	4m	F	B	S		Tenn	April		unknown	sudden
26	Jasper	5	M	B	S		Tenn	Sept		Inflamation of brain	2 weeks
27	John C. Brady	10	M				Tenn	Jan		Diarrhea	3 days
28	James Carver	54	M			M	S.C.	Jan	Farmer	Milk sick	1 week
29	Eliza W. Slaton	40	F			M	Va	Jan		Pneumonia	2 weeks
30	Agness	43	F	B	S	M	N.C.	March		Consumption	1 year
31	Thomas Pinson	50	M			M	Va	March	Farmer	Typhoid	4 weeks
32	Iverson Pinson	15					Tenn	Jan		Typhoid	2 weeks
33	Paralee	8	F	B	S		Tenn	Feb		S. fever	3 days
34	Mary C. Giles	20	F			M	Tenn	Sept		Inflamation of brain	3 days
35	Frances E. McAdoo	6	F				Tenn	Aug		Pneumonia	3 months

COUNTY OF CARTER, STATE OF TENNESSEE.

PAGE NO. 65 PERSONS WHO DIED DURING THE YEAR ENDING 1st JUNE, 1850.

10th Civil District
2nd Subdivision

No. of Visit	Name	Age	Sex	Color	Free or Slave	Married/Widowed	Place of Birth	Month Died	Occupation	Disease or Cause of Death	No. Days Ill
1	Orpha Jane Pierce	4	F	W	F	S	Tenn	March		Rheumatic	20 days
2	Joshua Frazier	75	M	W	F	M	S.C.	Sept-24	Farmer	unknown	5 years
3	Isaac Garland	1da	M	W	F	S	Tenn	June-1		unknown	1 hour
4	William Miller	11	M	W	F	S	Va	March		Dropsy	3 years
5	Rhoda Williams, Sr.	64	F	W	F	M	N.C.	May-1		Consumption	24 years
6	Mary Buckles	1da	F	W	F	S	Tenn	Oct-20		unknown	1 day

COUNTY OF CARTER, STATE OF TENNESSEE.

PAGE NO. 67 PERSONS WHO DIED DURING THE YEAR ENDING 1st JUNE, 1850.

9th Civil District

No. of Visit	Name	Age	Sex	Color	Free or Slave	Married/Widowed	Place of Birth	Month Died	Occupation	Disease or Cause of Death	No. Days Ill
1	William Thomas	1m	M	W	F		Tenn	July		unknown	1 day
2	James R. Crow	1m	M	W	F		Tenn	May		Croup	1 hour
3	Thomas Jenkins	28	M	W	F		Tenn	July	Farmer	T. fever	20 days

COUNTY OF CARTER, STATE OF TENNESSEE.

PAGE NO. 69 PERSONS WHO DIED DURING THE YEAR ENDING 1st JUNE, 1850.

8th Civil District
2nd Subdivision

No. of Visit	Name	Age	Sex	Color	Free or Slave	Married/Widowed	Place of Birth	Month Died	Occupation	Disease or Cause of Death	No. Days Ill
1	Joseph S. Humphries	1m	M	W	F	S	Tenn	7-27-49	none	unknown	10 days
2	Editha Hendrix	32	F	W	F	M	Tenn	10-15-49	____	Consumption	7 months
3	Eliza S. Houston	4	F	W	F	S	Tenn	9- -49	____	T. fever	7 days

COUNTY OF CARTER, STATE OF TENNESSEE.

PAGE NO. 71 PERSONS WHO DIED DURING THE YEAR ENDING 1st JUNE, 1850.

6th Civil District

No. of Visit	Name	Age	Sex	Color	Free or Slave	Married/Widowed	Place of Birth	Month Died	Occupation	Disease or Cause of Death	No. Days Ill
1	George Smith	72	M	W	F	M	N.C.	5-29-50	Farmer	unknown	4 weeks
2	Novilla M. Taylor	1m	F	W	F	S	Tenn	8- -49		Diarrhea	3 weeks
3	Clara Taylor	16	F	B	S	S	Tenn	10- -49		Typhoid	3 weeks
4	Margaret A. Taylor	19	F	W	F	S	Tenn	8- -49		Typhoid	3 weeks
5	Emaline Range	18	F	W	F	S	Tenn	7- -49		Typhoid	8 days
6	Enos McFall's child	—	M	W	F	S	Tenn	4- -50		Still born	
7	Eve Edens	73	F	W	F	M	N.C.	8- -50		Neuralgia	1 day
8	James W. Kite	24	M	W	F	M	Tenn	7- -49	Mex.Soldier	unknown	2 weeks
9	Eliza J. Cooper	13	F	W	F	S	Tenn	8- -49		T. fever	14 days

COUNTY OF CARTER, STATE OF TENNESSEE.

PAGE NO. 73 PERSONS WHO DIED DURING THE YEAR ENDING 1st JUNE, 1850.

7th Civil District

No. of Visit	Name	Age	Sex	Color	Free or Slave	Married/Widowed	Place of Birth	Month Died	Occupation	Disease or Cause of Death	No. Days Ill
1	William S. Smith	28m	M	W	F		Carter Co. TN	9- -49	none	Pneumonia	16 days
2	Mariah (C.H.Fitzmond)	26	F	M	S		Carter Co. TN	4- -50		Fever	60 days
3	Alford M. Carter	65	M	W	F		Carter Co. TN	5- 5-50	Iron manuf.	Epilepsy	15 years
4	Albert King	1m	M	W	F		Carter Co. TN	4- -50	none	Liver	3 days
5	James A. Tipton	22	M	W	F		Carter Co. TN	8-27-49	Farmer	Fever	23 days
6	Benjamin White	21	M	W	F		Carter Co. TN	5- 9-50	Hammerman	Pneumonia	65 days
7	Loucinda Jackson	25	F	W	F		Carter Co. TN	2- 8-50		Consumption	6 months
8	Nancy Ann Jackson	6m	F	W	F		Carter Co. TN	2- 7-50		Consumption	6 months

Remarks: I have 1 st since I commenced taking the Census seven weeks time on account of the sickness in my own family, my father having died on the 2nd and my dear daughter on the 26th day of September last (aged 15 years & 9 months).
(Refer to 1st page in this District) I had another desire with Cora and one born 31st Oct 1850.
C. W. Nelson, Assistant Marshal

COUNTY OF CARTER, STATE OF TENNESSEE.

PAGE NO. 75 PERSONS WHO DIED DURING THE YEAR ENDING 1st JUNE, 1850.

4th Civil District
2nd Subdivision

No. of Visit	Name	Age	Sex	Color	Free or Slave	Married/Widowed	Place of Birth	Month Died	Occupation	Disease or Cause of Death	No. Days Ill
1	George W. Dunkin	30	M	W	F	M	Tenn	4- -50	Christian Minister	Scrofula	2 years
2	Ann Britt	45	F	W	F	M	N.C.	5- -50	none	Cold	9 weeks
3	John Helton	80	M	W	F	M	N.C.	4- -50	Farmer	Consumption	2 years

COUNTY OF CARTER, STATE OF TENNESSEE.

PAGE NO. 77 PERSONS WHO DIED DURING THE YEAR ENDING 1st JUNE, 1850.

5th Civil District
2nd Subdivision

No. of Visit	Name	Age	Sex	Color	Free or Slave	Married/Widowed	Place of Birth	Month Died	Occupation	Disease or Cause of Death	No. Days Ill
1	Martha Rowe	1	F	W	F	S	Tenn	6- -50	none	Worms	3 days
2	C.P.Bereman's child	1da	M	W	F	S	Tenn	8- -49		unknown	
3	Rhoda Britt	5m	F	W	F	S	Tenn	8- -49		Whooping cough	6 weeks
4	Thomas Lyle	1m	M	W	F	S	Tenn	5- -50		unknown	3 weeks
5	Margarete J. Buck	1	F	W	F	S	Tenn	9- -49		Croup	7 days
6	Henry Carroll	18	M	W	F	S	Tenn	7- -49	Farmer	Chronic	12 days
7	Edmund H. Boyd	20m	M	W	F	S	Tenn	7- -49		Cholera infantum	3 days
8	Tom Tipton	70	M	B	S	—	Tenn	5- -50		unknown	3 days
9	Elizabeth Humphries	2m	F	W	F	—	Tenn	5- -50		unknown	3 days

Page 79 CARTER COUNTY, 3rd District Blank

COUNTY OF CARTER, STATE OF TENNESSEE.

PAGE NO. 81 PERSONS WHO DIED DURING THE YEAR ENDING 1st JUNE, 1850.

2nd Civil District

No. of Visit	Name	Age	Sex	Color	Free or Slave	Married/Widowed	Place of Birth	Month Died	Occupation	Disease or Cause of Death	No. Days Ill
1	Jacob Snider	45	M	W	F	M	Tenn	7- 4-49	Farmer	Fever	4 weeks
2	Tilton Sheffield	22	M	W	F	S	Tenn	7- 1-49		Fever	11 days
3	Martha J. Evins	21	F	W	F	S	Tenn	11- -49	Hireling (In N. Snider Family)	Cold	25 days
4	Michael Snider	1m	M	W	F	S	Tenn	2- -50	none	Croup	1 day
5	Margaret S. Snider	6	F	W	F	S	Tenn	7- -49		Croup	21 days
6	Finley Smith	20	M	W	F	S	Tenn	7- -49	Farmer	T. fever	11 days
7	Jackson Smith	17	M	W	F	S	Tenn	7- -49	Farmer	T. fever	12 days
8	Hila Smith	28	F	W	F	S	Tenn	7- -49	Farmer	T. fever	10 days
9	James Smith	26	M	W	F	M	Tenn	8- -49	Farmer	T. fever	15 days
10	Jacob Smith	54	M	W	F	M	Tenn	8- -49	Farmer	Palsy	9 years
11	Thomas Campbell	56	M	W	F	M	N.C.	4-29-50	Farmer	Cholic	17 days
12	Delila Julian	33	F	W	F	S	Tenn	9-28-49		Cold	6 days
13	Jonathan Cantrell	40	M	W	F	S	N.C.	6- -49	none	T. fever	10 days
14	Sarah Miller	30	F	W	F	M	Tenn	8- -49		T. fever	7 days
15	Adam Miller	12	M	W	F	S	Tenn	- -49		T. fever	18 days
16	Thomas Ingram	1m	M	W	F	S	Tenn	12- -49		Whooping cough	14 days
17	B. Nancy A. Ingram	7	F	W	F	S	Tenn	4-20-50		Drowned	sudden

Page 83
CARTER COUNTY, 1st Civil District

No. of Visit	Name	Age	Sex	Color	Free or Slave	Married/Widowed	Place of Birth	Month Died	Occupation	Disease or Cause of Death	No. Days Ill
1	Landon P. Moorland	3	M	W	F	S	Carter Co. TN	12- 2-49	none	White swelling	22 days
2	Lawson H. White	33	M	W	F	M	Carter Co. TN	10-27-49	none	Typhoid fever	5 weeks

COUNTY OF CLAIBORNE, STATE OF TENNESSEE.

PAGE NO. 85 PERSONS WHO DIED DURING THE YEAR ENDING 1st JUNE, 1850.

7th Subdivision

No. of Visit	Name	Age	Sex	Color	Free or Slave	Married/Widowed	Place of Birth	Month Died	Occupation	Disease or Cause of Death	No. Days Ill
1	Emeline Mullins	6	F				Tenn	March		Cold	C(100 da)
2	Jane Cloud	64	F			W	N.C.	April		Dropsy	C(100 da)
3	Joshua Davis	87	M			W	Maryland	Aug	none	Old age	
4	Ephraim	35	M	B	S		Tenn	March		Dropsy of the heart	40 days
5	Bethena	30	F	B	S		Va	Sept		Cold	C(100 da)
6	Betsy	1	F	M	S		Tenn	Nov		Whooping cough	10 days
7	John Maden	13	M				Tenn	Jan		unknown	C(100 da)
8	Nancy Webb	80	F			W	Va	May		Old age	
9	Mary Brooks	2m	F				Tenn	Dec		Croup	5 days
10	Elizabeth Hodges	85	F			M	Va	Dec		Old age	
11	Flemming Hodges	85	M			W	Va	Jan	none	Old age	
12	Olly Hodges	25	F			M	Tenn	Jan		Child birth	1 day
13	John Willis	5m	M				Tenn	March		unknown	14 days
14	Lewis M. Lynch	5m	M				Tenn	Jan		unknown	21 days
15	Elizabeth Sims	77	F			M	unknown	Sept		Old age	
16	McKinney Dooly	20	M			M	Tenn	May	Farmer	Fever	16 days
17	Eliza Wilson	23	F	M?		(M)	Tenn	Feb	Farmer	Fever	14 days
18	James W. Thompson	2	M				Tenn	Dec		Cancer	C(100 da)
19	William J. Belamy	20	M				Va	July	Laborer	Fever	15 days
20	Sarah Hodges	68	F			W	Tenn	Nov		Scrofula	C(100 da)
21	James C. Neil	18	M				Tenn	Nov	Farmer	Fever	21 days
22	David Chadwell	1	M				Tenn	May		Whooping cough	28 days

COUNTY OF CLAIBORNE, STATE OF TENNESSEE.

PAGE NO. 85 PERSONS WHO DIED DURING THE YEAR ENDING 1st JUNE, 1850.

7th Subdivision

No. of Visit	Name	Age	Sex	Color	Free or Slave	Married/Widowed	Place of Birth	Month Died	Occupation	Disease or Cause of Death	No. Days Ill
23	David McMahan	2m	M				Tenn	April		Whooping cough	14 days
24	Berton Southern	28	M				Tenn	Nov		unknown	8 days
25	Emily Hurst	2	F				Tenn	Dec		Burn	2 days
26	Bird Bussell	30	M			M	Va	March	Farmer	Drowned	____
27	George McHenry	19	M				Tenn	July		Affected from ch'hood, mentally & physically	
28	Joseph Hamilton	77	M			M	Ireland	July	Physician	Accident	____
29	Sarah Hamilton	88	F			W	N.C.	Sept		Old age	
30	Mary	38	F	B	S		Tenn	May		Dropsy	C(100 da)
31	Mary Epps	1	F				Tenn	March		Whooping cough	C(100 da)
32	Jim	1	F	M	S		Tenn	July		____	18 days
33	Susan Mays	65	F			W	Va	____		Dropsy	C(100 da)

Remarks: There is no disease known as an endemic of the region. Epidemic occassionally prevail. The principal of which is Dysentry. The great majority of cases of disease or sporadic: Pneumonia, Pleuricy, acute Rheumatism, and pseudo remittent fever. At particular spots on Rivers, pure intermittent and remittent fevers sometimes make their appearance in these years 1843-4-5 & 6. Typhoid Fever prevailed in 48 extensively.   George U. Cheek.

COUNTY OF CLAIBORNE, STATE OF TENNESSEE.

PAGE NO. 89 PERSONS WHO DIED DURING THE YEAR ENDING 1st JUNE, 1850.

7th Subdivision
E. District

No. of Visit	Name	Age	Sex	Color	Free or Slave	Married/Widowed	Place of Birth	Month Died	Occupation	Disease or Cause of Death	No. Days Ill
1	Charity Lane	1	F				Tenn	April		Whooping cough	14 days
2	Elizabeth Campbell	1	F				Tenn	May		unknown	1 day
3	Lucy N. Mise	27	F	M	F		Tenn	March		Fever	9 days
4	Samuel Wilson	38	M	M	F		Tenn	Feb	Farmer	Fever	13 days
5	Susan Wilson	17	F	M	F		Tenn	Feb		Fever	9 days
6	Levi Dobkins	18	M				Tenn	Sept	Laborer	unknown	6 days
7	Alexander Easter	9m	M				Tenn	April		Inflamation of liver	
8	Ananias Lyford	3m	M				Tenn	Oct		Croup	C(100 da)
9	Catharine Williams	36	F			M	Tenn	July		Consumption	C(100 da)
10	Jim	1	M	B	S		Tenn	Jan		unknown	14 days
11	Jacob Shaver	35	M				Va	May	Farmer	Indigestion	C(100 da)
12	Robert M. Ford	2m	M				Tenn	Dec		sudden	____
13	Juda Brock	65	F			W	unknown	July		Dropsy	C(100 da)
14	Penelope Mise	65	F	M	F	M	N.C.	Feb		Scrofula	25 days
15	Braxton Mise	25	M	M	F		N.C.	April	Farmer	Fever	20 days
16	John Owsley	28	M			M	Tenn	March	Farmer	Fever	9 days
17	James Mirse	65	M			M	N.C.	April	Farmer	unknown	4 days
18	Peny Sharp	9	F				Tenn	Sept		Fever	25 days
19	Franklin Berry	3m	M				Tenn	Aug		Croup	6 days
20	Tme	16	M	B	S		Tenn	Aug		Fever	9 days
21	Milly Brogans	22	F				Tenn	Aug		Fever	21 days
22	Henry Sharp	24	M				Tenn	Aug	Farmer	Fever	6 days
23	Luvicy Sharp	9	F				Tenn	Oct		Pleurisy	5 days
24	William Savage	84	M			M	N.C.	Oct	none	unknown	14 days
25	Jeremiah Eastridge	36	M			M	Tenn	April	Farmer	Cold	C(100 da)
26	Lewis	1	M	B	S		Tenn	March		Whooping cough	14 days
27	Louiza Jones	3	F				Tenn	March		Whooping cough	21 days
28	Harvy L. Goin	2	M				Va	March		Whooping cough	22 days
29	Charles	1	M				Tenn	Oct		Cholera morbus	7 days

COUNTY OF CLAIBORNE, STATE OF TENNESSEE.

PAGE NO. 89 PERSONS WHO DIED DURING THE YEAR ENDING 1st JUNE, 1850.

No. of Visit	Name	Age	Sex	Color	Free or Slave	Married/Widowed	Place of Birth	Month Died	Occupation	Disease or Cause of Death	No. Days Ill
30	Thomas Bruce	81	M			M	N.C.	Dec	Farmer	Rheumatism	C(100 da)
31	Rhoda Profit	2	F				Tenn	March		Fever	30 days
32	William Bowman	52	M			W	Tenn	Aug	Farmer	Fever	21 days
33	Tabitha Drummons	64	F			W	unknown	July		Palsy	5 days

Remarks: In the spring of 1850, a very fatal disease prevailed in a portion of the County, particularly among some free persons of color. The name of the disease, I have been unable to learn but presume it to have been Typhoid Fever. The carbonate of lime prodominates over every other mineral, in most of its various forms. Some Mountain ranges appear to be comprised principally of sandstone. The ores of

COUNTY OF CLAIBORNE, STATE OF TENNESSEE.

PAGE NO. 92 PERSONS WHO DIED DURING THE YEAR ENDING 1st JUNE, 1850.

7th Subdivision of E. District

No. of Visit	Name	Age	Sex	Color	Free or Slave	Married/Widowed	Place of Birth	Month Died	Occupation	Disease or Cause of Death	No. Days Ill
1	Smith Wilson	9m	M				Kentucky	Sept		Cholera morbus	9 days
2	Martha Laforce	2	F				Tenn	Sept		Cholera infantum	
3	Elizabeth Hays	31	F			M	unknown	Dec		unknown	4 days
4	William Johnson	38	M			M	Tenn	April		Fever	21 days
5	James W. Norton	2m	M				Tenn	Nov		Scrofula	4 days
6	Mary Lamar	44	F				Tenn	March		unknown	6 days
7	Alexander T. Hooper	10	M				Tenn	Jan		Disease of the bowels	10 days
8	Campbell A. Venable	10m	M				Tenn	June		Croup	6 days
9	David Huddleston	85	M			M	unknown	Dec		Old age	
10	Robert Southern	38	M			M	Tenn	Dec		Operation of the Knee joint	3 days

Remarks: (continued) lead is found sparingly, and some preparation of zinc fructiferous came sulphurite of ____ has been observed in this County. The grains resembling those of wheat. Spring of the purest limestone are found in great abundance. There are also a great number of mineral springs, some chalybeate and some sulphur wells are very scarce in the County, perhaps not more than a half dozen in the whole County. The soil is generally fertile but exceedingly mountainous.

COUNTY OF COCKE, STATE OF TENNESSEE.

PAGE NO. 93 PERSONS WHO DIED DURING THE YEAR ENDING 1st JUNE, 1850.

District No. 11

No. of Visit	Name	Age	Sex	Color	Free or Slave	Married/Widowed	Place of Birth	Month Died	Occupation	Disease or Cause of Death	No. Days Ill
1	Agnes Hampton	74	F			M	Va	Sept	Pauper	Old age	2 weeks
2	Nancy	3	F	B	S		Tenn	Feb		Croup	3 days
3	George	7	M	B	S		Tenn	March		Croup	1 week
4	Henry F. Carmichael	17	M				Tenn	Nov	Laborer	Inf. of brain and chills	6 weeks
5	Susan Carmichael	13	F				Tenn	Nov		Chills and fever	2 months
6	Benjamin D. Clark	27	M			M	Tenn	Nov	Farmer	Inflamation of kidneys	3 weeks
7	Jaily Palmer	13	F				Tenn	March		Congestive fever	2 days
8	Rachel D. Bulman	4m	F				N.C.	March		Bold hives	9 days
9	Sarah A. Ellis	16	F				Tenn	Nov		Pneumonia	4 days
10	Martin Kelly	11m	M				Tenn	March		Whooping cough	1 month
11	Isaac	1	M	B	S		Tenn	Jan		Worms	5 days
12	William Davis	1m	M				Tenn	Nov		unknown	3 weeks
13	Mary Castello	38	F			M	Tenn	Feb		Consumption	C(100 da)
14	William Davis, Sr.	50	M			M	Tenn	Aug	Laborer	Cramp Cholic	1 day
15	William V. Rodey	52	M			W	Tenn	March	Farmer	Pneumonia	3 weeks
16	Uriah Walden	50	M			M	unknown	Aug	Laborer	Cong. fever	2 days
17	Henry Wise	1m	M				Tenn	Feb		unknown	1 week
18	unnamed Nes	2	F				Tenn	Aug		Chills	1 week
19	James	55	M	B	S		Va	Aug		Apoplexy	sudden
20	unnamed Nes	1m	F				Tenn	Nov		Fits	7 days
21	unnamed Nes	1m	F				Tenn	Nov		Fits	9 days
22	Moses Linebarger	1m	M				Tenn	Sept		Croup	3 days
23	Christopher Blazer	47	M			M	Tenn	March	Farmer	Cancer	C(100 da)
24	Jacob Ottinger	66	M			M	Va	Nov	Farmer	Dec. Storm	2 months
25	Dolly A. Shepherd	5	F				Tenn	Jan		Inflamation of brain	1 week
26	Nancy Kelly	28	F			M	Tenn	Feb		unknown	sudden
27	Marion North	1	M				Tenn	Feb		Dropsy	C(100 da)
28	Crawford Epps	4m	M	B			Tenn	Feb		Disease of head	2 weeks
29	William Epps	2	M	M			Tenn	March		Fever	2 weeks
30	Lavina Lillard	2	F				Tenn	Sept		Fever	4 weeks
31	John Padget	2	M				Tenn	July		Fever	1 week
32	Matilda Harrison	4	F				Tenn	June		Scarlet fever	1 week
33	Sarah Dennis	1m	F				Tenn	Feb		Hives	1 day
34	unnamed McMahan	1da	F				Tenn	Dec		unknown	1 day
35	Jacob Webb	2	M				Tenn	May		..(illegible)..	2 weeks

Remarks: The County may be divided into two Districts, the high and the lowlands. The highlands are mountainous and healthy. The lowlands lie upon the Nolichucky and French Broad Rivers and are not so healthy, but very productive. Perhaps more so than any other portion of East Tennessee. The principal crop is Indian corn which the farmers feed to swine and horses for southern market.

COUNTY OF COCKE, STATE OF TENNESSEE.

PAGE NO. 96 PERSONS WHO DIED DURING THE YEAR ENDING 1st JUNE, 1850.

District No. 11

No. of Visit	Name	Age	Sex	Color	Free or Slave	Married/Widowed	Place of Birth	Month Died	Occupation	Disease or Cause of Death	No. Days Ill
1	William C. Broadman	65	M			W	Va	Aug	Merchant	Organic disease of heart	7 months
2	Thomas	10m	M	B	S		Tenn	March		unknown	6 months
3	Simon	1	M	B	S		Tenn	May		Diarrhea	2 months
4	unchristened	1m	M	B	S		Tenn	May		unknown	1 month
5	unchristened	2m	F	B	S		Tenn	May		Erysipelas	10 days
6	unchristened	1m	F	B	S		Tenn	Aug		unknown	1 day
7	Mahala	10	F	B	S		Tenn	Sept		Eating dirt	C(100 da)
8	Willis	52	M	B	S		Va	Jan		Pneumonia	10 days
9	Hector	57	M	B	S		Va	Nov		unknown	C(100 da)
10	Nancy Davis	45	F			W	N.C.	Dec		Pleurisy	1 month
11	Eliza Green	24	F				N.C.	July		Consumption	1 year
12	Jos. Anderson	14	M				Tenn	May		Liver complaint	C(100 da)
13	James Fenchem	2	M				Tenn	Sept		Croup	2 days
14	Mary O'Dell	69	F			W	Va	Jan		Old age	
15	Phebe Click	43	F			M	Tenn	Sept		Liver complaint	C(100 da)
16	Barbary Lotspeich	94	F			W	Va	May		Old age	
17	Elizabeth A. Hall	20	F				Tenn	Sept		Congestive chills	3 days
18	Anthony H. Cody	9m	M				Tenn	July		Cholera infantum	4 days
19	Lanten Beard	7m	M				Tenn	Nov		Chills	10 days
20	Matilda Finchem	38	F			M	S.C.	Jan		____ Albus	1 year
21	Sukey	65	F	B	S		Tenn	Jan		Pneumonia	10 weeks
22	John	9m	M	B	S		Tenn	May		Whooping cough	2 weeks
23	Wesley	19	M	B	S		Tenn	Sept		Congestive fever	1 week
24	Minerva	25	F	B	S		Tenn	Aug		Congestive fever	1 week
25	James Gray	39	M			M	Tenn	June	Farmer	Intemperance	C(100 da)
26	Amos Finney	2	M				Tenn	Nov		Croup	sudden
27	Delania Wood	30	F			M	Tenn	Jan		Child birth	1 day
28	William Romion(?)	4	M				Tenn	Jan		Croup	3 days
29	Dinah Allen	73	F	B			Va	May		Old age	C(100 da)
30	Sarah Hickey	38	F			M	Tenn	May		Pneumonia	9 days
31	unchristened, Lane	1m	F				Tenn	July		unknown	1 week
32	unchristened, Cole	1m	F				Tenn	July		unknown	1 day
33	John Rose	14	M				Tenn	March		unknown	3 days
34	Nancy Lewis	27	F			M	Tenn	May		Child birth	10 weeks
35	Sarah McLanhan	1da	F				Tenn	Aug		unknown	1 day

Remarks: The year ending 1st June 1850 was a healthy year compared with others proceeding it. The County of Cocke though not an unhealthy district is not so healthy as other portions of East Tennessee. The most common disease, chills and fever. The most fatal has, of late years, been congestive fever. The ____ typhoid fever and pneumonia also occassionally appear. I know of no local cause.

COUNTY OF COCKE, STATE OF TENNESSEE.

PAGE NO. 97 PERSONS WHO DIED DURING THE YEAR ENDING 1st JUNE, 1850.

District No. 11

No. of Visit	Name	Age	Sex	Color	Free or Slave	Married/Widowed	Place of Birth	Month Died	Occupation	Disease or Cause of Death	No. Days Ill
1	Mary	18	F	B	S		Tenn	Jan		Child birth	8 days
2	unnamed	1m	F	B	S		Tenn	Jan		unknown	2 days
3	Polly Faubian	39	F			M	Tenn	July		Child birth	1 day
4	unnamed, Faubian	1da	F				Tenn	July		unknown	1 day
5	unnamed, Faubian	1da	F				Tenn	July		unknown	1 day
6	Sarah Mantooth	6	F				Tenn	April		Whooping cough, effect of	3 years
7	Sarah	1m	F	B	S		Tenn	Nov		unknown	sudden
8	unchristened	1m	F	B	S		Tenn	Aug		unknown	sudden
9	Didannia McNabb	1	F				Tenn	Dec		Burned	3 weeks
10	George Praisewaters	7	M				Tenn	Oct		Croup	2 days
11	Robert Cooper	88	M			W	Penn	Oct	Farmer	Old age & hurt	1 week
12	Sarah Moore	6m	F				Tenn	Oct		unknown	1 week
13	Jos. H. Blazer	3	M				Tenn	Oct		Scarlet fever	5 days
14	James Clark	15	M				Tenn	July	Farmer	T. fever	2 weeks
15	Jane Clark	5	F				Tenn	March		Worms	1 week
16	Polly Guilliams	35	F			M	N.C.	June		Child birth	1 week
17	Thomas J. Guilliams	5m	M				Tenn	Oct		unknown	5 months
18	Albert H. Wittenburg	15	M				Tenn	May	Farmer	Inflamation of brain	3 days
19	Henry C. Scott	7	M				Tenn	April		Inflamation of brain	1 day
20	Jos. Menary	21	M				N.C.	June	Laborer	Consumption	C9100 da)
21	John Nichols	17	M				Tenn	Nov	Laborer	Fever of brain	3 days
22	Caroline Nichols	11	F				Tenn	Dec		Fever of brain	4 days
23	Stephen Stokley	3	M				Tenn	Feb		Burned	1 day
24	Nancy Williams	4	F				Tenn	April		Worms	2 days
25	John Price	1m	M				Tenn	March		Liver	C(100 da)

Remarks: Iron ore is abundant in the mountains and water power is almost without limit.
The principal rocks are the blue and black limestone and mountain boulders. There
are fine forests of white pine and the black pine is a common growth. The first
settlement was made about the close of the Revolution. The County has no commerce
by water. Driving and hauling are an only means of exchanging our staples for
articles of consumption.

COUNTY OF COFFEE, STATE OF TENNESSEE.

PAGE NO. 99 PERSONS WHO DIED DURING THE YEAR ENDING 1st JUNE, 1850.

District 5th & 2nd

No. of Visit	Name	Age	Sex	Color	Free or Slave	Married/Widowed	Place of Birth	Month Died	Occupation	Disease or Cause of Death	No. Days Ill
1	S. A. N. Barton	1	F				Tenn	Nov		Croup	4 days
2	Angeline	4	F	B	S		N.C.	May		Fits	sudden
3	Mary Stone	58	F			M	S.C.	Feb		Dropsy	sudden
4	Virginia Smith	8m	F				Tenn	Feb		Fits	sudden
5	Jenny	60	F	B	S		N.C.	Aug		unknown	C(100 da)
6	John Anthony	1m	M				Tenn	Oct		unknown	sudden
7	Robert	10m	M	B	S		Tenn	Sept		Teething	6 weeks
8	Thomas Blanton	1m	M				Tenn	Sept		Croup	1 day
9	Nancy Ann Lee	84	F			M	Va	Aug		Old age	1 week
10	Nancy Keele	70	F			M	New York	Nov		unknown	C(100 da)
11	Nancy J. Roach	10m	F				Tenn	Dec		Erysipelas	21 days
12	Cilla	7m	F	B	S		Tenn	April		unknown	6 weeks
13	William	3m	M	B	S		Tenn	Feb		unknown	sudden
14	Bob	70	M	B	S		N.C.	Dec		Old age	1 year

COUNTY OF COFFEE, STATE OF TENNESSEE.

PAGE NO. 99   PERSONS WHO DIED DURING THE YEAR ENDING 1st JUNE, 1850.

District 5th & 2nd

No. of Visit	Name	Age	Sex	Color	Free or Slave	Married/Widowed	Place of Birth	Month Died	Occupation	Disease or Cause of Death	No. Days Ill
15	Candes	38	F	B	S		Tenn	Aug		Scrofula	C(100 da)
16	Caroline	20	F	B	S		Tenn	Aug		Scrofula	5 years
17	Lucinda	16	F	B	S		Tenn	Aug		Scrofula	6 years
18	Bob	6	M	B	S		Tenn	Nov		Measles	7 days
19	Ned	63	M	B	S		S.C.	Nov		Consumption	C(100 da)
20	Elizabeth Dunkin	43	F			M	Tenn	Aug		Fever	1 month
21	Eliza	34	F	B	S		Va	April		unknown	6 days
22	Martha Ann	11m	F				Tenn	Feb		Fever	42 days
23	Elizabeth	6	F				Tenn	Aug		unknown	8 days
24	William Wilson	60	M			M	N.C.	Aug	Farmer	unknown	sudden
25	Henry	3	M	B	S		Tenn	July		T. fever	40 days
26	Mariah	40	F	B	S		Tenn	Oct		Consumption	8 days
27	Child	1m	F	B	S		Tenn	March		unknown	sudden
28	Child	1m	M	B	S		Tenn	July		unknown	sudden
29	Catharine Messic	2	F				Tenn	July		T. fever	21 days
30	Mucy Ann Messic	10m	F				Tenn	July		unknown	6 days
31	Adam Raburn	53	M			M	Va	Aug	Farmer	unknown	C(100 da)
32	George Raburn	2m	M	B	S		Tenn	Dec		smothered	sudden
33	Alston Hart	8	M				Tenn	Jan		Inflamation of brain	4 days
34	Jeremiah Lawrence	70	M			W	Va	April		Old age	C(100 da)
35	Amanda Jones	2m	F				Tenn	March		Hives	10 days

Remarks: No malady of a particular character. Limestone water is most abundant. The soil is of a black loamy character. Well adapted to the growth of hemp, corn, clover, blue grass & etc. Limestone rocks with a greatest of small free stone gravel. The natural growth of the timber is oak, ash, beech, poplar, walnut, hickory, maple, elm and etc.

COUNTY OF COFFEE, STATE OF TENNESSEE.

PAGE NO. 102   PERSONS WHO DIED DURING THE YEAR ENDING 1st JUNE, 1850.

Civil District 1st, 3rd, 4th & 6th

No. of Visit	Name	Age	Sex	Color	Free or Slave	Married/Widowed	Place of Birth	Month Died	Occupation	Disease or Cause of Death	No. Days Ill
1	Sarah Ann Ragsdale	29	F			W	Tenn	July		Consumption	3 years
2	Elizabeth Stephens	75	F			W	Va	June		Dropsy	1 year
3	Mary Floyd	19	F				Tenn	Aug		Fever	7 days
4	Elizabeth Floyd	19	F				Tenn	Aug		Fever	7 days
5	Amanda Teal	19	F			M	N.C.	May		unknown	3 weeks
6	Sarah Barnes	2	F				Tenn	Jan		Inflamation of brain	16 days
7	Emily Butler	40	F			M	N.C.	Aug		T. fever	13 days
8	John W. Butler	2	M				Tenn	Dec		Worms	5 weeks
9	Esther Carlisle	16	F				Ga	March		Fever	3 weeks
10	Nancy Carlisle	18	F				Ga	April		Fever	10 days
11	Mary A. Littleton	64	F				S.C.	Jan		Dropsy	1 year
12	John F. Burks	24	M				Tenn	Dec	Farmer	unknown	18 months
13	Artemucia Owens	2m	F				Tenn	March		Croup	1 month
14	Luther Johnson	28	M			M	unknown	Aug	Carpenter	Accident	sudden
15	Calaway D. Howard	11	M				Tenn	March		Dropsy	15 days
16	Mary Walker	13	F				Tenn	Feb		Fever	6 days
17	John W. Miccols	4	M				Tenn	Oct		Burned	8 days
18	Edmond	55	M	B	S		Va	July		unknown	2 months
19	Esther	7	F	B	S		Tenn	Aug		T. fever	1 month
20	Francisca Emerson	3	F				Tenn	Oct		Disease of bowels	2 months
21	Tom	50	M	B	S		Va	Jan		Dropsy	3 months

COUNTY OF COFFEE, STATE OF TENNESSEE.

PAGE NO. 102 PERSONS WHO DIED DURING THE YEAR ENDING 1st JUNE, 1850.

Civil District 1st, 3rd, 4th & 6th

No. of Visit	Name	Age	Sex	Color	Free or Slave	Married/Widowed	Place of Birth	Month Died	Occupation	Disease or Cause of Death	No. Days Ill
22	Mary Tanner	20	F				Tenn	Oct		T. fever	21 days
23	John Tanner	54	M			M	N.C.	March	Farmer	Dropsy	1 year
24	Virginia Taylor	8m	F				Tenn	Aug		Worms	8 days
25	Tom	8m	M	B	S		Tenn	July		Accident	sudden
26	Elizabeth	5m	F	B	S		Tenn	Jan		Inflamation of brain	8 days
27	Delpha Powers	45	F			M	N.C.	July		SC of the womb	6 months
28	Nancy J. Parker	5m	F				Tenn	Nov		Hives	7 days
29	James Vaughan	11m	M				Tenn	April		Croup	2 days
30	Eliga Croslin	6m	M				Tenn	Oct		Hives	1 month
31	Malinda Runnells	6	F				Tenn	July		Croup	3 days
32	Horace Bates	16	M				Tenn	Dec	Farmer	Accident	sudden
33	Rebecca McLemore	86	F			W	N.C.	Feb		Palsy	10 years
34	John Jones	78	M			W	Va	Sept	Carpenter	Old age	10 days
35	William Gilbert	1	M				Tenn	Jan		Inflamation of brain	2 weeks

Remarks: The First, Third and Fourth Districts are well adapted to the growth, hemp, corn, clover, blue grass, herds grass, & etc. The soil is of a black rich character intermixed with small gravel (in places), a great deal of lime stone rocks, limestone water generally. The natural growth of the timber is oak, ash, beech, hickory, poplar, walnut, & etc. The 6th District is a poor barren County.

COUNTY OF COFFEE, STATE OF TENNESSEE.

PAGE NO. 103 PERSONS WHO DIED DURING THE YEAR ENDING 1st JUNE, 1850.

Civil District 11th, 7th & 12th

No. of Visit	Name	Age	Sex	Color	Free or Slave	Married/Widowed	Place of Birth	Month Died	Occupation	Disease or Cause of Death	No. Days Ill
1	James Baker	17	M				Tenn	Sept	Laborer	Fever	2 weeks
2	Molly	85	F	B	S		S.C.	July		Old age	2 weeks
3	Reuben	25	M	B	S		Tenn	Feb		Fits	3 weeks
4	Alfred	50	M	B	S		unknown	May		Spinal affliction	6 months
5	Priscilla	35	F	B	S		Tenn	Sept		Cold	7 days
6	Infant	8m	M	B	S		Tenn	July		unknown	sudden
7	Dolly Price	80	F			W	Va	June		Dropsy	3 weeks
8	Isaac	45	M	B	S		Va	Sept		T. fever	3 weeks
9	Winny	28	F	B	S		S.C.	Aug		T. fever	2 weeks
10	Mary	11	F	B	S		Tenn	Aug		T. fever	2 weeks
11	Peter	8	M	B	S		Tenn	Sept		T. fever	2 weeks
12	Joseph	6m	M	B	S		Tenn	Sept		T. fever	7 days
13	William Richardson	5m	M				Tenn	Oct		unknown	2 weeks
14	George W. Thompson	55	M			M	N.C.	Oct	Farmer	Gravel	9 days
15	John	2	M	B	S		Tenn	Nov		Poisoned	3 days
16	Henry Cash	18	M				Tenn	Oct	Farmer	T. fever	8 days
17	Mary Ann Levins	22	F			M	Tenn	Aug		T. fever	8 days
18	Infant "	1m	M				Tenn	Jan		unknown	10 days
19	James Harris	12	M				Tenn	June		T. fever	3 months
20	Thomas Cunningham	7	M				Tenn	June		unknown	7 weeks
21	Hamilton Runnells	27	M			M	Tenn	Jan	Pedler	T. fever	7 weeks
22	Nancy Runnells	18	F			M	Tenn	Jan		T. fever	7 days
23	Jesse Runnells	60	M			M	Va	Jan	Farmer	T. fever	9 days
24	Henry Runnells	23	M				Tenn	Jan	Pedler	T. fever	3 weeks
25	Lucinda Runnells	18	F				Tenn	Feb		T. fever	4 weeks
26	Sarah C. Austil	36	F			M	S.C.	Jan		T. fever	6 weeks

COUNTY OF COFFEE, STATE OF TENNESSEE.

PAGE NO. 103   PERSONS WHO DIED DURING THE YEAR ENDING 1st JUNE, 1850.

Civil District 11th, 7th & 12th

No. of Visit	Name	Age	Sex	Color	Free or Slave	Married/Widowed	Place of Birth	Month Died	Occupation	Disease or Cause of Death	No. Days Ill
27	Henry Inman	21	M				N.C.	July	Laborer	unknown	5 weeks
28	Jane	21	F	B	S		Tenn	June		T. fever	8 days
29	Judy	3m	F	M	S		Tenn	June		Diarrhea	2 weeks
30	Jedaziah Payne	36	M			M	Tenn	May	Farmer	Consumption	11 weeks
31	Haney	60	F	B	S		unknown	March		unknown	2 days
32	John B. Holland	39	M			M	Va	March	Wagon-mkr	Dysentery	3 months
33	John L. Howard	10m	M				Tenn	Oct		Hives	sudden
34	John Charles	21	M				Tenn	Feb	Farmer	unknown	10 days
35	Richard J. Charles	18	M				Tenn	Nov	Farmer	T. fever	5 weeks

COUNTY OF COFFEE, STATE OF TENNESSEE.

PAGE NO. 106   PERSONS WHO DIED DURING THE YEAR ENDING 1st JUNE, 1850.

Civil District 8th, 9th & 10th

No. of Visit	Name	Age	Sex	Color	Free or Slave	Married/Widowed	Place of Birth	Month Died	Occupation	Disease or Cause of Death	No. Days Ill
1	Rachael J. Charles	13	F				Tenn	Nov		T. fever	5 weeks
2	Martha C. Charles	8	F				Tenn	Oct		T. fever	2 months
3	Mary B. Charles	3	F				Tenn	Oct		T. fever	2 weeks
4	Joseph Burruss	31	M			M	Va	July	Farmer	T. fever	3 weeks
5	Mahala Charles	29	F			M	N.C.	Sept		T. fever	2 weeks
6	Johannah C. Burg	1m	F				Tenn	Oct		Cholera infantum	4 days
7	John J. Burroughs	24	M			M	Alabama	March	Merchant	T. fever	3 weeks
8	Eliza Philips	34	F			M	Tenn	Feb		Spinal disease	C(100 da)
9	Joseph Pay	75	M			W	N.C.	Sept	Farmer	Old age	10 days
10	Manerva J. Foster	1m	F				Tenn	April		Croup	2 days
11	Manerva E. Bowen	2	F				Tenn	Aug		unknown	5 days
12	Margarett Carter	42	F			M	Va	Jan		Child bearing	4 days
13	Cleopatra Lane	1	F				Tenn	Oct		Flux	6 weeks
14	Frances Sparkman	1	F				Tenn	Sept		Flux	4 weeks
15	Mariah	25	F	B	S		unknown	Jan		T. fever	2 months
16	William Douglass	4	M				Tenn	Sept		Flux	6 weeks
17	Lewis	21	M	B	S		unknown	Jan		Dropsy	1 month
18	J. K. Cunningham	5	M				Tenn	Aug		Flux	18 days
19	Rachael Harpole	6	F				Tenn	Sept		Flux	2 weeks
20	Martha A. Banks	2	F				Tenn	Dec		Croup	1 day
21	James J. S. Bryan	28	M				Tenn	Oct	Farmer	Accident	18 days
22	Sarah Bryan	68	F			M	N.C.	Dec		unknown	7 days
23	David Scott	1	M				Tenn	Nov		Hives	sudden
24	Thomas Lynn	39	M			M	Tenn	Sept	Farmer	Consumption	9 years
25	Andrew Lynn	44	M			M	Tenn	Jan	Farmer	Consumption	5 years

COUNTY OF DAVIDSON, STATE OF TENNESSEE.

PAGE NO. 108 PERSONS WHO DIED DURING THE YEAR ENDING 1st JUNE, 1850.

Middle Tennessee No. 45
Subdivision No. 2

No. of Visit	Name	Age	Sex	Color	Free or Slave	Married/Widowed	Place of Birth	Month Died	Occupation	Disease or Cause of Death	No. Days Ill
1	Oney	15	F	B	S		Va	July		Dropsy	C(100 da)
2	Infant	1m	M	B	S		Tenn	May		Croup	1 day
3	Peggy	24	F	B	S		Tenn	June		Cholera	9 days
4	Joseph H. Scales	22	M				Tenn	Sept	none	Consumption	C(100 da)
5	Henderson	25	M	B	S		Va	April		Affected heart	C(100 da)
6	Anthony	1	M	B	S		Tenn	April		Inflamation of lungs	3 months
7	Eliza	1	F	B	S		Arkansas	Aug		unknown	10 days
8	Ellen	2	F	B	S		Tenn	May		Worms	6 days
9	Hannah	80	F	B	S		Va	Aug		unknown	10 days
10	Martha	25	F	B	S		Tenn	July		Consumption	C(100 da)
11	Mary Bell	4	F				Tenn	Oct		Inflamation of brain	3 weeks
12	Mary Owen	10	F				Tenn	June		Lock jaw	7 days
13	Susan Hart	7m	F				Tenn	Dec		Dropsy of brain	1 week
14	Fredonia	5m	F	B	S		Tenn	Dec		Whooping cough	21 days
15	Infant	2da	F	B	S		Tenn	Jan		Croup	1 day
16	Joe	6m	M	B	S		Tenn	Aug		Teething	3 days
17	Celia Wheeler	3	F				Tenn	Oct		unknown	C(100 da)
18	Phillis	25	F	M	S		Tenn	June		Disease of the womb	C(100 da)
19	Nicey	95	F	B	S		Maryland	Aug		Bil. fever	6 weeks
20	Eliza	10m	F	B	S		Tenn	Nov		Teething	14 days
21	Labon	2	M	B	S		Tenn	Jan		Measles	C(100 da)
22	Nancy Rhodes	50	F			W	N.C.	July		Consumption	C(100 da)
23	Martha Nye	50	F			W	N.C.	Nov		Disease of the womb	C(100 da)
24	Amanda Fitzhugh	25	F			M	Tenn	July		Liver complaint	C(100 da)
25	Mary Laceville	25	F			M	N.C.	July		Dropsy	C(100 da)
26	Rosana Laceville	1	F				Tenn	July		Inflamation of brain	1 month
27	John Wesley	18	M				Tenn	June	Farmer	Fever	4 weeks
28	Elizabeth Gray	70	F				Va	Jan		Inflamation of lungs	3 weeks
29	Job P. Dews	29	M			M	Va	Aug	Farmer	Bil. fever	12 days
30	Sally	90	F	B	S		Maryland	Aug		Old age	C(100 da)
31	Infant	1	F	B	S		Tenn	June		Teething	1 week
32	Frank	50	M	B	S		Tenn	June		Cholera	1 day
33	Mary	8	F	B	S		Tenn	March		unknown	C(100 da)
34	Henry	2	M	B	S		Tenn	July		Whooping cough	1 month
35	Wesley	1	M	B	S		Tenn	Aug		Whooping cough	1 month

Remarks: In that portion of Davidson County allotted to me, the soil (except on the gravelly sides) is very productive and except in the immediate vicinity of Nashville, covered with fine timber, consisting of oak, hickory, ash, poplar, sugar trees and beech. The water is strong limestone and is almost in every section of the County good particularly on the small streams in the most broken portions of the County. Gray and blue limestone is very abundant and in some parts of the District sand stone suitable for building.

COUNTY OF DAVIDSON, STATE OF TENNESSEE.

PAGE NO. 110 PERSONS WHO DIED DURING THE YEAR ENDING 1st JUNE, 1850.

No. of Visit	Name	Age	Sex	Color	Free or Slave	Married/Widowed	Place of Birth	Month Died	Occupation	Disease or Cause of Death	No. Days Ill
1	Ephraim	1m	M	B	S		Tenn	Aug		Whooping cough	2 weeks
2	Ann M. Gale	8m	F				Miss	Aug		Inflamation of brain	12 days
3	Cloe	45	F	B	S		Tenn	Aug		Cholera	1 day
4	Infant	7da	F	B	S		Tenn	May		unknown	4 days
5	Betsey	22	F	B	S		Va	July		Child bed	8 days
6	Dick	7da	M	B	S		Tenn	July		unknown	7 days
7	Caroline	1	F	B	S		Tenn	July		Worms	1 week
8	John	6m	M	B	S		Tenn	July		Inflamation of stomach	10 days
9	Robert Boyd	80	M			M	Ireland	Aug	Farmer	Fall from horse	C(100 da)
10	Tempe	21	F	B	S		Tenn	Sept		Croup	2 days
11	Louis	1	M	B	S		Tenn	July		Cholera infantum	1 week
12	Virginia Hill	1	F				Tenn	Nov		Erysipelas	8 days
13	Washington Hill	34	M				Tenn	Jan	Farmer	Fall from horse	C(100 da)
14	Pender	7	F	B	S		Tenn	July		unknown	C(100 da)
15	Jeff	1	M	B	S		Tenn	Sept		Diarrhea	1 week
16	Johnson Vaughn	22	M				Tenn	Sept	Farmer	Bil. fever	10 days
17	Alexander Waites	56	M				N.C.	May	none	Dropsy	C(100 da)
18	Bartley	50	M	B	S		Maryland	May		Fall from horse	1 month
19	Jim	60	M	B	S		Va	March		Pneumonia	2 weeks
20	Tennessee Haskins	3	F				Tenn	Oct		unknown	C(100 da)
21	Sarah Haskins	4da	F				Tenn	Sept		Hives	1 day
22	Abraham	3m	M	B	S		Tenn	July		Inflamation of brain	2 days
23	Jim	90	M	B	S		N.C.	Aug		Old age	C(100 da)
24	Richard	48	M	B	S		Tenn	Dec		Bil. Diarrhea	3 days
25	Mary Taylor	25	F	B			Tenn	Nov		unknown	21 days
26	Job Dawson	53	M			M	Kentucky	April	Farmer	unknown	C(100 da)
27	Virginia Laskins	24	F			M	Tenn	March		Scrofula	C(100 da)
28	Paninah Redd	1m	F				Tenn	Dec		Hives	1 day
29	Catharine	10m	F	B	S		Tenn	Sept		Teething	14 days
30	Infant of J.E. Newsom	7da	M				Tenn	Aug		Croup	1 day
31	Infant of R. Jannett	7da	F				Tenn	March		Croup	4 days
32	Joe	1	M	B	S		Tenn	April		Dropsy	C(100 da)
33	Hannah Green	42	F			M	Tenn	June		Consumption	C(100 da)
34	Elisha Rhodes	77	M			W	N.C.	July	Farmer	Fever	15 days
35	Lewis	96	M	B	S		Va	Sept		Old age	C(100 da)

Remarks: No causes can be assigned for the prevailance of Typhoid Fever which is unusual here and quite fatal. Making its appearance in Towns, high and dry locations and on margin of streams as clear as crystal. A negro woman, thirty five or forty, gave birth to twins, one black and the other light. The children are about 8 years of age and healthy. The mother is a dark copper color. Gen. William G. Harding has in his park 200 deer and 5 buffalo.

COUNTY OF DAVIDSON, STATE OF TENNESSEE.

PAGE NO. 112 PERSONS WHO DIED DURING THE YEAR ENDING 1st JUNE, 1850.

No. of Visit	Name	Age	Sex	Color	Free or Slave	Married/Widowed	Place of Birth	Month Died	Occupation	Disease or Cause of Death	No. Days Ill
1	Aaron Jones	81	M			W	N.C.	Feb	Carpenter	Dropsy	C(100 da)
2	Jim	3	M	B	S		Tenn	Aug		unknown	C
3	Peter	3	M	B	S		Tenn	Aug		unknown	C
4	Mary	2	F	B	S		Tenn	Feb		Scrofula	C
5	Infant	7da	F	B	S		Tenn	May		Hives	3 days
6	Mana Wyatt	2m	F				Tenn	July		Cholera	1 day
7	Jane Perkins	47	F			M	Va	Sept		unknown	C
8	George L. Thornton	25	M			M	Tenn	March	Farmer	Consumption	C
9	Almeida	1	F	B	S		Tenn	July		Inflamation of bowels	3 weeks
10	Thomas	10m	M	B	S		Tenn	Sept		Whooping cough	1 week
11	Nancy	7da	F	B	S		Tenn	March		Lock jaw	1 day
12	Jamison	14	M	B	S		La	July		Dropsy	C
13	Adelaid	13	F	B	S		Tenn	Aug		Scrofula	C
14	Joe Henry	1m	M	B	S		Tenn	June		Lock jaw	2 days
15	Infant	1m	M	B	S		Tenn	June		Thrash	4 days
16	Infant	1m	F	B	S		Tenn	June		Lock jaw	1 day
17	Will	53	M	B	S		Va	May		Scrofula	C
18	Welborne	5m	M	B	S		Tenn	Nov		Burn	sudden
19	Clarissa	50	F	M	S		Tenn	Oct		Dropsy	C
20	Joseph W. Easley	25	M				Tenn	March	Farmer	Consumption	C
21	Infant	1m	M	B	S		Tenn	Oct		Croup	23 days
22	Tom	4	M	B	S		Miss	Dec		Burn	3 days
23	Kate	1	F	B	S		Miss	Nov		Croup	3 days
24	Lewis	55	M	M	S		Maryland	June		Cholera	1 day
25	Samuel Crocker	1	M				Tenn	June		Cholera	1 day
26	Nancy	9	F	B	S		Tenn	Dec		T. fever	1 month
27	Thomas Newbern	17	M				Tenn	July	Clerk	Cholera	1 day
28	Thomas Frensley	9m	M				Tenn	Sept		unknown	6 weeks
29	Sarah Corbit	32	F			M	Tenn	June		Cholera	1 day
30	Ansill Turbinville	40	M				S.C.	June	Farmer	Cholera	1 day
31	William Haley	1	M				Tenn	June		unknown	9 weeks
32	Sarah Chilton	5	F				Tenn	June		Cholera	1 day
33	William Cobbs	31	M			M	Va	June	Carpenter	Cholera	1 day
34	Willie Cobbs	7	F				Va	June		Cholera	1 day
35	Martha Cobbs	5	F				Tenn	June		Cholera	6 hours

COUNTY OF DAVIDSON, STATE OF TENNESSEE.

PAGE NO. 117 PERSONS WHO DIED DURING THE YEAR ENDING 1st JUNE, 1850.

No. of Visit	Name	Age	Sex	Color	Free or Slave	Married/Widowed	Place of Birth	Month Died	Occupation	Disease or Cause of Death	No. Days Ill
1	Hampton	25	M	B	S		Tenn	July		Cholera	1 day
2	George	40	M	B	S		Tenn	Nov		unknown	C(100 da)
3	Joseph Stewart	50	M			M	S.C.	June	Blk-smith	Cholera	1 day
4	Matilda Rigsby	31	F				Kentucky	Aug		Erysipelas	1 week
5	Tennessee White	1	F				Tenn	July		Cholera	1 day
6	James Finch	52	M			M	Kentucky	Feb	Carpenter	Consumption	C(100 da)
7	Caroline	2	F	B	S		Tenn	July		Worms	5 days
8	Andrew	22	M	B	S		Tenn	May		T. fever	3 weeks
9	Daniel	50	M	B	S		Tenn	Dec		Cold	1 day
10	John	20	M	B	S		Tenn	July		Inflamation of bowels	10 days
11	Andrew	13	M	B	S		Tenn	July		Fever	10 days
12	Ellen	1	F	B	S		Tenn	July		Pneumonia	C
13	Walker	75	M	B	S		Va	April		Old age	C

COUNTY OF DAVIDSON, STATE OF TENNESSEE.

PAGE NO. 117   PERSONS WHO DIED DURING THE YEAR ENDING 1st JUNE, 1850.

No. of Visit	Name	Age	Sex	Color	Free or Slave	Married/Widowed	Place of Birth	Month Died	Occupation	Disease or Cause of Death	No. Days Ill
14	Frances	2	F	B	S		Tenn	June		Cholera	4 days
15	Eady	18	F	B	S		Tenn	Oct		Consumption	C
16	Margaret	7m	F	B	S		Tenn	July		Whooping cough	14 days
17	Sophia Childress	23	F			M	Tenn	July		Inflamation of bowels	7 days
18	Austin	54	M	B	S		Va	July		Cholera	8 hours
19	Margaret	16	F	B	S		Tenn	Sept		Consumption	C
20	Lavinia	13	F	B	S		Tenn	Oct		Consumption	C
21	Wesley	1	M	B	S		Tenn	July		Whooping cough	2 weeks
22	Salem	5m	M	B	S		Tenn	July		Whooping cough	2 weeks
23	Elizabeth Blane	35	F			M	La	Feb		Liver complaint	C
24	Jim	10	M	B	S		Tenn	May		Drowned	
25	Emily J. Hollis	40	F			M	Tenn	Jan		Child bed	sudden
26	Theney	33	F	B	S		Tenn	April		unknown	C
27	London	38	M	B	S		Kentucky	June		Cholera	4 days
28	Sally	45	F	B	S		Kentucky	Sept		Fever	2 weeks
29	Martha	14	F	B	S		Tenn	July		unknown	C
30	Solomon	40	M	B	S		Maryland	March		Pneumonia	11 days
31	William B. Joscelin	4	M				Tenn	July		unknown	C
32	Nancy J. Davidson	8m	F				Tenn	April		unknown	C
33	Nancy Elliott	1m	F				Tenn	June		unknown	C
34	Silvy	50	F	B	S		Va	June		Cholera	7 days
35	Nancy E. Johnson	53	F			W	Va	Oct		Dropsy	C

COUNTY OF DAVIDSON, STATE OF TENNESSEE.

PAGE NO. 119   PERSONS WHO DIED DURING THE YEAR ENDING 1st JUNE, 1850.

No. of Visit	Name	Age	Sex	Color	Free or Slave	Married/Widowed	Place of Birth	Month Died	Occupation	Disease or Cause of Death	No. Days Ill
1	Caroline Worke	33	F			M	Tenn	June		Cholera	1 day
2	John A. Worke	7	M				Tenn	June		Cholera	1 day
3	Samuel Worke	3	M				Tenn	June		Cholera	1 day
4	Silas Webb	60	M				Va	March	Clergyman	Consumption	C(100 da)
5	Isaac	30	M	B	S		Tenn	April		Inflamation of lungs	C
6	Rebecca	1	F	B	S		Tenn	March		Croup	2 days
7	Infant	1m	M	B	S		Tenn	April		unknown	1 day
8	Alice	6m	F	B	S		Tenn	June		Croup	4 days
9	Washington D. Campbell	40	M			M	Tenn	Feb	Laborer	Consumption	3 weeks

COUNTY OF DAVIDSON, STATE OF TENNESSEE.

PAGE NO. 121   PERSONS WHO DIED DURING THE YEAR ENDING 1st JUNE, 1850.

District No. 23rd

No. of Visit	Name	Age	Sex	Color	Free or Slave	Married/Widowed	Place of Birth	Month Died	Occupation	Disease or Cause of Death	No. Days Ill
1	Tennessee Hyde	23	F	W	F		Tenn	July		Pulmonary disease	180 days
2	Jane Hyde	20	F	W	F		Tenn	July		Pulmonary disease	90 days

Remarks: The number of death, less perhaps than for many years past. The fever not prevailing but in the mildest form and to a very limited extent. The cause unknown unless it might be attributed to the extensive prevailance of diarrhea in the country in a mild form.   A. G. Goodlet.

COUNTY OF DAVIDSON, STATE OF TENNESSEE.

PAGE NO. 123   PERSONS WHO DIED DURING THE YEAR ENDING 1st JUNE, 1850.

District No. 22nd.

No. of Visit	Name	Age	Sex	Color	Free or Slave	Married/Widowed	Place of Birth	Month Died	Occupation	Disease or Cause of Death	No. Days Ill
1	Edmond	65	M	B	S	M	Va	April	Servant	Bil. fever	15 days
2	Azilla Ramer	40	F	W	F	M	Tenn	Jan		Cong. fever	3 days
3	Allen	26	M	B	S		Tenn	Jan		Quinsy	9 days
4	Mary	18	F	B	S		Tenn	Jan		Cholera	2 days
5	Laura Marshall	1	F	W	F		Tenn	Oct		C. Diarrhea	60 days
6	Roda D. Thomson	5	F	W	F		Tenn	Dec		Croup	1 day

Remarks: The number of deaths less perhaps than many years past. The fever not prevailing but in the mildest form and to a very limited extent. The cause unknown unless it might be attributed to the extensive prevailance of diarrhea in the country in a mild form.   A. G. Goodlet.

COUNTY OF DAVIDSON, STATE OF TENNESSEE.

PAGE NO. 125   PERSONS WHO DIED DURING THE YEAR ENDING 1st JUNE, 1850.

District No. 21st.

No. of Visit	Name	Age	Sex	Color	Free or Slave	Married/Widowed	Place of Birth	Month Died	Occupation	Disease or Cause of Death	No. Days Ill
1	Lily	50	F	B	S	M	Va	Sept		Typhoid fever	49 days
2	George	1	M	B	S		Tenn	May		Consumption	60 days
3	Robert Harrison	44	M	W	F	M	Ireland	Oct	Shoe-Book mkr	Apoplexy	3 days
4	Charles	33	M	B	S		Tenn	Jan	Servant	Cholera	2 days
5	Milly	10	F	B	S		Tenn	July	Servant	Worms	20 days
6	Eliza A. Bowers	1	F	W	F		Tenn	Aug		Cholera	2 days
7	Eliza B. Sanders	1	F	W	F		Tenn	July		Cholera	14 days
8	Olevia Read	3	F	W	F		Tenn	May		Quinsy	14 days
9	William E. Morman	5	M	W	F		Tenn	Aug		Whooping cough	35 days
10	Martha T. Bowen	3	F	W	F		Tenn	Sept		Inflamation of brain	15 days

Remarks: The number of deaths less perhaps than for many years past. The fever not prevailing but in the mildest form and to a very limited extent. The cause unknown unless it might be attributed to the extensive prevalence of diarrhea in the country in a mild form.   A. G. Goodlet.

COUNTY OF DAVIDSON, STATE OF TENNESSEE.

PAGE NO. 127 PERSONS WHO DIED DURING THE YEAR ENDING 1st JUNE, 1850.

District No. 20th.

No. of Visit	Name	Age	Sex	Color	Free or Slave	Married/Widowed	Place of Birth	Month Died	Occupation	Disease or Cause of Death	No. Days Ill
1	Peter	60	M	B	S		Va	Sept	Servant	Dropsy	100 days
2	Pompey	23	M	B	S		Tenn	Feb	Servant	T. fever	15 days
3	Stanley	12	M	B	S		Tenn	Sept	Servant	Consumption	30 days
4	John McCallin	50	M	W	F	M	Tenn	July	Farmer	Dropsy	90 days
5	Manervy	22	F	B	S		Tenn	July	Servant	Dropsy	100 days

Remarks: (same as page 125).

COUNTY OF DAVIDSON, STATE OF TENNESSEE.

PAGE NO. 129 PERSONS WHO DIED DURING THE YEAR ENDING 1st JUNE, 1850.

District NO. 9.

No. of Visit	Name	Age	Sex	Color	Free or Slave	Married/Widowed	Place of Birth	Month Died	Occupation	Disease or Cause of Death	No. Days Ill
1	Essex	75	M	B	S		____	March		Old age	sudden
2	Lucy	65	F	B	S		____	April		Old age	10 days
3	Margaret Patterson	13	F				Tenn	March		Inflamation of bowels	6 days
4	Julia A. Hood	32	F			M	Tenn	June		Flux	9 days
5	Christiana Demumbrum	54	F			M	Tenn	March		T. fever	C(100 da)
6	Thorton	28	M	M	S		Tenn	June		Cholera	¼ day
7	Mary Sweeny	22	F			M	Tenn	June		Cholera	10/24 day
8	Harriet Sweeny	2	F				Tenn	July		Cholera	3 days
9	William Meadows	9m	M				Tenn	Aug		Teething	C(100 da)
10	John Moorhead	42	M			M	England	Aug	Grocer	Apoplexy	sudden
11	Sarah Moorhead	16	F				New York	July		Cholera	1 day
12	James Stewart	28	M			M	N.C.	June	Farmer	T. fever	21 days
13	J. T. Adcock	1m	M				Tenn	Sept		Hives	2 days
14	J. C. Davis	3	M				Tenn	Aug		Cholera	3 days
15	H. C. Davis	7m	M				Tenn	Aug		Flux	21 days
16	Infant	1m	M	B	F		Tenn	March		Whooping cough	14 days
17	Joseph Taylor	28	M			M	Tenn	June	Engineer	Cholera	8/24 day
18	Malinda Sumner	4	F	M	F		Tenn	Aug		Inflamation of lungs	21 days
19	Rhoda Anderson	26	F				unknown	Sept	none	Cholera	2 days
20	Charles Crandell	4	M				Ohio	June		Cholera	1 day
21	Ellen Crandell	6	F				Ohio	July		Cholera	21 days
22	Henry Haley	67	M			M	Va	July	Laborer	Cholera	3/24 day
23	Martha Haley	53	F			M	N.C.	July		Cholera	10 days
24	Foster Corbitt	3	M				Tenn	June		Whooping cough	21 days
25	W. P. Corbitt	9	(M)				Tenn	June		Cholera	1 day
26	John Cotton	53	M			M	N.C.	June	Carpenter	Cholera	1 day
27	Martha Cotton	52	F			M	N.C.	June		Cholera	2 days
28	James Cotton	1m	M				Tenn	June		Cholera	1 day
29	J. B. Carroll	19	M				Tenn	June	Carpenter	Cholera	1 day
30	Ellis	35	M	B	S		____	Jan		Cold	21 days
31	Washington	12	M	B	S		____	June		Consumption	C(100 da)
32	Henry	14	M	B	S		____	March		Cholera	1 day
33	Jane	50	F	B	S		____	June		Cholera	2 days
34	Mary	30	F	B	S		____	June		Cholera	2 days
35	Daniel	45	M	B	S		____	June		Cholera	1 day

COUNTY OF DAVIDSON, STATE OF TENNESSEE.

PAGE NO. 132 PERSONS WHO DIED DURING THE YEAR ENDING 1st JUNE, 1850.

District No. 2.

No. of Visit	Name	Age	Sex	Color	Free or Slave	Married/Widowed	Place of Birth	Month Died	Occupation	Disease or Cause of Death	No. Days Ill
1	Boy	6	M	B	S			Nov		Cold	14 days
2	Mary Baker	19	F				Tenn	Feb		T. fever	49 days
3	John T. Brooks	33	M			M	Tenn	May	Farmer	T. fever	28 days
4	Andrew Patterson	86	M			W	Va	Sept	Blk-smith	Old age	sudden
5	Bob	50	M	B	S			June		Cholera	3 days
6	Addison	30	M	B	S			June		Cholera	2 days
7	Infant	3	F	B	S			June		Cholera	1 day
8	Michael	1	M	B	S			Jan		unknown	21 days
9	Martha F. Lyons	28	F			M	Tenn	Jan		Bronchitis	C(100 da)
10	Mary J. Pennual	1	F				Tenn	Aug		Whooping cough	90 days
11	Mary H. Pennual	6	F				Tenn	June		T. fever	12 days
12	Hannah	8	F	B	S			Oct		unknown	sudden
13	Infant	1m	M	B	S			Sept		unknown	sudden
14	Silas	55	M	B	S			Feb		Consumption	C(100 da)
15	Mary D. Burton	21	F			M	Tenn	Oct		Pulmonary	C
16	Infant	4m	M	B	S			March		unknown	sudden
17	Synia	50	F	B	S			Sept		unknown	sudden
18	Infant	1m	F	B	S			Dec		Croup	sudden
19	Infant	1	F	B	S			Nov		unknown	C
20	Calvin	2	M	B	S			Oct		Whooping cough	35 days
21	Caesar	15	M	B	S			Dec		Consumption	C
22	Julia	35	F	B	S			Feb		unknown	C
23	Rachel Stewart	8m	F				Tenn	Nov		Inflamation of bowels	C
24	Josiah Green	54	M			M	Va	April	Farmer	Palsy	C
25	Thomas Rutherford	83	M			M	Va	Feb	Farmer	Old age	C
26	Susanna Card	1	F				Tenn	Dec		Burn	sudden
27	John Clarke	5m	M				Tenn	March		Croup	sudden
28	Lytle Dodson	22	M	B	F		Tenn	Feb	Painter	Consumption	C
29	S. G. Lowry	5	F	B	F		Tenn	Jan		Scrofula	C
30	William Fly	28	M			M	Tenn	July	Bricklayer	Consumption	C
31	Cupid	80	M	B	S			July		Old age	C
32	Thomas H. Estes	7m	M				Tenn	July		Inflamation of brain	20 days
33	Green	14	M	B	S			May		Consumption	C
34	Charles	1	M	B	S			Aug		Inflamation of brain	25 days
35	Sophia	2m	F	B	S			Oct		unknown	sudden

COUNTY OF DAVIDSON, STATE OF TENNESSEE.

PAGE NO. 133 PERSONS WHO DIED DURING THE YEAR ENDING 1st JUNE, 1850.

District No. 4.

No. of Visit	Name	Age	Sex	Color	Free or Slave	Married/Widowed	Place of Birth	Month Died	Occupation	Disease or Cause of Death	No. Days Ill
1	Maria K. Kerr	25	F				Kentucky	March		Cholera	7 days
2	Infant		M					June		unknown	sudden
3	Jim	90	M	B	S			Nov		Old age	C
4	Phillis	80	F	B	S			Nov		Angenia Pectoris	C

COUNTY OF DAVIDSON, STATE OF TENNESSEE.

PAGE NO. 136 PERSONS WHO DIED DURING THE YEAR ENDING 1st JUNE, 1850.

District NO. 4

No. of Visit	Name	Age	Sex	Color	Free or Slave	Married/Widowed	Place of Birth	Month Died	Occupation	Disease or Cause of Death	No. Days Ill
1	James	10	M	B	S		Tenn	Oct		Accident	sudden
2	Diana	14	F	B	S		Va	June		Inflamation of lungs	C
3	Infant	2m	M	B	S		Tenn	July		unknown	sudden
4	Caroline	28	F	B	S		Tenn	Dec		Consumption	C
5	Hard	3	M	B	S		Tenn	Feb		unknown	4 days
6	Frank	2	M	B	S		Tenn	March		Scrofula	C
7	Nancy Cherry	66	F			W	N.C.	June		Cholera	1 day
8	Marina	38	F	B	S			Sept		T. fever	10 days
9	Rachel	85	F	B	S			Aug		Old age	sudden
10	A. C. Airhart	30	M			M	Tenn	Oct	Wagon-mkr	Cholera	sudden
11	Infant	1m	M	B	S			Dec		unknown	sudden
12	Sarah J. Smith	11m	F				Tenn	Aug		Cholera	1/3 day
13	Sarah	25	F	B	S			July		Dropsy	14 days
14	Mary	30	F	B	S			May		Dropsy	C
15	Hollis Wright	70	M			M	N.C.	April	Farmer	T. fever	10 days
16	Infant	2m	F	M	F		Tenn	Dec		Hives	14 days
17	John Sturdevant	1	M				Tenn	Sept		Whooping cough	21 days
18	James Baker	1m	M				Tenn	Dec		Whooping cough	7 days
19	Sarah Johnson	47	F			M	N.C.	June		unknown	C
20	Parthenia Johnson	4m	F					Dec		Croup	sudden
21	James G. Martin	59	M			W	N.C.	July	Farmer	C. Diarrhea	28 days
22	Infant	1m	M	B	S			Sept		Lock jaw	sudden
23	Jenny	63	F	B	S			March		Apoplexy	sudden
24	Richard A. Turner	40	M			M	N.C.	July	Farmer	Cholera	3 days
25	Ady	36	F	B	S			July		Dysentery	7 days
26	Oscar	18	M	B	S			July		Dysentery	7 days
27	Rufus	8	M	B	S			July		Dysentery	7 days
28	Infant	3m	F	B	S			July		unknown	sudden
29	Ellen Marcum	1	F				Tenn	July		Dysentery	10 days
30	Lucy Marcum	2	F				Tenn	Aug		unknown	10 days
31	Jerry	90	M	B	S			July		Old age	C
32	Julius	8m	M	B	S			May		unknown	C
33	Infant	6m	F	B	S			July		unknown	C
34	Sylphia Overton	45	F	B	S		N.C.	May		T. fever	90 days
35	Mary	70	F	B	S			Sept		Apoplexy	sudden

Remarks: In this District stands the Hermitage. The Home of Andrew Jackson.
Charles M. Hays

COUNTY OF DAVIDSON, STATE OF TENNESSEE.

PAGE NO. 137   PERSONS WHO DIED DURING THE YEAR ENDING 1st JUNE, 1850.

District No. 3.

No. of Visit	Name	Age	Sex	Color	Free or Slave	Married/Widowed	Place of Birth	Month Died	Occupation	Disease or Cause of Death	No. Days Ill
1	Peter	90	M	B	S			Jan		Old age	C
2	Andrew Philips	3m	M				Tenn	Oct		Accident	sudden
3	Mary Chisholm	93	F			W	Va	May		Old age	C
4	Infant of J.W. Pugh	1m	F				Tenn	Sept		unknown	sudden
5	Infant of Jerry Ward	—	M				Tenn	Aug		unknown	sudden
6	Infant of M. Lovell	—	M				Tenn	May		unknown	sudden
7	Twins of James Garner	—	M/M				Tenn	March		Still born	
8	John H. Ellis	60	M			W	N.C.	Aug	Farmer	Consumption	C
9	Elizabeth Norvell	1m	F				Tenn	April		Dropsy of brain	30 days
10	Tennessee	6m	F	B	S		Tenn	Oct		Accident	sudden
11	Infant	2m	F	B	S		Tenn	March		unknown	sudden
12	Mary A. Goodrich	3	F				Tenn	July		Summer Croup	1 day
13	Ann Goodrich	3m	F				Tenn	March		Inflamation of brain	28 days
14	Mary A. Robinson	39	F			M	Tenn	Oct		Dropsy	C
15	Infant of J. Robinson	—	M				Tenn	Oct		unknown	sudden
16	Jane Vaugn	62	F			W	Va	June		Cholera	3 days
17	Martha Seat	65	F			W	Va	Dec		Old age	C
18	Emeline Grady	8	F				Tenn	June		T. fever	7 days
19	Daniel Patton	26	M			M	Tenn	Jan	Farmer	Apoplexy	sudden
20	Abram	40	M	B	S			Oct		Lock jaw	4 days
21	Mary Tennison	3	F				Tenn	Oct		unknown	C
22	Mary Baily	73	F			M	N.C.	Aug		Cancer	C
23	James Owens	3	M				Tenn	July		Inflamation of brain	14 days

COUNTY OF DAVIDSON, STATE OF TENNESSEE.

PAGE NO. 139   PERSONS WHO DIED DURING THE YEAR ENDING 1st JUNE, 1850.

District No. 5

No. of Visit	Name	Age	Sex	Color	Free or Slave	Married/Widowed	Place of Birth	Month Died	Occupation	Disease or Cause of Death	No. Days Ill
1	William Tynor	31	M				Illinois	June	Cigar-mkr	Congestive fever	5 days
2	Jim	1	M	B	S			Dec		Scrofula	C
3	William M. Morrison	16	M				Kentucky	Oct	Student	T. fever	14 days
4	Lydia	50	F	B	S			Dec		Disease of heart	C
5	Chloe	65	F	B	S			Dec		Inflamation of brain	14 days
6	Sarah A. West	45	F				N.C.	May		Consumption	C
7	Lewis	17	M	B	S			April		Cholera	4 days
8	Infant) Twins	—	M				Tenn	March		unknown	sudden
9	Infant)	—	M				Tenn	March		unknown	sudden
10	Henry Burnett	5	M	B	S		Tenn	March		T. fever	12 days

COUNTY OF DAVIDSON, STATE OF TENNESSEE.

PAGE NO. 142 PERSONS WHO DIED DURING THE YEAR ENDING 1st JUNE, 1850.

District No. 5.

No. of Visit	Name	Age	Sex	Color	Free or Slave	Married/Widowed	Place of Birth	Month Died	Occupation	Disease or Cause of Death	No. Days Ill
1	Ann E. Jackson	3	F				Tenn	Feb		Inflamation of brain	20 days
2	Sarah F. Floyd	11	F			S	Tenn	July		Cholera	1/6 day
3	Catharine Burnett	18	F	B	F		Tenn	May		Small pox	8 days
4	Abram Burnett	22	M	B	F		Tenn	May	none	Cholera	1 day
5	Permelia Seat	22	F			M	Tenn	July		Cholera	1 day
6	Thomas Stanfield	21	M				Tenn	Dec	Wagon-mkr	Pleurisy	7 days
7	John Warmoth	51	M				N.C.	July	Carpenter	Cholera	1/2 day
8	Mary	80	F	B	S		unknown	June		Old age	C
9	Matilda Searls	34	F			M	Tenn	Nov		Consumption	C
10	Lafayette	30	M	B	S		N.C.	July		Cholera	2 days
11	Isaac	25	M	B	S		N.C.	Aug		Consumption	C
12	Infant	1	M	B	S		Tenn	Aug		Cholera Infantum	14 days
13	Amanda Powers	28	F			M	Tenn	Dec		Fever	10 days
14	Benjamin Creech	56	M			M	N.C.	July	Farmer	T. fever	30 days
15	James Warmoth	12	M				Tenn	July		T. fever	27 days
16	Maria Rains	38	F			M	Tenn	July		Cholera	1 day
17	Amanda Rains	15	F				Tenn	Aug		Cholera	7 days
18	Maria F. Matlock	1	F				Tenn	April		Cholera infantum	30 days
19	John	25	M	B	S		unknown	July		Consumption	C
20	Jeremiah Shenick	38	M			M	Ireland	July	wagon yard keeper	Cholera	5 hours
21	Hannah Shenick	35	F			M	Ireland	July		Cholera	1 day
22	Hannah Shenick	6	F				America	July		Cholera	4 hours
23	Jerry Shenick	3	M				America	July		Cholera	6 hours
24	Felix Moss	40	M			M	unknown	July	Boarding house keeper	Cholera	2 days
25	Mrs. Moss	35	F			M	unknown	July		Cholera	1 day
26	Miss Moss	18	F				unknown	July		Cholera	1 day
27	____ Moss	4	M				unknown	July		Cholera	4 hours
28	____ Moss	8	M				unknown	July		Cholera	6 hours
29	____ Moss	6	M				unknown	July		Cholera	1 day
30	____ Moss	15	F				unknown	July		Cholera	4 days
31	Irishman, name unknown	25	M				Ireland	July	Laborer	Cholera	1 day
32	George Colman	20	M				Indiana	April	wagon-mkr	Accident	14 days
33	Joseph A. Bland	35	M				Tenn	June	Farmer	Cholera	4 hours
34	Susan Taylor	23	F				Va	Sept		Dyspepsia	C
35	Caleb Stovall	60	M			M	Va	July	Farmer	Cholera	5 days

COUNTY OF DAVIDSON, STATE OF TENNESSEE.

PAGE NO. 143 PERSONS WHO DIED DURING THE YEAR ENDING 1st JUNE, 1850.

District No. 6.

No. of Visit	Name	Age	Sex	Color	Free or Slave	Married/Widowed	Place of Birth	Month Died	Occupation	Disease or Cause of Death	No. Days Ill
1	William M. Battle	41	M			M	N.C.	Jan	Farmer	Cholera	2 days
2	name unknown	30	F	B	S		____	Jan		Cholera	3 days
3	name unknown	3	F	B	S		____	Jan		Cholera	sudden
4	name unknown	1	F	B	S		____	Jan		Cholera	sudden
5	name unknown	1	M	B	S		____	Jan		Accident	sudden
6	name unknown	25	M	B	S		Tenn	July		Cholera	sudden
7	name unknown	1	M	B	S		____	Jan		Inflamation of brain	3 days
8	Armstead Camp	71	M			M	Va	Aug	Farmer	Cholera	2 days
9	Benjamin Foster	19	M				Tenn	March	Laborer	Cholera	3 days
10	James G. Foster	58	M			W	Va	Aug	Peddler	Cholera	1 day
11	Nancy Harris	28	F			M	Tenn	June		Cholera	2 days
12	Elizabeth A. Gibson	45	F			M	Va	May		Consumption	C
13	Lafayette M. Vaugn	14	M				Tenn	Nov		Dropsy	C
14	Jane McFaddin	76	F			W	S.C.	Nov		Consumption	C
15	Nathan H. Lane	17	M				Tenn	March	Farmer	Inflamation of brain	27 days

COUNTY OF DAVIDSON, STATE OF TENNESSEE.

PAGE NO. 143   PERSONS WHO DIED DURING THE YEAR ENDING 1st JUNE, 1850.

District No. 6.

No. of Visit	Name	Age	Sex	Color	Free or Slave	Married/Widowed	Place of Birth	Month Died	Occupation	Disease or Cause of Death	No. Days Ill
16	Martha C. McFadden	2m	F				Tenn	Feb		Pneumonia	7 days
17	Emily	20	F	B	S		Tenn	Oct		Child birth	3 days
18	James A. Owens	22	M			M	Tenn	March	Farmer	Consumption	C

COUNTY OF DAVIDSON, STATE OF TENNESSEE.

PAGE NO. 146   PERSONS WHO DIED DURING THE YEAR ENDING 1st JUNE, 1850.

District No. 7

No. of Visit	Name	Age	Sex	Color	Free or Slave	Married/Widowed	Place of Birth	Month Died	Occupation	Disease or Cause of Death	No. Days Ill
1	William Hall	55	M			S	N.C.	March	Farmer	Inflamation of bowels	6 days
2	William A. Gunter	1	M				Tenn	June		Cholera	2 days
3	Alexander Jarrell	91	M			W	Maryland	Jan	Farmer	Old age	10 days
4	Louisa	4m	F	B	S		Tenn	Oct		Burn	14 days
5	Nathan J. Baker	1	M				Tenn	June		Cholera	2 days
6	Mary E. Jones	5	F				Tenn	June		Cholera	1 day
7	Margaret A. Quinn	18	F				Tenn	July		Cholera	2 days
8	Mary T. O. Goodrich	2	F				Tenn	May		Cholera	1 day
9	Ellen Creech	6m	F				Tenn	Oct		unknown	10 days
10	Thomas Shilcutt	82	M			M	Maryland	Jan	Farmer	Old age	8 days
11	John	2m	M	B	S		Tenn	April		unknown	sudden
12	James H. Cook	22	M				Tenn	Dec	Carpenter	Accident	10 days
13	Francis Houchins	24	M				Va	April	Laborer	Measles	C
14	Nancy Houchins	22	F				Va	April		T. fever	12 days
15	Washington	25	M	B	S		Tenn	Aug	Laborer	T. fever	15 days
16	Frank	9	M	B	S		Tenn	Jan		Dropsy	C
17	Elizabeth Carman	8m	F				Tenn	June		Brain fever	8 days
18	Pagitte Carman	1m	F				Tenn	Jan		unknown	sudden
19	Nancy	34	F	B	S		Alabama	June	Cook	Dysentery	C
20	Felix	6	M	B	S		Tenn	Sept		unknown	3 days
21	Amanda Fitzhugh	23	F			M	Tenn	July		Inf. of stomach & bowels	8 days
22	Daniel R. Watson	50	M			M	N.C.	May	Farmer	Drinking	sudden
23	Sarah E. Eason	1	F				Tenn	Aug		Inf. of bowels	14 days
24	Cynthia Taunt	30	F			M	unknown	May		Consumption	C
25	Samuel Reed	11	M				Tenn	Oct		Fall from horse	sudden
26	Infant of T. B. Bailey	1m	M				Tenn	Jan		Hives	5 days

Remarks: In the valley of Mill Creek, the cholera was prevalent from 1st June 1849 to 10th August 1849. The cause we cannot account for. Limestone water. Soil, fertile. Rock, limestone. Timber growing naturally, cedar, poplar, oak, hickory. Natural fertilizer, lime. Seasons cool and rainy.

Charles M. Hays.

COUNTY OF DAVIDSON, STATE OF TENNESSEE.

PAGE NO. 147 PERSONS WHO DIED DURING THE YEAR ENDING 1st JUNE, 1850.

Civil District, South Nashville

No. of Visit	Name	Age	Sex	Color	Free or Slave	Married/Widowed	Place of Birth	Month Died	Occupation	Disease or Cause of Death	No. Days Ill
1	Joseph	35	M	B	S			Aug		Consumption	C(100 da)
2	J. P. Sherrill	52	M				Va	April	none	Dropsy	C
3	W. Gould	8	M				Tenn	June		Cholera	sudden
4	Albert Gould	7	M				Tenn	June		Cholera	sudden
5	Rhoda A. Barnes	9m	F				Tenn	Aug		Inflamation of brain	C
6	Alfred Corbitt	5	M				Tenn	Dec		Accident	sudden
7	Margaret Whitlock	5m	F				Tenn	May		Whooping cough	14 days
8	Julia	22	F	B				Feb		Consumption	C
9	William	5	M	B				Jan		Cold	C
10	Martha Mallory	41	F			M	Tenn	June		Cholera	1 day
11	Wesley	28	M	B	S			July		Cholera	6/24 day
12	Ann Murray	2m	F				Tenn	Sept		unknown	sudden
13	Eliza	26	F	B	S			July		Cholera	1 day
14	Joseph Dougal	50	M			M	Penn	Sept	Tailor	Dropsy	C
15	Ella T. Green	2	F				Tenn	May		Cholera	4 days
16	Meranda Wells	1	F				Tenn	July		Inflamation of bowels	30 days
17	Infant of Slade	1m	M				Tenn	Feb		unknown	7 days
18	Hilia	19	M	B	S			Aug		Child birth	C
19	Robert Starkey	30	M			M	Tenn	June		Bil. fever	20 days

COUNTY OF DAVIDSON, STATE OF TENNESSEE.

PAGE NO. 149 PERSONS WHO DIED DURING THE YEAR ENDING 1st JUNE, 1850.

District Edgefield

No. of Visit	Name	Age	Sex	Color	Free or Slave	Married/Widowed	Place of Birth	Month Died	Occupation	Disease or Cause of Death	No. Days Ill
1	Edy	35	F	B	S			Jan		Consumption	C(100 da)
2	Infant	—	F	B	S		Tenn	Aug		Lock jaw	sudden
3	Infant		F	B	S		Tenn	Aug		Lock jaw	sudden
4	W. P. Maxey	53	M			M	Va	Sept	Farmer	Complicated	C
5	George	6m	M	B	S			Aug		Casualty	sudden
6	Beverly	2	M	B	S			Aug		Scrofula	C
7	Mary	30	F	B	S			Jan		unknown	sudden
8	Infant	4m	M	B	S			March		unknown	C
9	Mary E. Harris	25	F				N.C.	Aug		Consumption	C
10	Infant Fulrack	1m	M				Tenn	Jan		unknown	sudden
11	Isaac Clemmons	66	M			M	N.C.	Sept	Farmer	Casualty	sudden
12	Eliza	21	F	B	S			April		Complication	C
13	Boy	4	M	B	S			March		T. fever	30 days
14	Frances Obedience	27	F				Tenn	Feb		Consumption	C
15	Daniel	60	M	B				Feb		Pleurisy	14 days
16	W. P. Walker	62	M			M	Tenn	Aug	Farmer	Apoplexy	sudden
17	Jane Norment	70	F			W	Va	March		Cancer	C
18	George Looney	6	M				Tenn	March		Lungs	4 days
19	Easter	65	F	B	S			Sept		Apoplexy	sudden
20	Caroline	24	F	B	S			Jan		Consumption	C
21	Infant	1m	F	B	S			Feb		unknown	sudden
22	Vice	60	F	B	S			Feb		Apoplexy	sudden
23	Elizabeth	33	F	B	S			May		Prolapus Uterus	C
24	Louisa Anderson	34	F			M	Kentucky	May		Chronic Colic	7 days
25	Infant	1	M	B	S			March		Cold	21 days
26	Cherry	55	F	B	S			Sept		Dropsy	C

COUNTY OF DAVIDSON, STATE OF TENNESSEE.

PAGE NO. 152 PERSONS WHO DIED DURING THE YEAR ENDING 1st JUNE, 1850.

District Edgefield

No. of Visit	Name	Age	Sex	Color	Free or Slave	Married/Widowed	Place of Birth	Month Died	Occupation	Disease or Cause of Death	No. Days Ill
1	Susan	11	F	B	S		Tenn	July		Cholera	7 hours
2	Mary	70	F	B	S		Tenn	July		Cholera	10 days
3	Infant	6m	M	B	S		____	Aug		Accident	sudden
4	Mary E. Howerton	5m	F				Tenn	Dec		Croup	sudden
5	Pase	23	F	B	S		____	May		unknown	C
6	James R. Graves, Jr.	7m	M				Tenn	Dec		Infant, Throat	1 day
7	Mary Wallen	5	F				Tenn	June		Cholera	10 hours
8	Freelan Wallen	3	M				Tenn	June		Cholera	14 days
9	Ransom Wallen	1	M				Tenn	Oct		Cholera	7 days
10	James Chisenhall	25	M				Va	May	Blk-smith	T. fever	14 days
11	Richard	45	M	B	S		____	July		Cholera	5 days
12	Benjamin	60	M	B	S		____	July		Cholera	1 day
13	Jinny	60	F	B	S		____	July		Cholera	1 day
14	Rebecca	54	F	B	S		____	July		Cholera	1 day
15	Wesley	37	M	B	S		____	July		Cholera	5 days
16	Susan Shelton	25	F			M	Kentucky	Jan		Consumption	C
17	Harriet Wright	5	F				Tenn	July		Cholera	1/4 day
18	Sarah F. Wright	1	F				Tenn	Sept		Infl. of bowels	60 days
19	John Humphries	26	M				Tenn	Oct	Wagoner	Pleurisy	4 days
20	P. Smith	48	M			W	Va	March	Merchant	Disease of heart	C
21	Greenwood Paine	26	M				Tenn	Aug	Student	Consumption	21 days
22	Laura G. Payne	1	F				Tenn	Nov		Whooping cough	C
23	John Yeast	24	M			M	Germany	April	Milkman	Drowned	sudden
24	Prissa	70	F	B	S			June		Old age	C
25	Martha Mead	62	F				Va	May		Pneumonia	7 days
26	Mary A. Geturn	8	F				Tenn	Oct		Scarlet fever	42 days
27	Nancy	50	F	B	S		____	June		Cholera	2 days
28	Demas	25	M	B	S		____	June		Cholera	1/12 day
29	Jennings Lawrence	1	M				Tenn	Aug		Infl. of bowels	60 days
30	Edy	1	F	B	S		____	May		unknown	C
31	Nicholas	1	M	B	S		____	Aug		unknown	sudden
32	Harvey	2	M	B	S		____	Jan		unknown	sudden
33	Susan	30	F	B	S		____	Aug		Consumption	C
34	Orson	4	M	B	S		____	Oct		Consumption	C
35	Matilda	2	F	B	S		____	Dec		Consumption	C

COUNTY OF DAVIDSON, STATE OF TENNESSEE.

PAGE NO. 153 PERSONS WHO DIED DURING THE YEAR ENDING 1st JUNE, 1850.

City of Nashville

No. of Visit	Name	Age	Sex	Color	Free or Slave	Married/Widowed	Place of Birth	Month Died	Occupation	Disease or Cause of Death	No. Days Ill
1	George W. Watson	1	M				Tenn	Aug		Inflamation of bowels	2 days
2	Thomas Huffman	5	M				Tenn	July		Cholera	1 day
3	Nancy Besley	24	F	B	S	M	Tenn	July		Cholera	1 day
4	Samuel B. Besley	1	M	B	S		Tenn	July		Teething	2 weeks
5	Thomas J. Ensley	19	M				Tenn	July	none	Cholera	1 day
6	Gracy Ensley	51	F	B	S	M	N.C.	July		Cholera	1 day
7	Laura Ensley	1	F	B	S		Tenn	Nov		Burned	sudden
8	John Willis	52	M			M	Va	June		Cholera	2 weeks
9	John McClelland	43	M			M	Tenn	June		Cholera	1 day
10	S. E. Goodwin	1	F				Tenn	Oct		Y. thrash	5 months
11	Thomas Huffman	6	M				Tenn	July		Cholera	1 day
12	Mary J. Watkins	3	F				Tenn	July		Cholera	1 day
13	William Spain	1	M				Tenn	July		Lock jaw	3 days
14	Sarah Murray	1	F				Tenn	July		Cholera	5 days
15	James Keoff	35	M			W	Ireland	Oct	none	Consumption	4 months

COUNTY OF DAVIDSON, STATE OF TENNESSEE.

PAGE NO. 153 PERSONS WHO DIED DURING THE YEAR ENDING 1st JUNE, 1850.

City of Nashville

No. of Visit	Name	Age	Sex	Color	Free or Slave	Married/Widowed	Place of Birth	Month Died	Occupation	Disease or Cause of Death	No. Days Ill
16	John Kinney	24	M				Penn	April	Pilot	Cholera	1 week
17	George Boyd	50	M			M	Tenn	Oct		Fits	1 day
18	Sarah A. M. Manunerd	3	F				Kentucky	Nov		Diarrhea	1 week
19	Sarah Randolph	3	F				Tenn	Oct		Measles	1 week
20	Elizabeth Reed	35	F				Tenn	Oct		Fever	5 weeks
21	Richard Samuels	32	M			M	Va	July	Carpenter	Consumption	5 months
22	John Peabody	57	M			M	N.C.	July	Silver-smith	Cholera	1 day
23	Jacob Lentz	29	M			M	Germany	June	Merchant	Cholera	3 days
24	James Savage	2	M				Tenn	June		Cholera	1 day
25	Amanda Lattimore	16	F				Tenn	June		Cholera	5 weeks
26	William F. Shafer	42	M			M	Germany	July	Tailor	Cholera	1 day
27	William Doeherty	87	M			W	Ireland	July	Tailor	Cholera	1 day
28	Henry Winters	1	M				Tenn	Oct		Consumption	5 months
29	James M. Glenn	26	M				Tenn	Oct	Clerk	Cholera	1 day
30	Linda M. Woodward	54	F			M	Va	July		Consumption	2 years
31	M. G. Woodward	1	F				Tenn	Jan		Teething	1 day
32	Henry Ament	41	M			M	Kentucky	June		Cholera	1 day
33	Thaind Ament	27	F	B	S	M	Tenn	July		Cholera	5 days
34	William Smith	45	M			M	Va	Jan	Shoe-mkr	Consumption	8 weeks
35	John Smith	14	M				Tenn	June		Cholera	1 day

COUNTY OF DAVIDSON, STATE OF TENNESSEE.

PAGE NO. 156 PERSONS WHO DIED DURING THE YEAR ENDING 1st JUNE, 1850.

City of Nashville

No. of Visit	Name	Age	Sex	Color	Free or Slave	Married/Widowed	Place of Birth	Month Died	Occupation	Disease or Cause of Death	No. Days Ill
1	Thomas Fleming	33	M			M	Scotland	June	Painter	Cholera	1 day
2	John Fleming	7	M				Scotland	June		Cholera	1 day
3	E. Fleming	3	M				Scotland	June		Cholera	1 day
4	Huey Nowls	2	M	M			Tenn	June		Cholera	3 days
5	George R. Hundly	1	M				Tenn	June		Whooping cough	7 weeks
6	Sarah Johnson	67	F			W	Va	July		B. fever	1 week
7	H. M. Goldrich	30	F			W	Tenn	March		Consumption	6 weeks
8	John Bassy	60	M	B		M	Maryland	June		Cholera	2 weeks
9	Mary Bassy	28	F	B			Va	June		Cholera	1 day
10	William Squires	19	M			M	Tenn	July		Cholera	1 day
11	E. Hilsey	1	F				Tenn	Jan		Teething	6 weeks
12	Charles Farris	2	M				Tenn	Oct		Croup	1 week
13	Luke Foster	20	M	B			Tenn	April		Inflamation of lungs	3 weeks
14	Infant	1	F	M			Tenn	Feb		Teething	3 days
15	William E. Bilbo	1	M				Tenn	April		S. fever	3 weeks
16	Nancy Henry	56	F				N.C.	June		Cholera	1 week
17	Martha Henry	21	F				Tenn	June		Cholera	1 day
18	E. A. Henry	20	F				Tenn	June		Cholera	2 days
19	Susan A. Henry	18	F				Tenn	June		Cholera	2 days
20	Nancy Henry	16	F				Tenn	June		Cholera	2 days
21	Samuella Wilson	2	F				Tenn	June		Fever	1 day
22	William Winfield	75	M	B	S	W	Va	March		Inflamation of brain	8 weeks
23	Samuel Work	49	M			M	Tenn	June		Cholera	1 day
24	R. J. Cleveland	2	M				Tenn	July		Cholera	3 weeks
25	N. B. Cleveland	21	M				Tenn	Aug	Painter	Cholera	1 day
26	Catharine Allman	11	F				Tenn	July		Cholera	1 day
27	Unity Petty	41	F				Tenn	June		Cholera	1 day
28	George W. Petty	13	M				Tenn	June		Cholera	1 day
29	J. M. Petty	9	F				Tenn	June		Cholera	1 day
30	Tennessee Petty	6	F				Tenn	June		Cholera	1 day

COUNTY OF DAVIDSON, STATE OF TENNESSEE.

PAGE NO. 156 PERSONS WHO DIED DURING THE YEAR ENDING 1st JUNE, 1850.

City of Nashville

No. of Visit	Name	Age	Sex	Color	Free or Slave	Married/Widowed	Place of Birth	Month Died	Occupation	Disease or Cause of Death	No. Days Ill
31	James D. Petty	1	M				Tenn	June		Cholera	1 day
32	Nelson Donegan	19	M				Tenn	June	none	Cholera	1 day
33	Margaret A. Hagy	1	F				Tenn	June		Inflamation of brain	3 weeks
34	Frances Stump	1	F	B	S		Tenn	July		Cholera	1 day
35	Mary K. Fossett	53	F			W	Va	July		Cholera	2 days

COUNTY OF DAVIDSON, STATE OF TENNESSEE.

PAGE NO. 157 PERSONS WHO DIED DURING THE YEAR ENDING 1st JUNE, 1850.

City of Nashville

No. of Visit	Name	Age	Sex	Color	Free or Slave	Married/Widowed	Place of Birth	Month Died	Occupation	Disease or Cause of Death	No. Days Ill
1	Mary A. Johnson	4	F				Tenn	June		Cholera	1 week
2	Joseph Greene	82	M			W	England	Sept	Prof. Music	Cancer	1 week
3	H. J. G. Payne	1	M				Tenn	Nov		W. cough	4 weeks
4	Letty Crockett	17	F	B	S	M	Tenn	Dec		Child bed	1 week
5	William F. Everett	7m	M				Tenn	Jan		A. heart	1 day
6	F. W. Hunt	17	F(?)				Tenn	July	Merchant(?)	Cholera	1 day
7	George W. Everett	23	M				Tenn	July	Clerk	Cholera	1 day
8	Rachel Ford	55	F	B	S	W	N.C.	March		Pneumonia	10 days
9	John F. Kirkman	10	M				Tenn	June		Drowned	sudden
10	E. Hickman	27	F			M	Tenn	June		Child bed	2 months
11	John B. Snowdon	7	M				Tenn	Jan		unknown	2 weeks
12	K. Snowdon	8	F	B	S		Tenn	June		Lock jaw	1 month
13	Infant	7m	F				Tenn	June		Cholera	3 days
14	Ned	27	M	B	S	M	Va	July		Cholera	1 day
15	Susan Callender	16	F	B	S		Tenn	Dec		Consumption	3 weeks
16	M. Canin	50	F			M	Va	July		Consumption	2 years
17	Judia Patrick	60	F	B	S	M	Va	April		Consumption	3 weeks
18	Mariah Adams	43	F			W	Maryland	July		Cholera	9 days
19	Lewis Sigler	23	M	B	S	M	Tenn	July		Consumption	6 months
20	Clara Reed	24	F			M	Tenn	Jan		Child bed	5 weeks
21	H. S. Reed	6m	M				Tenn	July		B. fever	1 week
22	E. Johnson	40	M	B	S	M	Va	Aug		Croup	2 weeks
23	Susan A. Shields	27	F			M	Lousiana	Oct		Consumption	1 week
24	Elizabeth C. Stevenson	34	F			M	Tenn	July		Disease of heart	1 week
25	Sarah McIntosh	70	F			W	Va	July		Dropsy	6 months
26	C. Swanson	55	F			W	Europe	July		Cholera	1 day
27	David M. Brinkley	14	M				Alabama	July		Cholera	4 days
28	Infant		M	B	S		Tenn	Dec		Stillborn	
29	John Wright	72	M			M	Ireland	July		Cholera	2 days
30	Mariah Lea	10	F	B	S		Tenn	July		Cholera	1 week
31	C. H. Foster, 3rd		M				Tenn	July		Cholera	2 days
32	Elizabeth McNairy	12	F	B	S		Tenn	July		Cholera	2 days
33	William S. Rains	7	M				Tenn	June		B. fever	2 weeks
34	Lucy Smith	23	F	B	S	M	Tenn	July		Pneumonia	9 days
35	James K. Polk	55	M			M	N.C.	June	Lawyer	Voxcholerica	13 days

COUNTY OF DAVIDSON, STATE OF TENNESSEE.

PAGE NO. 160 PERSONS WHO DIED DURING THE YEAR ENDING 1st JUNE, 1850.

City of Nashville

No. of Visit	Name	Age	Sex	Color	Free or Slave	Married/Widowed	Place of Birth	Month Died	Occupation	Disease or Cause of Death	No. Days Ill
1	Matilda Polk	50	F	B		M	Tenn	June		Cholera	3 days
2	R. Horn	2	F				Tenn	Aug		B. fever	17 days
3	Rt. E. Cunningham	12	M				Tenn	June		B. fever	3 weeks
4	Sarah Cunningham	4m	F	B	S		Tenn	April		Inflamation of brain	1 day
5	George Greene	6m	M	B	S		Tenn	June		Cholera	2 days
6	Joseph D. Miller	20	M				Tenn	March	Mid-shipman	T. fever	5 days
7	E. Miller	3m	F	M	S		Tenn	July		Teething	3 days
8	Margaret W. Ewing	17	F				Tenn	March		T. fever	2 weeks
9	Infant		F	M	S		Tenn	Feb		Still-born	
10	William W. Goodwin	24	M				Tenn	July		Inflamation of brain	1 week
11	Anarchy Shuggs	50	F	B	S	M	Va	July		Dropsy	2 weeks
12	Margaret Moore	57	F				Ireland	June		Cholera	1 day
13	Thomas Chany	54	M			M	Maryland	July		Cholera	3 days
14	Paralee McEwen	15	F	B	S		Tenn	July		Cholera	1 day
15	William Batte	23	M	M	S		Va	July		Cholera	1 day
16	Austin Batte	21	M	B	S		Va	July		Cholera	1 day
17	Susan Batte	30	F	B	S	M	Tenn	July		Cholera	1 day
18	John Batte	6	M	M	S		Tenn	July		Cholera	1 day
19	W. Batte	1	M	M	S		Louisiana	July		Cholera	1 day
20	A. Roberts		M				Tenn	Feb		Croup	8 days
21	James C. Stevenson	57	M			M	Conn	July	Saddler	unknown	2 months
22	Mary Stevens	17	F	M	S		N.C.	June		Cholera	2 weeks
23	A. S. Marlin	25	F				Tenn	June		Inflamation of bowels	1 week
24	G. T. Leake	31	M			M	Tenn	May	Carpenter	Cholera	1 day
25	Rebecca Dorris	15	F				Tenn	July		Cholera	2 days
26	William Emison	61	M			M	France	June		Cholera	7 days
27	Elizabeth Moore	62	F			W	Va	July		Cholera	4 days
28	Orville James	1	M				Tenn	July		Cholera	1 day
29	Rufus James	3	M	B	S		Tenn	July		Cholera	3 days
30	Cymbert Fowbert	1	F				Ohio	Feb		Fits	1 day
31	Lewis Shores	31	M			M	Germany	July		Cholera	1 day
32	George Shores	10	M				Germany	July		Cholera	1 day
33	A. Dibrell	55	M	B	S	M	Maryland	Feb		Scrofula	6 months
34	John Kinchum	54	M			M	Kentucky	March	Saddler	Consumption	8 weeks
35	William Marks	1	M				Tenn	July		Cholera	2 days

COUNTY OF DAVIDSON, STATE OF TENNESSEE.

PAGE NO. 161 PERSONS WHO DIED DURING THE YEAR ENDING 1st JUNE, 1850.

City of Nashville

No. of Visit	Name	Age	Sex	Color	Free or Slave	Married/Widowed	Place of Birth	Month Died	Occupation	Disease or Cause of Death	No. Days Ill
1	William Seay	45	M	B	S	M	Tenn	July		Cholera	12 days
2	Sutton Walker	40	M	B	S		Va	July		Cholera	1 day
3	Frank Walker	20	M	M	S		Tenn	July		Cholera	1 day
4	William Walker	24	M	M	S		Tenn	July		Consumption	4 weeks
5	Samuel Walker	1	M	M	S		Tenn	Feb		Teething	1 week
6	W. W. Sullivan	45	M			M	Tenn	July		Cholera	1 week
7	Polly Lane	22	F	B	S	M	Tenn	Dec		Consumption	11 weeks
8	Nancy Allen	6	F				Tenn	July		Cholera	1 day
9	Josephine Allen	1	F				Tenn	July		Cholera	1 day
10	Robert Bell	5	M	M	S		Tenn	Aug		Cholera	3 days
11	Alexander Bell	4	M	M	S		Tenn	Aug		Cholera	3 days
12	William Irwin	9	M				Tenn	July		Cholera	1 day
13	Mary Merchant	6	F				England	July		Cholera	1 day
14	Joseph W. Merchant	1	M				Tenn	July		Inflamation of brain	4 days
15	Calvin Campbell	57	M			M	Kentucky	July	Printer	Cholera	1 day

COUNTY OF DAVIDSON, STATE OF TENNESSEE.

PAGE NO. 161   PERSONS WHO DIED DURING THE YEAR ENDING 1st JUNE, 1850.

City of Nashville

No. of Visit	Name	Age	Sex	Color	Free or Slave	Married/Widowed	Place of Birth	Month Died	Occupation	Disease or Cause of Death	No. Days Ill
16	John Ferguson	32	M				Ireland	July	none	Cholera	1 day
17	Fergus Hickey	27	M				Ireland	July	none	Cholera	1 day
18	Patrick Finney	25	M				Ireland	July	none	Cholera	7 days
19	Michael Monahan	25	M				Ireland	July	none	Cholera	1 day
20	Patrick Kenaday	25	M				Ireland	July	none	Cholera	1 day
21	James Kenaday	22	M				Ireland	July	none	Cholera	1 day
22	Mary Clinard	95	F				Ireland	Feb		Old age	3 years
23	E. C. Garrett	72	F			M	N.C.	July		Old age	2 months
24	Prymus Garrett	70	M	B	S	M	Va	July		Consumption	6 months
25	William Conn	40	M			M	N.C.	July	Carpenter	Cholera	2 days
26	William J. Conn	2	M				Tenn	March		Teething	1 week
27	Josephine Smith	12	F				Tenn	Dec		Bil. fever	2 weeks
28	Absalom Jarrett	27	M	M		M	Tenn	June		Cholera	1 day
29	Thomas Osburn	9	M				Tenn	July		Cholera	1 day
30	Samuella Jones	18	F				Tenn	July		Cholera	2 days
31	Marcus M. Jones	10	M				Tenn	June		Inflamation of brain	5 days
32	Sarah J. Mann	40	F			M	N.C.	Feb		T. fever	1 week
33	George Hanable	25	M			M	Tenn	June		Cholera	1 day
34	Solomon King	50	M			M	Va	Jan	Painter	Consumption	2 months
35	Jerry Conrad	22	M	B			Tenn	June	Barber	Cholera	1 day

COUNTY OF DAVIDSON, STATE OF TENNESSEE.

PAGE NO. 163   PERSONS WHO DIED DURING THE YEAR ENDING 1st JUNE, 1850.

City of Nashville

No. of Visit	Name	Age	Sex	Color	Free or Slave	Married/Widowed	Place of Birth	Month Died	Occupation	Disease or Cause of Death	No. Days Ill
1	Charles Trousdale	1	M	M	S		Tenn	Jan		Inflamation of lungs	2 weeks
2	David Lapsley	50	M	B	S	M	Tenn	Nov		Hemorrhage	1 day
3	Comford Moody	73	F	B	F	W	Va	March		Consumption	1 week
4	Frances McFarlan	25	F			M	Ireland	June		Consumption	5 months
5	John W. Gilliam	22	M				Ireland	July	Clerk	Ulcer	12 months
6	Polly Demorel	40	F	B	S	M	Va	June		Cholera	1 day
7	J. Moore	27	M	M	S	M	Tenn	July		Cholera	9 day
8	Samuel Hamilton	60	M	B	S	M	Va	July		Cholera	1 day
9	Peggy Tolbert	75	F	B	S	W	Va	June		Fall	3 weeks
10	Street Ball	23	M	B	S		Kentucky	June		Cholera	1 day
11	Mary E. Buch	1	F				Tenn	May		S. fever	9 days
12	Dinah Best	73	F	B	S	W	Va	June		Cholera	1 week
13	Frank Best	38	M	B	S	M	Maryland	June		Cholera	3 days
14	Margaret Mayors	37	F			M	Tenn	July		Cholera	1 day
15	Isabel Mayors	9	F				Tenn	July		Cholera	1 day
16	Nancy Corbett	3	F				Tenn	July		Lock jaw	2 weeks
17	B. Harrison	42	M				Tenn	Oct		Mercury	1 day
18	James Monroe	6m	M				Tenn	June		Cholera	3 days
19	James Hendrick	1	M				Tenn	June		Teething	1 week
20	Mary Mills	47	F			M	N.C.	July		Consumption	2 months
21	Mary A. Edwards	26	F				Tenn	Aug		Consumption	4 months
22	A. Craddock	45	M			M	Tenn	July		Cholera	1 day
23	Mary C. Orton	4	F				Tenn	July		Cholera	1 day
24	Jack Marston	31	M	M			Tenn	June		Cholera	1 day
25	Louisa Asewood	1	F				England	Nov		Teething	1 week
26	Charlotte J. Jackson	2	F				Tenn	July		Cholera	1 day
27	John Ewin	5	M	M	S		Tenn	June		Cholera	1 day
28	James H. Ewin	3	M	M	S		Tenn	July		Cholera	1 day
29	Robert Lynch	2	M				Tenn	July		Bil. fever	11 days
30	Mary F. Stearnes	3	F				Tenn	Sept		Flux	5 days

COUNTY OF DAVIDSON, STATE OF TENNESSEE.

PAGE NO. 163 PERSONS WHO DIED DURING THE YEAR ENDING 1st JUNE, 1850.

City of Nashville

No. of Visit	Name	Age	Sex	Color	Free or Slave	Married/Widowed	Place of Birth	Month Died	Occupation	Disease or Cause of Death	No. Days Ill
31	Infant	5m	M	B	S		Tenn	Aug		Diarrhea	2 days
32	M. Goulinham	35	M			M	Europe	July	Cashier in Bank	Cholera	3 days
33	John F. Snell	2	M				Tenn	June		Consumption	1 week
34	Edward Brown	2	M				Tenn	July		Inflation of bowels	1 month
35	William Hickman	25	M	B	S	M	Tenn	July		Cholera	1 day

COUNTY OF DAVIDSON, STATE OF TENNESSEE.

PAGE NO. 166 PERSONS WHO DIED DURING THE YEAR ENDING 1st JUNE, 1850.

City of Nashville

No. of Visit	Name	Age	Sex	Color	Free or Slave	Married/Widowed	Place of Birth	Month Died	Occupation	Disease or Cause of Death	No. Days Ill
1	Silvia Brown	45	F	M	S	M	Va	June		Cholera	1 day
2	Sarah Brown	45	F	M	S	M	Va	June		Cholera	1 day
3	William Harris	6	M	M			Tenn	June		Cholera	1 day
4	B. Parker	7m	M	B	F		Tenn	April		Inflation of brain	4 days
5	L. J. Manhal	1	F				Tenn	July		Teething	2 weeks
6	Thomas S. Ryan	13	M				Tenn	July		Cholera	1 day
7	John I. Manhal	26	M				Tenn	July	Physician	Cholera	1 day
8	Louisa Pecar	19	F				Ohio	July		Cholera	1 day
9	Albert Pecar	9m	M				Tenn	Sept		Teething	3 weeks
10	Mary A. Fortrell	2	F				Tenn	Dec		Croup	2 weeks
11	Margaret Kerby	3	F				Tenn	April		T. fever	1 week
12	William Kerby	10	M				Tenn	July		Cholera	1 day
13	Lewis Kerby	8	M				Tenn	July		Cholera	1 day
14	P. Irvin Kerby	2	M				Tenn	July		Cholera	1 day
15	Rachel Kerby	28	F				Tenn	July		Cholera	1 day
16	Sarah M. Wilcum	1	F				Tenn	July		Cholera	1 day
17	Mary Brown	50	F	B	S	W	Va	July		Cholera	1 day
18	W. W. Duff	23	M			M	Tenn	June		Cholera	1 day
19	William H. Jackson	9	M				Tenn	June		Cholera	1 day
20	Rachel Robertson	2	F				Tenn	March		Teething	1 week
21	Thomas Sullivant	39	M			M	Ireland	July		Killed	3 days
22	Thomas E. Sullivant	3	M				Va	July		Cholera	5 days
23	Caroline Smith	14	F	B	S		Tenn	June		Consumption	6 months
24	Albert Lewis	40	M	M		M	Tenn	Feb		Bil. fever	2 weeks
25	Lucinda Lewis	17	F	M			Tenn	July		Cholera	1 day
26	Mariah Lewis	8	F	M			Tenn	July		Cholera	1 day
27	Hucy Gordon	40	M	B	S	M	Tenn	June		Cholera	1 day
28	Frances Gordon	55	F	M	S	M	Va	June		Cholera	1 day
29	Thomas Grubbs	40	M			M	Tenn	July		Consumption	2 years
30	William Grubbs	3	M				Va	July		Cholera	2 days
31	Martha Mason	30	F			W	Tenn	July		Cholera	1 day
32	Jackson Travis	27	M			M	Alabama	Feb	Stone-cutter	Cholera	1 day
33	Martha Grodon	40	F	B	S	M	Tenn	July		Cholera	1 day
34	William T. Johnson	21	M				Tenn	July	Carpenter	Cholera	1 day
35	John D. Jacobs	6	M				Tenn	June		Cholera	2 days

COUNTY OF DAVIDSON, STATE OF TENNESSEE.

PAGE NO. 167 PERSONS WHO DIED DURING THE YEAR ENDING 1st JUNE, 1850.

City of Nashville

No. of Visit	Name	Age	Sex	Color	Free or Slave	Married/Widowed	Place of Birth	Month Died	Occupation	Disease or Cause of Death	No. Days Ill
1	Franklin W. Hite	30	M			M	Ga	April	none	Small pox	12 days
2	Richard A. Hite	1	M				Tenn	April		Small pox	90 days
3	Adaline Reed	—	M?				Tenn	May		Still born	sudden
4	Thomas Gilbert	21	M	B	F	M	Tenn	March		Consumption	90 days
5	Ann Hathaway	56	F			M	Va	Aug		Consumption	1 day
6	William H. T. Petit	3	M				Tenn	Aug		Cholera	6 days
7	Virginia Johnson	13	F				Va	May		T. fever	15 days
8	Franklin Roane	26	M				Tenn	May		Small pox	14 days
9	John H. Harris	40	M			M	Tenn	July	Merchant	Inflamation of lungs	29 days
10	Sarah Reives	22	F	M		M	Tenn	June		Cholera	1 day
11	Mary A. Shepard	56	F			M	Ireland	March		Consumption	8 days
12	F. C. Hart, Jr.	7m	M				Tenn	Dec		Disease of heart	210 days
13	Isaac F. Hart	2	M				Tenn	June		Teething	2 days
14	Elizabeth Herigus	54	F			M	Germany	June		Cholera	3 days
15	B. A. Herigus	20	F				Penn	June		Cholera	1 day
16	William Herigus	13	M				Penn	July		Cholera	1 day
17	Charles E. Shepard	2	M				Tenn	June		Cholera	14 days
18	Mary Blake	40	F			M	N.C.	June		Cholera	4 days
19	Martha E. Blake	1	F				Tenn	June		Cholera	1 day
20	Marinda Brooks	30	F	B	S	M	Tenn	June		Cholera	10 days
21	Mary J. Brooks	10m	F	B	S		Tenn	June		Cholera	28 days
22	M. B. Brooks	1	F				Tenn	June		Cholera	35 days
23	Joseph Carpenter	15	M				Alabama	June	Painter	Cholera	1 day
24	Sarah Hanks	10	F				Tenn	July		Cholera	1 day
25	James Owens	25	M				Tenn	June		Fever	9 days
26	William Owens	9	M				Tenn	July		Cholera	1 day
27	Philadelphia	50	F	B	S	M	Va	June		Cholera	sudden
28	Albert P. Reeves	44	M			M	Va	June	none	Cholera	1 day
29	Francis Smith	1	M	B	S		Tenn	June		Croup	3 days
30	Elmira Moore	1	F				Tenn	June		Teething	5 weeks
31	Infant	—	F	B			Tenn	April		Still born	sudden
32	Daniel Stout	33	M	B	S	W	Kentucky	June		Apoplexy	sudden
33	Angline Hall	17	F				Tenn	July		Cholera	2 days
34	Jane Ray	20	F	M		W	Tenn	July		Cholera	5 days
35	William Mallory	60	M	M		M	Va	Sept		Fever	2 weeks

COUNTY OF DAVIDSON, STATE OF TENNESSEE.

PAGE NO. 170 PERSONS WHO DIED DURING THE YEAR ENDING 1st JUNE, 1850.

No. of Visit	Name	Age	Sex	Color	Free or Slave	Married/Widowed	Place of Birth	Month Died	Occupation	Disease or Cause of Death	No. Days Ill
1	Samuel Ford	26	M			M	Va	Sept	Carpenter	Fever	2 weeks
2	Alexander Hannon	11	M				Tenn	May		unknown	1 day
3	John Cartwright	1	M				Tenn	Nov		unknown	21 days
4	Susan J. Thornhill	2	F				Tenn	May		Cholera	3 days
5	Susan C. Heyes	1	F				Tenn	Feb		Small pox	13 days
6	Infant	4m	F				Tenn	March		Small pox	10 days
7	Cordelia Grooms	3m	F				Tenn	June		Congestive fever	7 days
8	Thomas Dews	1	M				Tenn	March		Taking Laudanum	2 days
9	Infant	7m	M				Tenn	July		Bold hives	1 day
10	Infant	1m	M				Tenn	Aug		Dysentery	1 day
11	H. G. Bryant	46	M				Va	Sept	none	Fever	13 days
12	Henry Rye	49	M			M	Va	June	none	Cholera	1 day
13	William M. Smith	2	M				Tenn	Dec		S. Complaint	90 days
14	Andrew E. Smith	11	M				Tenn	May		Drowned	sudden
15	Rachel Smith	52	F	B	S	M	Va	Feb		Small pox	23 days

COUNTY OF DAVIDSON, STATE OF TENNESSEE.

PAGE NO. 170 PERSONS WHO DIED DURING THE YEAR ENDING 1st JUNE, 1850.

City of Nashville

No. of Visit	Name	Age	Sex	Color	Free or Slave	Married/Widowed	Place of Birth	Month Died	Occupation	Disease or Cause of Death	No. Days Ill
16	B. D. Hawkins, Jr.	1	M				Tenn	July		Inflamation of Brain	5 days
17	E. McGinnis	26	F				Tenn	June		Cholera	5 days
18	James Pew	20	M				Tenn	Sept	none	T. Fever	4 days
19	Leonard K. Massey	21	M				Tenn	Oct	Brick-mason	Fever	5 days
20	Frances Curtis	56	F	B	S	W	Tenn	May		Cancer	120 days
21	Mariah Stull	28	F			W	Kentucky	Feb		Small Pox	10 days
22	Infant	2m	F				Tenn	Feb		Small Pox	1 day
23	Infant		F				Tenn	July		Still born	6 hours
24	Thomas H. Parrish	37	M			M	Va	April	Dragman	Shot	sudden
25	Samuel Parrish	50	M	B	S	W	Va	June		Cholera	1 day
26	Francis M. Thompson	45	M			M	Va	Aug	Cooper	Nervous fever	8 days
27	Lucy Curley	63	F			W	Va	April		Conjestive chill	4 days
28	George Curley	5	M				Tenn	Sept		Pneumonia	11 days
29	Elizabeth Bankston	66	F			W	N.C.	Nov		Cholera	1 day
30	John T. Gant	3	M				Tenn	Aug		Croup	2 days
31	Moses Eakin	57	M			M	Va	June	Carpenter	T. Fever	18 days
32	Susan Parrish	43	F	M	S	M	Kentucky	June		Cholera	2 days
33	Harriett Bonville	48	F			W	France	April		Consumption	3 weeks
34	H. J. Ray	10m	F				Tenn	May		Inflamation of brain	30 days
35	William L. Newman	2	M				Tenn	June		Cholera	3 days

COUNTY OF DAVIDSON, STATE OF TENNESSEE.

PAGE NO. 171 PERSONS WHO DIED DURING THE YEAR ENDING 1st JUNE, 1850.

City of Nashville

No. of Visit	Name	Age	Sex	Color	Free or Slave	Married/Widowed	Place of Birth	Month Died	Occupation	Disease or Cause of Death	No. Days Ill
1	James Bledsoe	35	M			M	Tenn	April	Carpenter	Pleurisy	9 days
2	James Bledsoe, Jr.	7	M				Louisiana	July		B. Fever	3 weeks
3	Robert Woods	55	M	B	S	M	Tenn	Feb		Consumption	7 mos.
4	James Pew	36	M				Tenn	Feb	Pilot	Consumption	sudden
5	John Tarver	11	M				Tenn	July		Cholera	1 day
6	Infant		M				Tenn	May		Still born	
7	Infant		M				Tenn	May		Still born	
8	Poline Cox	26	F				Tenn	June		Consumption	8 weeks
9	Infant	8m	F				Tenn	June		unknown	1 day
10	Lewis Matlock	23	M	B	S	M	Tenn	Oct	Blk-smith	Poisoned	9 mos.
11	James Matlock	1	M				Tenn	June		Teething	1 week
12	Malinda Harrison	35	F	B	S	W	Tenn	June		Cholera	1 day
13	Infant		M	B	S		Tenn	June		unknown	7 days
14	Philip Calahan	60	M			M	Ireland	July	Grocer	Cholera	1 week
15	Nancy	12	F	B	S		Tenn	June		Cholera	1 day
16	John Singleton	6m	M	B	S		Tenn	June		Cholera	1 day
17	George Bangor	43	M			M	Germany	May	Confectioner	Dropsy	10 weeks
18	Infant	2m	F				Tenn	March		Fever	2 mos.
19	N. Carol	32	M				Germany	Sept	Prof - music	Cholera	1 day
20	A. Croll	1	M				Tenn	Sept		Inflamation of brain	2 weeks
21	John W. Montgomery	1	M				Tenn	July		Whooping cough	1 year
22	H. H. Wesling	1	M				Tenn	July		Teething	5 weeks
23	William Ewers	42	M			M	Germany	June	Tailor	Cholera	1 day
24	May Ewers	47	F			M	Germany	June		Cholera	1 day
25	Caroline Ewers	12	F				New York	June		Cholera	1 day
26	H. Hartman	28	M			M	Germany	July		Cholera	8 days
27	Elizabeth Hartman	8	F				New York	July		Cholera	1 day
28	Mary Hartman	5	F				Ohio	July		Cholera	8 days
29	Emity Hatman (Hartman)	3	F				Ohio	July		Cholera	8 days

COUNTY OF DAVIDSON, STATE OF TENNESSEE.

PAGE NO. 171 PERSONS WHO DIED DURING THE YEAR ENDING 1st JUNE, 1850.

No. of Visit	Name	Age	Sex	Color	Free or Slave	Married/Widowed	Place of Birth	Month Died	Occupation	Disease or Cause of Death	No. Days Ill
30	Ellen McGee	22	F				Penn	July		Cholera	1 day
31	Charles Mc. McGee	1	M				Tenn	July		Summer complaint	10 days
32	Elizabeth Byrne	1	F				Penn	July		Summer complaint	10 days
33	Joseph Metzell	36	M				Germany	July		Diarrhea	4 days
34	Agusta Foster	56	F			M	England	July		C. Diarrhea	5 months
35	Elizabeth Farnell	50	F			M	Ireland	Oct		B. Heart sting	14 months

COUNTY OF DAVIDSON, STATE OF TENNESSEE.

PAGE NO. 174 PERSONS WHO DIED DURING THE YEAR ENDING 1st JUNE, 1850.

City of Nashville

No. of Visit	Name	Age	Sex	Color	Free or Slave	Married/Widowed	Place of Birth	Month Died	Occupation	Disease or Cause of Death	No. Days Ill
1	Patrick Farnell	28	M				Ireland	June	Merchant	Cholera	5 days
2	George Allen	25	M	B	S		Tenn	July	Blk-smith	Cholera	4 days
3	A. Simms	46	F				Va	Aug		Dropsy	10 days
4	Robert Boyd	80	M				Ireland	Aug	Painter		sudden
5	E. N. Fraley	8m	F				Tenn	June		S. Complaint	5 weeks
6	Frederick Horn	80	M				Va	Dec	Farmer	Old age	3 weeks
7	Karian Donnel	30	M			W	New York	July	Shoe mkr	Cholera	2 days
8	Mary Ann Goss	19	F				Tenn	July		Cholera	1 day
9	Alexander	38	M	M	S		Tenn	June		Small Pox	10 days
10	William Seabury	32	M				New York	Feb	Engineer	Consumption	2 years
11	Margaret Waters	9m	F				Tenn	Aug		Cholera	4 days
12	Adolphus Markin	3m	M				Tenn	March		Lock Jaw	1 day
13	Kaziah	75	F	B	S	M	Tenn	June		Old age	6 months
14	Infant		M	B	S		Tenn	Aug		Lock Jaw	3 days
15	London	35	M	B	S	M	Va	Feb		Cholera	1 day
16	Rebecca Butler	28	F	B	S	M	Va	Feb		Consumption	6 months
17	Jane Robertson	1	F	B	S		Tenn	July		Teething	1 month
18	Mariah	1	F	M	S		Tenn	Oct		Hives	3 days
19	Infants	--	F	M	S		Tenn	Feb		Still born	
20	Daniel Burr	37	M			M	Ireland	Aug	Baker	Fever	3 weeks
21	Infant		M	B	S		Tenn	Dec		Still born	
22	Daniel	40	M	B	S	M	Tenn	July		Cholera	5 days
23	George Apple	36	M			M	Penn	July	Paper hanger	Cholera	1 day
24	J. B. W. Brown	35	M			M	Kentucky	May	Merchant	unknown	1 week
25	Elizabeth Brown	8	F				Tenn	May		Inf. Bowels	10 days
26	Sarah Dice	28	F			M	Ireland	May		Inf. Bowels	3 days
27	Ellen Brown	1	F				Tenn	June		Cholera	1 day
28	J. F. Zentzschel	28	F			M	Germany	June		Cholera	2 days
29	C. Zentzschel	4	M				Tenn	June		Cholera	2 days
30	William O. Zentzschel	1m	M				Tenn	July		Cholera	2 days
31	William Eakin	43	M				Ireland	Aug	Merchant	Inflamation of Bowels	1 day
32	Marinda	40	F	B	S	M	Tenn	July		Cholera	1 day
33	Elenor R. Nichols	4	F				Tenn	July		Cholera	1 day
34	A. Moss	43	M			M	Tenn	Feb	none	Consumption	5 weeks
35	Barbary Foster	3	F	B			Tenn	April		B. Fever	2 months

COUNTY OF DECATUR, STATE OF TENNESSEE.

PAGE NO. 175   PERSONS WHO DIED DURING THE YEAR ENDING 1st JUNE, 1850.

No. of Visit	Name	Age	Sex	Color	Free or Slave	Married/Widowed	Place of Birth	Month Died	Occupation	Disease or Cause of Death	No. Days Ill
1	John N. Turner	20	M				Tenn	March	Laborer	Cholera	5 days
2	William B. Jones	10m	M				Tenn	Dec	none	Croup	15 days
3	Parmelia Lancaster	44	F				Tenn	Nov	none	Fever	55 days
4	John Martin	6	M				Tenn	July	none	accident	sudden
5	Easter	15	F	B	S		Tenn	Nov	none	unknown	7 days
6	Samuel A. Williams	9m	M				Tenn	July	none	unknown	6 days
7	Infant Caudle	1m	M				Tenn	July	none	unknown	sudden
8	Infant Murphy	1m	M				Tenn	Aug	none	unknown	2 days
9	Hugh Vanada	55	M			W	N.C.	May	Blk-smith	B. Pleurisy	8 days
10	Infant	1m	M	B	S		Tenn	Mar		Hives	2 days
11	Nancy Brett	5	F				Arkansas	June	none	Dropsy	Chronic
12	John G. D. Stricklin	3	M				Tenn	Jan	none	Croup	1 day
13	Angeline Waldrum	13	F				Tenn	June	none	Fever	Chronic
14	John M. Veach	1m	M				Tenn	March	none	Hives	2 days
15	Daniel Boman	50	M			M	Tenn	June	none	Fever	6 days
16	Lucinda Boman	45	F			M	Tenn	June	none	Over heat	5 days
17	William Connell	33	M			M	Kentucky	July	Farmer	unknown	Chronic
18	Tyler O'Gwinn	38	M			M	Kentucky	Aug	Farmer	unknown	Chronic
19	Amy Johnson	11m	F				Mississippi	Dec	none	Cold	20 days
20	Hugh W. Long	51	M			M	N.C.	Nov	Farmer	unknown	15 days
21	Matilda Long	31	F			M	Tenn	March	none	Child Birth	sudden
22	Jack	2m	M	B	S		Tenn	June	none	unknown	sudden
23	Thomas M. Watson	4	M				Tenn	Dec	none	Scarlet Fever	7 days
24	William A. Watson	2	M				Tenn	Jan	none	Sc. Fever	9 days
25	Darcas	8	F	B	S		Tenn	July	none	Drowned	sudden
26	Eliza Houston	17	F				Tenn	Sept	none	Fever	19 days
27	Malvina Box	57	F			M	Tenn	Feb	none	Consumption	Chronic
28	Infant Rains	1m	M				Tenn	Nov	none	unknown	9 days
29	Infant slave	1m	M	B	S		Tenn	April	none	unknown	sudden
30	Sarah Wilson	25	F				N.C.	April	none	Child Birth	sudden
31	Samuel W. Hale	14	M				Tenn	Aug	none	Fever	3 days
32	John R. Henson	5	M				Tenn	Aug	none	Fever	3 days
33	Mary C. Watson	1	F				Tenn	Nov	none	Hives	15 days
34	Infant slave	—	M	B	S		Tenn	Dec	none	unknown	sudden

Remarks: Best quality. A great variety of timber, oak of various kinds, hickory in great abundance also poplar of all sizes and description, ash, walnut, gum of various kinds, beech, sugar tree, maple, birch, etc. There has been more overflows in the Tennessee River in the last three years than has been for twenty five years before so much so as to injure the crops maturity in the valley of the River and near the mouths of the creeks.

COUNTY OF DECATUR, STATE OF TENNESSEE.

PAGE NO. 178   PERSONS WHO DIED DURING THE YEAR ENDING 1st JUNE, 1850.

No. of Visit	Name	Age	Sex	Color	Free or Slave	Married/Widowed	Place of Birth	Month Died	Occupation	Disease or Cause of Death	No. Days Ill
1	George Findly	88	M			M	N.C.	June	Laborer	Old Age	9 days
2	John K. D. Goodnight	11m	M				Tenn	Feb	none	Pneumonia	15 days
3	Infant Lucy	___	F				Tenn	July	none	unknown	sudden
4	W. J. Welch	1	M				Tenn	July	none	unknown	6 days
5	Wilson	1	M	M	S		Tenn	July	none	Diarrhea	1 day
6	Holden White	12	M				Tenn	July	none	Fall of a limb	sudden
7	Stephen Harrel	55	M			W	N.C.	Dec	Farmer	Cholera	3 days
8	Mary Jane	1m	F	B	S		Tenn	July	none	unknown	sudden
9	Tennessee M. Wood	9	F				Tenn	June	none	unknown	9 days
10	Mary	2m	F	B	S		Tenn	Dec	none	Croup	1 day
11	Sarah Graham	63	F			W	N.C.	July	none	unknown	15 days
12	Samuel Condor	27	M			M	Tenn	March	Farmer	unknown	30 days
13	Robert Patterson	96	M			W?	Penn	Aug	Sch-teacher	Old Age	sudden
14	Infant Furguson	1m	F				Tenn	Jan	none	unknown	sudden
15	Infant	1m	M	B	S		Tenn	Feb	none	Croup	sudden
16	Rachael	14	F	B	S		Tenn	May	none	Fever	31 days
17	Mary	10m	F	B	S		Tenn	Jan	none	Cold	sudden
18	Samuel Roberts	2m	M				Tenn	Oct	none	Croup	sudden
19	Huldah W. J. Poar(Poor)	15	F				Tenn	June	none	Dropsy	Chronic
20	Holden W. Plunckett	47	M			M	N.C.	July	Farmer	Fever	? week
21	Samuel Amos	1	M				Tenn	May	none	Fever	8 days
22	M. R. Fisher	54	M			M	N.C.	June	Farmer	Consumption	Chronic
23	Nancy Fisher	15	F				Tenn	June	none	Cholera	6 days
24	Samuel Smith	14	M				Tenn	March	none	unknown	150 days
25	Isabella Smith	1	F				Tenn	Jan	none	Sc. Fever	11 days
26	Infant	___	M	B	S		Tenn	April	none	Died in Birth	sudden
27	Dewit C. Beaver	1m	M				Tenn	Feb	none	Croup	1 day
28	Celia A. Givins	2m	F				Tenn	June	none	Croup	5 days
29	James Croman	27	M				Alabama	April	Farmer	Fever	2 days
30	Henry H. Brown	1	M				Tenn	Feb	none	Fever	9 days
31	Calvin C. Roach	2	M				Tenn	Dec	none	Dropsy	Chronic
32	James Mahan	54	M			M	Tenn	Jan	Farmer	Inf. of the lungs	
33	James J. Burk	20	M				Virginia	July	Farmer	Congestive Chill	5 days
34	Infant Johnson	___	M				Tenn	Jan	none	Died in Birth	sudden
35	Infant Johnson	___	M				Tenn	Jan	none	Died in Birth	sudden

Remarks: In this County, there has been several cases of cholera during the spring and summer of 1849 without any apparent cause so far as the most expierenced Physicians were capable of judging. The character of the water is varied, principally limestone, some freestone and a number of fine sulphur springs. The soil is very good in the valleys. Quantity of mountainous poor land with great abundance of limestone rock with fine specimen of secondary marble, a quantity iron ore of the .....(not finished)

COUNTY OF DeKALB, STATE OF TENNESSEE.

PAGE NO. 179   PERSONS WHO DIED DURING THE YEAR ENDING 1st JUNE, 1850.

Civil District Nos. 4, 12, 7, & 14.

No. of Visit	Name	Age	Sex	Color	Free or Slave	Married/Widowed	Place of Birth	Month Died	Occupation	Disease or Cause of Death	No. Days Ill
1	William J. Scott	2	M				Tenn	Sept		Hives	sudden
2	Jesse Curtis	8	M				Tenn	July		Disease of Liver	7 days
3	William Williams	66	M			M	N.C.	June	Farmer	Gravel	C(100 days)
4	Infant of John Williams	1	M				Tenn	Oct		unknown	sudden
5	James Johnson	1	M				Tenn	July		unknown	sudden
6	Catharine Curtis	26	F			M	Tenn	Oct		Consumption	C
7	Amanda Driver	3	F				Tenn	June		Croup	sudden
8	Matilda Driver	7	F				Tenn	April		Worms	37 days
9	Silas of J. E. Priched	13	M	B	S		Tenn	June		unknown	C
10	Samuel of J. W. Allen	9m	M	B	S		Tenn	Aug		Scrofula	Chronic
11	Aggy of M. Simpson	1	F	B	S		Tenn	April		Diarrhea	30 days
12	Infant of Hullett	6da	F				Tenn	May		unknown	3 days
13	Mary H. Overall	3	F				Tenn	Oct		Croup	1 day
14	(unnamed) Taylor	1m	F				Tenn	Sept		unknown	4 days
15	Nicholas L. Lasater	1m	M				Tenn	Nov		Hives	sudden
16	Catharine Fowler	2	F				Tenn	Sept		Fall from tree	sudden
17	William A. Green	1	M				Tenn	Dec		Croup	90 days
18	Mary L. Cantrell	10	F				Tenn	May		unknown	Chronic
19	James H. Allen	65	M			M	Va	Aug	Farmer	Cancer	Chronic
20	Jane Hathaway	10	F				Tenn	Nov		unknown	3 days
21	Infant of N. B. Parker	4da	M				Tenn	Nov		unknown	4 days
22	Lot Adcock	16	M				Tenn	Jan	none	unknown	3 days
23	Edmund Judkins	45	M			M	Va	May	Shoemaker	Consumption	Chronic
24	John H. Cutler	26	M				Va	July	Clerking	Consumption	Chronic
25	Etheldred N. Durham	11m	M				Tenn	July		Pneumonia	7 days
26	William Allen	5	M				Tenn	June		Worms	3 days
27	Rachel	9	F	B	S		Tenn	April		Consumption	90 days
28	Ann	35	F	M	S		Tenn	May		Consumption	Chronic
29	Infant	11m	F	M	S		Tenn	May		unknown	5 days
30	Moses Lock	20	M				Tenn	June	Farmer	Affray	sudden
31	William Erwin	70	M			W	Va	March	none	Age	7 days
32	(not named) Willis	6m	M				Tenn	Aug		Hives	3 days
33	Houston, of J.E. Warren	1	M	B	S		Tenn	Oct		unknown	60 days
34	Daughter of William Barr	4 d	F				Tenn	Nov		unknown	4 days
35	William King	51	M			W	Va	Feb	Farmer	Consumption	60 days

COUNTY OF DeKALB, STATE OF TENNESSEE.

PAGE NO. 182   PERSONS WHO DIED DURING THE YEAR ENDING 1st JUNE, 1850.

Civil District No. 1 & 13.

No. of Visit	Name	Age	Sex	Color	Free or Slave	Married/Widowed	Place of Birth	Month Died	Occupation	Disease or Cause of Death	No. Days Ill
1	Martha E. Baird	—	F				Tenn	Nov		Infl of Brain	2 days
2	Infant of D. N. Estes	—	M				Tenn	Aug		Consumption	1 day
3	Pam Neal	36	F			M	Tenn	April		Consumption	C
4	Clarissa	45	F	B	S		Georgia	Feb		unknown	C
5	Ana, Infant not named	—	F				Tenn	Feb		Infl of Brain	5 days
6	Infant of William Jones	—	F				Tenn	July		unknown	7 days
7	Nancy P. Alexander	1	F				Tenn	July		Flux	10 days
8	William Tramel	15	M				Tenn	July	Farmer	Flux	8 days
9	James P. Hass	11	M				Tenn	Aug		Suicide by hanging	
10	Infant son of A.G. Hass	1 d	M				Tenn	May		unknown	1 day
11	Zizizy Burton	10d	F				Tenn	Jan		Hives	sudden
12	Thomas L. Rontsitt(?)	9	M				Tenn	June		Inf. Fever	12 days

COUNTY OF DeKALB, STATE OF TENNESSEE.

PAGE NO. 182 PERSONS WHO DIED DURING THE YEAR ENDING 1st JUNE, 1850.

Civil District No. 1 & 13.

No. of Visit	Name	Age	Sex	Color	Free or Slave	Married/Widowed	Place of Birth	Month Died	Occupation	Disease or Cause of Death	No. Days Ill
13	Mary Evans	65	F				Delaware	Dec		Apoplexy	
14	Henry	4	M	B	S		Tenn	Oct		unknown	C
15	Matilda Williams	21	F				Tenn	July		Fever	25 days
16	Octavo B. Gossett	14	F				Tenn	Sept		Consumption	C
17	a slave, not named	1m	F	B	S		Tenn	April		unknown	sudden
18	a slave, not named	1m	F	B	S		Tenn	May		Spasms	2 days
19	William T. Keaf	5m	M				Tenn	Dec		Inflamation of brain	13 days
20	not named, Derling	1d	F				Tenn	Feb		unknown	1 day
21	Anthony	18	M	B	S		Tenn	Nov	Farmhand	Consumption	C
22	Jane, slave of Grooms	1m	F	B	S		Tenn	Nov		Croup	sudden
23	not named, of J.Turney	1m	F	B	S		Tenn	Nov		unknown	1 day
24	not named, of J.W.Dodd	1m	M				Tenn	April		unknown	2 days
25	Elijah Truett	41	M				Tenn	Oct	Farmer	unknown	10 days
26	not named, Cradoc	1d	M				Tenn	Nov		unknown	1 day
27	William D. Parker	2m	M				Tenn	Sept		unknown	7 days
28	James Crook	46	M				Va	Oct	Farmer	Disease of liver	42 days
29	Mary Tune	25	F				Va	Oct		Fever	21 days
30	not named, of M. Fouch	1d	F	B	S		Tenn	July		unknown	1 day
31	Jordan Morford	14	M				Kentucky	Feb		Dropsy	C
32	Samuel Oakly	1m	M				Tenn	Aug		unknown	7 days
33	George Oakley	3d	M				Tenn	July		unknown	3 days
34	Matthew Parker	1m	M				Tenn	Dec		Hives	sudden
35	Infant of Jeargan	1d	M				Tenn	April		unknown	1 day

COUNTY OF DeKALB, STATE OF TENNESSEE.

PAGE NO. 183 PERSONS WHO DIED DURING THE YEAR ENDING 1st JUNE, 1850.

Civil District No. 9, 6, & 7

No. of Visit	Name	Age	Sex	Color	Free or Slave	Married/Widowed	Place of Birth	Month Died	Occupation	Disease or Cause of Death	No. Days Ill
1	James Johnson	6	M				Tenn	Nov		Scarlet Fever	35 days
2	Mary, of John Frazor	4m	F	B	S		Tenn	Dec		Scarlet Fever	sudden
3	Lemuel B. Whaley	3m	M				Tenn	June		Hives	20 days
4	Amanda Esthman	8m	F				Tenn	Sept		Scarlet Fever	15 days
5	McDowell		M					Dec		Small Pox	C
6	Burr Dosson	4m	M				Tenn	June		Jaundice	
7	Winfield Scott	5d	M				Tenn	April		unknown	sudden
8	John B. Capp	17	M				Tenn	Dec	Farmer	Fall from horse	sudden
9	William N. Martin	7	M				Tenn	Sept		Scarlet Fever	1 day
10	Elias Cantrell	21	M				Tenn	June	Farmer	Pleurisy	4 days
11	Jesse W. Taylor	6m	M				Tenn	Oct		Arazephaton	150 days
12	Henry Hicks	65	M			M	N.C.	May	Blk-smith	Dropsy	70 days
13	Letha Lewna	27	F			M	Alabama	June		Cholera	18 days
14	Mary A. L. Lewna	4m	F				Tenn	April		Hives	2 days
15	Joseph Rankham	89	M			W	N.C.	May	none	Age	15 days
16	Mary Bayn	2	F				Tenn	Aug		Croup	1 day

Remarks: McDowell No. 5, this page, died in this County within the year ending 1st June 1850, was not a permanent resident and is entered from the recollection of Asst. Marshal, no information having been given of his place of birth, name, or age by the family where he died. No. 15, Revolutionary Pensioner.

Note: I do certify that as assistant Marshal in and for the County of DeKalb, State of Tennessee, I have carefully collected the information required in accordance with the term of my oath of Office, that the foregoing is a full true and complete copying of schedule No. 3 statistics of mortality containing four pages, three of 35 lines each and one of sixteen. Total deaths 121. This 18th Dec. 1850.

Joseph Clarke, Asst. Marshal

COUNTY OF DeKALB, STATE OF TENNESSEE.

PAGE NO. 186 PERSONS WHO DIED DURING THE YEAR ENDING 1st JUNE, 1850.

Civil Districts No. 8, 11, & 15 & 9.

No. of Visit	Name	Age	Sex	Color	Free or Slave	Married/Widowed	Place of Birth	Month Died	Occupation	Disease or Cause of Death	No. Days Ill
1	Mary Sulivan	96	F			W	Penn	Feb		Age	14 days
2	Mary Parsley	28	F				Tenn	Oct		Milk Poison	9 days
3	Nancy E. Goss	1	F				Tenn	June		Hives	2 days
4	Jacob T. Tramel	1	M				Tenn	Dec		Hives	4 days
5	William Ellis	7	M				Tenn	July		Head Pleurisy	4 days
6	Adalin Page	1	F				Tenn	Aug		Croup	2 days
7	Mary E. McGinnis	2da	F				Tenn	Feb		unknown	1 day
8	John Spencer	9	M				Tenn	July		Dyspepsia	60 days
9	Alexander Taylor	1	M				Tenn	Aug		Inf. of Stomach	24 days
10	Pleasant W. Kerley	4	M				Tenn	Nov		Accident by rolling log	5 days
11	Linton Hale	70	M				Va	Sept	None	Consumption	Chronic
12	Infant of John Manon	1m	M				Tenn	Feb		unknown	30 days
13	Louson H. Trusty	25	M				Tenn	July		Disease of liver	21 days
14	Jacob Page	56	M				N.C.	Dec	Farmer	Fall from horse	sudden
15	Jane Page	45	F				unknown	March		Mortification	14 days
16	Jacob Page	2m	M				Tenn	May		unknown	60 days
17	Alfred Hendrixson	1	M				Tenn	May		unknown	14 days
18	Sarah Shoemaker	71	F			M	Va	May		Pleurisy	80 days
19	William Terrell	24	M				Tenn	Nov		Pneumonia	8 days
20	Frances Wallace	74	F				N.C.	April		Congestive fever	3 days
21	Solomon Goodman	3	M				Tenn	Feb		St. Anthony's fire	60 days
22	Mary Hays	1	F				Tenn	July		Worms	60 days
23	William H. Dosier	11	M				N.C.	June		Dropsy	6 days
24	Prescilla H. Dosier	9	F				N.C.	Aug		Dropsy	6 days
25	Richard Winnard	1m	M				Tenn	Feb		Croup	1 day
26	Sarah, slave of D.W.Brian	1	F	B	S		Alabama	Aug		Cholera Inf.	1 day
27	Edwin L. Stewart	7	M				Tenn	Sept		Scarlet fever	14 days
28	William Dunlap	3	M				Tenn	Sept		Scarlet fever	5 days
29	Infant of R. Cantrell	1m	M				Tenn	Oct		Croup	4 days
30	Calvin B. Gray	2	M				Tenn	Sept		Scarlet fever	28 days
31	Susan Johnson	35	F			M	Tenn	Aug		Cholera	1 day
32	N. L. Dearman	7	M				Tenn	Aug		Scarlet fever	5 days
33	Mary Combs	5	F				Indiana	Aug		Scarlet fever	2 days
34	Sharlotte A. Johnson	6m	F	B	S		Tenn	Sept		Croup	60 days
35	Levi Johnson	8	M				Tenn	Oct		Scarlet fever	4 days

COUNTY OF DICKSON, STATE OF TENNESSEE.

PAGE NO. 187 PERSONS WHO DIED DURING THE YEAR ENDING 1st JUNE, 1850.

Middle District

No. of Visit	Name	Age	Sex	Color	Free or Slave	Married/Widowed	Place of Birth	Month Died	Occupation	Disease or Cause of Death	No. Days Ill
1	Alfred Brown	40	M			M	Georgia	Nov	Farmer	Liver disease	42 days
2	Elizabeth Gray	1	F				Tenn	Sept		Teething	3 months
3	Mary Lampley	81	F			W	S.C.	April		unknown	4 weeks
4	Elizabeth Sullivan	40	F			W	N.C.	Aug		Infl. of stomach	9 days
5	Sarah McMurray	1	F	B	S		Tenn	Sept		unknown	3 months
6	Moses Dickson	14	M	B	S		Tenn	Jan		T. fever	4 weeks
7	Rosetta Stone	2	F	B	S		Tenn	June		Croup	3 months
8	Sarah Garrett	78	F			W	N.C.	Jan		unknown	1 week
9	Ned Napier	80	M	B	S		unknown	Dec		Old age	3 months
10	Parker Vanleer	22	M	B	S		Va	Jan		T. fever	17 days
11	Patrick Vanleer	35	M	B	S		unknown	Jan		Frozen	
12	William T. Crane	20	M				Tenn	Jan	Farmer	Pneumonia	7 days

COUNTY OF DICKSON, STATE OF TENNESSEE.

PAGE NO. 187 PERSONS WHO DIED DURING THE YEAR ENDING 1st JUNE, 1850.

Middle District

No. of Visit	Name	Age	Sex	Color	Free or Slave	Married/Widowed	Place of Birth	Month Died	Occupation	Disease or Cause of Death	No. Days Ill
13	Susan W. Patterson	24	F			W	Va	Jan		T. fever	1 month
14	William Bows	23	M				Tenn	May	Farmer	unknown	15 months
15	Edney Slayden	60	F				Va	May		Pneumonia	9 days
16	John Thorn	76	M			M	Maryland	Nov	Farmer	Infl of lungs	2 weeks
17	Joe Fentress	50	M	M	S		Tenn	Sept		unknown	1 year
18	George Fentress	24	M	M	S		Tenn	July		Infl of lungs	3 months
19	Charles Fentress	2	M	B	S		Tenn	Jan		Infl of bowels	1 week
20	Carter Fentress	6m	M	M	S		Tenn	March		Infl of bowels	1 week
21	Martha J. Adams	6m	F				Tenn	Aug		Hives	1 week
22	Allen Neesbit	6m	M	B	S		Tenn	Sept		Croup	1 day
23	Elizabeth Wells	32	F			W	Tenn	Feb		Cold	2 weeks
24	Eleanor Slayden	32	F	B	S		Tenn	Oct		Hemorage of lungs	6 weeks
25	Easter Slayden	17	F	B	S		Tenn	April		Pneumonia	4 months
26	German Dugger	3m	M				Tenn	Sept		Infl of brain	1 week
27	Joseph Thomas	17	M				Tenn	Jan	Farmer	Sudden fall of a tree	sudden
28	Samuel D. Glass	27	M				Tenn	Dec	Farmer	unknown	4 days
29	Bill Robertson	52	M	B	S		unknown	Nov		Neuralgia	2 years
30	Elijah Robertson	2	M	B	S		Tenn	April		Consumption	
31	Sam Robertson	52	M	B	S		unknown	May		Drowned	
32	Cave Patterson	2	M				Tenn	Sept		Worms	11 days
33	James Patterson	20	M				Tenn	March	Farmer	Consumption	9 months
34	Rhodella Ellis	2	F	B	S		Tenn	April		Consumption	2 years
35	Sarah E. Dickson	6m	F	B	S		Tenn	May		Smothered	

COUNTY OF DICKSON, STATE OF TENNESSEE.

PAGE NO. 190 PERSONS WHO DIED DURING THE YEAR ENDING 1st JUNE, 1850.

Middle District

No. of Visit	Name	Age	Sex	Color	Free or Slave	Married/Widowed	Place of Birth	Month Died	Occupation	Disease or Cause of Death	No. Days Ill
1	Mary C. Anderson	1	F				Tenn	July		Whooping cough	21 days
2	Georgiana Anderson	3	F	M	S		Tenn	July		Whooping cough	6 days
3	Henry Anderson	7m	M	B	S		Tenn	July		Whooping cough	7 days
4	Elisa A. Jones	12	F				Tenn	Sept		unknown	1 month
5	Josephine Smith	11m	F				Tenn	Dec		unknown	12 days
6	Thomas D. Bell	26	M				Alabama	July	Farmer	Cholera	2/24
7	Washington Bell	53	M	B	S		N.C.	Feb		unknown	3 months
8	Patience Hunter	74	F			W	N.C.	June		Dropsy	6 months
9	Caroline Sensing	4	F				Tenn	June		Phthisic	1 day
10	David Orsbrooks	53	M			M	N.C.	March	Farmer	Falling of a tree	sudden
11	Milly Jackson	30	F	B	S		Tenn	June		Lock jaw	3 days
12	Patsey Jackson	9m	F	B	S		Tenn	July		unknown	4 days
13	Anthony Cannon	41	M			M	Va	May	Collier	Cholera	4 days
14	John Bell	52	M			M	Tenn	Jan	Iron W.Mgr.	Fever	10 days
15	Sarah Cunningham	64	F			M	N.C.	Sept		Gastralgia	9 months
16	Charity Grymes	2m	F	B	S		Tenn	March		Smothered	sudden
17	Joe Leech	3	M	M	S		Tenn	May		Phthisic	1 day
18	William Brown	22	M				Kentucky	May	Farmer	Poisoned	2 days
19	Mary A. Mickle	3	F				Tenn	Dec		Pneumonia	2 weeks
20	Isabella Smith	65	F			M	Penn	Oct		Pneumonia	3 weeks
21	Rachael Crumpler	4	F				Tenn	Oct		Burnt	sudden
22	Emily Russell	3m	F				Tenn	Dec		Fever	1 month
23	William Brown	57	M				S.C.	Dec	Pauper	Dropsy (at Poor-house)	4 months
24	Elizabeth Willey	9	F				Tenn	June		Cholera Morbus	3 days

COUNTY OF DICKSON, STATE OF TENNESSEE.

PAGE NO. 190 PERSONS WHO DIED DURING THE YEAR ENDING 1st JUNE, 1850.

Middle District

No. of Visit	Name	Age	Sex	Color	Free or Slave	Married/Widowed	Place of Birth	Month Died	Occupation	Disease or Cause of Death	No. Days Ill
25	Henry H. Hutton	2m	M				Tenn	March		Croup	1 month
26	Infant of Aaron Laws	11m	M				Tenn	July		unknown	14 days
27	Martha Brown	80	F			M	Georgia	Nov		Infl of stomach	6 days
28	Ellen Karns	1m	F				Tenn	Nov		unknown	1 month
29	Rachael Berry	30	F	B	S		Tenn	May		Abscess on side	6 months
30	Mary E. Parrotte	7	F				Tenn	Feb		Pneumonia	8 days
31	Sarah Goodwin	80	F				Va	March		unknown	sudden
32	Nancy A. Rider	21	F				Tenn	April		Consumption	12 months
33	Garrett Hall	51	M			M	Georgia	Aug	Hse-carpenter	Congestive fever	6 days
34	Joshua Brown	40	M			M	Georgia	May	Farmer	Dropsy	3 months
35	Robert Nolen	30	M			M	S.C.	May	Farmer	T. fever	3 months

COUNTY OF DICKSON, STATE OF TENNESSEE.

PAGE NO. 191 PERSONS WHO DIED DURING THE YEAR ENDING 1st JUNE, 1850.

Middle District

No. of Visit	Name	Age	Sex	Color	Free or Slave	Married/Widowed	Place of Birth	Month Died	Occupation	Disease or Cause of Death	No. Days Ill
1	Serena Morris	73	F				Georgia	Dec		Deranged (unknown)	3 years
2	Zadok Patton	70	M				Maryland	Sept	Farmer	Dropsy	20 years
3	Martha Batthrop	1	F	B	S		Tenn	Aug		Pneumonia	10 days
4	Allen Neesbit	6m	M	B	S		Tenn	Jan		Croup	2 days
5	William H. May	1	M				Tenn	Aug		Inf of breast	2 days
6	Sarah J. Etheridge	1m	F				Tenn	May		unknown	1 day
7	S. Rutledge	21	F				Tenn	Feb		Rheumatism	7 years
8	William H. Monk	1	M				Tenn	May		Croup	3 days
9	Jessie Emory	15	M				N.C.	April		Inf of lungs	21 days

Remarks: This is to certify that this is a true copy of the mortality of Dickson County, State of Tennessee for the year ending on the 1st of June 1850 and that it has been taken in accordance with my oath and instruction to the best of my knowledge and belief.

George F. Raworth, Asst. Marshall
for the Dickson Cty, Subdivision.

COUNTY OF DYER, STATE OF TENNESSEE.

PAGE NO. 193   PERSONS WHO DIED DURING THE YEAR ENDING 1st JUNE, 1850.

No. of Visit	Name	Age	Sex	Color	Free or Slave	Married/Widowed	Place of Birth	Month Died	Occupation	Disease or Cause of Death	No. Days Ill
1	Charity Ferrell	53	F			M	N.C.	Dec		Pneumonia	14 days
2	Dent Ferrell	55	M			W	N.C.	Dec		Pneumonia	21 days
3	Samuel	2	M	B	S		Tenn	April		Consumption	C
4	James	33	M	M	S	S	Va	Jan		Pneumonia	18 days
5	Rossa	1	F	B	S		Tenn	unknown		Croup	20 days
6	J. B. Dearman	5m	M				Tenn	Dec		unknown	21 days
7	Eli Hendricks	15	M				Tenn	Dec	Farmer	Pneumonia	15 days
8	L. Canady	1m	F				Tenn	April		unknown	7 days
9	Willis Ferrell	58	M			M	N.C.	Jan	Farmer	Inflamation, etc.	C
10	A. Holland	1m	M				Tenn	March		Fits	2 days
11	Thomas Curtis	20	M				Tenn	Oct	Farmer	Consumption	C
12	Henry	3	M	B	S		Tenn	April		Inflamation of brain	10 days
13	William Curtis	1m	M				Tenn	Oct		Croup	4 days
14	Frances Bagget	22	F			M	Tenn	Feb		Liver disease	C
15	W. F. Sawyer	8	M				Tenn	June		Risings	C
16	V. Foster	14	F				Tenn	June		Consumption	C
17	Solomon	50	M	B	S		Va	Aug		Consumption	C
18	W. H. Duke	2m	M				Tenn	Nov		Cholera	2 days
19	Lewis	18	M	B	S		Kentucky	Oct		Pneumonia	7 days
20	C. L. Thurman	3	F				Tenn	April		Pneumonia	18 days
21	S. Simmons	1	F				Tenn	Aug		unknown	6 weeks
22	W. H. Atkins	1	M				Tenn	Sept		Croup	1 day
23	Delila	3m	F	B	S		Tenn	Oct		Overlaid	sudden
24	Flora	4	F	B	S		Tenn	Aug		Fever	4 days
25	H. McCullock	2	F				Tenn	Aug		Fever	4 days
26	B. Tarrent	2	F				Tenn	Sept		Pneumonia	20 days
27	Henry Reed	23	M				Tenn	Feb	Farmer	Pneumonia	14 days
28	Margaret Turner	32	F				Tenn	Jan		Pneumonia	6 days
29	J. Scoby	79	M				N.C.	Oct	Farmer	Pneumonia	10 days
30	E. Thomas	84	M				N.C.	Dec		Pneumonia	14 days
31	Susan	33	F	B	S		N.C.	Jan		Pneumonia	10 days
32	M. Wyatte	6	M				N.C.	Dec		Dropsy	C
33	M. Tucker	31	F				N.C.	Jan		Pleurisy	3 days
34	J. M. McCorkle	46	M				N.C.	Dec	Farmer	Pneumonia	11 days
35	A. Pierce	18	M				Tenn	Aug	Farmer	Poison	4 days

COUNTY OF DYER, STATE OF TENNESSEE.

PAGE NO. 196   PERSONS WHO DIED DURING THE YEAR ENDING 1st JUNE, 1850.

No. of Visit	Name	Age	Sex	Color	Free or Slave	Married/Widowed	Place of Birth	Month Died	Occupation	Disease or Cause of Death	No. Days Ill
1	M. L. Eason	4	F				Tenn	April		T. fever	28 days
2	W. W. Shelton	3m	M				Tenn	May		W. Cough	20 days
3	Susan E. Murder	4	F				Tenn	Oct		Milk tick	4 days
4	Jane Miller	3m	F				Tenn	July		Cholera infantum	9 days
5	Mary E. Loveing	20	F				Tenn	March		Cancer	4 years
6	Susan Meredith	1m	F				Tenn	July		Hives	3 days
7	Amanda	2	F	B	S		Tenn	June		Rickets	5 months
8	Mary	1	F	B	S		Tenn	Oct		Croup	1 day
9	Crisey Tetton	67	F			M	N.C.	May		unknown	sudden
10	J. T. Moore	1	F				Tenn	Sept		Chills	14 days
11	Archey	1	M	B	S		Tenn	Jan		unknown	3 weeks
12	L. V. Turnage	1m	M				Tenn	Feb		Croup	2 days

COUNTY OF DYER, STATE OF TENNESSEE.

PAGE NO. 196 PERSONS WHO DIED DURING THE YEAR ENDING 1st JUNE, 1850.

No. of Visit	Name	Age	Sex	Color	Free or Slave	Married/Widowed	Place of Birth	Month Died	Occupation	Disease or Cause of Death	No. Days Ill
13	E. J. Harrell	1	F				Tenn	April		Disease of lungs	25 days
14	J. B. Moss	1m	M				Tenn	March		Jaundice	4 days
15	H. Robeson	2m	F				Tenn	Feb		Shingles	21 days
16	Mary	23	F	B	S		Tenn	Feb		Consumption	C
17	Issabella	3	F	B	S		Tenn	Nov		Consumption	C
18	John Goodlow	1m	M				Tenn	Oct		Croup	2 days
19	M. J. Mills	3m	F				Tenn	Nov		unknown	4 days
20	Volentine Pierce	17	M				Tenn	May	Farmer	Pneumonia	2 days
21	L. B. McBride	1m	F				Tenn	July		unknown	6 days
22	Lewis	21	M	B	S		N.C.	Oct		Drowning	sudden
23	John H. Light	40	M				Va	Oct	none	unknown	7 days
24	Matilda	8m	F	M	S		Tenn	March		W. Cough	20 days
25	James	14	M	B	S		Tenn	Oct		unknown	sudden
26	Mary	3m	F	B	S		Tenn	Feb		W. Cough	10 days
27	T. T. Webster	1	M				Tenn	Aug		B. fever	5 weeks
28	William	1	M	B	S		Tenn	March		Croup	15 days
29	Charles	2	M	B	S		Tenn	Aug		unknown	15 days
30	Boland	4	M	B	S		Tenn	July		W. Cough	14 days
31	Mary E. Wright	2	F				Tenn	Aug		unknown	9 days
32	P. Henson	4m	F				Tenn	Sept		Hives	23 days
33	F. C. Smith	22	M				N.C.	Oct	Farmer	Pneumonia	8 days
34	E. P. Hamilton	27	F			M	Tenn	Dec		unknown	sudden
35	W. E. Hamilton	7m	F				Tenn	Jan		Pneumonia	20 days

COUNTY OF DYER, STATE OF TENNESSEE.

PAGE NO. 197 PERSONS WHO DIED DURING THE YEAR ENDING 1st JUNE, 1850.

No. of Visit	Name	Age	Sex	Color	Free or Slave	Married/Widowed	Place of Birth	Month Died	Occupation	Disease or Cause of Death	No. Days Ill
1	M. J. Bailey	1	F				Tenn	Sept		Croup	2 days

COUNTY OF FAYETTE, STATE OF TENNESSEE.

PAGE NO. 199 PERSONS WHO DIED DURING THE YEAR ENDING 1st JUNE, 1850.

Civil District No. 1

No. of Visit	Name	Age	Sex	Color	Free or Slave	Married/Widowed	Place of Birth	Month Died	Occupation	Disease or Cause of Death	No. Days Ill
1	Thomas D. Greer	58	M			M	Penn	April	Farmer	Consumption	2 years
2	L. F. Lacy	11m	F				Tenn	March		Inflamation of brain	10 days
3	Mary	1	F	M	S		Va	April		Pneumonia	8 days
4	Fredrick	66	M	B	S		Va	April		Pneumonia	20 days
5	Mary	1	F	B	S		Tenn	May		Pneumonia	20 days
6	Sam	1	M	B	S		Tenn	Sept		Diarrhea	Chronic
7	Wiley Parks	48	M				S.C.	July	none	Fever	21 days
8	Rose	20	F	M	S		N.C.	Jan		Fever	10 days
9	Roselean	2	F	M	S		Tenn	Dec		Diarrhea	7 days
10	Washington	6m	M	B	S		Tenn	Feb		Diarrhea	7 days
11	Harriett	6m	F	B	S		Tenn	April		Diarrhea	7 days

COUNTY OF FAYETTE, STATE OF TENNESSEE.

PAGE NO. 199 PERSONS WHO DIED DURING THE YEAR ENDING 1st JUNE, 1850.

Civil District No. 1

No. of Visit	Name	Age	Sex	Color	Free or Slave	Married/Widowed	Place of Birth	Month Died	Occupation	Disease or Cause of Death	No. Days Ill
12	Clara	42	F	B	S		N.C.	Sept		Consumption	5 years
13	David	15	M	B	S		Va	Dec		Dropsy	4 months
14	Sarah J. Stewart	3m	F				Tenn	March		unknown	sudden
15	John Ozier	55	M			M	N.C.	Oct	Farmer	Consumption	3 years
16	Howell	1	M	B	S		Tenn	Aug		unknown	sudden
17	Clara	19	F	M	S		Tenn	Feb		Burn	8 weeks
18	Juda	4m	F	M	S		Tenn	July		Scrofula	4 months
19	Daniel	4m	M	M	S		Tenn	Sept		Scrofula	4 months
20	Charles	2	M	M	S		Tenn	June		Diarrhea	Chronic
21	Lucy	5	F	B	S		Tenn	March		Fever	20 days
22	Silva	30	F	B	S		N.C.	Nov		Dropsy	5 months
23	Mathew Parish	47	M			M	N.C.	April	Farmer	T. fever	18 days
24	Baker Hudson	67	M			M	Va	May	Farmer	Consumption	3 years
25	Andrew	10	M	B	S		Tenn	Feb		Burn	3 weeks
26	Elvin	25	M	B	S		Tenn	July		Pneumonia	6 months
27	Henrietta	3	F	M	S		Va	Aug		unknown	sudden
28	James Martin	46	M			M	Tenn	Feb	Farmer	Consumption	1 year
29	Hardtimes	1	M	M	S		Tenn	Aug		unknown	Chronic
30	Kitty	70	F	B	S		Va	June		T. fever	2 months

COUNTY OF FAYETTE, STATE OF TENNESSEE.

PAGE NO. 202 PERSONS WHO DIED DURING THE YEAR ENDING 1st JUNE, 1850.

Civil District No. 2

No. of Visit	Name	Age	Sex	Color	Free or Slave	Married/Widowed	Place of Birth	Month Died	Occupation	Disease or Cause of Death	No. Days Ill
1	Margarett A. Long	23	F				Tenn	Sept		Consumption	8 months
2	Thomas J. Cullum	1	M				Tenn	May		Pneumonia	16 days
3	Jim	10	M	B	S		N.C.	May		Pneumonia	4 weeks
4	Manda	12	F	B	S		N.C.	July		Consumption	6 months
5	Margarett Walker	45	F				Tenn	April		Consumption	3 years
6	Samuel K. Willson	27	M				Alabama	June	Farmer	Fever	9 days
7	Sophronia C. Minor	18	F				Tenn	Feb		Spasms	17 years
8	William Bond	2m	M				Tenn	July		unknown	Chronic
9	Looney	1	M	B	S		Tenn	Dec		Pneumonia	6 weeks
10	William	7m	M	B	S		Tenn	July		Pneumonia	2 weeks
11	Frances	7m	F	B	S		Tenn	July		Pneumonia	2 weeks
12	Alfred	1	M	B	S		Tenn	Jan		Fever	5 days

COUNTY OF FAYETTE, STATE OF TENNESSEE.

PAGE NO. 203 PERSONS WHO DIED DURING THE YEAR ENDING 1st JUNE, 1850.

Civil District No. 3

No. of Visit	Name	Age	Sex	Color	Free or Slave	Married/Widowed	Place of Birth	Month Died	Occupation	Disease or Cause of Death	No. Days Ill
1	Jane Read	71	F				Va	Aug		Palsy	8 months
2	Easter	8m	F	B	S		Tenn	March		Croup	2 days
3	Wesley	9m	M	B	S		Tenn	Aug		Inflamation of bowels	8 days
4	Caty	17	F	B	S		Alabama	Oct		Pneumonia	7 days
5	Mary	2m	F	B	S		Tenn	March		unknown	sudden
6	Ann	4m	F	B	S		Tenn	Jan		unknown	sudden
7	William E. Bridgewater	1	M				Tenn	Oct		Diarrhea	Chronic
8	John Wright	56	M				N.C.	July	Hse-carpenter	Laryngitis	4 weeks
9	Tom	6	M	B	S		Tenn	Dec		Spasms	sudden
10	Jinney	84	F	B	S		N.C.	Oct		Consumption	15 months
11	Tom	65	M	B	S		N.C.	Jan		Consumption	12 months
12	James	3	M	B	S		N.C.	Aug		Croup	3 days
13	Henry	2	M	B	S		N.C.	Dec		Dropsy	21 days
14	Fillis	6m	F	B	S		Tenn	July		Diarrhea	7 days
15	Isreal	5m	M	B	S		Tenn	July		unknown	sudden
16	Polly	20	F	B	S		Tenn	May		Rheumatism	14 days

COUNTY OF FAYETTE, STATE OF TENNESSEE.

PAGE NO. 206 PERSONS WHO DIED DURING THE YEAR ENDING 1st JUNE, 1850.

Civil District No. 4

No. of Visit	Name	Age	Sex	Color	Free or Slave	Married/Widowed	Place of Birth	Month Died	Occupation	Disease or Cause of Death	No. Days Ill
1	Celistia Terry	10m	F				Tenn	March		Pneumonia	7 days
2	Emily	10m	F	B	S		Tenn	Sept		Pneumonia	7 days
3	Nelson	1m	M	B	S		Tenn	Oct		unknown	7 days
4	Tennessee	5	F	B	S		Tenn	March		Diarrhea	Chronic
5	Ned	8m	M	B	S		Tenn	Dec		Inflamation of brain	21 days
6	Anderson	5	M	B	S		Tenn	May		unknown	sudden
7	Henry	12	M	B	S		Tenn	July		Congestive fever	9 days
8	Delia	1	F	B	S		Tenn	March		unknown	Chronic
9	Huell	5	M	B	S		Tenn	Jan		unknown	sudden
10	William C. Burt	49	M			M	N.C.	March	Physician	Cholera	4 days
11	Isaac	60	M	B	S		Va	Jan		Pneumonia	10 days
12	Ann E. Stanley	1	F				Tenn	July		Croup	21 days
13	Henry	3	M	B	S		Tenn	April		Burn	1 day
14	Ann	1	F	B	S		Tenn	Aug		Diarrhea	Chronic
15	Charity	47	F	B	S		N.C.	May		Pneumonia	7 days
16	Jiney	35	F	B	S		Va	April		Dropsy	21 days
17	Nat	1	M	B	S		Tenn	May		Pneumonia	5 days
18	Maranda	35	F	B	S		N.C.	May		Appoplexy	sudden
19	Bennett H. Henderson	67	M			M	Va	Oct	Farmer	Diarrhea	Chronic
20	Silvetta A. B. Henderson	28	F			M	Va	March		T. Fever	21 days
21	Gilbert	55	M	B	S		Va	April		Dropsy	5 years
22	Major	27	M	B	S		Tenn	March		Inflamation of bowels	Chronic
23	William	1	M	B	S		Tenn	Dec		unknown	Chronic
24	Rutha W. Trotter	22	F			M	Tenn	Nov		Consumption	1 year
25	Amy	90	F	B	S		Tenn(?)	March		Asphyxia	10 days
26	James K. P. Hazlewood	5	M				Tenn	April		Congestion	3 days
27	Dick	5	M	B	S		Tenn	Dec		unknown	Chronic

COUNTY OF FAYETTE, STATE OF TENNESSEE.

PAGE NO. 207   PERSONS WHO DIED DURING THE YEAR ENDING 1st JUNE, 1850.

Civil District No. 5

No. of Visit	Name	Age	Sex	Color	Free or Slave	Married/Widowed	Place of Birth	Month Died	Occupation	Disease or Cause of Death	No. Days Ill
1	Henson	18	M	B	S		Va	Feb		Spasms	2 days
2	Stephen	95	M	B	S		N.C.	July		Old age	
3	Roxana	7	F	B	S		Tenn	Feb		Dropsy	Chronic
4	Jinney	2	F	B	S		Tenn	March		Worms	1 month
5	Lousey	1	M	B	S		Tenn	Nov		Diarrhea	Chronic
6	Buckner Harvell	25	M				Tenn	June	Physician	Consumption	5 years
7	Bargella	45	M	B	S		Va	April		Pneumonia	4 weeks
8	Lidda	60	F	B	S		Va	March		Consumption	1 year
9	Angeline	3	F	B	S		Tenn	Dec		unknown	sudden
10	Mary	1	F	B	S		Tenn	Sept		Pneumonia	4 days
11	Tom	6m	M	B	S		Tenn	Oct		Pneumonia	2 days
12	Susan	9m	F	B	S		Tenn	July		Pneumonia	7 days
13	Kasiah	10	F	B	S		Tenn	July		Drowned	sudden
14	William D. Hilliard	5	M				Tenn	Oct		Congestive fever	5 days
15	Sam	5	M	B	S		Tenn	Jan		White swelling	14 days
16	Joe	6m	M	B	S		Tenn	Feb		Inflamation of brain	7 days
17	Mariah	6m	F	B	S		Tenn	April		Croup	2 days
18	Patience	3m	F	B	S		Tenn	Aug		Croup	1 day
19	Nancy	40	F	B	S		unknown	Aug		Dropsy	1 year
20	Martha	3	F	B	S		Tenn	March		unknown	Chronic
21	Rebecca Harris	4m	F				Alabama	April		Diarrhea	Chronic
22	Mariah	23	F	B	S		Va	May		Fever	21 days
23	Solomon	1	M	B	S		Tenn	Oct		Croup	1 day
24	Wesley	4m	M	B	S		Tenn	July		unknown	5 days
25	Elizabeth C. Shaw	4m	F				Tenn	July		unknown	sudden
26	Eliza	22	F	B	S		Va	Nov		Consumption	5 years
27	Wallice	10m	M	B	S		Tenn	Oct		Pneumonia	7 days
28	Lewis	21	M	B	S		Va	Feb		Consumption	4 months
29	Joe	3m	M	B	S		Tenn	July		Diarrhea	14 days
30	Molly	80	F	B	S		Va	April		Old age	

COUNTY OF FAYETTE, STATE OF TENNESSEE.

PAGE NO. 210   PERSONS WHO DIED DURING THE YEAR ENDING 1st JUNE, 1850.

Civil District No. 6

No. of Visit	Name	Age	Sex	Color	Free or Slave	Married/Widowed	Place of Birth	Month Died	Occupation	Disease or Cause of Death	No. Days Ill
1	Joanna Melton	45	F				Tenn	June		Diarrhea	14 days
2	William Melton	14	M				Tenn	June		Gravel	Chronic
3	Marion Melton	7	M				Tenn	June		T. fever	21 days
4	Laura	9m	F	B	S		Tenn	Aug		Diarrhea	Chronic
5	Martha	8m	F	B	S		Tenn	Aug		Diarrhea	Chronic
6	Harriett	2	F	B	S		Tenn	Feb		unknown	1 week
7	Manerva	1	F	B	S		Tenn	May		unknown	1 week
8	M. W. Hunt	11m	F				Tenn	July		Gastric --	10 days
9	Lotta	80	F	B	S		Va	July		Old age	
10	B. W. Guinn	23	M				Va	July	Wagon-maker	T. fever	14 days
11	Julia	2	F	B	S		Tenn	July		Worms	Chronic
12	John	6m	M	B	S		Tenn	March		Burn	sudden
13	Eloweze	4m	F	B	S		Tenn	Aug		Croup	2 days
14	Robert McCraw	1	M				Tenn	Sept		Diarrhea	Chronic
15	Mary B. McCraw	25	F				Tenn	Feb		Consumption	3 years
16	Easter	1m	F	B	S		Tenn	Aug		Diarrhea	Chronic
17	William A. Cothran	1	M				Tenn	July		Diarrhea	Chronic

COUNTY OF FAYETTE, STATE OF TENNESSEE.

PAGE NO. 210 PERSONS WHO DIED DURING THE YEAR ENDING 1st JUNE, 1850.

Civil District No. 6

No. of Visit	Name	Age	Sex	Color	Free or Slave	Married/Widowed	Place of Birth	Month Died	Occupation	Disease or Cause of Death	No. Days Ill
18	Willson	1	M	B	S		Tenn	Jan		Diarrhea	4 days
19	Lucy D. Jammeson	4	F				Tenn	Sept		Burn	sudden
20	Malinda F. L. Burrow	1	F				Tenn	April		unknown	Chronic
21	Francis Lowring	38	M			M	Maryland	Sept	Physician	Pneumonia	10 days
22	Paul	1	M	B	S		Tenn	Feb		Negro Consumption	Chronic
23	Fanny	2m	F	B	S		Tenn	Feb		unknown	Chronic
24	Henry	2	M	B	S		Tenn	Dec		unknown	Chronic
25	Adam	1m	M	B	S		Tenn	March		unknown	sudden
26	Charles	4m	M	B	S		Tenn	Nov		unknown	sudden
27	Jno. W. Rochaels	2	M				Alabama	Sept		Croup	2 days
28	Archabald Wiggins	18	M				N.C.	Sept	none	T. fever	19 days
29	Isaac	12	M	B	S		Tenn	June		Scrofula	2 years
30	Hannah	27	F	B	S		N.C.	Aug		T. fever	19 days
31	Henry	4	M	B	S		Tenn	Sept		T. fever	12 days
32	Samuel Herron	10m	M				Tenn	June		Diarrhea	28 days
33	William M. Rochaels	11m	M				Tenn	Oct		Diarrhea	Chronic
34	Margarett A. Hughes	11m	F				Tenn	Nov		Inflamation of brain	8 days

COUNTY OF FAYETTE, STATE OF TENNESSEE.

PAGE NO. 211 PERSONS WHO DIED DURING THE YEAR ENDING 1st JUNE, 1850.

Civil District No. 7

No. of Visit	Name	Age	Sex	Color	Free or Slave	Married/Widowed	Place of Birth	Month Died	Occupation	Disease or Cause of Death	No. Days Ill
1	Indiana	1	F	B	S		Tenn	Oct		unknown	Chronic
2	William	10	M	B	S		Tenn	Sept		Inflamation of brain	sudden
3	Milly	3	F	B	S		Tenn	May		Whooping cough	6 weeks
4	Thompson	1	M	B	S		Tenn	May		Whooping cough	3 weeks
5	Jim	17	M	B	S		N.C.	Feb		Asthma	Chronic
6	Alice	3	F	B	S		Tenn	Feb		Whooping cough	3 days
7	Wesley	18	M	B	S		Alabama	Jan		Dropsy	7 months
8	William	1	M	B	S		Tenn	April		unknown	Chronic
9	Amanda Robertson	38	F			M	Va	Oct		T. fever	2 weeks
10	Henry	3m	M	B	S		Tenn	Oct		unknown	sudden
11	Charles Hughes	10m	M				Tenn	May		White swelling	6 weeks
12	Fanny	2	F	B	S		Tenn	June		Thrast	2 months
13	Sarah	2	F	B	S		Tenn	March		Whooping cough	1 month
14	John R. Carr	19	M				N.C.	June	Farmer	unknown	Chronic
15	Rose	70	F	B	S		Va	March		Dropsy	1 year
16	Precilla	60	F	B	S		Va	Sept		Accident	sudden
17	John T. Oats	19	M				N.C.	Sept	none	T. fever	12 days
18	John Exum	49	M			M	Va	May	Farmer	Pneumonia	3 months
19	Abigal Monroe	13	F				Va	Sept		T. fever	6 weeks
20	Sarah J. Green	2	F				Tenn	Sept		Diarrhea	7 days
21	Frances	1	F	B	S		Tenn	Aug		Consumption	1 year
22	Peter	8m	M	B	S		Tenn	Oct		Diarrhea	6 weeks
23	Alice	1	F	B	S		Tenn	Aug		Diarrhea	Chronic
24	Charlotte	42	F	B	S		N.C.	March		unknown	Chronic
25	Rebecca Dupree	63	F			M	Va	Aug		Pneumonia	5 weeks

COUNTY OF FAYETTE, STATE OF TENNESSEE.

PAGE NO. 214 PERSONS WHO DIED DURING THE YEAR ENDING 1st JUNE, 1850.

Civil District No. 8

No. of Visit	Name	Age	Sex	Color	Free or Slave	Married/Widowed	Place of Birth	Month Died	Occupation	Disease or Cause of Death	No. Days Ill
1	Elizabeth Gordon	84	F				N.C.	May		Consumption	25 years
2	Susan	6m	F	B	S		Tenn	May		Accident	sudden
3	Mary	2	F	B	S		Tenn	Dec		Whooping cough	2 months
4	Henry	1	M	B	S		Tenn	March		Croup	2 days
5	Mariah	1	F	B	S		Tenn	March		Croup	4 days
6	Sally	9m	F	B	S		Tenn	March		Croup	5 days
7	Mornen	1	F	B	S		Tenn	March		Croup	1 day
8	Ann H. Langley	1	F				Tenn	May		Apoplexy	11 hours
9	Cherry	40	F	B	S		N.C.	March		unknown	Chronic
10	Frank	24	M	B	S		N.C.	Dec		T. fever	6 weeks
11	Sam	26	M	B	S		Va	Aug		T. fever	20 days
12	Jno. L. Hardy	16	M				Va	Nov		T. fever	28 days
13	Hellen	18	F	B	S		Va	March		unknown	Chronic
14	Katy	8	F	B	S		Tenn	April		unknown	Chronic
15	Nancy	1m	F	B	S		Tenn	Nov		unknown	Chronic
16	Louiza Cross	1	F	B	S		Tenn	Sept		Diarrhea	Chronic
17	Joe	28	M	B	S		Tenn	Jan		unknown	Chronic
18	Jery	50	M	B	S		N.C.	Feb		Consumption	6 weeks
19	Finis	2m	M	B	S		Tenn	Feb		Whooping cough	2 weeks
20	Gabe	4	M	B	S		Tenn	Feb		Whooping cough	1 week
21	Marshall	1m	M	B	S		Tenn	March		unknown	7 days
22	Green	22	M	B	S		Va	Sept		Negro Consumption	6 weeks
23	Lucky	38	F	B	S		N.C.	Sept		Pneumonia	10 days
24	Martha	25	F	B	S		Alabama	March		Burn	1 week
25	Elbert	8	M	B	S		Tenn	July		unknown	Chronic
26	Rear	50	F	B	S		Va	Nov		Dropsy	8 weeks
27	Lunn	27	M	B	S		N.C.	Nov		Cholera	2 days
28	Moses	4	M	B	S		Tenn	Feb		Whooping cough	1 week
29	Harry	2m	M	B	S		Tenn	Feb		Whooping cough	3 days
30	Husen	1	M	B	S		Tenn	June		Inflamation of bowels	2 days
31	Frances	4m	F	B	S		Tenn	Sept		Inflamation of bowels	6 days

COUNTY OF FAYETTE, STATE OF TENNESSEE.

PAGE NO. 215 PERSONS WHO DIED DURING THE YEAR ENDING 1st JUNE, 1850.

Civil District No. 10-15(?)

No. of Visit	Name	Age	Sex	Color	Free or Slave	Married/Widowed	Place of Birth	Month Died	Occupation	Disease or Cause of Death	No. Days Ill
1	Delcy	22	F	B	S		S.C.	Aug		Dropsy	12 months
2	Eve	43	F	B	S		S.C.	Aug		Dropsy	24 months
3	Fanny	1	F	B	S		Tenn	July		Cholera Inf.	4 months
4	Wyatte	35	M	B	S		N.C.	July		unknown	2 days
5	Henry	7m	M	B	S		Tenn	July		Diarrhea	Chronic
6	Isaac	40	M	B	S		Va	June		Pneumonia	14 days
7	Davy	21	M	B	S		Va	Jan		Consumption	12 months
8	Andrew L. Gates	14	M				Tenn	April		Inflamation of brain	7 days
9	Tames	15	F	B	S		Tenn	Nov		unknown	3 days
10	Ruben T. Owens	2	M				Tenn	July		Dropsy	28 days
11	Murrell	34	M	B	S		N.C.	Dec		Pneumonia	14 days
12	Fanny	1	F	B	S		Tenn	Dec		unknown	Chronic
13	Billy	1	M	B	S		Tenn	Aug		Diarrhea	Chronic
14	John	11m	M	B	S		Tenn	Aug		Diarrhea	Chronic
15	Chaney	35	F	B	S		N.C.	May		Pneumonia	10 days

COUNTY OF FAYETTE, STATE OF TENNESSEE.

PAGE NO. 217 PERSONS WHO DIED DURING THE YEAR ENDING 1st JUNE, 1850.

Civil District No. 11

No. of Visit	Name	Age	Sex	Color	Free or Slave	Married/Widowed	Place of Birth	Month Died	Occupation	Disease or Cause of Death	No. Days Ill
1	James Manus	63	M			M	Tenn	June	Merchant	————	Chronic
2	George	17	M	B	S		Va	June		Dropsy	Chronic
3	Malissa	1	F	B	S		Tenn	July		Diarrhea	7 days
4	Ann L. Neal	33	F				N.C.	Feb		unknown	10 days
5	Benjamin O. Neal	3m	M				Tenn	May		unknown	1 day
6	Jno. F. Presley	1	M				Tenn	July		Pneumonia	21 days
7	Mary	13	F	B	S		Missouri	March		Scrofula	Chronic
8	Isabel	1	F	B	S		Tenn	April		unknown	Chronic
9	Eliza D. Plummer	29	F			M	N.C.	July		Fever	21 days
10	William F. Mathews	1	M				Tenn	Oct		Diarrhea	11 days
11	Thomas Allen	21	M				N.C.	June	Student	T. fever	35 days
12	John Allen	63	M				N.C.	Jan	Farmer	Diarrhea	12 days
13	Louiza Burnett	15	F				Tenn	Jan		Consumption	6 months
14	Alexander Coleman	43	M				N.C.	Jan	Farmer	Congestion	3 days
15	Margarett E. Coleman	2	F				Tenn	March		unknown	Chronic
16	Arthur Williams	55	M				N.C.	March	Farmer	Pneumonia	8 days
17	Beverly	28	M	B	S		Va	April		Pneumonia	21 days
18	Harriett	1	F	B	S		Tenn	Aug		unknown	3 days
19	James T. P. Baird	5	M				Tenn	June		Scrofula	2 years

COUNTY OF FAYETTE, STATE OF TENNESSEE.

PAGE NO. 220 PERSONS WHO DIED DURING THE YEAR ENDING 1st JUNE, 1850.

Civil District No. 12

No. of Visit	Name	Age	Sex	Color	Free or Slave	Married/Widowed	Place of Birth	Month Died	Occupation	Disease or Cause of Death	No. Days Ill
1	Olivia Smith	8	F				Mississippi	Sept		T. fever	20 days
2	Lucinda A. George	1	F				Tenn	Jan		Teething	21 days
3	Phillips	37	M	B	S		Va	March		Cancer	3 months
4	James M. Duke	22	M				N.C.	Oct	Farmer	Pneumonia	12 days
5	Isabella Vanssett	7	F				Tenn	Oct		Pneumonia	21 days
6	Josephine	8m	F	B	S		Tenn	Nov		Pneumonia	14 days
7	Lewis	1	M	B	S		Tenn	Nov		Pneumonia	28 days
8	James W. Richerson	6m	M				Tenn	July		Scarletine	10 days
9	Ambrose Carter	52	M			M	N.C.	Jan	Farmer	Cholera	1 day
10	Carolina	28	F	B	S		Alabama	July		unknown	90 days
11	Henry	3m	M	B	S		Tenn	Dec		unknown	sudden
12	Cornelius W. Lovings	1	M				Tenn	Sept		Diarrhea	Chronic
13	Catherine Appleton	45	F				Tenn	May		Diarrhea	3 days
14	William Scott	60	M			M	S.C.	May	Farmer	Diarrhea	14 days
15	Henry	6m	M	B	S		Tenn	Sept		unknown	sudden
16	Harriett	11	F	B	S		Tenn	March		Scrofula	12 months
17	Ransom	6	M	B	S		Tenn	May		Pneumonia	1 month
18	Andrew	3	M	B	S		Tenn	May		Pneumonia	1 month
19	Mary M. Willson	60	F			M	Louisiana	May		unknown	Chronic
20	Fanny	1	F	B	S		Tenn	Jan		Diarrhea	Chronic

COUNTY OF FAYETTE, STATE OF TENNESSEE.

PAGE NO. 221   PERSONS WHO DIED DURING THE YEAR ENDING 1st JUNE, 1850.

Civil District No. 9

No. of Visit	Name	Age	Sex	Color	Free or Slave	Married/Widowed	Place of Birth	Month Died	Occupation	Disease or Cause of Death	No. Days Ill
1	Kitty	20	F	B	S		Missouri	Sept		Dropsy	4 months
2	Elijah Hart	58	M			M	Va	Feb	Farmer		Chronic
3	Nervason	4m	M	B	S		Tenn	Nov		Croup	2 days
4	Thomas J. Bailey	33	M			M	Va	July		T. fever	8 weeks
5	Elizabeth O. Bailey	27	F				Va	July		T. fever	3 weeks
6	William A. Bailey	1	M				Va	June		Cholera Inf.	1 week
7	Virginia A. Falwell	10	F				Tenn	Feb		unknown	5 days
8	Mary	1	F	B	S		Tenn	May		Burn	sudden
9	George	1	M	B	S		Tenn	June		unknown	Chronic
10	Dennis	2	M	B	S		Tenn	July		Diarrhea	7 days
11	Isaac	1	M	B	S		Tenn	April		Diarrhea	Chronic
12	Henry Landreth	9	M				N.C.	Nov		Spasms	7 days
13	Jim	23	M	B	S		N.C.	Nov		T. fever	21 days
14	Alph	5	M	B	S		Tenn	Oct		Scrofula	12 months
15	Robert Anthony	2	M				Tenn	July		unknown	Chronic
16	Jincy	29	F	B	S		N.C.	March		Pneumonia	4 months
17	Fanny	2m	F	B	S		Tenn	March		unknown	sudden
18	Fillis	33	F	B	S		Va	July		Cholera	2 days
19	Lucy	1m	F	B	S		Tenn	July		Diarrhea	14 days
20	Hance	2	M	B	S		Tenn	Aug		Teething	7 days
21	Jno. B. Waller	1	M				Tenn	Sept		Diarrhea	7 days
22	Robert	8	M	B	S		Tenn	March		Fever	6 weeks
23	Edmond	6	M	B	S		Mississippi	Aug		Fever	4 weeks
24	Narcissa A. Elder	5m	F				Tenn	May		Diarrhea	5 days
25	Sally	3m	F	B	S		Tenn	April		Thrash	10 days
26	Beattus J. Conway	2m	F				Tenn	July		unknown	sudden
27	Mason	1	M	B	S		Tenn	May		Inflamation of brain	7 days
28	Paralee	6	F	B	S		Tenn	July		Whooping cough	6 weeks

COUNTY OF FAYETTE, STATE OF TENNESSEE.

PAGE NO. 224   PERSONS WHO DIED DURING THE YEAR ENDING 1st JUNE, 1850.

Civil District No. 10

No. of Visit	Name	Age	Sex	Color	Free or Slave	Married/Widowed	Place of Birth	Month Died	Occupation	Disease or Cause of Death	No. Days Ill
1	Margarett	45	F	B	S		Unknown	Jan		unknown	Chronic
2	Mary Glenn	72	F				Va	April		Apoplexy	sudden
3	William S. Kee	4	M				Mississippi	May		Fever	2 weeks
4	Incas	7	M	B	S		Tenn	Sept		Diarrhea	Chronic
5	Amanda P. Baker	3	F				Tenn	Aug		unknown	3 months
6	Ben	6m	M	B	S		Tenn	March		unknown	2 weeks
7	John B. Johnson	2	M				Tenn	Aug		Croup	1 week
8	Ben	34	M	B	S		S.C.	Nov		Pneumonia	3 months
9	Martha	25	F	B	S		Va	July		Pneumonia	6 months
10	Henry	8	M	M	S		Tenn	Aug		Fever	1 month
11	Sarah	1	F	B	S		Tenn	Feb		unknown	Chronic
12	Clarinda Woods	25	F			M	Kentucky	Oct		unknown	3 days
13	Daniel	35	M	B	S		Alabama	Aug		unknown	sudden
14	George	1	M	B	S		Tenn	March		Teething	Chronic
15	Abram	70	M	B	S		Maryland	Nov		Old age	
16	Agy	60	F	B	S		Georgia	Nov		Pneumonia	10 days
17	Mary Capps	50	F			M	N.C.	Feb		Dropsy	5 years
18	William Baucom	5m	M				Tenn	July		Hives	3 days
19	Maxaline J. Woodard	19	F			M	N.C.	Oct		unknown	1 day

COUNTY OF FAYETTE, STATE OF TENNESSEE.

PAGE NO. 224   PERSONS WHO DIED DURING THE YEAR ENDING 1st JUNE, 1850.

Civil District No. 10

No. of Visit	Name	Age	Sex	Color	Free or Slave	Married/Widowed	Place of Birth	Month Died	Occupation	Disease or Cause of Death	No. Days Ill
20	Cassa	29	F	B	S		Kentucky	July		unknown	Chronic
21	Pheba	17	F	B	S		Tenn	Oct		Scrofula	10 months
22	Eliza J. Rosser	1	F				Tenn	July		Inflamation of brain	1 month
23	Alcester Baldwin	1	F				Tenn	Sept		unknown	1 week
24	Eli	1	M	B	S		Tenn	Aug		Diarrhea	Chronic
25	Mary A. Hudson	1	F				Tenn	July		Diarrhea	21 days

COUNTY OF FAYETTE, STATE OF TENNESSEE.

PAGE NO. 225   PERSONS WHO DIED DURING THE YEAR ENDING 1st JUNE, 1850.

Civil District No. 3 - 13(?)

No. of Visit	Name	Age	Sex	Color	Free or Slave	Married/Widowed	Place of Birth	Month Died	Occupation	Disease or Cause of Death	No. Days Ill
1	Grace	60	F	B	S		Va	Dec		Consumption	1 week
2	Daniel Stafford	5	M				Tenn	July		Dropsy	21 weeks
3	Richard E. Branch	7m	M				Tenn	Dec		Pneumonia	21 days
4	Ritsa	35	F	B	S		Va	May		Pneumonia	10 days
5	Osburn	3	M	B	S		Mississippi	Feb		Worms	14 days
6	Mariah	8m	F	B	S		Tenn	March		Worms	14 days
7	Juda	1	F	B	S		Tenn	Jan		unknown	sudden
8	Nancy	6m	F	B	S		Tenn	Aug		unknown	sudden
9	Alice	2	F	B	S		Mississippi	Aug		unknown	Chronic
10	Spencer	50	M	B	S		S.C.	May		unknown	1 day
11	Mary Stafford	13	F				N.C.	May		Inflamation of brain	7 days
12	Jesse Stafford	19	M				N.C.	Jan		Small Pox	9 days
13	Martha Stafford	57	M			M	N.C.	Feb		Small Pox	29 days
14	Stephen	1	M	B	S		Tenn	Dec		Burn	2 days
15	Laura M. Mayo	1	F				Tenn	Aug		Fever	60 days
16	Sally E. M. D. Mayo	45	F			W	N.C.	March		Consumption	10 years
17	Orenge	4m	M	B	S		Tenn	May		Fever	7 days
18	Laura	4m	F	B	S		Tenn	May		Fever	7 days
19	Bob	1m	M	B	S		Tenn	May		unknown	sudden
20	George W. Mitchell	1	M				Tenn	Aug		Diarrhea	Chronic
21	Sam	2m	M	B	S		Tenn	Dec		Croup	2 days
22	Mariah	17	F	B	S		Tenn	March		unknown	2 days
23	Sarah Woodson	27	F			M	Va	June		Diarrhea	Chronic
24	Antney	2	M	B	S		Tenn	Nov		unknown	Chronic
25	Stephen S. Swift	1	M				Tenn	Nov		Thrash	Chronic

COUNTY OF FAYETTE, STATE OF TENNESSEE.

PAGE NO. 228   PERSONS WHO DIED DURING THE YEAR ENDING 1st JUNE, 1850.

Civil District No. 14

No. of Visit	Name	Age	Sex	Color	Free or Slave	Married/Widowed	Place of Birth	Month Died	Occupation	Disease or Cause of Death	No. Days Ill
1	Abner Clark	14	M				Va	Oct		Accident	sudden
2	Harriett	18	F	B	S		S.C.	Dec		T. fever	20 days
3	Mary Ann	10	F	B	S		Tenn	Aug		Diarrhea	7 days
4	Agnes L. Miller	3	F				Tenn	April		Burn	sudden
5	Mary	1	F	B	S		Tenn	Oct		unknown	sudden
6	Margarett	10m	F	B	S		Tenn	Jan		Burn	3 days
7	Richard	1	M	B	S		Tenn	Feb		unknown	Chronic
8	Jim	3m	M	B	S		Tenn	July		Diarrhea	Chronic
9	James Parks	40	M				N.C.	Dec	Farmer	Consumption	2 years
10	Mary Robinson	47	F				Tenn	July		unknown	Chronic
11	Richard	30	M	B	S		N.C.	April		Pneumonia	10 days
12	John Brison	2	M				N.C.	Jan		Fever	8 days
13	Perry Tomlin	55	M			M	N.C.	Aug		T. fever	21 days
14	Eliza	13	F	B	S		N.C.	Aug		T. fever	20 days
15	Columbus Tomblin	8	M				N.C.	June		T. fever	28 days
16	Jane R. Nealey	25	F				N.C.	July		Consumption	7 months
17	Nancy	2m	F	B	S		Tenn	May		Scrofula	Chronic
18	Simeon	1	M	B	S		Tenn	July		Inflamation of brain	1 day
19	Susan	24	F	B	S		Tenn	March		Consumption	12 months
20	Malinda M. Lookey	18	F				Tenn	July		Consumption	3 years
21	Frances Faris	4	F				Tenn	March		Scarletina	2 days
22	Mark A. Stroghn	17	M				Tenn	July		Drowned	sudden
23	Martha England	3	F				Tenn	Aug		Burn	14 days
24	Jno. N. Palmour	3m	M				Tenn	Sept		Whooping cough	14 days
25	James S. Brown	3m	M				Tenn	July		Inflamation of brain	Chronic
26	Richard	10	M	B	S		Tenn	July		Accident	14 days
27	Ellen	17	F	B	S		Tenn	March		Consumption	12 months
28	Cornelia	23	F	B	S		Tenn	May		unknown	sudden
29	Julia Pater	30	F				Tenn	Dec		Fever	5 months
30	David	11	M	B	S		Tenn	March		Dropsy	5 months
31	Elizabeth Putney	38	F			W	Tenn	June		Consumption	6 months
32	Polly	30	F	B	S		Tenn	June		unknown	sudden
33	Joe	14	M	B	S		Tenn	May		Whooping cough	14 days
34	Stephen	3	M	B	S		Tenn	May		Whooping cough	14 days
35	Mary	8m	F	B	S		Tenn	Sept		Whooping cough	21 days

COUNTY OF FENTRESS, STATE OF TENNESSEE.

PAGE NO. 229   PERSONS WHO DIED DURING THE YEAR ENDING 1st JUNE, 1850.

No. of Visit	Name	Age	Sex	Color	Free or Slave	Married/Widowed	Place of Birth	Month Died	Occupation	Disease or Cause of Death	No. Days Ill
1	Darca Grooms	2	F				Kentucky	Jan		Worms	8 days
2	Sally Campbell	21	F	B	S		Kentucky	May		Chronic	8 months
3	Margaret Davidson	28	F			M	Tenn	May		Dropsy	7 days
4	Penelope Payne	9m	F				Tenn	June		Worms	4 days
5	Anna Ragan	45	F			M	Kentucky	Sept		Chronic Cancerous	380 days
6	Shaw Wright	10	M				Tenn	Aug		Fever	1 month
7	Green Murphy	3	M				Tenn	Aug		Inflamation of brain	2 weeks
8	Rose Morris	7m	F				Tenn	Oct		Cholera Inf.	7 days
9	Parker Young	1m	M				Tenn	June		Whooping cough	9 days
10	John Wincham	1m	M				Tenn	April		unknown	9 days
11	Thomas Cooper	86	M				Penn	June	Farmer	Chronic Rheumatism	2 years
12	George Smith	3	M				Tenn	March		Worms	3 days

COUNTY OF FENTRESS, STATE OF TENNESSEE.

PAGE NO. 229   PERSONS WHO DIED DURING THE YEAR ENDING 1st JUNE, 1850.

No. of Visit	Name	Age	Sex	Color	Free or Slave	Married/Widowed	Place of Birth	Month Died	Occupation	Disease or Cause of Death	No. Days Ill
13	Anna Baty	22	F				Tenn	March		Cold	4 days
14	Betty Choat	17	F				Tenn	Aug		Bil. fever	4 weeks
15	Rebeca Alred	34	F				Tenn	April		Palsy	4 years
16	Margaret Morris	8	F				Tenn	March		Sc. fever	6 days
17	Mary Morris	1m	F				Tenn	April		Sc. fever	4 days
18	Darca Gorney	23	F				Tenn	March		Dropsy	3 days
19	Jane Gorney	25	F				Tenn	March		Cold	7 days
20	Polk Gorney	3	M				Tenn	April		unknown	4 months
21	Moses Brooks	7	M				Tenn	Jan		Dropsy	1 year
22	Jas. Sutton	13	M				Tenn	June		Dropsy	6 months
23	Daniel Sutton	9	M				Tenn	July		Dropsy	4 months
24	Eliza Sutton	7	F				Tenn	July		Dropsy	4 months
25	Polly Sutton	5	F				Tenn	Aug		Dropsy	7 months
26	Josephine Randolph	1	F				Ohio	July		Teething	6 weeks
27	Elenor Kinkston	83	F			W	Va	Jan		Old age	6 days
28	Coonrod Piles	84	M			W	N.C.	Oct	Farmer	Old age	5 weeks
29	Becca Moody	45	F	B	S		Tenn	Jan		Fever	2 weeks
30	Jerry Moody	8	M	B	S		Tenn	Oct		Fever	2 weeks
31	Winy Paty	4m	F				Tenn	Jan		Hives	1 day
32	John Stewart	4m	M				Tenn	Aug		Hives	2 days
33	J. Price	38	M			M	Tenn	July	Farmer	Fever	2 weeks

Remarks: No. 21 to 26, these persons reported as having died of dropsy. The predisposing cause was dirt eating. 2 other members of the same family have since died of the same disease.

COUNTY OF FENTRESS, STATE OF TENNESSEE.

PAGE NO. 231   PERSONS WHO DIED DURING THE YEAR ENDING 1st JUNE, 1850.

Civil District No. 6 & 13

No. of Visit	Name	Age	Sex	Color	Free or Slave	Married/Widowed	Place of Birth	Month Died	Occupation	Disease or Cause of Death	No. Days Ill
1	Betsy (Taylor)	26	F	B	S		Tenn	Aug		Typhoid	9 days
2	Tom	1	M	B	S		Tenn	Sept		Debility	2 days
3	Peter (Turners)	27	M	B	S		Va	April	Farmer	Typhoid	3 weeks
4	George (")	26	M	B	S		Va	May	Farmer	Typhoid	15 days
5	Allick	1	M	B	S		Tenn	March		Croup	2 days
6	James Winkler	13	M				Tenn	March	Laborer	Typhoid	6 days
7	Wilson Chausteen	13	M				Tenn	June	Student	Cholera	1 day
8	Mary L. Chausteen	6	F				Tenn	Nov		Inflamation of brain	3 days
9	John Muse	35	M				Tenn	Feb	Laborer	sudden	sudden
10	Green Travis	19	M	B	S		Tenn	Jan	Laborer	Typhoid	25 days
11	Ann Weddington	11m	F	B	S		Tenn	Jan		Croup	2 days
12	Thomas J. Parks	10m	M				Tenn	Dec		Croup	8 days
13	Julian Brandon	11m	F				Tenn	Jan		sudden	sudden
14	Z. Taylor	11m	M				Tenn	Aug		unknown	4 days
15	Emily Connell	9m	F				Tenn	July		Inflamation of brain	12 days
16	Charles Daniel	5m	M				Tenn	Nov		Bold Hives	6 weeks
17	John Poe	82	M				Maryland	Nov	Farmer	sudden	sudden
18	William D. Cherry	11	M				Tenn	March		Small Pox	22 days
19	William Lynch	2	M				Tenn	July		Worms	12 days

COUNTY OF FENTRESS, STATE OF TENNESSEE.

PAGE NO. 231 PERSONS WHO DIED DURING THE YEAR ENDING 1st JUNE, 1850.

Civil District No. 6 & 13

No. of Visit	Name	Age	Sex	Color	Free or Slave	Married/Widowed	Place of Birth	Month Died	Occupation	Disease or Cause of Death	No. Days Ill
20	Rachael Davis	55	F				Tenn	Sept		Bil. fever	6 days
21	William A. Crabtree	11	M				Tenn	Nov		Typhoid	9 days
22	Elizabeth Wilkinson	42	F				Tenn	Jan		Small pox	10 days
23	William Wilkinson	20	M				Tenn	Jan		Small pox	13 days
24	Frances Ann Wilkinson	18	F				Tenn	Feb		Small pox	12 days
25	John West	63	M				Tenn	Oct		Typhoid	26 days
26	Simeon Putnum	74	M				Tenn	Oct		Old age	9 days
27	Peter	1	M	B	S		Tenn	May		Croup	8 days

COUNTY OF FRANKLIN, STATE OF TENNESSEE.

PAGE NO. 233 PERSONS WHO DIED DURING THE YEAR ENDING 1st JUNE, 1850.

Civil District No. 8, 9, 10 & 12

No. of Visit	Name	Age	Sex	Color	Free or Slave	Married/Widowed	Place of Birth	Month Died	Occupation	Disease or Cause of Death	No. Days Ill
1	Elizabeth (O'Rear)	22	F	B	S		Tenn	Aug		Scrofula	6 months
2	Alfred (Perkins)	3m	M	B	S		Tenn	Aug		Croup	2 days
3	Nancy Hopper	25	F				Tenn	Nov		Consumption	12 months
4	John (Bells)	80	M	B	S		Va	Aug		Old age	2 months
5	Anderson D. Swan	19	M				Tenn	Oct	Farmer	sudden	
6	Seabray Swan	75	F				Maryland	Feb		Consumption	2 months
7	William Swan	2m	M				Tenn	Oct		Hives	2 weeks
8	Caroline Baker	6m	F				Tenn	Sept		Typhoid	6 days
9	Elizabeth Ikard	26	F			M	Va	Oct		Consumption	12 months
10	Parthana Travis	17	F				Tenn	June		Cholera	38 hours
11	William Farris	16	M				Tenn	June		Cholera	1 day
12	Sarah E. Farris	9	F				Tenn	June		Cholera	12 hours
13	Columbus	11	M	B	S		Tenn	Feb		Typhoid	6 days
14	John Z. Miller	32	M			M	Tenn	March	Farmer	Typhoid	7 days
15	Darcus Brakfield	30	F				Tenn	June		Consumption	6 months
16	Nancy	5	F	B	S		Tenn	Aug		Typhoid	7 days
17	Winny	1	F	B	S		Tenn	Aug		Typhoid	6 days
18	David	13	M	B	S		Tenn	June		Typhoid	4 weeks
19	Angeline Sargant	17	F				Va	Feb		Measles	14 days
20	Sarah (")	2	F	B	S		Tenn	Feb		Measles	10 days
21	Winston (")	2	M	B	S		Tenn	Feb		Measles	10 days
22	Elvira (")	2	F	B	S		Tenn	Feb		Measles	8 days
23	Josephine	1	F	B	S		Tenn	May		Debility	10 days
24	Maria	46	F	B	S		Tenn	July		Typhoid	15 days
25	Elizabeth Elliott	30	F			M	Kentucky	Oct		Bronchitis	8 days
26	Lawson Elliott	4	M				Tenn	Oct		Bronchitis	8 days
27	Jack (Heny)	3m	M	B	S		Tenn	June		Debility	3 days
28	Lewis Steel	1	M	B	S		Tenn	Oct		Croup	3 hours
29	Margaret Steel	30	F	B	S		Tenn	Oct		Typhoid	12 days
30	Winford D. Strother	60	F				Georgia	July		Inflamation	4 weeks
31	Bird Franklin	9	M				Tenn	April		Dropsy	3 months
32	David Garner	3m	M				Tenn	June		Croup	1 day
33	William C. Rose	3	M				Tenn	Dec		Worms	6 days
34	James Reggins	3	M				Tenn	Aug		Croup	6 hours
35	Susan C. Crabtree	25	F				Tenn	March		Child birth	8 days

COUNTY OF FRANKLIN, STATE OF TENNESSEE.

PAGE NO. 236 PERSONS WHO DIED DURING THE YEAR ENDING 1st JUNE, 1850.

Civil District No. 7 & 8

No. of Visit	Name	Age	Sex	Color	Free or Slave	Married/Widowed	Place of Birth	Month Died	Occupation	Disease or Cause of Death	No. Days Ill
1	Sarah (Daniel)	42	F	B	S		N.C.	June		Dropsy	7 months
2	Grant Hamilton	36	M			M	Tenn	July	Farmer	Cholera	1½ days
3	Nancy Hamilton	28	F			M	Tenn	July		Cholera	8 days
4	A. J. Hamilton	2	M				Tenn	July		Cholera	8 hours
5	William L. Hamilton	6	M				Tenn	July		Cholera	8 hours
6	Lucy Turner	40	F			M	Tenn	March		Cholera	12 hours
7	Milly Ladd	46	F				Tenn	April		Dropsy	2 months
8	Gressy Read	30	F			M	Tenn	July		Cholera	1 day
9	John Read	6	M				Tenn	July		Cholera	1 day
10	Cicely Cheevers	45	F			M	Tenn	July		Breast Complaint	3 years
11	Nancy Emery	4m	F				Tenn	Jan		St. Anthony's fire	3 months
12	Charles (Hamilton)	15	M	B	S		Tenn	Sept		Typhoid	10 days
13	Edmond (Holder)	11m	M	B	S		Tenn	Dec		Debility	9 days
14	Maria (")	4m	F	B	S		Tenn	Jan		unknown	1 day
15	John (")	1da	M	B	S		Tenn	April		Debility	1 day
16	Peter (")	1m	M	B	S		Tenn	April		Debility	36 hours
17	John (Howard)	38	M	B	S		Va	July		Cholera	3 days
18	Minerva (")	40	F	B	S		Kentucky	Oct		Apoplexy	sudden
19	Mitchell	26	M	B	S		Tenn	May		Typhoid	12 days
20	Easther J. O'Rear	5	F				Tenn	Nov		Measles	18 days
21	John H. Rawlins	1m	M	) Twins			Tenn	July		Thrash	12 days
22	T. E. Rawlins	1m	M	)			Tenn	July		Thrash	12 days
23	Addison Knight	25	M	B	S		Va	Dec	Blk-smith	Typhoid	4 weeks
24	Elizabeth	50	F	B	S		Va	July		Consumption	6 months
25	Pamelia Corn	48	F				Va	Aug		Inflamation of bowels	10 days
26	Catharine Hale	89	F				Va	Nov		Chill & Fever	8 weeks
27	Nancy J. McNeill	8m	F				Tenn	Aug		Inflamation	18 days
28	B. B. Knight	5m	M				Tenn	March		Inflamation of brain	8 days
29	Morgan Taylor	68	M				Tenn	Feb	Farmer	C. Consumption	3 days
30	William G. Taylor	37	M				Tenn	March	Farmer	Fits	8 years
31	Henry	20	M	B	S		Tenn	Aug	Laborer	Cholera	16 days
32	Elizabeth Coaker	1	F				Tenn	Aug		Hives	8 days
33	Elizabeth Miller	23	F				Tenn	Aug		Typhoid	7 days
34	Eliza	4	F	B	S		Tenn	Nov		Typhoid	18 days
35	Edward H. Martin	18	M				Tenn	May		Typhoid	15 days

COUNTY OF FRANKLIN, STATE OF TENNESSEE.

PAGE NO. 237 PERSONS WHO DIED DURING THE YEAR ENDING 1st JUNE, 1850.

Civil District No. 3, 4 & 5

No. of Visit	Name	Age	Sex	Color	Free or Slave	Married/Widowed	Place of Birth	Month Died	Occupation	Disease or Cause of Death	No. Days Ill
1	Vinery	10	F	B	S		Tenn	May		Worms	2 days
2	Leathy	15	F	B	S		Tenn	March		Typhoid	2 weeks
3	Jefferson	1	M	B	S		Tenn	Aug		Bowel Complaint	8 days
4	Asa D. Oakley	53	M			M	Va	Sept	Farmer	Liver Complaint	4 weeks
5	Martha Ann Syler	3	F				Tenn	June		Drowned	sudden
6	Eliza Syler	3	F				Tenn	June		Burnt	sudden
7	Maria Jane Syler	6	F				Tenn	Feb		unknown	sudden
8	Jonathan Houston	52	M			M	Tenn	Feb	Farmer	Consumption	2 months
9	Lucy M. Hall	11m	F				Tenn	April		Winter fever	7 days
10	Isaac VanZant	69	M			M	N.C.	Jan	Farmer	Palsy	5 days
11	Sophia (Trigg)	3m	F	B	S		Tenn	March		Debility	3 days
12	Mary (Trigg)	3m	F	B	S		Tenn	July		Debility	5 days
13	William Patrick	38	M				Kentucky	Oct	Merchant	Typhoid	10 days
14	Z. Taylor	1m	M				Tenn	June		Debility	3 days
15	Elizabeth	1	F	B	S		Tenn	July		Flux	6 days
16	Sarah Hunt	21	F				Tenn	Aug		Typhoid	9 days
17	John Miller	1	M				Tenn	Nov		Debility	4 hours
18	Jane	6	F	B	S		Tenn	Sept		Typhoid	26 days
19	Alfred	20	M	B	S		Tenn	July		Bil. fever	6 days
20	Emily	18	F	B	S		Tenn	Aug		Bil. fever	8 days
21	Lucinda	46	F	B	S		Va	July		Typhoid	6 days
22	Ann Stovall	99	F			W	Va	Oct		Old age	3 years
23	Henry	10	M	B	S		Tenn	Oct		Consumption	5 days
24	Harris Perry	18	M				Tenn	Feb	Laborer	Typhoid	10 days
25	Mary	33	F	B	S		Tenn	March		Child birth	10 days
26	Rice Robbins	17	M				Tenn	June	Laborer	Inflamation	13 days
27	Garland Miller	3m	M				Tenn	Sept		Debility	1 day
28	Col. Richard Calloway	80	M				Kentucky	July	Farmer	Liver Complaint	3 weeks
29	Dock	3	M	B	S		Tenn	March		Debility	3 weeks
30	John Barkly	82	M				New Jersey	Aug	Sch-teacher	Old age	4 weeks
31	Jefferson	3m	M	B	S		Tenn	Aug		Debility	1 day
32	Lucy	3	F	B	S		Tenn	Feb		Sc. fever	3 days
33	Samuel	17	M	B	S		Tenn	April		Typhoid	9 days
34	Lewis	4m	M	B	S		Tenn	Jan		Croup	1 day
35	Samuel Robinson	14	M				Tenn	June		Killed in a storm	sudden

COUNTY OF FRANKLIN, STATE OF TENNESSEE.

PAGE NO. 240   PERSONS WHO DIED DURING THE YEAR ENDING 1st JUNE, 1850.

No. of Visit	Name	Age	Sex	Color	Free or Slave	Married/Widowed	Place of Birth	Month Died	Occupation	Disease or Cause of Death	No. Days Ill
1	Caleb	33	M	B	S		Va	March	Wagoner	Typhoid	12 days
2	John	20	M	B	S		Tenn	Dec	Wagon-mkr	Poison	9 weeks
3	Maria	80	F	B	S		Maryland	May		Old age	3 weeks
4	Isaac	36	M	B	S		Va	July	Laborer	Cholera	4 days
5	Jamima	1	F	M	S		Tenn	Aug		Liver disease	8 months
6	Lewis	45	M	B	S		Va	July	Laborer	Cholera	3 days
7	Margaret Raines	47	F			M	Tenn	Sept		Bronchitis	10 months
8	Robert Francis	2m	M				Tenn	Aug		Hives	2 weeks
9	Bob	2	M	B	S		Va	May		Sc. fever	4 days
10	Harriett	40	F	B	S		Va	Dec		Pleurisy	6 days
11	Juddy	60	F	B	S		Va	April		Pleurisy	8 days
12	Emily	2m	F	B	S		Tenn	Oct		Debility	2 months
13	William A. Bates	45	M				Maryland	July	Clerk at tunnel	Cholera	4 days
14	Alfred	19	M	B	S		Tenn	May	Laborer	Typhoid	8 days
15	Caroline	17	F	B	S		Tenn	Aug		Typhoid	8 days
16	Hester Ann	2	F	B	S		Tenn	Oct		Debility	2 weeks
17	Mrs. Susan Turner	77	F			M	Va	Aug		T.	2 weeks
18	Eliza	27	F	B	S		Va	June		T.	2 weeks
19	Martha	26	F	B	S		Tenn	July		T.	10 days
20	Edmond F. Upton	19	M				Tenn	May	Farmer	Inflamation of brain	4 days
21	Milly	18	F	B	S		Tenn	March		Consumption	6 months
22	William Turney	14	M				Tenn	Jan	son (Hokkins L. Turney)	Congestion	4 days
23	Mary Ellen Turney	3m	F				Tenn	Aug		Croup	4 days
24	Eliza Garner	5m	F				Tenn	Sept		Debility	5 months
25	Susan	4m	F	B	S		Tenn	Sept		Croup	3 months
26	Elmira	18	F	B	S		Tenn	March		T.	8 days
27	Delila	17	F	B	S		Tenn	March		T.	15 days
28	Hayden	1	M	B	S		Tenn	May		Bowel Complaint	2 months
29	Racheal	55	F	B	S		Va	June		Dropsy	6 months
30	Robert P. Young	2	M				————	Nov		Croup	2 days
31	Sarah Young	60	F				unknown	May		Cholera	3 months
32	John Morris	49	M			M	N.C.	Oct	Farmer	Heart disease	5 weeks
33	Jackson	1	M	B	S		Tenn	Dec		unknown	3 months
34	Maria	18	F	B	S		Tenn	Aug		T.	9 days
35	Jim	1	M	B	S		Tenn	July		Sc. fever	2 weeks

COUNTY OF GIBSON, STATE OF TENNESSEE.

PAGE NO. 241   PERSONS WHO DIED DURING THE YEAR ENDING 1st JUNE, 1850.

No. of Visit	Name	Age	Sex	Color	Free or Slave	Married/Widowed	Place of Birth	Month Died	Occupation	Disease or Cause of Death	No. Days Ill
1	L. B. Cary	3	M				Tenn	Sept		unknown	2 weeks
2	Mary E. Cary	2m	F				Tenn	March		unknown	sudden
3	Chaney	40	F	B	S		Tenn	April		unknown	sudden
4	Easter	48	F	B	S		N.C.	Feb		Fever	20 days
5	Feliciana	13	F	B	S		Tenn	Oct		Dropsy	6 months
6	Elizabeth Wood	19	F			M	N.C.	Sept		Child bed	4 weeks
7	M. D. Dolason	9m	M				Tenn	Jan		Winter fever	3 weeks
8	William R. Wade	9m	M				Tenn	April		Sc. fever	3 days
9	Joe	1	M	B	S		Tenn	March		Sc. fever	4 days
10	Mary	20	F	B	S		Tenn	April		Chronic disease	2 years
11	Wesley	6m	M	B	S		Tenn	Jan		unknown	1 day
12	Drury Ingram	7m	M				Tenn	April		Sc. fever	12 days
13	Lewis McDougald	1	M				Tenn	April		Sc. fever	8 days
14	James Bowers	60	M				N.C.	July		Fits	40 years
15	Thomas Bowers	1m	M				Tenn	March		Sc. fever	1 month
16	Allen McDougald	4m	M				Tenn	April		Sc. fever	10 days
17	Mary Russell	1m	F				Tenn	May		unknown	sudden
18	William Porter	7m	M				Tenn	Feb		Sc. fever	1 month
19	Mary	22	F	B	S		Tenn	June		Fever	6 weeks
20	John	1	M	B	S		Tenn	Nov		Croup	sudden
21	Ben	1m	M	B	S		Tenn	March		Croup	sudden
22	John Holder	82	M			W	N.C.	Jan	Farmer	unknown	sudden
23	Jas. T. Barnes	5	M				Tenn	Aug		Worms	4 weeks
24	Alfred	10m	M	M	S		Tenn	Nov		Cold	17 days
25	Thomas Woodson	40	M			M	S.C.	Dec	Farmer	Rheumatism	5 months
26	Caroline	23	F	B	S		Tenn	April		unknown	1 week
27	George	9m	M	B	S		Tenn	Nov		Sc. fever	2 weeks
28	Matilda	28	F	B	S		Tenn	Feb		Poison	8 months
29	M. W. Hopkins	20	M				N.C.	Aug		Dropsy	2 years
30	William S. Walker	1	M				Tenn	April		Diarrhea	4 weeks
31	Joseph M. Casthell	33	M			M	Georgia	Aug		D---illegible	2 years
32	Mary L. Jones	6	F				Tenn	Feb		Hives	1 day
33	Jacob Goins	12	M				Tenn	Sept		Pl risy	1 year
34	James Goins	9	M				Tenn	Feb		Pleurisy	10 months
35	Peter Glascock	70	M			M	N.C.	Dec	Farmer	Intemperance	2 weeks

COUNTY OF GIBSON, STATE OF TENNESSEE.

PAGE NO. 244 PERSONS WHO DIED DURING THE YEAR ENDING 1st JUNE, 1850.

No. of Visit	Name	Age	Sex	Color	Free or Slave	Married/Widowed	Place of Birth	Month Died	Occupation	Disease or Cause of Death	No. Days Ill
1	Hosea Parker	37	M			M	Tenn	Dec	Tailor	Consumption	6 months
2	Frances	1	F	B	S		Tenn	Oct		unknown	sudden
3	Sarah M. Edwards	25	F			M	N.C.	May		Apoplexy	sudden
4	Infant "	3m	F				Tenn	March		unknown	sudden
5	T. J. Edwards	2	M				Tenn	Aug		Congestive chill	sudden
6	Infant	1m	F	B	S		Tenn	Dec		unknown	sudden
7	William Gibson	51	M			M	Va	Oct	Shoemaker	Chronic disease	6 months
8	Thomas Pearce	75	M				Va	May		Intemperance	
9	A. Patterson	80	M			M	N.C.	Feb	Farmer	Dropsy	2 years
10	Lawson McDaniel	1	M				Tenn	Jan		Cholera morbus	sudden
11	Antony	21	M	B	S		Tenn	Nov		Scrofula	4 months
12	S. A. Ray	2m	F				Tenn	Sept		unknown	2 days
13	Joe	12	M	B	S		Tenn	March		Dropsy	1 month
14	John Craddock	47	M			M	Va	April	Farmer	Fever	2 weeks
15	Eliza J. Raines	7	F				Tenn	Feb		Pneumonia	2 weeks
16	B. F. Harris, Jr.	1m	M				Tenn	Sept		unknown	1 day
17	Anna M. Hill	2	F				Tenn	May		Inflamation of brain	sudden
18	Margaret D. Williams	26	F				Alabama	Feb		Chronic disease	3 years
19	William Sale	60	M				N.C.	July	Farmer	Dropsy	10 months
20	Louisa Lane	1	F				Tenn	Dec		Pneumonia	4 weeks
21	George W. Sale	14	M				Tenn	Sept		Chronic disease	1 month
22	William H. Sale	12	M				Tenn	March		Dropsy	6 months
23	Dorchas Andrews	36	F			M	N.C.	April		Consumption	2 months
24	Jos. M. Davidson	9m	M				Tenn	Jan		Sc. fever	2 weeks
25	Collin G. Mobley	1	M				Tenn	March		Pneumonia	14 days
26	Infant	2m	M				Tenn	March		Sc. fever	2 weeks
27	Lucinda Rankin	3	F				Tenn	April		Sc. fever	2 weeks
28	George Fisher	39	M			M	N.C.	March	Farmer	Pneumonia	3 weeks
29	Abel Hall	9	M				Tenn	Oct		T. fever	2 weeks
30	Infant	6m	M				Tenn	Aug		unknown	2 weeks
31	Hester Cooper	78	F			W	N.C.	Nov		unknown	7 days
32	William C. Gibson	30	M			M	Tenn	Jan	Farmer	Pneumonia	2 days
33	Hannah	33	F	B	S		Va	Dec		unknown	4 days
34	H. Z. B. McWhorter	2	M				Tenn	Dec		Sc. fever	6 days
35	Lean Nance	41	F			M	Alabama	Sept		Cancer	1 year

COUNTY OF GIBSON, STATE OF TENNESSEE.

PAGE NO. 245 PERSONS WHO DIED DURING THE YEAR ENDING 1st JUNE, 1850.

No. of Visit	Name	Age	Sex	Color	Free or Slave	Married/Widowed	Place of Birth	Month Died	Occupation	Disease or Cause of Death	No. Days Ill
1	Nancy E. Altman	18	F				Tenn	May		T. fever	3 weeks
2	Jas. F. Altman	16	M				Tenn	May	Farmer	T. fever	2 months
3	Nancy	60	F	B	S		Va	July		Cancer	10 years
4	H. Weatherspoon	66	M			W	N.C.	Nov	Farmer	Dropsy	5 years
5	Henry Price	9	M				Tenn	April		Inflamation	2 weeks
6	Sarah E. West	1m	F				Tenn	July		unknown	5 days
7	M. J. E. McClure	11m	F				Tenn	Aug		Chronic disease	1 month
8	William Richardson	86	M			W	Va	Nov	Farmer	Chronic disease	3 months
9	Hannah	1m	F	B	S		Tenn	Dec		unknown	sudden
10	George W. Malone	22	M				N.C.	Nov	Farmer	Cholera	3 days
11	Infant	1m	M	B	S		Tenn	Sept		unknown	sudden
12	Carroll	19	M	B	S		Tenn	April		Chronic disease	2 years
13	A. D. Fletcher	70	F			M	N.C.	Nov		Consumption	1 year
14	Matilda A. Clements	4	F				Tenn	May		T. fever	2 weeks
15	Joseph W. Richardson	28	M			M	Tenn	Nov	Farmer	Pneumonia	3 weeks
16	Lewis	75	M	B	S		N.C.	March		Pneumonia	5 days
17	Rhoda	5m	F	B	S		Tenn	July		Croup	10 hours
18	Laura V. Hardison	4	F				Tenn	Sept		Cholera M.	12 hours
19	Robert	3	M	B	S		Tenn	Feb		Chronic disease	6 months
20	Mary	1	F	B	S		Tenn	Aug		Dropsy	2 months
21	Levi Bradford	1	M				Tenn	Feb		unknown	2 days
22	E. W. Woods	19	F				N.C.	Nov		T. fever	4 weeks
23	Susan E. Ragan	5	F				Tenn	Oct		Croup	2 days
24	C. A. Harpole	1	M				Tenn	Nov		unknown	sudden
25	R. L. Pennington	1	F				Tenn	Aug		unknown	12 months
26	Cinda	1	F	B	S		Tenn	Nov		unknown	all life
27	Mary A. Russell	1m	F				Tenn	May		unknown	sudden
28	Sally	9m	F	B	S		Tenn	Jan		unknown	12 days
29	Benjamin Booth	1m	M				Tenn	May		unknown	sudden
30	William W. Bills	1m	M				Tenn	April		unknown	sudden
31	James K. McCaleb	43	M				N.C.	Sept	Farmer	Pneumonia	9 days
32	Nancy Simmons	20	F				Tenn	June		Chronic disease	sudden
33	Visty	43	F	B	S		Tenn	May		unknown	9 days
34	Caroline Avery	6m	F				Tenn	April		unknown	3 days
35	James M. Wilson	1	M				Tenn	May		Congestive chill	1 day

COUNTY OF GIBSON, STATE OF TENNESSEE.

PAGE NO. 248 PERSONS WHO DIED DURING THE YEAR ENDING 1st JUNE, 1850.

No. of Visit	Name	Age	Sex	Color	Free or Slave	Married/Widowed	Place of Birth	Month Died	Occupation	Disease or Cause of Death	No. Days Ill
1	William E. Daniel	3	M				Tenn	Nov		Burn	10 days
2	Infant	1m	F				Tenn	Dec		unknown	sudden
3	A. Glisson	62	M			W	N.C.	Nov	Farmer	Consumption	2 years
4	David Briant	45	M			M	N.C.	April	Farmer	Consumption	1 year
5	Henry Cook	20	M				N.C.	May	Laborer	Fever	4 days
6	Lithia L. Dibrell	47	F			M	N.C.	July		Consumption	6 months
7	A. F. Dibrell	20	M				Tenn	Nov	Farmer	Consumption	5 months
8	P. A. McKenzie	19	F				Tenn	Feb		Consumption	4 months
9	Robert McKenzie	11m	M				Tenn	Sept		Scrofula	6 weeks
10	Matilda Trooper	10	F				Tenn	June		unknown	2 months
11	Robert Harrison	32	M			M	Tenn	May	Farmer	Pneumonia	2 weeks
12	Infant	1m	F	B	S		Tenn	Feb		Burn	7 days
13	Charles Yates	44	M			M	N.C.	May	Farmer	Intemperance	2 weeks
14	John Yates	18	M				N.C.	April	Farmer	T. fever	4 days
15	Charles Lawrence	50	M			M	N.C.	May	Farmer	Dropsy	2 months
16	Laura D. Yates	5m	F				Tenn	March		unknown	10 days
17	G. A. Lock	14	M				Tenn	March		Dropsy	3 years
18	Mary A. Davis	75	F			W	N.C.	Nov		Consumption	1 year
19	Frances C. Casey	32	F			M	Tenn	April		Consumption	3 years
20	William Motherell	45	M			M	Tenn	March		Pneumonia	8 weeks
21	Tabby	16	F	B	S		Tenn	June		Pneumonia	1 week
22	Joseph M. White	30	M			M	Kentucky	June		Consumption	1 year
23	Martha Hancock	24	F				Tenn	July		Consumption	6 months
24	Robert D. McCallister	5m	M				Tenn	Feb		--illegible--	4 months
25	William M. Martin	1m	M				Tenn	Jan		unknown	sudden
26	James M. Pounds	25	M			M	N.C.	Feb		T. fever	3 weeks
27	G. H. Martin	26	M				Va	March		Dyspepsia	7 months
28	G. W. Bell	31	M				N.C.	Dec		Pneumonia	8 days
29	James G. Williams	2	M				Tenn	Dec		Sc. fever	2 weeks
30	Martha J. Rutledge	26	F				Tenn	Dec		unknown	4 months
31	James A. Perry	4m	M				Tenn	Sept		unknown	1 week
32	Joe	80	M	B	S		Va	Sept		Gravel	7 years
33	Lilly	37	F	B	S		N.C.	Oct		Congestive chill	4 days
34	Amy	1m	F	B	S		Tenn	April			sudden
35	L. C. Hutchinson	9	M				Tenn	Dec		Sc. fever	2 weeks

COUNTY OF GILES, STATE OF TENNESSEE.

PAGE NO. 250 PERSONS WHO DIED DURING THE YEAR ENDING 1st JUNE, 1850.

Civil District No. 2

No. of Visit	Name	Age	Sex	Color	Free or Slave	Married/Widowed	Place of Birth	Month Died	Occupation	Disease or Cause of Death	No. Days Ill
1	William Jones	74	M			M	Va	Nov	Farmer	Cancer	20 years
2	Susannah	2m	F	B	S		Tenn	Dec		Croup	2 days
3	Thomas Brown	3m	M	B	S		Tenn	Oct		Croup	1 day
4	Henry Beasley	6m	M	B	S		Tenn	Feb		unknown	sudden
5	-- no name given --	1da	F				Tenn	May		unknown	1 day
6	John W. Harvell	3	M				Tenn	Sept		Scrofula	17 days
7	John W. Erwin	18	M				Tenn	Oct	Farmer	Fever	2 months
8	Infant of A. Brown	1hr	F	B	S		Tenn	May		unknown	½ hour
9	Jeffrey Adkins	90	M	B	S		Va	Noc		Old age	unknown
10	Mary Ford	16	F				Tenn	June		Congestive chills	2 days
11	Thomas Swift	13	M				Tenn	Dec		Nervous	6 weeks
12	Josaphine	8m	F	B	S		Tenn	Nov		Inflamation of brain	1 day
13	Two infants of Dougherty	died a few minutes after birth									
14	Harvy Whitfield	40	M	B	S		unknown	June		unknown	sudden
15	Backus Keer	35	M	B	S		N.C.	April		Consumption	C
16	John Shields	45	M			M	unknown	Aug	Carpenter	Mortification of broken limb	7
17	Martha Reed	12	F	B	S		Tenn	April		killed by fall of a tree	sudden
18	Moses Brown	55	M	B	S		Va	Aug		unknown	C
19	Martha Garret	6	F				Tenn	Sept		Croup	14 days
20	Elias Mitchall	47	M			M	S.C.	Nov	Farmer	T. fever	C

Remarks: The climate in this District is very healthful, nothing like an annual visitation of disease or epidemic has ever afflicted its inhabitants. The soil, especially that upon the various streams, water flow through it is exceedingly productive. No minerals have yet been found embedded within its bosom. There is nothing of traditionary interest connected with this part of the County and nothing particular striking in the scenery to amiss the attention of the traveler.   James H. Brooks.

COUNTY OF GILES, STATE OF TENNESSEE.

PAGE NO. 251 PERSONS WHO DIED DURING THE YEAR ENDING 1st JUNE, 1850.

Civil District No. 3

No. of Visit	Name	Age	Sex	Color	Free or Slave	Married/Widowed	Place of Birth	Month Died	Occupation	Disease or Cause of Death	No. Days Ill
1	Robert Beard	78	M			M	S.C.	March	Farmer	Diarrhea	C
2	Alley Hughs	40	F			M	S.C.	July		Disease of the womb	1 month
3	Betsy Edmondson	1m	F	B	S		Tenn	Feb		unknown	12 days
4	Jane Kimbrough	7	F	B	S		Tenn	Aug		Falling of a tree	
5	Sirena Gatlin	35	F			M	Tenn	May		Chronic Bronchitis	2 weeks
6	Amanda Gatlin	4	F				Tenn	May		Worms	3 days
7	John Coughran	9	M				Tenn	May		Dropsy	7 days
8	Child of D. Gooch	2wk	F	B	S		Tenn	May		Croup	7 days
9	Amie Keer	52	F			M	N.C.	Sept		unknown	14 days
10	Franklin Harwell	10	M				Tenn	Sept		T. fever	24 days
11	Child of Barrenton Jackson	1m	M				Tenn	Aug		unknown	30 days
12	Rachel Smith	25	F	B	S		Tenn	Dec		Poisoned	C

COUNTY OF GILES, STATE OF TENNESSEE.

PAGE NO. 251 PERSONS WHO DIED DURING THE YEAR ENDING 1st JUNE, 1850.

Civil District No. 3

Remarks: A large portion of this District is still unsettled. Wonderously hilly and poor. It would seem that almost all the tillable lands were occupied, so much so that many are complaining of want room and have started for the far west to seek them freer homes. It is a well watered County. All the streams remarkable for their cleanness. I have been informed by the oldest inhabitant, "That no people have been healthier until the present summer. Where a very fatal disease (probably Typhoid Fever) made its appearance, and has caused much distress, no legends coming to as from olden times, are related here nothing particular attractive in nature or in art." James H. Brooks.

COUNTY OF GILES, STATE OF TENNESSEE.

PAGE NO. 254 PERSONS WHO DIED DURING THE YEAR ENDING 1st JUNE, 1850.

The Town of Pulaski

No. of Visit	Name	Age	Sex	Color	Free or Slave	Married/Widowed	Place of Birth	Month Died	Occupation	Disease or Cause of Death	No. Days Ill
1	_____ McMillen	1	F				Kentucky	Aug		Teething	6 weeks
2	Eliza	8	F	B	S		Kentucky	June		Dropsy	1 year
3	Martha Faris	6m	F				Tenn	Feb		Milk-crust	3 months
4	Infant of John Shephard	1m	F	M			Tenn	June		unknown	1 month
5	Amos Richardson	3	M				Tenn	Feb		Accident (firing pistol)	1 day
6	Elizabeth Pearce	44	F				Tenn	May		unknown	1 day
7	John Ervin	1	M				Tenn	July		Teething	2 hours
8	Infant of Cyrus Cofer	1m	F				Tenn	Feb		unknown	1 day
9	Younger	17	F	B	S		Tenn	Oct		T. fever	6 weeks
10	Joseph Budd	29	M				Va	May	Plasterer		7 days
11	Negro of Albert Morris	1m	M	B	S		Tenn	Jan		unknown	3 days
12	Harriet Perkins	50	F				Va	May		Consumption	3 months
13	THIS CLOSES THE CENSUS OF THE TOWN OF PULASKI:										
14	Ephraim W. Bass	1m	M				Tenn	Sept		Inflamation of bowels	15 days
15	Alexander Black	72	M				Kentucky	Nov		Palsy	2 weeks
16	Albert, of A. C. White	22	M	M	S		Missouri	March		Winter fever	10 days
17	Amanda, of A. C. White	24	F	B	S		Tenn	March		Winter fever	2 weeks
18	Mary, of A. C. White	15	F	B	S		Tenn	March		Winter fever	9 days
19	James, of A. C. White	3	M	B	S		N.C.	April		Winter fever	10 days
20	Amanda, of A. C. White	15	F	B	S		N.C.	June		Cramp Cholic	1 day
21	Infant of Spencer Clack	1m	F	B	S		Tenn	May		unknown	1 week
22	Negro of John Phillips	1m	F	B	S		Tenn	Dec		Croup	2 days
23	Infant	6m	F	B	S		Tenn	Sept		Pleurisy	4 weeks
24	Basil	26	M	B	S		Tenn	May		Drown	
25	Samuel	35	M	B	S		unknown	Aug		Killed by a tree	
26	Nancy Ann Anderson	3m	F				Tenn	Sept		Bronchitis	18 days
27	Sarah Jane Jemison	2	F				Tenn	June		Croup	9 days
28	Slave of F. H. Wilkinson	1m	M	B	S		Tenn	April		unknown	1 day
29	John Jackson	2m	M	B	S		Tenn	May		Smothering	
30	James Lynch	1m	M				Tenn	Feb		unknown	7 days
31	Zachary T. Page	8m	M				Tenn	July		Inflamation of brain	3 months
32	Alexander	70	M	B	S		N.C.	Dec		Dropsy	2 months
33	Thomas Evans	20	M				Tenn	Oct	Farmer	T. fever	6 days
34	Anthony	20	M	B	S		Tenn	May		Breast Complaint	3 months
35	John Bailey	35	M				Tenn	Dec	Farmer	Cold	3 months

COUNTY OF GILES, STATE OF TENNESSEE.

PAGE NO. 254   PERSONS WHO DIED DURING THE YEAR ENDING 1st JUNE, 1850.

The Town of Pulaski

No. of Visit	Name	Age	Sex	Color	Free or Slave	Married/Widowed	Place of Birth	Month Died	Occupation	Disease or Cause of Death	No. Days Ill

Remarks: These two Districts are generally hilly and are very rich and productive and is also as finely watered as any portion of middle Tennessee. The society is as good as can be found in any county. The price of land in these districts have advanced in the last five years from on an average from 25 to 50 per cent. There is a large cotton mill situated in the immediate vicinity of Pulaski, which is now about being completed, to be run by steam, which probably will give employment to some sixty or eighty laborers. There has been no visitation of disease or epidemic raging in our midst to cause distress amoungst our inhabitants. Nothing like minerals or mines in either of these Districts have as yet been unbosomed.
James H. Brooks.

COUNTY OF GILES, STATE OF TENNESSEE.

PAGE NO. 255   PERSONS WHO DIED DURING THE YEAR ENDING 1st JUNE, 1850.

Civil District No. 14

No. of Visit	Name	Age	Sex	Color	Free or Slave	Married/Widowed	Place of Birth	Month Died	Occupation	Disease or Cause of Death	No. Days Ill
1	Elizabeth Palina Webb	7	F				Tenn	Oct		Chronic	8 months
2	Thomas Lovel	51	M				unknown	Dec	Farmer	Cholera	15 days
3	Infant of William Fry	1m	F				Tenn	Sept		Hives	2 days
4	John Y. Abernathy	48	M				N.C.	Oct	Farmer	Pneumonia	6 weeks
5	Infant of Wm. C. Stewart	1m	M				Tenn	July		unknown	1 day
6	Infant	1m	M	B	S		Tenn	May		unknown	
7	William Boatright	24	M				Tenn	Oct	Farmer	Inter. fever	8 days
8	Cicero	3m	M	B	S		Tenn	1 June		unknown	6 weeks
9	William T. Joins	1m	M				Tenn	Sept		unknown	3 days
10	Franklin Wilks	1	M				Tenn	Oct		Cholera	4 weeks
11	Margaret H. English	1	F				Tenn	Nov		Sc. fever	21 days
12	John Haile	85	M				Va	April	Farmer	Old age	8 days
13	John Silvester Gilmore	30	M				Tenn	Jan	Farmer	Chronic Consumption	
14	Henry Duncan	1m	M				Tenn	May		Hives	3 days
15	Lorenzo Lovel	43	M				Kentucky	May	Farmer	Dropsy	3 months
16	Nancy C. Locke	39	F				Tenn	Oct		T. fever	14 days
17	Andrew J. Yokley	8m	M				Tenn	June		Inf. of brain	12 hours
18	James Hannah	68	M				Ireland	Dec	Farmer	T. fever	15 days
19	Lydia	45	F	B	S		Tenn	Dec		T. fever	18 days
20	Rachel	4m	F	B	S		Tenn	Sept		Croup	2 weeks
21	Robert Rea	76	M				N.C.	May	Farmer	Dropsy	3 months
22	Isabella	53	F	B	S		Georgia	Jan		Breast Complaint	Chronic
23	Mary Rackley	14	F				Tenn	Jan		Pneumonia	5 weeks
24	William McDaniel	70	M				N.C.	May	Farmer	unknown	Chronic
25	Thomas A. Collins	2	M				Tenn	June		Worms	10 days
26	Mary Compton	33	F				Kentucky	Aug		T. fever	8 days
27	Nancy A. Smith	20	F				Tenn	May		Breast Complaint	Chronic
28	Anna Gilmore	73	F				Va	April		Inflamation of brain	Chronic
29	Eliza	37	F	B	S		Va	Feb		unknown	sudden
30	Alexander Parker	17	M				Tenn	April		Consumption	6 weeks

COUNTY OF GILES, STATE OF TENNESSEE.

PAGE NO. 255 PERSONS WHO DIED DURING THE YEAR ENDING 1st JUNE, 1850.

Civil District No. 14

Remarks: This District is very thickly settled and is also very broken but is remarkably rich and well watered with creeks and springs. It is one of the best adapted districts in the County for raising stock and corn and grass. On the various streams which flow through this district, there is a great many excellent sites for mills and other machinery and at some of them, there are some very excellent saw and grist mills, it is also very healthy and it would seem from the face of the County and from the character of the water, that man might live as long as he could wish. Nothing like minerals and mines in this district has as yet been found.   John McGrew.

COUNTY OF GILES, STATE OF TENNESSEE.

PAGE NO. 257 PERSONS WHO DIED DURING THE YEAR ENDING 1st JUNE, 1850.

Civil District No. 13

No. of Visit	Name	Age	Sex	Color	Free or Slave	Married/Widowed	Place of Birth	Month Died	Occupation	Disease or Cause of Death	No. Days Ill
1	Catharine	7	F	B	S		Va	Aug		unknown	C
2	Susan H. Gillum	25	F				Tenn	July		Congestive chills	1 week
3	Allen Y. Wilkerson	57	M				N.C.	April	Farmer	Palsy	30 hours
4	Slave of A. Y. Wilkerson	2m	M	B	S		Tenn	July		unknown	7 days
5	Susan Ann	18	F	B	S		Tenn	Aug		Winter fever	8 days
6	Joseph	10	M	B	S		Tenn	Sept		Winter fever	2 months
7	Sarow (Sarah)	3	F	B	S		Tenn	Jan		unknown	24 hours
8	Maria	5	F	B	S		Tenn	June		Sc. fever	13 days
9	Hanner	3	F	B	S		Tenn	June		Sc. fever	14 days
10	Julia Ann Petty	23	F				Tenn	Nov		Cause heart	18 months
11	Granville Bratton	21	M				Tenn	April	Farmer	Slow fever	14 days
12	Slave of Thomas Buford	2m	F	B	S		Tenn	Dec		Smothered	
13	William Bowenn	6m	M				Va	June		Risen in head	4 weeks
14	William M. Scott	4	M				Tenn	May		Worms	4 days
15	Babe Scott	1m	M				Tenn	June		unknown	3 hours
16	Clairy Scott	2	F				Tenn	March		Inflamation of brain	7 days
17	Malinda Scott	19	F				Tenn	July		Consumption	C
18	Granville	3m	M	B	S		Tenn	July		unknown	2 months
19	David	10m	M	B	S		Tenn	Feb		Inflamation of brain	4 days
20	General Allen Gines	3m					Tenn	Dec		Sc. fever	6 weeks
21	Spicey Carpenter	40	F				Va	Feb		unknown	C

Remarks: This district, has in general, a healthful climate, and a rich fertile soil and a diversified surface, hill and vales. The lands are very rich and productive. The people, generally intelligent and enterprising. A large portion of this district is owned by wealthy people and will command a fine price, being rated so high that several persons who were farmers and have large families, are compelled to sell their lands and move. For want of room, some of whom have already gone to the far west. I had the pleasure of conversing with an old Revolutionary Soldier, by the name of Baker, who has since died. He informed me that he was 104 years old on the 4th day of May last and served in and at the Battle of Bunker Hill, also at Guilford Court House and at Stoney Point and that he had never drawn a pension, nor would not, and that he had received what he had fought for, which was all that he desired, which was .....   John McGrew.

COUNTY OF GILES, STATE OF TENNESSEE.

PAGE NO. 260 PERSONS WHO DIED DURING THE YEAR ENDING 1st JUNE, 1850.

Civil District No. 5

No. of Visit	Name	Age	Sex	Color	Free or Slave	Married/Widowed	Place of Birth	Month Died	Occupation	Disease or Cause of Death	No. Days Ill
1	Nancy E. Tucker	1m	F				Tenn	May		Inflamation of bowels	14 days
2	Spencer Beavers	71	M				Tenn	June		Gravel	4 weeks
3	Babe	1m	F				Tenn	Oct		unknown	sudden
4	Lydia	56	F	B	S		N.C.	June		Cancer	2 years
5	James M. Bodenheimer	4m	M				Tenn	April		unknown	C
6	Stephen	27	M	B	S		Tenn	June		Stricture of bowels	C
7	Sarah E. Buchanan	22	F				Tenn	April		Dropsy	8 months
8	Babe Smith	1m	F				Tenn	Oct		unknown	sudden
9	Sarah Owens	90	F				Maryland	June		Dropsy	6 weeks
10	David M. D. L. Gooch	7	M				Tenn	Aug		unknown	5 days
11	John	60	M	B			unknown	March		unknown	C
12	Thomas W. Rhea	28	M				Illinois	April		unknown	2 weeks
13	Babe	1m	M				Tenn	July		Inflamation of bowels	1 week
14	Eliza Jane Waller	22	F				Tenn	May		Dropsy	2 months
15	Nancy Faught	80	F				Va	Jule		unknown	2 months
16	Jasper Chapman	3m	M				Tenn	May		unknown	10 days
17	John W. Innman	1	M				Tenn	Aug		Flux	5 days
18	James Lock	2	M				Tenn	Aug		Flux	2 weeks

Remarks: This District is very broken and hilly and nearly or quite all of the table lands are clear. It is a well watered District and is thickly settled. There is no manufacturing establishments of any cause, importance in this district and as yet no minerals have been discovered. I find some of the inhabitants very much displeased with the free schools, and say that instead of their existance being a blessing that they are a misfortune. As a goodly number of persons depend on them entirely to have their children educated, and frequently their teachers are not competent, because the school commissioners employ ones who will teach for the smallest price.   John McGrew.

COUNTY OF GILES, STATE OF TENNESSEE.

PAGE NO. 261 PERSONS WHO DIED DURING THE YEAR ENDING 1st JUNE, 1850.

Civil District No. 12

No. of Visit	Name	Age	Sex	Color	Free or Slave	Married/Widowed	Place of Birth	Month Died	Occupation	Disease or Cause of Death	No. Days Ill
1	Mary	27	F	B	S		Tenn	June		Lock jaw	3 days
2	Babe	1m	M	B	S		Tenn	April		unknown	1 day
3	Elizabeth	1m	F	B	S		Tenn	June		unknown	6 hours
4	Charles	9m	M	B	S		Tenn	Sept		Cholera Inf.	4 days
5	Marcus	32	M	B	S		Tenn	June		unknown	30 days

Remarks: This District, particularly the western portion, is some what uneven and hilly, is very rich and productive, and is remarkable healthy, and well watered and is blessed with as good society as any district in the County. Nothing like an epidemic or disease have affected its inhabitants. No minerals or mines of any kind have as yet been found in this district.   John McGrew.

COUNTY OF GILES, STATE OF TENNESSEE.

PAGE NO. 264 PERSONS WHO DIED DURING THE YEAR ENDING 1st JUNE, 1850.

Civil District No. 4

No. of Visit	Name	Age	Sex	Color	Free or Slave	Married/Widowed	Place of Birth	Month Died	Occupation	Disease or Cause of Death	No. Days Ill
1	Francis M. Cosbey	24	M				N.C.	May	Farmer	T. fever	26 days
2	Joseph L. Kincaide	6m	M				Tenn	Aug		unknown	2 days
3	Mary G. Griffin	43	F				Tenn	July		unknown	C
4	Babe Dixon	1m	M				Tenn	June		unknown	1 day
5	Findus Noblet	1m	M				Tenn	June		unknown	6 days
6	Babe of John Hogan	1m	M				Tenn	Feb		unknown	1 day
7	Infant of Permenus P. Cox	1m	M	M	S		Tenn	May		unknown	8 days
8	Mary F. Walker	3m	F				Tenn	Dec		Hives	2 months
9	Sarah M. Shields	37	F				unknown	Feb		Liver complaint	5 weeks
10	Baby Shields	1m	F				Tenn	Feb		unknown	1 day
11	Martha F. Wood	5	F				Tenn	Oct		Burned	1 day
12	Joseph Jones	90	M				unknown	Sept	Farmer	Chills and fever	2 weeks

Remarks: A large portion of this District is still unsettled. It is generally very poor and broken, except on the various streams, which is very productive and is composed of a black and gravely soil. It is an extremely healthy section of country and is principally settled by poor people. The water is very clear and on a good many of the different streams which flow through the District, is to be found several very excellent sites for the erection of Cotton Mills and other kinds of machinery. John McGrew.

COUNTY OF GILES, STATE OF TENNESSEE.

PAGE NO. 265 PERSONS WHO DIED DURING THE YEAR ENDING 1st JUNE, 1850.

Civil District No. 18

No. of Visit	Name	Age	Sex	Color	Free or Slave	Married/Widowed	Place of Birth	Month Died	Occupation	Disease or Cause of Death	No. Days Ill
1	Robert F. Shelton	20	M				Tenn	Jan	Farmer	Killed by a tree	sudden
2	Elizabeth Johnston	65	F				Penn	Jan		Consumption	Chronic
3	Babe Curtis	1m	F				Tenn	June		unknown	sudden
4	Elizabeth Hillhouse	70	F				S.C.	March		Dropsy	6 weeks
5	Mary Laramore	83	F				Maryland	Dec		Old age	sudden
6	Levi	8m	M	B	S		Tenn	Jan		Pneumonia	4 weeks
7	Hugh Smith	1m	M				Tenn	Nov		unknown	1 month
8	Rachel H. Davenport	38	F				Tenn	July		Hung herself, idiot	1 day
9	Harriet Roberts	46	F				Va	May		unknown	sudden
10	Susan E. Harwell	7	F				Tenn	July		Fits, deaf and dumb	Chronic
11	Samuel Harwell	76	M				Va	Oct		Flux	3 months
12	Molly	80	F				Va	June		Old age, most blind	Chronic
13	Babe Spaulding	1m	M				Tenn	Sept		Croup	13 days
14	King	9m	M	B	S		Tenn	Sept		Croup	3 days
15	Infant	1m	M	B	S		Tenn	May		unknown	1 week
16	Sarah H. Potter	47	F				Kentucky	Sept		T. fever	6 weeks
17	Infant	1m	F				Tenn	Nov		unknown	1 day

Remarks: At least three fourths of this District is wonderously hilly and very poor, and in some parts of it very thinly settled and it seems that it cannot even be, from the fact, that no man of an enterprising disposition, who wish to cultivate the land or would settle on it, because they could not more than make a support, but along on the creeks, it is generally very rich and general in small bodies, except in the north eastern portion where it is very rich and productive and valuable. The District is well watered and is as healthy as any portion of the County. No minerals or mines have been discovered. Nothing very interesting in the scenery to attract the attention of the traveler. John McGrew.

COUNTY OF GILES, STATE OF TENNESSEE.

PAGE NO. 268 PERSONS WHO DIED DURING THE YEAR ENDING 1st JUNE, 1850.

Civil District No. 6

No. of Visit	Name	Age	Sex	Color	Free or Slave	Married/Widowed	Place of Birth	Month Died	Occupation	Disease or Cause of Death	No. Days Ill
1	William	5	M	B	S		Tenn	Nov		Killed in Cotton Gin	sudden
2	Infant	1m	M	B	S		Tenn	Sept		unknown	sudden
3	William Davenport	63	M				Va	May	Farmer	Palsy	Chronic
4	Felix	5	M	M	S		Tenn	March		unknown	Chronic
5	Dilsey	60	F	B	S		Va	March		unknown	Chronic
6	Ann	1	F	B	S		Tenn	Aug		Inflamation of bowels	1 week
7	Katharine Barnett	18	F				Tenn	Oct		Dropsy	Chronic
8	Infant of James Martin	1m	F				Tenn	July		unknown	3 weeks
9	Malcomb B. Gibson	40	M				Tenn	Nov		Congestive fever	9 weeks
10	Susan A. Craig	28	F				Tenn	Aug		Chronic disease	3 months
11	Richard J. Craig	5m	M				Tenn	Sept		Chronic disease	3 months
12	Livenia	1	F	B	S		Tenn	April		unknown	6 months
13	William Hancock	73	M				N.C.	Sept		unknown	4 weeks
14	Maria	2	F	B	S		Tenn	Aug		Worms	2 weeks
15	Rachel	1	F	B	S		Tenn	Aug		Worms	3 weeks
16	Marion	6m	M	B	S		Tenn	May		Worms	2 days
17	Slave of Jas. B. Kimbrough	1m	M	B	S		Tenn	May		unknown	sudden
18	Slave of Jas. B. Kimbrough	1m	F	M	S		Tenn	April		unknown	sudden
19	Slave of Jas. B. Kimbrough	2m	M	M	S		Tenn	May		Thrash	3 days
20	Infant of Jas.B.Kimbrough	1m	F				Tenn	Feb		unknown	1 day
21	Babe of Jerome Black	1	M				Tenn	April		Inflamation of brain	1 month
22	Charlotte	36	F	B	S		Tenn	Dec		T. fever	15 days
23	Infant slave	1m	F	B	S		Tenn	Sept		unknown	
24	Reubin, of Calvin Reynolds	6m	M	B	S		Tenn	Oct		unknown	3 months
25	Albert, of Calvin Reynolds	1m	M	B	S		Tenn	Sept		Smothered	
26	Nice, of Calvin Reynolds	3m	F	B	S		Tenn	Sept		Croup	6 days

Remarks: This District is thickly settled and about one half is cleared up and in cultivation, and the lands on the creeks and branches seem to be very much worn in places from the fact that it has been planted in cotton so long that it needs to be seeded or cleared. There is a good deal of this District very rocky and broken and in some portions of it timber is very scarce. The people have generally been very healthy, although there has been more slave deaths in it, in the last year in porportion to its size than any other District that I have visited. The water is generally limestone, but is generally very good. John McGrew.

COUNTY OF GILES, STATE OF TENNESSEE.

PAGE NO. 269 PERSONS WHO DIED DURING THE YEAR ENDING 1st JUNE, 1850.

No. of Visit	Name	Age	Sex	Color	Free or Slave	Married/Widowed	Place of Birth	Month Died	Occupation	Disease or Cause of Death	No. Days Ill
1	Sarah Young	102	F				Va	Jan		Old age	C
2	D. H. Cunningham	43	F				N.C.	Dec		Child birth	30 days
3	Lucretia	20	F	B	S		Tenn	Oct		Burn	C
4	Catharine	1	F	B	S		Tenn	Sept		Worms	4 days
5	Felix M. McCallum	20	M				Tenn	Feb		Fever	7 days
6	Nancy Roberts	65	F				Tenn	Sept		--illegible--	C
7	Rebecca Hill	71	F				N.C.	June		Cancer	C
8	Richard Wilks	48	M				Va	Nov		Fever	20 days
9	Clarinda Ursery	2	F				Tenn	March		unknown	C
10	Elijah	10	M	B	S		Tenn	June		Worms	2 days
11	Jerry	3	M	B	S		Tenn	Dec		Worms	4 days
12	William	2m	M	B	S		Tenn	Sept		unknown	sudden
13	Amos London	80	M				New Jersey	Feb	Farmer	Dropsy	14 days
14	Martin M. Wade	2	F(?)				Tenn	May		Fever	5 days

COUNTY OF GILES, STATE OF TENNESSEE.

PAGE NO. 272 PERSONS WHO DIED DURING THE YEAR ENDING 1st JUNE, 1850.

No. of Visit	Name	Age	Sex	Color	Free or Slave	Married/Widowed	Place of Birth	Month Died	Occupation	Disease or Cause of Death	No. Days Ill
1	Mary Frazier	52	F				Va	July		Cancer	C
2	Elizabeth Kidwell	8m	F				Tenn	July		unknown	C
3	Nancy	2	F	B	S		Tenn	Aug		Croup	sudden
4	Sarah	5	F	B	S		Tenn	April		unknown	14 days
5	Sally Johnson	5	F				Tenn	July		Croup	4 days
6	Nancy	4	F	B	S		Tenn	July		unknown	8 days
7	--(not named)--	2m	F	B	S		Tenn	Aug		Smothered	sudden
8	James McMillian	3m	M				Tenn	July		Croup	3 days
9	Frances	12	F	M	S		Tenn	Sept		Fever	21 days
10	Agnes	4m	F	M	S		Tenn	May		Smothered	sudden
11	Thomas	14	M	B	S		Alabama	April		Dropsy	90 days
12	Benj. J. Hill	2	M				Tenn	July		unknown	C
13	John	16	M	B	S		Maryland	Jan		Drowned	
14	Jane	8	F	B	S		Alabama	Dec		unknown	35 days
15	Joseph	3	M	M	S		Tenn	Aug		unknown	sudden
16	Jesse	50	M	B	S		Va	Feb		Pleurisy	7 days
17	John	8	M	B	S		Tenn	March		Rheumatism	7 days
18	Rachel	45	F	B	S		Va	March		Phthisic	C
19	Jane	3m	F	B	S		Tenn	Nov		Smothered	
20	Matthew Walker	4	M				Tenn	Sept		Jaundice	35 days
21	Richard Roberts	42	M				Va	Aug		Cholera	1 day
22	Ruth J. Holder	3	F				Tenn	Dec		Croup	1 day
23	Thomas	8	M	B	S		Tenn	Feb		Worms	3 days
24	John	2	M	B	S		Tenn	Jan		Whooping cough	14 days
25	Jane	2	F	B	S		Tenn	Oct		Teething	5 days
26	Inf.	1m	M	B	S		Tenn	Sept		unknown	C
27	not named Infant	1da	M				Tenn	March		unknown	
28	James L. Vick	3m	M				Tenn	July		unknown	10 days
29	Sarah McDonald	1m	F				Tenn	Sept		Hives	3 days
30	Sarah A. Plot	80	F				Va	July		Dropsy	C
31	Elisha Dodson	70	M				N.C.	May		Cancer	C
32	Uriah Compton	15	M				Tenn	Dec		Fever	35 days
33	not named	1m	F				Tenn	Oct		unknown	7 days
34	Thomas	55	M	B	S		Maryland	Sept		Fever	14 days

COUNTY OF GILES, STATE OF TENNESSEE.

PAGE NO. 273 PERSONS WHO DIED DURING THE YEAR ENDING 1st JUNE, 1850.

No. of Visit	Name	Age	Sex	Color	Free or Slave	Married/Widowed	Place of Birth	Month Died	Occupation	Disease or Cause of Death	No. Days Ill
1	Pressley W. Stephenson	1	M				Tenn	July		Fits	C
2	Abigail Brown	38	F				N.C.	Oct		Cholera	6 days
3	Grace	45	F	B	S		S.C.	Sept		Dropsy	C
4	John	38	M	B	S		Tenn	April		Pneumonia	14 days
5	Tomazine McDonald	6m	M				Tenn	March		Inflamation of brain	5 days
6	Elizabeth Garret	48	F				S.C.	April		unknown	C
7	Wiley Neal	57	M				S.C.	April	Farmer	unknown	C
8	Thomas W. Grubbs	55	M				Va	April		Palsy	C
9	Sarah E. Abernathy	7	F				Tenn	Aug		unknown	10 days
10	Mary J. Abernathy	28	F				Tenn	Dec		Fever	33 days
11	John	6m	M	B	S		Tenn	Oct		Inflamation of brain	3 days
12	Martha A. Adkins	40	F				Tenn	Nov		Fever	21 days
13	Joe	45	M	B	S		Tenn	Aug		Hung himself	sudden
14	Sophia	14	F	B	S		Tenn	July		Fever	7 days
15	Wiley	2	M	B	S		Tenn	Aug		Cholic	1 day
16	Constantine	9m	M	B	S		Tenn	Feb		Croup	1 day

COUNTY OF GILES, STATE OF TENNESSEE.

PAGE NO. 273   PERSONS WHO DIED DURING THE YEAR ENDING 1st JUNE, 1850.

No. of Visit	Name	Age	Sex	Color	Free or Slave	Married/Widowed	Place of Birth	Month Died	Occupation	Disease or Cause of Death	No. Days Ill
17	Sarah A. Harwell	21	F				Tenn	March		Consumption	C
18	Jesse	15	M	B	S		Tenn	May		unknown	C
19	Benj. F. Butler	20	M				Tenn	Oct	Farmer	Pneumonia	12 days
20	Francis Macklin	3m	M				Tenn	Aug		unknown	C
21	James Macklin	1m	M				Tenn	Sept		unknown	C
22	Joe	2m	M	B	S		Tenn	July		unknown	2 days
23	Sarah Chambliss	60	F				Va	April		unknown	4 days
24	Ann H. Burgess	2	F				Tenn	Oct		Cholera	C
25	Nancy Young	27	F				Tenn	April		Consumption	C
26	Hannah	24	F	B	S		Tenn	Feb		Child birth	3 days
27	Victoria Young	2	F				Tenn	Feb		Croup	2 days
28	Mary Sutton	22	F				Tenn	June		Child birth	6 days
29	Elem	73	M	B	S		Va	June		Dropsy	C
30	Isham	25	M	B	S		Tenn	Jan		Fever	7 days
31	Neill L. Brown Holly	7m	M				Tenn	March		Croup	1 day
32	Mary J. W. Craig	3da	F				Tenn	Feb		Croup	1 day
33	Sarah Harwell	58	F				Tenn	May		Scrofula	C
34	Samuel Gamble	77	M				Georgia	Sept	Farmer	Consumption	C
35	Wiley P. M. Brittain	9m	M				Tenn	March		Hydrocephalus	4 days

COUNTY OF GILES, STATE OF TENNESSEE.

PAGE NO. 276   PERSONS WHO DIED DURING THE YEAR ENDING 1st JUNE, 1850.

No. of Visit	Name	Age	Sex	Color	Free or Slave	Married/Widowed	Place of Birth	Month Died	Occupation	Disease or Cause of Death	No. Days Ill
1	Catharine Stivers	50	F			M	Kentucky	Feb		unknown	C
2	Hortense Bearden	8m	F				Tenn	Nov		Cholera	4 days
3	Boyd Wilson	70	M				N.C.	July	Farmer	unknown	C
4	Sinai H. Johnson	1	F				Tenn	Dec		Cholera	2 days
5	John	29	M	B	S		Tenn	July		Killed	sudden
6	Nancy	19	F	B	S		Tenn	March		Pneumonia	10 days
7	John W. York	2	M				Tenn	July		Fever	90 days
8	Lydia A. York	8m	F				Tenn	March		Cold	28 days
9	Fanny	8m	F	B	S		Tenn	July		unknown	C
10	William Y. Crenshaw	5m	M				Alabama	Sept		Congestion of brain	C
11	Jane	40	F	B	S		Tenn	March		unknown	C
12	Elizabeth A. Stone	33	F				Va	Aug		Consumption	C
13	John	8	M	B	S		Tenn	Sept		Sore throat	10 days
14	Jesse	1	M	B	S		Tenn	Jan		unknown	C
15	Jane	1	F	B	S		Tenn	May		Whooping cough	6 days
16	Thomas	6m	M	B	S		Tenn	Sept		Croup	1 day
17	Jane	4	F	B	S		Tenn	Sept		Whooping cough	20 days
18	Joseph	2	M	B	S		Tenn	Sept		Whooping cough	14 days
19	Wyat F. Swinny	4m	M				Tenn	April		unknown	5 days
20	Eleanor Smith	1	F				Tenn	Aug		unknown	1 day
21	Mary Peebles	56	F				Va	Aug		Palsy	30 days
22	Luke Watkins	10m	M				Tenn	April		Hives	28 days
23	Jane	1	F	B	S		Tenn	May		Bronchitis	10 days
24	Meshack Boyce	69	M				Delaware	Sept	Farmer	unknown	C
25	John W. Ledbetter	2	M				Alabama	Nov		Inflamation of brain	6 days
26	Thomas	134	M	B	S		Va	Oct		Old age	C
27	David	12	M	B	S		Tenn	March		Killed by Gin	sudden
28	James Abernathy	52	M				Va	April	Merchant	Bronchitis	C
29	John	56	M	B	S		Africa	May		unknown	14 days
30	Juda	47	F	B	S		Tenn	Sept		Henorrhage of lungs	C
31	Davy	13	M	B	S		Tenn	Aug		Fever	7 days

COUNTY OF GILES, STATE OF TENNESSEE.

PAGE NO. 276 PERSONS WHO DIED DURING THE YEAR ENDING 1st JUNE, 1850.

No. of Visit	Name	Age	Sex	Color	Free or Slave	Married/Widowed	Place of Birth	Month Died	Occupation	Disease or Cause of Death	No. Days Ill
32	——————	6m	F	B	S		Tenn	Jan		Fever	6 days
33	——————	6m	F	B	S		Tenn	Feb		Cold	7 days
34	——————	3m	F	B	S		Tenn	March		Smothered	sudden
35	Edmund Shelton	40	M				N.C.	Jan	Farmer	Drowned	sudden

Remarks: The negro man, Thomas, represented as 134 years old, was no douby that age as he had descendants from one generation to another of the same family, his age is well authenticated.   Rees W. Porter.

COUNTY OF GRAINGER, STATE OF TENNESSEE.

PAGE NO. 277 PERSONS WHO DIED DURING THE YEAR ENDING 1st JUNE, 1850.

Civil District No. 1, 3, 4, 5 & 6

No. of Visit	Name	Age	Sex	Color	Free or Slave	Married/Widowed	Place of Birth	Month Died	Occupation	Disease or Cause of Death	No. Days Ill
1	Laura Bell	10m	F				Tenn	Feb		Yellow gum	300 days
2	Josiah Shipley	1hr	M				Tenn	Jan		Premature birth	15 days
3	Sarah Garretson	40	F			M	Tenn	Aug		Congestive fever	90 days
4	Rutha A. Robertson	16	F				Tenn	March		Winter fever	21 days
5	Martha M. Morelock	2½	F				Tenn	Sept		unknown	70 days
6	Asenath Rice	51	F			M	Tenn	Jan		Pneumonia	5 days
7	Welford C. Ludd	10m	M				Kentucky	Aug		Cholera	3 days
8	Henry Boatman	40	M			M	Tenn	Dec	Laborer	Consumption	150 days
9	John Garretson	50	M			M	Tenn	April	Cabinet mkr	Pneumonia	21 days
10	William Barren	45	M				Indiana	March	Laborer	T. fever	7 days
11	Susannah Stansbury	93	F			W	Va	April		Old age	365 days
12	Phebe M. J. Trase	2m	F				Tenn	Nov		Bold hives	14 days
13	Barbary Spoon	75	F			W	N.C.	March		unknown	9 days
14	Elizabeth Perkepile	62	F			W	N.C.	June		Palsy	7 days
15	Louisa J. Lowe	23	F			M	Tenn	Aug		unknown fever	12 days
16	Harriet J. Taylor	29	F			M	Tenn	May		Inflamation of stomach	7 days
17	Thom	19	M	B	S		Tenn	March		Pneumonia	9 days
18	Azariah Barton	16	M				Tenn	Aug	Laborer	unknown	6 days
19	David Barton	9m	M				Tenn	Feb		unknown	6 days
20	Elijah Barton	4½m	M				Tenn	Sept		Croup	6 days
21	Henry Barton	3	M	B	S		Tenn	Nov		Worms	unknown
22	James O. Howell	82	M			W	N.C.	Nov		Pneumonia	15 days
23	Matilda	23	F	B	S		N.C.	Feb		Inflamation of womb	5 days
24	Milly	6	F	B	S		Tenn	Feb		T. fever	35 days
25	Samuel Harben	20	M				Tenn	Sept	Laborer	Consumption	
26	Lavina Hodge	15m	F				Tenn	Dec		Worms	3 days
27	Jemima McAnally	9m	F				Tenn	Nov		inflamation of lungs	60 days
28	Benjamin Mitchel	52	M			M	Va	March	Farmer	Pneumonia	15 days
29	Pleasant Young	4	M				Tenn	April		Inflamation of brain	3 days
30	Pierce Cody	49	M			M	N.C.	Dec	Farmer	Cholera	1 day
31	Alice	22	F	B	S		Tenn	July		Scrofula	120 days
32	Samuel Snider	4m	M				Tenn	Dec		Croup	5 days
33	Josiah Cox	1	M				Tenn	Oct		Inflamation of brain	10 days
34	Rachel H. Manson	18m	F				Tenn	Nov		Bold hives	2 days
35	Delila	45	F	B	S		Tenn	Nov		T. fever	21 days

Remarks: The individual above mentioned who died with cholera had just returned from a region of country where that disease was prevailing.   William M. Williams.

COUNTY OF GRAINGER, STATE OF TENNESSEE.

PAGE NO. 280 PERSONS WHO DIED DURING THE YEAR ENDING 1st JUNE, 1850.

Civil District No. 6, 7, 8, 9, 10 & 11

No. of Visit	Name	Age	Sex	Color	Free or Slave	Married/Widowed	Place of Birth	Month Died	Occupation	Disease or Cause of Death	No. Days Ill
1	Juda Mitchel	80	F			W	Va	July		Palsy	91 days
2	Hetta Witlock	41	F				unknown	Feb		Rheumatism	54 days
3	Mary J. Roach	1m	F				Tenn	Dec		Bold hives	8 days
4	Mary J. Bradly	15	F				Tenn	Feb		Breast Complaint	36 days
5	John W. Summer	2	M				Tenn	April		sudden	2 hours
6	Mary Smith	25	F				Tenn	Dec		Burn	21 days
7	William Chase	40	M				Tenn	Feb	Farmer	Winter fever	9 days
8	Corbin Jackson	57	M			M	Va	Nov	Farmer	sudden	1 day
9	Jane Shields	84	F			W	Penn	Dec		Old age	300 days
10	Matthew Campbell	74	M			M	Tenn	Nov	Farmer	Chronic	36 days
11	Adeline Jones	6	F				Tenn	June		Flux	13 days
12	Margaret Jones	6	F				Tenn	June		Flux	11 days
13	Martha Duvall	11	F				N.C.	July		Flux	13 days
14	Lemuel Floid	15	M				Tenn	Jan	Laborer	Pneumonia	4_ days
15	John Floid	13	M				Tenn	Jan		unknown	99 days
16	Mahala Henderson	40	F				Tenn	Oct		Fever	7 days
17	Mary A. Shields	22	F				Va	June		Disease of the heart	60 days
18	Pompy	70	M	B	S		N.C.	June		Old age	7 days
19	Dick	17	M	B	S		Tenn	Feb		Whooping cough	10 days
20	Elizabeth	4m	F	B	S		Tenn	Feb		Whooping cough	10 days
21	John Staly	4m	M				Tenn	Jan		unknown	7 days
22	Mary Dyer	50	F				unknown	June		Chronic	547 days
23	Stephen T. Godwin	18	M				Tenn	Aug	Farmer	Hurt	9 days
24	Emeline Miles	17	F				Va	July		Pneumonia	14 days
25	James	1	M	B	S		Tenn	April		Scrofula	3 days
26	Goodin Solomon	56	M			M	Va	April	none	Pneumonia	8 days
27	Jack	7m	M	B	S		Tenn	Sept		Whooping cough	
28	Richard Collins	10m	M				Tenn	Nov		Dropsy in head	20 days
29	Delphia Dalton	49	F				N.C.	Aug		Inflamation of the throat	sudden
30	Louisa Dalton	1	F				Tenn	Jan		Whooping cough	20 days
31	Mary J. Dalton	3	F				Tenn	April		Whooping cough	60 days
32	Riley Dalton	2m	M				Tenn	Feb		Whooping cough	35 days
33	Claborn McCoy	38	M			M	Tenn	Sept	Farmer	Bil. fever	12 days
34	Elvira	14	F	B	S		Tenn	Sept		Bil. fever	10 days
35	Anderson	17	M	B	S		Tenn	Aug		Bil. fever	15 days

COUNTY OF GRAINGER, STATE OF TENNESSEE.

PAGE NO. 281 PERSONS WHO DIED DURING THE YEAR ENDING 1st JUNE, 1850.

Civil District No. 11, 12, 13, 14 & 15

No. of Visit	Name	Age	Sex	Color	Free or Slave	Married/Widowed	Place of Birth	Month Died	Occupation	Disease or Cause of Death	No. Days Ill
1	Lucindy Bull	1	F				Tenn	May		Whooping cough	21 days
2	Thomas P. McAnally	34	M			M	Tenn	Nov	Farmer	Pneumonia	4 days
3	Harriett McAnally	11	F				Tenn	April		Pneumonia	49 days
4	Henry Holt	78	M				Va	Oct	Sch-teacher	Carbuncle	28 days
5	Esquire Collins	40	M				Tenn	April	Farmer	T. fever	14 days
6	Susan McGinis	36	F			M	Tenn	Dec		Pneumonia	9 days
7	Jaily Bullen	46	F				Tenn	June		Dropsy	365 days
8	Dicy Bullen	2m	F				Tenn	June		Premature birth	14 days
9	Marvel Dodson	10m	M				Tenn	Aug		Bowel complaint	8 days
10	William J. Crawford	1m	M				Tenn	March		Bold hives	1 day
11	Elizabeth Ash	1m	F				Tenn	March		Whooping cough	21 days
12	Martha Arvine	2m	F				Tenn	unknown		Croup	¼ day
13	Milly Dyer	16	F				Tenn	March		Pneumonia	55 days
14	Vestina Idel	7	F				Tenn	March		Burn	2 days
15	Elizabeth Acuff	1	F				Tenn	March		Inflamation of brain	7 days

COUNTY OF GRAINGER, STATE OF TENNESSEE.

PAGE NO. 281 PERSONS WHO DIED DURING THE YEAR ENDING 1st JUNE, 1850.

Civil District No. 11, 12, 13, 14 & 15

No. of Visit	Name	Age	Sex	Color	Free or Slave	Married/Widowed	Place of Birth	Month Died	Occupation	Disease or Cause of Death	No. Days Ill
16	Mary Dodson	1	F				Tenn	April		Whooping cough	60 days
17	Nicholas Acuff	10m	M				Tenn	Feb		Hair lip	30 days
18	Elizabeth Clark	49	F				Tenn	May		Fall from chair	sudden
19	Martin Cleveland	41	M			M	N.C.	June	Farmer	Palp. of the heart	sudden
20	David Merit	21	M				Tenn	Sept	Farmer	Blind piles	16 days
21	Harriet Adkins	25	F				Tenn	March		Dropsy	Chronic
22	John Hukman	100	M			W	N.C.	Dec	Farmer	Old age	Chronic
23	Mary Collet	36	F				Tenn	May		Consumption	300 days
24	Louisa Vitito	1m	F				Tenn	Sept		Whooping cough	21 days
25	Anna Needham	29	F				Tenn	Dec		Pneumonia	21 days
26	Nancy Holland	7	F				Tenn	Jan		Pain in head and bowels	3 days
27	Simeon Coffman	12	M				Tenn	Jan		Pain in head and bowels	3 days
28	George Nikly	1	M				Tenn	Feb		Cold	50 days
29	Parasine Dennis	15	F				Tenn	March		Breast complaint	365 days
30	Aaron Dennis	8m	M				Tenn	Feb		Bold hives	42 days
31	Rebeca B. Vitito	30	F				Tenn	Aug		Inf. of kidneys	270 days
32	Leroy Damewood	17	M				Tenn	May	Farmer	Winter fever	21 days
33	Mary J. Clapp	2m	F				Tenn	Nov		Bold hives	2 days
34	Child of N. Gibbs	5m	F				Tenn	July		Milk) supposed	30 days
35	Child of N. Gibbs	5m	M				Tenn	July		Milk) supposed	30 days

COUNTY OF GRAINGER, STATE OF TENNESSEE.

PAGE NO. 284 PERSONS WHO DIED DURING THE YEAR ENDING 1st JUNE, 1850.

Civil District No. 15

No. of Visit	Name	Age	Sex	Color	Free or Slave	Married/Widowed	Place of Birth	Month Died	Occupation	Disease or Cause of Death	No. Days Ill
1	James E. Leach	6m	M				Tenn	July		Bold hives	2 days
2	Orlina Monroe	26	F				Tenn	Nov		Pul. Consumption	210 days
3	Tabitha L. Sexton	1	F				Tenn	May		Whooping cough	? days
4	Eda Smith	29	F				Tenn	May		Suffocation	sudden
5	Gracy	55	F	B	S		N.C.	May		Cancer	Chronic
6	Thomas Hannly	10	M				Tenn	June		Drowned	sudden
7	Elijah Evans	3	M				Tenn	May		Fever	3 days
8	Rebecca A. Yaden	2m	F				Tenn	Feb		Whooping cough	21 days

COUNTY OF GREENE, STATE OF TENNESSEE.

PAGE NO. 286 PERSONS WHO DIED DURING THE YEAR ENDING 1st JUNE, 1850.

The 9th Division, Eastern Dist.

No. of Visit	Name	Age	Sex	Color	Free or Slave	Married/Widowed	Place of Birth	Month Died	Occupation	Disease or Cause of Death	No. Days Ill
1	William L. Harris	21	M				S.C.	Aug	Law Student	Typhoid	14 days
2	Ruth Brannon	32	F				Tenn	Sept		Congestion	7 days
3	G. W. Foute, Jr.	3	M				Tenn	July		Pertussis	33 days
4	Hannah Farnsworth	1	F	M	F		Tenn	May		unknown	10 days
5	Nancy J.	1	F		F		Tenn	July		Pertussis	58 days
6	Eliza Van Vactor	21	F	M	F		Tenn	May		Pulmonary	Chronic
7	John Gwinn	52	M			M	Va	Aug	Saddler	Accident	1 day
8	Jacob D. Bell	26	M			M	N.C.	Nov	Carpenter	Typhoid	23 days
9	Esaw Morrow	70	M			W	unknown	Jan		Pulmonary	Chronic
10	James A. Oliphant	6	M				Tenn	June		Pertussis	25 days
11	Eve E. Gridner	60	F				Penn	Jan		Carditis	21 days
12	William Brotherton	6	M				Tenn	June		Drowned	
13	Infant		M				Tenn	Dec		Cholera	4 days
14	S. M. Ricker	2	M				Tenn	Sept		Cholera	Chronic
15	Margaret Foster	5	F				Tenn	Sept		Pertussis	60 days
16	Jack	65	M	B	S		Tenn	July		Apoplexy	sudden
17	William Barkly	65	M			W	Va	April	Farmer	Neuralgia	sudden
18	Henry H. Ballew	8	M				N.C.	Aug		Cholera	14 days
19	Charly	4m	M	B	S		Tenn	May		Bronchitis	Chronic
20	Letty Chapman	2	F				Tenn	April		Bronchal	Chronic
21	Moses Reeves	82	M			M	Va	April	Cooper	Angina Pec.	30 days
22	Joseph L. Arlshil	1m	M				Tenn	June		Hives	1 day
23	Compton J. P. Dawson	2	M				Tenn	June		Pertussis	30 days
24	Infant Malory	1m	M				Tenn	July		Hives	7 days
25	Jane McFarland	20	F	B			Tenn	March		Plumonary	14 days
26	Martha J. McDaniel	17	F				N.C.	May		Congestion	4 days
27	Sarah Goss	26	F				Tenn	July		Pulmonary	Chronic
28	Jemima Casteel	72	F				Penn	July		Pulmonary	Chronic
29	John A. Payne	7m	M				Tenn	Jan		unknown	Chronic
30	Elizabeth Runnels	50	F			M	Tenn	May		Pneumonia	36 days
31	Prescilla M. Fincher	11m	F				Tenn	July		Pertussis	21 days
32	Margarett McAmish	56	F			M	Tenn	Dec		Pulmonary	Chronic
33	Alfred C. Swatzell	1	M				Tenn	March		Deformed	
34	Elizabeth Stewart	1	F				Tenn	May		Pneumonia	14 days
35	George Fortner	6	M				Tenn	Oct		Pneumonia	5 days

Remarks: The geology and mineralogy of Green County is as follows: Two formations, primitive and transitions, cover the County of Green. White and Smoky Mountains (the line between North Carolina and Tennessee) is primitive. This formation extend on a line parallel with that range from eight to ten miles north, there ending in a northern range of Mountains corresponding with the Chilhowee Mountain, a line at which the
......
Jesse Henderson.

COUNTY OF GREENE, STATE OF TENNESSEE.

PAGE NO. 288   PERSONS WHO DIED DURING THE YEAR ENDING 1st JUNE, 1850.

The 9th Division, East District

No. of Visit	Name	Age	Sex	Color	Free or Slave	Married/Widowed	Place of Birth	Month Died	Occupation	Disease or Cause of Death	No. Days Ill
1	Charles	42	M	B	S		Tenn	June		Pulmonary	Chronic
2	Samuel E. Johnson	6m	M				Tenn	July		Pertussis	7 days
3	Malinda Willis	19	F				Tenn	Dec		Pulmonary	Chronic
4	Jonah Marsh	5m	M				Tenn	May		--illegible--	21 days
5	Barbara E. Fellers	1	F				Tenn	Dec		Idiot	sudden
6	John Odel	34	M			M	Tenn	July	Farmer	Typhoid	42 days
7	Thomas C. Odel	18	M				Tenn	Aug	Farmer	Typhoid	50 days
8	Eather	20	F	B	S		Tenn	Aug		Typhoid	28 days
9	Harriet	35	F	M	S		Tenn	Aug		Pulmonary	Chronic
10	Alfred	25	M	B	S		Tenn	Dec		Pneumonia	14 days
11	Infant	1m	M				Tenn	Sept		Bronchal	5 days
12	John Muncher	60	M			M	Tenn	Jan	Farmer	Jaundice	Chronic
13	Nancy Painter	60	F			M	Tenn	July		Gastritis	Chronic
14	Jordan Marshall	14	M				Tenn	Jan		Dropsy	Chronic
15	Martha J. Oler	5m	F				Tenn	July		Pertussis	8 days
16	Infant	1m	F				Tenn	May		Fits	sudden
17	John W. Fanning	4	M				Tenn	Jan		Burned	1 day
18	Ruth M. L. Jennings	2	F				Tenn	Feb		Scalded	9 days
19	Mary E. Jackson	18	F				Tenn	Aug		Pneumonia	54 days
20	John Bowers, Sr.	77	M				Penn	July	Farmer	Apoplexy	sudden
21	John Ren	1	M				Tenn	Oct		Scarletina	9 days
22	George Easterly	68	M				Va	March	Luth. Minister	Angina Pec.	sudden
23	Infant		F					Feb			birth
24	Jacob Miller	86	M			M	Penn	Aug	Farmer	Rupture	Chronic
25	Philip Erard	87	M				Penn	Jan	Farmer	Pulmonary	Chronic
26	Infant	1m	M				Tenn	Sept		unknown	sudden
27	Clarissa	10m	F	B	S		Tenn	April		Pneumonia	5 days
28	William G. Myers	3	M				Tenn	April		Typhoid	21 days
29	John Cranes	39	M			M	Tenn	Feb	Farmer	Pulmonary	Chronic
30	Aladin Rollins	12	M	M			Tenn	Dec		Accident	
31	William H. Rambo	22	M			M	Tenn	April	Farmer	Knee joint	Chronic
32	John Fellers	17	M				Tenn	June	Farmer	Fever	35 days
33	Adolphus Fellers' infant		F				Tenn	Feb		Deformed	6 days
34	Mary Fellers	38	F			M	Tenn	March		Dropsy	Chronic
35	Mary A. Dunsmore	33	F			M	Tenn	Jan		--illegible--	9 days

Remarks: (continued from previous page) first traces of vegetable and organic ____ are discoverable. Thence, further north, the formation, to the extent of the County is transition. The first mentioned formation is Mountainous running in range north-east and south-west, mostly very fertile, covered with valuable timber, abounding in abundance of ____ iron ore and the ore of zinc in the same range is found beds of fine clay, most of which is beautifully white, such as ores of manganese fine graines grindstone... (continued)

COUNTY OF GREENE, STATE OF TENNESSEE.

PAGE NO. 290 PERSONS WHO DIED DURING THE YEAR ENDING 1st JUNE, 1850.

The 10th Sub-Division, East Div.

No. of Visit	Name	Age	Sex	Color	Free or Slave	Married/Widowed	Place of Birth	Month Died	Occupation	Disease or Cause of Death	No. Days Ill
1	Francis Snider	14	M				Tenn	April		Drowned	
2	John Kisser	88	M				Penn	Oct	Farmer	Old age	5 days
3	Abraham Snider	77	M			M	Va	Feb	Farmer	Palsy	4 days
4	Margaret H. Whittenburg	15	F				Tenn	Aug		Fever	14 days
5	Adam Dunwoody	29	M			M	Tenn	Dec	Farmer	Fever	35 days
6	Thomas H. Russell	6	M				Tenn	Feb		Fever	3 days
7	Francis Russell	16	F				Tenn	Sept		Fever	7 days
8	Elam Russell	14	M				Tenn	Sept		Fever	21 days
9	Fredrick Russell	12	M				Tenn	Oct		Fever	14 days
10	Wilson Willet	1	M				Tenn	Aug		Croup	21 days
11	Mary Swatsell	50	F			W	Tenn	July		Palsy	11 days
12	Rufus Lane	9	M				N.C.	June		Worms	1 day
13	Sarah Russell	57	F			M	Tenn	Oct		--illegible--	3 days
14	Harvey Russell	31	M			M	Tenn	Nov	Farmer	Rheumatism	14 days
15	Martha Jane Harrison	1m	F				Tenn	Jan		Croup	3 days
16	Catharine Laughner	77	F				Penn	Jan		Palsy	70 days
17	Lawson Bowers	1	M				Tenn	Dec		Cholera	sudden
18	Fredrick S. Melser	63	M				Va	March	Farmer	Piles	60 days
19	Mary Lafollet	5	F				Tenn	July		Diarrhea	30 days
20	Anna Masoner	22	F				Tenn	June		Consumption	14 days
21	Sarah Ann Phipps	1	F				N.C.	July		Whooping cough	28 days
22	Robert M. Nelson	1	M				Tenn	July		Drowned	
23	George	53	M	B	S		S.C.	Sept		Dropsy	7 days
24	Gracy	52	F	B	S		Va	April		Consumption	21 days
25	Mary Ann Feasel	2m	F				Tenn	Aug		Croup	9 days
26	Anna Cobble	17	F				Tenn	Jan		Palsy	sudden
27	Margaret Lowry	73	F				Va	June		Palsy	5 days
28	Lorenzo D. Lowe	4	M				Tenn	June		Gravel	14 days
29	Nancy E. Walker	1	F				Tenn	Oct		Croup	14 days
30	Jacob Bibb	58	M			M	Tenn	May	Farmer	Fever	12 days
31	Mary McMillen	8m	F				Tenn	Jan		Croup	sudden
32	Thompson Black	24	M				Tenn	Feb	none	By a fall	30 days
33	Jacob Litrel	12	M				Tenn	Sept		Chills	26 days
34	James Hale	10	M				Tenn	Aug		sudden	
35	John Hale	5m	M				Tenn	Aug		Chills	31 days

Remarks: No sickness in this part of the County except one case of fever and six cases of chills, more healthy than usual. Water and land is of different qualities, some limestone, some slate of inferior quality. The limestone water is generally good. The southern part of the district, the land is generally good of a limestone nature produces well, the middle and northern part is more broken and of a slate quality. Production not so good. These remarks is for the time taking down the above. James Craig.

COUNTY OF GREENE, STATE OF TENNESSEE.

PAGE NO. 291 PERSONS WHO DIED DURING THE YEAR ENDING 1st JUNE, 1850.

The 10th Sub-Division, East Dist.

No. of Visit	Name	Age	Sex	Color	Free or Slave	Married/Widowed	Place of Birth	Month Died	Occupation	Disease or Cause of Death	No. Days Ill
1	Zachariah Turley	69	M			M	Maryland	Nov	Farmer	Consumption	11 days
2	Daniel J. Kesterson	23	M				Tenn	June	Farmer	Fever	15 days
3	Amy	85	F	B	S		Va	Nov		Old age	
4	Juda	50	F	B	S		Tenn	Jan		Pneumonia	15 days
5	Allen	50	M	M	S		Tenn	Feb		Pneumonia	7 days
6	Maria	6	F	B	S		Tenn	Feb		Pneumonia	10 days
7	Samuel	48	M	B	S		Va	April		unknown	90 days
8	Orpha Pitts	35	F				S.C.	March		Inflamation of bowels	6 days
9	Allice	30	F	B	S		Tenn	Aug		sudden	
10	Louisa Ann Jenkins	26	F				Tenn	Aug		Consumption	1 year
11	Mary Jenkins	4m	F				Tenn	July		unknown	7 days
12	James Bryant	11	M				Tenn	Nov		Fever	1 day
13	John Bryant	11	M				Tenn	Nov		Fever	3 days
14	Oliver M. Lody	16	M				Tenn	Jan	Farmer	Nervous Disease	4 days
15	Martha Woods	23	F				Tenn	May		Liver complaint	42 days

Remarks: The timber varies according to the quality of land. Where the land is good the timber is hickory, walnut, oak, pine, poplar, sugar tree, and where the land is broken and thin, the timber is mostly scrubby oak and hickory. Iron ore is plenty in the southern part of the district. No other ores or minerals known. James Craig.

COUNTY OF GREENE, STATE OF TENNESSEE.

PAGE NO. 293 PERSONS WHO DIED DURING THE YEAR ENDING 1st JUNE, 1850.

The 9th Division, East Dist.

No. of Visit	Name	Age	Sex	Color	Free or Slave	Married/Widowed	Place of Birth	Month Died	Occupation	Disease or Cause of Death	No. Days Ill
1	William Ou	1	M				Tenn	July		Rheumatic	7 days
2	George M. D. Broyles	25	M				N.C.	Oct	Lawyer	--illegible--	Chronic
3	Lucy M. Nelson	5m	F				Tenn	July		Inflamatory	10 days
4	Lucinda Dugger	36	F				Va	Dec		Bronchitis	Chronic
5	Phebe A. Hatley	2	F				Tenn	Aug		Croup	2 days
6	Serephina Weems	2	F				Tenn	July		Phrenitis	7 days
7	Sarah J. Earls	2m	F				Tenn	Sept		Pertussis	27 days
8	Elizabeth Kinney	60	F			W	Va	April		Pulmonary	Chronic
9	Robert McGee	2	M				Tenn	Oct		Drowned	
10	Infant	1m	M				Tenn	Jan		unknown	2 days
11	William Philips	19	M				Tenn	Feb	Teacher	Spinal	Chronic
12	Lucy Self	1	M?				Tenn	Jan		Pneumonia	3 days
13	Sella Tarrant	82	F			W	Va	Jan		unknown	22 days
14	Nancy Thompson	18	F				Tenn	Dec		Pulmonary	Chronic
15	Nancy McLaughlin	75	F				N.C.	Sept		unknown	Chronic
16	David Wallenberger	2	M				Tenn	Sept		Croup	4 days
17	Amos Davis	45	M			M	Tenn	Sept	Farmer	Parotitis	21 days
18	Ellen Dyke	4m	F				Tenn	April		Abscess	14 days
19	Margarett Otherton	19	F				Tenn	Oct		Pulmonary	Chronic
20	Eliza A. Philips	2	F				Tenn	April		Phrenitis	5 days
21	Christian Fincher	29	F			W	Penn	Oct		Pneumonia	42 days
22	Diana J. Crawford	2	F				Tenn	Dec		Phrenitis	7 days
23	William N. Robertson	3m	M				Tenn	Nov		Croup	3 days
24	James McGee	1	M				Tenn	May		Croup	3 days
25	Nancy McMackin	19	F			M	Tenn	April		Child bed	2 days
26	Leander McMackin	1	M				Tenn	Sept		Croup	2 days
27	Lucinda Dickerson	6m	F				Tenn	Sept		unknown	Chronic

COUNTY OF GREENE, STATE OF TENNESSEE.

PAGE NO. 293   PERSONS WHO DIED DURING THE YEAR ENDING 1st JUNE, 1850.

The 9th Division, East Dist.

No. of Visit	Name	Age	Sex	Color	Free or Slave	Married/Widowed	Place of Birth	Month Died	Occupation	Disease or Cause of Death	No. Days Ill
28	Levi Hartman	69	M			M	Va	June	Farmer	Dropsy	Chronic
29	Rancelor Smith	23	M				Tenn	Sept	Carpenter	_ fever	42 days
30	William DeFord	2	M				Tenn	Jan		Worms	77 days
31	Infant		M				Tenn	Feb		Still born	
32	Nancy	1m	F	M	S		Tenn	Oct		unknown	
33	Elbert S. Tullock	23	M				Tenn	May	Blk-smith	Typhoid	28 days
34	Eliza Smith	40	F			M	Tenn	July		Pulmonary	Chronic
35	Mary Lewis	40	F				Tenn	May		Typhoid	40 days

Remarks: ... of a greenish hue not unlike the ____ ____ stones near the top of Smoky Mountains, is found a strong veil of _____ iron ore throughout the secondary formation above mentioned. The County is undulating in places, hilly, rocks, principally Mountain limestone in most of its vicinities. The land on Nolachucky River and Lick Creek are fertile. In some portions of the County are found clay-slate.   Jesse Henderson.

COUNTY OF GREENE, STATE OF TENNESSEE.

PAGE NO. 295   PERSONS WHO DIED DURING THE YEAR ENDING 1st JUNE, 1850.

The 9th Division, East Dist.

No. of Visit	Name	Age	Sex	Color	Free or Slave	Married/Widowed	Place of Birth	Month Died	Occupation	Disease or Cause of Death	No. Days Ill
1	Rachel Lewis	18	F				Tenn	May		Typhoid	60 days
2	Daniel Crabtree	33	M				Tenn	March	Farmer	Bronchitis	90 days
3	Jacob F. McAmish	2	M				Tenn	March		Pneumonia	14 days

Remarks: The kinds of timber, oaks of all kinds, hickory, black walnut, chestnut, sugar tree, locust, sweet and black gum. In Mountains, white wild cherry and sugar maple of unusual size. White pine in abundance, yellow poplar, most in profussion and yet not used being, to a want of a proper knowledge of its application. No particular malady prevailent.

Remarks: Striped with small streams of calcareous spur seams of Gypsum are found in this State reached in sinking wells along Lick Creek. Small veins of lead with Carbonate of zinc are found in the north side of Bays Mountains near Kinney. Lead is spoken of in other places but of these there has been no exploration. Dark colored marble is found in some places embedded in green slate sulphate of Barytes is also found in some places. The common level of the County is about 1600 feet above sea level. Springs are abundant and the air is pure.   Jesse Henderson.

COUNTY OF GRUNDY, STATE OF TENNESSEE.

PAGE NO. 297   PERSONS WHO DIED DURING THE YEAR ENDING 1st JUNE, 1850.

Michael Hoover
District No. 1, 4, 5, 6, & 7

No. of Visit	Name	Age	Sex	Color	Free or Slave	Married/Widowed	Place of Birth	Month Died	Occupation	Disease or Cause of Death	No. Days Ill
1	Elizabeth Sack	19	F			M	Tenn	May		Dropsy	C
2	Patsey Janson	16	F				Tenn	Dec		Small pox	14 days
3	Jesse Wooton	1m	M	B	S			Oct			1 day
4	Daniel Sain	68	M			M	N.C.	Jan	Blk-smith	Dropsy	6 months
5	George A. Webb	1m	M				Tenn	Aug		Bold hives	4 days
6	Joseph Davis	1	M				Tenn	June		Canker	1 year
7	Susan Price	7m	F				Tenn	June		Inflamation	1 month
8	Isaac Roberts	85	M			M	N.C.	June	Farmer	Old age	6 months
9	Frances Benson	92	F				Va	Aug		Old age	5 months
10	Eli Cleveland	65	M			M	unknown	April	Farmer	Palsy	sudden
11	Philip Roberts	6m	M	B	S			July		Diarrhea	3 weeks
12	John Phips	80	M			M	Va	May	Farmer	Old age	1 month
13	Margaret Roberts	7m	F				Tenn	May			3 months
14	Davidson Cox	10m	M				Tenn	March			2 weeks
15	Alexander M. Blair	44	M			M	N.C.	Aug	Farmer	Gastric fever	2 weeks
16	Chansey McMellan	35	M				unknown	July	Pill Pedler	T. fever	1 week
17	Martha A. Simmons	23	F			M	Tenn	Feb		Female Cramp	33 days
18	Mary F. Mullins	1	F				Tenn	Jan			6 days
19	Joseph H. Smith	6m	M				Tenn	Sept		T. fever	10 days
20	Mahaly Fults	26	F				Tenn	May		Fits	sudden

COUNTY OF GRUNDY, STATE OF TENNESSEE.

PAGE NO. 299   PERSONS WHO DIED DURING THE YEAR ENDING 1st JUNE, 1850.

Civil District No. 2, 3, & 8

No. of Visit	Name	Age	Sex	Color	Free or Slave	Married/Widowed	Place of Birth	Month Died	Occupation	Disease or Cause of Death	No. Days Ill
1	George D. Cullender	31	M			M	Tenn	Oct	Physician	T. fever	22 days
2	Salina Patton	34	F			M	Georgia	Aug		T. fever	10 days
3	Virginia Burrell	15	F				Tenn	May		T. fever	9 days
4	Samuel Sutherland	55	M			M	S.C.	July	Farmer	Inflamation of brain	9 days
5	Anna Jane Pattie	30	F			M	Alabama	April		Consumption	C
6	Bill, slave of J.D.Pattie	4	M	B	S		Tenn	Dec		T. fever	8 days
7	Sam, slave of W.G.Greenn	8m	M	B	S		Tenn	Nov		By fall	3 days
8	Nancy J. Paterson	3m	F				Tenn	Nov		Croup	1 day
9	Margaret E. Paterson	9m	F				Tenn	April		Teething	6 days
10	Ezekiel Hobbs	74	M			M	unknown	March	Farmer	Diarrhea	5 weeks

Remarks: This County has throughout the year ending 1st June 1850, unusually healthy, no disease of maglignant character has been known here, during the year, unless Typhoid Fever may be so considered. This disease was most prevalent in District 6 & 7 and 8 and most fatal in the month of September 1849. The Physicians of Pelham do not assign any local cause for its exsistance in that region. The Valley of Elk River, embracing the above Districts, is generally low and flat and in winter and spring, a great portion of the land is covered with water which, in summer and autumn, causes fever and other diseases, peculiar to such situations. The soil near Elk River is very fertile and where it has not been cleared for tillage, is covered with poplar, walnut, oak, hickory, ash, and sugar tree. The water is generally limestone in the valley and the mountain it is generally freestone, sometimes chalybeate, limestone is very ____ in the valley and on the sides of the mountains half way to the ....   W. H. Thompson.

COUNTY OF HAMILTON , STATE OF TENNESSEE.

PAGE NO. 302 PERSONS WHO DIED DURING THE YEAR ENDING 1st JUNE, 1850.

District No. 27   R. P. Jones

No. of Visit	Name	Age	Sex	Color	Free or Slave	Married/Widowed	Place of Birth	Month Died	Occupation	Disease or Cause of Death	No. Days Ill
1	Elizabeth Sivley	49	F			M	Tenn	Aug		Fever	3 weeks
2	Rebecca Sivley	17	F				Tenn	Aug		Fever	6 weeks
3	Martha Shadric	18	F				Tenn	April		unknown	5 months
4	Clary Evans	30	F	B	S		unknown	Aug		Fever	2 weeks
5	Nancy Vandergriff	20	F			M	Va	Aug		Fever	5 days
6	Robert Bean	3	M				Tenn	April		Winter fever	4 months
7	Sarah Wiley	72	F			M	Va	Oct		Dropsy	6 months
8	John Wiley	72	M			M	Va	May	Farmer	Palsy	5 weeks
9	Sarah Wiley	38	F			M	Va	June		sudden	sudden
10	Mary Hughs	35	F	B	S		Tenn	July		Cold	2 weeks
11	Elizabeth Hughs	27	F				Tenn	June		Consumption	C
12	Samuel Hughs	25	M				Tenn	July	Farmer	Consumption	2 years
13	Charles Adams	1	M				Tenn	Aug		Dysentery	6 weeks
14	Charlotta Cozby	18	F	B	S		Tenn	May		Fever	4 days
15	Hezekiah Renow	60	M			M	Tenn	April	Farmer	T. fever	4 days
16	Jane Puckett	1	F				Tenn	Nov		Cancer	2 months
17	Sarah Campbell	62	F			W	Tenn	Feb		Cold	2 months
18	Rosana Simpson	13	F				Tenn	July		Fever	5 weeks
19	Nancy Shepherd	50	F	B	S		N.C.	Oct		Erupture	2 weeks
20	George Luttrell	22	M			M	Tenn	Jan	Farmer	Fever	3 weeks
21	Phillip Raines	21	M			M	Tenn	Oct	Farmer	Fever	47 days
22	Matilda Raines	15	F				Tenn	Nov		Fever	48 days
23	John Camren	1	M				Tenn	Aug		Diarrhea	7 weeks
24	Mary Hill	4	F	M	S		Alabama	Aug		Fever	5 weeks
25	Rindia Henderson	28	F	B	S		Tenn	Sept		Dropsy	6 months
26	Pheriba Glass	25	F	B	S		Georgia	March		Measles	2 weeks
27	George McMillion	14	M	B	S		Tenn	Nov		Consumption	6 months
28	Joseph Williams	10	M				N.C.	Dec		Fever	3 weeks
29	Marshall Swimm	1	M				N.C.	Sept		Fever	2 weeks
30	Wiley Turman	2	M				Tenn	Dec		Scalded	3 weeks
31	Thomas Crutchfield	48	M			M	Va	March	Brickmason	T. fever	7 days
32	William Piburn	10	M				Tenn	April		Gravel	2 years
33	Elizabeth Willson	90	F			W	Penn	Nov		Old age	
34	George Mitchel	10	M				Tenn	March		Pneumonia	3 days
35	Pheraby Massey	25	F				Tenn	Feb		Fever	4 weeks

Remarks: The general character of water is limestone. Limestone rocks most generally in the valley and sandstone in the mountains. A variety of timber: black oak, white oak, spanish oak, red oak, post oak, poplar, pine, chestnut and locust. The mountains abound with iron ore and inexhaustable bids of stove coal.

R. P. Jones.

COUNTY OF HAMILTON, STATE OF TENNESSEE.

PAGE NO. 303 PERSONS WHO DIED DURING THE YEAR ENDING 1st JUNE, 1850.

District No. 27 R. P. Jones

No. of Visit	Name	Age	Sex	Color	Free or Slave	Married/Widowed	Place of Birth	Month Died	Occupation	Disease or Cause of Death	No. Days Ill
1	Joseph M. Burk	2	M				Tenn	April		unknown	3 months
2	Charles M. Evitt	42	M			M	Va	Sept		Scrofula	2 years
3	Ivin Davis	57	M			M	N.C.	July	Farmer	Consumption	C
4	Jesse Roberts	4m	M				Tenn	Oct		Hives	1 day
5	Houston Nowlen	8m	M				Tenn	Feb		Croup	2 days
6	Prudence Reed	70	F			W	S.C.	July		Old age	
7	George Lock	6m	M				Tenn	Oct		Dysentery	2 months
8	Susan Cavender	11	F				Tenn	April			sudden
9	William Fitzgerall	72	M			M	Va	March	Farmer	Dropsy	6 months
10	Anderson Hunter	29	M			M	Tenn	Dec	Farmer	Fever	6 days
11	Tennessee More	20	F				Tenn	Jan		Fever	1 month
12	Elizabeth Savage	72	F				Tenn	Aug		Fever	10 days
13	Nicholas Dorharity	5	M				Georgia	May		Dropsy	1 month

COUNTY OF HANCOCK, STATE OF TENNESSEE.

PAGE NO. 305 PERSONS WHO DIED DURING THE YEAR ENDING 1st JUNE, 1850.

33rd Subdivision, East Dist.

No. of Visit	Name	Age	Sex	Color	Free or Slave	Married/Widowed	Place of Birth	Month Died	Occupation	Disease or Cause of Death	No. Days Ill
1	Sneed Brewer	6m	M				Tenn	Aug	Infant	Dysentery	14 days
2	Martha Thornton	66	F			W	N.C.	July	Weaver	Dropsy	2½ years
3	William Vannoy	21	M				Kentucky	Aug	none	Fever	8 days
4	Mary Jane Gipson	1½	F				Tenn	Oct	Infant	King's evil	7 weeks
5	Robert Gipson	8da	M				Tenn	Dec	Infant	unknown	5 days
6	Sarah E. Perkey	2m	F				Tenn	June	Infant	Hives	3 days
7	Son of Joshuah Givins	1da	M				Tenn	Sept	Infant	accident	1 day
8	Son of Joshuah Givins	1da	M				Tenn	Sept	Infant	accident	1 day
9	Zachariah Jones	39	M			M	Tenn	June	Farmer	Shot	1 day
10	Barthena Brewer	2	F				Tenn	Jan	Infant	Hives	3 days
11	Sarah Elrod	60	F			W	N.C.	Dec		sudden	sudden
12	Catharine Jackson	1	F				Tenn	June	Infant	unknown	1 day
13	William Barnard	11m	M				Tenn	April	Infant	Whooping cough	6 days
14	Volentine Singleton	1	M				Tenn	Dec	Infant	unknown	1 day
15	George Barnard	33	M			M	Kentucky	July	Farmer	Consumption	8 months
16	William Testament	52	M			M	N.C.	April	Farmer	Gravel	2 years
17	Manela Edons	2	F				Tenn	April	Infant	Burnt	1 day
18	John Sullavin	60	M			W	Tenn	Feb	Farmer	Fever	9 days
19	Mariah Nichols	50	F	B	S	M	Tenn	March	Slave	Consumption	1 year
20	Thomas J. Warren	15	M				Tenn	Feb	Farmer	Fall from horse	5 days
21	Plesant Overton	25	M	B	S	M	Tenn	April	Farmer	Colic Cramp	3 days
22	Thursey Minton	40	F				Tenn	Oct		Cold	6 months
23	Sarah Burk	2	F				Va	March	Infant	Whooping cough	6 weeks
24	Orphy Gilbert	28	F			M	Tenn	Nov		Consumption	7 weeks
25	Nancy M. Gilbert	4m	F				Tenn	Feb	Infant	Hives	1 day
26	Sousanah Denum	16	F				Tenn	Nov		Fever	3 weeks
27	Charlotta Gipson	1	F				Tenn	Aug	Infant	Croup	4 days

Remarks: No. 9th, it appears that Zachariah Jones had escaped from Court of Justice of Hawkins County while on trial of a charge for murder and in June 1849 was shot in Retakin in Hancock County.   William S. Rose.

COUNTY OF HANCOCK, STATE OF TENNESSEE.

PAGE NO. 308 PERSONS WHO DIED DURING THE YEAR ENDING 1st JUNE, 1850.

No. of Visit	Name	Age	Sex	Color	Free or Slave	Married/Widowed	Place of Birth	Month Died	Occupation	Disease or Cause of Death	No. Days Ill

Remarks: Hancock County: (no names)
Hancock County, Tennessee is a new and small County. The valleys and Creek bottoms is rich and fertile. Clinch and Powell Rivers enters throughout and numerous _____ Wollins Ridge and Powell Mountains exist ends through the County as are M____ of Mountains. Limestone and chalybeate Springs in abundance. Iron ore and vein lead is found. The growth is sugar maple, oaks, poplar & etc.
                                                        William S. Rose.

COUNTY OF HANCOCK, STATE OF TENNESSEE.

PAGE NO. 309 PERSONS WHO DIED DURING THE YEAR ENDING 1st JUNE, 1850.

32 Subdivision, East Dist.

No. of Visit	Name	Age	Sex	Color	Free or Slave	Married/Widowed	Place of Birth	Month Died	Occupation	Disease or Cause of Death	No. Days Ill
1	Simon Mills	29	M				Tenn	April	Agriculture	Fever	5 weeks
2	Holland Mills	20	M				Tenn	May	Agriculture	Fever	3 days
3	Ally Mills	24	F				Tenn	May		Fever	3 days
4	John Bolin	1m	M				Tenn	Feb		Hives	1 day
5	Perlina Trail	40	F			M	Va	April		Abortion	1 day
6	George Tucker	58	M			M	N.C.	March	Blk-smith	Fever	4 weeks
7	Sarah	34	F	B	S		N.C.	Dec		Fever	3 weeks
8	Juda	30	F	B	S		N.C.	Jan		Fever	4 weeks
9	Joshua	16	M	B	S		N.C.	Oct		Fever	2 weeks
10	Lydia	14	F	B	S		Tenn	Feb		Fever	1 week
11	Nancy	3	F	B	S		Tenn	March		Whooping cough	3 weeks
12	Matilda	3	F	B	S		Tenn	April		Whooping cough	4 weeks
13	Eliza	12	F	B	S		Tenn	Jan		Fever	3 weeks
14	John	1m	M	B	S		Tenn	April		Whooping cough	4 weeks
15	Caroline	6m	F	B	S		Tenn	April		Erysipelas	8 days
16	Lewis	2	M	B	S		Tenn	Nov		Croup	1 day
17	Cyntha	1m	F	B	S		Tenn	July		Croup	30 days
18	Sarah Winkler	1m	F				Tenn	May		Hives	12 days
19	Edward McCoy	23	M				Tenn	Oct	Laborer	Fever	9 days
20	Ruetna Bradley	2	F				Tenn	Nov		Hives	1 day
21	James Willis	2	M				Tenn	Dec		Inflamation	5 weeks
22	Catharine Herd	35	F			M	Tenn	Nov		Fever	2 weeks
23	Ruth Wells	68	F			M	Va	March		Palsy	6 years

Remarks: My division is generally rough and hilly. Limestone springs abound in great plenty. This region is generally healthy, no epidemic ever prevails to any extent. There are a few mineral springs. The growth consists of oak, poplar, ash, beech, sugar maple, etc. The soil is generally fertile. L.T. Wells.

COUNTY OF HARDEMAN, STATE OF TENNESSEE.

PAGE NO. 313 PERSONS WHO DIED DURING THE YEAR ENDING 1st JUNE, 1850.

No. of Visit	Name	Age	Sex	Color	Free or Slave	Married/Widowed	Place of Birth	Month Died	Occupation	Disease or Cause of Death	No. Days Ill
1	Eve McClarie	73	F			W	Va	Oct	Midwife	Inflamation of stomach	3 weeks
2	Martha	5m	F	B	S		Tenn	Aug		Inflamation of bowels	2 weeks
3	James Butler	64	M				N.C.	April	Carpenter	Dropsy	9 weeks
4	Charles	35	M	B	S		N.C.	Nov	Laborer	T. fever	5 weeks
5	Martha E. Grantham	19	F				Tenn	Dec		T. fever	3 weeks
6	Elizabeth Grantham	11	F				Tenn	Dec		T. fever	3 weeks
7	Minta	35	F	B	S		N.C.	April		T. fever	2 weeks
8	Arthur	17	M	B	S		Tenn	Feb		T. fever	7 weeks
9	Mary Brantly	7	F				Tenn	May		Scrofula	13 weeks
10	John Powell	25	M			M	N.C.	Feb	Farmer	T. fever	4 weeks
11	George Reasons	20	M				N.C.	April	Student	T. fever	4 weeks
12	Martha J. Ledford	1	F				Georgia	Nov		Teething	4 weeks
13	Almira G. Haise	17	F				Tenn	Nov		T. fever	3 weeks
14	Aiden Moore	13	M				Tenn	April		T. fever	2 weeks
15	J. T. Hansby	36	M				N.C.	July	Farmer	Dropsy	11 years
16	Kimbro Hornsly	40	M			M	N.C.	May	Farmer	T. fever	8 weeks
17	Z. Mulligan	37	M			M	N.C.	April	Brk-mason	Pneumonia	1 week
18	Everline Mulligan	6m	F				Tenn	April		Inflamation of brain	1 week
19	M. Scott	24	M				Ireland	Oct	Farmer	T. fever	2 wk-2da
20	Martha J. Kirly	5m	F				Tenn	July		T. fever	8 weeks
21	Eaton T. Rook	25	M				Tenn	June	Farmer	T. fever	3 weeks
22	Elizabeth Cowen	85	F			W	Va	June		Old age	5 months
23	Sarah E. Brown	1	F				Tenn	Aug		Flux	3 days
24	Henry J. Currin	14	M				Tenn	Feb		T. fever	3 weeks
25	Peter M. Wilson	2	M				Tenn	Aug		Flux	3 weeks
26	E. W. Ross	2m	M				Tenn	April		Smothered	sudden
27	Elizabeth Wilkins	26	F			M	N.C.	Nov		Inflamation of stomach	2 weeks
28	Francis	5	F	B	S		Tenn	Oct		T. fever	3 weeks
29	Christiana Combs	88	F			W	Va	May		Palpitation of heart	4 days
30	Lydia Reaves	55	F			M	N.C.	June		Pleurisy	4 years
31	Eliza E. Myrick	3	F				Tenn	Sept		Inflamation of brain	2 weeks
32	Mansol Crisp	86	M			M	N.C.	May	Saddler	Neuralgia	10 days
33	Tom	1	M	B	S		Tenn	March		Burnt	10 days
34	John	1	M	B	S		Tenn	Aug		Inflamation of bowels	3 months
35	Ophlia	7	F	B	S		Tenn	Jan		Whooping cough	4 days

Remarks: The Typhoid Fever has raised to more extent than usual in this County and there is no particular cure known to the Physicians for the same. Other fevers have been less prevailent than usual. The water is free stone, slightly impregnated in places with soap stone. Springs and Wells are both used mostly of the later. Well water is found from 15 to 18 feet deep. There is occassionally a chalybeate spring to be found.   M. A. Trice.

COUNTY OF HARDEMAN, STATE OF TENNESSEE.

PAGE NO. 316 PERSONS WHO DIED DURING THE YEAR ENDING 1st JUNE, 1850.

No. of Visit	Name	Age	Sex	Color	Free or Slave	Married/Widowed	Place of Birth	Month Died	Occupation	Disease or Cause of Death	No. Days Ill
1	John	4	M	B	S		Tenn	Jan		Whooping cough	1 week
2	Martha	3	F	B	S		Tenn	Jan		Whooping cough	1 week
3	Judy	45	F	B	S		Va	Oct		Crippled	2 days
4	James	16	M	B	S		Tenn	Sept	Laborer	Congestive chills	3 days
5	George	4m	M	B	S		Tenn	May		Smothered	sudden
6	Mary Jane	32	F	B	S		Tenn	Dec		Fever	4 days
7	John	1m	M	B	S		Tenn	July		Eruption of skin	3 weeks
8	Mary	2	F	B	S		Tenn	June		Teething	2 months
9	Ann	4m	F	B	S		Tenn	Aug		Smothered	sudden
10	Lucy	17	F	B	S		Tenn	June		Dropsy	7 weeks
11	Amelia Irons	52	F			M	Georgia	July		Disease of Kidney	4 months
12	Moses	31	M	B	S		Va	Sept	Laborer	T. fever	6 weeks
13	Sopha	29	F	B	S		Alabama	June		Hemorrhage of lungs	2 weeks
14	Elizabeth	12	F	B	S		Georgia	May		T. fever	2 weeks
15	Emily	37	F	B	S		N.C.	Oct		Consumption	18 months
16	Isaac	30	M	B	S		N.C.	July		Homicide	sudden
17	Sarah	1	F	B	S		Tenn	May		Pneumonia	6 months
18	Austin	9m	M	B	S		Tenn	Oct		Croup	3 days
19	Sam	10m	M	B	S		Tenn	Feb		Whooping cough	6 weeks
20	Eliza White	58	F				N.C.	March		Erysipelas	5 days
21	Sarah Ham	56	F			W	S.C.	March		Dropsy	6 months
22	Mary J. Shearn	14	F				N.C.	Sept		T. fever	3 weeks
23	Mildred M. Avent	1	F				Tenn	Jan		Inflamation of bowels	5 days
24	Jerry	45	M	B	S		Va	April		T. fever	1 week
25	Susand	4m	F	B	S		Tenn	Sept		Smothered	sudden
26	William W. Shackleford	81	M			M	Va	Nov	Farmer	Old age	2 months
27	William G. Dodson	51	M			M	N.C.	Sept	Farmer	T. fever	10 days
28	Nathaniel Moore	40	M			M	N.C.	Oct	Farmer	Consumption	2 months
29	Joseph	60	M	B	S		Va	June	Laborer	Inflamation of bowels	2 months
30	Julia	2m	F	B	S		Tenn	April		Smothered	sudden
31	Candice	5m	F	B	S		Tenn	April		Cold	2 weeks
32	Talitha White	50	F			W	N.C.	March		T. fever	8 days
33	Jane	75	F	B	S		S.C.	July		Old age	5 days
34	Caroline	26	F	B	S		Tenn	Aug		T. fever	5 days
35	Susand Moore	23	F			M	Va	June		Diarrhea	15 days

Remarks: There are few places in the County where cestern water is used. Big Hatchie River runs through this County from eastwardly to a westwardly direction and there is much swamp land that is too low for cultivation. Most of the high land is productive and where it lies level, it is generally in cultivation. There are but few rocks to be seen in this County and they are generally what is termed sandrocks. There ..... M. A. Trice.

COUNTY OF HARDEMAN, STATE OF TENNESSEE.

PAGE NO. 317   PERSONS WHO DIED DURING THE YEAR ENDING 1st JUNE, 1850.

No. of Visit	Name	Age	Sex	Color	Free or Slave	Married/Widowed	Place of Birth	Month Died	Occupation	Disease or Cause of Death	No. Days Ill
1	Mina	30	F	B	S		Alabama	Feb		Costive	3 months
2	Daniel	10m	M	B	S		Tenn	March		--illegible--	4 months
3	John	1m	M	B	S		Tenn	July		Smothered	sudden
4	Mancel	1	F	B	S		Tenn	Aug		Bil. fever	2 months
5	Stephen Tilmon	5	M				Tenn	Feb		Croup	2 weeks
6	Louisa McCommon	25	F				Tenn	July		unknown	5 days
7	Thomas Joiner	53	M			M	N.C.	Dec	Farmer	Cholera	2 days
8	A. J. Macon	3m	M				Tenn	Feb		Whooping cough	1 week
9	A. Parker	33	M			M	Tenn	May	Farmer	Liver complaint	7 weeks
10	Henry	25	M	B	S		N.C.	Dec		T. fever	3 weeks
11	Louisa	21	F	B	S		Tenn	Jan		T. fever	2 weeks
12	H. Pepkins	36	M			M	N.C.	April	Farmer	Kicked by horse	sudden
13	Martha J. Macon	3m	F				Tenn	Feb		Smothered	sudden
14	Joshua Hopkins	71	M			M	Maryland	Oct	Farmer	Rheumatism	2 months
15	Franklin Minter	26	M				Tenn	Sept	Farmer	Consumption	4 years
16	Isabella G. Ruddle	20	F				Tenn	May		Consumption	6 months
17	John H. Mitchell	18	M				Tenn	Sept	Laborer	Liver disease	6 weeks
18	William B. Raigen	33	M			M	Tenn	Oct	Farmer	Poisoned	5 days
19	Sam	24	M	B	S		S.C.	Feb		Burnt	6 months
20	Richard Pugh	1	M				Tenn	June		Flux	4 days
21	Thomas	6m	M	B	S		Tenn	April		unknown	sudden
22	Fanney	6m	F	B	S		Tenn	Feb		Inflamation of lungs	1 week
23	John W. Oliver	5	M				N.C.	June		Croup	5 days
24	Counsel Beard	45	M			M	N.C.	Jan		Dropsy	10 months
25	Catherine Mangrum	60	F			M	N.C.	April		Hemorrhage of lungs	10 days
26	John Bogus	27	M				Tenn	May		Disease of heart	10 years
27	Elizabeth	17	F	B	S		Va	April		F. disease	4 months
28	Justice Lake	60	M			M	Georgia	May		Consumption	6 months
29	Arthur	11	M	B	S		Tenn	Aug		Thrown from horse	sudden
30	Stephen	40	M	B	S		Va	Dec		--illegible--	2 months
31	Kerley	6m	M	B	S		Tenn	Sept		Bowel effect	3 months
32	Joseph Franklin	1m	M	B	S		Tenn	May		Croup	5 minutes
33	Jack	2	M	B	S		N.C.	April		Scrofula	4 months
34	King	1	M	B	S		Tenn	April		Croup	1 month
35	Jack	1	M	B	S		Tenn	April		Croup	1 day

Remarks: Ore of any kind except iron and but slight appearance of that. The timber on high lands are oak, hickory, poplar, gum, dogwood, and pine. On the Low lands, beech, hickory, walnut, and cypress and gum. The last season was unusually wet. There is a large portion of the land that is in cultivation that is very much exhusted, owing chiefly to a bad state of cultivation but little or no pains has been taken.....   M. A. Trice.

COUNTY OF HARDEMAN, STATE OF TENNESSEE.

PAGE NO. 320   PERSONS WHO DIED DURING THE YEAR ENDING 1st JUNE, 1850.

No. of Visit	Name	Age	Sex	Color	Free or Slave	Married/Widowed	Place of Birth	Month Died	Occupation	Disease or Cause of Death	No. Days Ill
1	Peter	1	M	B	S		Tenn	Jan		Croup	1 day
2	Isaah Caviness	40	M			M	N.C.	Nov		Pneumonia	7 days
3	Elenn	1	M	B	S		Tenn	April		unknown	8 weeks
4	Josiah Shoes	4	M				N.C.	Sept		Croup	1 week
5	Laura McCarley	6m	F				Tenn	Sept		Teething	1 month
6	Sarah Nedham	12	F				Tenn	March		T. fever	12 days
7	Franklin Commings	14	M				Tenn	March		Dropsy	6 months
8	Frank	1	M	B	S		Tenn	June		unknown	1 week
9	Jacob	1	M	B	S		Tenn	June		unknown	1 week
10	Manervy Mayfield	1	F				Tenn	Feb		Abscess	2 months
11	Mary Simpson	84	F			W	S.C.	Aug		Old age	2 weeks
12	William D. Bishop	3	M				Tenn	Jan		Cholera Inf.	9 days
13	Elizabeth	2	F	B	S		Tenn	Nov		unknown	1 week
14	William	1	M	B	S		Tenn	Dec		unknown	1 month
15	Edmond	4	M	B	S		Tenn	April		Smothered	sudden
16	John Pulley	8	M				Alabama	April		Drowned	sudden
17	Joseph Sharp	77	M			M	N.C.	May	Farmer	Consumption	12 weeks
18	G. Furgerson	3	M				N.C.	Oct		Croup	2 weeks
19	Henry	1	M	B	S		Tenn	March		Cold	1 day
20	Lewis	1	M	B	S		Tenn	Nov		Dropsy	8 months
21	Caroline Bryant	28	F			M	N.C.	May		Child birth	7 months
22	Susand A. Wellings	27	F			M	Tenn	June		T. fever	2 weeks
23	Rebecca	1	F	B	S		Tenn	May		Croup	1 week
24	William Dunn	35	M			M	N.C.	Nov	Farmer	T. fever	2 months
25	Joseph Sellers	37	M			M	N.C.	Oct	Farmer	Cholera	1 day
26	Rachell Rodgers	10m	F				Tenn	Aug		T. fever	9 days
27	Francis Lee	83	F			W	Maryland	Nov		Old age	2 years
28	R. L. Young	9	M				Tenn	June		Bowel complaint	6 weeks
29	John Holliday	88	M				Va	Sept	Farmer	Thrown from horse	12 days
30	Cager	1	M	B	S		Tenn	Jan		Inflamation of brain	1 week
31	Mitchell Johnson	90	M			M	N.C.	Aug	Farmer	Apoplexy	sudden
32	Hugh McLean	21	M				S.C.	Oct	Farmer	Congestive Chill	5 days
33	V. King	1	F				Tenn	Oct		Bowel complaint	12 weeks
34	Joseph Neighbors	30	M			M	Tenn	Aug	Farmer	Flux	2 weeks
35	M. Hottom	45	F			M	N.C.	Oct		T. fever	4 weeks

Remarks: ....as yet to reinstate the same. There has been some few deaths reported from cholera but they were citizens who had been below on boats. M.A.Trice.

COUNTY OF HARDEMAN, STATE OF TENNESSEE.

PAGE NO. 321 PERSONS WHO DIED DURING THE YEAR ENDING 1st JUNE, 1850.

M. A. Trice

No. of Visit	Name	Age	Sex	Color	Free or Slave	Married/Widowed	Place of Birth	Month Died	Occupation	Disease or Cause of Death	No. Days Ill
1	Edmond	14	M	B	S		N.C.	June		Abscess	3 months
2	Sam	22	M	B	S		Tenn	Jan	Laborer	T. fever	14 days
3	Robert	11	M	M	S		Missouri	April		Drowned	sudden
4	John W. Clayton	8m	M				Tenn	Sept		Disease of spine	3 weeks
5	Regal	1	M	B	S		Tenn	June		Rickets	6 months
6	George	1	M	B	S		Tenn	June		Rickets	6 months
7	Anthony	40	M	B	S		N.C.	Dec	Laborer	Pneumonia	5 days
8	Elizabeth F. Jackson	1	F				Tenn	June		Abscess	2 months
9	K. Jackson	2	M				Tenn	Aug		Flux	2 weeks
10	Mariah	1	F	B	S		Tenn	May		Croup	2 weeks
11	Caroline	8	F	B	S		Tenn	Sept		Inflamation of brain	2 days
12	Thomas	1m	M	B	S		Tenn	Sept		Smothered	sudden
13	Fanney	2m	F	B	S		Tenn	Sept		Smothered	sudden
14	Saley	90	F	B	S		Africa	April		Old age	7 months
15	Malinda	14	F	B	S		Tenn	July		Cancer	2 months
16	Isaac	13	M	B	S		Tenn	Oct		Dropsy	3 months
17	Mary	2m	F	B	S		Tenn	April		unknown	3 days
18	Manervy	15	F	B	S		Tenn	Aug		T. fever	3 weeks
19	William	1m	M	B	S		Tenn	Nov		Disease of spine	2 days
20	Louisa	6m	F	M	S		Tenn	June		Thrash	1 month
21	Amanda	2	F	B	S		Tenn	July		Worms	14 days
22	Louisa	1m	F	B	S		Tenn	Dec		Croup	2 days
23	Jesse F. Thompson	1	M				Tenn	July		Hives	6 months
24	William	1	M	B	S		Tenn	May		Hives	2 days
25	Mary Roberson	80	F			W	N.C.	July		Old age	1 year
26	Henry	10m	M	B	S		Va	Aug		Teething	3 months
27	Judy	3m	F	B	S		Tenn	Feb		Smothered	sudden
28	Frank	13	M	B	S		Tenn	Oct		T. fever	9 days
29	Sanford	16	M	B	S		Tenn	Oct		T. fever	4 days
30	Jane T. Anderson	16	F				Va	March		T. fever	3 weeks
31	Mary S. Elmoore	25	F				Va	June		Consumption	2 years
32	William	21	M	B	S		N.C.	Aug		White swelling	8 years
33	William	2m	M	B	S		Tenn	June		Bowel complaint	1 month
34	Patience	12	F	B	S		Tenn	Feb		Burnt	sudden
35	Doctor	1	M	B	S		Tenn	Dec		Chills	4 months

COUNTY OF HARDEMAN, STATE OF TENNESSEE.

PAGE NO. 324 PERSONS WHO DIED DURING THE YEAR ENDING 1st JUNE, 1850.

M. A. Trice

No. of Visit	Name	Age	Sex	Color	Free or Slave	Married/Widowed	Place of Birth	Month Died	Occupation	Disease or Cause of Death	No. Days Ill
1	Austin	4m	M	B	S		Tenn	Dec		Whooping cough	2 days
2	Aulsey	1	M	B	S		Tenn	Jan		Smothered	sudden
3	Jane	5m	F	B	S		Tenn	Sept		Whooping cough	2 months
4	Eliza	6m	F	B	S		Tenn	Sept		Whooping cough	1 month
5	Charlott	1	F	B	S		Tenn	Dec		Dropsy	5 months
6	Marrick	1	M	B	S		Tenn	Oct		Flux	1 week
7	John	1	M	B	S		Tenn	June		Inflamation of bowels	5 days
8	Parthenia	1	F	B	S		Tenn	Dec		Whooping cough	5 days
9	Spencer	22	M	B	S		S.C.	April		T. fever	1 week
10	Lewis	20	M	B	S		N.C.	April		Disease of spine	6 months
11	Allice	1	F	B	S		Tenn	Oct		Whooping cough	2 weeks
12	Silver	2	F	B	S		Tenn	Oct		Pneumonia	1 week
13	Albert	6m	M	B	S		Tenn	Oct		Pneumonia	2 weeks
14	Jesse	8m	M	B	S		Tenn	Jan		Pneumonia	1 week
15	William A. Mastin	3m	M				Tenn	March		Whooping cough	4 weeks

COUNTY OF HARDEMAN, STATE OF TENNESSEE.

PAGE NO. 324   PERSONS WHO DIED DURING THE YEAR ENDING 1st JUNE, 1850.

M. A. Trice

No. of Visit	Name	Age	Sex	Color	Free or Slave	Married/Widowed	Place of Birth	Month Died	Occupation	Disease or Cause of Death	No. Days Ill
16	Frank	22	M	B	S		Va	July		T. fever	8 days
17	Mary	1	F	B	S		Tenn	June		Pneumonia	8 days
18	Nancy	30	F	B	S		N.C.	Jan		Child bed	1 month
19	Lewis	18	M	B	S		N.C.	Oct		Abscess	5 months
20	James Crews	1m	M				Tenn	Oct		Fits	1 day
21	William B. Roberson	4	M				Tenn	May		T. fever	4 weeks
22	Robert	1	M	B	S		Tenn	Dec		Smothered	sudden
23	Violet	3	F	B	S		Tenn	Dec		Consumption	6 months
24	Caroline	1	F	B	S		Tenn	Oct		Croup	1 week
25	Richard	3m	M	B	S		Tenn	June		Croup	1 week
26	Lucy	2m	F	B	S		Tenn	Dec		Smothered	sudden
27	Sarah	5m	F	B	S		Tenn	May		Burnt	3 weeks
28	Mary	1m	F	B	S		Tenn	June		Croup	2 days
29	John G. McAulty	6	M				Tenn	July		Putrid Sore throat	1 week
30	Lewis	1	M	B	S		Tenn	March		unknown	3 months
31	Wiley	7m	M	B	S		Tenn	May		Pneumonia	2 weeks
32	George	2	M	B	S		Tenn	June		Pneumonia	1 week
33	Sam	4m	M	B	S		Tenn	March		Whooping cough	3 weeks
34	W. H. McGee	9	M				Tenn	Nov		Flux	1 week
35	Mary Shields	70	F			W	N.C.	May		Consumption	5 months

COUNTY OF HARDEMAN, STATE OF TENNESSEE.

PAGE NO. 325   PERSONS WHO DIED DURING THE YEAR ENDING 1st JUNE, 1850.

M. A. Trice

No. of Visit	Name	Age	Sex	Color	Free or Slave	Married/Widowed	Place of Birth	Month Died	Occupation	Disease or Cause of Death	No. Days Ill
1	Elizabeth Richardson	18	F				N.C.	May		T. fever	3 weeks
2	Jane Daniel	55	F				Va	Sept		unknown	1 year
3	Mary Davis	22	F				Tenn	Nov		T. fever	3 weeks
4	Sarah J. Herriman	3	F				Tenn	March		Croup	1 day
5	James Eavans	1	M				Tenn	Oct		Croup	3 days
6	Sollomon Willeby	67	M			M	N.C.	April	Farmer	T. fever	3 weeks
7	Vencin Willeby	70	M			M	N.C.	Jan	Farmer	T. fever	2 weeks
8	Mahulda Yarbrough	4	F				Tenn	Dec		Scrofula	7 days
9	M. Yarbrough	2	F				Tenn	Dec		Scrofula	3 days
10	Calvin C. Anderson	1	F?				Tenn	Feb		Quinsy	2 weeks
11	Emberson	6	M	B	S		Tenn	Aug		Inflamation of brain	4 days
12	Elizabeth	9	F	B	S		Tenn	Sept		Flux	3 days
13	William Moore	3m	M				Tenn	Feb		Eruption of skin	6 weeks

COUNTY OF HARDIN, STATE OF TENNESSEE.

PAGE NO. 327 PERSONS WHO DIED DURING THE YEAR ENDING 1st JUNE, 1850.

Civil District No. 12, 2 & 3

No. of Visit	Name	Age	Sex	Color	Free or Slave	Married/Widowed	Place of Birth	Month Died	Occupation	Disease or Cause of Death	No. Days Ill
1	Nancy D. Karns	10m	F				Tenn	Sept		Infant fever	10 days
2	Elizabeth C. Kincannon	13	F				Illinois	Oct		T. fever	23 days
3	Mary	1m	F				Tenn	Oct		Croup	3 days
4	George W. Nichols	23	M				Tenn	March	Boatsman	Cholera	5 days
5	Seanah Alexander	6m	F				Tenn	Sept		Croup	1 day
6	John O. Pool	35	M			M	Tenn	June	Boatsman	Cholera	2 days
7	Redick White	28	M			M	N.C.	Dec	Farmer	Cholera	5 days
8	Alexander Russell	27	M				Tenn	Jan	Laborer	Cholera	4 days
9	John Russell	20	M				Tenn	May	Laborer	Cholera	3 days
10	Robert Russell	61	M			W	N.C.	May	M.E.Clergy	T. fever	4 weeks
11	Ezekiel Alexander	72	M			M	N.C.	May	Farmer	T. fever	4 weeks
12	Elizabeth Hardin	25	F			M	Tenn	April		Pneumonia	5 weeks
13	Edy E. Byrd	4m	F				Tenn	Feb		unknown	1 week
14	Frank	8	M	B	S		____	Feb		unknown	1 day
15	Rachael Hurley	1m	F				Tenn	July		unknown	sudden
16	Elizabeth Hurley	27	F				N.C.	July		Dropsy	3 months
17	William R. Welch	13	M				Tenn	March		Congestive fever	2 days
18	Philip W. Frie	21	M			M	Tenn	Feb	Laborer	Pneumonia	12 days
19	Precilla White	40	F				Tenn	Jan		__ fever	10 days
20	Mary Bain	77	F				N.C.	March		Hydrothorax	2 months
21	Azubra Andrews	29	F				Tenn	April		Consumption	1 year
22	Hugh McCares	70	M				S.C.	Aug	Farmer	Consumption	3 months
23	Susannah Perkins	10	F				Tenn	Oct		T. fever	8 weeks
24	Mary E. Mundy	20	F			M	Tenn	March		Phlebites	1 year
25	Elizabeth A. Mundy	5m	F				Tenn	July		unknown	1 week
26	James Criuse	69	M			M	Va	Dec		Hydrothorax	1 year

Remarks: State of Tennessee, Hardin County. I, George D. Morrow, certify that the foregoing schedule contains three pages and is made and filled up in accordance to my oath and instruction to the best of my knowledge and belief. This the 28th day of February, 1851.
George D. Morrow, Asst. Marshal

Sworn to and subscribed before me on the 28 day of Februarym 1851.
James D. Martin, J.P.
Hardin County.

COUNTY OF HARDIN, STATE OF TENNESSEE.

PAGE NO. 329 PERSONS WHO DIED DURING THE YEAR ENDING 1st JUNE, 1850.

Geo. D. Morrow

Civil District No. 4 & 6

No. of Visit	Name	Age	Sex	Color	Free or Slave	Married/Widowed	Place of Birth	Month Died	Occupation	Disease or Cause of Death	No. Days Ill
1	Sarah J. Cherry	25	F			M	Tenn	Feb		T. fever	6 weeks
2	Anderson	22	M	M	S		Tenn	Jan		Pneumonia	10 days
3	Sweeny	1m	M				Tenn	June		unknown	5 days
4	Sarah E. Porter	1m	F				Tenn	Oct		Croup	3 days
5	Mahala	28	F	B	S		Tenn	Aug		Peu. fever	5 days
6	Daniel	2m	M	M	S		Tenn	Sept		Infant fever	1 week
7	Esther	2m	F	B	S		Tenn	Aug		unknown	sudden
8	Mary C. Maxwell	6	F				Tenn	July		Congestive fever	3 days
9	A. E. Shell	35	M				Va	Sept	Tailor	Intemperance	9 weeks
10	Reuben	3m	M	B	S		____	Dec		unknown	sudden
11	Caroline	2	F	B	S		Tenn	Feb		Croup	4 days
12	Thomas P. Payne	33	M			M	Georgia	June	Tailor	T. fever	6 weeks
13	Martha Jane Payne	13	F				Tenn	Sept		T. fever	10 days
14	Charles Baker	18	M				Tenn	July	Clerk	T. fever	2 weeks

COUNTY OF HARDIN, STATE OF TENNESSEE.

PAGE NO. 329 PERSONS WHO DIED DURING THE YEAR ENDING 1st JUNE, 1850.

Civil District No. 4 & 6

Geo. D. Morrow

No. of Visit	Name	Age	Sex	Color	Free or Slave	Married/Widowed	Place of Birth	Month Died	Occupation	Disease or Cause of Death	No. Days Ill
15	Riley	18	M	B	S			March		Pneumonia	4 weeks
16	Jesse	1m	M	B	S			April		Croup	1 day
17	Alexander M. Hardin	42	M			M	Tenn	March	Lawyer	Inf. fever	9 days
18	Nancy M. S. C. Daniel	1	F				Tenn	Sept		Cholera Inf.	8 weeks
19	_____ Daniel	1m	M				Tenn	May		Croup	1 day
20	Milly	44	F	B	S			May		Child bed	sudden
21	Alexander T. Anderson	11	M				Tenn	March		Inflamation of brain	1 week
22	Celia Greer	22	F				Tenn	May		Laryngitis	3 weeks
23	Thomas J. Hodgen	46	M				N.C.	Oct		Congestive fever	2 days
24	Sarah Ann Easely	13	F				Tenn	March		T. fever	11 days
25	Nancy C. Warren	2	F				Tenn	Sept		Whooping cough	3 months
26	Infant	4m	F	B	S			Oct		Smothered	sudden
27	John Wood	1	M				Tenn	Sept		Bowel complaint	1 month
28	George Byrd	24	M				Tenn	March	Laborer	Inft. fever	1 week
29	Sarah J. Johnson	73	F				N.C.	April		Fungus Hematoid	6 months
30	Sarah Ann Franks	15	F				Alabama	April		T. fever	1 week
31	Joseph Finis Palmer	2m	M				Tenn	Sept		Croup	3 days
32	Polly Ann Milam	1m	F				Tenn	April		Croup	3 days
33	Niniam A. Sted	20	M				Tenn	May	Laborer	Consumption	1 year
34	Sarah E. Franks	2m	F				Tenn	July		Cholera Inf.	1 day
35	Mahala I.(J) Milam	17	F				Tenn	April		Consumption	2 years

COUNTY OF HARDIN, STATE OF TENNESSEE.

PAGE NO. 332 PERSONS WHO DIED DURING THE YEAR ENDING 1st JUNE, 1850.

Civil District No. 11, 9, 10, 13 & 12

Geo. D. Morrow

No. of Visit	Name	Age	Sex	Color	Free or Slave	Married/Widowed	Place of Birth	Month Died	Occupation	Disease or Cause of Death	No. Days Ill
1	Sarah Robertson	55	F				Va	Jan		Congestive chills	8 hours
2	Pamelia V. Barnett	1m	F				Tenn	Feb		Croup	1 day
3	_____ Hitchock	1m	M				Tenn	Aug		unknown	sudden
4	John P. Waters	6m	M				Louisiana	June		Enteritis	3 months
5	Edward	2	M	M	S		Tenn	July		Inflamation of brain	5 days
6	Young B. Smith	6	M				Tenn	March		Fever	8 days
7	Jane Lanon	53	F				Tenn	Feb		Erysipelas	6 days
8	Thomas I. Norwood	3	M				Tenn	March		Inft. fever	2 weeks
9	Thomas Williamson	1	M				Tenn	July		Cholera Inf.	2 weeks
10	Nathaniel Armstrong	13	M				Tenn	Feb		Congestive brain	4 days
11	Margaret Simpson	82	F			M	S.C.	April		Old age	Chronic
12	Robert Grisholm	83	M			W	N.C.	May		unknown	sudden
13	Jonathan J. H. Pedigo	2	M				Alabama	Feb		Diabetes	Chronic
14	Elizabeth E. Robertson	5m	F				Tenn	June		Cholera Inf.	6 weeks
15	Judy Wyatt	67	F				S.C.	April		Pneumonia	1 week
16	Susan	6m	F	B	S			March		Croup	2 days
17	Dolphin	4m	M	B	S			Sept		Convulsions	3 months
18	_____ Mathews	1m	M				Tenn	July		unknown	2 days
19	John Johnson	12	M				Tenn	Jan		Rickets	Chronic
20	Barbara A. Redden	2	F				Tenn	June		Burned	2 weeks
21	Malinda J. Akins	1m	F				Tenn	Jan		Croup	1 day
22	Tennessee C. Hooks	1	F				Tenn	March		Whooping cough	3 months
23	Thankful Fisher	44	F				Tenn	Oct		Consumption	Chronic
24	Margaret J. Clark	5m	F				Tenn	Dec		Croup	5 days
25	Lucy	37	F	B	S			June		Cramp Cholic	1 day
26	William	2	M	M	S			Sept		Inflamation of brain	8 days
27	John W. Armstrong	6m	M				Tenn	April		unknown	1 week
28	Rebecca A. Morris	1m	F				Tenn	July		Yellow gum	10 days
29	William S. Flatt	10m	M				Tenn	Aug		Hydrocephalus	4 months

COUNTY OF HARDIN, STATE OF TENNESSEE.

PAGE NO. 332 PERSONS WHO DIED DURING THE YEAR ENDING 1st JUNE, 1850.

Civil District No. 11, 9, 10, 13 & 12

Geo. D. Morrow

No. of Visit	Name	Age	Sex	Color	Free or Slave	Married/Widowed	Place of Birth	Month Died	Occupation	Disease or Cause of Death	No. Days Ill
30	William Meek	56	M				S.C.	Dec		Consumption	Chronic
31	William Seaton	24	M				Alabama	Feb		Epilepsy	Chronic
32	James E. Morris	24	M				N.C.	Feb		Pneumonia	23 days
33	Margaret Spencer	1m	F				Tenn	July		Yellow gum	4 days

COUNTY OF HARDIN, STATE OF TENNESSEE.

PAGE NO. 333 PERSONS WHO DIED DURING THE YEAR ENDING 1st JUNE, 1850.

Civil District No. 1st, 5th, 7th & 8th.

Thos. Maxwell

No. of Visit	Name	Age	Sex	Color	Free or Slave	Married/Widowed	Place of Birth	Month Died	Occupation	Disease or Cause of Death	No. Days Ill
1	Mary Ann Lackey	10m	F				Tenn	July		Ulceration	9 days
2	Ben	19	M	M	S		Tenn	April		Consumption	50 days
3	Clara	38	F	B	S		Tenn	April		unknown	Chronic
4	Joseph N. Dowdy	1m	M				Tenn	Oat		Fever	14 days
5	Nancy Allen	2	F				Tenn	Nov		Accidental	unknown
6	Catherine E. Allen	5m	F				Tenn	Dec		Hives	unknown
7	Francis W. Randolph	1d	M				Tenn	March		unknown	unknown
8	Josanna Anglin	2m	F				Tenn	Aug		unknown	1 day
9	Rosanna Anglin	2m	F				Tenn	Aug		unknown	1 day
10	Joseph F. Basye	24	M				Tenn	Sept	Farmer	Diarrhea	unknown
11	Joseph West	3m	M				Tenn	July		unknown	unknown
12	Nelson	27	M	B	S		Tenn	Aug		unknown	sudden
13	James T. Boatwright	1	M				Tenn	Aug		Accidental	sudden
14	William D. Fleming	31	M			M	Tenn	Jan	Farmer	Pneumonia	7 days
15	John H. Low	9m	M				Tenn	Dec		Accidental	3 days
16	Harriet	28	F	B	S		N.C.	Jan		Inflamation of brain	11 days
17	Zylpha Nisbett	22	F			M	Tenn	Feb		Pneumonia	9 days
18	Sarah E. Campbell	8m	F				Tenn	Nov		unknown	60 days
19	John Strickland	65	M			M	N.C.	Oct	Farmer	unknown	Chronic
20	Harriet	30	F	B	S		Va	Sept		unknown	10 days
21	Alvira	25	F	B	S		Tenn	Sept		unknown	8 days
22	Elizabeth Loyd	56	F			M	unknown	March		Pleurisy	17 days
23	Solomon Roane	60	M			M	N.C.	Aug	Farmer	C. fever	10 days

Remarks: State of Tennessee, Hardin County. I, Thomas Maxwell, certify that the above schedule has been filled up and made according to my oath and instruction to the best of my knowledge and belief. This thirteenth day of February, 1851. Sworn to and subscribed before me this 13th February, 1851

Thos. Maxwell, Asst. Marshal

George D. Morrow (Seal)
J.P. for Hardin County.

I do certify that these is 1 page in the foregoing schedule. February 13th, 1850. Thos. Maxwell.

In the first Civil District, the soil is rich and productive. Fine limestone water and the seventh and eighth Civil District, rocky, broken and hilly with little tillable land. Freestone water and remarkably healthy and is said to abound with iron ore. Fine water power for machinery.

Thomas Maxwell, Asst. Marshal.

COUNTY OF HAWKINS, STATE OF TENNESSEE.

PAGE NO. 335 PERSONS WHO DIED DURING THE YEAR ENDING 1st JUNE, 1850.

All of District

No. of Visit	Name	Age	Sex	Color	Free or Slave	Married/Widowed	Place of Birth	Month Died	Occupation	Disease or Cause of Death	No. Days Ill
1	Caroline Miller	52	F	B	S		Tenn	Aug		Dropsy	40 days
2	Frances Moore	19	F	F			Tenn	May		Hepatitis	365 days
3	Peter	65	M	B	S		Tenn	July		sudden	
4	Sarah Sullenbarger	3	F	F			Tenn	Sept		Croup	1 day
5	Lucy Bear	66	F	F		M	Tenn	Feb		Pneumonia	14 days
6	Mary Paschal	85	F	F		W	N.C.	Feb		Old age	40 days
7	Emeline	5	F	B	S		Tenn	May		Fever	10 days
8	Will	36	M	M	S		Tenn	Feb		Pneumonia	15 days
9	Willie Arny	35	M	F			Tenn	Feb	Laborer	Antrum Maxilla	150 days
10	Barsheba	3	F	F			Tenn	Jan		Croup	4 days
11	William Wiggins	1m	M	F			Tenn	Oct		Croup	1 day
12	James Baker	2	M	F			Tenn	Aug		Cholera Inf.	14 days
13	George	40	M	B	S		Tenn	Oct	Laborer	Fever	31 days
14	Lavina Long	9m	F	F			Tenn	Sept		Croup	5 days
15	Sylva Hamilton	45	F	F		M	N.C.	April		Fever	40 days
16	Josiah Mooney	3	M	F			Tenn	April		Croup	3 days
17	Margaret	3	F	B	S		Tenn	Sept		Croup	5 days
18	Jas. Headrick	2	M	F			Tenn	Oct		Croup	5 days
19	Mary Headrick	3	F	F			Tenn	Oct		Croup	4 days
20	William West	49	M	F		M	Tenn	June	Farmer	Fever	60 days
21	James West	22	M	F			Tenn	June	Laborer	Fever	40 days
22	Robert Draper	25	M	F			Tenn	April	Laborer	Fever	24 days
23	Mary Spires	3	F	F			Tenn	March		King's evil	41 days
24	Margaret M. Herd	2	F	F			Tenn	Oct		Croup	14 days
25	James Brown	2m	M	F			Tenn	April		Croup	5 days
26	Manerva Hickman	4	F	F			Tenn	Feb		Hydrocephalus	100 days
27	Elizabeth Smith	40	F	F		M	Tenn	Jan		Thesis Pulmonatus	2 days
28	Sarah	3	F	B	S		Tenn	Aug		Croup	15 days
29	Jack Burem	55	M	B	S		Tenn	April	Laborer	Pneumonia	10 days
30	Scip Burem	57	M	B	S		Tenn	May	Laborer	Cold	3 days
31	John Burem	2	M	B	S		Tenn	May		Croup	8 days
32	Margaret Luster	11m	F	F			Tenn	Nov		Still	
33	Samuel Light	10m	M	F			Tenn	May		Cold	14 days
34	Sarah Ball	60	F	F		W	Va	Nov		Jaundice	50 days
35	Paralee Talent	1	F	F			Tenn	Nov		Pneumonia	40 days

COUNTY OF HAWKINS, STATE OF TENNESSEE.

PAGE NO. 338 PERSONS WHO DIED DURING THE YEAR ENDING 1st JUNE, 1850.

All of the Districts
R. P. Kyle

No. of Visit	Name	Age	Sex	Color	Free or Slave	Married/Widowed	Place of Birth	Month Died	Occupation	Disease or Cause of Death	No. Days Ill
1	Isaac Arterburn	48	M	F		M	Tenn	Jan	Farmer	Fever	14 days
2	Thomas J. Christian	38	M	F		M	Tenn	March	Farmer	Pneumonia	11 days
3	Jane Skelton	80	F	F		W	Va	Aug		Flux	8 days
4	Hanibald Crigler	11m	M	F			Tenn	Oct		Croup	2 days
5	Elizabeth Pratt	50	F	F		M	Tenn	April		Cold	21 days
6	Jane Pratt	26	F	F			Tenn	Aug		T. fever	150 days
7	Mary Pratt	11m	F	F			Tenn	Aug		Still	
8	James M. Belamy	25	M	F			Va	July	Laborer	T. fever	20 days
9	Francis Couley	51	F	B	F		Va	Jan		Gastritis	3 days
10	Preston Couley	30	M	B	F	M	Tenn	Feb		Accident	sudden
11	David Phipps	60	M	M	S		Tenn	Oct	Laborer	Fever	14 days
12	Stephen Phipps	17	M	M	S		Tenn	Oct	Laborer	Fever	14 days
13	Jane Phipps	11m	F	B	S		Tenn	Nov		Still	
14	King Phipps	1	M	B	S			Nov		Croup	10 days
15	Nancy Tartar	3m	F	F			Tenn	Feb		Croup	24 days
16	Thomas Surgenes	10m	M	F			Tenn	Oct		Croup	7 days
17	Robert Vaughn	11m	M	F			Tenn	Nov		Croup	3 days
18	Sarah Larkins	30	F	B	S		Tenn	Sept		Thesis Pulmonatus	150 days
19	Robert Waitman	11m	M	F			Tenn	May		Croup	7 days
20	John Shipley	6	M	F			Tenn	Nov		Fever	42 days
21	Samuel Hale	4	M	B	S		Tenn	Sept		Scrofula	365 days
22	Jesse Hale	2	M	B	S		Tenn	Feb		Croup	2 days
23	Sarah Leeper	6	F	B	S		Tenn	Aug		Hydrocephalus	3 days
24	Delila Housewright	1	F	F			Tenn	Aug		Croup	6 days
25	Cornelia Barret	4m	F	F			Tenn	Feb		Still	
26	Joseph Hord	70	M	B	S		N.C.	Feb		Old age	14 days
27	Edwin Herald	11m	M	F			Tenn	Aug		Still	
28	Mary Brice	74	F	F		M	Va	Oct		Diarrhea	28 days
29	Nancy Shoat	69	F	F		W	N.C.	March		Thesis Pulmonatus	60 days
30	Mary Campbell	2	F	F			Tenn	Jan		Hydrocephalus	28 days
31	Columbus Campbell	4m	M	F			Tenn	April		Cold	14 days
32	Mary Watterson	40	F	M	S		Tenn	Feb		Thesis Pulmonatus	150 days
33	James Y. Crawford	57	M	F			Tenn	May	Meth. Mins.	Hydrothorax	15 days
34	Lucien Young	6m	M	B	S		Tenn	Dec		King's evil	40 days
35	Leonard Miller	18	M	B	S		Tenn	May		Thesis Pulmonatus	150 days

COUNTY OF HAYWOOD, STATE OF TENNESSEE.

PAGE NO. 340 PERSONS WHO DIED DURING THE YEAR ENDING 1st JUNE, 1850.

Civil District No. 7 & 8
John D. Ware

No. of Visit	Name	Age	Sex	Color	Free or Slave	Married/Widowed	Place of Birth	Month Died	Occupation	Disease or Cause of Death	No. Days Ill
1	Edwin H. Peete	1	M				Tenn	Aug		Teething	45 days
2	Mary E. Nixon	6m	F				Tenn	Jan		Croup	6 days
3	Joshua Farrington	77	M				N.C.	Sept	Gin-maker	Inflamation	8 days
4	Ro L. Thomas Randal	26	M	B	S		Tenn	Sept		C	
5	William Sevier	1	M				Tenn	March		Pneumonia	16 days
6	Mary E. Bennett	7m	F				Tenn	Aug		Bowel complaint	2 days
7	Emma V. Peebles	1	F				Tenn	Aug		unknown	60 days
8	George M. Trimble	8m	M				Tenn	March		Pulmonary	60 days
9	Mansfield Ware	68	M				Va	July	Trader	C	
10	R.B.Langley's Emily	16	F	B	S		____	July		C	
11	Emeline McCormick	32	F				Tenn	April		Fever	14 days
12	James L. Tugwell	14	M				Tenn	March		Pleurisy	6 days
13	Joel D. Coleman	27	M				Tenn	Dec	Clerk	Cholera	1 day
14	Elizabeth Burton	3	F				Tenn	Sept		Dysentery	10 days
15	E.Richmond's Peggy	60	F	B	S		____	Sept		Dysentery	1 day
16	E. Richmond's Lucy	6m	F	B	S		____	Jan		unknown	3 days
17	E. Richmond's John	17	M	B	S		____	Feb		unknown	3 days
18	Aridra J. Wood	27	F			M	Indiana	March		C	90 days
19	William P. Wood	27	M			W	N.C.	April	Farmer	C	180 days
20	J. Carlton's John	10	M	B	S		____	Aug		Fever	3 days
21	J. Carlton's William	11	M	B	S		____	Sept		Fever	21 days
22	E. Well's George	22	M	B	S		____	Dec		C	110 days
23	N.T.Perkin's Harriet	38	F	B	S		____	Feb		C	110 days
24	N.T.Perkin's Phillis	66	F	B	S		____	Jan		Cholic	14 days
25	John O. Neal	87	M			M	unknown	March	Farmer	C	90 days
26	Samuel Green's Aciy	32	F	B	S		____	Nov		C	
27	William H. Haralson, Jr.	6	M				Tenn	Dec		Fever	5 days
28	Victoria M. Sanders	10	F				Tenn	April		Dyspepsia	90 days
29	Avarilla Fortner	28	F			M	Tenn	Dec		Inflamation	90 days
30	J. Taliaferro's Susan	20	F	B	S		____	Feb		C	170 days
31	J. Taliaferro's Mererve	5m	M	B	S		____	May		Fever	14 days
32	A. Mann's Ann	65	F	B	S		____	Oct		unknown	10 days
33	A. Mann's Billy	17	M	M	S		____	Nov		Pneumonia	7 days
34	W. Mann's Tom	7	M	M	S		____	May		C	
35	W. Mann's Archer	7	M	B	S		____	Aug		Fever	3 days

COUNTY OF HAYWOOD, STATE OF TENNESSEE.

PAGE NO. 341 PERSONS WHO DIED DURING THE YEAR ENDING 1st JUNE, 1850.

Civil District No. 10, 11 & 12

No. of Visit	Name	Age	Sex	Color	Free or Slave	Married/Widowed	Place of Birth	Month Died	Occupation	Disease or Cause of Death	No. Days Ill
1	R. Neal's Lyrus	40	M	B	S		—	April		C	
2	A.M. Estes' Ann	2	F	B	S		—	Sept		Chills	2 days
3	William Neal	1	M				Tenn	April		Dropsy	56 days
4	Mildred Estes	31	F			M	Va	Dec		Fever	14 days
5	Rebecca Johnson	30	F			M	Va	Dec		Paralytic	60 days
6	Jesse Cobb's Margaret	1	F	B	S		—	May		Bowel complaint	60 days
7	Jesse Cobb's Abram	1	M	B	S		—	April		Bowel complaint	60 days
8	John T. Moore's Mary	21	F	B	S		—	April		C	170 days
9	John Drisdale's Lavenia	8m	F	B	S		—	May		Inflamation	30 days
10	John Drisdale's Archer	8m	M	B	S		—	April		Inflamation	30 days
11	Mary S. Anthony's Rosetta	1	F	B	S		—	April		unknown	
12	Mary S. Anthony's Lewis	4m	M	B	S		—	March		unknown	
13	H.W. Bennet's Jarret	18	M	B	S		—	May		Scrofula	150 days
14	James H. Perkin's Maria	1	F	B	S		—	Oct		Brain affected	
15	James Bond's Penny	75	F	B	S		—	May		Paralysis	4 days
16	J.C. Coggeshalle's Mary	85	F	B	S		—	Dec		C	
17	J.C. Coggeshalle's Betsey	60	F	B	S		—	July		C	
18	William W. Williams	3	M				Tenn	April		Tumor	90 days
19	Seth William's Jim	17	M	B	S		—	April		C	90 days
20	John L. Thomas' Louisa	1	F	B	S		—	Dec		Pneumonia	7 days
21	E. G. Young's Ann	6m	F	B	S		—	March		sudden	
22	H. J. Anderson's Joana	2	F	B	S		—	Jan		Pneumonia	14 days
23	H. J. Anderson's Jefferson	16	M	B	S		—	April		unknown	60 days
24	Lavina Rickman	4m	F				Tenn	Feb		sudden	
25	James L. Green's Spencer	28	M	B	S		—	June		C	
26	Eason White	8	M				Tenn	Feb		Fever	35 days
27	Reuben Robinson	69	M				N.C.	Jan	Farmer	Fever	120 days
28	M. A. Clay's Sally	18	F	B	S		—	Aug		Dropsy	unknown
29	M. A. Clay's John	3m	M	B	S		—	Aug		unknown	unknown
30	M. A. Clay's Jef	3m	M	B	S		—	Aug		unknown	unknown
31	William Porter	9m	M				Tenn	Feb		Fever	14 days
32	Martha A. Green	4	F				Tenn	Sept		Sore throat	4 days
33	Ellen Smothers	2	F				Tenn	May		Inflamation	10 days
34	James Parmenter	8m	M				Tenn	Oct		Inflamation	8 days
35	John K. Parmenter	20	M				N.C.	Jan	Farmer	Pneumonia	2 days

COUNTY OF HAYWOOD, STATE OF TENNESSEE.

PAGE NO. 344 PERSONS WHO DIED DURING THE YEAR ENDING 1st JUNE, 1850.

Civil District No. 1, 2, 3 & 4

No. of Visit	Name	Age	Sex	Color	Free or Slave	Married/Widowed	Place of Birth	Month Died	Occupation	Disease or Cause of Death	No. Days Ill
1	H. Green's Ben	1	M	B	S			Sept		Cold	120 days
2	R. Stott's George	6m	M	B	S			Oct		Inflamation	21 days
3	W. Newsom's Mary	6m	F	B	S			March		Cold	14 days
4	John Ragsdale	7m	M				Tenn	Dec		unknown	28 days
5	Gustavus B. Hill	2	M				Tenn	March		Fever	21 days
6	Rebecca Hill	4m	F				Tenn	May		Whooping cough	20 days
7	James C. Booth	1	M				Tenn	Aug		Congestion	10 days
8	Joseph Stokley's Eliza	7	F	B	S			Nov		Fits	3 days
9	Mary A. Smith	4	F				Tenn	Feb		Dropsy	200 days
10	Wm. B. Thomas' Daniel	24	M	B	S			March		Dropsy	50 days
11	Joseph T. Hart	30	M				N.C.	Jan		C	
12	Samuel Hunter's Adeline	22	F	B	S			Jan		Pneumonia	6 days
13	Shelly Currie's Temperance	9	F	B	S			May		Fever	70 days
14	Mary Jones	3m	F				Tenn	April		Whooping cough	21 days
15	A. Hunter's Watson	18	M	B	S			Feb		Fever	8 days
16	Leah Christian	82	F			W	S.C.	July		Dropsy	60 days
17	Frances A. Pewett	30	F			M	N.C.	Aug		C	
18	Wm. B. Pewett's Cyrus	50	M	B	S			Feb		Heart disease	60 days
19	Hiram Burford	51	M			M	N.C.	Sept	Farmer	Fever	7 days
20	Mary A. Marshall	28	F				N.C.	Aug		Spinal affected	130 days
21	James Payree's Louisa	1	F	B	S					unknown	30 days
22	Wm. Ware's Peggy	60	F	B	S			Dec		sudden	
23	John H. Ware	16	M				Tenn	July		Drowned	
24	G. G. Ware's George	70	M	B	S			Nov		Pleurisy	21 days
25	G. G. Ware's Anderson	6m	M	B	S			Nov		sudden	
26	G. G. Ware's Tempy	6m	F	B	S			Nov		Fever	14 days
27	Martha F. Osborne	17	F				Tenn	July		Cholera	1 day
28	R.M. Osborne's Chainey	45	F	B	S			July		Cholera	1 day
29	R.M. Osborne's Mary	1	F	B	S			July		Cholera	1 day
30	Lucy Ashe's William	1	M	B	S			Sept		Cold	60 days
31	Lucy Ashe's Infant	3m	F	B	S			Sept		unknown	
32	Sophia Chandler	36	F			M	N.C.	May		Pneumonia	8 days
33	A. Batchelor's Martin	24	M	B	S			March		Pneumonia	8 days
34	Ro. H. Rose's John	30	M	B	S			Jan		Pneumonia	14 days
35	William Christie	67	M				N.C.	Feb	Farmer	Fever	21 days

COUNTY OF HAYWOOD, STATE OF TENNESSEE.

PAGE NO. 345 PERSONS WHO DIED DURING THE YEAR ENDING 1st JUNE, 1850.

Civil District No. 4, 5 & 6
John D. Ware

No. of Visit	Name	Age	Sex	Color	Free or Slave	Married/Widowed	Place of Birth	Month Died	Occupation	Disease or Cause of Death	No. Days Ill
1	Elizabeth Gordon	60	F			M	N.C.	March		Palpatation of heart	98 days
2	Nancy Powers	50	F			M	N.C.	Nov		Fever	56 days
3	A. Gray's Adelia	6m	F	B	S			Dec		unknown	
4	John L. Cobb	7	M				N.C.	June		unknown	5 days
5	Jas. Musgraves' Green	6m	M	B	S			March		unknown	
6	Jos. J. Newborn's Ned	6m	M	B	S			Jan		Croup	1 day
7	John P. Perkins' Tom	90	M	B	S			April		sudden	
8	M. Shaw's Lundy	75	M	B	S			March		C	180 days
9	_ Richardson's Allen	23	M	B	S			Sept		Fever	5 days
10	Phineas Thomas	49	M			M	Va	April	Brk-mason	C	
11	Joseph Castelow	4	M				Tenn	Aug		Croup	3 days
12	James T. Britt	4m	M				Tenn	Nov		Croup	6 days
13	John Y. Taylor's Mary Jane	1	F	B	S			Sept		Fever	20 days
14	H.W. Cottor's Harriet	6m	F	B	S			May		unknown	
15	William Jones	1	M				Tenn	Aug		Fever	21 days
16	L. Boyd's Peggy	80	F	B	S			Nov		unknown	21 days
17	L. Boyd's Fanny	6m	F	B	S			Dec		Pneumonia	30 days
18	Rebecca Bond	37	F			M	N.C.	Aug		Diarrhea	15 days
19	Wm. P. Bond's Mary	55	F	B	S			Aug		Fever	30 days
20	Wm. P. Bond's Matilda	40	F	B	S			Oct		Dropsy	30 days
21	Wm. P. Bond's Andrew	14	M	B	S			Dec		Fever	15 days

Remarks: State of Tennessee, Haywood County. I, John D. Ware, Assistant Marshal, certify that the foregoing returns are true copies of the original and that they are made according to my oath and instruction, to the best of my knowledge and belief.   John D. Ware
Sworn to and subscribed before me,
This 24th December, 1850, C. P. Taliaferro, J.P.

COUNTY OF HENDERSON, STATE OF TENNESSEE.

PAGE NO. 347 PERSONS WHO DIED DURING THE YEAR ENDING 1st JUNE, 1850.

Civil District No. 1
C. M. Harman

No. of Visit	Name	Age	Sex	Color	Free or Slave	Married/Widowed	Place of Birth	Month Died	Occupation	Disease or Cause of Death	No. Days Ill
1	Catharine Hudson	40	F				N.C.	Dec		Brain Fever	3 days
2	Malvina Gullett	14	F				Tenn	Feb		Winter fever	2 days
3	Mary Hendricks	67	F			W	S.C.	Feb		Killed by fall	87 days
4	Lewis Waller	39	M			M	N.C.	June	Farmer	T. fever	5 days
5	Harriet	3	F	M	S		Tenn	Aug		Croup	7 days
6	Elisha Woodward	35	M				N.C.	May	Shoemaker	Congestive fever	5 days
7	Abigail Roberts	3	F				Tenn	March		Death by burn	
8	John W. Seymore	7m	M				Tenn	Aug		Congestive fever	4 days
9	Silas Davidson	1m	M				Tenn	Jan		Croup	1 day
10	Elisha Mims	28	M				N.C.	May	Farmer	Consumption	90 days
11	James J. Copeland	21	M				Tenn	April	Farmer	Consumption	180 days
12	Clary	2m	F	B	S		Tenn	Dec		Cold	3 days

COUNTY OF HENDERSON, STATE OF TENNESSEE.

PAGE NO. 350 PERSONS WHO DIED DURING THE YEAR ENDING 1st JUNE, 1850.

Civil District No. 2

No. of Visit	Name	Age	Sex	Color	Free or Slave	Married/Widowed	Place of Birth	Month Died	Occupation	Disease or Cause of Death	No. Days Ill
1	Starling Taylor	26	M				N.C.	July	Farmer	Gravel	4 days
2	Sarah Oneal	77	F				Penn	Nov		Cold	12 days
3	John Brownin(g)	1	M				Tenn	July		Croup	1 day
4	Jeptha Weathers	55	M			M	S.C.	Jan	Farmer	Consumption	180 days

COUNTY OF HENDERSON, STATE OF TENNESSEE.

PAGE NO. 351 PERSONS WHO DIED DURING THE YEAR ENDING 1st JUNE, 1850.

Civil District No. 3

No. of Visit	Name	Age	Sex	Color	Free or Slave	Married/Widowed	Place of Birth	Month Died	Occupation	Disease or Cause of Death	No. Days Ill
1	Milly Green	87	F			W	N.C.	May		Old age	
2	Darcus	51	F	B	S		N.C.	Aug		Consumption	180 days
3	Infant	4m	F	B	S		Tenn	July		unknown	10 days
4	Infant	4m	F	B	S		Tenn	Sept		unknown	10 days
5	Frank	1	M	B	S		Tenn	Feb		Pneumonia	8 days
6	Infant	1m	M	B	S		Tenn	Sept		unknown	7 days
7	William W. Collins	29	M			M	Tenn	Sept	Farmer	Epeleptic Fits	1 day
8	Martha	18	F	B	S		Tenn	Sept		Intermittent Fever	18 days
9	Stephen Hearn	54	M			M	N.C.	April	Farmer	Consumption	540 days
10	Joshua Carter	12	M				Tenn	Aug		Fits	3 days

COUNTY OF HENDERSON, STATE OF TENNESSEE.

PAGE NO. 354 PERSONS WHO DIED DURING THE YEAR ENDING 1st JUNE, 1850.

Civil District No. 4

No. of Visit	Name	Age	Sex	Color	Free or Slave	Married/Widowed	Place of Birth	Month Died	Occupation	Disease or Cause of Death	No. Days Ill
1	Friona Parchman	1m	F				Tenn	Sept		Croup	1 day
2	Hollensbury Parchman	6m	F				Tenn	March		Croup	180 days
3	Arcadia	9m	F	B	S		Tenn	Aug		Diarrhea	21 days
4	John H. Blankenship	9	M				Tenn	March		Dropsy	21 days

COUNTY OF HENDERSON, STATE OF TENNESSEE.

PAGE NO. 355 PERSONS WHO DIED DURING THE YEAR ENDING 1st JUNE, 1850.

Civil District No. 5

No. of Visit	Name	Age	Sex	Color	Free or Slave	Married/Widowed	Place of Birth	Month Died	Occupation	Disease or Cause of Death	No. Days Ill
1	Peter	1	M	B	S		Tenn	Sept		Whooping cough	21 days
2	John	4m	M	B	S		Tenn	Sept		Whooping cough	21 days
3	Samuel	1m	M	B	S		Tenn	Sept		Smothered	
4	Hugh Ross	82	M			W	Scotland	Nov		Chill	3 days
5	Mary L. Smith	10m	F				Tenn	Dec		Burnt	
6	Sarah Stewart	22	F			M	Tenn	Nov		Consumption	30 days
7	Nicy Attaway	47	F			W	S.C.	June		Pneumonia	7 days
8	Martha Hasting	77	F			W	Va	Aug		Consumption	120 days
9	Emma C. Key	5m	F				Tenn	Sept		Yellow Jaundice	7 days

COUNTY OF HENDERSON, STATE OF TENNESSEE.

PAGE NO. 358 PERSONS WHO DIED DURING THE YEAR ENDING 1st JUNE, 1850.

Civil District No. 6

No. of Visit	Name	Age	Sex	Color	Free or Slave	Married/Widowed	Place of Birth	Month Died	Occupation	Disease or Cause of Death	No. Days Ill
1	Sarah	45	F	B	S		Va	Feb		Dropsy	365 days
2	William Arnold	3	M				Tenn	June		Whooping cough	12 days
3	Adolphus F. O. Watson	18	M				Va	Aug	Farmer	Drowned	

COUNTY OF HENDERSON, STATE OF TENNESSEE.

PAGE NO. 359 PERSONS WHO DIED DURING THE YEAR ENDING 1st JUNE, 1850.

Civil District No. 7

No. of Visit	Name	Age	Sex	Color	Free or Slave	Married/Widowed	Place of Birth	Month Died	Occupation	Disease or Cause of Death	No. Days Ill
1	Anna Threadgell	52	F			M	N.C.	April		Dropsy	65 days
2	Abner Brown	72	M			M	N.C.	Jan	Farmer	Gravel	30 days
3	Hannah Bray	66	F			W	N.C.	June		Dropsy	60 days
4	Moses	33	M	M	S		N.C.	Aug		Consumption	363 days
5	Sterling Johnson	56	M			M	Va	March	Farmer	Dropsy	6 days
6	Thomas Hill Williams	6	M				Tenn	March		unknown	11 days

COUNTY OF HENDERSON, STATE OF TENNESSEE.

PAGE NO. 362 PERSONS WHO DIED DURING THE YEAR ENDING 1st JUNE, 1850.

Civil District No. 8

No. of Visit	Name	Age	Sex	Color	Free or Slave	Married/Widowed	Place of Birth	Month Died	Occupation	Disease or Cause of Death	No. Days Ill
1	Cherry	7	F	B	S		Tenn	March		Fever	14 days
2	Caesar	7m	M	B	S		Tenn	April		Worms	10 days
3	George	2	M	B	S		Tenn	May		Bronchitis	90 days
4	Louis	1	M	M	S		Tenn	March		Diarrhea	5 days
5	Mary Hendricks	80	F			M	Ireland	Jan		Dropsy	90 days
6	John Grant	84	M			W	N.C.	Feb	Farmer	Cancer	365 days

COUNTY OF HENDERSON, STATE OF TENNESSEE.

PAGE NO. 363 PERSONS WHO DIED DURING THE YEAR ENDING 1st JUNE, 1850.

Civil District No. 9

No. of Visit	Name	Age	Sex	Color	Free or Slave	Married/Widowed	Place of Birth	Month Died	Occupation	Disease or Cause of Death	No. Days Ill
1	Matilda C. Wilson	6	F				Tenn	June		unknown	240 days
2	James Barger	2	M				Tenn	Aug		Scarlet fever	9 days
3	Patsy	42	F	B	S		Tenn	Aug		unknown	90 days
4	Rachael	1m	F	B	S		Tenn	June		unknown	14 days
5	Elizabeth McClerkin	70	F			M	Va	May		Liver disease	
6	Henderson Clark	44	M			M	N.C.	July		Rheumatism	150 days
7	Phil	45	M	B	S		Va	March		Erysipelas	4 days
8	Matthew Allen	4m	M				Tenn	Feb		Hives	21 days
9	Jane Davis	65	F				N.C.	Sept		Fall from horse	30 days
10	Arden Taylor	63	M			M	N.C.	April		T. fever	12 days
11	Josiah Taylor	20	M				Tenn	Jan		T. fever	9 days

COUNTY OF HENDERSON, STATE OF TENNESSEE.

PAGE NO. 366 PERSONS WHO DIED DURING THE YEAR ENDING 1st JUNE, 1850.

Civil District No. 10

No. of Visit	Name	Age	Sex	Color	Free or Slave	Married/Widowed	Place of Birth	Month Died	Occupation	Disease or Cause of Death	No. Days Ill
1	Rose	35	F	-	S		Va	Aug		--illegible--	
2	Sarah	18	F	-	S		Tenn	Aug		T. fever	365 days
3	Jane	29	F	M	S		Tenn	Dec		Winter fever	90 days
4	Samuel Appleby	58	M			M	Georgia	May		Pneumonia	15 days
5	Annanias Boatright	64	M			M	N.C.	June		Cholera	8 days
6	Hezekiah	21	M	B	S		Tenn	Aug		Consumption	120 days
7	Mary	15	F	B	S		Tenn	Oct		Consumption	1 day
8	Jenny	4m	F	B	S		Tenn	Jan		Killed by fall	1 day
9	Stephen	1	M	B	S		Tenn	Feb		Smothered	10 days
10	Martha Bird	19	F			M	Tenn	Oct		T. fever	9 days
11	Maletha Philips	18	F				Tenn	Dec		unknown	30 days
12	Lizella Yates	6m	F				Tenn	Aug		unknown	90 days
13	Milly J. Baily	1m	F				Tenn	April		Whooping cough	8 days

COUNTY OF HENDERSON, STATE OF TENNESSEE.

PAGE NO. 367 PERSONS WHO DIED DURING THE YEAR ENDING 1st JUNE, 1850.

C. M. Harman

No. of Visit	Name	Age	Sex	Color	Free or Slave	Married/Widowed	Place of Birth	Month Died	Occupation	Disease or Cause of Death	No. Days Ill
1	Zachariah Jordan	6m	M				Tenn	Dec		--illegible--	9 days
2	Caroline Patterson	24	F			M	N.C.	Aug		Liver disease	60 days
3	Alcy King	3m	F				Tenn	Nov		Hives	7 days
4	John T. Gillam	13	M				Tenn	Sept		unknown	4 days
5	Martha Carter	26	F			M	Tenn	Aug		Cholera	

COUNTY OF HENDERSON, STATE OF TENNESSEE.

PAGE NO. 370   PERSONS WHO DIED DURING THE YEAR ENDING 1st JUNE, 1850.

Civil District No. 12

No. of Visit	Name	Age	Sex	Color	Free or Slave	Married/Widowed	Place of Birth	Month Died	Occupation	Disease or Cause of Death	No. Days Ill
1	Sarenus Galbraith	1	M				Tenn	Dec		Sc. fever	20 days
2	Nancy McNatt	7	F				Tenn	July		Fever	9 days

COUNTY OF HENDERSON, STATE OF TENNESSEE.

PAGE NO. 371   PERSONS WHO DIED DURING THE YEAR ENDING 1st JUNE, 1850.

Civil District No. 13

No. of Visit	Name	Age	Sex	Color	Free or Slave	Married/Widowed	Place of Birth	Month Died	Occupation	Disease or Cause of Death	No. Days Ill
1	Benjamine	60	M	B	S		N.C.	Feb		Pneumonia	17 days
2	Polly	24	F	B	S		Va	June		Cholera	1 day
3	John	1	M	B	S		Tenn	June		Whooping cough	90 days
4	Matilda Lamb	14	F				Tenn	March		Pleurisy	7 days
5	Malinda Holly	2	F				Tenn	Sept		Croup	1 day
6	Hannah	1	F	B	S		Tenn	Feb		Whooping cough	3 days
7	Mary A. Morris	30	F			M	N.C.	July		Pneumonia	7 days

COUNTY OF HENDERSON, STATE OF TENNESSEE.

PAGE NO. 374   PERSONS WHO DIED DURING THE YEAR ENDING 1st JUNE, 1850.

Civil District No. 14

No. of Visit	Name	Age	Sex	Color	Free or Slave	Married/Widowed	Place of Birth	Month Died	Occupation	Disease or Cause of Death	No. Days Ill
1	Mary J. McKinsay	3m	F				Tenn	Dec		Hydrocephalus	1 day
2	Malinda Moreland	51	F			M	Kentucky	March		unknown	
3	Jackson Powers	8	M				Tenn	Nov		Infl. fever	30 days
4	James White	46	M			M	Georgia	April	Farmer	unknown	
5	Dorcus Powers	29	F			M	N.C.	Jan		Consumption	120 days
6	John Deer	5m	M				Tenn	Dec		Hives	7 days

COUNTY OF HENDERSON, STATE OF TENNESSEE.

PAGE NO. 375   PERSONS WHO DIED DURING THE YEAR ENDING 1st JUNE, 1850.

Civil District No. 15

No. of Visit	Name	Age	Sex	Color	Free or Slave	Married/Widowed	Place of Birth	Month Died	Occupation	Disease or Cause of Death	No. Days Ill
1	David L. Moore	2m	M				Tenn	Dec		unknown	60 days

COUNTY OF HENDERSON, STATE OF TENNESSEE.

PAGE NO. 378   PERSONS WHO DIED DURING THE YEAR ENDING 1st JUNE, 1850.

Civil District No. 16

No. of Visit	Name	Age	Sex	Color	Free or Slave	Married/Widowed	Place of Birth	Month Died	Occupation	Disease or Cause of Death	No. Days Ill
1	John L. Scott	3m	M				Tenn	Sept		Erysipelas	5 days
2	Ann E. Mackey	82	F			W	Va	Sept		T. fever	20 days

COUNTY OF HENDERSON, STATE OF TENNESSEE.

PAGE NO. 379   PERSONS WHO DIED DURING THE YEAR ENDING 1st JUNE, 1850.

Civil District No. 17

No. of Visit	Name	Age	Sex	Color	Free or Slave	Married/Widowed	Place of Birth	Month Died	Occupation	Disease or Cause of Death	No. Days Ill
1	John Coffee	72	M			W	Tenn	Dec	Farmer	unknown	
2	Nancy E. Blair	17	F				Tenn	April		Tumorous Gland	14 days
3	Caroline	3	F	B	S		Tenn	Dec		Worms	14 days
4	James Kizer	2	M				Tenn	Oct		Enlargement of spleen	60 days
5	William Trice	2	M				Tenn	Oct		Dropsy	60 days
6	Feraby	17	F	B	S		Tenn	Feb		Winter fever	14 days
7	Charlotte Dalton	8	F				Tenn	April		T. fever	35 days
8	Infant	1m	M	B	S		Tenn	Feb		Catarrah	
9	James Stewart	58	M			M	N.C.	April	Farmer	Whiskey	90 days

COUNTY OF HENDERSON, STATE OF TENNESSEE.

PAGE NO. 382   PERSONS WHO DIED DURING THE YEAR ENDING 1st JUNE, 1850.

Civil District No. 18

No. of Visit	Name	Age	Sex	Color	Free or Slave	Married/Widowed	Place of Birth	Month Died	Occupation	Disease or Cause of Death	No. Days Ill
1	Elizabeth Hendricks	58	F			M	Georgia	Aug		Remittent fever	10 days
2	John Hinson	5	M				Tenn	Aug		Diarrhea	4 days
3	Margaret E. C. Dodd	17	F			M	S.C.	July		Palsy	8 days

COUNTY OF HENRY, STATE OF TENNESSEE.

PAGE NO. 383   PERSONS WHO DIED DURING THE YEAR ENDING 1st JUNE, 1850.

T. Cooney

No. of Visit	Name	Age	Sex	Color	Free or Slave	Married/Widowed	Place of Birth	Month Died	Occupation	Disease or Cause of Death	No. Days Ill
1	S.C.Love's Elizabeth	1	F	B	S		Tenn	Sept		Bowel complaint	21 days
2	William F. Greer	2	M				Tenn	Jan		Sc. fever	1 day
3	John Clark	63	M			W	Penn	March	Laborer	Consumption	7 years
4	Const. Fagan's Lucy	68	F	B	S		Va	March		Phlebites	C
5	Sarah Arnn	65	F			M	Va	June		Dropsy	21 days
6	William Carrol Chilton	1	M				Tenn	June		Eruption	2 months
7	Sarah Ann Edwards	71	F				Kentucky	Sept		T. fever	14 days
8	Robert R. Steely	5	M				Tenn	April		Sc. fever	7 days
9	Henry Allen	41	M			M	N.C.	July	Farmer	Inflamation of lungs	11 days
10	Lewis Whitnell Finley	5m	M				Tenn	Sept		Water on brain	12 days
11	Amanda B. Conyars	8m	F				Tenn	Feb		Decline	3 months
12	Charley Sharman	6	M				Tenn	June		Fever	30 days
13	William G. Craig	10m	M				Kentucky	Aug		Inflamation of brain	30 days
14	Mary Anderson	61	F			M	N.C.	Jan		Dropsy	15 days
15	Juliana Holland	2	F				Tenn	July		Sc. fever	12 days
16	Mary J. Harmon	22	F			M	Tenn	Sept		Child bed fever	10 days
17	William Wright	48	M			M	Tenn	Jan	Farmer	Pneumonia	8 days
18	Mary Jane Edwards	25	F			M	N.C.	April		Congestive chills	3 days
19	Mary Ann Smith	35	F			M	Alabama	May		Child birth	12 days
20	Sarah Bevel	43	F			M	N.C.	Aug		Tumor	12 hours
21	William Thompson	66	M			W	Va	March	Farmer	Chronic Diarrhea	3 hours
22	Rebecca Boden	7	F				Tenn	Jan		Brain fever	10 days
23	Clara Nance	2	F				Tenn	Jan		Croup	12 hours
24	J. Young's Peter	3	M	B	S		Tenn	Oct		Dropsy	10 months
25	William Burk	83	M	B	S	M	N.C.	Feb	Farmer	Consumption	30 days
26	Infant of Mrs. Atkins	1m	F								
27	Josiah Alderson	68	M			M	Va	Aug	Trader	Cholic	2 days
28	Alabama McConnell	1	F				Tenn	Feb		Croup	7 days
29	Jacob Mortons	84	M			W	N.C.	Dec	Pauper	Consumption	3 months
30	Jackson Barton	16	M				Tenn	April	Pauper	Fits	2 days
31	Susanna Hogg	86	F			W	Va	Sept		Old age	2 years
32	Adam Alexander Harmon	2m	M				Tenn	Oct		Fever	30 days
33	Elisha Harmon	36	M			M	Tenn	Aug	Farmer	Liver disease	10 months
34	Thomas Harmon	9	M				Tenn	March		Liver disease	3 months
35	Emma H. Depriest	11	F				Tenn	July		Consumption	2 years

COUNTY OF HENRY, STATE OF TENNESSEE.

PAGE NO. 386 PERSONS WHO DIED DURING THE YEAR ENDING 1st JUNE, 1850.

T. Cooney

No. of Visit	Name	Age	Sex	Color	Free or Slave	Married/Widowed	Place of Birth	Month Died	Occupation	Disease or Cause of Death	No. Days Ill
1	Miles J. Graves	1	M				Tenn	Nov		Croup	3 days
2	George W. Davis	24	M			M	Tenn	Sept	Laborer	Bil. fever	6 days
3	Matilda Cunningham	28	F			M	Tenn	April		Pneumonia	2 months
4	Harriet Walker	29	F			M	N.C.	April		Pneumonia	8 days
5	Sarah Causey	39	F			M	N.C.	Jan		Child birth	1 day
6	Lucinda Gardner	26	F			W	Tenn	Aug		Puerperal fever	3 months
7	Betsey, J. Grainger's	30	F	B	S		Va	Feb		Scrofula	years
8	Lucy Ann, J. Grainger's	7	F	B	S		Va	Dec		Burnt	sudden
9	Marietta, W.B.Pryor's	6m	F	B	S		Tenn	April		Croup	2 days
10	Francis Blakemore	5	F				Tenn	Dec		Cholera Inf.	4 weeks
11	Charlotta, Capt. Sallie's	1	F	B	S		Tenn	Feb		suddenly	
12	Lge, J. H. Vandyke's	19	M	B	S		Va	Nov		Pneumonia	21 days
13	Caroline, Wm.H.Vandyke's	2	F	B	S		Tenn	Nov		suddenly	
14	James C. Winn	21	M				Tenn	May		a helpless idiot from birth	
15	Oliver H. P. Russell	22	M				Tenn	July	Farmer	T. fever	5 days
16	George Simmons	16	M				N.C.	Aug		Bil. fever	
17	Luther, Eli Kendall's	9m	M	B	S		Tenn	Dec		Croup	3 days
18	Martin Neese, Sen.	90	M			W	Penn	July	Farmer	Old age	
19	Martin Neese, Jur.	50	M			M	N.C.	Oct	Farmer	Inflamation of brain	35 days
20	Tabby, E. McGehee's	28	F	B	S		Va	June		Dropsy of the heart	10 days
21	Mary, E. McGehee's	3m	F	B	S		Tenn	March		Croup	sudden
22	Thomas Norton	70	M				Penn	Feb	Farmer	Paralysis	sudden
23	Samuel J. Freeland	18	M				Tenn	March		Abscess	30 days
24	Elizabeth Roper	50	F			W	Va	Jan		Inflamation of brain	28 days
25	Horace Daniel	4	M				Tenn	Feb		Sc. fever	15 days
26	Francesco Whittington	8	M				Tenn	July		Fever	21 days
27	James K. Rogers	27	M			M	Tenn	Sept	Merchant	Chronic desentery	6 months
28	Josiah Emery	5	M				Tenn	Dec		Burn	30 days
29	Isaac, Benj. Bowden's	22	M	B	S		Tenn	June		Negro consumption	6 months
30	Green, Benj. Bowden's	20	M	B	S		Tenn	Aug		Negro consumption	6 months
31	Henry, Benj. Bowden's	14	M	B	S		Tenn	Oct		Negro consumption	2 months
32	Martha, Benj. Bowden's	10	M	B	S		Tenn	Oct		Inflamation of bowels	5 weeks
33	Landrum, Benj. Bowden's	3	M	B	S		Tenn	Jan		Worms	7 days
34	Delila A. E. Moore	1	F				Tenn	Feb		Inflamation of brain	14 days

COUNTY OF HENRY, STATE OF TENNESSEE.

PAGE NO. 387   PERSONS WHO DIED DURING THE YEAR ENDING 1st JUNE, 1850.

T. Cooney

No. of Visit	Name	Age	Sex	Color	Free or Slave	Married/Widowed	Place of Birth	Month Died	Occupation	Disease or Cause of Death	No. Days Ill
1	Geraldine Cooper	7	F				Tenn	Sept		Inflamation of brain	6 days
2	Peter, Jas. R. Randles'	2	M	B	S		Tenn	Jan		Worms	7 days
3	Martha Ann Carter	9m	F				Tenn	June		Cholera	3 days
4	Jeremiah Moody	91	M			M	Va	Oct	Farmer	Old age	14 days
5	not named, Watkin's	1m	F				Tenn	June		Spasm	11 days
6	Violet, W.A.Tharpe's	60	F	B	S		N.C.	Dec		unknown	40 days
7	Jim, W.A.Tharpe's	19	M	B	S		N.C.	May		Negro consumption	3 months
8	Mary Ann, W.A.Tharpe's	4	F	B	S		Tenn	March		unknown	21 days
9	not named, W.A.Tharpe's	3m	F	B	S		Tenn	April		accidental smothered	1 day
10	not named, W.A.Tharpe's	4m	M	B	S		Tenn	Jan		unknown	1 day
11	not named, W.A.Tharpe's	6m	F	B	S		Tenn	Feb		unknown	1 day
12	not named, W.A.Tharpe's	8m	M	B	S		Tenn	July		unknown	1 day
13	not named, W.A.Tharpe's	1m	F	B	S		Tenn	Aug		unknown	1 day
14	not named, Childress'	1m	M				Tenn	June		unknown	2 weeks
15	Eliza Childress	4	F				Tenn	Nov		Bowel complaint	2 weeks
16	Mary Crews	42	F			M	Va	April		Milk leg	1 week
17	Samantha Love	5m	F				Tenn	Nov		Croup	10 days
18	Jefferson Jno.Dillahanty	1	M	B	S		Tenn	Jan		Whooping cough	7 days
19	Berry, Samuel Swarengin's	25	M	B	S		Tenn	Dec		Flux	5 days
20	not named, Jas.Denwiddie's	1m	M	B	S		Tenn	Sept		Croup	7 days
21	James Robert	2	M				Tenn	Nov		Croup	2 days
22	Bloof, Allison T.Carter's	28	M	B	S		Tenn	Dec		unknown	7 days
23	Mary, David Petty's	6m	F	B	S		Tenn	Dec		Croup	3 days
24	Jerry, Ambrose Mitchell's	1m	M	B	S		Tenn	Dec		Smothered	sudden
25	Aaron, David Petty's	45	M	B	S		Kentucky	May		Fits	14 months
26	Carter, Nancy Wallace's	30	M	B	S		Tenn	Aug		fever	30 days
27	Erasmus Harris	20	M				Tenn	March	Law	Consumption	7 months
28	Elizabeth Forrest	84	F			W	Va	April		Old age	4 days
29	William G. Myrick	1	M				Tenn	Feb		Sc. fever	4 days
30	Mary, Wm. R. Hamm's	1	F	B	S		Tenn	Aug		Diarrhea	10 days
31	Howell A. Myrick	20	M			W	Tenn	July	Farmer	Flux	3 weeks
32	Adalie, P. G. Haynes'	7	F	B	S		Tenn	Feb		Whooping cough	2 weeks
33	Mack, P. G. Haynes'	3	M	M	S		Kentucky	Sept		Worms	5 weeks
34	George, P. G. Haynes'	1	M	B	S		Tenn	Aug		Dropsy of the brain	3 weeks
35	Angaline, P. G. Haynes'	8m	F	B	S		Tenn	Oct		Smothered	sudden

COUNTY OF HENRY, STATE OF TENNESSEE.

PERSONS WHO DIED DURING THE YEAR ENDING 1st JUNE, 1850.

T. Cooney

No. of Visit	Name	Age	Sex	Color	Free or Slave	Married/Widowed	Place of Birth	Month Died	Occupation	Disease or Cause of Death	No. Days Ill
1	Dave, John Hall's	35	M	B	S		Tenn	March		Inflamation of bowels	9 days
2	not named, Cal Dargans'	1m	M	B	S		Tenn	Nov		unknown	1 day
3	Sarah Matilda Atkins	1	F				Tenn	Sept		Congestive chills	6 days
4	Nancy Elizabeth Rawls	5	F				Tenn	Aug		Croup	7 days
5	Joseph McYates	16	M				Tenn	May	Farmer	Fits	all life
6	not named, Yates'	1m	M				Tenn	Feb		Deformity	all life
7	Elizabeth Lafayette	26	F			M	Tenn	Jan		Congestive chills	2 days
8	George Washington Hill	1m	M				Tenn	Nov		unknown	4 days
9	Clementine Lemmons	1m	F				Tenn	Oct		Croup	8 days
10	Julia Webster	1	F				Tenn	Oct		Sc. fever	14 days
11	not named, Bradley	1m	F				Tenn	Nov		unknown	10 days
12	Margaret Dunlap	63	F			W	Va	Aug		Dysentery	3 months
13	James B. Crowder	3m	M				Tenn	July		unknown	8 days
14	Margaret Crowder	3m	F				Tenn	July		unknown	8 days
15	Elias Bowden	21	M				Tenn	Sept	Farmer	Bil. Pneumonia	8 days
16	David Albert Archer	7	M				Tenn	Nov		Sc. fever	7 days
17	Sarah Ann Bland	9m	F				Tenn	Sept		Sc. fever	18 days
18	John Willis Weldroup	6	M				Tenn	Oct		Sc. fever	8 days
19	Alfred Weldroup	3	F(M)				Tenn	Oct		Sc. fever	7 days
20	John Bumpass	14	M				Tenn	Feb		Injury to chest	14 days
21	America Humphrys	1	F				Tenn	Sept		Fever	14 days
22	Nancy H. Jones	35	F				Va	March		Winter fever	35 days
23	Josiah Monroe	45	M				Va	Nov	Farmer	Small pox	13 days
24	Elisha Jones	39	M			M	S.C.	May	Farmer	Accidental posioned	3 hours
25	John Phillips	40	M				N.C.	March		Pneumonia	21 days
26	Elizabeth Duke	26	F			M	Tenn	April		Consumption	25 days
27	Manerva Stewart	8m	F				Tenn	Aug		Cholera Inf.	1 day
28	unnamed, Alfred Hartsfields	1m	M	B	S		Tenn	April		Debility	5 days
29	Lucy Taylor VanCleve	6m	F				Tenn	July		Diarrhea	5 days
30	Elizabeth Holiday	27	F			M	Tenn	July		Dropsy	7 months
31	Tennessee Routen	5m	F				Tenn	May		unknown	4 weeks
32	Billy, J.L.Haglar's	21	M	B	S			July		Negro consumption	3 months
33	Eveline Finch	9m	F				Tenn	Oct		Fits	1 day
34	Marie L. Porter	43	F			M	Kentucky	Dec		Inflamation of bowels	21 days
35	William Blont Cooper	4m	M				Tenn	Oct		Inflamation of bowels	4 days

COUNTY OF HENRY, STATE OF TENNESSEE.

PAGE NO. 391 PERSONS WHO DIED DURING THE YEAR ENDING 1st JUNE, 1850.

T. Cooney

No. of Visit	Name	Age	Sex	Color	Free or Slave	Married/Widowed	Place of Birth	Month Died	Occupation	Disease or Cause of Death	No. Days Ill
1	Maria, Wm. Tharpe's	22	F	B	S		N.C.	Mar		Child bed	3 days
2	Louisa, W. A. Tharpe's	19	F	B	S		Tenn	April		Hemorhage of lungs	1 day
3	Mary, D. Looney's	6m	F	B	S		Tenn	Dec		Teething	1 day
4	Nathaniel, Chs. Clarke's	25	M	B	S		Tenn	Dec		unknown	4 days
5	Nancy Diggs	23	F			M	N.C.	July		Congestive chills	4 days
6	Julida C. Dinwiddie	3	M				Tenn	June		Worms	14 days
7	Milbery Atkins	46	M			W	N.C.	April		Bil. fever	21 days
8	Rebecca Atkins	7	F				Tenn	April		Bil. fever	28 days
9	Frances L. Cooper	6	F				Tenn	Feb		Pulmonary	120 days
10	unnamed, M.L.Dinwiddie's	1m	M				Tenn	Jan		unknown	5 days
11	William C. Granada	2m	M				Tenn	Sept		Hives	5 days
12	Thomas Moor	7	M				Tenn	Sept		Inflamation of brain	16 days
13	Nathan Moor	5m	M				Tenn	Sept		Inflamation of brain	5 days
14	Jane D. Dennings	1	M?				Tenn	June		Fever	42 days
15	Cale, John Manly's	42	M	B	S		N.C.	March		Pheumatism	3000 days
16	Charles, Charles J.Roger's	23	M	B	S		Tenn	June		Bil. fever	5 days
17	Jim, Charles J. Roger's	1m	M	B	S		Tenn	June		unknown	10 days
18	Jackson Crawley	28	M			M	Va	April	Farmer	Bleeding of the lungs	40 days
19	Daniel, R. S. Thomason	9	M	B	S		N.C.	July		Pneumonia	210 days
20	Neley Clark	49	M				Tenn	Nov		Inflamation of bowels	21 days
21	unnamed, Golden	2m	F				Tenn	Aug		unknown	1 day
22	William Paynter	1m	M				Tenn	Sept		Tumor complaint	45 days
23	John Marberry	2	M				Tenn	June		unknown	1 day
24	Jane Hunt	50	F				Va	Oct		Drowned	
25	Robert, Hunt's Estate	1	M	B	S		Tenn	Sept		Congestive chills	8 days
26	Charles Whitlock	40	M				N.C.	March		unknown	90 days
27	Charles, J.Dillahunty's	1	M	B	S		Tenn	April		Fever	120 days
28	John Cunningham	26	M				Tenn	July	Farmer	Whooping cough	5 days
29	Casy, Jas. Cowans'	70	F	B	S		N.C.	Sept		Diarrhea	28 days
30	Rebecca, Jas. Cowans'	15	F	B	S			Oct		Abscess of lungs	35 days
31	Hannibal, Jas. Cowans'	1	M	B	S			Oct		Consumption	120 days
32	Jesse, Jas. Cowans'	1	M	B	S			Oct		--illegible--	28 days
33	unnamed, Jas. Cowans'	1m	M	B	S			May		unknown	21 days
34	John, Jas. Cowans'	25	M	B	S			Oct		never well	30 days
35	Elizabeth Brogden	1	F					Aug		Pleurisy	90 days

Remarks: The County has been extremely healthy, no epidemics has prevailed, chills and fever, which have been troublesome in this County, have not prevailed to any extent for the last 3 or 4 years. No cases of cholera was ever known to one or not in this County.   T. Cooney, Asst. Marshal
December 28, 1850

COUNTY OF HENRY, STATE OF TENNESSEE.

PAGE NO. 394 PERSONS WHO DIED DURING THE YEAR ENDING 1st JUNE, 1850.

T. Cooney

No. of Visit	Name	Age	Sex	Color	Free or Slave	Married/Widowed	Place of Birth	Month Died	Occupation	Disease or Cause of Death	No. Days Ill
1	William Asa Barn	14	M				Tenn	April		Typhoid fever	21 days
2	George, T. T. Thomas's	64	M				S.C.	Nov		--illegible--	25 years
3	Ohella Rodes	2m	F				Tenn	Oct		unknown	never well
4	Harrison, B.T.Campbell's	8	M				Tenn	Sept		Scrofula	180 days
5	Rowan Parish	4	M				Tenn	Dec		Cholera Inf.	4 days
6	Eliza Priscilla Parish	8	F				N.C.	Dec		Cholera Inf.	3 days
7	James A. Parrish	9	M				Tenn	Jan		Cholera Inf.	3 days
8	Carrol Wren	19	M				Tenn	Sept		unknown	28 days
9	Sarah McCampbell	40	F			M	N.C.	April		Pneumonia	90 days
10	Erasmus Harris	—	M				Tenn	——		Consumption	——

COUNTY OF HICKMAN, STATE OF TENNESSEE.

PAGE NO. 395 PERSONS WHO DIED DURING THE YEAR ENDING 1st JUNE, 1850.

Edwin M. Baird

No. of Visit	Name	Age	Sex	Color	Free or Slave	Married/Widowed	Place of Birth	Month Died	Occupation	Disease or Cause of Death	No. Days Ill
1	Samuel J. Studdart	8	M				Tenn	Oct		Congestive fever	5 days
2	James Barnhill	85	M				N.C.	March	Blk-smith	unknown	14 days
3	Margarette Arnold	2m	F				Tenn	Feb		Croup	4 days
4	Infant	1m	F				Tenn	Feb		unknown	sudden
5	Cairy	2	M	B	S		Tenn	May		Croup	3 days
6	Solomon	1	M	B	S		Tenn	Dec		Croup	2 days
7	Albert Vincent	1m	M				Tenn	Jan		unknown	sudden
8	Sarah Cates	80	F				N.C.	July		unknown	3 days
9	Infant	2m	M	M	S		Tenn	Nov		unknown	5 days
10	Infant	1m	M				Tenn	Jan		unknown	sudden
11	Jonathan Reeves	17	M				Tenn	June	Farmer	C	80 days
12	Infant	1m	F				Tenn	June		unknown	sudden
13	Infant	1m	M				Tenn	June		unknown	sudden
14	Nelly	50	F	B	S		S.C.	Nov		Dropsy	100 days
15	John L. Humble	32	M				Tenn	May	Farmer	disease of kidneys	45 days
16	James	26	M	B	S		Tenn	June		Fever	20 days
17	Milly	2	F	B	S		Tenn	Oct		Cholera Inf.	24 days
18	Richard M. Graham	8m	M				Tenn	April		Pneumonia	10 days
19	Infant	1m	M	B	S		Tenn	Feb		Pneumonia	2 days
20	Jane	22	F	B	S		Tenn	March		Pneumonia	3 days
21	Mahulda Chappel	3	F				Tenn	July		Croup	3 days
22	Minerva Minor	21	F			M	Tenn	Nov		C	60 days
23	Elizabeth Griffin	22	F				Tenn	March		unknown	sudden
24	Infant	1m	M				Tenn	March		unknown	sudden
25	William Lawrence	67	M				Va	Sept	Farmer	Dropsy	14 days
26	James W. McMinn	26	M			M	Tenn	March	Farmer	T. fever	21 days
27	Isabella McMinn	1m	F				Tenn	Sept		unknown	sudden
28	Delia	30	F	B	S		Maryland	Aug		unknown	35 days
29	Nelly Walker	57	F				N.C.	Oct		C	60 days
30	Infant	1m	M				Tenn	June		unknown	sudden
31	Benjamin McAdoo	10m	M				Tenn	Oct		unknown	7 days
32	Lucretia Martin	72	F			W	N.C.	March		Dropsy	90 days
33	Infant	1m	F				Tenn	March		unknown	sudden
34	Mary Worley	90	F			W	unknown	Feb		unknown	C
35	Drewry Gossett	6m	M				Tenn	Jan		Croup	sudden

Remarks: The water, freestone, mostly springs. The rocks, limestone, sufficient for all practable purposes. The soil in the river and creek bottom, deep rich loam and very productive. Heavy timbered such as oak, elm, beech, ash, poplar, etc. The ridges thin gray soil, heavy timbered principally small black oak. The iron ore is the only ore yet discovered. In the spring of 1849, heavy frosts, great damage to the wheat crops. Edwin M. Baird.

COUNTY OF HICKMAN, STATE OF TENNESSEE.

PAGE NO. 398 PERSONS WHO DIED DURING THE YEAR ENDING 1st JUNE, 1850.

Edwin M. Baird

No. of Visit	Name	Age	Sex	Color	Free or Slave	Married/Widowed	Place of Birth	Month Died	Occupation	Disease or Cause of Death	No. Days Ill
1	Melissa A. Jones	1	F				Tenn	Sept		Inflamation of brain	7 days
2	Mary A. Vickory	43	F				Georgia	May		C	70 days
3	Infant	1m	M				Tenn	Oct		unknown	sudden
4	Edward Hailey	10	M				N.C.	Aug		Diarrhea	8 days
5	Infant	1m	F				Tenn	June		unknown	sudden
6	Infant	1m	M				Tenn	Oct		unknown	sudden
7	William A. Lancaster	3	M				Tenn	April		Drowned	
8	-- blank --	--	-				----	-----		-------	------
9	Angeline Morgan	1	F				Tenn	Sept		Cholera Inf.	12 days
10	Infant	1m	F				Tenn	March		unknown	sudden
11	Charles Adkinson	1m	M				Tenn	Feb		unknown	sudden
12	Willie	6m	M	B	S		Tenn	Jan		unknown	7 days
13	Martha Howard	6m	F				Tenn	May		unknown	4 days
14	Infant	3m	M				Tenn	July		Diarrhea	30 days
15	Isaac Skelton	30	M			M	Tenn	May	Farmer	C	90 days
16	Anna Skelton	66	F			M	S.C.	Dec		C	70 days
17	Drurinda Skelton	13	F				Tenn	March		T. fever	5 days
18	Malinda J. Depriest	7	F				Tenn	May		Inflamation of brain	4 days
19	Elizabeth Joyce	38	F				Tenn	April		unknown	8 days
20	Washington	1	M	B	S		Tenn	July		Croup	sudden
21	Josiah P. Harder	50	M			M	N.C.	Feb		C	56 days

COUNTY OF HICKMAN, STATE OF TENNESSEE.

PAGE NO. 399 PERSONS WHO DIED DURING THE YEAR ENDING 1st JUNE, 1850.

Edwin M. Baird

No. of Visit	Name	Age	Sex	Color	Free or Slave	Married/Widowed	Place of Birth	Month Died	Occupation	Disease or Cause of Death	No. Days Ill
1	Infant	1m	M				Tenn	April		unknown	sudden
2	Dudley Clymer	75	M			W	Va	Feb	Hatter	Erysipelas	7 days
3	Andrew Clymer	36	M			M	Tenn	Feb	Farmer	unknown	8 days
4	William H. Dunlap	2	M				Tenn	Jan		Scalded	12 days
5	Infant	1m	M				Tenn	April		unknown	sudden
6	William Young	2m	M				Tenn	Dec		unknown	6 days
7	Pawhatten	9m	M	B	S		Tenn	Aug		C	
8	Infant	1m	M				Tenn	June		unknown	sudden
9	Infant	4m	F	B	S		Tenn	Feb		unknown	sudden
10	Florida Nix	1m	F				Tenn	April		Jaundice	3 days
11	Josiah Cook	80	M			M	Louisiana	Jan	Farmer	C	
12	Dorcus E. Baker	17	F			M	Tenn	Sept		A hurt	9 days
13	Simon	70	M	B			Va	March		Dropsy	90 days
14	John D. Sadler	21	M				Illinois	April	Carpenter	T. fever	9 days
15	Pernina Savage	1	F				Tenn	Sept		Croup	12 days
16	Exselda	1	F	B	S		Tenn	May		unknown	9 days
17	Lewis	37	M	B	S		Tenn	Feb		Pneumonia	4 days
18	Nicholas E. Moton	5m	M				Tenn	Nov		unknown	10 days
19	Fortisque	5m	M	B	S		Tenn	Oct		Croup	8 days
20	Robert	3m	M	B	S		Tenn	Nov		Croup	sudden
21	Julian Grimes	9	F				Tenn	March		unknown	4 days
22	William Harrington	5	M				Tenn	Oct		Sc. fever	2 days
23	Nancy Harrington	69	F				N.C.	June		T. fever	14 days
24	Kizziah	23	F	B	S		Tenn	Jan		C	35 days
25	Emily Richards	5	F				Tenn	Sept		unknown	sudden
26	Samuel Brooks	30	M			M	Tenn	Jan	Farmer	Cholera	sudden
27	Granderson	50	M	B	S		Maryland	April		C	50 days
28	Jesse R. Tatum	20	M			M	Tenn	March	Farmer	C	40 days
29	Infant	2m	M				Tenn	March		unknown	4 days

COUNTY OF HICKMAN, STATE OF TENNESSEE.

PAGE NO. 399 PERSONS WHO DIED DURING THE YEAR ENDING 1st JUNE, 1850.

Edwin M. Baird

No. of Visit	Name	Age	Sex	Color	Free or Slave	Married/Widowed	Place of Birth	Month Died	Occupation	Disease or Cause of Death	No. Days Ill
30	Lydia Parker	39	F			M	Tenn	June		Bil. fever	30 days
31	Willie Malugen	26	M			M	Tenn	March	Blk-smith	T. fever	8 days
32	Nace	38	M	B	S		Maryland	March		Winter fever	15 days
33	Infant	3m	F	B	S		Tenn	Oct		unknown	sudden
34	Harriett	10m	F	B	S		Tenn	Jan		unknown	30 days
35	Joseph Alexander	10m	M				Tenn	Aug		Cholera Inf.	6 days

COUNTY OF HICKMAN, STATE OF TENNESSEE.

PAGE NO. 402 PERSONS WHO DIED DURING THE YEAR ENDING 1st JUNE, 1850.

Edwin M. Baird

No. of Visit	Name	Age	Sex	Color	Free or Slave	Married/Widowed	Place of Birth	Month Died	Occupation	Disease or Cause of Death	No. Days Ill
1	William G. Reed	30	M				Tenn	March	Carpenter	C	30 days
2	Rebecca Prince	55	F				S.C.	April		unknown	17 days
3	Infant	1m	F				Tenn	May		unknown	1 day
4	Mary Simmons	15	F				Tenn	Jan		T. fever	13 days
5	Priscilla Aydlott	1m	F				Tenn	July		unknown	sudden
6	Infant	1m	M				Tenn	Oct		unknown	sudden
7	Clarke	9m	M	B	S		Miss	July		unknown	8 days
8	Susan Richards	3	F				Tenn	Sept		T. fever	10 days
9	Roena	13	F	B	S		Tenn	March		Scrofula	12 days
10	Infant	4m	M	B	S		Tenn	March		unknown	sudden
11	Elizabeth Roberts	12	F				Tenn	May		unknown	2 days
12	John Roberts	7	M				Tenn	May		T. fever	15 days
13	Vanburen George	19	M				Tenn	Oct	Farmer	T. fever	15 days
14	Hardin Williams	11	M				Tenn	Oct		Dropsy	40 days
15	Armsted Alderson	33	M			M	Tenn	Oct	Farmer	Congestive fever	8 days
16	Juda	10m	F	B	S		Tenn	Oct		Croup	7 days
17	Hezekiah Ross	25	M				Kentucky	April	Farmer	Cholera	2 days
18	George Clymer	49	M				N.C.	Feb	Laborer	C	3 days
19	William Bird	61	M			M	Tenn	May	none	Rheumatism	4 days
20	Susan McClannahan	7	F				Tenn	Nov		Whooping cough	20 days
21	Johnny McClannahan	1	M				Tenn	Oct		Burn	8 days
22	Infant	1m	M				Tenn	Aug		unknown	sudden
23	Infant	1m	M				Tenn	June		unknown	sudden
24	Bersana Walker	1m	F				Tenn	March		unknown	sudden
25	Bird Easley	3m	M				Tenn	Jan		Inflamation of brain	40 days
26	Emily Easley	10	F				Tenn	Aug		Sc. fever	8 days
27	Seborn Grunnett	20	M				Tenn	July	Farmer	Congestive fever	5 days
28	Sarah P. Lovelace	9m	F				Tenn	Dec		Inflamation of brain	4 days
29	Infant	1m	F				Tenn	Sept		unknown	sudden
30	Infant	1m	F				Tenn	Sept		unknown	sudden
31	Matilda	27	F	B	S		Tenn	Dec		Burn	12 days
32	Green	1	M	B	S		Tenn	Dec		Burn	10 days
33	Philis	45	F	B	S		Tenn	Feb		Cold	42 days
34	Rebecca C. Primm	1m	F				Tenn	April		unknown	sudden
35	George W. Horton	5	M				Tenn	March		Fits	5 days

COUNTY OF HUMPHREY, STATE OF TENNESSEE.

PAGE NO. 403   PERSONS WHO DIED DURING THE YEAR ENDING 1st JUNE, 1850.

A. J. Saunders

No. of Visit	Name	Age	Sex	Color	Free or Slave	Married/Widowed	Place of Birth	Month Died	Occupation	Disease or Cause of Death	No. Days Ill
1	James W. Owens	5m	M				Tenn	April		H. Pleurisy	11 days
2	John W. Crockett	2	M				Tenn	Aug		Fits	½ day
3	Philip Luten	26	M			M	Tenn	Aug	Farmer	Fever	7 days
4	George	16	M	B	S		Tenn	Jan		W. fever	21 days
5	Wesley	7	M	B	S		Tenn	May		Pleurisy	8 days
6	Freeman Yates	40	M				N.C.	Oct	Grocer	Consumption	6 months

Remarks: The above is a complete return of all the persons who died in the year ending 1st June 1850, as enumerated by me, in the County of Humphrey, State of Tennessee, amounting to 76 souls.   A. J. Saunders, Asst. Marshal.

COUNTY OF HUMPHREY, STATE OF TENNESSEE.

PAGE NO. 405   PERSONS WHO DIED DURING THE YEAR ENDING 1st JUNE, 1850.

A. J. Saunders

No. of Visit	Name	Age	Sex	Color	Free or Slave	Married/Widowed	Place of Birth	Month Died	Occupation	Disease or Cause of Death	No. Days Ill
1	Martha Larkins	1	F				Tenn	Oct		Scald	1 week
2	James H. Pearce	1	M				Tenn	Dec		Dropsy of brain	3 weeks
3	William Mayfield	45	M				unknown	March	Boatsman	Bil. Cholic	4 weeks
4	John Miller	43	M				Tenn	Oct	Idiotic	unknown	Chronic
5	Sarah Kirkland	28	F			M	Tenn	Aug		Child birth	2 days
6	Joseph	13d	M	B	S		Tenn	Jan		Bold hives	8 days
7	Hiram B. Traylor	39	M			M	Tenn	May	Farmer	Consumption	12 months
8	Viley Cooley	11	F				Tenn	Nov		Fever	2 weeks
9	Rebecca Cooley	20	F				Tenn	Aug		T. fever	11 days
10	Sebourn Cooley	19	M				Tenn	Sept	Farmer	T. fever	33 days
11	Joseph Hooper	73	M			M	unknown	Sept	Farmer	Old age	
12	Rachael	19	F	B	S		Tenn	Nov		T. fever	3 weeks
13	J. T. Turner	10m	M				Tenn	March		Inflamation of bowels	6 days
14	Jane Hudson	25	F			M	Tenn	Nov		Palsy	Chronic
15	Elizabeth Hudson	65	F			M	Va	Nov		Dropsy	12 months
16	Mary	3	F	B	S		Tenn	Nov		T. fever	4 weeks
17	Netty	5m	F	B	S		Tenn	Nov		Fits	3 days
18	Robert	22	M	B	S		Tenn	Aug		Killed, fray	
19	John Mathews	5	M				Tenn	April		Killed by horse	
20	Lucinda Pain	50	F			M	Va	Nov		L. complaint	3 months
21	Joel Ridens	51	M			M	N.C.	April	Farmer	Drowned	
22	Isabel Rushing	53	F			W	N.C.	June		Cancer	6 months
23	C. O'Barr	4	M				Tenn	April		Worms	10 days
24	Babe, Collier	5m	M				Tenn	Aug		B. complaint	7 days
25	Samuel Self	73	M			W	Va	Jan	Farmer	Dropsy	22 days
26	F. Ross	32	M				N.C.	Feb	Farmer	Consumption	2 months
27	William Cimbrod	1	M				Tenn	Jan		Winter fever	2 weeks
28	Minor Curtis	20	M				Tenn	March	Farmer	Diarrhea	1 week
29	John Crafton	1	M				Tenn	Aug		Hives	2 days
30	C. A. Watts	10	M				Kentucky	Dec		Quinsy	7 days
31	Nicy Ann Watts	13	F				Tenn	Jan		C. chills	4 days
32	John W. Crockett	2	M				Tenn	Aug		Fits	½ day
33	H. O. Donloe	52	M			W	Va	Aug	Farmer	P. sore throat	5 weeks
34	John	1	M	B	S		Tenn	June		Fever	4 days
35	Lee Hendrix	25	M			M	Tenn	Nov	Farmer	unknown	6 weeks

COUNTY OF HUMPHREY, STATE OF TENNESSEE.

PAGE NO. 408 PERSONS WHO DIED DURING THE YEAR ENDING 1st JUNE, 1850.

A. J. Saunders

No. of Visit	Name	Age	Sex	Color	Free or Slave	Married/Widowed	Place of Birth	Month Died	Occupation	Disease or Cause of Death	No. Days Ill
1	Joel Smith	64	M			M	N.C.	July	Farmer	Liver complaint	7 weeks
2	Rosa	70	F	B	S		Va	Oct		Dropsy of head	3 weeks
3	Isaac Ray	55	M			M	S.C.	Nov	Farmer	Spider bitten	9 days
4	Michael McInroe	11m	M				Tenn	June		Fever	7 days
5	William Kirkland	6m	M				Tenn	April		Bold hives	sudden
6	H. H. Washbourn	50	M			M	Tenn	July	Wheelwright	Liver complaint	4 months
7	Roger	80	M	B	S	M	Va	Jan		Old age	
8	Felix	2	M	M	S		Tenn	March		Inflamation of brain	7
9	George Saunders	9m	M				Tenn	May		Worms	4 days
10	David Russell	1	M				Tenn	Nov		Inflamation of bowels	10 days
11	Elizabeth Spann	74	F			W	Va	July		Diarrhea	10 days
12	Leamond Bivens	28	M				Tenn	June	none	Dropsy	Chronic
13	Susan Binkley	7	F				Tenn	Aug		Inflamation of brain	4 days
14	Freedona Beasley	8d	F				Tenn	Feb		Croup	2 days
15	Martha Ellis	16	F				Tenn	Dec		Paralysis	5 months
16	Narcissa White	2	F				Tenn	March		Consumption	Chronic
17	Sarah Hobbs	16d	F				Tenn	March		Fits	16 days
18	Polly	32	F	B	S		Tenn	Feb		Child bed	3 months
19	Jack	17	M	B	S		Tenn	Feb		Consumption	6 weeks
20	William Reeves	35	M			M	Tenn	Feb	Farmer	Cold	1 month
21	Samuel Dunlap	27	M			M	Tenn	Dec	Farmer	Cholera	2 days
22	James Fortner	9m	M				Tenn	Oct		Inflamation of lungs	2 months
23	John	2m	M	B	S		Tenn	Oct		unknown	2 weeks
24	Lewis	3m	M	B	S		Tenn	Nov		Bold hives	sudden
25	Isaac Jackson	17w	M				Tenn	Nov		Bold hives	4 days
26	Thomas McMurtry	6	M				Tenn	Sept		Fever	3 days
27	William McMurtry	1	M				Tenn	Sept		Fever	2 days
28	William Brody	21	M				Tenn	April	Laborer	P. sore throat	2 weeks
29	Erastus Simmons	7	M				Tenn	May		Sc. fever	2 days
30	Pitman Simmons	4	M				Tenn	May		Sc. fever	16 days
31	Henry Simmons	1	M				Tenn	June		Sc. fever	28 days
32	Erasmus King	3	M				Tenn	July		Sc. fever	sudden
33	Richard Terrald	53	M			M	Va	Fev	Sch-teacher	Apoplexy	sudden
34	John Smith	32	M			M	Tenn	March	Farmer	Winter fever	10 days
35	Elvira	16	F	B	S		Tenn	May		Consumption	3 weeks

COUNTY OF JACKSON, STATE OF TENNESSEE.

PAGE NO. 409 PERSONS WHO DIED DURING THE YEAR ENDING 1st JUNE, 1850.

Civil District No. 10
James R. Kerr

No. of Visit	Name	Age	Sex	Color	Free or Slave	Married/Widowed	Place of Birth	Month Died	Occupation	Disease or Cause of Death	No. Days Ill
1	Frances J. Burton	11	F				Tenn	Dec		Fever	9 days
2	Sarah E. Huddleston	17	F				Tenn	Jan		unknown	30 days
3	Marth(a) Clinton	1m	F				Tenn	Oct		unknown	3 days
4	Milly M. Brown	1	F				Tenn	Jan		Fever	12 days
5	Sarah J. Erwin	24	F				Tenn	May		Dropsy	35 days
6	Joseph Brown	31	M			M	Tenn	Feb	Farmer	Fever	45 days
7	Edward Anderson	6	M				Tenn	Aug		Fever	3 weeks
8	Sarah Hale	20	F				Tenn	May		Fever	3 weeks
9	Ann	4m	F	M	S		Tenn	March		Croup	1 day
10	Marena Hughs	29	F			M	Tenn	April		Consumption	3 months
11	Anna M. Brown	3m	F				Tenn	Sept		Fever	8 days
12	Jane Boyd	1m	F				Tenn	Aug		Croup	20 days
13	Elizabeth Sanger	6m	F				Tenn	Jan		unknown	2 weeks
14	John F. Reed	1	M				Tenn	Jan		Inflamation	14 days
15	George Medley	55	M			M	Va	Jan	Farmer	unknown	sudden
16	Carroll Brown	10m	M				Tenn	Sept		Fever	3 days
17	William Odom	3	M				Tenn	Sept		Worms	14 days
18	Wiley Fann	50	M			M	unknown	Sept	Farmer	Dropsy	8 weeks
19	Benjamin Brown	65	M			M	Tenn	Sept	Farmer	Cramp Cholic	7 days
20	Martha Allcorn	17	F				Tenn	Dec		--illegible--	4 weeks
21	Sarah K. McCalup	6m	F				Tenn	Feb		Croup	sudden
22	John Ellet	8	M				Tenn	April		Fever	4 days
23	Mary Ellet	4	F				Tenn	May		Fever	4 days
24	Rolan Madden	3	M				Tenn	Oct		Fever	3 days
25	Ann Madden	5	F				Tenn	Oct		Fever	3 days
26	Margaret Cooke	58	F			M	S.C.	Dec		Pleurisy	12 days
27	Henry Harpool	64	M			M	Maryland	Aug		Fever	17 days
28	Caroline L. Terry	9	F				Tenn	Nov		Fever	9 days
29	Sarah E. Carrolton	6	F				Tenn	Dec		Fever	4 days
30	Jackson Carrolton	3	M				Tenn	Sept		Fever	3 days
31	Nancy Sims	13	F				Tenn	Oct		Fever	20 days
32	Carroll D. Sims	4	M				Tenn	March		Accident	sudden
33	William Terry	28	M			M	Tenn	Nov	Farmer	Cholera	sudden
34	Elizabeth Terry	6	F				Tenn	Nov		Cholera	sudden
35	Mabery T. Hale	24	M			M	Tenn	Jan	Farmer	Consumption	5 months

COUNTY OF JACKSON, STATE OF TENNESSEE.

PAGE NO. 412 PERSONS WHO DIED DURING THE YEAR ENDING 1st JUNE, 1850.

Civil District No. 10
James R. Kerr

No. of Visit	Name	Age	Sex	Color	Free or Slave	Married/Widowed	Place of Birth	Month Died	Occupation	Disease or Cause of Death	No. Days Ill
1	Daniel E. Tesdel	1	M				Tenn	Aug		Croup	14 days
2	Mary Harpool	1m	F				Tenn	Oct		unknown	10 days
3	Lucinda Anderson	31	F			W	Tenn	Oct		Fever	28 days
4	Jesse Mansel	43	M			M	Tenn	May	Farmer	Consumption	21 days
5	Walter Evans	74	M			W	Tenn	July	none	Old age	4 months
6	Samuel Baker	77	M			M	Va	Oct	none	Old age	7 days
7	Jonathan Bennett	26	M				Tenn	Jan	Farmer	Consumption	3 months
8	Selina McDaniel	8	F				Tenn	Nov		Cold	4 months
9	Martha E. Grisham	3	F				Tenn	Dec		Fever	14 days
10	Altamery F. Young	10m	F				Tenn	May		unknown	7 days
11	Armstrong A. Bush	2	M				Tenn	June		Inflamation	8 days
12	Elizabeth E. Williamson	1	F				Tenn	Aug		Inflamation	8 days
13	Red Pippen	1m	M				Tenn	March		Croup	3 days
14	David Harboard	83	M			W	Va	Aug	none	Cancer	30 days
15	Robert Shadon	50	M			W	Va	July	none	Palsy	3 days

COUNTY OF JACKSON, STATE OF TENNESSEE.

PAGE NO. 412 PERSONS WHO DIED DURING THE YEAR ENDING 1st JUNE, 1850.

Civil District No. 10
James R. Kerr

No. of Visit	Name	Age	Sex	Color	Free or Slave	Married/Widowed	Place of Birth	Month Died	Occupation	Disease or Cause of Death	No. Days Ill
16	Catharine Stevens	1m	F				Tenn	Nov		Croup	7 days
17	James Carter	74	M				Va	Oct	Physician		
18	Pheby	40	M	B	S		Tenn	Sept		Child birth	sudden
19	Allis McKindley	2	F				Tenn	Jan		Fever	7 days
20	Lucinda Wade	22	F			M	Tenn	May		Consumption	3 months
21	Elvina S. Slaughter	15	F				Tenn	Feb		Dropsy	2 months
22	Amanda Morgan	8m	F				Tenn	May		Croup	4 days
23	Jane Caver	29	F				Tenn	April		--illegible--	1 day
24	Jasper Bryant	7	M				Tenn	April		Fever	7 days
25	Matilda Bryant	5	F				Tenn	April		Fever	11 days
26	Nash	12	M	B	S		Tenn	Jan		Dropsy	3 months
27	Welran	45	M	B	S		Tenn	Nov		Bleeding	5 months
28	Barbry Serca	1	F				Tenn	Nov		unknown	14 days
29	Margaret Sercy	21	F			M	Tenn	July		Mis-carriage	2 days
30	Nancy Phillips	1m	F				Tenn	Aug		Croup	2 days
31	Mary Duke	3	F				Tenn	Jan		Inflamation	7 days
32	Elizabeth Browning	27	F			M	Tenn	Feb		--illegible--	4 months
33	James D. Smith	51	M			W	N.C.	April	Farmer	Consumption	4 months
34	William	10	M	B	S		Tenn	May		Consumption	2 months
35	Rose	12	F	B	S		Tenn	Feb		Sc. fever	3 days

COUNTY OF JACKSON, STATE OF TENNESSEE.

PAGE NO. 413 PERSONS WHO DIED DURING THE YEAR ENDING 1st JUNE, 1850.

Civil District No. 11
James R. Kerr

No. of Visit	Name	Age	Sex	Color	Free or Slave	Married/Widowed	Place of Birth	Month Died	Occupation	Disease or Cause of Death	No. Days Ill
1	Burrel L. Wright	1	M				Tenn	Oct		Inflamation	10 days
2	Elisa Spurlock	50	F			M	Kentucky	May		Consumption	4 months
3	John Brown	9m	M				Tenn	Oct		Sc. fever	14 days
4	Nancy Smith	8m	F				Tenn	Nov		Fever	28 days
5	Polly A. Duncan	4	F				Kentucky	Sept		Fever	21 days
6	Jesse McClelen	77	M			M	N.C.	May	Farmer	Old age	21 days
7	John R. Stout	1m	M				Tenn	May		Croup	2 days
8	Mary J. Tacket	22	F				Tenn	Jan		Spleen	1 year

COUNTY OF JACKSON, STATE OF TENNESSEE.

PAGE NO. 415 PERSONS WHO DIED DURING THE YEAR ENDING 1st JUNE, 1850.

Civil District No. 1 & 17
A. H. Morgan

No. of Visit	Name	Age	Sex	Color	Free or Slave	Married/Widowed	Place of Birth	Month Died	Occupation	Disease or Cause of Death	No. Days Ill
1	James S. Smith	35	M			M	Tenn	March	Farmer	Congestive fever	6 days
2	Samuel T. Smith	5m	M				Tenn	March		Congestive fever	
3	Jemima Richard	56	F			W	N.C.	Sept		Diarrhea	15 days
4	John Armer	101	M			M	N.C.	Jan	Farmer	Old age	sudden
5	Mary Clements	45	F			M	Tenn	Sept		Fever	9 days
6	Missouri Stith	3	F				Tenn	Dec		Fever	8 days
7	Martha J. Keeth	11	F				Tenn	April		Congestive fever	
8	Jesse Vinson	58	M			M	N.C.	Feb		Consumption	6 days
9	Martha Vinson	50	F			M	N.C.	March		Diarrhea	12 days
10	Elizabeth Comer	23	F			M	Tenn	Aug		Congestive fever	5 days
11	Simpson Skipworth	1m	M				Tenn	April		Smothered in bed	

Remarks: I have made a mark thus + opposite the name of each person that has died since June 1850. There was some 14 deaths with cholera in July last in Gainston (Gainesboro) or in the vicinity of the Town. It is a hard matter to know what disease was the cause of several deaths. November the 13th, 1850.
A. H. Morgan.

(NOTE: The margin in which the enumerator put his mark thus +, was not on the micro-film. Eds.)

COUNTY OF JACKSON, STATE OF TENNESSEE.

PAGE NO. 417 PERSONS WHO DIED DURING THE YEAR ENDING 1st JUNE, 1850.

Civil District No. 1 & 17
A. H. Morgan

No. of Visit	Name	Age	Sex	Color	Free or Slave	Married/Widowed	Place of Birth	Month Died	Occupation	Disease or Cause of Death	No. Days Ill
1	Nancy Stafford	24	F			M	Tenn	Feb		Consumption	C
2	Simeon H. Hail	1	M				Tenn	Oct		Croup	22 days
3	Sarah Carlisle	1m	F				Tenn	Jan		unknown	1 day
4	Sarah Stafford	21	F			M	Tenn	May		Child bed fever	
5	Mary Stafford	1m	F				Tenn	May		unknown	15 days
6	Joseph Stafford	3m	M				Tenn	Dec		unknown	1 day
7	Sarah Stafford	7	F				Tenn	April		Sc. fever	3 days
8	Sarah Winneham	20	F			M	Tenn	Jan		Consumption	C
9	Nancy Patton	20	F				Tenn	June		Fever	10 days
10	William Right	30	M				N.C.	July	Farmer	Fever	15 days
11	Susanna Murry	66	F				N.C.	Sept		Female disease	C
12	James Handcock	76	M			W	S.C.	March	Farmer	Dropsy	C
13	Sarah Buckhannon	5	F				N.C.	July		Ricketts	6 days
14	Edward Walker	54	M			M	Kentucky	March	Blk-smith	Drowned	sudden
15	Sally Hall	40	F			M	Tenn	July		Consumption	C
16	Jane Smith	1m	F				Tenn	Jan		--illegible--	1 day
17	Sally Carlisle	28	F			M	Tenn	May		Consumption	C
18	Zurelda Sadler	29	F			M	Tenn	Sept		Consumption	C
19	Martha A. Flin	12	F				Tenn	March		Fever	3 days
20	Sarah Carlisle	27	F			M	Tenn	March		Consumption	C
21	Elizabeth Carlisle	5	F				Tenn	Feb		Winter fever	20 days
22	Burnettie Carlisle	1m	F				Tenn	March		unknown	8 days
23	Jesse Gentry	70	M			M	N.C.	May		Consumption	C
24	Clarenda Maberry	20	F			M	Tenn	April		Child bed fever	
25	Celina B. Hicks	1	F				Tenn	March		Sc. fever	2 days
26	Edward E. Mehanay	1	M				Tenn	Aug		Sc. fever	10 days
27	Ruben Gentry	3	M				Tenn	April		Sc. fever	8 days
28	William Davidson, slave	60	M	B	S		N.C.	Feb		Dumb Palsy	90 days
29	Alice Chilton	1	F				Tenn	April		unknown	3 days
30	John Perry	1	M		S		Tenn	April		Croup	15 days
31	Burton, a slave	1	M		S		Tenn	July		Teething	20 days

COUNTY OF JACKSON, STATE OF TENNESSEE.

PAGE NO. 417   PERSONS WHO DIED DURING THE YEAR ENDING 1st JUNE, 1850.

Civil District No. 1 & 17
A. H. Morgan

No. of Visit	Name	Age	Sex	Color	Free or Slave	Married/Widowed	Place of Birth	Month Died	Occupation	Disease or Cause of Death	No. Days Ill
32	Eliza Caderage	37	F			M	Tenn	Feb		unknown	40 days
33	Elizabeth Quarles	22	F			M	Tenn	March		Child bed fever	
34	Esther J. Sizemore	20	F			M	Tenn	April		fever	6 days
35	Sally A. Manard	7	F				Tenn	Sept		Chills	

Remarks: You see from this list the most of the deaths was females and the most of them was at or in a short time after delivery. This portion of Jackson County, very broken and not convenient to a "Doctor", is one reason why there was so many deaths among the female, though we have had two very healthy seasons in this portion of Jackson County. We have some cholera in this County.

COUNTY OF JACKSON, STATE OF TENNESSEE.

PAGE NO. 420   PERSONS WHO DIED DURING THE YEAR ENDING 1st JUNE, 1850.

Civil District No. 1 & 17
A. H. Morgan

No. of Visit	Name	Age	Sex	Color	Free or Slave	Married/Widowed	Place of Birth	Month Died	Occupation	Disease or Cause of Death	No. Days Ill
1	Robert Manard	3	M				Tenn	Oct		Fits	sudden
2	Anna Burris	59	F			M	S.C.	Aug		Consumption	
3	Rhoda, slave	6m	F	B			Tenn	March		Croup	3 hours
4	Sarah Long	1	F				Tenn	Aug		Flux	4 days
5	Malinda Scisco	1	F				Tenn	June		Flux	8 days
6	Martha Sittings	7	F				Tenn	Jan		Pleurisy	1 day
7	Eliza Purcell	15	F				Tenn	May		Congestive fever	1 day
8	Artemace Lovelady	4m	F				Tenn	April		Croup	1 day
9	Nancy Purcell	14	F				Tenn	April		sudden	1 day
10	Mahala Scisco	9m	F				Tenn			Croup	1 day
11	Susanna Parrish	2	F				Tenn	July		Flux	9 days
12	James Proctor	10	M				Tenn	May		Congestive fever	8 days
13	Katharine Fagg	35	F			M	Tenn	May		Delivery	12 hours
14	Telitha Wilson	22	F				Tenn	June		Consumption	6 days
15	Elizabeth Hail	25	F			M	Kentucky	Nov		Consumption	C
16	William McCaughan	7	M				Tenn	Jan		unknown	22 days
17	Hannor,	70	F		S		N.C.	May		Consumption	C
18	Moses	4m	M		S		Tenn	June		unknown	C
19	William Mastress	35	M			M	Tenn	Jan	Farmer	Consumption	C
20	Margara Mastress	15	F			M	Tenn	Dec		Consumption	C
21	Elizabeth Mastress	1m	F				Tenn	Jan		Consumption	5 days
22	Cyntha McCarver	45	F			M	N.C.	Aug		Apoplexy	1 day
23	Benjamin Whitehead	63	M			M	Va	June		Pleurisy	1 day
24	Zachariah Martin	2	M				Tenn	July		Croup	½ day
25	Hillery Martin	9	M				Tenn	Dec		Diarrhea	15 days
26	Jefferson P. Roberts	4m	M				Tenn	Jan		King's evil	60 days
27	Michael Stocton	42	M		S		N.C.	March		Colera	C
28	Polly Meirath	60	F				Va	June		Cholera	1 day
29	Charles Davis	37	M				N.C.	March	Farmer	Cholera	1 day
30	Hugh Roberts	15	M				Tenn	Feb		unknown	1 day
31	Squire Block	7m	M		S		Tenn	April		Croup	18 days
32	James S. Smith	33	M			M	Tenn	March		Consumption	C
33	Sarah Hughes	4	F				Tenn	Oct		Burn to death	
34	James Burdwell	73	M			M	N.C.	Feb		Consumption	C
35	John Fredrick	65	M				Va	Aug		unknown	C

COUNTY OF JACKSON, STATE OF TENNESSEE.

PAGE NO. 420   PERSONS WHO DIED DURING THE YEAR ENDING 1st JUNE, 1850.

Civil District No. 1 & 17
A. H. Morgan

No. of Visit	Name	Age	Sex	Color	Free or Slave	Married/Widowed	Place of Birth	Month Died	Occupation	Disease or Cause of Death	No. Days Ill

Remarks: I have been careful to point out the number and case of deaths and the number that died. It will be and is strange how many more females died in 1849 and the most of the females on delivery or in a short time after in the bounds. I took, there has been some 50 deaths since June 1850 on the 17th July the cholera broke out in Gainsboro and there was some 14 deaths there.

COUNTY OF JEFFERSON, STATE OF TENNESSEE.

PAGE NO. 421   PERSONS WHO DIED DURING THE YEAR ENDING 1st JUNE, 1850.

Civil District No. 13
James Baker

No. of Visit	Name	Age	Sex	Color	Free or Slave	Married/Widowed	Place of Birth	Month Died	Occupation	Disease or Cause of Death	No. Days Ill
1	Lucy	28	F	B	S		Tenn	May		Cold	6 days
2	John Griffin	49	M			M	Va	April	Hse-carpenter	Pneumonia	9 days
3	Harriet McDaniel	17	F				Tenn	Aug		Bil. fever	28 days
4	Sevina Jones	25	F			M	Tenn	April		Bil. fever	35 days
5	Susan	30	F	B	S		Va	April		Child bed	2 days
6	Benjamin	13	M	B	S		Va	May		Fever	21 days
7	Samuel Lackey	30	M			M	Tenn	April	Laborer	Pneumonia	5 days
8	George Weaver	71	M			W	Penn	June	Farmer	Dropsy	150 days
9	Nancy J. Hann	1m	F				Tenn	Dec		Erysipelas	18 days
10	George W. Linch	14	M				Tenn	May		Pal. of heart	150 days
11	William Kirkpatrick	43	M			M	Tenn	March	Farmer	Liver	8 days
12	Elizabeth Stipling	63	F			W	S.C.	July		Paralysis	Chronic
13	John Watkins	65	M			W	Va	Sept	Laborer	Fever	16 days
14	John Sawyers	24	M			M	Tenn	July	Hse-carpenter	Fever	9 days
15	William Austin	73	M			M	S.C.	Dec	Farmer	Fever	14 days
16	Alexander	30	M	B	S		Tenn	Sept		Fever	4 days
17	William Henderson	59	M			M	unknown	Aug	Farmer	Fever	14 days
18	Joel W. Cowen	54	M			M	Tenn	May	Farmer	Fever	2 days
19	James Brown	11	M				S.C.	Dec		Chronic	
20	Barbary Brimer	55	F			M	Va	April		Dyspepsia	35 days
21	Abel McCarter	60	M			M	N.C.	March	Laborer	Chills	150 days
22	Henry Chamber	60	M			W	S.C.	March	Laborer	Piles	60 days
23	Ann Linzy	80	F			W	Va	April		Sore leg	10 days
24	Casey Baker	5	F				Tenn	Feb		Cholera inf.	2 days
25	Martha A. Carman	4	F				Tenn	Feb		Fever	6 days
26	Margaret A. Thomas	20	F				Tenn	Nov		Cold	21 days
27	Tabitha	45	F	B	S		unknown	Sept		Chronic	
28	Elizabeth Elmore	62	F				N.C.	Feb		Chronic	
29	Frederic Snider	55	M			M	Maryland	Feb	Sch-teacher	T. fever	5 days
30	Robert McSpadden	9	M				Tenn	April		Fever	13 days
31	Lettitia Gawt	81	F			W	Penn	Oct		Palsy	150 days
32	Duke Kimbrough	87	M			M	Va	Sept	Clergy,M.B.	Cholera	150 days
33	Cyndrilla Caldwell	5	F				Tenn	April		Croup	10 days
34	Jane Hammond	24	F				Tenn	Feb		Consumption	180 days
35	Nancy Stone	25	F			M	Tenn	Nov		Child bed	1 day

Remarks: In my District or County, the most prevailing disease is intermitttent fever, which doubtless is owning to malaria arising from the decay of vegetable matter as well as stagnent sinks of water which are to be found interpsersed generally over the whole surface of the country. Occasionally, we have fevers of a very malignant character. Partaking (continued),...

COUNTY OF JEFFERSON, STATE OF TENNESSEE.

PAGE NO. 424 PERSONS WHO DIED DURING THE YEAR ENDING 1st JUNE, 1850.

Civil District No. 13
James Baker

No. of Visit	Name	Age	Sex	Color	Free or Slave	Married/Widowed	Place of Birth	Month Died	Occupation	Disease or Cause of Death	No. Days Ill
1	Eliza Hogan	60	F				N.C.	Sept		Fever	12 days
2	Lettitia McBride	75	F			W	N.C.	Oct		Chronic	
3	Henry Davis	63	M			M	Va	Feb	Farmer	Inflamation of bowels	9 days
4	Elvira Chandler	19	F			M	S.C.	May		Child bed	2 days
5	John Dunwoody	57	M			M	Tenn	Sept	Farmer	Fever	9 days
6	Aaron R. Lewis	3	M				Tenn	Oct		Croup	3 days
7	Preston	25	M	B	S		Va	March		Pneumonia	14 days
8	Samuel C. Waters	18	M				Tenn	Sept	Laborer	Fever	18 days
9	Mary	8m	F				Tenn	Feb		Scalded	4 days
10	Thomas Shephard	8m	M				Tenn	unknown		Croup	2 days
11	Gibson	9m	M	B	S		Tenn	Feb		Pneumonia	12 days
12	John G. Bewly	31	M			M	Tenn	Feb	Law	Dyspepsia	90 days
13	Ellen Yokely	7	F				Tenn	May		Worms	5 days
14	Richard White	59	M			M	Tenn	Oct	Farmer	Chronic	
15	Curtis	3m	M	M	S		Tenn	Sept		unknown	5 days
16	Agi	55	F	B	S		unknown	Sept		Fever	10 days
17	Mary	17	F	B	S		N.C.	Oct		Fever	30 days
18	James D. Dedrick	1m	M				Tenn	April		Croup	2 days
19	George Witt	55	M			M	Va	Aug	Farmer	Cholera mor.	40 days
20	Joseph	2	M	B	S		Tenn	Feb		Dropsy	28 days
21	Nancy A. Cooper	1	F				Tenn	June		Cholera inf.	5 days
22	Joseph Williams	22	M				Tenn	July	Farmer	Bil. fever	14 days
23	John E. Fane	8m	M				Tenn	Sept		Croup	8 days
24	John B. Renion	5m	M				Tenn	Jan		Chills	3 days
25	Anna Elliott	70	F			W	Maryland	Sept		Old age	
26	James Love	1	M				Tenn	Oct		Croup	9 days
27	James Scruggs	56	M			M	Tenn	May	Farmer	Chronic	
28	Thomas Haynes	50	M			M	Tenn	Aug	Shoemaker	Breast complaint	150 days
29	Moses	1m	M				Tenn	Oct		Croup	8 days
30	James D. Chandler	1	M				Tenn	Oct		Chill	10 days
31	William E. Henderson	1	M				Tenn	Jan		Burned	5 days
32	Abraham Sunderland	66	M			M	Va	Nov	Farmer	Accident	
33	Allens Brown	1da	M				Tenn	July		unknown	
34	Hannah Parsley	11m	F				Tenn	July		Diarrhea	30 days
35	Alice	11m	F				Tenn	Aug		Diarrhea	50 days

Remarks: (continued) of the pneumonia and typhoid type, which almost universally proves fatal. We have a variety of water, such as limestone, black and white sulphur and chalybeate, all of considerable purity. We have the limestone which produces us any quality of lime as a fertilizer of our soil. As to ores, we have some lead and (continued)......

COUNTY OF JEFFERSON, STATE OF TENNESSEE.

PAGE NO. 425 PERSONS WHO DIED DURING THE YEAR ENDING 1st JUNE, 1850.

Civil District No. 13
James Baker

No. of Visit	Name	Age	Sex	Color	Free or Slave	Married/Widowed	Place of Birth	Month Died	Occupation	Disease or Cause of Death	No. Days Ill
1	Philip M. Hodge	12	M				Tenn	March		unknown	5 days
2	Samuel Carson	82	M			W	Va	March	Farmer	Plen.	12 days
3	Jesse Neal	70	M			W	Va	March	Farmer	Consumption	20 years
4	Joseph H. Peck	27	M				Tenn	Dec	Clergy, M.E.	Pulmonary	3 months
5	Phillis	40	F	B	S		Tenn	May		unknown	35 days
6	James H. Goss	47	M			M	Tenn	Feb	Clergy,P.N.S.	Pulmonary	35 days
7	Charlott Howel	5	F				Tenn	Sept		Sore throat	7 days
8	Wilson Orr	63	M			M	Va	April	Farmer	Fever	11 days
9	Margaret Skane	20	F			M	Tenn	April		Cold	10 days
10	Julia A. Moor	35	F			M	Tenn	May		--illegible--	12 months
11	Sarah Moses	72	F			W	Penn	July		Chills	28 days
12	Seth Rogers	45	M			M	Tenn	May	Farmer	Fever	15 days
13	James Cupp	30	M			M	Tenn	Oct	Laborer	Consumption	12 months
14	Mary Miles	35	F			M	Tenn	April		Consumption	6 months
15	Catharine Crider	85	F			W	Va	July		Old age	
16	John Carson	76	M			M	Va	Feb	Farmer	Old age	
17	Rebecca Morris	62	F			W	S.C.	Oct		Dropsy	3 months
18	Phillis	85	F	B	S		unknown	April		Old age	
19	Spence Watkins	99	M			M	Va	Sept	Wheel wright	Old age	
20	William P. Jones	47	M			M	Tenn	Feb	Merchant	Pneumonia	8 days
21	Manda	20	F	B	S		Tenn	March		Pneumonia	28 days
22	Calvin	9m	M	B	S		Tenn	Aug		Chills	2 days
23	Sarah	3m	F	B	S		Tenn	Oct		unknown	2 days
24	William	1m	M	B	S		Tenn	April		unknown	1 day
25	James H. Jones	47	M			M	Tenn	July	Merchant	Pulmonary	3 months
26	Peter	38	M	B	S		Tenn	April		Pulmonary	14 days
27	John Dickey	1	M				Tenn	March		unknown	2 days

Remarks: (continued) iron, but perhaps not in sufficient quantities to justify manufacturies for these. Our soil, especially upon the rivers, are of an alluvial character and very productive. Our uplands are of clay substratum, and also productive and capable of being made very fertile. Our winters are long and severe and our springs, consequently late, but our summers are very warm and congeniel to the rapid growth of vegetation. As to natural phenomenia, we have known which deserves a notice, except one or two extensive caves which abound in a good many curious deposite interesting doubtley to mineralogist and others engaged in investegating the curiosities of nature. We have every variety of timber, pine, oak, chestnut and poplar, with almost every growth common to any country and abounding in large quantities. Upon the whole, we have a county abounding in natural resourses of every character which only need industry and capital to fully develope them.

James Baker, Asst. Marshal
13th District, Jefferson County.

COUNTY OF JOHNSON, STATE OF TENNESSEE.

PAGE NO. 427 PERSONS WHO DIED DURING THE YEAR ENDING 1st JUNE, 1850.

Alexander D. Smith

No. of Visit	Name	Age	Sex	Color	Free or Slave	Married/Widowed	Place of Birth	Month Died	Occupation	Disease or Cause of Death	No. Days Ill
1	Orpha Flannagan	19	F			M	Tenn	March	none	Pain in the head	3 months
2	slave of B. Showns	1m	F	M	S		Tenn	March		Hives	sudden
3	Roena A. Duff	1m	F				Tenn	Jan		unknown	sudden
4	William H. Duff	1m	M				Tenn	Jan		unknown	sudden
5	Lewis J. Johnson	4m	M				Tenn	Sept		unknown	2 months
6	_____ Mulwie	1m	F				Tenn	March		unknown	sudden
7	_____ McQueen	1m	M				Tenn	Sept		unknown	sudden
8	Isaac Osborn	52	M			M	N.C.	April	Farmer	T. fever	3 months
9	Sarah Osborn	53	F			W	Tenn	May		unknown	sudden
10	_____ Wilson	1m	F				Tenn	April		Inflamation of bowels	2 weeks
11	Abner Smith	68	M			M	N.C.	May	Farmer	unknown	3 weeks
12	Winna E. Olliver	3	F				N.C.	Sept		Burnt	1 day
13	Dicy Davis	52	F			M	Tenn	Feb	Hse-keeper	Consumption	7 years
14	Daniel Reese	54	M			W	Tenn	Oct	Farmer	unknown	6 months
15	Sarah Brown	3	F				N.C.	April		Whooping cough	8 days
16	_____ Wilson	1m	F				Tenn	Oct		unknown	sudden
17	Nicholas Moreland	21	M			M	Tenn	Jan	Farmer	T. fever	4 weeks
18	Isaac T. Howard	3	M				N.C.	April		Drowned	sudden
19	William B. Howard	2	M				N.C.	April		Drowned	sudden
20	Nancy C. Wagner	2m	F				Tenn	March		Hives	5 days
21	Samuel E. Lewis	2m	M				Tenn	Sept		unknown	1 month
22	Thomas Kidd	18	M				Tenn	March	Hammerman	Nervous fever	1 month
23	Elizabeth Rainbolt	59	F			M	Tenn	Jan		T. fever	10 days
24	Susan	13	F	B	S		Tenn	Sept		T. fever	8 days
25	Anna Burns	76	F			W	N.C.	Nov	Seamstress	Affection of the spine	4 months
26	Slave of Mich. Smithpeter	2	M	B	S		Tenn	April		unknown	2 weeks
27	_____ Loyd	5m	F				Tenn	March		Whooping cough	10 weeks
28	Thomas Rogers	30	M				Tenn	Oct	Farmer	Fever	2 weeks
29	Patterson Sharp	60	M			M	Va	Sept	Co.Register	Bil. fever	2 weeks

Remarks: As most mountainous counties. The principal malad maladies are typhous and billious fevers, pneumonia, bronchitus and rheumatism. The water is abundant, pure and fresh, principally soft interspersed however with a little hard in the (S.W.) Springs are numerous and bold, the features rough and broken, being essentially valley and mountains, the latter are lofty and ragged, with dense forests and a large portion of the ____, the ____ of fogs and mists. The principle stone are the square and cornered and large massive ledges of Mountain rocks, with occasional beds of both red and blue slate, the valleys are low and lie along the streams, which are full of rapids, offering the greatest facilities to water power. The soil of this portion generally alluvial with some bids of marl. The up or hill is primitive, interspersed with clay and occassional beds of limestone. Oak and pine of three varieties.......... hickory, wild cherry, walnut, ash, poplar, buckeye, lynn, sugartree, etc..... The whole country lies high and is envisioned by lofty mountains. communicating with neighboring regions by only ...(in margin, not on film).

COUNTY OF KNOX, STATE OF TENNESSEE.

PAGE NO. 429 PERSONS WHO DIED DURING THE YEAR ENDING 1st JUNE, 1850.

31st Subdivision, East District
S. M. Cammron

No. of Visit	Name	Age	Sex	Color	Free or Slave	Married/Widowed	Place of Birth	Month Died	Occupation	Disease or Cause of Death	No. Days Ill
1	Robert H. Crews	3	M				Tenn	Oct		Fever	40 days
2	Martha J. Brown	2	F				Tenn	May		Croup	1 day
3	Isabella Green	85	F			M	Penn	Nov		Suddenly	
4	Albert Hill	33	M			M	Tenn	Aug	Farmer	Consumption	6 days
5	Infant of Thos. McNutt	5d	M				Tenn	Feb		Croup & Hives	1 day
6	John Cole	72	M			M	N.C.	Aug	Farmer	Dropsy	C
7	Infant of Moses Webb	1d	F				Tenn	March		unknown	sudden
8	Elizabeth Pratt	1d	F				Tenn	Aug		unknown	sudden
9	Sarah McLemore	16	F				Tenn	June		Fever	9 days
10	Adam Like	1	M				Tenn	May		Fever	21 days
11	Mias Wilson	50	F			W	Tenn	May		Consumption	C
12	Jacob Like	1m	M				Tenn	May		Croup	30 days
13	Simes A. Crawford	43	M			M	N.C.	March	Farmer	unknown	3326 days
14	Jane Haggard	42	F			M	Va	March		unknown	2 days
15	Harriett, Wm. Wright's	1	F	B	S		Tenn	Nov		unknown	2 days
16	Jane, Wm. Wright's	1	F	B	S		Tenn	Nov		unknown	2 days
17	Nancy, Wm. Wright's	1	F	B	S		Tenn	Jan		unknown	2 days
18	John Reynolds	67	M			M	N.C.	May	Wagon-mkr	Dropsy	40 days
19	Infant of C. Sheberly	1d	M				Tenn	April		unknown	1 day
20	George Sheberly	46	M			M	Tenn	Aug	Farmer	Bil. diarrhea	8 days
21	Martha Jane Propes	29	F			M	Tenn	May		Dropsy	90 days
22	Stephen Boyd	35	M	B	S		Tenn	June		Pneumonia	14 days
23	Pleasant J. Temple	36	M			M	Louisiana	Jan	Sch-teacher	Fever	56 days
24	John Mabry	1	M	B	S		Tenn	Oct		Croup	1 day
25	Margaret J. Sterling	33	F			M	Tenn	Feb		Consumption	C
26	Silas Scott	71	M			M	Va	Oct	Farmer	unknown	C
27	James H. B. Sherwood	2m	M				Tenn	Oct		Croup	5 days
28	Sarah Wheeler	76	F			W	Va	April		Dropsy	1 day
29	Atlas Story	1m	M				Tenn	July		Croup	1 day
30	Annirva Smith	6	F				Tenn	May		Croup	

Remarks: No particular disease prevailing in the County Knox during the last year. This County is principally limestone water finely watered. Timber, the principal growth is white, black and red oak, pine and hickory, poplar, etc.

S. M. Cammron, Asst. Marshal

COUNTY OF KNOX, STATE OF TENNESSEE.

PAGE NO. 432 PERSONS WHO DIED DURING THE YEAR ENDING 1st JUNE, 1850.

Subdivision No. 15
Daniel McCallam

No. of Visit	Name	Age	Sex	Color	Free or Slave	Married/Widowed	Place of Birth	Month Died	Occupation	Disease or Cause of Death	No. Days Ill
1	Jane Snead	37	F	B	S		Tenn	Jan		Pneumonia	2 weeks
2	William Wetherford	50	M			W	Va	Feb	Shoemaker	Inflamation of lungs	1 week
3	Abraham Bonns	27	M	B	S		Tenn	Jan	Laborer	Consumption	7 weeks
4	Chambles Hill	94	M			M	Va	Aug	Laborer	Old age	3 months
5	Priscilla Deton(Denton)	28	F			W	Tenn	Sept		Dropsy	3 days
6	Infant of P. Denton	4d	F				Tenn	Sept		unknown	sudden
7	Name not known, Denton	10	F				Tenn	Sept		T. fever	8 days
8	Margaret King	1m	F				Tenn	Aug		Jaundice	8 days
9	Malinda Bearden	14	F	M	S		Tenn	May		Dropsy	4 months
10	James J. Montgomery	1	M				Tenn	July		Whooping cough	2 days
11	Mary A. Piper	1	F				Tenn	Oct		Whooping cough	6 days
12	George Kiben	63	M				Penn	Aug	Tailor	Intemperance	2 weeks
13	Delia Jackson	65	F				Va	Jan		Pneumonia	6 days
14	French Jackson	51	M				Va	May		Inflamation of lungs	11 days
15	Russel Paxton	1	M	M	S		Tenn	March		Bronchitis	1 day
16	Susan Gillum	40	F	M	F	M	Tenn	June		Inflamation of lungs	12 weeks
17	Mary E. White	7	F				Tenn	Sept		Pneumonia	2 weeks
18	Thomas Branch	41	M	B	F	M	Tenn	Feb	Shoemaker	Consumption	2 months
19	Jacob W. Willis	40	M			M	Tenn	June	none	Fits	sudden
20	Mary J. Smith	19	F	M			Tenn	May		Pneumonia	2 weeks
21	William Smith	18	M	B			Tenn	March	Laborer	Drowned	sudden
22	Oliver S.--illegible--	10	M	B	S		Tenn	March		Inflamation of throat	2 weeks
23	Anna Williams	30	F	B	S		Tenn	Sept		Consumption	6 months
24	James Moody	20	M	M	S		Alabama	Jan		Consumption	6----
25	Lucy Williams	1	F	B	S		Tenn	Aug		Consumption	1----
26	Henry Morgan	1	M	M	S		Tenn	March		Consumption	2----
27	John M. Bowen	30	M				Tenn	June	Merchant	Dropsy	3----
28	Rebecca Daniel	8	F				Va	May		Bil. fever	2 weeks
29	Jane Strong	3m	F				Tenn	Sept		Croup	1----
30	Charles W. Myres	25	M				Va	Nov	Teacher of	deaf & Dumb Asylum, T.fever	1 day
31	Adelia Kenida	3m	F	M	S		Tenn	Nov		Fits	sudden
32	Frederick Farmer	40	M	B	F	M	Tenn	Oct	Blk-smith	Consumption	2 weeks
33	John Dudly	80	M			W	Va	Feb		Pneumonia	2 weeks
34	An Infant	1m	M	M	S		Tenn	March		unknown	1 week
35	Thomas McSwan	23	M				Tenn	Jan	Clerk	Consumption	6----

Remarks: There has been no particular disease prevalent in my County during the last year. The water is limestone. The pricipal growth of timber consists of black, red and white oak, pine, poplar, hickory and walnut. The surface of the County is broken (continued)

COUNTY OF KNOX, STATE OF TENNESSEE.

PAGE NO. 433 PERSONS WHO DIED DURING THE YEAR ENDING 1st JUNE, 1850.

Subdivision No. 15
Daniel McCallum

No. of Visit	Name	Age	Sex	Color	Free or Slave	Married/Widowed	Place of Birth	Month Died	Occupation	Disease or Cause of Death	No. Days Ill
1	Moses M. Swan, Jr.	12	M				Tenn	Oct		Spinal eff.	4 days
2	Milly Swan	35	F	B	S		Tenn	Sept		Inflamation of lungs	4 weeks
3	John McGhee	1	M				Tenn	Aug		Inflamation of brain	1 week
4	Elizabeth J. Rutherford	45	F			M	Tenn	June		Ulcer of lung	10 years
5	Sophia E. Craighead	27	F			M	Tenn	June		Pulmonary disease	3 months
6	John Pinckney	35	M				Georgia	Jan	Bricklayer	Typhus	6 weeks
7	O. P. Hill	22	M				Tenn	June		Diarrhea	2 months
8	Hannah Boyd	24	F	B	S		Tenn	July		Inflamation of lungs	6 weeks
9	John W. Knox	22	M				Tenn	Nov	Farmer	Bil. fever	9 days
10	James M. Crippen	38	M			M	Tenn	May	Shoemaker	White swelling	2 weeks
11	Josephine Knox	2	F				Tenn	April		Pneumonia	2 days
12	Robert H. Love	2	M				Tenn	Sept		Sc. fever	2 weeks
13	James Scott	1m	M	B	S		Tenn	Feb		Croup	sudden
14	Infant of Benj. Arnold	1d	M				Tenn	April		unknown	1 day
15	Robert M. Murphy	99	M			W	Ireland	May	Weaver	Old age	8 weeks
16	Thomas J. Graves	23	M				Tenn	Nov	Farmer	unknown	15 months
17	Joseph D. Anderson	23	M				Tenn	April	none	Spinal eff.	5 years
18	Rose E. Anderson	19	F				Tenn	Dec		Spinal eff.	4 days
19	Mary Anderson	19	F	M	S		Tenn	March		Abscess of lungs	8 weeks
20	Lewis C. Charchule	1m	M	B	S		Tenn	June		Gravel	4 days
21	Peggy C. McKinley	40	F				Va	Oct		Abortion	sudden
22	William H. Smith	39	M			M	Tenn	Dec	Farmer	Dropsy	8 months
23	Mary Coffman	75	F			M	Va	March		Phthisic	4 days
24	Joseph Elledge	19	M				Tenn	April	none	Bil. fever	17 days
25	Drucilla J. Anderson	1m	F				Tenn	May		unknown	1 month
26	John Ingram	84	M			W	Va	Nov	Farmer	Dropsy	2 weeks
27	James H. Scruggs	17	M				Tenn	Feb	Student	Congestion	sudden
28	John Lonas	50	M				Tenn	Jan	Cabinet-mkr	Fits	6 days
29	Elvin Minton	1	M				Tenn	Jan		Diarrhea	3 weeks
30	Mary Atkins	5m	F	M	S		Tenn	Sept		Whooping cough	8 days
31	Jesse Harmon	75	M	B	S		Va	March		Old age	7 days
32	Martha Holoway	10m	F				Tenn	Jan		Teething	5 days
33	Rebecca Tillery	53	F				Tenn	June		Flux	4 days
34	Permelia C. Fowler	4	F				Tenn	June		Diarrhea	12 days
35	Josiah Fowler	2	M				Tenn	Oct		Croup	3 days

Remarks: (continued) and hilly. The finest portion of the farming land lying on the River, French Broad and Holston. The only fertilizers we have is that of lime which os obtained by burning the limestone which is very abundant.

COUNTY OF KNOX, STATE OF TENNESSEE.

PAGE NO. 436 PERSONS WHO DIED DURING THE YEAR ENDING 1st JUNE, 1850.

15th Subdivision, East District
Daniel McCallum

No. of Visit	Name	Age	Sex	Color	Free or Slave	Married/Widowed	Place of Birth	Month Died	Occupation	Disease or Cause of Death	No. Days Ill
1	Philis Davis	5m	F	B	S		Tenn	Dec		unknown	sudden
2	Sarah S. Gentry	9m	F				Tenn	July		Diarrhea	1 month
3	James E. Gentry	8	M				Tenn	Aug		Diarrhea	4 days
4	Elizabeth Rochat	29	F				Switzerland	Oct		Nervous fever	6 weeks
5	Nathaniel Nave	29	M				Tenn	March	Farmer	Drowned	sudden
6	Mary Ann Keyhill	19	F				Tenn	Jan		Pneumonia	17 days
7	Joseph King	44	M			M	Tenn	Aug	Farmer	Dropsy	9 months
8	Jesse Simpson	73	M			W	Va	May	Farmer	unknown	sudden
9	James A. Currier	2	M				Tenn	Sept		Croup	4 days
10	Esther Kirkam	75	F				unknown	May		unknown	10 days
11	Infant of James Porter	9d	M				Tenn	June		Inflamation of bowels	6 days
12	Peter Wheeler	9m	M				Tenn	June		unknown	13 days
13	John Wheeler	16d	M				Tenn	Nov		Croup	sudden
14	Elijah Howell	86	M			W	Va	Feb	Carpenter	Dropsy	4 weeks
15	Mary Ferguson	75	F			M	Va	May		Consumption	2 years
16	Mariah J. McClellan	24	F			M	Tenn	Nov		Child bed	5 days
17	James C. McClellan	2wk	M				Tenn	Nov		unknown	4 days
18	Manervy Maxwell	79	F				Tenn	July		Affection of breast	3 months
19	Jesse Wells	65	M			M	Va	May	Farmer	Liver complaint	3 weeks
20	Vina Cotrell	16	F				Tenn	Jan		Fever	3 days
21	Rebecca A. Caton	11m	F				Tenn	March		unknown	16 days
22	Elizabeth Lutrell	91	F			W	Va	Sept		unknown	4 months
23	Tamsey McKimmy	49	F			M	N.C.	March		Breast complaint	18 months
24	Janie Carter	67	F			W	N.C.	Jan		T. fever	2 weeks
25	Infant of Prior S. Hoggs	1wk	M				Tenn	March		unknown	sudden
26	Thomas Magget	7	M				Tenn	July		Bil. fever	8 days
27	Gainum Magget	25	M				Tenn	July	Farmer	Bil. fever	2 weeks
28	Samuel Magget	23	M				Tenn	Aug	Farmer	Bil. fever	27 days
29	Elizabeth Jones	9m	F				Tenn	July		unknown	3 days
30	Henry Foster	84	M			W	S.C.	July	Shoemaker	Sore legs	12 weeks
31	Aggy Looney	48	F	B	S		N.C.	Nov		Dropsy	2 months
32	Joseph S. Reed	10m	M				Tenn	Nov		Croup	4 days
33	Stephen Love	1m	M				Tenn	Jan		unknown	sudden
34	Mary Jane Varner	3	F				Tenn	Oct		Dropsy	3 months
35	Samuel Love	2m	M				Tenn	Feb		unknown	sudden

COUNTY OF KNOX, STATE OF TENNESSEE.

PAGE NO. 437 PERSONS WHO DIED DURING THE YEAR ENDING 1st JUNE, 1850.

15th Subdivision, East District
Daniel McCallum

No. of Visit	Name	Age	Sex	Color	Free or Slave	Married/Widowed	Place of Birth	Month Died	Occupation	Disease or Cause of Death	No. Days Ill
1	William S. Mowery	7m	M				Tenn	March		Croup	3 days
2	Jacob Ingram	52	M			W	N.C.	June	Farmer	Inflamation of liver	2 weeks
3	Elizabeth Aires	18	F				Tenn	Sept		Cholera Morbus	7 days
4	Angus Lamonds	26	M			M	N.C.	Oct	Farmer	T. fever	3 weeks
5	Walker Richardson	55	M	B	S		Tenn	March		Inflamation of lungs	4 weeks
6	Polly P. Armstrong	33	F				Tenn	May		Affection of liver	2 years
7	John Brown	70	M			W	unknown	Aug	Farmer	Pneumonia	4 weeks
8	Catharine Pugh	40	F			M	Tenn	Dec		Typhus fever	4 months
9	Abner Pugh	16	M				Tenn	Nov	Laborer	Typhus fever	2 weeks
10	Martha Pugh	2	F				Tenn	Feb		Worms	1 day
11	Benjamin Ezell	70	M			M	N.C.	-illeg.		Dropsy	3 weeks
12	Rapheal Crippen	1m	M				Tenn	Nov		Croup	3 days
13	Susan Barnwell	18	F				Tenn	April		Consumption	sudden
14	John H. Gibbs	1	M				Tenn	Sept		Cholera Inf.	2 weeks
15	Absolem Rutherford	45	M			M	Tenn	Jan	Farmer	Consumption	10 months
16	Charles Y. Oliver	68	M			M	Va	Aug	Farmer	Affection of liver	2 years
17	Andrew Copeland	62	M			M	N.C.	Nov	Farmer	Fall from wagon	7 days
18	John Majors	1	M				Tenn	Sept		Croup	4 days
19	William P. Smith	4	M				Tenn	Oct		Burn	19 days
20	Nicholas Majors	2	M				Tenn	Sept		Cholera Morb.	1 week
21	Julia Ann Smith	30	F			M	Tenn	June		Consumption	7 months
22	Michael Kirkpatrick	15	M				Tenn	Sept	Laborer	Bil. fever	3 days
23	Moses Cocks	10	M				Tenn	Oct		Typhus fever	2 months
24	Harriet Weaver	1m	F				Tenn	May		Croup	sudden
25	Phebe S. Smith	4	F				Tenn	Nov		Typhus fever	10 days
26	Infant of Benj. Hartley	5d	M				Tenn	May		unknown	5 days
27	Sophiah Blackburn	67	F			M	N.C.	Oct		Dropsy	2 months
28	Leander Shelton	5	M				Tenn	Jan		unknown	1 year
29	Nancy Wadlington	60	F				Va	May		unknown	6 weeks
30	Delila Parker	30	F			M	N.C.	March		Inflamation of brain	4 months
31	Nancy Bell	22	F				Tenn	July		Convulsions	5 days
32	Veleria Warwick	25	F				Tenn	May		Consumption	2 months
33	William B. Lucy	1	M				Tenn	Oct		Dropsy	6 days
34	Prior L. Turner	18	M				Tenn	March	Farmer	Typhus fever	23 days
35	Terry Cobb	28	M	M	S		Tenn	Oct		Consumption	2 months

COUNTY OF KNOX, STATE OF TENNESSEE.

PAGE NO. 440 PERSONS WHO DIED DURING THE YEAR ENDING 1st JUNE, 1850.

15th Subdivision, East District
Daniel McCallum

No. of Visit	Name	Age	Sex	Color	Free or Slave	Married/Widowed	Place of Birth	Month Died	Occupation	Disease or Cause of Death	No. Days Ill
1	Sarah E. Peters	1m	F				Tenn	Aug		unknown	2 days
2	Martha Cobb	11m	F	M	S		Tenn	May		unknown	3 weeks
3	William G. Hordon	8m	M				Tenn	Dec		Pneumonia	10 days
4	Mark Hordon	3m	M	M	S		Tenn	Oct		Cold	2 weeks
5	Seanah A. Williams	2m	F				Tenn	Nov		unknown	2 months
6	Elizabeth West	5	F				Tenn	Feb		Drowned	sudden
7	John Holder	38	M			M	N.C.	April	Farmer	Pneumonia	5 weeks
8	Lucy F. Davon	15	F				Va	May		Dropsy	3 months
9	Abner Ellis	76	M			M	S.C.	June	Farmer	Dropsy	29 months
10	Martha Dickey	3	F				Tenn	Aug		Catarrh fever	8 days
11	Alfred Cox	1	M				Tenn	June		Mumps	2 weeks
12	Moses Roylston	72	M			M	Va	March	Farmer	Breast complaint	3 days
13	Henry Harmon	38	M			M	Tenn	May	Laborer	Drowned	sudden
14	Sarah Brien	32	F				Va	June		Consumption	8 months
15	Infant of James M. Harris	1m	M				Tenn	Sept		Hives	3 days
16	Robert A. Scott	1	M				Tenn	Jan		Diarrhea	4 days
17	Matilda Lesenby	38	F			M	S.C.	April		Dropsy	4 months
18	Nelly Pearson	16	F				Tenn	April		Bil. fever	2 weeks
19	Ann E. Fowler	11m	F				Tenn	March		Whooping cough	2 months
20	Catharine Hasken	76	F			W	Va	Nov		Palsy	2 years
21	Marvail C. Childress	2	M				Tenn	March		Croup	2 weeks
22	James Childress	35	M				Tenn	Dec	Laborer	Consumption	3 months
23	Fanny E. Jenkins	4d	F				Tenn	Aug		Croup	1 day
24	Solomon Branson	41	M				Tenn	Dec	Farmer	Pneumonia	11 days
25	Margaret E. Murphy	1	F				Tenn	Aug		Whooping cough	3 weeks
26	Rebecca Regans	52	F			M	Va	Jan		Consumption	1 year
27	Elizabeth Smith	42	F			M	Tenn	April		Consumption	1 year
28	Jack Lyon	70	M	B	S		unknown	Oct		Rheumatism	1 month

COUNTY OF LAUDERDALE, STATE OF TENNESSEE.

PAGE NO. 441 PERSONS WHO DIED DURING THE YEAR ENDING 1st JUNE, 1850.

Isaac M. Steele

No. of Visit	Name	Age	Sex	Color	Free or Slave	Married/Widowed	Place of Birth	Month Died	Occupation	Disease or Cause of Death	No. Days Ill
1	Dorcas	9m	F	B	S		Tenn	Sept		Worms	4 days
2	unnamed	1m	M	B	S		Tenn	April		unknown	3 days
3	unnamed	6m	F	B	S		Tenn	Nov		unknown	7 days
4	Martha	24	F	B	S		Va	May	Fieldhand	Inflamation	7 days
5	Gideon Hankins	65	M			W	unknown	Nov		Bil. fever	40 days
6	Claussa	20	F	B	S		S.C.	Sept	Fieldhand	Cold	6 days
7	unnamed	1m	M	B	S		Tenn	Sept		unknown	sudden
8	Delilah	23	F	B	S		Tenn	April		Consumption	3 years
9	John Barnes	60	M			M	N.C.	Sept	Farmer	Dropsy & Fever	40 days
10	Susameon	50	F	B	S		Va	Feb		unknown	3 days
11	Ellis	14	M	B	S		N.C.	May		Consumption	7 months
12	Infant	3m	F	B	S		Tenn	Feb		Croup	1 day
13	_____ Fitzpatrick	2m	F				Tenn	July		Croup	15 days
14	George W. Tatum	36	M				N.C.	March	Farmer	Drinking	suddenly
15	Francis A. Henry	25	M				Georgia	Oct	Farmer	T. fever	30 days
16	Phil	57	M	B	S		Va	June		Dropsy	20 days
17	Bird	3d	F				Tenn	July		unknown	2 days
18	George Matthew	11	M				Tenn	July		Fits	
19	Walker Mathis	6	M				Tenn			Croup	7 days
20	George B. G. Henning	9	M				Tenn	Sept		T. fever	30 days
21	Sarah A. Henning	1	F				Tenn	Oct		T. fever	
22	Augustus	6m	M	B	S		Tenn	Feb		unknown	sudden

COUNTY OF LAUDERDALE, STATE OF TENNESSEE.

PAGE NO. 441   PERSONS WHO DIED DURING THE YEAR ENDING 1st JUNE, 1850.

Isaac M. Steele

No. of Visit	Name	Age	Sex	Color	Free or Slave	Married/Widowed	Place of Birth	Month Died	Occupation	Disease or Cause of Death	No. Days Ill
23	Vina	2	F	B	S		Tenn	Aug		Measles	12 months
24	Tom	2	M	B	S		Tenn	Oct		Whooping cough	28 days
25	Haley Burton	1m	M				Tenn	June		Phlogosis from birth	
26	_____ Boydston	6m	M				Tenn	April		unknown	sudden
27	Mary Jane Massey	2	F				Tenn	Dec		unknown	8 days
28	Emily L. Acuff	17	F				Tenn	April		unknown	77 days
29	Sumerson	6m	F				Tenn			unknown	4 days
30	John W. Luma	2	M				Tenn	Aug		Worms	14 days

Remarks: Remain as it now is, or retake the Census of my whole County.
Isaac M. Steele, Asst. Marshal

COUNTY OF LAUDERDALE, STATE OF TENNESSEE.

PAGE NO. 444   PERSONS WHO DIED DURING THE YEAR ENDING 1st JUNE, 1850.

No. of Visit	Name	Age	Sex	Color	Free or Slave	Married/Widowed	Place of Birth	Month Died	Occupation	Disease or Cause of Death	No. Days Ill
1	Angeline Braden	22	F			M	Tenn	Oct		Child birth	sudden
2	Belfield	28	M				unknown	June		Dropsy	2 months
3	Fanny	4m	F	B	S		Tenn	May		unknown	10 months
4	Dick	1	M	B	S		Tenn	June		Smothered	sudden
5	Henry	22	M	B	S		Kentucky	May		Dropsy	2 months
6	Mary Anthony	3m	F				Tenn	Feb		Bronchitis	7 days
7	Martha J. Davenport	1	F				Tenn	March		unknown	8 days
8	John	10m	M	B			Va	June		Teething	2 months
9	Infant	1	M	B			Tenn	July		unknown	3 days
10	Infant	1m	F				Tenn	July		Croup	4 days
11	Charles J. McFarlin	3m	M				Tenn	March		unknown	1 day
12	_____ Sanders	1d	M				Tenn	Oct		Congestion	4 days
13	Elizabeth Price	13	F				Tenn	Dec		Congestion	
14	William Strain	74	M			M	S.C.	Sept	Farmer	Carbuncle	1 year
15	Slave,	1m	F	B	S		Tenn	March		Croup	3 days
16	Margaret Williams	37	F			M	N.C.	April		unknown	6 days
17	Henry W. Willard	25	M				Penn	Nov	Farmer	Pneumonia	5 days
18	Mary E. Harris	4	F				Tenn	Sept		Bil. fever	10 days
19	Sarah Walton	21	F				Tenn	Oct		unknown	12 days
20	Stephen Howard	54	M			M	N.C.	May	Farmer	unknown	sudden
21	John Russell	50	M				Kentucky	Oct	Farmer	Cold	12 days
22	Infant	1m	F				Tenn	Feb		unknown	7 days
23	Lydia Walpole	31	F			M	Tenn	March		unknown	sudden
24	_____ Walpole	1m	F				Tenn	April		unknown	21 days
25	Milville	16	M	B	S		Va	May		unknown	6 days
26	Nancy Brady	43	F				Tenn	Feb		Bronchitis	15 years
27	Jno. J. Carnall	3m	M				Tenn	Oct		unknown	21 days
28	Slave, not named	1m	F	B	S		Tenn			unknown	21 days
29	Elizabeth Reynolds	17	F				Tenn	July		Congestive chill	3 days
30	_____ Polk	3	F				Tenn	Aug		Congestive chill	sudden
31	Julia H. Leet	3	F				Ireland	Sept		Worms	sudden
32	John Langly	3	F?				Tenn	Sept		Bil. fever	9 days
33	Harriet A. Turner	4	F				Tenn	July		Worms	3 days
34	John W. Turner	2	M				Tenn	Aug		Worms	14 days
35	Dick	7m	M	B			Tenn	March		Croup	2 days

Remarks: I had nearly completed the Census of my County before I received the circular from the Census Office directing me to fill up the heading of my County or deceased with the Civil Subdivision thereof, I was then unable to seperate it from memory and had not obtained, but to let a ....(unfinished)....

COUNTY OF LAWRENCE, STATE OF TENNESSEE.

PAGE NO. 445 PERSONS WHO DIED DURING THE YEAR ENDING 1st JUNE, 1850.

J. L. Smith

No. of Visit	Name	Age	Sex	Color	Free or Slave	Married/Widowed	Place of Birth	Month Died	Occupation	Disease or Cause of Death	No. Days Ill
1	Unas F. Johnson	3m	M				Tenn	Aug		unknown	10 days
2	James Maler	36	M				Va	Sept	Carpenter	Compl. Cold	C
3	Margaret Horne	21	F				Tenn	Aug		Fits	14 weeks
4	William E. Evans	7	M				Tenn	Jan		Pneumonia	17 days
5	Jas. M. Holcomb	1	M				Tenn	March		Pneumonia	21 days
6	William Williams	7	M				N.C.	June		Yellow Jaundice	C
7	Elizabeth Defoe	15	F				Tenn	April		Pneumonia	21 days
8	Amanda L. Dickson	13	F				Tenn	July		King's evil	21 days
9	Oney	33	F	B	S		Tenn	June		Pneumonia	12 days
10	Dilsy	60	F	B	S		Va	Feb		Paralysis	2 days
11	Judy	36	F	B	S		Mi. (Miss)	July		Cholera M.	4 days
12	Sylva	6	F	B	S		Mi. (Miss)	Nov		Burnt	sudden
13	John	5	M	B	S		N.C.	April		Winter fever	30 days
14	Henry	1m	M	B	S		N.C.	April		Over laid	sudden
15	Julia	13	F	B	S		Tenn	April		Pneumonia	28 days
16	James H. Tuller	7m	M				Tenn	Aug		Bil. fever	9 days
17	Samuel McLean, Sr.	75	M			M	N.C.	April	Farmer	unknown	sudden
18	Infant of R.C. Chennault	1m	F				Tenn	Jan		unknown	sudden
19	William Jas. Clifton	10	M				Tenn	Feb		Dropsy	C
20	Sidney Payne	1	M				Tenn	April		Inflamation	8 days
21	Emily Tracy	18	F				Tenn	May		Consumption	12 months
22	Martha Johnson	94	F			W	England	Aug		Old age	
23	Adaline	4	F	B	S		unknown	Aug		Worms	21 days
24	Infant	1m	M				Tenn	Sept		unknown	sudden
25	William M. Moor	4	M				Tenn	Jan		Winter fever	21 days
26	John M. Killiam	22	M			M	Tenn	March	Farmer	Pneumonia	8 days
27	Artemus Killiam	22	F			W	Tenn	March		Pneumonia	10 days
28	Infant	1m	F				Tenn	March		unknown	sudden
29	Mary A. V. Crews	21	F			M	Tenn	June		Child bed fever	17 days
30	Infant Sanders	1m	F				Tenn	Aug		unknown	sudden
31	Infant Vaughn	1m	F				Tenn	May		unknown	sudden
32	Thomas Vaughn	15	M				Tenn	March	Laborer	Pleurisy	7 days
33	James G. Ingram	1m	M				Tenn	July		Summer complaint	sudden
34	Frances J. Moore	17	F				Tenn	July		Typhoid	14 days
35	William T. Bassham	3m	M				Tenn	Dec		Croup	22 days

COUNTY OF LAWRENCE, STATE OF TENNESSEE.

PAGE NO. 448 PERSONS WHO DIED DURING THE YEAR ENDING 1st JUNE, 1850.

J. L. Smith

No. of Visit	Name	Age	Sex	Color	Free or Slave	Married/Widowed	Place of Birth	Month Died	Occupation	Disease or Cause of Death	No. Days Ill
1	David Klyen	45	M	B	S		Maryland	April	Wagon-mkr	Wound	12 days
2	Infant Klyen	1m	M	B	S		Tenn	Jan		Cold	1 day
3	Elenor E. Meek	21	F			M	Tenn	Sept		Consumption	C
4	Mary M. Meek	4m	F				Tenn	Jan		Inflamation of brain	20 days
5	Susan C. Austin	28	F			M	Kentucky	Dec		Dropsy	C
6	Salina Austin	5m	F				Tenn	Dec		Inflamation of the heart	24 days
7	Infant	1m	M	B	S		Tenn	M		Croup	4 days
8	B. R. Ryan	45	M				Tenn	Oct	Speculator	Mania --illegible--	8 days
9	Sarah J. C. Mason	9m	F				Tenn	Jan		Sc. fever	9 days
10	William H. Allen	3	M				Tenn	May		Inflamation of brain	18 days
11	Jefferson O. Tarkington	3	M				Tenn	Oct		Croup	8 days
12	Mathew Love	70	M				Ireland	Oct	Shoemaker	unknown, sudden	4 days
13	Jas. F. Henderson, Jr.	9m	M				Tenn	March		Consumption	C
14	Jas. F. Henderson, Sr.	30	M			M	Tenn	Oct	Physician	Consumption	C
15	Ethelinda J. Buchanan	17	F				Tenn	Aug		Complicated	C
16	Henry Eaton	7	M				Tenn	Sept		Inflamation	8 days
17	Mary Melton	2	F				Tenn	May		Congestion	9 days
18	Milton T. Cunningham	26	M				Tenn	Jan	Hse-carpenter	Consumption	12 months
19	Frances Carter	63	F				N.C.	Jan		Complicated	3 months
20	William C. Green	26	M				Tenn	June	Farmer	T. fever	8 days
21	Infant	1m	F				Tenn	Feb		Flux	10 days
22	Infant	1m	M				Tenn	July		Bold hives	2 days
23	Elizabeth Spencer	95	F				Va	Aug		Old age	
24	Martha M. Baird	18	F				Alabama	July		Congestion	8 days
25	Infant	1m	M				Tenn	Dec		unknown	sudden
26	Andy Smith	4	M				Tenn	Oct		Liver, gravel	1 month
27	Myrna	28	F	M	S		Tenn	Feb		Consumption	4 months
28	Infant	1m	F	M	S		Tenn	Feb		unknown	sudden
29	William F. Tayse	1	M				Tenn	Oct		Croup	4 days
30	Cornelious S. Wester	1	M				Tenn	March		Flux	8 days
31	Jeremiah Jackson	4	M	B	S		Tenn	Dec		Sc. fever	8 days
32	Willis H.	2	M	B	S		Tenn	unknown		unknown	7 days
33	Infant	1m	F	B	S		Tenn	unknown		unknown	8 days
34	Sarah Myers	90	F			M	S.C.	Nov		Old age	
35	Lucinda A. Trobaugh	25	F			M	Alabama	Oct		Complicated	2 months

COUNTY OF LAWRENCE, STATE OF TENNESSEE.

PAGE NO. 449 PERSONS WHO DIED DURING THE YEAR ENDING 1st JUNE, 1850.

T. M. Scott

No. of Visit	Name	Age	Sex	Color	Free or Slave	Married/Widowed	Place of Birth	Month Died	Occupation	Disease or Cause of Death	No. Days Ill
1	Infant	4m	F	B	S		Tenn	April		Croup	3 days
2	Julia	30	F	B	S		N.C.	Sept		C	30 days
3	Ned	1	M	M	S		Tenn	Aug		Flux	8 days
4	Gorge	1	M	B	S		Tenn	Aug		Flux	4 days

COUNTY OF LAWRENCE, STATE OF TENNESSEE.

PAGE NO. 452 PERSONS WHO DIED DURING THE YEAR ENDING 1st JUNE, 1850.

T. M. Scott

No. of Visit	Name	Age	Sex	Color	Free or Slave	Married/Widowed	Place of Birth	Month Died	Occupation	Disease or Cause of Death	No. Days Ill
1	John M. A. Mason	1	M				Tenn	Aug		Pneumonia	7 days
2	Andrew Jackson	10m	M				Tenn	Aug		unknown	3 days
3	Lucy A. Bumpass	6m	F				Tenn	Aug		Inflamation	20 days
4	Jas. Arnold	85	M			W	unknown	Oct	Farmer	Old age	8 days
5	Andrew J. Parham	8	M				Tenn	Sept		--illegible--	15 days
6	Obediance Hill	82	F			W	N.C.	May		Cancer	12 days
7	Martha T. Snow	3	F				Tenn	June		Burnt	15 days
8	E. W. Gowen	27	M				Tenn	May	Farmer	Diarrhea	5 days
9	Mary Mitchel	35	F			M	Tenn	May		Dropsy	3 days
10	John W. Mitchel	10m	M				Tenn	Jan		Croup	2 days
11	Henrietta C. Morris	21	F			M	Tenn	Aug		Bil. fever	8 days
12	Infant	1m	F				Tenn	Aug		Bil. fever	sudden
13	Mariah Christian	14	F				Tenn	June		Pneumonia	12 days
14	R. E. Stuart	1m	F				Tenn	Sept		Bold hives	1 day
15	Elizabeth Lawderdale	37	F			M	N.C.	June		Congestive chills	5 days
16	Willis Lawderdale	10	M				Tenn	March		Dropsy	90 days
17	John W.	3m	M	B	S		Tenn	Dec		Croup	8 days
18	Simon C. Pippin	4	M				Tenn	Nov		Flux	18 days
19	Ann L.	2	F	B	S		Tenn	Oct		Flux	10 days
20	Ben	34	M	B	S		Tenn	Oct		By a saw log	sudden
21	Rebecca F. Penington	1	F				Tenn	Aug		Flux	7 days
22	July A. Letsinger	38	F			M	N.C.	May		Congestive chills	sudden
23	Infant Walker	1m	F				Tenn	July		Flux	1 day
24	William H. McKnight	9	M				Tenn	March		Phthisic	6 days
25	John F. Williams	5	M				Tenn	July		Flux	15 days
26	Ann Gilmore	72	F			M	Va	April		Old age	C
27	Lavira L. Ashmore	34	F			M	Tenn	Dec		Dropsy	28 days
28	Mary Ashmore	1m	F				Tenn	Jan		unknown	6 days
29	John W. Ashmore	1m	M				Tenn	Jan		unknown	7 days
30	Effy Patterson	95	F			W	Scotland	Feb		Old age	C
31	Jas. Stuart	76	M			M	N.C.	Feb	Farmer	Old age	50 days
32	John H. Polk	6	M				Tenn	Oct		Diarrhea	15 days
33	William	2m	M	B	S		Tenn	Feb		Croup	sudden
34	Jas.	19	M	B	S		Tenn	March		Scrofula	C
35	Gilbreath F. Lemorton	10m	M				Tenn	May		Disease of the heart	6 days

Remarks: Timbers, principally oaks, chestnut, etc. Rocks, flint and lime stone. Water, principally freestone, some chalybeate and limestone. Iron ore is the principal ore.

COUNTY OF LAWRENCE, STATE OF TENNESSEE.

PAGE NO. 453 PERSONS WHO DIED DURING THE YEAR ENDING 1st JUNE, 1850.

T. L. Smith

No. of Visit	Name	Age	Sex	Color	Free or Slave	Married/Widowed	Place of Birth	Month Died	Occupation	Disease or Cause of Death	No. Days Ill
1	Infant	1m	M	M	S		Tenn	Nov		unknown	6 days
2	William J. White	2	M				Tenn	Sept		Croup	8 days
3	Nancy Miles	47	F			M	S.C.	Sept		Chronic	10 days
4	Rhoda L. Ayres	6	M?				Tenn	July		Flux	13 days
5	William Meredith	3	M				Tenn	Aug		Typhoid	14 days
6	Eliza T. Hardiston	1	F				Tenn	June		Flux	8 days
7	Sarah A. Gibson	14	F				Tenn	May		Disease of heart	4 days
8	Silas A. Mathews	12	M				Tenn	Feb		Typhoid	90 days
9	James Wilsford	77	M			M	Va	June	Farmer	Wound	C

COUNTY OF LEWIS, STATE OF TENNESSEE.

PAGE NO. 455 — PERSONS WHO DIED DURING THE YEAR ENDING 1st JUNE, 1850.

Civil District No. ? & 2
John C. Johnston

No. of Visit	Name	Age	Sex	Color	Free or Slave	Married/Widowed	Place of Birth	Month Died	Occupation	Disease or Cause of Death	No. Days Ill
1	_____ Stockard	5d	M		F		Tenn	May		Lockjaw	3 days
2	Sarah Langly	57	F		F	M	N.C.	Nov		Consumption	7 days
3	Dolly Gordon	40	F	B	S		Tenn	Dec		Poison	14 days
4	Caroline Smith	2	F	B	S		Tenn	May		Fever	5 days
5	Elizabeth Duke	84	F		F	W	N.C.	Aug		Palsy	2 y, 5m
6	John W. Cecil	39	M		F	M	Va	June	Farmer	Consumption	270 days
7	Haywood Cecil	2	M	B	S		Tenn	March		Disease of lungs	7 days
8	_____ Harris	1m	M		F		Tenn	Nov		unknown	4 days
9	Frances J. Nowlen	4	F		F		Tenn	Sept		Sc. fever	14 days
10	Mary A. Nowlen	5m	F		F		Tenn	July		Sc. fever	8 days
11	Lethe W. Nowlen	8m	F		F		Tenn	July		Sc. fever	20 days
12	_____ Nixon	2m	F		F		Tenn	Dec		Fever	14 days

COUNTY OF LEWIS, STATE OF TENNESSEE.

PAGE NO. 458 — PERSONS WHO DIED DURING THE YEAR ENDING 1st JUNE, 1850.

Civil District No. 5, 6, 10, 7, 8, 1, 3, 9 & 4

No. of Visit	Name	Age	Sex	Color	Free or Slave	Married/Widowed	Place of Birth	Month Died	Occupation	Disease or Cause of Death	No. Days Ill
1	Robert Nichols	74	M			W	N.C.	July	Farmer	Superanuated)	42 days
2	Elizabeth J. Brashears	1	F				Tenn	July		Bold hives)	5 days
3	Young Kirk	63	M			M	N.C.	March	Farmer	Gravel) District	390 days
4	Benjamin W. Tanant	4	M				Tenn	Nov		Burn) 5	20 days
5	_____ Sharp	1d	M				Tenn	July		unknown)	1 day
6	Levi Johnston	24	M	B	S	M	Tenn	June	Farmer	Consumption)	150 days
7	Samuel Venable	32	M	B	S	M	Tenn	March	Farmer	Negro disease)	90 days
8	Jane Farrar	70	F			M	N.C.	Jan		Dropsy) District	365 days
9	_____ Cre-o-	1d	F				Tenn	Aug		unknown) 6	1 day
10	_____ Morris	1d	M				Tenn	May		unknown)	1 day
11	Michael Goodwin	63	M			M	N.C.	July	Farmer	Dropsy) District 10	
12	James A. Keeling	5	M				Tenn	July		Scrofula)	340 days
	Joseph M. Keeling	7	M				Tenn	Jan		unknown) District	3 days
13	Mary C. Brock	11	F				Tenn	July		Infl. of brain) 7	90 days
14	_____ Brock	1m	F				Tenn	May		Bowel Disease)	
15	Elizabeth Sellars	64	F			M	N.C.	Jan		Dropsy) District 8	180 days
16	Priscilla Anderson	80	F	B	S	M	unknown	March		Superanuated)	1 day
17	Moses Kennedy	1m	M	B	S		Tenn	Sept		Smothered) District	
18	Barret Owens	45	M			M	N.C.	Sept		Lung disease) 1	30 days
19	John Bullock	82	M			M	N.C.	Feb	Farmer	Lung disease)	23 days
20	Nancy Wilson	50	F				Va	Feb		unknown)	365 days
21	Minerva, a slave	29	F	B	S	M	Tenn	June		Dropsy)	60 days
22	_____ Blackburn	2m	F				Tenn	May		Bowel disease)	40 days
23	George W. Isom	36	M			M	Tenn	Feb	Farmer	T. fever)District	13 days
24	Margaret A. Dickson	34	F			M	S.C.	May		Rheumatism) 3	10 days
25	Elizabeth Hobson	11m	F	M	S		Tenn	Jan		Spasms)	11 days
26	Matilda Flowers	48	F			W	N.C.	May		Palsy) District 9	9 days
27	_____ Borgus	1d	M				Tenn	April		unknown)	1 day
28	_____ Borgus	1d	M				Tenn	April		unknown)	1 day
29	Samuel E. Durham	18	M				Tenn	Aug	Farmer	T. fever)	28 days
30	James W. King	1m	M				Tenn	July		Disease of head)	1 day
31	Allen King	28	M				Tenn	July	Farmer	T. fever)District	20 days
32	John A. King	2	M				Tenn	Dec		Cold) 4	14 days
33	Martha G. Shaw	36	F				Tenn	March		Child birth)	2 hours
34	Sarah A. Holmes	22	F				Tenn	Aug		Dyspepsia)	365 days

COUNTY OF LINCOLN, STATE OF TENNESSEE.

PAGE NO. 474 PERSONS WHO DIED DURING THE YEAR ENDING 1st JUNE, 1850.

Subdivision No. 2
Alfred Bearden

No. of Visit	Name	Age	Sex	Color	Free or Slave	Married/Widowed	Place of Birth	Month Died	Occupation	Disease or Cause of Death	No. Days Ill
1	Lucinda Daniel	44	M			M	S.C.	Jan		T. fever	7 days
2	Infant	1m	M	B	S		Tenn	Jan		Inflamation	sudden
3	Eliza Brown	5m	F	B	S		Tenn	June		Diarrhea	2 months
4	Elizabeth Speck	26	F				Tenn	Jan		Consumption	18 months
5	Infant	1m	M	B	S		Tenn	April		Croup	2 days
6	Wiliam F. Newman	1	M				Tenn	March		T. fever	3 weeks
7	Terry	32	M	B	S		Tenn	April		Inflamation of lungs	8 days
8	Jonathan Trip	45	M			M	N.C.	Dec	Lawmaker	unknown	6 months
9	Marshel	9m	M	B	S		Tenn	July		Diarrhea	6 months
10	Charlot	45	F	B	S		Tenn	June		Hanging	sudden
11	Fenton Gregory	38	M				Tenn	Aug	Farmer	Bil. fever	14 days
12	A. E. Hattishill	44	M				N.C.	March	Farmer	Dropsy	4 years
13	James M. George	31	M				Tenn	May	Farmer	T. fever	2 days
14	Martha J. Perry	4	F				Tenn	May		Croup	3 months
15	Andrew J. Talor (Taylor)	20	M				Tenn	April	Farmer	T. fever	22 days
16	Melissa Finnings	1m	F				Tenn	Dec		Croup	1 month
17	Samuel Mikel	22	M				Ohio	March	Farmer	T. fever	1 month
18	Jacob Lenord	72	M			M	N.C.	Oct	Farmer	Gravel	2 weeks
19	Mary Leonard	72	F			M	N.C.	Oct		unknown	4 months
20	Charlot Arnold	76	F			W	S.C.	Oct		Dropsy	2 years
21	Nancy Foster	63	F			W	Kentucky	Oct		Congestive chills	8 days
22	Mariah Scot	2	F				Tenn	April		Fever	21 days
23	Fanny	35	F	B	S		Tenn	Feb		Inflamation of lungs	2 months
24	Nelson	14	M	B	S		Tenn	July		Fever	14 days
25	Lurinda Harbon	35	F				S.C.	Dec		Congestive chills	3 days
26	Sarah Berrier	3	F				Tenn	May		unknown	7 days

Remarks: extent, it in some cases terminates soon, in others its progress is very slow, but from what I could learn, it put on all the signatures of the nervous fever described in the old books.

COUNTY OF LINCOLN, STATE OF TENNESSEE.

PAGE NO. 459 PERSONS WHO DIED DURING THE YEAR ENDING 1st JUNE, 1850.

Subdivision No. 1
O. W. Higgins

No. of Visit	Name	Age	Sex	Color	Free or Slave	Married/Widowed	Place of Birth	Month Died	Occupation	Disease or Cause of Death	No. Days Ill
1	Patrick Kennon	60	M	B	S	W		March		Pulmonary	90 days
2	Isabella Kennon	25	F				Tenn	March		Pulmonary	90 days
3	Marcus Askins	60	M	B	S	M		Feb		Cholic	7 days
4	Henry Askins	4	M	B	S			June		Drowned	
5	Samuel Tweed	35	M			M	Ireland	April	Farmer	Inflamation	10 days
6	Elizabeth Ennis	22	F				Tenn	Aug		Spasms	5 days
7	Rebecca Hedgepeth	9m	F				Tenn	Oct		Inflamation	8 days
8	Daniel R. Moores	61	M			M	N.C.	July	Farmer	Bil. fever	9 days
9	Elizabeth Shelton	35	F			M	N.C.	April		unknown	3 years
10	Andy Whitaker	2	M		S		Tenn	Feb		unknown	35 days
11	Dick Twitty	18	M		S		Tenn	Aug		T. fever	12 days
12	Charlotte	1	F		S		Tenn	June		Bowel	6 days
13	John	2	M		S		Tenn	Aug		Worms	20 days
14	Harper	8m	M		S		Tenn	Sept		Worms	6 days
15	Jim Cole	1	M		S		Tenn	April		Worms	2 days
16	Phillis Cole	1	F		S		Tenn	April		Worms	2 days
17	William O. Butler	1	M				Tenn	Jan		Worms	10 days
18	J. O. Nelson	21	M		S		Tenn	July		Lungs	18 days

COUNTY OF LINCOLN, STATE OF TENNESSEE.

PAGE NO. 459 PERSONS WHO DIED DURING THE YEAR ENDING 1st JUNE, 1850.

Subdivision No. 1
O. W. Higgins

No. of Visit	Name	Age	Sex	Color	Free or Slave	Married/Widowed	Place of Birth	Month Died	Occupation	Disease or Cause of Death	No. Days Ill
19	Josephine Nelson	1	F		S		Tenn	Jan		Smothered	1 day
20	Philamel Higgins	2m	M				Tenn	Sept		--illegible--	10 days
21	Joel Sharp	42	M				Tenn	Oct	Farmer	Drowned	
22	Thomas Grant	72	M				Va	May	Farmer	Chronic	
23	Henry Russell	2	M		S		Tenn	Aug		Cholera	1 day
24	Nancy Rives	31	F			M	Tenn	May		Inflamation	6 days
25	Martha Ann Devers	1	F				Tenn	May		Worms	6 days
26	Alfred Hurley	1m	M		S		Tenn	Dec		Smothered	
27	Isaac Swinebroad	70	M		S			Nov		Pneumonia	5 days
28	Polly Moore	4	F		S			Jan		Lockjaw	30 days
29	Louiza Wilson	9m	F		S			March		Croup	10 days
30	Eliza Wilson	1m	F		S			July		Croup	3 days
31	W. B. Wright	43	M				Tenn	June	Farmer	Cong. fever	15 days
32	Edith Summers	30	F				Tenn	June		Int. fever	15 days
33	Ally Davis	80	F				Va	April		Old age	
34	Elizabeth Holbert	4m	F		S		Tenn	July		Worms	10 days
35	William Huckaby	78	M				N.C.	March		Gravel	15 days

COUNTY OF LINCOLN, STATE OF TENNESSEE.

PAGE NO. 462 PERSONS WHO DIED DURING THE YEAR ENDING 1st JUNE, 1850.

Subdivision No. 1
O. W. Higgins

No. of Visit	Name	Age	Sex	Color	Free or Slave	Married/Widowed	Place of Birth	Month Died	Occupation	Disease or Cause of Death	No. Days Ill
1	E. Randolph	1m	F				Tenn	Aug		unknown	1 day
2	John Moore	84	M				S.C.	April	Farmer	Cancer	12 months
3	Titus McDonald	3	M				Tenn	Oct		Chills	12 days
4	Joseph B. Starnes	10	M				Tenn	March		Dropsy	3 days
5	Benjamin Starnes	14	M				Tenn	May		Dropsy	30 days
6	Alexander J. Wiley	3	M				Tenn	Dec		Fits	2 days
7	Sarah E. Good	1	F				Tenn	Nov		Inflamation of brain	3 days
8	William Randolph	60	M	B	S			July		Cold	8 days
9	Rufus Griffith	15	M	B	S			Aug		Pneumonia	12 days
10	George Caldwell	55	M	B	S			March		Pneumonia	4 days
11	Nancy Stray	1m	F					Jan		Hives	7 days
12	Phillip Fagan	75	M				S.C.	Nov	Farmer	Gravel	6 days
13	Jane Ransom	16	F				Tenn	Jan		Pneumonia	14 days
14	Infant of S. Wilson	1m	F				Tenn	April		Croup	1 day
15	Mary Templeton	64	F				Kentucky	April		Old age	10 days
16	Infant Templeton	1m	F				Tenn	Aug		Croup	12 days
17	Sarah Leatherwood	3	F				Tenn	Dec		Worms	5 days
18	Lewis C. McCown	35	M				Tenn	Nov	Farmer	Lungs	12 days
19	Eliza Smith	1	F				Tenn	July		Cholera Inf.	15 days
20	Elizabeth Henderson	34	F	B	S			March		Killed by (blank)	30 days
21	Malinda Henderson	15	F	B	S			Jan		Measles	12 days
22	Dick Patterson	40	M	B	S			May		Hanged	
23	Rebecca Sherrel	25	F	B	S			April		T. fever	8 days
24	Rebecca Sherrel	1m	F	B	S			May		Croup	8 days
25	Isaac McCown	65	M				Georgia	April		Intemperence	4 days
26	Mary S. Wallace	35	F				Tenn	Nov		Chronic	
27	William Jackson	21	M				unknown	March	Farmer	Pleurisy	35 days
28	Margaret B. Blue	12	F				Tenn	Oct		Rheumatism	1 year
29	John Gines	14	M				Tenn	Jan		Dropsy	27 days
30	Jane Blair	1m	F	B	S			Dec		Croup	3 days
31	Jane Neely	1m	F				Tenn	April		Croup	
32	Nancy Bottoms	17	F		S			July		T. fever	30 days
33	Cephus Bottoms	6m	M		S			March		Croup	12 days
34	Fanny Blucher	54	F				S.C.	June		Brain	50 days

COUNTY OF LINCOLN, STATE OF TENNESSEE.

PAGE NO. 463   PERSONS WHO DIED DURING THE YEAR ENDING 1st JUNE, 1850.

Subdivision No. 1

O. W. Higgins

No. of Visit	Name	Age	Sex	Color	Free or Slave	Married/Widowed	Place of Birth	Month Died	Occupation	Disease or Cause of Death	No. Days Ill
1	Martha McPhail	2	F	B	S		Tenn	July		Diarrhea	14 days
2	Haney Morgan	50	M	B	S		Maryland	June		Dropsy	25 days
3	Tabitha Kennedy	5	F	B	F		Tenn	June		Cholera Morbus	30 days
4	John V. McKinney	65	M			M	Kentucky	Aug	Doctor	Dyspepsia	60 days
5	Berry	__	M		S		Tenn	June		Disease brain	14 days
6	Emma Shapard	17	F	B	S		Tenn	Dec		Consumption	10 years
7	Archibald Woods	2	M				Tenn	Jan		Fever	2 years
8	Fanny	3	F	B	S		Tenn	Feb		Worms	8 weeks
9	Jonas	1	M	B	S		Tenn	Feb		Liver disease	14 days
10	George	1m	M	B	S		Tenn	Feb		Liver disease	2 days
11	Frances Neeld	2	F				Tenn	Aug		Cholera inf.	5 days
12	Rachael Gray	96	F				Maryland	Nov		Old age	17 months
13	Rebecca Formalt	2	F				Tenn	Sept		Inflamation of brain	2 months
14	Jame	inf	M	B	S		Tenn	April		Burn	42 days
15	Conway Anny	2	M	B	S		Tenn	March		unknown	1 day
16	Henry McLane	38	M			M	Tenn	Aug	Farmer	Congestion	4 days
17	Jacob Bagley	55	M	B	S	M	N.C.	April	Laborer	Palsy	120 days
18	Hillard Stone	22	M	B	S		N.C.	March		T. fever	14 days
19	Stephen Small	57	M	B	S	W	Va	Nov	Blk-smith	Paralysis	inst.
20	George Cole	35	M	B	S		Va	Aug		T. fever	28 days
21	William McKenzie	87	M			M	Scotland	June	Farmer	Nervous, Old age	90 days
22	Margaret McKinzie	75	F			M	Georgia	Sept		Chronic	
23	William Stokes	21	M				Tenn	Dec	Hse-carpenter	T. fever	30 days
24	Harriet Stephenson	25	F	B	S	M	Kentucky	Aug		Congestive fever	12 days
25	Virginia Clark	1	F	B	S		Tenn	June		Measles	100 days
26	Cynthia Carter	24	F			M	unknown	Sept		Fits	10 days
27	John Beaty	86	M			W	Penn	Aug	Farmer	Old age	40 days
28	James Kimes	26	M	M	S	M	Tenn	March		T. fever	10 days
29	William D. Blake	52	M			M	N.C.	May	Farmer	Inflamation of brain	10 days
30	Mary Angelina Fremont	11m	F				Tenn	May		unknown	12 days
31	William Bearden	35	M			M	Va	July	Gunsmith	Dyspepsia	5 days
32	Thomas Blacknel	52	M			M	N.C.	March	Farmer	Dyspepsia	5 days
33	Edward Crunk	1m	M				Tenn	May		unknown	3 days
34	James Greer	60	M	B	S	M	unknown	Jan		Scrofula	12 days
35	Catharine Jane	1	F				Tenn	April		Dropsy	24 days

COUNTY OF LINCOLN, STATE OF TENNESSEE.

PAGE NO. 466 PERSONS WHO DIED DURING THE YEAR ENDING 1st JUNE, 1850.

Subdivision No. 16
O. W. Higgins

No. of Visit	Name	Age	Sex	Color	Free or Slave	Married/Widowed	Place of Birth	Month Died	Occupation	Disease or Cause of Death	No. Days Ill
1	Erasmus Smith	9m	M	B	S		Tenn	March		Inflamation of brain	6 days
2	S. W. Carmack	47	M			M	Tenn	Dec	Lawyer	Consumption	12 years
3	Thomas N. Scott	2	M				Tenn	July	Infant	Flux	45 days
4	John McCoy	22	M				Tenn	May	Blk-smith	Inf. fever	9 days
5	Elizabeth Crawford	61	F			W	Va	July	Seamstress	Cancer	Lingering
6	Infant of A. A. Tate		M				Tenn	Sept		Spasm	2 days
7	George Smith	1	M	B	S		Tenn	Sept		Croup	1 day
8	Lilly Talley	4m	F				Tenn	Sept		Hives	30 days
9	Nancy C. Buchanan	18	F				Tenn	Nov		Consumption	60 days
10	John Crabtree	2	M				Tenn	Oct		Fits	18 days
11	William M. Davis	32	M			W	Tenn	June	Farmer	Consumption	30 days
12	Bennet Mason	7	M				Alabama	Feb		Measles	8 days
13	Elisha Bradford	7	M				Tenn	Sept		Flux	8 days
14	Susan Crabtree	20	F				Tenn	Aug		Consumption	50 days
15	Louiza Crabtree	10	F				Tenn	May		Consumption	90 days
16	Henry Beck, Sr.	62	M			M	N.C.	April	Farmer	Gout	15 days
17	Infant of T. Massey	16d	M				Tenn	Oct		7 month child	6 days
18	Cyntha Smith	48	F			W	Va	Dec		Consumption	3 months
19	William A. Cathey	20	M				N.C.	May	Sch-teacher	Chronic	15 days
20	D---- Rayborn	5	F				Tenn	May		Congestion	6 days
21	Aley Davis	85	F			W	--illegible--	April		Bil. fever	24 days
22	Thomas Summers	7m	M				Tenn	Nov		Bil. fever	16 days
23	John Davis	70	M			M	N.C.	June	Farmer	Cancer	sudden
24	Andrew Sawyers	19	M	—	S		Tenn	Sept		Pneumonia	60 days
25	Martha Sawyers	14	F	—	S		Tenn	July		Measles	60 days
26	Calvin Sawyers	13	M	—	S		Tenn	Sept		Measles	120 days
27	Sally Eastland	24	F			M	Tenn	May		Inflamation	2 days
28	Louiza Commons	16	F				Tenn	May		Black tongue	8 days
29	Mima	65	F		F			May		Black tongue	8 days
30	Thomas	30	M		F			May		Black tongue	8 days
31	Robert Fullerton	30	M				Tenn	Sept	Sch-teacher	Congestive fever	10 days
32	Richard West	29	M			M	Tenn	Oct	Farmer	Fits	1 day
33	Richard Compton	70	M			M	Va	Feb	Farmer	Consumption	2 days
34	John Barnes	6	M				Tenn	Dec		Inflamation	2 days
35	Archibald McMillen	100	M			W	Ireland	March	Farmer	Old age	10 days

COUNTY OF LINCOLN, STATE OF TENNESSEE.

PAGE NO. 467 PERSONS WHO DIED DURING THE YEAR ENDING 1st JUNE, 1850.

Subdivision No. 2
Alfred Bearden

No. of Visit	Name	Age	Sex	Color	Free or Slave	Married/Widowed	Place of Birth	Month Died	Occupation	Disease or Cause of Death	No. Days Ill
1	Eveline	6m	F	B	S		Tenn	March		Croup	1 day
2	Mary	10	F	B	S		Tenn	Nov		Sc. fever	4 days
3	Jane Cammell	19	F			M	Tenn	Dec		Child bed	14 days
4	Berry S. Woodard	16	M				Tenn	Oct	Farmer	Dropsy	5 days
5	James McNatt	2	M				Tenn	April		Whooping cough	13 days
6	Hannah Ford	53	F			M	Tenn	July		Dyspepsia	21 days
7	Andrew J. Easlick	30	M			M	Tenn	Dec		Drowned	sudden
8	Bird Glidewell	50	M			M	Va	Dec	Farmer	--illegible--	sudden
9	John Taylor	41	M			M	N.C.	April	Farmer	T. fever	10 days
10	Simeon Nix	40	M			M	unknown	May	Farmer	T. fever	21 days
11	Tabitha Lions	80	F			W	N.C.	Feb	Farmer	unknown	5 weeks
12	Baker(Raker) Luttrell	29	M			M	Tenn	Aug	Farmer	Congestive fever	2 months
13	William H. Stokes	22	M				Tenn	Dec	Carpenter	T. fever	2 days
14	Henry F. Stokes	18	M				Tenn	Jan	Farmer	T. fever	1 month
15	Finetta Cariger	18	F				Tenn	Sept		Sc. fever	5 days
16	Margaret Carigar	12	F				Tenn	Sept		Sc. fever	5 days
17	Mary A. Crigar	10	F				Tenn	Sept		Sc. fever	4 days
18	Christine Carigar	7	F				Tenn	Sept		Sc. fever	2 days
19	Catharine Carigar	80	F				Penn	Oct		Old age	4 months
20	Mary J. Smith	23	F				Tenn	Aug		Child bed	16 days
21	Thomas Holt	5m	M				Tenn	Oct		Sc. fever	5 days
22	Joseph Ede	20	M	B	S		Tenn	May		unknown	5 months
23	Elizabeth Runels	24	F			M	Penn	Oct		Bil. fever	17 days
24	Bissy Kirklin	5m	M				Tenn	Jan		unknown	2 weeks
25	Joel Norris	40	M			M	N.C.	Oct	none	Shot	sudden
26	Thomas Talor (Taylor)	1m	M				Tenn	Aug		unknown	sudden
27	Joseph Keller	2	M				Illinois	June		Inflamation of brain	1 month
28	John T. Berry	10m	M				Tenn	Sept		Cholera Inf.	3 months
29	Sarah F. Berry	5	F				Tenn	July		Erysipelas	11 days
30	Sarah Webb	86	F			W	Va	Oct		Old age	23 days
31	Rose	16	F	B	S		Tenn			Child bed	sudden
32	Sarah Dance	80	F			W	Va	Sept		Old age	1 month
33	George	27	M	B	S		Tenn	May		Drowned	sudden
34	Kitty	1	F	B	S		Tenn	Jan		Diarrhea	2 days
35	Infant	1m	M	B	S		Tenn	Jan		Stillborn	

Remarks: and stimulants, but all the skill of the physicians seemed to have but little effect. The family spoken of lived near a creek, a place that had been settled some fifty years. The County around is hilly with limestone region. Near the mouth of the same creek and bordering on E.(Elk) River in a hilly limestone region during the latter part of last winter and spring and summer, a fever called Typhoid has raged to a considerable.....

COUNTY OF LINCOLN, STATE OF TENNESSEE.

PAGE NO. 470   PERSONS WHO DIED DURING THE YEAR ENDING 1st JUNE, 1850.

Subdivision No. 2
Alfred Bearden

No. of Visit	Name	Age	Sex	Color	Free or Slave	Married/Widowed	Place of Birth	Month Died	Occupation	Disease or Cause of Death	No. Days Ill
1	Winney	15	F	B	S		————	Jan		T. fever	1 month
2	Boler	16	F	B	S		————	April		unknown	1 month
3	Manerva	20	F	B	S		————	March		unknown	1 month
4	Wiliam Woodrough	59	M				Kentucky	Jan	Farmer	Fever	2 days
5	Elizabeth M. Beard	2	F				Tenn	April		unknown	2 days
6	Ruths Rone	78	F			W	N.C.	April		Cancer	9 years
7	Susan Blankenship	13	F				Alabama	Jan		White swelling	11 months
8	Driscal Beverly	4m	M				Tenn	Sept		Croup	6 days
9	Martilda	30	F	B	S		Tenn	June		Inflamation of lungs	
10	Mary L. Rease	27	F			M	Tenn	Oct		Cancer	10 years
11	James Shepard	16	M				Tenn	July	Farmer	Erysipelas	28 days
12	John Jonson	2	M				Tenn	Aug		Dysentery	7 days
13	William Brown	90	M			W	Va	Dec	Farmer	Old age	16 days
14	Mary A. Brown	84	F			M	Maryland	July		Old age	3 years
15	Martha J. Jonson	4	F				Tenn	July		Croup	8 days
16	Peter S.	60	M	B	S		N.C.	Sept		unknown	3 months
17	Moses Harding	78	M			M	N.C.	Oct	Farmer	Old age	5 months
18	Marion Thompson	1	M				Tenn	Feb		Sc. fever	5 months
19	Julia	36	F	B	S		Va	April		Child bed	2 months
20	Sion M. C. Bates	1m	M				Tenn	Aug		Whooping cough	5 days
21	Henry H. Pamplin	53	M				Va	Oct	Farmer	Consumption	9 days
22	Delinda Pamplin	46	F			W	Va	Feb		Apoplexy	sudden
23	George Wright	10m	M				Tenn	Sept		Cholera Inf.	7 days
24	Mariah	8	F	B	S		Tenn	Nov		Disease of liver	6 months
25	Martha	25	F	B	S		Va	Feb		T. fever	3 days
26	Louise	3	F	B	S		Va	Feb		T. fever	5 days
27	Pina	25	F	B	S		Tenn	Feb		T. fever	14 days
28	Eliza	1	F	B	S		Tenn	Nov		Croup	3 days
29	John Poke	1	M				Tenn	Oct		Diarrhea	14 days
30	Robert J. Sively	10	M				Tenn	Nov		Scrofula	21 days
31	Mary J. Wells	1	F				Tenn	Feb		Consumption	2 weeks
32	John B. Bagley	4	M				Tenn	Oct		Croup	5 days
33	Wiliam Renegar	1m	M				Tenn	Jan		Croup	3 days
34	Sarah Smith	68	F				Va	Oct		Old age	14 days
35	George M. D. Moor	6	M				Tenn	Jan		unknown	3 days

Remarks: with the exception of some two or three neighborhoods, this County has been remarkably healthy for the last year. On Mulberry Creek, some ten miles north of Elk River, in one neighborhood, a scarlet fever in its most malignant form prevailed. In Sept 1849, in one family, there was four deaths in a short time, almost everyone that was attached, died, in from two or five days. The disease was treated in various ways, both with mercurials and ....

COUNTY OF LINCOLN, STATE OF TENNESSEE.

PAGE NO. 471   PERSONS WHO DIED DURING THE YEAR ENDING 1st JUNE, 1850.

Subdivision No. 2
Alfred Bearden

No. of Visit	Name	Age	Sex	Color	Free or Slave	Married/Widowed	Place of Birth	Month Died	Occupation	Disease or Cause of Death	No. Days Ill
1	Winney	15	F	B	S		————	Jan		T. fever	1 month
2	Boler	16	F	B	S		————	April		unknown	1 month
3	Minerva	20	F	B	S		————	March			

COUNTY OF McMINN, STATE OF TENNESSEE.

PAGE NO. 475 PERSONS WHO DIED DURING THE YEAR ENDING 1st JUNE, 1850.

23rd Subdivision, E. District
H. M. McElrath

No. of Visit	Name	Age	Sex	Color	Free or Slave	Married/Widowed	Place of Birth	Month Died	Occupation	Disease or Cause of Death	No. Days Ill
1	Mary Civels	12	F				Tenn	Oct	none	Croup	7 days
2	Justina Riddle	1	F				Tenn	Oct	none	Croup	7 days
3	Coleman Dennis	22	M				Tenn	June	Farmer	Fever	20 days
4	Crigton Dennis	20	M				Tenn	Aug	Farmer	Fever	20 days
5	H. H. Sheppard	11	M	B	S		N.C.	Aug	none	Worms	21 days
6	Susan Wood	33	F			M	N.C.	Aug	none	Fever	14 days
7	Mary Wood	70	F			W	N.C.	Aug	none	Old age	
8	Infant of Susan Wood	1	F				Tenn	Aug	none	Fever	14 days
9	John Owens	52	M			M	N.C.	Dec	Farmer	Drowned	
10	John Otterly	6m	M				Tenn	Dec	none	Croup	7 days
11	Elizabeth Grissom	52	F			M	Tenn	April	none	Consumption	C
12	Nancy J. Dennis	19	F				Tenn	June	Hse-work	Fever	14 days
13	Nancy Axley	3	F				Tenn	June	none	Pneumonia	7 days
14	Thomas Birch	6m	M				Tenn	Dec	none	unknown	6 days
15	James Rutherford	84	M			M	Va	Dec	Farmer	Dropsy	6 days
16	Mary Shearman	1	F				Tenn	May	none	Fever	7 days
17	Ann Coghill	60	F			M	Va	July	unknown	unknown	C
18	Rhoda Day	24	F			M	Tenn	Nov	Spinster	unknown	C
19	Martha Pettit	50	F			M	N.C.	Jan	Spinster	unknown	C
20	Levi Stratton	22	M				Tenn	July	Farmer	Fever	5 days
21	Arch Day	1	M				Tenn	July	none	unknown	40 days
22	Pheba Smith	83	F			W	Va	Nov	none	Disease of heart	5 days
23	Robert Stanfield	9m	M				Tenn	March	none	Cold	15 days
24	Margaret Search	5	F				N.C.	Aug	none	unknown	9 days
25	Slave of E. Rice's	8m	M	M	S		Tenn	Aug	none	Croup	1 day
26	Slave of Penelope Ivines'	1	F	M	S		Tenn	Feb	none	unknown	1 day
27	Mary Martin	50	F			W	Tenn	Aug	none	Congestive fever	14 days
28	Catharine Lea	23	F			M	Tenn	May	none	Consumption	14 days
29	A. P. Workman	4m	M				Tenn	April	none	Erysipelas	4 days
30	Lavinia, A. McClatchey's	40	F	B	S		N.C.	Aug	Cook	Cancer	C
31	Lavinia, A. McClatchey's	4m	F	B	S		Tenn	Dec	none	suffocated	
32	Infant of Mrs. Sanford	1m	F				Tenn	Aug	none	Fever	4 days
33	Dina, W. P. McDermot's		F	M	S		Tenn	June	Laborer	Fever	9 days
34	James	17	M	B	S		Tenn	Aug	Laborer	Fever	26 days
35	Van	10	M	M	S		Tenn	Aug	Laborer	Fever	6 days

COUNTY OF McMINN, STATE OF TENNESSEE.

PAGE NO. 478 PERSONS WHO DIED DURING THE YEAR ENDING 1st JUNE, 1850.

23rd Subdivision, East District

H. M. McElrath

No. of Visit	Name	Age	Sex	Color	Free or Slave	Married/Widowed	Place of Birth	Month Died	Occupation	Disease or Cause of Death	No. Days Ill
1	Slave of W. P. McDermot	1m	M	M	S		Tenn	Dec	none	Croup	1 day
2	Charity Ward	24	F			W	Kentucky	March	none	Consumption	C
3	Jacob Shook	1m	M				Tenn	July	none	Flux	36 days
4	Thomas Crutchfield	59	M			M	Tenn	Dec	Brk-mason	Fever	14 days
5	George, J. S. Bridges'	20	M	B	S		Tenn	March	Laborer	Scrofula	C
6	Temps, J. S. Bridges'	35	F	B	S		Tenn	April	Hse-girl	unknown	14 days
7	John Boyer	7	M				Tenn	May	none	Pneumonia	C
8	Mary R. Stover	1m	F				Tenn	June	none	Croup	1 day
9	V. M. Campbell	41	M			M	Tenn	Jan	Bank cashier	Consumption	C
10	Isaac Wallen	32	M				unknown	Dec	none	Dyspepsia	C
11	James Davis	3	M				Tenn	July	none	Fever	4 days
12	Rachel VanDyke	30	F			M	Tenn	Nov	Spinster	Consumption	C
13	James Lowry	78	M			M	Va	Oct	Farmer	Gravel	C
14	Martha Rice	53	F			W	Tenn	Oct	unknown	Liver complaint	35 days
15	William Ballen	74	M			M	N.C.	April	Farmer	Old age	
16	Sarah Heaton	56	F			W	S.C.	April	none	Fever	9 days
17	Jane Hale	51	F			M	Tenn	Sept	Spinster	Cancer	C
18	Nancy L. Hale	17	F				N.C.	July	none	Chills, Fever	C
19	Mary L. Step	36	F			M	Va	Oct	none	Liver complaint	C
20	Elizabeth Morris	60	F			M	Va	Oct	none	Liver complaint	C
21	Lavinia Wheely	15	F				Tenn	Oct	none	Cold	C
22	John Belcher	1	M				Tenn	June	none	Hives	7 days
23	Ruthy Dennis	20	F				Tenn	Aug	none	Fever	21 days
24	Mary T. Zegler	7	F				Tenn	March	none	unknown	C
25	Infant Lawson	2	M				Tenn	Oct	none	unknown	7 days
26	John Ellis	45	M			M	Tenn	Oct	Farmer	Dyspepsia	C
27	Mary Willis	30	F			M	Tenn	Oct	Spinster	Suicide by hanging	
28	Turner Sharp	80	M			M	unknown	Jan	Farmer	Cancer	C
29	Nimrod Hays	13	M				Tenn	April	none	Worms	7 days
30	William Hays	4	M				Tenn	Jan	none	Consumption	C
31	James Hays	27	M			M	Tenn	Dec	Farmer	Consumption	C
32	Arthur Newman	27	M			M	Tenn	Oct	Farmer	Fever	7 days
33	Sarah T. Rector	9	F				Tenn	Aug	none	---- of the mucus membrane	C
34	Jessee Carter	75	M			M	Va	Aug	Farmer	Fever	8 days
35	Martin Cook	50	M			M	Tenn	Dec	Farmer	Fever	6 days

COUNTY OF McMINN, STATE OF TENNESSEE.

PAGE NO. 479 PERSONS WHO DIED DURING THE YEAR ENDING 1st JUNE, 1850.

23rd Subdivision, East District
H. M. D. McElrath

No. of Visit	Name	Age	Sex	Color	Free or Slave	Married/Widowed	Place of Birth	Month Died	Occupation	Disease or Cause of Death	No. Days Ill
1	Elizabeth Haynes	28	F			M	Tenn	Dec	none	Child bed fever	14 days
2	Winefred Burnet	17	F				Tenn	June	none	Fever	8 days
3	James M. Hambright	19	M				Tenn	Dec	Student	T. fever	14 days
4	Benjamin F. Hambright	13	M				Tenn	Jan	Student	T. fever	14 days
5	Mary Courtney	64	F			W	Tenn	June	none	T. fever	14 days
6	Eliza Haywood	4	F				Tenn	June	none	unknown	42 days
7	Margaret Melton	10	F				Tenn	April	none	Fever	3 days
8	Martha Hardy	60	F			M	Va	Jan	none	Consumption	C
9	George Long	77	M			M	N.C.	Jan	Farmer	Old age	C
10	Samuel Connon	1	M				Tenn	Feb	none	Worms	24 days
11	James Walter	13	M				Tenn	Sept	none	Scrofula	18 days
12	Mathew H. Grills	1m	M				Tenn	June	none	unknown	7 days
13	John Sibert	75	M			W	Va	Nov	Farmer	Liver complaint	C
14	John W. Copeland	21	M				Tenn	Feb	Farmer	Fever	21 days
15	Infant of J. Thompson	1	M				Tenn	Oct	none	unknown	36 days
16	Joseph H. McSpoon	9m	M				Tenn	June	none	Cholera Inf.	4 days
17	Washington L. Cook	7	M				Tenn	Feb	none	Inflamation of brain	5 days
18	Sarah Hoil	30	F			M	Tenn	May	none	Winter fever	6 days
19	Nancy Hoil	5m	F				Tenn	May	none	Croup	2 days
20	Jacob Balinger	80	M			W	N.C.	June	Farmer	Old age	10 days
21	Meridith Balinger	77	M			M	N.C.	Aug	Farmer	Old age	10 days
22	Beersheba Harris	2m	F				Tenn	March	none	Fits	sudden
23	Elizabeth R. Galbreath	45	F			W	Tenn	Oct	none	Fever	10 days
24	Rispy Cobb	4	F				Tenn	Sept	none	Worms	7 days
25	Richard, J. Hoil's	25	M	M	S		Tenn	July	Laborer	Fever	4 days
26	Sam, J. Hoil's	23	M	M	S		Tenn	Sept	Laborer	Spinal affect.	C
27	Emily, J. Hoil's	31	F	M	S		Tenn	Aug	Laborer	Consumption	C
28	Mary Rutherford	1m	F				Tenn	Jan	none	unknown	1 day
29	George Fleming	9m	M				Tenn	March	none	Fever	21 days
30	Gabriel Cantrell	50	M			M	Tenn	Dec	Farmer	Suicide by hanging	
31	Salina Reynolds	28	F			M	Tenn	July	none	Liver complaint	C
32	Emily Terry	19	F				Tenn	Nov	none	Fever	21 days
33	Infant of Joe Smith	9m	F				Tenn	Nov	none	Thrash	2 days

Remarks: No particular malady prevalent in our County during the past year. Occasional chills and fever. Limestone water, with here and there a chalybeate spring. Timber of pine, oak, poplar, chestnut, hickory and walnut exsist in abundance. Lime in a natural state very abundant.

COUNTY OF McNAIRY, STATE OF TENNESSEE.

PAGE NO. 482 PERSONS WHO DIED DURING THE YEAR ENDING 1st JUNE, 1850.

B. B. Adams

No. of Visit	Name	Age	Sex	Color	Free or Slave	Married/Widowed	Place of Birth	Month Died	Occupation	Disease or Cause of Death	No. Days Ill
1	James Burtwell	50	M			W	Conn.	March	Deg. Artist	Rheumatism	3 years
2	Henry	35	M	B	S		unknown	Nov		Dead Palsy	9 months
3	Felix S. Braden	2	M				Tenn	April		Inflamation of brain	3 weeks
4	Charles	3	M	B	S		Tenn	Feb		Bronchitis	3 weeks
5	Polly Ann Benson	4m	F				Tenn	April		St. Anthony's fever	3 months
6	Jackson	8	M	M	S		Tenn	May		Inflamation of bowels	1 week
7	Sarah J. Hill	1m	F				Tenn	Feb		unknown	1 month
8	Prudence Inman	69	F			M	S.C.	April		Winter fever	3 months
9	Louise Bell	40	F			M	Tenn	July		Consumption	10 years
10	Amanda McCann	4	F				Tenn	May		Whooping cough	3 weeks
11	Esther Willoby	58	F			M	N.C.	June		Ulcer	15 years
12	Martha Ann Anderson	5	F				Tenn	Sept		Fever	2 weeks
13	Arilla Adams	24	F			M	N.C.	Aug		Consumption	18 months
14	Bolivar Adams	3m	M				Tenn	Sept		unknown	2 weeks
15	Nancy McAfee	22	F				Tenn	Oct		Consumption	3 months
16	Malci	1m	M	B	S		Tenn	May		unknown	3 weeks
17	Jefferson	3m	M	B	S		Tenn	April		unknown	4 weeks
18	Rachel Prather	65	F			M	Maryland	April		Dropsy	3 months
19	Tom	9m	M	B	S		Tenn	Sept		Worms	1 week
20	Salina Wardlow	8m	F				Tenn	Dec		unknown	2 months
21	Jasper Ham	17	M				Tenn	Sept	Farmer	Killed by horse	sudden
22	Sarah J. Huggins	1	F				Tenn	Sept		Cholera Inf.	1 week
23	Louisa Garret	3m	F				Tenn	Dec		unknown	sudden
24	Samuel	2m	M	B	S		Tenn	Jan		unknown	sudden
25	William R. Henderson	40	M			W	unknown	Feb	Farmer	Consumption	6 months
26	James Henderson	4	M				Tenn	unknown		unknown	unknown
27	Frank	6m	M	B	S		Tenn	Dec		unknown	sudden
28	Matthew	4m	M	B	S		Tenn	Jan		unknown	sudden
29	Zirnenah	3m	M	B	S		____	Jan		unknown	sudden
30	John Reid	3	M				Tenn	July		unknown	2 months
31	Eliza Gossett	45	F			M	unknown	Nov		Gravel	1 year
32	George McVey	1m	M				Tenn	April		unknown	3 weeks
33	Ellen	35	F	B	S		Va	July		Cholera	sudden
34	Booker Wynn	4	M				Tenn	July		Cholera Inf.	sudden
35	Albert McNairy	11m	M				Tenn	May		Congestive fever	3 weeks

COUNTY OF McNAIRY, STATE OF TENNESSEE.

PERSONS WHO DIED DURING THE YEAR ENDING 1st JUNE, 1850.

B. B. Adams

No. of Visit	Name	Age	Sex	Color	Free or Slave	Married/Widowed	Place of Birth	Month Died	Occupation	Disease or Cause of Death	No. Days Ill
1	Joseph Gage	8	M				—	March		T. fever	3 weeks
2	Elizabeth Sutton	1	F				Tenn	Aug		Inflamation	1 week
3	Susannah Parks	27	F				Tenn	July		Cholera	sudden
4	Benjamin Suiter	100	M			M	S.C.	Nov	Farmer	Cholera	sudden
5	Eli Sykes	28	M			M	unknown	Nov	Farmer	T. fever	2 weeks
6	Malinda Ramer	10m	F				Tenn	Aug		unknown	sudden
7	John R. Helms	8	M				N.C.	May		unknown	3 months
8	Susan Clifton	21	F				N.C.	Oct		T. fever	6 weeks
9	Eliza Laughlin	5m	F				Tenn	Jan		unknown	sudden
10	Jane Valient	83	F			W	Maryland	Oct		Congestive chill	sudden
11	Isaac N. Coleman	19	M				N.C.	Nov	Farmer	T. fever	4 weeks
12	Cicero H. Hendrix	4	M				N.C.	Oct		unknown	3 months
13	Thomas McCalpin	82	M			M	Georgia	Jan	Farmer	unknown	6 months
14	F. P. Owens	4	M				Tenn	Sept		Bil. fever	2 weeks
15	Nancy Whitley	20	F				N.C.	Oct		T. fever	1 week
16	Sally Whitley	16	F				N.C.	Oct		T. fever	1 week
17	Betsey Whitley	19	F				N.C.	Nov		T. fever	1 month
18	William H. King	9m	M				Tenn	Nov		T. fever	1 month
19	Aleyan Stovall	4	F				Miss	Sept		Inflamation of brain	sudden
20	Emeline	18	F	B	S		Alabama	Oct		T. fever	1 month
21	Anna	1	F	B	S		Tenn	Dec		Quinsy	5 days
22	Natt	2	M		S		—	July		Burnt	sudden
23	Martha McKinney	35	F			M	N.C.	April		Pelvis disease	sudden
24	John Lacefield	6	M				Tenn	Dec		T. fever	11 days
25	Martin Kirkman	8	M				N.C.	Feb		Dropsy	2 months
26	Susan Lockman	13	F				N.C.	Jan		unknown	1 week
27	Lemuel Sanders	50	M			M	N.C.	Nov	Farmer	T. fever	6 weeks
28	Mary Simpson	84	F			M	S.C.	Aug		T. fever	10 days
29	Rachel Maxwell	38	F				Tenn	Nov		T. fever	6 weeks
30	Eli Herrel	2	M				Arkansas	July		Dropsy	6 months
31	Martha Franks	1	F				Tenn	Oct		Croup	2 weeks
32	Harman Armfield	47	M			M	N.C.	July	Farmer	Bil. fever	1 month
33	Louisa Potter	10m	F				Tenn	May		unknown	2 weeks
34	Pleasant Holyfield	22	M				Tenn	Nov	Farmer	T. fever	2 months
35	Thomas Beeny	20	M				N.C.	Nov	Blk-smith	T. fever	1 month

COUNTY OF McNAIRY, STATE OF TENNESSEE.

PAGE NO. 485 PERSONS WHO DIED DURING THE YEAR ENDING 1st JUNE, 1850.

B. B. Adams

No. of Visit	Name	Age	Sex	Color	Free or Slave	Married/Widowed	Place of Birth	Month Died	Occupation	Disease or Cause of Death	No. Days Ill
1	James	3m	M	B	S		Tenn	Dec		Accident	sudden
2	Reubin Ross	12	M				Tenn	Sept		T. fever	5 weeks
3	Sarah Smith	12	F				Tenn	Sept		Inflamation fever	4 weeks
4	Lucinda Maness	4	F				Tenn	Oct		T. fever	4 weeks
5	Alonzo Thomas	1m	M				Tenn	Feb		unknown	1 month
6	Randle McDaniel	58	F			M	N.C.	July	Farmer	Pleurisy	3 months
7	Laviny Randolph	5	F				Tenn	Jan		T. fever	1 week
8	Willis	18	M	B	S			June		Consumption	3 years
9	Nelson	5m	M	B	S			Nov		Phthisic	sudden
10	John Williams	1	M				Tenn	July		Inflamation of brain	1 week
11	Thomas Muse	55	M			M	N.C.	April	Carpenter	Cholera	sudden
12	Kenneth McKenzie	80	M			M	N.C.	April	Farmer	Chronic	4 years
13	William Davis	10	M				Tenn	Feb		T. fever	3 weeks
14	Ira Rama	28	M				Tenn	Nov	Farmer	T. fever	3 weeks
15	Elizabeth Mitchell	30	F			M	S.C.	Nov		Dropsy	12 months
16	Nancy Pike	33	F			M	N.C.	Oct		Congestive Chill	3 weeks
17	Catharine Plunk	73	F			W	N.C.	Nov		Old age	1 week
18	Eliza Sypes	18	F				Tenn	Nov		T. fever	1 month
19	Abner Rhodes	55	M			M	N.C.	Dec	Carpenter	Consumption	2 years
20	Jackson Luny	24	M			M	Tenn	Jan	Farmer	Consumption	2 years
21	James Whitman	9m	M				Tenn	Jan		Croup	1 week
22	Adam Ruth	66	M			W	S.C.	Jan	Farmer	unknown	2 months
23	John Plunk	1m	M				Tenn	April		Whooping cough	12 days
24	Priscilla Melton	1m	F				Tenn	Nov		unknown	1 week
25	Nancy Lee	18	F				Tenn	Feb		Winter fever	9 days
26	Mary Ann Lee	20	F				Tenn	Feb		Winter fever	3 weeks
27	George Hightower	9m	M				Tenn	Dec		unknown	2 weeks
28	Nancy Dunn	42	F			M	Alabama	Jan		Congestive fever	2 weeks
29	Louisa Shelton	18	F				Va	Sept		Yellow Jaundice	2 weeks
30	Ellender Thompson	95	F			W	N.C.	Oct		Old age	2 weeks
31	Amy	68	F	B	S			Oct		Phthisic	2 weeks
32	Mary Odum	1	F				Tenn	Oct		unknown	sudden
33	John Sewell	19	M				Tenn	Feb	Farmer	Consumption	3 months
34	Porter McLaughlin	14	M				Tenn	Dec		Congestive fever	10 days
35	Nathan Kemp	11m	M				Tenn	Jan		Inflamation of brain	2 weeks

COUNTY OF McNAIRY, STATE OF TENNESSEE.

PAGE NO. 487 PERSONS WHO DIED DURING THE YEAR ENDING 1st JUNE, 1850.

B. B. Adams

No. of Visit	Name	Age	Sex	Color	Free or Slave	Married/Widowed	Place of Birth	Month Died	Occupation	Disease or Cause of Death	No. Days Ill
1	William Adams	18	M				Tenn	March	Idiotic	Pleurisy	sudden
2	Margaret Ingle	2m	F				Tenn	Dec		Whooping cough	1 week
3	Harriet Farmer	11m	F				Tenn	July		unknown	sudden
4	Polly Ann Willet	21	F				Tenn	Jan		Consumption	1 year
5	Catherine Jones	1m	F				Tenn	Nov		unknown	1 week
6	Elizabeth Jones	1m	F				Tenn	Nov		unknown	2 weeks
7	Charles Picket	52	M			M	Kentucky	Dec	Farmer	Accident	3 weeks
8	Susan Cobb	17	F				Alabama	March		T. fever	4 weeks
9	Caroline Perkins	31	F			M	Tenn	Jan		Consumption	1 year
10	Amanda Layton	21	F				Tenn	March		Dropsy	3 months
11	Louisa	18	F	B	S			July		Dropsy	9 months
12	Ann	2	F	B	S		———	July		unknown	1 week
13	Caledonia Ursery	17	F				Tenn	March		Consumption	9 months
14	Elijah Mills	3m	M				Tenn	Sept		unknown	2 months
15	William Walker	34	M				Illinois	Nov	Farmer	T. fever	3 weeks
16	Caledonia Mickie	9m	F				Tenn	Aug		Cholera Inf.	2 weeks
17	Susan Stephenson	30	F			M	Tenn	March		Consumption	2 years
18	Claiborn Harris	35	M			M	N.C.	Oct	Mechanic	Inflamation of bowels	4 days

Remarks: The most prevalent malady in my District was Typhoid Fever in a very malignant form. The general character of water is freestone. Some portions of the County abounded with Shell(Shale), when water is found from one to three hundred feet in depth. Soil sandy, mixed with marl and clay. Timber of the most abundance, natural growth are oakm black-jack, hickory, chestnut and pine.

COUNTY OF MACON, STATE OF TENNESSEE.

PAGE NO. 489 PERSONS WHO DIED DURING THE YEAR ENDING 1st JUNE, 1850.

Civil District No. 1

H. S. Young

No. of Visit	Name	Age	Sex	Color	Free or Slave	Married/Widowed	Place of Birth	Month Died	Occupation	Disease or Cause of Death	No. Days Ill
1	Daniel Smith Weems	2	M				Tenn	March		Croup	1 week
2	Solanda J. Weems	1	F				Tenn	Jan		unknown	3 weeks
3	Mary Thomas	87	F			W	Penn	April		Dead Palsy	3 days
4	Harriet Holland	20	F	M	S		Tenn	Aug		Fever	1 week
5	Mahulda Holland	14	F	M	S		Tenn	Aug		Fever	1 week
6	Lewis Holland	12	M	M	S		Tenn	Aug		Fever	1 week
7	John A. Dreury	1	M				Tenn	Oct		unknown	2 months
8	Samuel Freeman	10m	M				Tenn	Nov		Sc. fever	2 months
9	William Chamberlain	68	M			M	Tenn	Nov	Saddler	Dropsy	1 year
10	Ellen Adkinson	5	F				Tenn	Feb		Cold	10 days
11	Aron Fuqua	11	M				Va	Jan		Dropsy	15 months
12	Lucinda Meadow	15	F				Tenn	May		Fever	16 days
13	not named	2d	F				Tenn	Nov		unknown	1 day
14	Jane	2	F	B	S		Tenn	April		Burnt	3 days
15	John Adams	2	M				Tenn	Dec		unknown	9 days
16	Hulet Lane	2	M				Tenn	Sept		Worms	3 weeks

COUNTY OF MACON, STATE OF TENNESSEE.

PAGE NO. 492 PERSONS WHO DIED DURING THE YEAR ENDING 1st JUNE, 1850.

Civil District No. 3
H. S. Young

No. of Visit	Name	Age	Sex	Color	Free or Slave	Married/Widowed	Place of Birth	Month Died	Occupation	Disease or Cause of Death	No. Days Ill
1	unnamed	1d	F				Tenn	March		unknown	1 hour
2	Jesse Coker	65	M			M	N.C.	Nov	Farmer	Apoplexy Fits	sudden
3	John Vance	22	M				Tenn	Sept	Farmer	Congestive fever	6 days
4	Benjamin Mills	1	M				Tenn	July		Inflamation of brain	5 days
5	Prudence Adams	30	F				Tenn	May		Fever	30 days
6	Delila Rouse	40	F	B		M	Tenn	Aug		Chronic	5 years
7	(no name)	1	F				Tenn	March		unknown	1 day
8	Andrew Prock	26	M				Tenn	Oct	Farmer	Consumption	12 months
9	John Reid	32	M			M	Tenn	Dec	Farmer	Consumption	2 years
10	John Mitchel	1	M				Tenn	April		Worms	4 days
11	Solomon Morris	12	M				Tenn	June		Milk sick	9 days
12	Wilkinson Sutton	33	M			M	Tenn	March	Farmer	Milk sick	3 days
13	Elias Stewart	18	M	B			Tenn	Dec	Farmer	Consumption	6 months
14	Sarah Smothers	27	F				Tenn	Nov		Chol. Bil.	30 days
15	Cymantha Hammock	1	F				Tenn	Oct		unknown	7 days
16	Mary A. Vaughan	18	F			M	Va	Feb		unknown	3 days
17	Elmira J. Kerly	7	F				Tenn	June		--illegible--	14 days
18	Ira Meadow	59	M			M	Va	Oct	Farmer	T. fever	21 days
19	Isaac Hatchet	40	M			M	Tenn	April	Farmer	Fever	14 days
20	Elijah Adams	84	M			W	N.C.	April	Farmer	T. fever	40 days
21	(no name)	1d	M				Tenn	June		unknown	1 day
22	Elizabeth Jones	38	F			M	Va	Jan		D. Palsy	12 months
23	Charles Alvis	1	M				Tenn	Nov		Inflamation of brain	7 days
24	James A. Sloan	11m	M				Tenn	Jan		Inflamation of brain	14 days
25	Cyntha A. Gaines	18	F				Tenn	Sept		Fever	1 week
26	Angeline Carter	12	F				Tenn	Feb		Pleurisy	6 days
27	Elizabeth Parrish	1	F				Tenn	Sept		Fever	2 weeks
28	James M. Dalton	2m	M				Tenn	Nov		Croup	2 weeks
29	Benja. Haines	103	M			W	Va	Jan	Farmer	Dropsy	5 weeks
30	Susanna Haines	85	M?			M	Va	Oct		Accident	4 weeks
31	not named, Smith	1d	M				Tenn	Jan		unknown	1 day
32	not named, Smith	1d	M				Tenn	Jan		unknown	1 day
33	not named, Goodall	1d	F				Tenn	Nov		unknown	1 day
34	John R. Gibbs	14	M				Tenn	Oct		Congestive Chill	10 days
35	Mariah Carter	3m	F				Tenn	Feb		unknown	5 days

COUNTY OF MACON, STATE OF TENNESSEE.

PAGE NO. 493 PERSONS WHO DIED DURING THE YEAR ENDING 1st JUNE, 1850.

Civil District No. 7
20th day of Aug 1850 by Halery S. Young

No. of Visit	Name	Age	Sex	Color	Free or Slave	Married/Widowed	Place of Birth	Month Died	Occupation	Disease or Cause of Death	No. Days Ill
1	Fielding Bell	1	M				Tenn	Jan		Sc. fever	5 days
2	Samuel G. McConehay	70	M				Tenn	Feb		Chronic	1 year
3	no name	1d	M				Tenn	Dec		Premature	
4	Negro child	2m	M	M	S			March		unknown	1 day
5	Franklin	4m	M	M	S		Tenn	June		unknown	1 day
6	Hannah	30	F	M	S		Tenn	Dec		Fever	40 days
7	Nancy Brandon	40	F			M	Kentucky	July		unknown	12 months
8	no name	10d	M				Kentucky	April		unknown	10 days
9	Daniel Decker	38	M				Tenn	July	Farmer	Fever	25 days
10	Caison, slave	23	F	B	S			May		Poison	5 weeks
11	Lucy Ann	2m	F				Tenn	Oct		Fever	10 days
12	Jefferson Wallace	39	M				Kentucky	Feb	Shoemaker	Cancer	19 years
13	Felix G. Rusor	15	M				Kentucky	Feb	Farmer	Fever	3 months
14	Anna Andrews	5	F				Tenn	July		Dropsy	3 months
15	Amanda Andrews	17	F				Tenn	Jan		Consumption	12 months
16	Nancy Linville	9m	F				Tenn	Nov		Yellow thrash	4 weeks
17	Andrew Burrow	13	M				Tenn	March		Dropsy	18 months
18	no name, Burrow	2m	M	M	S		Tenn	Sept		unknown	1 day
19	Sarah Burrow	4	F	M	S		Tenn	Oct		Accident	2 weeks
20	Louis Cap	8m	M	M	S		Tenn	Aug		Smothered	sudden
21	Matthew Burrow	20	M	M	S		Tenn	Feb		Poison	2 weeks
22	Sabra E. Holland	1m	F				Tenn	March		unknown	1 month
23	Moses G. Ford	52	M			M	Tenn	May	Farmer	Dead Palsy	3 years
24	not named	1w	F				Tenn	Feb		unknown	1 day
25	Lucy Woodcock	77	F			M	N.C.	Feb		Accident	1 year
26	Jerome Gregory	1m	M				Tenn	Feb		Hives	1 hour
27	Abner Owen	37	M			M	Va	Aug		Dropsy	2 years
28	Susanah Stinson	30	F				Va	Aug		Dropsy	2 months
29	Hugh Roark	4m	M				Tenn	July		Fall, head	1 week
30	not named	1	F					Sept		unknown	1 hour
31	E. Sutton	81	M				N.C.	April	Farmer	Old age	9 days
32	Hannah Wakefield	54	F	M	S		Tenn	May			6 months
33	John Barker	43	M			M	Va	Dec	Farmer	Consumption	7 weeks
34	Marshall Barker	10m	M				Tenn	Nov		unknown	3 months
35	Cora Bandy	80	F			W	Va	Dec	Farmer	Old age	6 months

COUNTY OF MADISON, STATE OF TENNESSEE.

PAGE NO. 495 PERSONS WHO DIED DURING THE YEAR ENDING 1st JUNE, 1850.

Jo. M. Parker

No. of Visit	Name	Age	Sex	Color	Free or Slave	Married/Widowed	Place of Birth	Month Died	Occupation	Disease or Cause of Death	No. Days Ill
1	Margaret B. Faulkner	1	F				Tenn	Nov			sudden
2	Mary A. B. Phillips	1	F				Tenn	Oct			sudden
3	Andrew	1	M	B	S		Tenn	May		unknown	C
4	Joseph	1	M	B	S		Tenn	March		unknown	C
5	Ann E. Hart	17	F				N.C.	Jan		Con.	C
6	Elizabeth	18	F	B	S		Tenn	Feb		Con.	C
7	Monroe	1	M	B	S		Tenn	Dec			sudden
8	Thomas	3	M	B	S		Tenn	June		unknown	C
9	David	3	M	B	S		Tenn	July		unknown	C
10	Ann	1	F	B	S		Tenn	Sept		unknown	12 days
11	Mary A. McCrory	37	F			M	Tenn	Feb		Fever	8 days
12	Frances McCrory	1	F				Tenn	Jan		Chicken pox	30 days
13	Amy	50	F	B	S		N.C.	Oct		unknown	C
14	Martha E. Watson	14	F				Tenn	Oct		unknown	
15	Ann	18	F	B	S		Tenn	Aug		Cholera Mor.	6 days
16	Eliza	17	F	B	S		Va	Aug		Cholera Mor.	21 days
17	George	90	M	B	S		Va	March		Old age	
18	Mary Crowell	42	F				N.C.	Aug		unknown	
19	Adelia Horton	1	F				Tenn	Feb		Pneumonia	30 days
20	Daniel	3	M	B	S		Tenn	Feb		Burned	sudden
21	Thomas	45	M	B	S		N.C.	Nov		Pneumonia	4 days
22	Doctor	20	M	B	S		N.C.	Feb		Pneumonia	2 days
23	Helen Jones	30	F				N.C.	Sept		Congestive chill	6 days
24	Mrs. Moore	20	F				Alabama	June		Child bed	3 days
25	Martha	10	F	B	S		Tenn	March		Dropsy	14 days
26	Cary	8	M	B	S		Tenn	April		Scrofula	25 days
27	Martha H. Hall	3m	F				Tenn	Dec		Hives	15 days
28	Frederick	39	M	B	S		Tenn	Jan		Pneumonia	12 days
29	James	1	M	B	S		Tenn	April		Fever	12 days
30	Amy	19	F	B	S		N.C.	April		unknown	
31	Rachel	4	F	B	S		Tenn	Feb		Scrofula	
32	Isham	10m	M	B	S		Tenn	Dec		unknown	
33	John D. Boon	1	M				Tenn	April		unknown	
34	D. Jones	62	F			M	Va	Nov		Con.	C
35	Malinda	31	F	B	S		N.C.	March		unknown	C

COUNTY OF MADISON, STATE OF TENNESSEE.

PAGE NO. 498 PERSONS WHO DIED DURING THE YEAR ENDING 1st JUNE, 1850.

J. M. Parker

No. of Visit	Name	Age	Sex	Color	Free or Slave	Married/Widowed	Place of Birth	Month Died	Occupation	Disease or Cause of Death	No. Days Ill
1	Jane	16	F	B	S		Kentucky	Feb		Con.	C
2	A. J. Robards	18	M				Va	Feb	Farmer	unknown	
3	Margaret Bratton	89	F			W	N.C.	Oct		Old age	
4	Nancy Montgomery	48	F			W	Tenn	March		unknown	C
5	E. R. McAdoo	2	F				Tenn	Nov		Asthma	C
6	Zachary Taylor	1	M				Tenn	Nov		unknown	C
7	Henry	5m	M	B	S		Tenn	Nov		unknown	C
8	Jas. McWilliams	60	M				Tenn	Jan	Farmer	unknown	
9	Martha J. Gibbs	1	F				Tenn	Aug		unknown	
10	Mary Ingram	21	F			M	N.C.	May		Con.	C
11	Thomas	22	M	B	S		N.C.	Jan		Cold	6 days
12	Harriet	23	F	B	S		Tenn	Feb		Fever	12 days
13	John McNatt	6	M				N.C.	Jan		Croup	12 days
14	Dilsy	40	F	B	S		Va	July		Fits	6 days
15	Sarah Hardage	30	F			M	Tenn	June		Con.	C
16	Jane Williamson	2	F				Tenn	May		unknown	
17	James T. Walsh	3m	M				Tenn	March		Cholera Inf.	6 days
18	Jos. E. Browder	47	M			M	Va	Dec	Farmer	Fits	21 days
19	Nelson	16	M	B	S		Tenn	Nov		Con.	C
20	Cymantha	7m	F	B	S		Tenn	Dec		unknown	
21	Henry Norton	73	M			M	Penn	Jan	Farmer	Dropsy	C

COUNTY OF MADISON, STATE OF TENNESSEE.

PAGE NO. 499 PERSONS WHO DIED DURING THE YEAR ENDING 1st JUNE, 1850.

J. M. Parker

No. of Visit	Name	Age	Sex	Color	Free or Slave	Married/Widowed	Place of Birth	Month Died	Occupation	Disease or Cause of Death	No. Days Ill
1	Jinsy	2	F	B	S		Tenn	Aug		Bowel complaint	21 days
2	William Miller	20	M				Tenn	Feb	none	Con.	C
3	Jane	8	F	B	S		Tenn	May		Scrofula	C
4	John Lynch	40	M				Va	Dec	Farmer	Con.	C
5	Rachel	85	F				Va	Dec		Old age	
6	Jane E. Campbell	42	F			M	Tenn	Dec		Pneumonia	8 days
7	George	11	M	B	S		Tenn	April		unknown	3 days
8	George	1	M	B	S		Tenn	July		Ricketts	C
9	Allice D. Parker	1	F				Tenn	April		Dropsy of brain	21 days
10	E. Gardner	1m	F				Tenn	Jan		Pneumonia	1 day
11	Bobb	2m	M	B	S		Tenn	May		unknown	4 days
12	Dick	40	M	B	S		Va	Nov		Pneumonia	14 days
13	Cornelius	5	M	B	S		Tenn	Jan		Dropsy	12 days
14	James	75	M	B	S		Va	July		Old age	
15	Fanny W. Collins	2	F				Tenn	Aug		Fever	1 month
16	Dennis	2	M	B	S		Tenn	July		Diarrhea	2 months
17	Eliza J. Edwards	10m	F				Tenn	Sept		Brain fever	1 month
18	G. Anderson	75	M			M	S.C.	Jan	Farmer	unknown	C
19	Kizza	50	F	B	S		unknown	April		Dropsy	C
20	Patience	62	F	B	S		unknown	April		Dropsy	C
21	G. M. Longmire	9m	M				Tenn	Aug		Scalded	sudden
22	Alex. Johnson	35	M			M	N.C.	Sept	Farmer	Fever	7 days
23	Stephen	20	M	B	S		unknown	Feb		Hemorrhage	7 days
24	Louisa Artist	16	F	B	S		unknown	April		T. fever	C
25	Caroline	5	F				Tenn	April		Scalded	sudden
26	Fanny	1	F	B	S		Tenn	Dec		Pneumonia	10 days
27	Allethia	1	F	B	S		Tenn	May		Fits	3 days
28	Lany Tyson	52	F				N.C.	April		Scruvey	C
29	S. W. Dunaway	2	F				Tenn	Sept		Croup	4 days

COUNTY OF MADISON, STATE OF TENNESSEE.

PAGE NO. 499 PERSONS WHO DIED DURING THE YEAR ENDING 1st JUNE, 1850.

J. M. Parker

No. of Visit	Name	Age	Sex	Color	Free or Slave	Married/Widowed	Place of Birth	Month Died	Occupation	Disease or Cause of Death	No. Days Ill
30	Adeline	5m	F	B	S		Tenn	Aug		Pleurisy	4 days
31	Peter Swink	3	M				Tenn	Aug		Violence	sudden
32	W. H. Parker	1	M				Tenn	Nov		Bronchitis	10 days
33	Rachel	26	F	B	S		N.C.	March		unknown	10 days
34	Louisa J. Marsh	1m	F				Tenn	Oct		unknown	30 days
35	Jasper Newton	7m	M	B	S		Tenn	Feb		unknown	C

COUNTY OF MADISON, STATE OF TENNESSEE.

PAGE NO. 502 PERSONS WHO DIED DURING THE YEAR ENDING 1st JUNE, 1850.

J. M. Parker

No. of Visit	Name	Age	Sex	Color	Free or Slave	Married/Widowed	Place of Birth	Month Died	Occupation	Disease or Cause of Death	No. Days Ill
1	Sarah Bickers	10m	F				Tenn	Aug		unknown	30 days
2	Sarah Thompson	1	F				Tenn	Sept		Diarrhea	C
3	E. Merony	63	F			W	N.C.	Dec		Pleurisy	C
4	Margaret York	58	F			W	S.C.	Dec		unknown	14 days
5	George	8m	M	B	S		Tenn	Sept		Smothered	sudden
6	Frank	6m	M	B	S		Tenn	Sept		unknown	
7	Mary	8m	F	B	S		Tenn	Aug		Fever	21 days
8	Mary E. Read	7m	F				Tenn	July		Cholera Inf.	C
9	Olivia Henry	33	F				N.C.	Sept		Dropsy	C
10	Mat. Deberry	21	M			M	Tenn	March	Farmer	Fever	6 weeks
11	Martha	21	F	B	S		Tenn	Oct		Fever	8 days
12	Peter	50	M	B	S		Georgia	March		Dyspepsia	C
13	Harriett	17	F	B	S		Tenn	May		unknown	2 days
14	Joshua Lawrence	38	M			M	N.C.	Jan	Farmer	Pneumonia	10 days
15	Joshua Glenn	25	M				Tenn	Nov	Farmer	Cholera	3 days
16	Sarah S. Bond	25	F			M	N.C.	Oct		Fever	15 days
17	Allen Weatherly	41	M			M	N.C.	July	Farmer	Fever	21 days
18	Jas. McMahon	10	F?				Tenn	Dec		Brain fever	8 days
19	Handy	20	M	B	S		Tenn	Dec		Con.	C
20	Gilla	35	F	B	S		Tenn	Sept		Deranged	C
21	E. J. Matthews	13	F				Tenn	Nov		Fever	31 days
22	John	1	M	B	S		Tenn	April		Pneumonia	14 days
23	Wilson	12	M	B	S		Tenn	Feb		Killed	sudden
24	Emily	2	F	B	S		Tenn	Oct		Croup	3 days
25	Isaac	2	M	B	S		Tenn	May		S	sudden
26	Jane	66	F	B	S		S.C.	Feb		Con.	C
27	Endora Witherspoon	6m	F				Tenn	March		Diarrhea	3 days
28	Reuben	6m	M	B	S		Tenn	March		Diarrhea	6 days
29	Elizabeth Hunter	4m	F				Tenn	June		Diarrhea	30 days
30	Caroline	20	F	B	S		Tenn	March		Child bed	7 days
31	Benjamin	8m	M	B	S		Tenn	March		Pleurisy	C
32	Rebecca	20	F	B	S		unknown	Nov		unknown	6 days
33	Mary A. Vantreese	18	F			M	Tenn	June		Dropsy	25 days
34	Charlott	25	F	B	S		S.C.	Feb		Pneumonia	7 days
35	G. B. Medlin	45	M			M	Tenn	July	Farmer	Con.	C

COUNTY OF MARION, STATE OF TENNESSEE.

PAGE NO. 503 PERSONS WHO DIED DURING THE YEAR ENDING 1st JUNE, 1850.

Different Districts
J. A. Hargis

No. of Visit	Name	Age	Sex	Color	Free or Slave	Married/Widowed	Place of Birth	Month Died	Occupation	Disease or Cause of Death	No. Days Ill
1	Abigal Stone	50	F			M	Va	Dec		Pneumonia	19 days
2	Martha J. Rankin	19	F			M	Tenn	March	Meth.Church	unknown	13 days
3	Elizabeth Steel	11m	F				Tenn	July		unknown	14 days
4	Charles Webe	17	M				Tenn	May		Consumption	M 2
5	Andrew Onley	41	M			M	Ireland	April	R.E.Church	unknown	5 days
6	Sarah Auston	43	F			M	S.C.	April		Pneumonia	10 days
7	Andrew Jackson	2	M				Tenn	Aug		unknown	7 days
8	Mary Brooks	16	F				Tenn	Nov		unknown	7 days
9	John Willson	68	M			M	S.C.	April	Farmer	Fever	7 weeks
10	Mary D.	70	F	B	S		Va	Nov		Cholic	14 days
11	George A. Brooks	62	M				Tenn	Jan	C.P.Church	unknown	6 years
12	Constintine Ladd	53	M			M	N.C.	Feb	Farmer	Fever	17 days
13	Mary Byers	28	F				Alabama	June	Meth. Church	Nervous	5 days
14	George W. Doss	5	M				Tenn	March		Croup	3 days
15	Thomas Hargis	2	M				Tenn	Dec		Nervous	10 days
16	Manon Austin	1	M				Tenn	July		Fever	30 days
17	Larinda Newsom	22	F				Tenn	Aug	Meth.	unknown	8 days
18	Mary E. Pearson	3	F				Tenn	April		Dropsy	6 weeks
19	Elizabeth Colewell	11	F				Georgia	Oct		unknown	sudden
20	Jasper McCoy	2m	M				Tenn	Jan		Hives	6 days
21	Nancy Clark	50	F			M	Tenn	Jan		Spasms	6 days
22	James Willson	18	M				S.C.	May		unknown	6 days
23	Andrew Willson	16	M				S.C.	Sept		unknown	10 days
24	Helen Torbett	19	F				Tenn	May	C.P.Church	Mumps	3 weeks
25	Susan Burnett	1m	F				Tenn	Feb		unknown	8 days
26	Catharine Burnett	1m	F				Tenn	Feb		unknown	10 days
27	Sarah McDaniel	1m	F				Tenn	April		unknown	1 day
28	Stephen Oyens	1	M				Tenn	April		unknown	8 days

Total amount of deaths 61

Remarks: State of Tennessee, Marion County. I, J. A. Hargis, Asst. Marshal of the East District of East Tennessee, do hereby certify that the foregoing schedule is a correct copy of the original as was taken by from the instruction and order of oath taken by me, this 12th day of November, 1850.

J. A. Hargis, Asst. Marshal
East District, East Tennessee.

COUNTY OF MARION, STATE OF TENNESSEE.

PAGE NO. 506 PERSONS WHO DIED DURING THE YEAR ENDING 1st JUNE, 1850.

Different Districts
J. A. Hargis

No. of Visit	Name	Age	Sex	Color	Free or Slave	Married/Widowed	Place of Birth	Month Died	Occupation	Disease or Cause of Death	No. Days Ill
1	Sarah Bridges	11m	F				Tenn	Sept		Pneumonia	3 days
2	Phillip Jonson	1	M				Tenn	Sept		C. fever	8 days
3	Nancy Manvill	6	F				Tenn	Aug		Pneumonia	6 days
4	William Ketner	5	M				Tenn	Aug		Pneumonia	14 days
5	John McKee	5	M				N.C.	Dec		unknown	4 days
6	Jehew Griffith	38	M				Tenn	Aug	Merchant	Cholera Morbus	6 days
7	Francis Tabers	16	M				Tenn	March	Farmer	Pneumonia	4 days
8	Benjamin Condra	51	M			M	Tenn	March	Farmer	Pneumonia	5 days
9	Calvin L. Swoferd	1	M				Tenn	Sept		Burned	14 days
10	Elizabeth Jack	18	F			M	Tenn	Sept		unknown	9 days
11	Frederick Farmer	78	M			M	Va	April	Farmer	Pneumonia	9 days
12	Charles P. Griffith	21	M			M	Tenn	April	Farmer	Pneumonia	2 days
13	Louransey Gray	10	M				Tenn	Oct		unknown	3 months
14	Rebeca Smith	22	F				Tenn	July	Meth.	Cholera Morbus	7 days
15	Benjamin Miser	32	M				Tenn	Dec		unknown	6 days
16	A-ah Miser	2m	F				Tenn	Dec		Consumption	46 days
17	Jane Fredrick	80	F				N.C.	Dec	Baptist	Old age	15 days
18	Sarah Stewart	82	F			W	Va	Sept	C.Presby.	Old age	30 days
19	Barbery Meritt	94	F			W	unknown	Dec	Methodist	Old age	9 days
20	Thomas Clining	57	M			W	Tenn	Feb	Bapt-Farmer	Consumption	6 months
21	Jane Graham	14	F				Tenn	Feb		Pneumonia	30 days
22	Hall Ridge	24	M				Tenn	July	Farmer	Pneumonia	8 days
23	George Shelton	14	M				Tenn	Feb	Farmer	Pneumonia	29 days
24	Elizabeth Shelton	52	F			M	Va	July	C.P.Church	Pneumonia	14 days
25	William Kelley	63	M			M	unknown	July	Farmer	Pneumonia	9 days
26	Harrison Woodley	47	M			M	Va	Oct	Farmer	Accident	21 days
27	William Thurmin	3m	M				Tenn	March		Croup	5 days
28	Obedience Martin	4	F				Tenn	July		Croup	17 days
29	Susan Brown	1m	F				Tenn	Sept		unknown	5 days
30	Manervey Daim	1m	F				Tenn	May		Croup	2 days
31	John Daim	19	M				Tenn	July	Farmer	unknown	5 days
32	Cintha Gord	1m	F				Tenn	April		Cold	6 days
33	Andrew McQuest	1m	M				Tenn	May		unknown	1 day

COUNTY OF MARSHALL, STATE OF TENNESSEE.

PAGE NO. 507 PERSONS WHO DIED DURING THE YEAR ENDING 1st JUNE, 1850.

Civil District No. 15
A. A. Johnson

No. of Visit	Name	Age	Sex	Color	Free or Slave	Married/Widowed	Place of Birth	Month Died	Occupation	Disease or Cause of Death	No. Days Ill
1	Margaret Houston	22	F	W	F	M	Tenn	March		unknown	10 days
2	Rhoda Morris	55	F	W	F	M	Va	Jan		Consumption	10 days
3	Infant	2m	F	B	S		Tenn	Feb		unknown	6 weeks
4	Zilla Yowell	8m	F	W	F		Tenn	Aug		Cholera Inf.	2 weeks
5	Preston	20m	M	B	S		Tenn	June		Diarrhea	1 year
6	William Benn Caudle	1	M	W	F		Tenn	Nov		Sc. fever	5 days
7	Margaret Record	6	F	W	F		Tenn	May		Inflamation of brain	17 days
8	Infant, G. W. Record's	1m	M	M	S		Tenn	June		Croup	2 days
9	Sarah Hammonds	2	F	W	F		Tenn	Aug		Consumption	6 months
10	Albert	11	M	B	S		Tenn	Jan		Congestive fever	8 hours
11	Julia	24	F	M	S	M	N.C.	Aug		T. fever	5 days
12	Laura F. Holbrook	7m	F	W	F		Texas	July		Fever	3 weeks
13	James M. Bowden	39	M	W	F	M	Tenn	July	Carpenter	Tetanus	2 weeks
14	Levander	1m	M	M	S		Tenn	June		Accident	sudden
15	Martha J. Clarke	1m	F	W	F		Tenn	July		Whooping cough	6 days
16	George Capps	3	M	W	F		Tenn	July		unknown	3 weeks
17	James	2	M	W	F		Tenn	July		unknown	2 weeks
18	Joseph M. Cloud	13	M	W	F		Tenn	Dec		Accident	sudden
19	Rachael	24	F	B	S	M	Tenn	Oct		Fever	4 months
20	Ryan Seaton	45	M	W	F		unknown	Oct	Shoemaker	Congestive chills	1 week
21	Presley Hopwood	23	M	W	F		Tenn	Oct	no trade	Fever	9 days
22	Cleopatra Jones	2	F	W	F		Tenn	July		Croup	1 day
23	Infant of David Bigham	1m	M	W	F		Tenn	Sept		unknown	1 day
24	Wilson P. Davis	1	M	W	F		Tenn	June		Diarrhea	6 days
25	Franklin W. White	2	M	W	F		Tenn	Aug		Croup	6 days
26	Slave, Martin S. Jones'	1m	F	M	S		Tenn	Dec		unknown	2 days
27	George Tomblinson	60	M	W	F	W	N.C.	June	Farmer	Liver disease	2 months
28	Andrew Lawrance	35	M	W	F	M	Tenn	Aug	Farmer	Dropsy of chest	2 months
29	Infant	11m	M	B	S		Tenn	May		unknown	2 months
30	Ambrose F. Fowler	1m	M	W	F		Tenn	June		unknown	3 days
31	Infant of Irvin Duncan	4m	M	W	F		Tenn	July		Diarrhea	4 days
32	Sarah Stephens	45	F	W	F	M	Va	July		Consumption	1 year
33	Edward P. Stephens	1	M	W	F		Tenn	June		Consumption	1 year
34	Jefferson	4m	M	M	S		Tenn	March		unknown	2 weeks
35	Infant	4m	M	M	S		Tenn	Feb		unknown	2 weeks

COUNTY OF MARSHALL, STATE OF TENNESSEE.

PAGE NO. 509 PERSONS WHO DIED DURING THE YEAR ENDING 1st JUNE, 1850.

Civil District No. 14
A. A. Johnson

No. of Visit	Name	Age	Sex	Color	Free or Slave	Married/Widowed	Place of Birth	Month Died	Occupation	Disease or Cause of Death	No. Days Ill
1	Lillus M. Bills	3m	F	W	F		Tenn	Aug		Thrash	2 months
2	Margaret H. Lincoln	6m	F	W	F		Tenn	Aug		Croup	sudden
3	Infant slave	1m	M	B	S		Tenn	Sept		unknown	sudden
4	Lewis Harris	79	M	W	F		Va.	Sept		Dropsy	6 months
5	William H. Evans	20	M	W	F		Tenn	Oct	Farmer	T. fever	2 weeks
6	Infant of W. H. Osborne	4m	F	W	F		Tenn	March		unknown	sudden
7	Elizabeth H. London	16	F	W	F		Tenn	Aug		Fever	5 days
8	Eliza Roberts	5	F	W	F		Alabama	Oct		Croup	sudden
9	James K. Hill	13	M	W	F		Tenn	Sept		Accident	sudden
10	Richard	19	M	B	S		Kentucky	March		unknown	2 weeks

COUNTY OF MARSHALL, STATE OF TENNESSEE.

PAGE NO. 511 PERSONS WHO DIED DURING THE YEAR ENDING 1st JUNE, 1850.

Civil District No. 4

No. of Visit	Name	Age	Sex	Color	Free or Slave	Married/Widowed	Place of Birth	Month Died	Occupation	Disease or Cause of Death	No. Days Ill
1	John M. Luna	8m	M	W	F		Tenn	July		unknown	8 months
2	John C. Holland	7m	M	W	F		Tenn	May		Hives	3 days
3	Infant	6m	M	B	S		Tenn	April		Hives	1 week
4	Malinda	32	F	B	S	M	Va	Feb		Cholera	2 months
5	John T. Craig	6m	M	W	F		Tenn	May		Croup	4 months
6	Thomas Blacknell	53	M	W	F	M	N.C.	March	Farmer	Consumption	10 years
7	Moses Curtiss	70	M	W	F	M	S.C.	June	Farmer	Dropsy	2 years
8	Mary Adams	80	F	W	F	W	N.C.	Jan		Old age	sudden
9	Henry C. Bagley	85	M	W	F	M	N.C.	Nov	Carpenter	Dropsy	1 month
10	Arena S. M. A. Brents	1	F	W	F		Tenn	Jan		Cholera Inf.	3 days
11	Margaret C. Houston	22	F	W	F	M	Tenn	March		Excessive labor(Childbirth)	8 days
12	Infant Houston	1d	M	W	F		Tenn	March		unknown	sudden

COUNTY OF MARSHALL, STATE OF TENNESSEE.

PAGE NO. 513 PERSONS WHO DIED DURING THE YEAR ENDING 1st JUNE, 1850.

Civil District No. 1

No. of Visit	Name	Age	Sex	Color	Free or Slave	Married/Widowed	Place of Birth	Month Died	Occupation	Disease or Cause of Death	No. Days Ill
1	Susan Davis	8m	F	W	F		Tenn	Sept		Cholera Inf.	1 month
2	William King	60	M	W	F	M	N.C.	Aug	Farmer	unknown	2 months
3	Sarah	1	F	B	S		Tenn	March		unknown	2 months
4	Infant slave	1m	M	B	S		Tenn	April		Thrash	1 month
5	William W. Nichols	88	M	W	F	W	N.C.	April	Farmer	Old age	8 days
6	Martha	28	F	B	S	M	Tenn	Sept		unknown	3 months
7	Thomas	2	M	B	S		Tenn	March		Croup	12 months
8	Meredith	20	M	B	S		Tenn	May		Dropsy	1 month
9	Isabella Kanier (Caneer)	80	F	W	F	W	Ireland	Dec		Old age	sudden
10	Infant Kanier) Twins	7m	M	W	F		Tenn	May		unknown	1 week
11	Infant Kanier)	6m	F	W	F		Tenn	March		unknown	sudden
12	Infant	6m	M	B	S		Tenn	Dec		unknown	sudden
13	Margaret Shires	95	F	W	F	W	Kentucky	March		unknown	sudden

COUNTY OF MARSHALL, STATE OF TENNESSEE.

PAGE NO. 515 PERSONS WHO DIED DURING THE YEAR ENDING 1st JUNE, 1850.

Civil District No. 13

No. of Visit	Name	Age	Sex	Color	Free or Slave	Married/Widowed	Place of Birth	Month Died	Occupation	Disease or Cause of Death	No. Days Ill
1	Samuel D. Mitchel	2m	M	W	F		Tenn	Nov		unknown	2 months
2	Infant of Seaborn Jones	3m	M	W	F		Tenn	Nov		unknown	sudden
3	William Dickson	63	M	W	F	M	N.C.	June	Farmer	Consumption	2 years
4	William E. Douglas	2	M	W	F		Tenn	Nov		Measles	7 days
5	James W. Jones	1	M	W	F		Tenn	Oct		Croup	1 day
6	Caledonia	7m	F	B	S		Tenn	July		Overlaid	sudden

COUNTY OF MARSHALL, STATE OF TENNESSEE.

PAGE NO. 517 PERSONS WHO DIED DURING THE YEAR ENDING 1st JUNE, 1850.

Civil District No. 9
John Venable

No. of Visit	Name	Age	Sex	Color	Free or Slave	Married/Widowed	Place of Birth	Month Died	Occupation	Disease or Cause of Death	No. Days Ill
1	Benjamin Lanier	53	M			M	Va	Sept	Farmer	Fever	5 weeks
2	Sarah L.--illegible--	1	F				Tenn	June		Cholera	1 day
3	Elizabeth Pharris	1	F				Tenn	Sept		Consumption	6 days
4	Mary Dawdy	20	F				Tenn	Aug		Fever	4 weeks
5	Catharine Wells	4	F	B	S		Tenn	Jan		Scrofula	C
6	Theodocia Gentry	87	F			W	N.C.	Jan		Old age	_____
7	Nancy Gentry	12	F	B	S		Va	March		Pneumonia	2 months
8	John Gentry	65	M	B	S		Va	April		unknown	2 weeks
9	Sarah Clark	18	F			M	Tenn	May		Consumption	4 months
10	Sarah Jones	2	F	B	S		Tenn	July		Phthisic	1 year
11	John Manear	52	M				Tenn	Aug	Farmer	Fever	3 months
12	James Davis	64	M			M	Va	March	Shoemaker	Cancer	1 year
13	Mary E. Cathey	1	F				Tenn	March		Worms	21 days

COUNTY OF MARSHALL, STATE OF TENNESSEE.

PAGE NO. 519 PERSONS WHO DIED DURING THE YEAR ENDING 1st JUNE, 1850.

Civil District No. 8
John Venable

No. of Visit	Name	Age	Sex	Color	Free or Slave	Married/Widowed	Place of Birth	Month Died	Occupation	Disease or Cause of Death	No. Days Ill
1	Jane Bullock	2	F	B	S		Tenn	April		Smothered	
2	Mary Dawdy	20	F				Tenn	Aug		Cholera	14 days
3	Elizabeth Biggars	4	F				Tenn	Oct		Fever	3 months
4	Susanah Smotherman	3	F				Tenn	Oct		Croup	5 days
5	Jno. W. Smotherman	6m	M				Tenn	Feb		Croup	6 days
6	Jas. Davis	76	M				N.C.	March	Shoemaker	Cancer	18 months
7	Moses Wilson	84	M				N.C.	July	none	Cholic	7 days
8	Ellen Graves	6	F				Tenn	Aug		Flux	5 days

COUNTY OF MARSHALL, STATE OF TENNESSEE.

PAGE NO. 521 PERSONS WHO DIED DURING THE YEAR ENDING 1st JUNE, 1850.

Subdivision No. 24

No. of Visit	Name	Age	Sex	Color	Free or Slave	Married/Widowed	Place of Birth	Month Died	Occupation	Disease or Cause of Death	No. Days Ill
1	Nancy Blake	9m	F				Tenn	April		unknown	4 weeks
2	Malvina McCaul	23	F				Tenn	May		Consumption	1 year
3	William Shires	8	M				Tenn	May		Fever	5 days
4	James Adams	34	M			M	S.C.	April	Farmer	Fever	1 month
5	Elizabeth Cathey	64	F			M	N.C.	Sept		Consumption	1 year
6	George Neil	33	M			M	Tenn	Dec	Farmer	Consumption	2 years
7	Calitha Martin	7	F	B	S		Tenn	July		Consumption	4 months
8	Newton Powell	1m	M				Tenn	Nov		unknown	3 days
9	Daniel Rosson	20	M	B	S		Tenn	July		Fever	1 month
10	Granville Gentry	19	M	B	S		Tenn	Feb		unknown	3 months
11	Alfred McLane	17	M	B	S		Tenn	Aug		Fever	3 weeks
12	Mary Street	73	F			W	Va	Dec		Dropsy	1 year
13	Robert Epperson	1m	M				Tenn	Feb		Hives	2 days
14	Hetty Ellington	5m	F	B	S		Tenn	March		Smothered	
15	Sarah Reed	37	F			M	Tenn	Sept		Consumption	5 months
16	Elizabeth Knight	1	F	B	S		Tenn	Dec		Croup	2 days
17	Mason Jones	1	M	B	S		Tenn	March		unknown	1 day
18	Sarah Sutton	20	F			M	Tenn	Jan		Fits	1 day
19	Huldah Hill	40	F			M	Tenn	June		Consumption	6 months
20	John Rone	3m	M				Tenn	Dec		Croup	3 days
21	Mary Hayes	1	F				Tenn	July		Fever	24 days
22	Mary Anderson	6	F				Tenn	Nov		Dropsy	60 days
23	Elizabeth McLeary	82	F			W	Penn	Jan		Old age	
24	Ewing McLeary	19	M				Tenn	Dec	Student	Fever	2 days
25	James Neil	40	M			M	Tenn	Sept	Physician	Consumption	1 year
26	James Neil	6m	M				Tenn	Oct		Consumption	60 days
27	Morton Roberts	2	M				Tenn	Dec		Dropsy	3 months
28	Linsley Weaver	12	M				Tenn	May		Fits	2 years
29	Jane Fisher	27	F			M	Tenn	Sept		unknown	1 year
30	Eveline Liggett	36	F			M	N.C.	July		Childbirth	1 day
31	Napoleon Ewing	4m	M	B	S		Tenn	May		Smothered	
32	Jane Ewing	4m	F	B	S		Tenn	July		unknown	4 months
33	Jackson Liggett	48	M			M	N.C.	Feb	Farmer	Palsy	1 year
34	Mary Helton	1	F				Tenn	Aug		unknown	1 year
35	Lucinda Hardison	35	F	B	S		N.C.	April		Consumption	8 years
1	Tiney Fox	46	F	B	S		N.C.	Nov		Cancer	6 years
2	Margaret McLean	1m	F	M	S		Tenn	June		unknown	2 weeks

COUNTY OF MARSHALL, STATE OF TENNESSEE.

PAGE NO. 525 PERSONS WHO DIED DURING THE YEAR ENDING 1st JUNE, 1850.

Civil District No. 2
R. A. Williams

No. of Visit	Name	Age	Sex	Color	Free or Slave	Married/Widowed	Place of Birth	Month Died	Occupation	Disease or Cause of Death	No. Days Ill
1	Richard Rainey	1d	M	W			Tenn	Jan		Premature	
2	Robert J. Gant	3	M	W			Tenn	Sept		Croup	5 days
3	Mahaley	7	F	B	S		Tenn	Dec		Cramp cholic	1 day
4	Rebecca Stilwell	30	F	W	F	M	S.C.	Nov		Fever	8 days
5	Margaret McGahey	93	F	W	F	W	Penn	Oct		Old age	
6	Thomas Harris	35	M	W	F	M	Va	April	Farmer	Bil. fever	10 days

COUNTY OF MARSHALL, STATE OF TENNESSEE.

PAGE NO. 528 PERSONS WHO DIED DURING THE YEAR ENDING 1st JUNE, 1850.

No. of Visit	Name	Age	Sex	Color	Free or Slave	Married/Widowed	Place of Birth	Month Died	Occupation	Disease or Cause of Death	No. Days Ill
1	Thomas P. Finly	5	M	W			Tenn	June		Inflamation	6 months
2	Margaret A. Finly	1m	F	W			Tenn	Nov		Hives	8 days
3	Mary A. Spencer	90	F	W			Va	April		Cancer	20 years
4	Harriett Finly	50	F	W			Tenn	Oct		Dropsy	12 years
5	Lucy Hobes	75	F	B	S		Va	Oct		Old age	2 years
6	Jerry	22	M	B	S		Tenn	Feb	Blk-smith	Pleurisy	2 weeks
7	Infant	½m	F	B	S		Tenn	Nov		Smothered	
8	Mary Spencer	90	F	W	F	W	Va	Feb		Cancer	20 years
9	Infant	1	F	W	F		Tenn	May		Spasms	1 year
10	July Maulden	40	F	W	F	W	N.C.	June		Fever	9 days

COUNTY OF MARSHALL, STATE OF TENNESSEE.

PAGE NO. 529 PERSONS WHO DIED DURING THE YEAR ENDING 1st JUNE, 1850.

Civil District No. 5
R. A. Williams

No. of Visit	Name	Age	Sex	Color	Free or Slave	Married/Widowed	Place of Birth	Month Died	Occupation	Disease or Cause of Death	No. Days Ill
1	William J. Null	3	M	W			Tenn	Nov		Worms	7 days
2	Infant Null	3d	M	W			Tenn	Dec			
3	Fletcher Blackwell	10m	M	W			Tenn	May		Fever	7 days
4	Wesley N. Cummings	6m	M	W			Tenn	Nov		unknown	6 days
5	Thomas J. Cummings	7m	M	W			Tenn	Oct		unknown	5 days
6	Sarah	35	F	B	S		N.C.	Dec		unknown	1 week
7	Jane	40	F	B	S		Kentucky	Jan		Spinal	10 days
8	Sarah N. Fowler	41	F	M	F	S	Va	May		Pneumonia	23 months
9	Johana	36	F	B	S		Tenn	Dec		Apoplexy	½ hour
10	Elizabeth Garrison	45	F	W	F	M	Georgia	April		Spasms	3 weeks
11	John Burgess	12	M	W	F	S	Tenn	April		Spasms	2 weeks

COUNTY OF MAURY, STATE OF TENNESSEE.

PAGE NO. 531 PERSONS WHO DIED DURING THE YEAR ENDING 1st JUNE, 1850.

Civil District No. 23
T. W. Rainey

No. of Visit	Name	Age	Sex	Color	Free or Slave	Married/Widowed	Place of Birth	Month Died	Occupation	Disease or Cause of Death	No. Days Ill
1	Slave of Wiley Brown	1	M	B	S		Tenn	May		Consumption	4 months
2	Harriet Lockridge	35	F			W	Tenn	Oct		Inflamation of brain	3 days
3	Slave of R.B.Hardison	15	F	B	S		Tenn	June		Phthisic	6 weeks
4	N. D. Dixon	70	F				N.C.	May		Consumption	4 months
5	Jno. Booker	1	M				Tenn	July		unknown	1 week
6	Slave of S. Caruthers	1m	F	B	S		Tenn	Aug		unknown	1 week
7	Slave of P. Akin	10	M	B	S		Tenn	Aug		Hemorrhage	2 months
8	Slave of P. Akin	1m	F	B	S		Tenn	July		Miscarried	
9	Slave of Jas. Southall	60	F	B	S		Va	Feb		unknown	4 months
10	Slave of J. Cooper	3m	F	B	S		Tenn	Sept		Fever	1 week
11	Anna Adkinson	50	F			M	Kentucky	March		Consumption	1 year
12	Slave of P. Akin	1m	M	B	S		Tenn	July		Miscarried	
13	Slave of Thos. Stone	10	F	B	S		Tenn	March		Fever	6 weeks
14	Rachael Crawford	2	F				Tenn	June		Teething	3 weeks
15	Slave of Leticia Wortham	17	F	B	S		Tenn	Jan		Fever	10 days
16	Slave of Leticia Wortham	1m	F	B	S		Tenn	Jan		Premature birth	3 days
17	Slave of Jno. M. Francis	2	F	B	S		Tenn	May		Diarrhea	2 months
18	Sarah Lester	7	F				Tenn	Feb		Disease of lungs	6 weeks
19	William Elmore	46	M			M	N.C.	March	Grocer	Inflamation of brain	1 week
20	Jno. F. Hall	3	M				Tenn	Aug		Disease of lungs	1 week
21	Robert McCord	2	M				Tenn	Sept		Disease of lungs	10 days
22	A. M. Hammer	45	M			M	Va	Sept	Physician	Consumption	6 months
23	Slave of W. D. Davis	17	F	B	S		Va	Oct		unknown	10 days
24	Elmira Warren	31	F			M	Tenn	June		Consumption	3 months
25	Slave of Thomas Warren	5	F	B	S		Tenn	Oct		unknown	6 weeks
26	Slave of W. P. Martin	60	M	B	S		Va	Feb		unknown	3 days
27	Martha Hamilton	9	F				Tenn	Nov		Disease of heart	10 days
28	Slave of F. G. Smith	5	F	B	S		Tenn	Dec		Fever	2 weeks
29	Josephine Shaw	8	F				Tenn	May		Fever	2 weeks
30	Mary Sandford	1	F				Tenn	Aug		Diarrhea	3 months
31	Slave of W. A. Sanford	18	M	B	S		Alabama	Sept		Pneumonia	1 week
32	Slave of W. A. Sanford	1	F	B	S		Tenn	Aug		Diarrhea	2 weeks
33	Slave of Gray P. Webb	22	M	B	S		Tenn	Jan		Pneumonia	10 days
34	P. G. Franklin	39	M			M	Va	Feb	Merchant	Fever	2 weeks
35	Slave of Rebecca D.--	18	F	B	S		Tenn	Feb		Fever	3 weeks

Remarks: willow and numerous other small and less important growth. Trees, large and forest dense.

T. W. Rainey.

COUNTY OF MAURY, STATE OF TENNESSEE.

PAGE NO. 534 PERSONS WHO DIED DURING THE YEAR ENDING 1st JUNE, 1850.

Civil District No. 22
T. W. Rainey

No. of Visit	Name	Age	Sex	Color	Free or Slave	Married/Widowed	Place of Birth	Month Died	Occupation	Disease or Cause of Death	No. Days Ill
1	Virginia Tomlinson	8	F				Tenn	June		Fever	5 days
2	Wesley	1	M	B	S		Tenn	July		Teething	2 months
3	Negro child	3m	M	B	S		Tenn	Feb		Croup	sudden
4	Infant	1m	M	B	S		Tenn	June		Diarrhea	4 days
5	Infant	1	M	B	S		Tenn	Aug		unknown	2 months
6	Infant	1	M	B	S		Tenn	Aug		Diarrhea	2 weeks
7	Infant	9m	F	B	S		Tenn	May		Scalded	2 weeks
8	Slave of M. F. Cheaires	1m	F	B	S		Tenn	March		Croup	2 days
9	Slave of M. F. Cheaires	1m	F	B	S		Tenn	unknown		unknown	sudden
10	Slave of M. F. Cheaires	1	M	B	S		Tenn	unknown		unknown	unknown
11	Slave of M. F. Cheaires	1m	F	B	S		Tenn	unknown		unknown	unknown
12	Slave of M. F. Cheaires	1m	F	B	S		Tenn	unknown		unknown	unknown
13	Negro child	2	M	B	S		Tenn	May		Worms	unknown
14	Negro child	6m	M	B	S		Tenn	Oct		Smothered	sudden
15	Slave of J. McKissick	47	M	B	S		Tenn	Feb		Overeating	1 day
16	Slave of A. Turner	3m	M	B	S		Tenn	Feb		Smothered	sudden
17	Judy Lester	79	F			W	Va	Sept		Dropsy	1 year
18	Emeline Matthews	20	F			M	Tenn	Jan		Child bed	10 days
19	Slave of J. Howard	2	F	B	S		Tenn	May		Accident	3 weeks
20	Slave of D. C. Kinnard	4	F	B	S		Tenn	Oct		Accident	sudden
21	Slave of Jas. F. Byers	80	F	B	S		Va	May		Old age	
22	Samuel Lockridge	43	M			M	Tenn	April	Farmer	Hemorrhage	sudden
23	Slave of H. Brown	1m	F	B	S		Tenn	May		Hives	2 days
24	Slave of J. W. Brown	36	F	B	S		Tenn	March		Scrofula	2 months
25	Slave of Albert Bailey	7	F	B	S		Tenn	April		Inflamation of brain	sudden
26	Slave of Jas. C. Stephenson	22	M	B	S		Tenn	July	Farmer	Diarrhea	2 weeks
27	Slave of J.W.Lockridge	33	F	B	S		Tenn	Dec		unknown	3 months
28	Slave of Tabitha Hardin	4	F	B	S		Tenn	July		Hives	1 day
29	Slave of Tabitha Hardin	1m	F	B	S		Tenn	May		Accident	sudden
30	Charlotte Shepherd	36	F				N.C.	Sept		Hemorrhage	1 week
31	Slave of Wiley Brown	28	F	B	S		Tenn	Dec		Consumption	2 weeks
32	Slave of Wiley Brown	4	F	B	S		Tenn	Feb		Consumption	2 months
33	Slave of Wiley Brown	22	F	B	S		Tenn	March		Consumption	2 months
34	Slave of Wiley Brown	21	M	B	S		Tenn	March		Consumption	6 weeks
35	Slave of Wiley Brown	1	M	B	S		Tenn	April		Consumption	6 weeks

Remarks: There is no known local causes of disease. Soil rich limestone. Natural growth, ash, (black, white and red) beech, boxelder, buckeye, blackgum, chestnut, cherry, cedar, dogwood, elm(red), hickory, hackberry, hornbeam, holly, haw, locust (honey), iron-wood, linn, locust (black), maple (sugar and white), mulberry, oak (black and white, red post chestnut), poplar, pine, persimmon, pawpaw, red bud, sycamore, sassafras, slippery elm, sumack, sweetgum, walnut (white and black),....

COUNTY OF MAURY, STATE OF TENNESSEE.

PAGE NO. 535 PERSONS WHO DIED DURING THE YEAR ENDING 1st JUNE, 1850.

Civil District No. 6
T. W. Rainey

No. of Visit	Name	Age	Sex	Color	Free or Slave	Married/Widowed	Place of Birth	Month Died	Occupation	Disease or Cause of Death	No. Days Ill
1	Slave of W. H. Ramsey	6m	M	B	S		Tenn	April		Accident	sudden
2	Infant of David Mills	1m	M				Tenn	Jan		Fits	2 weeks
3	Infant of M. P. Crain	8m	M				Tenn	Sept		unknown	1 week
4	Slave of Mary Warden	20	M	B	S		Tenn	Nov		unknown	4 days
5	Infant of Samuel Grigg	1m	M				Tenn	Feb		Died at birth	
6	Slave of M. M. Law	1m	M	B	S		Tenn	Jan		unknown	1 week
7	Slave of Jno. D. Ramsey	4	M	B	S		Tenn	Jan		Accident	sudden
8	Infant of W.S.T.Wilkes	1m	F				Tenn	July		unknown	
9	Charles Cates	60	M			W	N.C.	June	Laborer	Fits	1 month
10	Slave of A. P. Hughes	1	F	B	S		Tenn	Feb		Cold	1 week
11	Elizabeth Thurman	33	F			M	Tenn	March		unknown	7 months
12	Reuben Bray	90	M			W	N.C.	May	Farmer	Old age	
13	Melinda Bray	80	F			M	N.C.	Jan		Phthisic	1 year
14	Slave of J. A. Thompson	35	F	B	S		Tenn	April		unknown	2 weeks
15	Infant of J. B. Stockard	1m	F				Tenn	March		unknown	sudden
16	O. H. Perry	1m	M				Tenn	Jan		Inflamation of brain	1 day
17	Infant of G. C. Stockard	1m	M				Tenn	Feb		Died at birth	
18	Slave of Wm. Pillow	20	M	B	S		Tenn	Jan		Heart disease	2 weeks
19	Slave of Wm. Pillow	40	F	B	S		Tenn	Jan		Inflamation of brain	2 weeks
20	Slave of R. R. Mathews	25	M	B	S		Tenn	Oct		T. fever	1 month
21	Mary Dugger	20	F			M	Tenn	Dec		Child bed	
22	Slave of J. H. Wilkes	6m	M	B	S		Tenn	Dec		Measles	1 week
23	Slave of W.D.Benderman	5	F	B	S		Tenn	May		Cold	3 days
24	Slave of Burchett T.Macon	59	M	B	S		Tenn	March		Consumption	3 months
25	Slave of Burchett T.Macon	14	F	B	S		Tenn	Oct		Lockjaw	sudden
26	Slave of Burchett T.Macon	1m	F	B	S		Tenn	Nov		Died at birth	
27	Infant of Nancy McFall	1m	M				Tenn	Sept		Inflamation of brain	3 days
28	Slave of G. W. Polk	1	F	B	S		Tenn	Nov		Apoplexy	sudden
29	Nicholas T. Long	53	M			W	N.C.	May	Farmer	Pneumonia	2 months
30	Slave of M. Dawson	50	F	B	S		Tenn	April		Lockjaw	sudden
31	Slave of M. H. Williams	1m	F	B	S		Tenn	Dec		Dropsy	2 yrs(?)
32	Slave of M. H. Williams	5	F	B	S		Tenn	Dec		Lockjaw	sudden
33	Slave of Mary W. Ridley	1m	F	B	S		Tenn	May		Scrofula	6 mo (?)
34	Slave of Nancy Terry	7	M	B	S		Tenn	May		Lockjaw	sudden
35	Slave of J.W.S.Ridley	1m	F	B	S		Tenn	May		unknown	3 months

COUNTY OF MAURY, STATE OF TENNESSEE.

PAGE NO. 538 PERSONS WHO DIED DURING THE YEAR ENDING 1st JUNE, 1850.

Civil District No. 11
T. W. Rainey

No. of Visit	Name	Age	Sex	Color	Free or Slave	Married/Widowed	Place of Birth	Month Died	Occupation	Disease or Cause of Death	No. Days Ill
1	Zachariah Hickman	1	M				Tenn	Dec		Sc. fever	2 weeks
2	Cenith Gargues	25	F				Tenn	Aug		Pneumonia	2 weeks
3	Jas. F. Scott	1	M				Tenn	Dec		Sc. fever	8 days
4	Jefferson Coffey	11	M				Tenn	Aug		T. fever	2 months
5	Slave of F.B.Hackney	3m	M	B	S		Tenn	May		unknown	1 day
6	Mary Ellis	30	F				Tenn	Sept		Consumption	6 years
7	Jas. M. Bryson	47	M			M	N.C.	July	Farmer	Consumption	3 months
8	Slave of Jane Bryson	8	F	B	S		Tenn	Dec		Dropsy	1 year
9	Slave of Jane Bryson	16	F	B	S		Tenn	Dec		Consumption	1 year
10	Slave of Jane Bryson	15	F	B	S		Tenn	Jan		Fever	6 months
11	Slave of Jane Bryson	6	M	B	S		Tenn	June		Scrofula	1 year
12	Mary T. Bryson	18	F				Tenn	June		Dropsy	5 months
13	Narcissa Overstreet	46	F			M	Tenn	May		Consumption	2 years
14	Slave of Wm. C. Acuff	2m	M	B	S		Tenn	March		unknown	2 months
15	Slave of Wm. C. Acuff	10m	M	B	S		Tenn	Dec		Accident	2 weeks
16	Slave of W. W. Young	1m	M	B	S		Tenn	Dec		Fits	1 day
17	Slave of J. J. Bryant	4m	F	B	S		Tenn	Dec		Cold	1 month
18	Slave of J. J. Bryant	23	F	B	S		N.C.	Feb		Inflamation of brain	1 week
19	Slave of J. J. Bryant	3m	F	B	S		Tenn	April		Smothered	
20	Slave of M. Kittrell	42	F	B	S		N.C.	Oct		T. fever	3 weeks
21	Slave of M. Kittrell	50	M	B	S		N.C.	Jan		Cholic	3 days
22	Slave of S.T.Lawrence	14	M	B	S		Tenn	June		Fever	2 weeks
23	Slave of H. Hoge	16	F	B	S		Tenn	Nov		unknown	2 weeks
24	Moses Sprinkles	83	M			W	N.C.	March	Farmer	Gravel	1 month
25	Infant of R.T.Sprinkles	1m	F				Tenn	April		Hives	sudden
26	Franklin F. Booker	2	M				Tenn	April		Drowned	
27	Slave of R.C.Whiteside	3m	F	B	S		Tenn	April		Hereditary disease	3 months
28	Slave of Nancy Terry	70	F	B	S		N.C.	Nov		Cholic	sudden
29	Slave of J. J. Wortham	6	M	B	S		Tenn	July		Lockjaw	sudden
30	Infant of Solomon Forshee	1m	M				Tenn	Aug		Died at birth	
31	Infant of Solomon Forshee	1m	M				Tenn	Aug		unknown	2 days
32	Delila Taylor	62	F			M	N.C.	June		unknown	2 years
33	Polly Hickman	32	F			M	Kentucky	Sept		Cancer	2 months

COUNTY OF MAURY, **STATE OF TENNESSEE.**

PAGE NO. 539 **PERSONS WHO DIED DURING THE YEAR ENDING 1st JUNE, 1850.**

Civil District No. 9
T. W. Rainey

No. of Visit	Name	Age	Sex	Color	Free or Slave	Married/Widowed	Place of Birth	Month Died	Occupation	Disease or Cause of Death	No. Days Ill
1	Slave of Mary Booker	2	F	B	S		Tenn	May		Croup	1 day
2	Slave of Ellen Booker	12	F	B	S		Tenn	Feb		Inflamation of brain	3 weeks
3	Slave of Ellen Booker	10m	M	B	S		Tenn	Jan		Heredity Disease	10 months
4	Slave of Ellen Booker	2	M	B	S		Tenn	Dec		Inflamation of lungs	3 weeks
5	John Booker	2	M				Tenn	Nov		Inflamation of lungs	3 weeks
6	Slave of F.F.Rankin	50	M	B	S		Kentucky	Jan		Dropsy	10 years
7	Slave of F.F.Rankin	40	F	B	S		Va	May		Dropsy	5 months
8	Slave of C. C. Martin	3m	M	B	S		Tenn	May		Accident	sudden
9	Mary Harrison	65	F			M	N.C.	Oct		Consumption	6 months
10	Infant of Edwin Lee	1m	F				Tenn	Sept		unknown	1 day
11	Slave of A. Booker	1m	M	B	S		Tenn	Feb		Hives	sudden
12	Slave of Wm.Offnt (?)	80	M	B	S		N.C.	Jan		Old age	
13	Drusilla Nichol	74	F			W	N.C.	Nov		Palsy	10 years
14	Infant of John Edgin	1m	F				Tenn	Feb		Died at birth	
15	William Nicholson	3m	M				Tenn	July		Liver disease	2 weeks
16	Slave of Stephen Hancock	1	M	B	S		Tenn	Dec		Fever	10 days
17	Slave of T. F. Bain	1m	F	B	S		Tenn	Feb		Died at birth	
18	Slave of Josh Hardison	2	F	B	S		Tenn	Aug		Worms	1 week
19	Infant of Wm. Perry	1m	M				Tenn	Dec		Died at birth	
20	Mary Rowe	100	F			W	Va	Oct		Dropsy	1 year
21	Slave of Sarah Fitzgerald	20	M	B	S		Tenn	Oct		Consumption	6 months
22	Slave of Sarah Fitzgerald	18	M	B	S		Tenn	Dec		Consumption	1 year
23	Slave of Samuel Matthews	35	M	B	S		Tenn	Aug		Toothache	5 days
24	Slave of Samuel Matthews	19	F	B	S		Tenn	Feb		Rheumatism	1 week
25	Slave of Samuel Matthews	3m	F	B	S		Tenn	Sept		Croup	1 day
26	Slave of J. B. Pillow	40	M	B	S		Tenn	May		Dropsy	3 months
27	Slave of J. B. Pillow	2m	F	B	S		Tenn	March		Accident	sudden
28	Slave of G. J. Pillow	1	M	B	S		Tenn	unknown		Whooping cough	2 weeks
29	Slave of G. J. Pillow	3	F	B	S		Tenn	May		Croup	sudden
30	Martha Estes	67	F			M	S.C.	July		unknown	10 years
31	Slave of Wilkerson Barnes	4	F	B	S		Tenn	May		Whooping cough	1 month
32	Slave of Wilkerson Barnes	3m	M	B	S		Tenn	Jan		unknown	sudden
33	Slave of George Maxwell	1m	M	B	S		Tenn	Sept		unknown	sudden
34	Sarah E. Mack	25	F			M	Tenn	July		Fever	1 week
35	Nathan P. Mack	1m	M				Tenn	July		Fever	1 week

COUNTY OF MAURY, STATE OF TENNESSEE.

PAGE NO. 542 PERSONS WHO DIED DURING THE YEAR ENDING 1st JUNE, 1850.

Civil District No. 8
T. W. Rainey

No. of Visit	Name	Age	Sex	Color	Free or Slave	Married/Widowed	Place of Birth	Month Died	Occupation	Disease or Cause of Death	No. Days Ill
1	Jerome B. Yancey	7	M				Tenn	Dec		Accident	sudden
2	Slave of Mary Porter	6m	M	B	S		Tenn	May		unknown	6 months
3	Slave of Evan Young	1	M	B	S		Tenn	Aug		Diarrhea	1 week
4	Slave of Evan Young	6m	M	B	S		Tenn	Aug		Diarrhea	1 week
5	Ann Wallace	3	F				Louisiana	Aug		Croup	10 days
6	John T. Taylor	1	M				Tenn	Nov		Compl. disease	1 year
7	Samuel Parsons	10	M				Tenn	Oct		Sore throat	3 weeks
8	Slave of Elizabeth Smith	11m	F	B	S		Tenn	July		Inflamation of brain	2 weeks
9	Slave of G. W. Kerr	26	F	B	S		Tenn	Dec		Child bed	
10	Jas. H. Holland	40	M				N.C.	June		Bil. fever	9 days
11	Slave of Jane Mangrum	5	M	B	S		Tenn	Oct		unknown	12 days
12	Martha Burnett	52	F			M	N.C.	June		Consumption	5 months
13	Slave of Jas. Baldridge	3m	M	B	S		Tenn	Feb		unknown	sudden
14	Slave of Isaac J. Thomas	1	M	B	S		Tenn	May		Inflamation of brain	2 days
15	Sarah Dean	9m	F				Tenn	Dec		Croup	1 day
16	A. J. Gates	8	M				Tenn	Aug		Fever	5 days
17	Slave of Catharine McCrory	60	M	B	S		Va	Feb		Cold	2 weeks
18	Jas. R. Fisher	1	M				Tenn	Oct		Worms	1 week
19	Slave of Jas. M. Jones	3m	M	B	S		Tenn	June		Poisoned	1 day
20	Charlotte Dean	2m	F				Tenn	May		Hives	1 day
21	Susan A. Johnson	17	F				Tenn	Jan		Consumption	3 years
22	William Collins	1	M				Tenn	Feb		Compl. disease	1 month
23	Slave of S. Deamand	1	M	B	S		Tenn	July		T. fever	11 days
24	Eliza Revis	40	F			M	N.C.	Nov		Consumption	2 months
25	Ann Smith	70	F			M	Georgia	Aug		Fever	3 weeks
26	Harriet Smith	18	F				Tenn	Aug		Fever	5 days
27	Melissa Cockrum	28	F			M	Tenn	Aug		Consumption	6 years
28	Martha Kirks	39	F			M	Va	June		Consumption	6 months
29	Robert Westmoreland	33	M			M	Va	Oct	Farmer	Consumption	6 months
30	Slave of Robt. Westmoreland	5m	F	B	S		Tenn	May		Croup	4 weeks
31	Virginia E. Mack	5	F				Tenn	May		Worms	1 week
32	Margaret Freeland	55	F			W	S.C.	Nov		Consumption	10 months
33	Samuel Wells	39	M			M	Va	Aug	Farmer	Accident	sudden
34	Slave of Richard Tidwell	1	F	B	S		Tenn	April		unknown	3 weeks
35	Slave of Robt.T.Matthews	1	M	B	S		Tenn	Feb		Sc. fever	2 weeks

COUNTY OF MAURY, STATE OF TENNESSEE.

PAGE NO. 543 PERSONS WHO DIED DURING THE YEAR ENDING 1st JUNE, 1850.

G. C. Gordon

No. of Visit	Name	Age	Sex	Color	Free or Slave	Married/Widowed	Place of Birth	Month Died	Occupation	Disease or Cause of Death	No. Days Ill
1	Washington	1	M	M	S		Tenn	July	none	Scalded	10 days
2	Infant	1m	F	B	S		Tenn	Oct	none	Smothered	sudden
3	Mary Johnson	22	F			M	Tenn	Oct	none	Pneumonia	6 days
4	Mary A. Johnson	27	F				N.C.	Aug	none	Congestive fever	8 days
5	Olive	4	F	B	S		Tenn	Jan	none	Accident	sudden
6	Jane	55	F	B	S	M	Tenn	May	none	Dropsy of chest	1 year
7	James Arnell	42	M			M	New York	March	Pres. Minister	Pneumonia	8 days
8	Jane	1	F	B	S		Tenn	July	none	Whooping cough	10 days
9	Emily	1	F	B	S		Tenn	July	none	Whooping cough	9 days
10	Jerry	6m	M	B	S		Tenn	July	none	Whooping cough	10 days
11	Lawrence	2	M	B	S		Tenn	Sept	none	Inflamation of lungs	4 days
12	Infant	1m	M	B	S		Tenn	Oct	none	Croup	1 day
13	Rebecca McKey	56	F			M	S.C.	Feb	none	Old age	
14	Susan	6	F	B	S		Tenn	Feb	none	T. fever	5 days
15	John Hill	72	M			M	N.C.	Aug	none	Apoplexy	7 days
16	Wallace	1	M	B	S		Tenn	Feb	Farmer (?)	unknown	1 day
17	Margaret	1	F	B	S		Tenn	March	none	Inflamation of brain	2 weeks
18	Henry	8m	M	B	S		Tenn	Sept	none	Hydrocephalus	10 days
19	Mary J. McKey	5	F				Tenn	Dec	none	Fever	7 days
20	Elias Passmoore	23	M				Tenn	Nov	Teacher	T. fever	14 days
21	David	12	M	B	S		N.C.	Nov	none	T. fever	21 days
22	Adaline	6	F	B	S		Tenn	March	none	Pneumonia	8 days
23	Margaret N. Thomas	39	F			M	Va	June	none	Complicated	3 years
24	Sarah E. Looney	1	F				Tenn	Jan	none	Teething	9 days
25	Joe	4	M	B	S		Tenn	Jan	none	Worms	1 month
26	Infant	1m	F	B	S		Tenn	July	none	unknown	1 day
27	Charles Keezee	7	M				Tenn	April	none	Croup	1 day
28	J. B. Polk	26	F			M	S.C.	Aug	none	Enl. of heart	9 days
29	Lawrence	50	M	B	S	M	Va	Sept	none	Cold	3 months
30	Caroline	18	F	B	S	M	Tenn	Aug	none	Accident	sudden
31	Infant	2m	M	M	S		Tenn	Oct	none	unknown	2 days
32	Sam	13	M	B	S		Tenn	Sept	none	Fever	3 weeks
33	John W. Gamblin	34	M			M	Tenn	July	Tailor	Inflamation of lungs	4 days
34	Dennis	30	M	B	S		Tenn	March	none	Dropsy	6 months
35	Harriet	40	F	B	S	M	Tenn	Oct	none	Consumption	12 years

COUNTY OF MAURY, STATE OF TENNESSEE.

PAGE NO. 546 PERSONS WHO DIED DURING THE YEAR ENDING 1st JUNE, 1850.

Columbia
G. C. Gordon

No. of Visit	Name	Age	Sex	Color	Free or Slave	Married/Widowed	Place of Birth	Month Died	Occupation	Disease or Cause of Death	No. Days Ill
1	Henderson	16	M	B	S		Tenn	June	none	Fever	3 weeks
2	Infant	3m	F	B	S		Tenn	Nov	none	unknown	2 months
3	Infant	3m	M	B	S		Tenn	Dec	none	unknown	4 weeks
4	James Owens	50	M			W	Tenn	March	Waggoner	Whiskey	3 weeks
5	Minny	10	F	B	S		Tenn	Aug	none	unknown	1 week
6	Moses	2	M	B	S		Tenn	April	none	unknown	1 year
7	Joyce Hill	80	F			W	Va	May	none	Consumption	15 years
8	Susan Parten	23	F				Tenn	May	none	Consumption	2 months
9	Louisa Jones	3	F				Tenn	Oct	none	Croup	2 days
10	Martha A. Jaggers	18	F				Tenn	Nov	none	Consumption	5 months
11	Sarilda C.M.J.Dooley	3m	F				Tenn	June	none	Dropsy	3 years
12	Laura	3m	F	B	S		Tenn	March	none	Erysipelas	2 months
13	C. W. Webster	1	F				Tenn	June	none	Inflamation of brain	12 days
14	Peggy	30	F	B	S	M	Tenn	Dec	none	Cold	1 day
15	Robert A. Frierson	3	M				Tenn	Feb	none	Accident	sudden
16	James C. O'Riley	74	M			M	Ireland	Sept	Physician	Abscess	2 years
17	Prince	2	M	B	S		Tenn	July	none	Consumption	2 months
18	Adaline Goodloe	2	F				Tenn	Nov	none	Quinsy	2 weeks
19	Willis	2	M	B	S		Tenn	March	none	unknown	6 days
20	Infant	1m	F	B	S		Tenn	Aug	none	unknown	3 days
21	Sarah E. Ricketts	3	F				Tenn	Jan	none	unknown	1 month
22	Richard Stockerd	59	M			M	N.C.	June	Blk-smith	Pneumonia	12 months
23	Elizabeth Jennings	44	F			M	Va	Feb	none	Consumption	4 months
24	January	75	M	B	S	W	S.C.	Feb	none	Dropsy	6 months
25	Fanny	16	F	B	S		Tenn	May	none	Consumption	1 month
26	Beny	3	M	B	S		Tenn	Feb	none	unknown	2 days
27	Infant	1m	F	B	S		Tenn	March	none	in birth	
28	Infant	1m	F	B	S		Tenn	Dec	none	Accident	sudden
29	Infant	2m	F	B	S		Tenn	Jan	none	in birth	
30	Infant	1m	M	B	S		Tenn	Nov	none	Hives	7 days
31	Infant	1m	M	B	S		Tenn	Nov	none	in birth	
32	Infant	1m	M	B	S		Tenn	Jan	none	in birth	
33	Amanda J. Allen	9m	F				Tenn	July	none	Diarrhea	5 days
34	Judy	30	F	B	S	M	Tenn	Jan	none	Lockjaw	2 days
35	Ebenezer	30	M	B	S	M	Tenn	Aug	none	T. fever	16 days

COUNTY OF MAURY, STATE OF TENNESSEE.

PAGE NO. 547 PERSONS WHO DIED DURING THE YEAR ENDING 1st JUNE, 1850.

G. C. Gordon

No. of Visit	Name	Age	Sex	Color	Free or Slave	Married/Widowed	Place of Birth	Month Died	Occupation	Disease or Cause of Death	No. Days Ill
1	Thomas C. Gordon	4m	M				Tenn	June	none	Croup	3 weeks
2	Jane	18	F	B	S	M	Tenn	Oct	none	Congestive fever	1 month
3	Margaret	18	F	B	S	M	Tenn	April	none	Congestive fever	1 month
4	Tom	21	M	B	S	M	Tenn	April	none	Congestive fever	3 weeks
5	Infant	1m	F				Tenn	Feb	none	unknown	3 days
6	Sarah A. Woody	4	F				Tenn	Oct	none	Croup	2 days
7	Eliza A. Davis	1m	F				Tenn	Jan	none	unknown	1 day
8	Patience Griffin	74	F			W	N.C.	July	none	Chronic	2 years
9	Infant	1m	F				Tenn	July	none	unknown	1 day
10	John A. Wilkins	48	M			M	N.C.	Feb	Farmer	Cholera	3 days
11	Jeremiah Oakley	49	M			M	N.C.	Sept	Shoemaker	Chills	5 days
12	Elizabeth Oakley	60	F			W	N.C.	July	none	T. fever	10 days
13	Eliza J. Harbison	21	F				Tenn	Aug	none	Dropsy	16 months
14	Judith	42	F	B	S	M	Tenn	Sept	none	T. fever	1 month
15	Mary	1	F	B	S		Tenn	May	none	unknown	3 months
16	Margaret A. Russell	4	F				Tenn	Dec	none	Croup	5 days
17	James K. P. Olephint	9	M				Tenn	Feb	none	Croup	2 days
18	Leander	3	M	M	S		Tenn	Dec	none	Croup	5 days
19	Violet	45	F	M	S	M	Tenn	Dec	none	Chronic	
20	Lemuel Sherod	58	M			M	N.C.	April	Farmer	Chronic	
21	Margaret Gray	86	F			W	Va	May	none	Chronic	
22	James G. Hudspeth	10	M				Tenn	Sept	none	T. fever	12 days
23	W. F. M. Johnson	5	M				Tenn	March	none	Croup	6 days
24	J. S. Johnson	4	M				Tenn	Feb	none	Croup	20 days
25	M. A. Watkins	17	F				Tenn	Feb	none	Pneumonia	13 days
26	E. Watkins	40	F			M	Va	July	none	Inflamation of stomach	8 days
27	L. H. Watkins	20	M				Tenn	Aug	Farmer	Diarrhea	5 days
28	R. E. Harris	17	F			M	Tenn	April	none	Dyspepsia	5 months
29	Haywood Partee	6	M				Tenn	Oct	none	Fever	3 weeks
30	Infant	6m	M	B	S		Tenn	June	none	unknown	1 day
31	Crecy	5	F	B	S		Tenn	April	none	Inflamation	2 weeks
32	Infant	1m	M	B	S		Tenn	Dec	none	in birth	2 weeks
33	Harriet	14	F	B	S		Tenn	Dec	none	Croup	1 day
34	Infant	2m	F	B	S		Tenn	Dec	none	Croup	4 days
35	Jefferson	4m	M	B	S		Tenn	Feb	none	Croup	10 days

COUNTY OF MAURY, STATE OF TENNESSEE.

PAGE NO. 550 PERSONS WHO DIED DURING THE YEAR ENDING 1st JUNE, 1850.

G. C. Gordon

No. of Visit	Name	Age	Sex	Color	Free or Slave	Married/Widowed	Place of Birth	Month Died	Occupation	Disease or Cause of Death	No. Days Ill
1	Martha	25	F	B	S	M	Tenn	May	none	Consumption	1 year
2	Sarah West	24	F			M	Tenn	Feb	none	in child birth	1 day
3	Nathaniel Smithson	18	M				Tenn	May	Farmer	unknown	6 months
4	Serena E. Ashworth	17	F				Tenn	Sept	none	T. fever	11 days
5	Mary Warren	5	F				Tenn	Jan	none	sudden	
6	Martha Lockhart	80	F			W	N.C.	Sept	none	Chills	3 days
7	Honour Prowell	39	M			M	Kentucky	March	Farmer	Fever	2 weeks
8	Sarah Caughran	43	F			M	Kentucky	May	none	Chronic	
9	Infant	1m	M				Tenn	May	none	in birth	
10	Edy	1	F	B	S		Tenn	Oct	none	unknown	
11	William C. Barnes	35	M			M	Kentucky	Feb	Farmer	Cholera	4 days
12	Infant	2m	M	B	S		Tenn	March	none	unknown	2 days
13	Rachael Harbison	45	F			M	N.C.	Oct	none	Ulcer	8 months
14	Sampson	1m	M	B	S		Tenn	May	none	Croup	1 day
15	Mary	20	F	B	S	M	Tenn	May	none	Child birth	
16	Infant	1m	M				Tenn	Jan	none	in birth	
17	Darcas Akin	75	F			W	S.C.	Sept	none	Old age	
18	Milley	1	F	B	S		Tenn	Dec	none	Complicated	7 days
19	Armstead	30	M	B	S		Tenn	Jan	none	T. fever	8 days
20	Margaret	4	F	B	S		Tenn	April	none	Inflamation of stomach	3 weeks
21	James P. Sharber	1	M				Tenn	Aug	none	Pneumonia	5 days
22	Frances W. Porter	63	F			W	N.C.	March	none	Dropsy	1 day
23	Nelly	40	F	B	S		Tenn	Sept	none	Complicated	8 weeks
24	Harriet L. Howard	26	F			M	N.C.	July	none	Fever	3 days
25	William L. Howard	5m	M				Tenn	Sept	none	Complicated	2 months
26	George	1	M	B	S		Tenn	July	none	Scrofula	1 week
27	Gordon	1	M	B	S		Tenn	Oct	none	Pneumonia	1 week
28	Eli	7	M	B	S		Tenn	May	none	Consumption	6 months
29	Joseph Malone	14	M				N.C.	July	none	T. fever	3 weeks
30	Bitha	20	F	B	S		Tenn	June	none	Diarrhea	1 month
31	Infant	4m	F	B	S		Tenn	June	none	unknown	2 weeks
32	Infant	4m	F	B	S		Tenn	July	none	Croup	1 week
33	Infant	4m	F	B	S		Tenn	July	none	unknown	2 days
34	Jim	68	M	B	S	M	N.C.	April	none	Old age	
35	Jourdan	80	M	B	S		N.C.	Jan	none	Old age	

COUNTY OF MAURY, STATE OF TENNESSEE.

PAGE NO. 551   PERSONS WHO DIED DURING THE YEAR ENDING 1st JUNE, 1850.

Civil District No. 19
G. C. Gordon

No. of Visit	Name	Age	Sex	Color	Free or Slave	Married/Widowed	Place of Birth	Month Died	Occupation	Disease or Cause of Death	No. Days Ill
1	Infant	1m	F	B	S		Tenn	Sept	none	Spasms	1 day
2	Sarah Blakely	68	F			W	S.C.	March	none	Apoplexy	sudden
3	Judy	37	F	B	S	M	Tenn	Aug	none	Consumption	5 months
4	Virginia C. Hunter	1	F				Tenn	Aug	none	Teething	3 months
5	Infant	3m	F	B	S		Tenn	Sept	none	Croup	10 days
6	Prince	20	M	B	S		Tenn	June	none	Poisoned	7 days
7	Tom	80	M	B	S	M	S.C.	Jan	none	Old age	
8	Elijah G. Adkinson	3m	M				Tenn	Oct	none	Croup	7 days
9	Gracy Edminson	75	F			M	N.C.	April	none	Dropsy of chest	4 years
10	Lucy	45	F	B	S		Va	June	none	Fever	1 year
11	Infant	1m	F				Tenn	May	none	Hives	3 days
12	Harriet J. Jones	30	F			M	Tenn	June	none	Inflamation of lungs	1 month
13	Infant Jones	1m	M				Tenn	Sept	none	at birth	
14	Infant	1	M	B	S		Tenn	Feb	none	unknown	3 months
15	Susan Halcomb	2	F				Tenn	May	none	Croup	5 days
16	James D. Irvine	38	M			M	Va	Feb	Farmer	Consumption	5 years
17	Abram Ferguson	50	M			M	Va	Aug	none	Consumption	2 months
18	John Arnold	1	M				Tenn	July	none	Croup	3 days
19	Mary Arnold	5m	F				Tenn	May	none	unknown	
20	Newman	68	M	B	S	M	N.C.	April	none	Gravel	12 months
21	R. W. Ferguson	1m	M				Tenn	May	none	Croup	3 days
22	Frances McFinley	24	M			M	Tenn	Aug	none	Consumption	3 months
23	Betty	1	F	B	S		Tenn	Jan	none	Pneumonia	15 days
24	Argentine A. Sowell	10	F				Tenn	Dec	none	unknown	10 days
25	Joseph	18	M	B	S		Tenn	Dec	none	T. fever	
26	Lucinda	26	F	B	S	M	Tenn	Feb	none	Chronic	
27	Jim	23	M	B	S	M	S.C.	July	none	Cholera	1 day
28	Ellis	8m	M	B	S		Tenn	Sept	none	Worms	6 days
29	Roena	5	F	B	S		Tenn	Sept	none	Burn	2 days
30	Mary Brinn	20	F			M	N.C.	Sept	none	unknown	2 months
31	J. E. Harris	29	F			M	N.C.	Aug	none	unknown	1 year
32	R. W. Brinn	2m	M				Tenn	Aug	none	unknown	2 months
33	Rainey	1m	M				Tenn	July	none	unknown	1 month
34	Emily B. Russell	14	F				Tenn	March	none	T. fever	12 days
35	Ned	3m	M	B	S		Tenn	Sept	none	Diarrhea	2 months

COUNTY OF MAURY, STATE OF TENNESSEE.

PAGE NO. 554 PERSONS WHO DIED DURING THE YEAR ENDING 1st JUNE, 1850.

Civil District no. 19
G. C. Gordon

No. of Visit	Name	Age	Sex	Color	Free or Slave	Married/Widowed	Place of Birth	Month Died	Occupation	Disease or Cause of Death	No. Days Ill
1	J. S. Fly	2	M				Tenn	Oct	none	Accident	sudden
2	Ned	2	M	B	S		Tenn	Aug	none	Influenza	5 days
3	Frances Lavender	19	F			M	Tenn	June	none	T. fever	35 days
4	John Morton	73	M			W	Va	Aug	Min.Mis.Bapt.	Consumption	3 years
5	George Gantt	58	M			M	Maryland	Feb	Min. Bapt.	Pneumonia	10 days
6	Infant	1m	M				Tenn	Sept	none	unknown	1 day
7	William	1	M	B	S		Tenn	May	none	unknown	1 day
8	Infant	1m	M	B	S		Tenn	Oct	none	unknown	1 day
9	Infant	1m	F	B	S		Tenn	March	none	unknown	1 day
10	Jethro Howell	46	M			M	N.C.	May	Farmer	Cramp	1 day
11	John	40	M	B	S	M	Tenn	March	none	Consumption	8 months

COUNTY OF MEIGS, STATE OF TENNESSEE.

PAGE NO. 555 PERSONS WHO DIED DURING THE YEAR ENDING 1st JUNE, 1850.

22nd Subdivision
William L. Adams

No. of Visit	Name	Age	Sex	Color	Free or Slave	Married/Widowed	Place of Birth	Month Died	Occupation	Disease or Cause of Death	No. Days Ill
1	Harriet	22	F	B	S		Tenn	June	Housegirl	unknown	
2	Martha E. Simpson	30	F	W	F	1839	Tenn	Feb	Hse-keeping	unknown	2 days
3	Ravenia S. Covington	1	F	W	F		Tenn	Feb	none	unknown	8 days
4	Mary Pettit	23	F	W	F		Kentucky	Oct	-illegible-	Congestive Chills	28 days
5	William J. Pettit	1	M	W	F		Tenn	Oct	none	Croup	3 days
6	Isaac Moore	2	M	W	F		Tenn	Dec	none	Whooping cough	8 days
7	John W. Moore	1	M	W	F		Tenn	Nov	none	Whooping cough	6 days
8	Mary	10	F	B	S		Tenn	Jan	none	T. fever	5 days
9	Nancy A. Gamble	30	F	W	F	1830	Tenn	Oct	Hse-keeping	Fever	15 days
10	Reuben L. McKenzie	17	M	W	F		Tenn	April	Farmer	Fever	3 days
11	Easter	2	F	B	S		Tenn	Jan	none	unknown	0
12	Rachael	1	F	B	S		Tenn	Oct	none	Croup	2 days
13	James McCowan	0	M	W	F		Tenn	July	none	unknown	0
14	Maddison B. Johnson	38	M	W	F	1832	Tenn	Aug	Farmer	Fever	15 days
15	Andrew R. Johnson	7	M	W	F		Tenn	Sept	none	Fever	10 days
16	Lucy	2	F	B	S		Tenn	Jan	none	unknown	15 days
17	Frank	6	M	B	S		Tenn	March	none	Quinsy	8 days
18	Plesant Price	11	M	W	F		Tenn	Oct	none	Croup	5 days
19	Mary Colbaugh	2	F	W	F		Tenn	Oct	none	Flux	6 days
20	Elizabeth Stokes	32	F	W	F		Tenn	April	none	Fever	7 days
21	Louisa Stokes	18	F	W	F		Tenn	April	none	Fever	7 days
22	John Elder	1	M	W	F		Tenn	April	none	Croup	8 days
23	George Carell	14	M	W	F		Tenn	July	Farmer	Pneumonia	6 days
24	John C. Bivins	14	M	W	F		Tenn	March	Farmer	T. fever	35 days
25	Thomas Hunter	65	M	W	F	W	Va	Feb	Farmer	Pneumonia	5 days
26	Mary Little	80	F	W	F	W	Va	Oct	none	Fits & age	
27	George W. Wood	22	M	W	F		Tenn	April	Blk-smith	Fever	10 days
28	Andrew R. Cate	21	M	W	F		Tenn	Feb	Farmer	Fever	6 days
29	Thomas R. Wade	20	M	W	F		Tenn	April	Farmer	Pneumonia	15 days
30	Sarah Neil	15	F	W	F		Tenn	June	School	Vaccination	14 days
31	Mary E. Wells	3	F	W	F		Tenn	Feb	none	Burnt	3 days
32	Mahala Snider	24	F	W	F	1846	Tenn	Nov	Hse-keeping	Pneumonia	10 days
33	Rhoda Day	28	F	W	F	1842	Tenn	Nov	Hse-keeping	Pneumonia	11 days

COUNTY OF MEIGS, STATE OF TENNESSEE.

PAGE NO. 558   PERSONS WHO DIED DURING THE YEAR ENDING 1st JUNE, 1850.

22nd Subdivision

William L. Adams

No. of Visit	Name	Age	Sex	Color	Free or Slave	Married/Widowed	Place of Birth	Month Died	Occupation	Disease or Cause of Death	No. Days Ill
1	Julia Farris	11	F	W	F		Tenn	Oct	none	Fever	21 days
2	William Prewet	90	M	W	F	1835	Va	Aug	Farmer	Old age	
3	William Prewet	4	M	W	F		Tenn	Feb	none	Whooping cough	30 days
4	Catharine Romaines	5	F	W	F		Tenn	Sept	none	Fever	20 days
5	James Coffer	0	M	W	F		Tenn	Sept	none	Croup	2 days
6	Elizabeth Grigsby	32	F	W	F	1842	Tenn	May	Hse-keeping	Consumption	6 months
7	Polly Ann Farrar	21	F	W	F		Tenn	Nov	Spinster	Pneumonia	3 days
8	James C. Farrar	18	M	W	F		Tenn	Nov	Farmer	Pneumonia	4 days
9	Jefferson	1	M	B	S		Tenn	Nov	none	unknown	2 days
10	Sidney	—	F	B	S		Tenn	June	none	unknown	7 days
11	Fanny	—	F	B	S		Tenn	June	none	unknown	1 day
12	Thomas	—	M	B	S		Tenn	June	none	unknown	8 days
13	Quentinena Riddle	1	F	W	F		Tenn	Nov	none	Croup	8 days
14	John M. C. Vincent	11	M	W	F		Tenn	Nov	none	Pneumonia	4 days
15	Rhoda S. Edington	0	F	W	F		Tenn	April	none	unknown	10 days
16	Martin Cook	27	M	W	F	1847	Tenn	Jan	Farmer	T. fever	16 days
17	Richard	6	M	B	S		Tenn	May	none	Whooping cough	15 days
18	Charles	4	M	B	S		Tenn	Nov	none	Fever	16 days
19	Andrew J. McAllen	29	M	W	F	1843	Tenn	Feb	Farmer	Inflamation of brain	3 months
20	Martha Wood	7	F	W	F		Tenn	May	none	Pneumonia	8 days
21	Frederick Green	58	M	W	F	1814	Va	May	Farmer	Chills & Fever	8 days
22	Mary Green	24	F	W	F		Tenn	Feb	Spinster	Consumption	6 weeks
23	Zachary T. Green	4	M	W	F		Tenn	Feb	none	Inflamation of bowels	5 days
24	Mary A. McAllen	53	F	W	F	1818	Tenn	Feb	Hse-keeping	T. fever	23 days
25	Jacob M. Butler	45	M	W	F	1845	Va	March	Farmer	unknown	3 years
26	Richard R.-illegible-	9	M	W	F		Tenn	Dec	none	Thrown from horse	2 days
27	Elizabeth Fernfro	19	F	W	F	1849	Tenn	April	Spinster	Fever	12 days
28	John Brown	30	M	W	F		Tenn	May	Farmer	Murdered	5 days
29	Uriah S. Huff	32	M	W	F	1837	Tenn	March	Farmer	unknown	8 days
30	Enoch C. Alferd	1	M	W	F		Tenn	April	none	unknown	4 days
31	Lucinda Alferd	—	F	W	F		Tenn	Oct	none	Fever	6 days
32	Angaline	2	F	B	S		Tenn	Dec	none	unknown	0
33	William Branum	22	M	W	F		Tenn	May	Farmer	T. fever	14 days
34	John M. Duffer	1	M	W	F		Alabama	Feb	none	unknown	6 days
35	Elizabeth Young	65	F	W	F	1800	N.C.	April	Hse-keeping	Dropsy	12 days

COUNTY OF MONROE, STATE OF TENNESSEE.

PAGE NO. 559   PERSONS WHO DIED DURING THE YEAR ENDING 1st JUNE, 1850.

M. Clibourne

No. of Visit	Name	Age	Sex	Color	Free or Slave	Married/Widowed	Place of Birth	Month Died	Occupation	Disease or Cause of Death	No. Days Ill
1	Orange	22	M	B	S		Tenn	Oct	Laborer	T. fever	8 days
2	not named	1	F					July		Born dead	
3	John Woods	1	M				Tenn	July		Disease of head	14 days
4	William Tailor	24	M				Tenn	June	Farmer	B.C. Lungs	Chronic
5	not named		F				Tenn	Nov		Born dead	
6	Samuel Cartwright	28	M				Tenn	April	Farmer	T. fever	14 days
7	Alvira Berdit	24	F				Tenn	April		T. fever	5 weeks
8	Scott	11	M	B	S		Tenn	Jan		Fever	1 month
9	Henry Newton	18	M				Tenn	Aug	Farmer	Murdered	
10	Nat Willson	1d	M				Tenn	Oct		unknown	1 day
11	Jane Woolridge	55	F			M	Tenn	Nov		Dropsy	3 years
12	John Hicks	1	M				Tenn	Aug		Sc. fever	17 days
13	William Blair	24	M				Tenn	Nov	Farmer	Fever	2 weeks
14	Houston Vanzant	28	M			M	Tenn	May	Farmer	Cholera	2 days
15	not named	1d	F				Tenn	March		unknown	1 day
16	Mary Freeman	2	F				Tenn	Dec		Croup	3 days
17	James Henderson	70	M			W	Ireland	April	Farmer	Diabetes	3 days
18	Henderson Hensley	17	M				Tenn	Oct	Farmer	Stab in thigh	3 weeks
19	Eliza King	8m	F				Tenn	June		Liver disease	9 days
20	James F. Walker	6	M				Tenn	Oct		Palsy	2 years
21	George G. Hart	3	M				Tenn	Nov		Croup	3 days
22	not named	1d	M				Tenn	Oct		unknown	1 day
23	William Bandy	10m	M				Tenn	July		Croup	5 days
24	Russell Witt	1	M				Tenn	Nov		Drowned	
25	John W. Crowder	5	M				Tenn	April		Burnt	9 days
26	Margaret	39	F			M	N.C.	May		Dropsy	1 week
27	Samuel Roddy	52	M			M	Tenn	Sept	Farmer	Fever	4 weeks
28	Samuel Thornburg	4	M				Tenn	July		Worms	3 weeks
29	William Tailor	3m	M				Tenn	June		Croup	1 day
30	John Bright	45	M			M	N.C.	June	Farmer	Cholera Mor.	2 years
31	Richard Presley	1m	M				Tenn	Nov		Croup	4 days
32	George Scruggs	3	M				Tenn	Oct		Inflamation of bowels	3 weeks
33	James T. Williams	1	M				Tenn	Nov		Inflamation of bowels	2 weeks
34	Elizabeth Henson	1	F				Tenn	March		unknown	1 day
35	Robert Doherty	11	M				Tenn	June		unknown	4 days

Remarks: There are gold mines in the southwest portion of County which have been a good deal and profitable worked but at present, very little is being done at them. The timber comprises nearly all the species of oak, chestnut, poplar, sugar maple, pitch pine, hemlock, sweet and black gums, walnut, and beech, hickory, etc.

COUNTY OF MONROE, STATE OF TENNESSEE.

PAGE NO. 562 PERSONS WHO DIED DURING THE YEAR ENDING 1st JUNE, 1850.

Civil District No. 11
M. Clibourne

No. of Visit	Name	Age	Sex	Color	Free or Slave	Married/Widowed	Place of Birth	Month Died	Occupation	Disease or Cause of Death	No. Days Ill
1	Nabednago Hargus	29	M				Tenn	July	Farmer	Bil. fever	6 days
2	Alfred	1m	M	B	S		Tenn	Nov		unknown	7 days
3	Elizabeth Gipson	35	F				Tenn	March		unknown	sudden
4	Oliver Doak	1m	M				Tenn	July		Disease of heart	1 day
5	Ann G. Steel	44	F				Rhode Island	Feb		T. fever	7 days
6	James N. Stokley	5m	M				Tenn	July		Cholera Inf.	150 days
7	Lydia Ann Meek	3	F				Tenn	June		unknown	12 days
8	Adison A. Abernathy	1	M				Tenn	July		Diarrhea	15 days
9	Thomas Day	11m	M				Tenn	Feb		Whooping cough	30 days
10	No name, Day	1	M				Tenn	May		unknown	1 day
11	No name, Day	1	F				Tenn	May		unknown	1 day
12	Andrew A. White	14	M				Tenn	Aug	Farmer	T. fever	4 weeks
13	Mary E. McCoy	3	F				Tenn	Sept		Fever	1 week
14	Thomas Douglass	3m	M				Tenn	Feb		Croup	2 hours
15	Nancy Alexander	69	F			M	Va	June		Consumption	C hours
16	Sarah Alexander	46(1)	F				S.C.	April		Consumption	C hours
17	George Alexander	10	M	M	S		Tenn	Feb		T. fever	20 days
18	Jane Alexander	1	F	M	S		Tenn	Aug		Dysentery	30 days
19	Elizabeth Maddy	84	F			W	Va	May		Old age	long time
20	Susanah H. Brown	3	F				Tenn	April		unknown	60 days
21	Phebe Vann	2	F				Tenn	July		Disease of liver	4 months
22	Betsey Allen	89	F				N.C.	July		Old age	
23	Rebecca Tucker	58	F			M	Tenn	Oct		Cancer	27 months
24	Sarah Kerby	1m	F				Tenn	June		Whooping cough	1 month
25	Joshua Hartsell	2	M	M			Tenn	Oct		Worms	2 days
26	Madison M. Jones	29	M				N.C.	Oct	Sch-teacher	Stabbed	sudden
27	James Kile	3	M				Tenn	Feb		Diabetes	14 days
28	Elendor Hall	73	F				S.C.	Aug		unknown	sudden
29	Eliza Ann Parks	21	F			M	Tenn	April		Black lung fever	8 days
30	James Tucker	91	M			W	unknown	Nov	Farmer	Old age	Chronic
31	Jane	6	F	B	S		Tenn	May		Fever	5 days
32	George Selvage	64	M			M	Tenn	Nov	Farmer	Kidneys	Chronic
33	Frank	60	M	B	S	M	Tenn	Oct	Laborer	unknown	12 months
34	David	3	M	M	S		Tenn	Oct		_____	sudden
35	Sarah Grubb	10	F				Tenn	Dec		T. fever	8 days

Remarks: The most prevalent disease have been typhoid fever and pneumonia. The face of the County is high and rolling in part and in part very mountainous. The great cause of disease are the frequent and great _____ in the temperature of the atmosphere and the vast amount of vegetable debries in the unburnt woods. The geological formation is of the secondary mo---- after there are large quanities of limestone and some marl. There are intense beds of iron ore, lead ore in one or two places.

COUNTY OF MONROE, STATE OF TENNESSEE.

PAGE NO. 563   PERSONS WHO DIED DURING THE YEAR ENDING 1st JUNE, 1850.

M. Clibourne

No. of Visit	Name	Age	Sex	Color	Free or Slave	Married/Widowed	Place of Birth	Month Died	Occupation	Disease or Cause of Death	No. Days Ill
1	Presley	2m	M				Tenn	Jan		Croup	4 days
2	Joseph Ragsdale	1	M				Tenn	April		Inflamation	5 weeks
3	Ann	1	F				Tenn	March		unknown	1 year

COUNTY OF MONTGOMERY, STATE OF TENNESSEE.

PAGE NO. 565   PERSONS WHO DIED DURING THE YEAR ENDING 1st JUNE, 1850.

Jordan Neblett

No. of Visit	Name	Age	Sex	Color	Free or Slave	Married/Widowed	Place of Birth	Month Died	Occupation	Disease or Cause of Death	No. Days Ill
1	Sterling Jordan	1	M	B	S		Tenn	Feb		Pneumonia	28 days

Remarks: No. of page 1. The foregoing page as first named is correct and was well and truly made according to the tenor of my oath of office.
J. Neblett, Asst. Marshal.

COUNTY OF MONTGOMERY, STATE OF TENNESSEE.

PAGE NO. 567   PERSONS WHO DIED DURING THE YEAR ENDING 1st JUNE, 1850.

No. of Visit	Name	Age	Sex	Color	Free or Slave	Married/Widowed	Place of Birth	Month Died	Occupation	Disease or Cause of Death	No. Days Ill

Remarks: Schedule 3 - Persons who died during the year ending 1st June, 1850. In the County of Montgomery, State of Tennessee, enumerated by me.
T. Ramey, Asst. Marshal.

COUNTY OF MONTGOMERY, STATE OF TENNESSEE.

PAGE NO. 568 PERSONS WHO DIED DURING THE YEAR ENDING 1st JUNE, 1850.

Jordan Neblett

No. of Visit	Name	Age	Sex	Color	Free or Slave	Married/Widowed	Place of Birth	Month Died	Occupation	Disease or Cause of Death	No. Days Ill
1	Robert Cothron	1	M	B	S		Tenn	March		unknown	unknown
2	Alford Alison	7	M	B	S		Tenn	Nov		unknown	C
3	Ariminta Pain	40	F				Tenn	Oct		Female disease	11 days
4	Pheba Marshall	12	F	B	S		Tenn	June		unknown	C
5	James Bryan	2	M	B	S		Tenn	Sept		unknown	21 days
6	Thomas Johnson	65	M	B	S		Va	Jan		Dropsy	C
7	Quintina Pain	18	F	B	S		Tenn	May		Child bed	10 days
8	Loucinda Penny	43	F				Va	March		Child bed	3 days
9	Sarah Shaw	90	F	B	S		N.C.	Sept		Old age	15 days
10	Lagrand Hiten	3	M				Tenn	May		unknown	10 days
11	William Fortson	95	M	B	S		N.C.	June		Old age	C
12	Edwin M. Johnson	12	M				Tenn	March		unknown	10 days
13	Victora Johnson	1	F	B	S		Tenn	Nov		of cold	unknown
14	Silua Moody	103	F	B	S		N.C.	Feb		Old age	sudden
15	Robert Moody	52	M	B	S		Tenn	March		Pneumonia	15 days
16	Henry Collins	1	M	B	S		Tenn	Sept		unknown	unknown
17	John Reaves	8m	M	B	S		Tenn	April		Pneumonia	28 days
18	Amy Gold	60	F	B	S		Va	July		unknown	30 days
19	Columbus Weatherford	11	M				Tenn	Jan		Worms	6 days
20	Francis Abney	2	F				Tenn	March		Drown	sudden
21	Mildred Abney	1	F	B	S		Tenn	Oct		unknown	6 days
22	Stephen Boling	65	M	B	S		N.C.	May		Old age	age
23	Ann Wathington	70	F				Maryland	May		Old age	age
24	Harriet Royster	2	F	B	S		Tenn	Nov		Croup	3 days
25	Horace Smith	8m	M	B	S		Tenn	July		Croup	30 days
26	Moses Johnson	31	M	B	S		N.C.	May		Rupture	9 days
27	Infant Yancy	6m	F				Tenn	Nov		unknown	unknown
28	Infant Yancy	6m	F				Tenn	Nov		unknown	unknown
29	John Herndon	27	M				Va	Jan	Carpenter	Pleurisy	unknown
30	Sarah Herndon	22	F				Va	Jan		T. fever	unknown
31	John P. Ligon	8	M				Tenn	March		Lung disease	unknown
32	William Norsworthy	6m	M	B	S		Tenn	Feb		unknown	3 days
33	John Hatcher	30	M				Tenn	Dec	none	unknown	C
34	William Jordan	81	M				Scotland	Aug	Farmer	Fall	sudden
35	Mary Jordan	29	F	B	S		Va	Aug		T. fever	40 days

COUNTY OF MONTGOMERY, STATE OF TENNESSEE.

PAGE NO. 569 PERSONS WHO DIED DURING THE YEAR ENDING 1st JUNE, 1850.

No. of Visit	Name	Age	Sex	Color	Free or Slave	Married/Widowed	Place of Birth	Month Died	Occupation	Disease or Cause of Death	No. Days Ill
	No names listed										

COUNTY OF MONTGOMERY, STATE OF TENNESSEE.

PAGE NO. 570 PERSONS WHO DIED DURING THE YEAR ENDING 1st JUNE, 1850.

T. Ramey

No. of Visit	Name	Age	Sex	Color	Free or Slave	Married/Widowed	Place of Birth	Month Died	Occupation	Disease or Cause of Death	No. Days Ill
1	T. E. Pollard	40	F	B	S		Tenn	April		Measles	10 days
2	H. F. Beaumont	50	F	B	S		unknown	June '49		Cholera	2 days
3	C. Bailey	35	M	B	S		Va	June		Scrofula	2 years
4	M. E. Poston	30	F			M	Kentucky	Feb		unknown	4 days
5	Infant Hill	1m	M	B	S		Tenn	May		Lockjaw	5 days
6	Alick Wheatley	37	M	B	S		Va	Dec	Cooper	Cholera	1 day
7	Infant Herring	4m	F	B	S		Tenn	Jan		unknown	4 days
8	Infant Haskins	1	M	B	S		Tenn	May		Bronchitis	20 days
9	Infant Castner	6m	M				Tenn	Jan		Bronchitis	18 days
10	Clara Russell	22	F			M	Va	Dec		Consumption	C
11	Margaret Chilton	58	F			M	Va	June		unknown	C
12	Dick Chilton	25	M	B	S		Va	Aug		Drowned	sudden
13	Sally Chilton	21	F	B	S		Tenn	Aug		unknown	C
14	Infant Chilton	2m	F	B	S		Tenn	Sept		unknown	sudden
15	Joseph Rogers	45	M	B	S		Tenn	Feb		Pneumonia	20 days
16	Harry Rogers	40	M	B	S		Tenn	Feb		Pneumonia	20 days
17	Thomas Lyle	42	M			M	Tenn	Feb	Farmer	unknown	C
18	Martha Jenkins	13	F				Tenn	May		Sc. fever	10 days
19	J. C. Bailey	15	M				Tenn	Feb		unknown	30 days
20	Samuel Barnet	1m	M				Tenn	April		unknown	1 day
21	Infant Barnet		M	B	S		Tenn	Oct		unknown	6 months
22	Elisa Brodie	4	F	B	S		Tenn	July		Cong. of lungs	1 day
23	Harriet Stewart	12	F				Kentucky	April		Pneumonia	12 days
24	Edmond Lockert	42	M	B	S		S.C.	Nov	Miller	unknown	12 days
25	Aggy McKaine	25	F	B	S		unknown	April		unknown	20 days
26	Louis Cass	1	M	B	S		Tenn	March		unknown	20 days
27	Mary McCulloch	1	F	B	S		Tenn	March		unknown	21 days
28	Vass Munford	75	M	B	S		unknown	June	Gardener	Cholera	1 day
29	Edmund Peacher	26	M	B	S		Va	April		Pneumonia	1 day
30	Arthur H. Hirst	28	M				Tenn	Dec		Consumption	9 months
31	George Read	14	M	M	S		Kentucky	July		Drowned	sudden
32	Willie Niblett	4m	M	B	S		Tenn	March		unknown	12 days
33	Charity Anglen	7	F	B	S		Tenn	Feb		Burned	1 day
34	Infant Anglen	3m	F	B	S		Tenn	unknown		unknown	unknown
35	Amy Johnson	25	F	B	S		Tenn	unknown		unknown	unknown

COUNTY OF MONTGOMERY, STATE OF TENNESSEE.

PAGE NO. 571 PERSONS WHO DIED DURING THE YEAR ENDING 1st JUNE, 1850.

T. Ramey

No. of Visit	Name	Age	Sex	Color	Free or Slave	Married/Widowed	Place of Birth	Month Died	Occupation	Disease or Cause of Death	No. Days Ill
1	Laura Donaldson	4	F				Tenn	Oct		unknown	3 days
2	Sandy Woods	25	M	B	S		Tenn	March	Blk-smith	Cholera	3 days
3	Mary Herington	24	F				Kentucky	Jan		Consumption	32 days
4	Judy Barton	62	F			M	N.C.	Feb		Cancer	C
5	Nancy Walthall	18	F	B	S		Tenn	Nov		Pneumonia	C
6	Polly Walthall	2	F	B	S		Tenn	April		unknown	30 days
7	Infant Walthall	6m	M	B	S		Tenn	Sept		unknown	20 days
8	Joseph Milton	9m	M				Tenn	March		unknown	20 days
9	Norah Herring	2	F	B	S		Tenn	unknown		unknown	unknown
10	B. Satterlee	37	M				New York	March	Merchant	Consumption	14 months
11	Thomas Parker	1m	M				Tenn	Feb		unknown	30 days
12	Catharine W. Johnson	27	F			M	Tenn	Oct		Paralysis	C
13	Henry Waters	14	M				Tenn	Oct		Chills	2 days
14	Louisa Thomas	13	F	B	S		Tenn	Sept		unknown	1 day
15	Nelson Brown	2	M				Tenn	Aug		Disease of bowels	60 days
16	Tennessee Brown	2m	F				Tenn	Jan		Hives	1 day
17	Sarah Williams	35	F			M	Tenn	Sept		unknown	C
18	Harriet A. Smith	3m	F				Tenn	Aug		Affect. lungs	7 days
19	Nathaniel Weakley	1	M				Tenn	Aug		Affect. lungs	7 days
20	John Cane	3m	M				Tenn	May		Hives	1 day
21	Jane Maguffey	5	F				Kentucky	July		Disease of head	C
22	Shelby Maguffey	4	M				Kentucky	Aug		Chills	30 days
23	Abram Stewart	67	M	B	S		N.C.	March		unknown	C
24	Mary Atkins	33	F			M	Penn	June		Apoplexy	sudden
25	William D. Morgan	1m	M				Penn	Nov		unknown	10 days
26	Amanda P. Pace	1	F				Tenn	May		unknown	1 day
27	Green Hudgens	6	M	B	S		Tenn	May		Measles	unknown
28	Milly Chisenhall	37	F			M	N.C.	Oct		unknown	sudden
29	Sarah A. Mitchell	6m	F	B	S		Tenn	Dec		unknown	sudden
30	Fanny Irby	65	F				Va	July		unknown	12 days
31	Edith Barbee	42	F				Georgia	Jan		unknown	unknown
32	Mary Killibrew	2	F	B	S		Tenn	June		unknown	5 days
33	James Bradley	8m	M	B	S		Tenn	Feb		unknown	30 days
34	Wallace Willis	40	M	B	S		Tenn	June		Consumption	C
35	Priscilla Humphreys	76	F			W	N.C.	Dec		Old age	

COUNTY OF MONTGOMERY, STATE OF TENNESSEE.

PAGE NO. 574 PERSONS WHO DIED DURING THE YEAR ENDING 1st JUNE, 1850.

T. Ramey

No. of Visit	Name	Age	Sex	Color	Free or Slave	Married/Widowed	Place of Birth	Month Died	Occupation	Disease or Cause of Death	No. Days Ill
1	Lucinda Herring	35	F	B	S		Tenn	June		unknown	sudden
2	Infant Herring	3m	F	B	S		Tenn	June		unknown	sudden
3	Elisa Smith	27	F	B	S		Tenn	Feb		unknown	C
4	Jack Foster	5m	M	B	S		Va	May		unknown	14 days
5	Elisa Foster	21	F	B	S		Tenn	March		unknown	14 days
6	Infant Foster	10m	F	B	S		Tenn	Aug		unknown	14 days
7	Thomas Elder	20	M	B	S		Tenn	unknown		unknown	unknown
8	Infant Johnson	1m	M	B	S		Tenn	Sept		unknown	unknown
9	Washington Dunlap	13	M	B	S		Tenn	unknown		unknown	————
10	Dick Dunlap	19	M	B	S		Tenn	unknown		unknown	C
11	Dicey Manson	1m	F	B	S		Tenn	unknown		unknown	14 days
12	Jasper Martin	8	M				Va	March		unknown	8 days
13	Serina V. Rye	2	F				Tenn	July		unknown	1 day
14	Harriet Jones	4	F				Tenn	Aug		Croup	3 days
15	Uriah Tyson	72	M			M	N.C.	Dec	Farmer	unknown	60 days
16	Chaney Barbee	6m	F				Tenn	unknown		unknown	unknown
17	Sylvia Edmondson	57	F	B	S		Va	May		Cancer	C
18	J. Hail	1m	M				Tenn	Dec		unknown	sudden
19	Charles Carlace	62	M	B	S		N.C.	March		Pleurisy	8 days
20	Lewis Stewart	60	M	B	S		Tenn	Feb		Cholera	7 days
21	Presley Lynes	23	M				Tenn	May		Inflamation of bowels	sudden
22	Jacob Helm	42	M	B	S		Va	March		Cut by axe	sudden
23	Judith Walker	36	F	B	S		Tenn	Sept		unknown	unknown
24	Sarah Walker	4	F	B	S		Tenn	Aug		unknown	unknown
25	Julius Johnson	56	M				N.C.	Dec	Farmer	unknown	6 days
26	Sophronia Frasier	2m	F				Tenn	July		unknown	unknown
27	Edward Beck	47	M				N.C.	Feb	Mechanic	unknown	unknown
28	Fanny Perdue	16	F	B	S		Tenn	April		unknown	unknown
29	Isar Perdue	1	M	B	S		Tenn	Oct		unknown	unknown
30	Thomas W. Shearron	22	M				Tenn	Nov		Disease of lungs	unknown
31	Randal Mallory	6m	M	B	S		Tenn	Aug		Bowel Complaint	14 days
32	Sarah C. Smith	4	F				Tenn	Nov		unknown	sudden
33	George Conrad	1	M				Tenn	Sept		unknown	30 days
34	George Landon	8m	M	B	S		Tenn	Feb		unknown	unknown
35	Barry Quarles	24	M	B	S		Tenn	June		T. fever	9 days

COUNTY OF MONTGOMERY, STATE OF TENNESSEE.

PAGE NO. 575 PERSONS WHO DIED DURING THE YEAR ENDING 1st JUNE, 1850.

T. Ramey

No. of Visit	Name	Age	Sex	Color	Free or Slave	Married/Widowed	Place of Birth	Month Died	Occupation	Disease or Cause of Death	No. Days Ill
1	Chaney Johnson	57	F	B	S		Va	Feb		Pneumonia	2 days
2	Richard Rogers	35	M	B	S		Va	March	Blk-smith	Consumption	6 months
3	Brum Rogers	51	M	B	S		N.C.	June		unknown	C
4	David Lynch	85	M				N.C.	April	Farmer	unknown	sudden
5	Betsey Powers	46	F				Tenn	unknown		unknown	C
6	Infant Wilson	6m	F	B	S		Tenn	unknown		unknown	unknown
7	Silla Pace	75	F	B	S		N.C.	May		Old age	
8	Infant Chilton	3m	M	B	S		Tenn	unknown		unknown	unknown
9	Lucy A. Ferrell	14	F				Tenn	March		unknown	unknown
10	Thomas A.J.L.Tutor	4	M				Tenn	April		T. fever	60 days
11	John W. High	35	M				Tenn	Aug	Farmer	Stabbed	28 days
12	Mary L. Gardner	75	F				Va	March		unknown	21 days
13	Fanny Neblett	23	F	B	S		Tenn	unknown		unknown	unknown
14	Emily Neblett	21	F	B	S		Tenn	unknown		unknown	unknown
15	Violet Neblett	40	F	B	S		Tenn	unknown		unknown	unknown
16	Thomas Neblett	12	M	B	S		Tenn	unknown		unknown	unknown
17	Lewis Neblett	1	M	B	S		Tenn	unknown		unknown	unknown
18	Infant McCauley	5m	M				Tenn	unknown		unknown	unknown
19	John Cocke	4	M				Tenn	Nov		unknown	9 days
20	Louisa L. Gaines	35	F				Tenn	March		unknown	1 day
21	Samuel A. Morrison	10m	M				Tenn	Feb		Fever	28 days
22	Thomas Smith	60	M	B	S		N.C.	April		unknown	sudden
23	Jacob Black	55	M				Tenn	March	Farmer	T. fever	21 days
24	Reuben Fort	76	M	B	S		N.C.	unknown		Inflamation of bowels	7 days
25	Catharine Kyle	26	F				Tenn	Jan		unknown	unknown
26	Crecy Vaughan	25	F	B	S		Tenn	March		Pneumonia	12 days
27	Peter Fort	78	M	B	S		N.C.	unknown		Inflamation of bowels	7 days
28	Barrett Herring	50	M	B	S		N.C.	Dec		unknown	90 days
29	Margaret Farrier	18	F	B	S		Tenn	Aug		T. fever	21 days
30	Infant Farrier	1	F	B	S		Tenn	Sept		T. fever	21 days
31	Minerva Erwin	28	F	B	S		Tenn	March		Cold	8 days
32	Thomas Erwin	12	M	B	S		Tenn	April		Chills	2 days
33	Green Erwin	2	M	B	S		Tenn	April		Cholera Inf.	2 days
34	Infant Erwin	11m	F	B	S		Tenn	April		Cholera Inf.	2 days
35	Peter Williamson	1	M	B	S		Tenn	unknown		unknown	unknown

COUNTY OF MONTGOMERY, STATE OF TENNESSEE.

PAGE NO. 578 PERSONS WHO DIED DURING THE YEAR ENDING 1st JUNE, 1850.

T. Ramey

No. of Visit	Name	Age	Sex	Color	Free or Slave	Married/Widowed	Place of Birth	Month Died	Occupation	Disease or Cause of Death	No. Days Ill
1	Siddy Jamison	55	F				Kentucky	unknown		unknown	sudden
2	Jack Willis	2	M	B	S		Tenn	Oct		unknown	sudden
3	John B. Harvy	25	M				N.C.	Aug	Farmer	unknown	sudden
4	Absolom Odom	70	M				S.C.	March	Farmer	Old age	unknown
5	Mary S. Marable	1	F				Tenn	Nov		Cholera Inf.	6 days
6	Louisa Jackson	13	F				Tenn	unknown		unknown	unknown
7	York Jorden	60	M	B	S		N.C.	unknown	Farmer	unknown	unknown
8	Henry McFall	58	M				N.C.	unknown	Farmer	unknown	unknown
9	Hocksena Marable	2	F	B	S		Tenn	unknown		unknown	unknown
10	Rebecca Allen	45	F	B	S		Tenn	June		unknown	unknown
11	Keziah Stone	69	F				N.C.	unknown		unknown	unknown
12	Martha Henderson	18	F	B	S		Tenn	June		unknown	unknown
13	Catherine Kyle	25	F				Tenn	April		unknown	unknown
14	Mary E. Vaughn	9m	F				Tenn	unknown		unknown	unknown
15	Robert Baxter	65	M				New Jersey	April	Iron Master	Pneumonia	20 days
16	Dick Baxter	50	M	B	S		Va	April	Blk-smith	Rupture	C
17	Rack Williams	47	M				unknown	Jan	Farmer	unknown	C
18	George McCauley	7	M				Tenn	March		unknown	C
19	America F. McCauley	2m	F				Tenn	Nov		unknown	sudden
20	Joan Batson	5	F				Tenn	Dec		Croup	sudden
21	James Swift	5	M				Tenn	unknown		Killed, accident	sudden
22	Isam Crockett	39	M	B	S		Tenn	Dec		Pleurisy	6 days
23	Mariah McCauley	6m	F	B	S		Tenn	Dec		Croup	1 day
24	Elizabeth Louis	70	F				S.C.	unknown		Old age	21 days
25	Fredonia Easley	15	F	B	S		Tenn	Feb		Measles	3 months
26	Elizabeth S. Kennady	4	F				Tenn	Nov		Burned	sudden
27	Susan Copeland	14	F	B	S		Tenn	Oct		Female disease	C
28	Isam T. Dawson	12	M				Tenn	Jan		unknown	4 months
29	Florrance Dawson	6	F				Va	unknown		unknown	6 days
30	Henry Tally	2	M	B	S		Tenn	unknown		unknown	unknown
31	Harry Tally	2	M	B	S		Tenn	unknown		unknown	unknown
32	James A. Ramey	27	M				Tenn	Nov	Farmer	T. fever	21 days
33	Allen Ramey	60	M				N.C.	Jan	Farmer	unknown	14 days
34	Infant Ramey	7m	M	B	S		Tenn	Nov		Croup	sudden
35	John Daniel	2m	M				Tenn	March		unknown	sudden

COUNTY OF MONTGOMERY, STATE OF TENNESSEE.

PAGE NO. 579 PERSONS WHO DIED DURING THE YEAR ENDING 1st JUNE, 1850.

T. Ramey

No. of Visit	Name	Age	Sex	Color	Free or Slave	Married/Widowed	Place of Birth	Month Died	Occupation	Disease or Cause of Death	No. Days Ill
1	Lizy Hodges	35	F	B	S		Tenn	unknown		Cholera	sudden
2	Polly Ann Shelton	4m	F				Tenn	July		Cholera Inf.	20 days
3	Catherine M. Larmon	27	F				Kentucky	Nov		Consumption	C
4	Infant Allen	3m	M	B	S		Tenn	unknown		unknown	unknown
5	Infant Allen	2m	F	B	S		Tenn	unknown		unknown	unknown
6	Nancy Ann Bradbery	1	F				Tenn	Jan		Croup	sudden
7	Sarah Thurston	25	F	B	S		Tenn	Dec		Consumption	C
8	Josephine Thurston	6m	F	B	S		Tenn	Jan		unknown	sudden
9	Edwin Thompkins	20	M	M	S		Tenn	March	Farmer	Brain fever	8 days
10	Moses London	60	M	B	S		N.C.	April	Laborer	Paralysis	12 days
11	Violet Cross	70	F	B	S		Va	unknown		Old age	C
12	Ned Pettus	22	M	B	S		Tenn	Aug		T. fever	10 days
13	Mary Pollard	19	F	B	S		Tenn	Aug		T. fever	14 days
14	Sally Trice	50	F	B	S		Tenn	unknown		unknown	C
15	Green McCauley	20	M	B	S		Tenn	Nov		T. fever	16 days
16	Squire McCauley	18	M	B	S		Tenn	Nov		T. fever	25 days
17	Daniel McCauley	16	M	B	S		Tenn	Nov		T. fever	12 days
18	John McCauley	14	M	B	S		Tenn	Nov		T. fever	8 days
19	Moses McCauley	2	M	B	S		Tenn	Nov		T. fever	21 days
20	James McCauley	9m	M	B	S		Tenn	Nov		T. fever	sudden
21	Sampson McCauley	8m	M	B	S		Tenn	Nov		T. fever	sudden
22	Aniliza McCauley	12	F	B	S		Tenn	Nov		T. fever	14 days
23	Rebecca Stewart	12	F	B	S		Tenn	Feb		Dropsy	C
24	Drury Allen	41	M			M	Tenn	March	Farmer	Consumption	C
25	Abner P. Bowers	38	M			M	Tenn	April	Farmer	Diarrhea	30 days
26	Sarah Bowers	6	F				Tenn	Sept		Croup	4 days
27	James Edmonds	38	M			M	Tenn	Sept	Farmer	Fever	30 days
28	Ann Newell	70	F	B	S		Va	Jan		Old age	20 days
29	Fanny Newell	40	F	B	S		N.C.	May		Milk leg	300 days
30	George Newell	1	M	B	S		Tenn	Jan		unknown	sudden
31	Sally A. Welsh	27	F			M	Kentucky	May		Liver complaint	30 days
32	Nelson Welsh	22	M	B	S		Tenn	May		Fever	10 days
33	Newton Welsh	7	M	B	S		Tenn	May		Fever	20 days
34	George Phillips	13	M	B	S		Tenn	Feb		unknown	10 days
35	Phillip Huggins	55	M			M	N.C.	Sept		Dropsy	40 days

COUNTY OF MONTGOMERY, STATE OF TENNESSEE.

PAGE NO. 582 PERSONS WHO DIED DURING THE YEAR ENDING 1st JUNE, 1850.

T. Ramey

No. of Visit	Name	Age	Sex	Color	Free or Slave	Married/Widowed	Place of Birth	Month Died	Occupation	Disease or Cause of Death	No. Days Ill
1	Thomas Dodd	87	M			W	S.C.	June	Farmer	Urine disease	19 days
2	Mary E. Landrom	1	F				Kentucky	Aug		unknown	3 days
3	Randolph A. Trice	5	M				Tenn	Jan		unknown	4 days
4	Hezekiah Lisenby	6	M				Tenn	May		Kill by cart	sudden
5	Mary Gollady	45	F				Kentucky	March		unknown	unknown
6	Winder Brown	70	F	B	S		N.C.	April		unknown	unknown
7	Frances Hart	60	F			W	N.C.	May		unknown	24 days
8	Robert G. Johnson	11	M				Tenn	Oct		Fever	60 days

Remarks: No. 6¼ pages. The number of pages above stated is correct of the foregoing copy and they were well and truly made according to the tenor of my oath of office.   T. Ramey, Asst. Marshal
I have no very particular remarks to make as it respects the sickness in my County the last year, ending the 1st of June 1850. There has been no particular malady in my County. Chills and fevers is more common than any other disease. The water in my County generally limestone. We have a variety of soil and rocks and also.....

Remarks: Page 583. The growth generally is oak, hickory, poplar, black gum, sweet gum, and some few blackjack, sassafras, chestnut, black and white walnut and cherry. There is several kinds of the maple sugar, elm and almost any other kind of growth of timber that grows in Tennessee. Iron ore beds inexhaustable.

Remarks: Page 586. Schedule 5. Products of Industry in the County of Montgomery, State of Tennessee, during the year ending June 1st 1850, as enumerated by me.
    T. Ramey, Asst. Marshal.

COUNTY OF MORGAN **, STATE OF TENNESSEE.**

PAGE NO. 587 **PERSONS WHO DIED DURING THE YEAR ENDING 1st JUNE, 1850.**

19th Subdivision, East Tenn District
A. H. Hendrix

No. of Visit	Name	Age	Sex	Color	Free or Slave	Married/Widowed	Place of Birth	Month Died	Occupation	Disease or Cause of Death	No. Days Ill
1	John Stephen	22	M				Morgan Co.	Dec	Farmer	Diarrhea	400 days
2	Shadrack Stephens, Jr.	5	M				Morgan Co.	June		unknown	26 days
3	Matilda Stephens	9m	F				Morgan Co.	June		Flux	3 days
4	Joseph	18	M	B	S		Morgan Co.	March		unknown	2 days
5	Sarah Hall	35	F			M	Overton Co.	March		unknown	30 days
6	Katharine Adkinson	50	F			M	Va	May		unknown	sudden
7	Isaac Reece	25	M				Tenn	June	Laborer	Diarrhea	180 days
8	Mary Green	8	F				Morgan Co.	Nov		Fever	5 days
9	Anderson Howard	14	M				Morgan Co.	Nov		Fever	6 days
10	Mary Cook	21	F				Morgan Co.	June		Dropsy	130 days
11	Elvira Ann Bownier	3m	F				Morgan Co.	Feb		unknown	4 days
12	Katharine Hodge	30	F				Germany	May		Consumption	130 days
13	Oleon Benica	1m	M				Morgan Co.	Jan		unknown	2 days
14	John Stenner	1m	M				Morgan Co.	Aug		unknown	7 days
15	Robert Buseton	15	M				Morgan Co.	June	Farmer	unknown	18 days
16	Willis Buseton	7	M				Morgan Co.	April		unknown	3 days
17	Elizabeth Hollaway	18	F				Morgan Co.	May		Consumption	300 days
18	Rebecca Hollaway	86	F			W	unknown	March		Age	8 days
19	Margaret Haneycut	18	F				Tenn	April		Fits	1 day
20	Mary A. Sims	14	F				Morgan Co.	May		unknown	3 days
21	Sarah A. Buent	38	F				Tenn	Oct		Dropsy	300 days
22	Henry V. Buent	1	M				Morgan Co.	June		Croup	6 days

Remarks: Morgan is a high elevated County, entirely mountainous, very healthy. The soil very broken, fine mineral springs besides the other kinds of timber that is common in East Tennessee. There is white and Spruce pine and land in abundance which is not common in mountain Countys like this, and so.....

COUNTY OF OBION, STATE OF TENNESSEE.

PAGE NO. 589 PERSONS WHO DIED DURING THE YEAR ENDING 1st JUNE, 1850.

Wm. B. Gibbs

No. of Visit	Name	Age	Sex	Color	Free or Slave	Married/Widowed	Place of Birth	Month Died	Occupation	Disease or Cause of Death	No. Days Ill
1	Elizabeth White	36	F			M	Va	Sept		Cholera Mur.	7 days
2	Rosella Warren	7	F				Tenn	March		Cholera	12 hours
3	Jonas Meadows	26	M			M	Tenn	Jan	Farmer	Drown	sudden
4	Benjamin Logan	40	M			M	Tenn	Nov	Farmer	Pneumonia	8 days
5	Mary Childress	39	F				Tenn	Oct		From a burn	C
6	James Mafas	1	M				Tenn	Feb		Croup	2 days
7	Abigail Calhoun	5	F				Tenn	Feb		Pneumonia	16 days
8	Samuel Campbell	40	M			M	Va	March	Blk-smith	Cholera	3 days
9	Susan Nix	8m	F				Tenn	Aug		Fever	8 days
10	unnamed	2d	F				Tenn	Dec			
11	Louisa	1m	F	B	S		Tenn	Jan			
12	Mary Allen	16	F				Tenn	April		Consumption	C
13	John Piney	45	M			M	unknown	Feb	Farmer	Fever	14 days
14	unnamed	1d	M				Tenn	Sept			
15	Jane Rickman	3	F				Indiana	Dec		Whooping cough	60 days
16	Sarah Rickman	2	F				Kentucky	March		Scrofula	C
17	David Templeton	41	M				Tenn	July	Farmer	Congestive fever	4 days
18	Sarah Box	13	F				Illinois	Dec		Pneumonia	4 days
19	Franklin Bill	2	M				Tenn	Oct		Inflamation of brain	
20	Sarah Graham	52	F			M	Kentucky	April		Consumption	C
21	Sarah Graham	4m	F				Tenn	Dec		Whooping cough	10 days
22	Solomon Stevenson	20	M				Illinois	April	Farmer	Rheumatism	14 days
23	Moses Cassion	10m	M				Tenn	Oct		Inflamation of brain	4 days
24	Louissa Murray	5	F				Tenn	Dec		Whooping cough	
25	Sarah McGee	6	F				Tenn	Nov		Whooping cough	
26	Rufus Carroll	1	M				Tenn	Oct		Croup	2 days
27	Judith Davidson	24	F			M	Tenn	Oct		Child bed	4 days
28	Elizabeth Hughes	20	F				unknown	Oct		Consumption	C
29	Edgar Williamson	1	M				Tenn	Nov		Thrash	30 days
30	John	5	M	B	S		Va	Nov		Worms	3 days
31	Nancy	7m	F	B	S		Tenn	Nov		Thrash	10 days
32	Tilman Hogan	3	M				Tenn	Feb		Croup	2 days
33	Rubin McWhirter	39	M			M	Kentucky	July	Farmer	Fever	15 days
34	Franklin McWhirter	40	M			M	Kentucky	March	Farmer	Fever	17 days

COUNTY OF OBION, STATE OF TENNESSEE.

PERSONS WHO DIED DURING THE YEAR ENDING 1st JUNE, 1850.

Wm. B. Gibbs

No. of Visit	Name	Age	Sex	Color	Free or Slave	Married/Widowed	Place of Birth	Month Died	Occupation	Disease or Cause of Death	No. Days Ill
1	Littleton Ward	41	M			M	S.C.	Nov	Farmer	Accident	sudden
2	George Mathis	7m	M				Tenn	Dec		Small pox	10 days
3	Maston Brockwell	23	M				Va	Nov	Brickmason	Small pox	15 days
4	Allen Walker	25	M			M	Tenn	Sept	Farmer	Congestive fever	17 days
5	Daniel Walker	23	M			M	Tenn	July	Farmer	Congestive fever	6 days
6	Billy	60	M	B	S		N.C.	June		Consumption	C
7	Elbert Reed	1	M				Tenn	Oct		unknown	30 days
8	Charley	1m	M	B	S		Tenn	Oct		Consumption	4 weeks
9	John M. Brockwell	34	M			M	Va	Dec	Brickmason	Small pox	23 days
10	Jane House	4	F				Tenn	Oct		Fever	6 days
11	Jane Philips	33	F			M	N.C.	May		Child bed	3 days
12	Carrol Washam	16	M				Tenn	April	Farmer	Fever	7 days
13	Moundville	104	M	B	S		Va	July		Old age	
14	John Reeves	9m	M				Tenn	May		Cholera Inf.	14 days
15	Nancy Davis	70	F				N.C.	Oct		unknown	C
16	Francis Nudery	18	M				Tenn	Jan	Farmer	Consumption	C
17	unnamed	1m	M				Tenn	Oct		Fits	sudden
18	John Donnelson	23	M				Tenn	Oct	Farmer	Fever	7 days
19	George	1	M	B	S		Tenn	Jan		Croup	sudden
20	William	18	M	B	S		N.C.	March		Fits	sudden
21	Kate	2	F	B	S		Tenn	July		unknown	C
22	Joseph Tipton	22	M				Tenn	Nov	Farmer	Cholera	4 days
23	Moses Edwards	35	M				Ohio	Dec	Woodchopper	Small pox	12 days
24	William Teran	22	M				Georgia	Dec	Woodchopper	Cholera	3 days
25	Carca	1	F	M	S		Tenn	May		Whooping cough	60 days
26	Linsey Reeves	1m	M				Tenn	July		unknown	
27	Harriet	22	F	B	S		Va	Nov		Consumption	C
28	Toby	1	M	B	S		Tenn	Dec		Worms	14 days
29	Lewis Ragan	60	M			M	N.C.	Dec	Farmer	Pneumonia	6 days
30	Fliphem Mitchel	52	M			M	Missouri	March	Farmer	Congestive Chill	4 days
31	unnamed	1d	F				Tenn	May			
32	unnamed	1d	F				Tenn	June			
33	Louisa Raibram	11m	F				Tenn	Sept		unknown	C
34	Edward Jones	4	M				Tenn	Jan		Cholera	4 hours
35	Sarah Auston	22	F				Tenn	March		Consumption	C

COUNTY OF OBION, STATE OF TENNESSEE.

PAGE NO. 593 PERSONS WHO DIED DURING THE YEAR ENDING 1st JUNE, 1850.

Wm. B. Gibbs

No. of Visit	Name	Age	Sex	Color	Free or Slave	Married/Widowed	Place of Birth	Month Died	Occupation	Disease or Cause of Death	No. Days Ill
1	William	1	M	B	S		Tenn	Sept		Whooping cough	3 days
2	unnamed	1d	M				Tenn	April			
3	Moses Moultrie	24	M			M	N.C.	Feb	Fisherman	Fever	9 days
4	Nancy Gentry	67	F			W	unknown	Jan		Fever	7 days
5	Sarah McElroy	21	F				Tenn	Aug		Fever	20 days
6	Silus Stroud	28	M			M	Tenn	Aug	Tanner	Fever	35 days
7	Henderson Pickerd	38	M			M	Tenn	May	Tanner	Pneumonia	8 days
8	William Bean	62	M			M	S.C.	May	Tanner	Consumption	C
9	Margaret Wright	62	F			W	N.C.	June		Congestion	2 days
10	William Whiteside	87	M			W	S.C.	March	none	Old age	
11	Synthia Hagan	49	F			M	S.C.	June		Fever	9 days
12	Paulina Shore	18	F				N.C.	March		Dropsy	C
13	Sarah	25	F	B	S		N.C.	Jan		Fever	21 days
14	William Helms	75	M			M	Va	Aug	Farmer	Gravel	C
15	Winney	2	F	B	S		Tenn	April		Rickets	C
16	unnamed	6m	F				Tenn	Sept		unknown	C
17	Caroline Reeves	37	F			W	S.C.	June		Consumption	C
18	Mary	12	F	B	S		Tenn	March		Fever	16 days
19	Martha Letton	1m	F				Tenn	April		Hives	1 day
20	unnamed	1d	F				Tenn	June		unknown	

COUNTY OF OVERTON, STATE OF TENNESSEE.

PAGE NO. 595 PERSONS WHO DIED DURING THE YEAR ENDING 1st JUNE, 1850.

A. Cullom

No. of Visit	Name	Age	Sex	Color	Free or Slave	Married/Widowed	Place of Birth	Month Died	Occupation	Disease or Cause of Death	No. Days Ill
1	John C. Bilbrey	2	M				Tenn	Aug		Cholera Inf.	10 days
2	Margaret Murphey	5	F				Tenn	April		Fever	21 days
3	John White	2	M				Tenn	April		Croup	4 days
4	Liddy Norris	41	F			M	Tenn	Oct		Fever	28 days
5	James Harp	42	M			M	Tenn	Nov	Farmer	Fever	21 days
6	Calvin B. Ely	22	M				Tenn	Sept	Sch-teacher	Fever	21 days
7	Nancy A. Stocton	34	F			M	N.C.	May		Fever	2 months
8	Celina Ely	12	F				Tenn	Oct		Fever	21 days
9	William Wilmoth	25	M			M	Tenn	Nov	Farmer	Fever	21 days
10	Malicy E. Bilbrey	1m	_				Tenn	Sept		Croup	1 day
11	Michael C. A. Hall	65	M			W	Va	Jan	Cabinet-mkr	Cold	11 days
12	Katy Cannon	23	F				Tenn	Sept		Fever	17 days
13	Andrew Cannon	21	M				Tenn	April	Tanner	Fever	17 days
14	Mary Gilliland	1	F				Tenn	June		Fever	9 days
15	William Gray	30	M			M	Tenn	Sept	Merchant	Fever	9 days
16	Mary Lee	85	F			W	Va	Jan		unknown	28 days
17	James G. Carmack	30	M				Tenn	Nov	Farmer	Consumption	9 years
18	Abraham Canatswer	68	M			M	unknown	Dec	Farmer	unknown	1 day
19	Easter Canatswer	62	F			W	unknown	May		unknown	7 days
20	Samuel Boswell	76	M			M	Va	Feb	Farmer	Dropsy	1 year
21	Ann Allred	35	F			M	Tenn	Oct		Asthma	2 years
22	Polly Allred	1m	F				Tenn	Dec		Hives	4 days
23	Polly A. Stanton	9	F				Tenn	May		unknown	4 months
24	Charles Stanton	6	M				Tenn	March		unknown	1 year
25	Julius Stanton	4	M				Tenn	Aug		Worms	4 months
26	Nancy Stanton	1m	F				Tenn	April		Hives	2 days
27	Jackson Smith	2	M				Tenn	Jan		F. Measles	3 days
28	Elizabeth Douglass	21	F				N.C.	Oct		Fever	27 days
29	John P. Douglass	13	M				Tenn	Oct		Fever	12 days
30	Henry C. Douglass	5	M				Tenn	Nov		Fever	15 days
31	Polly Harris	16	F				Tenn	June		Dropsy	3 years

COUNTY OF OVERTON, STATE OF TENNESSEE.

PAGE NO. 598 PERSONS WHO DIED DURING THE YEAR ENDING 1st JUNE, 1850.

Alvon Cullom

No. of Visit	Name	Age	Sex	Color	Free or Slave	Married/Widowed	Place of Birth	Month Died	Occupation	Disease or Cause of Death	No. Days Ill
1	Mary Copeland	1m	F				Tenn	April		unknown	1 day
2	Martha Copeland	1m	F				Tenn	April		unknown	1 day
3	Nancy Eldridge	26	F			M	Tenn	Nov		Fever	14 days
4	Martha Colquitt	8m	F				Tenn	Dec		Meningitis	60 days
5	Jediah C. Herriford	16	M				Kentucky	Oct	Student	Fever	15 days
6	Becky D. Jestice	7m	F				Tenn	Aug		Croup	30 days
7	Washington Shomake	32	M			M	Tenn	Feb	Farmer	unknown	6 months
8	Louisa A. Allison	2	F				Tenn	Sept		Croup	1 day
9	Hiram Howard	1	M				Tenn	Aug		unknown	5 days
10	Elizabeth Boles	82	F			M	Va	April		Old age	
11	Sarah Alberson	60	F				S.C.	July		Dropsy	————
12	Jesse Hunt	28	M				Tenn	Oct	Farmer	Accident	————
13	Ruben Padgett	1	M				Tenn	April		unknown	21 days
14	William Huddleston	6m	M				Tenn	July		Fever	4 months
15	Field Huddleston	1m	M				Tenn	Aug		Nettle rash	9 days
16	Calvin Miller	1m	M				Tenn	April		unknown	1 day
17	Thomas Cash	38	M			M	Tenn	April	Merchant	Diabetes	4 days
18	Mariah Carlock	40	F	B	S		Kentucky	July		Dropsy	8 months
19	Polly Hooks	95	F			W	N.C.	unknown		Old age	————
20	Joseph Woody	2	M				Tenn	March		Croup	4 days
21	Nancy Chainy	8m	F				Tenn	Sept		unknown	2 months
22	Green Presley	1m	M				Tenn	Nov		Cancer	1 month
23	Sarah McCully	40	F			M	Tenn	March		Child bed	5 days
24	Jones McCully	6	M				Tenn	March		Fever	4 days
25	Mary A. Peaters	19	F				Tenn	Sept		Fever	12 days
26	Benjamin J. J. Jetton	3	M				Tenn	Sept		Fever	35 days
27	Benjamin E. Jetton	23	M				N.C.	Aug	Farmer	Fever	17 days
28	Mary M. Jetton	19	F				N.C.	Aug		Fever	15 days
29	Mary J. Peak	8	F				Tenn	Dec		Fever	8 days
30	Jane Webb	44	F			M	Tenn	Oct		Fever	24 days
31	Bartlet Gentry	17	M				Alabama	Oct	Farmer	Fever	12 days
32	Letta Breeding	60	F			M	N.C.	Oct		Fever	20 days
33	Henry L. Breeding	4	M				Tenn	Oct		Fever	17 days
34	Elizabeth Gardenhier	7m	F				Tenn	April		Fever	7 days
35	John H. Chapin	46	M			M	N.C.	Oct	Farmer	Fever	49 days

Remarks: It appears that one half of all the deaths in this report have been from fever (typhoid), which is not a common disease in this County. We are perhaps, blessed with more good springs than almost any County in the State, principally lime, with several chalybeate and sulphur spring. The surface of the County is rather uneven. The character of the soil, various....

COUNTY OF OVERTON, STATE OF TENNESSEE.

PAGE NO. 599 PERSONS WHO DIED DURING THE YEAR ENDING 1st JUNE, 1850.

Civil District Nos. 12th, 7th, 8th, 4th, 3rd, & 2nd.

Henry Young

No. of Visit	Name	Age	Sex	Color	Free or Slave	Married/Widowed	Place of Birth	Month Died	Occupation	Disease or Cause of Death	No. Days Ill
1	Joyce Felkins	43	F			M	Va	Nov		Child bed	1 day
2	Henry Dillen	88	M			W	Va	Aug	Farmer	Old age	8 days
3	Mary Reeves	23	F			M	Tenn	May		T. fever	6 days
4	Mary Lahorn	4m	F				Tenn	Nov		Croup	4 days
5	George Heard	5	M				Tenn	Feb		Croup	2 days
6	Susan Taylor	53	F				Tenn	May		C	25 years
7	Susan Mullens	5	F				Tenn	Nov		Sc. fever	17 days
8	Jane Eldridge	50	F			M	Va	Sept		Inflamation	16 days
9	Mordica Smith	35	M			M	Tenn	Jan	Farmer	Rheumatism	5 months
10	Thomas Johnson	5	M				Tenn	Aug		Croup	4 days
11	William Green	1m	M				Tenn	March		unknown	
12	Mary Keen	14	F				Tenn	July		Sc. fever	4 days
13	Catharine McLusky	35	F			M	Kentucky	Sept		Dropsy	13 days
14	Mildred Stewart	6	M				Tenn	Sept		unknown	15 days
15	Isaac	10m	M	B	S		Tenn	Feb		Burned	5 days
16	Betsy	84	F	B	S		S.C.	Jan		Old age	
17	Mary Jewett	5	F	B	S		Tenn	Feb		Sc. fever	8 days
18	Angeline Edens	10m	F				Tenn	March		unknown	3 days
19	George	3	M	B	S		Tenn	April		Scrofula	12 days
20	Martha Harrison	67	F			M	N.C.	May		unknown	40 days
21	Elizabeth Johnson	95	F				N.C.	Sept		Old age	
22	Sarah Harp	93	F				Va	Aug		Old age	
23	Lucinda Davis	25	F			M	Tenn	June		Consumption	60 days
24	Sarah Maxwell	21	F			M	Tenn	April		Quinsy	1 day
25	Mary Maxwell	28	F				Tenn	Oct		unknown	100 days
26	Alfred Ridge	9	M				Tenn	May		Dirt eating	5 days
27	Julian Wilson	2	M				Tenn	Nov		Quinsy	4 days
28	Jane Goldsby	85	F			W	Va	May		Old age	6 days
29	Ellen Coffman	5m	F				Tenn	Feb		unknown	1 day
30	Parilla Johnson	20	F			M	Tenn	Aug		T. fever	14 days
31	Agnes Matthews	6m	F				Tenn	Sept		Croup	1 day
32	Elizabeth Cherry	12	F				Tenn	Oct		Fever	14 days

Remarks: Personally appeared, Henry Young, before me and made oath that this copy agrees to the original taken by him, Oct 22, 1850. Thomas C. Parris, (J.P.)

COUNTY OF PERRY, STATE OF TENNESSEE.

PAGE NO. 601 PERSONS WHO DIED DURING THE YEAR ENDING 1st JUNE, 1850.

R. M. Thomas

No. of Visit	Name	Age	Sex	Color	Free or Slave	Married/Widowed	Place of Birth	Month Died	Occupation	Disease or Cause of Death	No. Days Ill
1	Mary Evans	84	F	W	F	M	Va	Aug		Old age	90 days
2	Thomas L. Lamberson		M	W	F		Tenn	Aug		Infant	
3	Malinda Lane	12	F	W	F		Tenn	May		unknown	3 days
4	Infant	21d	M	W	F		Tenn	May		Whooping cough	
5	George Taylor	3	M	W	F		Tenn	Aug		Fever	35 days
6	Richard Cragg	78	M	W	F	M	N.C.	June	Farmer	Gravel	30 days
7	Pleasant Murray	22	M	W	F		Tenn	April	Farmer	Fever	35 days
8	James Marrs	63	M	W	F	M	Va	Sept	Farmer	Fever and age	21 days
9	Cristeane Compen	2	F	W	F		France	April		Cholera	2 days
10	Wesley Daniel	23	M	W	F		Tenn	Nov	D.Sheriff	Cholera	1 day
11	Elijah Dailey	47	M	W	F		N.C.	Sept	Farmer	Fever	10 days
12	Peggy Townsend	40	F	B	S		N.C.	Sept		Fever	14 days
13	Warren Nix	46	M	W	F	M	Tenn	Dec	Farmer	Cholera	1 day
14	James McGouder	1	M	W	F		Tenn	July		unknown	15 days
15	John Thompson	35	M	M	F		Kentucky	April	Blk-smith	Dropsy	90 days
16	Lydia Morrison	69	F	W	F	M	N.C.	Nov		Dropsy	8 months
17	Jane Campbell	26	F	W	F		Tenn	April		unknown	6 years
18	John	23	M	B	S		Tenn	April		Whipped to death	6 days
19	Mary J. Cude	1	F	W	F		Tenn	May		Croup	2 days

COUNTY OF PERRY, STATE OF TENNESSEE.

PAGE NO. 604 PERSONS WHO DIED DURING THE YEAR ENDING 1st JUNE, 1850.

No. of Visit	Name	Age	Sex	Color	Free or Slave	Married/Widowed	Place of Birth	Month Died	Occupation	Disease or Cause of Death	No. Days Ill
1	Jasper Shepard	2	M	W	F		Tenn	June	Infant	Cholera	4 days
2	Infant unnamed	2d	F	W	F		Tenn	Jan	Infant	unknown	
3	Infant unnamed		F	W	F		Tenn	July	Infant	unknown	
4	Ann H. Freeman	41	F	W	F	M	Tenn	July	Tailoress	Weakness	2 days
5	Jesse Cragg	4	M	W	F		Tenn	July	Infant	Fever	10 days
6	Rebecca Sullivan	16	F	W	F		Tenn	Oct		Fever	15 days
7	William Grooves	55	M	W	F	M	Va	March	Farmer	Drunkard	42 days
8	Alexander Goodman	60	M	W	F	M	S.C.	July	Farmer	Fever	18 days
9	Minerva Ward	17	F	W	F		Tenn	July		Consumption	150 days
10	Elizabeth Moore	7m	F	W	F		Tenn	June		unknown	10 days
11	Thomas James	1	M	W	F		Tenn	May		Croup	1 day
12	Robert Thompson	12	M	W	F		Tenn	Nov		unknown	90 days
13	Florence Adkinson	1m	F	W	F		Tenn	Jan	Infant	unknown	10 days
14	Levi Adkinson	2m	M	W	F		Tenn	Feb	Infant	Rising	14 days
15	James M. Sluder	1	M	W	F		Tenn	Aug	Infant	Fever	9 days
16	James H. Smith	4	M	W	F		Tenn	Oct	Infant	Fever	7 days
17	Samuel Turnbow	51	M	W	F	M	N.C.	Aug	Farmer	Fever	10 days
18	Joel Smith	53	M	W	F	M	Kentucky	March	Farmer	Consumption	60 days
19	John F. Fowler	1	M	W	F		Tenn	July		By a fall	21 days
20	Haywood Nichol	22	M	W	F		Tenn	March	Boatsman	Cholera	6 days
21	Elizabeth J. Aford	11m	F	W	F		Tenn	Aug		unknown	
22	Sarah Green	28	F	W	F	M	Tenn	July		Consumption	30 days
23	Milly A. Green	18	F	W	F	M	Tenn	Jan		Inflamation of brain	
24	Mary Green	30	F	W	F	-	Tenn	March		unknown	200 days
25	Martha L. Green	10	F	W	F		Tenn	Oct		Fever	12 days
26	Mahala Armstrong	48	F	W	F	M	Tenn	April		Child birth	1 day
27	Mary A. Anderson	18	F	W	F	M	Tenn	Feb		Cold	2 days
28	Martha McCullough	16	F	W	F		S.C.	July		Cholera	2 days
29	Sarah A. Ary	4m	F	W	F		Tenn	Aug		St. Anthony's fire	7 days
30	John Kimble	18	M	W	F		Tenn	Dec	Farmer	Consumption	30 days
31	Hugh White	2	M	W	F		Tenn	Oct		Inflamation of brain	7 days

COUNTY OF PERRY, STATE OF TENNESSEE.

PAGE NO. 604 PERSONS WHO DIED DURING THE YEAR ENDING 1st JUNE, 1850.

R. M. Thomas

No. of Visit	Name	Age	Sex	Color	Free or Slave	Married/Widowed	Place of Birth	Month Died	Occupation	Disease or Cause of Death	No. Days Ill
32	Joel A. White	1	M	W	F		Tenn	Oct		Inflamation of brain	
33	Elizabeth Bone	11	F	W	F		Tenn	July		Fever	3 days
34	John Panny	15	M	W	F		Tenn	Feb	Laborer	unknown	30 days
35	Jane Baker	8	F	W	F		Tenn	Dec		unknown	34 days

COUNTY OF POLK, STATE OF TENNESSEE.

PAGE NO. 605 PERSONS WHO DIED DURING THE YEAR ENDING 1st JUNE, 1850.

25th Subdivision, E. District

John Shields

No. of Visit	Name	Age	Sex	Color	Free or Slave	Married/Widowed	Place of Birth	Month Died	Occupation	Disease or Cause of Death	No. Days Ill
1	James Freeman	5	M				Tenn	June		Cholera Mor.	4 days
2	Infant Freeman	1	M				Tenn	June		Cholera Mor.	5 days
3	Infant Pearson	1m	M				Tenn	Sept		Ulcer	30 days
4	John Cain	13	M				Georgia	June		Cholera Mor.	7 days
5	Infant Johnson	1	M				Tenn	June		Flux	7 days
6	John Blackwell	22	M				Tenn	June		Accident	14 days
7	James Carter	16	M				Tenn	March	Farmer	Consumption	12 months
8	William Russell	2	M				Tenn	Dec	Farmer	Quinsy	5 days
9	Jefferson Russell	2	M				Tenn	Dec		Quinsy	11 days
10	_____ Childress	1	F				Tenn	Aug		Worms	7 days
11	Easter Carter	39	F			M	Tenn	April		Consumption	4 years
12	Infant Fain	4m	M				Georgia	April		Croup	28 days
13	Infant Pearson	1m	M				Tenn	Aug		unknown	
14	James Goss	12	M				Georgia	May		Rheumatism	14 months
15	Infant Stillwell	1m	M				Georgia	April		Croup	2 days
16	Mary McFarland	88	F			W	Tenn	Dec		Old age	
17	Fanny Carter	92	F				Va	April		Old age	
18	Hiram Jenkins	4	M				Tenn	Oct		Worms	
19	John Cowden	28	M			M	Tenn	April	Wheelwright	Fever	
20	Almsted Ashley	5	M				Tenn	Sept		Inflamation	2 days

COUNTY OF POLK, STATE OF TENNESSEE.

PAGE NO. 608   PERSONS WHO DIED DURING THE YEAR ENDING 1st JUNE, 1850.

25th Subdivision
John Shields

No. of Visit	Name	Age	Sex	Color	Free or Slave	Married/Widowed	Place of Birth	Month Died	Occupation	Disease or Cause of Death	No. Days Ill
1	J. H. Alexander's slave	1	F	B	S		Tenn	Aug		Croup	4 days
2	James Gordon	26	M				S.C.	May	Farmer	Liver complaint	12 days
3	Nancy Kerr	31	F			M	Tenn	Jan		P. fever	17 days
4	Infant of T. Rodden	1m	M				Tenn	March		Hives	9 days
5	George W. Crittenden	1m	M				S.C.	July		unknown	1 day
6	Wm. Dockery	50	M			M	Tenn	Aug	Farmer	Fever	14 days
7	Phebe Woniger	6m	F				Tenn	June		Cholera Mor.	14 days
8	Infant of H. London	1	F				Tenn	Sept		Croup	2 days
9	Ann Johnston	40	F			M	Tenn	June		Fever	7 days
10	Infant of Jas. Smith	7m	F				Tenn	June		Fever	14 days
11	S. M. Reid's slave	8m	F	B	S		Tenn	May		unknown	21 days
12	E. H. Dunn's slave	4m	F	B	S		Georgia	July		Mumps	20 days
13	Mary Weaver	9	F				Tenn	Nov		Accident	2 days
14	Jesse Ramsey	7	M				Tenn	Aug		Croup	1 day
15	Mary Evans	33	F				Tenn	May		Consumption	Chronic
16	Susanna Pains	25	F				Tenn	Nov		Fits	Chronic
17	John Williams	15	M				Tenn	Oct	Farmer	Bleeding lungs	1 day
18	Infant of E. Williams	1	M				Tenn	Sept		Diarrhea	90 days
19	Jane Kimbrough	34	F				Tenn	March		unknown	Chronic
20	Infant of A. Hannah	5m	F				Tenn	June		Hives	5 days
21	Infant of W. Hannah	3m	F				Tenn	Aug		Croup	7 days
22	John Harris	12	M				Tenn	Nov		Pleurisy	4 days
23	Mary Bedwell	75	F			M	N.C.	May		Dropsy	Chronic
24	Martha Washburn	67	F			W	N.C.	April		Asthma	Chronic
25	Sarah Brown	50	F			M	Tenn	April		Consumption	4 weeks
26	Elizabeth Washburn	4	F				Tenn	March		Cholic	2 days
27	Jane Stinnett	7	M(?)				Tenn	April		Burnt	46 days
28	J. C. Kennedy's slave	80	F	B	S		S.C.	May		Hepatitis	6 months
29	J. C. Kennedy's slave	27	M	B	S		Tenn	Dec		Drowned	
30	S. R. Gwinn's slave	44	F		S		N.C.	Aug		Liver Complaint	2 months
31	Infant of T. Skelton	1	M				Tenn	Sept		Cholera Inf.	1 day
32	Infant of Holderfield	3d	F				Tenn	April		unknown	3 days
33	Elizabeth Bond	17	F				Tenn	July		Fever	4 months
34	R. P. Epperson	61	M			M	N.C.	Aug	Farmer	Liver Complaint	14 days
35	James Freeman	7	M				Tenn	June		Cholera Mor.	7 days

COUNTY OF RHEA, STATE OF TENNESSEE.

PAGE NO. 609 PERSONS WHO DIED DURING THE YEAR ENDING 1st JUNE, 1850.

21st Subdivision, E. District
W. T. Goss

No. of Visit	Name	Age	Sex	Color	Free or Slave	Married/Widowed	Place of Birth	Month Died	Occupation	Disease or Cause of Death	No. Days Ill
1	Mary A. E. C. Ellison	3	F				Tenn	Feb		Burn	1 day
2	Jane W. Thompson	57	F			W	Tenn	June		Apoplexy	6 years
3	Jacob Roddy	19	M	B	S		Tenn	July		Fever	20 days
4	Leroy Harris	12	M				Tenn	Feb		Liver complaint	6 months
5	Nancy Garrison	49	F			M	Tenn	April		Consumption	2 years
6	Joseph Long	61	M				Va	April	Farmer	Murdered	
7	William Bean	22	M				Tenn	Sept	Farmer	Consumption	5 years
8	Emily Roser	4	F				Tenn	July		Flux	40 days
9	William F. Lowry	10m	M				Tenn	Aug		Cold	3 months
10	Priscilla Thompson	1	F				Tenn	July		Inflamation of brain	3 days
11	Cumberland Rector	75	M			M	Va	Jan	Farmer	Gravel	9 days
12	Sarah McCaleb	8	F	B	S		Tenn	Sept		Fever	30 days
13	Mary Cozly	1	F	B	S		Tenn	Feb		Accident	sudden
14	James M. Williams	1/24	M					unknown		Croup	2 days
15	John Torbet	75	M			M	Va	Nov	Farmer	Diabetes	C
16	Eliza J. Ellison	4m	F				Tenn	Nov		unknown	9 days
17	Franklin Locke	3	M				Tenn	Nov		Flux	6 weeks
18	Jemima Smith	65	F	B	S		Tenn	April		Gout	21 days
19	John T. West	1	M				Tenn	Aug		unknown	6 weeks
20	Mary Hoyle	21	F	M	S		Tenn	April		Fever	3 months
21	George Ryan	2m	M	B	S		Tenn	Aug		unknown	sudden
22	John A. Cook	23	M				Tenn	Nov	Clerk	Fever	19 days
23	William Peterson	27	M			M	Tenn	April	Blk-smith	Bil. Cholic	3 days
24	Alfred Caldwell	30	M			M	Tenn	Aug	Tailor	Consumption	4 years
25	Jane Crow	15	F				Tenn	April		Fever	9 days
26	Nicholas G. Frazier	37	M			M	Tenn	May	Physician	Consumption	4 years
27	James Ryan	21	M				Tenn	Jan	Farmer	Liver complaint	4 days
28	Jesse W. Bandy	1	M				Tenn	Dec		Burn	17 days
29	Byron Griffith	15	M				Tenn	July		Cold	6 days
30	Sarah Martin	78	F			W	unknown	Dec		Old age	
31	Sarah A. Smith	10	F				Tenn	Nov		Pleurisy	5 days

COUNTY OF ROANE, STATE OF TENNESSEE.

PAGE NO. 611 PERSONS WHO DIED DURING THE YEAR ENDING 1st JUNE, 1850.

20th Subdivision
B. F. Melcher

No. of Visit	Name	Age	Sex	Color	Free or Slave	Married/Widowed	Place of Birth	Month Died	Occupation	Disease or Cause of Death	No. Days Ill
1	Barnett Hill	37	M			M	Tenn	Jan	Farmer	Inflamation of bowels	7 days
2	John F. Sevier	10	M				Tenn	July		Flux	21 days
3	Van	18	M	B	S		Tenn	Sept		Flux	3 months
4	Delilah Greene	31	F			M	Tenn	June		Prefered fever	10 days
5	Infant	4m	F	B	S		Tenn	Jan		Croup	5 days

COUNTY OF ROANE, STATE OF TENNESSEE.

PAGE NO. 614 PERSONS WHO DIED DURING THE YEAR ENDING 1st JUNE, 1850.

20th Subdivision
B. F. Melcher

No. of Visit	Name	Age	Sex	Color	Free or Slave	Married/Widowed	Place of Birth	Month Died	Occupation	Disease or Cause of Death	No. Days Ill
1	Wilson Burkett	27	M				Tenn	Jan	Farmer	Consumption	6 months
2	Jane	37	F	B	S		Tenn	July		Disease of lungs	12 months
3	Robert M. Reynolds	48	M			M	Va	May	Blk-smith	Cold	7 days
4	Sarah Moore	74	F			W	S.C.	Jan		Fever	14 days
5	Infant Huffman	5m	F				Tenn	May		unknown	8 days
6	Jacob Purkey	1m	M				Tenn	Oct		Croup	7 days
7	Malindy	17	F	B	S		Tenn	Jan		Fever	14 days
8	Robert Long	73	M			W	Va	Oct	Wagon-mkr	unknown	28 days
9	Delia Jackson	62	F			M	Va	Jan		Pneumonia	23 days
10	Lawson	2	M	B	S		Tenn	Jan		Dropsy	3 months
11	Rose	70	F	B	S		Va	Dec		Old age	20 days
12	John M. Davis	2	M				Tenn	March		Inflamation of bowels	20 days
13	Hezekiah G. Adams	3m	M				Tenn	Oct		unknown	11 days
14	Martha Wright	35	F				Tenn	March		Liver complaint	7 days
15	James Soward	32	M				Tenn	Jan		Consumption	9 months
16	Jane Spradley	44	F				Tenn	April		P. fever	1 day
17	Crump	21	M	B	S		Tenn	Jan		unknown	12 months
18	Francis	18	M	B	S		Tenn	March		Fever	6 days
19	Matilda	6m	F	B	S		Tenn	Jan		Fever	3 days
20	John	3	M	M	S		Tenn	Aug		Fever	1 month
21	George Cook	37	M			M	Tenn	March	Farmer	Fever	10 days
22	Lucindy E. Turpin	1m	F				Tenn	Oct		Fever	5 days
23	Elizabeth J. Magill	1	F				Tenn	Sept		Accident	instantly
24	Nancy Roberts	78	F			W	S.C.	Sept		Dropsy	2 years
25	Francis R. Robinson	36	F			M	Tenn	Feb		Fever	3 months
26	Sarah A. Robinson	14	F				Tenn	Feb		Fever	5 days
27	James N. Robinson	1m	M				Tenn	Feb		Fever	1 day
28	Mary J. Butler	2m	F				Tenn	Oct		Croup	4 days
29	Mary Benge	40	F			W	Kentucky	June		P. fever	10 days
30	Ann E. Tedder	5m	F				Tenn	Oct		Hives	7 days
31	Hugh F. Crumless	9m	M				Tenn	March		Hives	1 day
32	Elijah Isham	54	M				Tenn	Feb	Farmer	Quinsy	1 day
33	John S. C. Baker	5m	M				Tenn	March		Croup	4 days
34	George W. Baker	1m	M				Tenn	Dec		Croup	2 days
35	Moses S. Millican	51	M			M	S.C.	April	Farmer	Consumption	18 months

COUNTY OF ROANE, STATE OF TENNESSEE.

PAGE NO. 615 PERSONS WHO DIED DURING THE YEAR ENDING 1st JUNE, 1850.

20th Subdivision
B. F. Melcher

No. of Visit	Name	Age	Sex	Color	Free or Slave	Married/Widowed	Place of Birth	Month Died	Occupation	Disease or Cause of Death	No. Days Ill
1	Infant of S. King	2m	M				Tenn	Oct		unknown	3 days
2	Mariah Messmore	3	F				Tenn			Fits	1 day
3	Benjamin Clark	87	M			W	N.C.	April	Farmer	Old age	1 year
4	Margarette J. Miller	18	F				Tenn	Oct		Diarrhea	9 days
5	Ortes Miller	13	M				Tenn	May		Liver complaint	1 year
6	Sarah C. Nipper	12	F				Tenn	Jan		Fever	3 days
7	G. F. Smith	22	M				Va	May		Pleurisy	2 days
8	George C. Tuter	6	M				Tenn	May		Neuralgia	8 days
9	Patsy Marly	56	F			W	N.C.	Dec		Fever	42 days
10	Mary Selvage	63	F			M	N.C.	April		Old age	5 days
11	Jas. A. Wilson	6m	M				Tenn	March		Fever	21 days
12	Rebecca J. Elkins	24	F				Tenn	Aug		Cold	8 days
13	Peggy	45	F	B	S		Tenn	Nov		Consumption	1 year
14	Malinda A. Osborn	23	F			M	Tenn	July		Consumption	4 months
15	May J. Edwards	42	F			M	Tenn	April		Fever	2 days
16	Elisha P. Melson	1	M				Tenn	July		Worms	7 days
17	Sarah Anderson	1	F				Tenn	Aug		Flux	7 days
18	Polly Allison	57	F				Va	Aug		Fever	28 days
19	John Campbell	77	M			W	Va	Aug	Farmer	Gravel	1 year
20	Margarette Campbell	66	F			M	Va	July		Consumption	1 year
21	Robert Morgan	12	M				Tenn	July		Consumption	2 months
22	Buckner Walker	67	M				N.C.	Dec	Farmer	Congestive fever	9 days
23	Mahala E. Walker	3	F				Tenn	Feb		Burn	instantly
24	Sarah Ezell	2	F				Tenn	March		Inflamation of bowels	14 days
25	James	5	M	B	S		Tenn	Dec		Fever	35 days
26	Hannah Harrison	85	F				Maryland	Oct		Erysipelas	8 days
27	Fanny	21	F	B	S		Tenn	Feb		Fever	14 days
28	Philip Melson	51	M				Va	Feb	Blk-smith	unknown	12 hours
29	Hosanah Breazeale	44	F			M	Tenn	May		Consumption	5 years
30	Mary Bogart	41	F			M	Tenn	June		unknown	sudden
31	John Fry	2	M				Tenn	Dec		Worms	3 days
32	Lucindy Findly	35	F			M		April		Consumption	6 months
33	Nancy E. Mead	7	F				Tenn	Oct		unknown	½ day
34	Nancy Ball	28	F			?	Tenn	Jan		Consumption	1 year
35	Infant Henderson	1m	F				Tenn	April		unknown	1 day

COUNTY OF ROANE, STATE OF TENNESSEE.

PAGE NO. 618 PERSONS WHO DIED DURING THE YEAR ENDING 1st JUNE, 1850.

20th Subdivision
B. F. Melcher

No. of Visit	Name	Age	Sex	Color	Free or Slave	Married/Widowed	Place of Birth	Month Died	Occupation	Disease or Cause of Death	No. Days Ill
1	Mariah Nicholson	29	F			M	Tenn	April		Consumption	5 months
2	Julia Shahara	1	F				Tenn	Nov		Chills & Fever	25 days
3	Harriet Chapman	7	F				Tenn	July		Accidently	13 days
4	Alfred	1	M	B	S		Tenn	May		Fever	5 days
5	Minty	1m	F	B	S		Tenn	April		Croup	1 day
6	Peter Berry	64	M				S.C.	Feb		Fever	7 days
7	Susannah Johnson	10m	F				Tenn	Feb		Fever	12 days
8	Margarette	5m	F	B	S		Tenn	Jan		Accidental	instantly
9	Infant	1m	F	B	S			Feb		Accidental	instantly
10	Jonathan Bagwell	55	M			M	N.C.	June	Farmer	Dyspepsia	6 years
11	Margarette M. Carrol	10m	F				Tenn	Dec		unknown	7 days
12	Mary J. Winston	15	F				Tenn	Aug		Fever	8 days
13	Susan McPherson	95	F				Va	June		Dead Palsy	12 days
14	Aggy	40	F	B	S		Georgia	June		unknown	21 days
15	John Rentfro	34	M				Tenn	July		Drunkness	9 days
16	Sarah E. Irvine	1m	F				Tenn	Oct		Fever	3 days
17	Michael Cook	75	M				unknown	May		Old age	3 days
18	Infant J. Kingcades	1m	F				Tenn	Feb		unknown	1 day
19	Pernia Delozin	66	F			M	Va	Oct		Cancer	9 days
20	William Rose	7	M				Tenn	April		Fever	9 days
21	Edward Rose	1m	M				Tenn	March		Fits	10 days
22	Isaac Burk	27	M				Tenn	Aug		Diarrhea	1 year
23	Mary	11	F				Tenn	Aug		Fever	10 days
24	John H. Smally	33	M				Tenn	April	Farmer	Fever	15 days
25	William Christian	3	M				Tenn			Dropsy	1 year
26	Martha J. Galvan	12	F				Tenn	Jan		Fever	5 days
27	Eliza	5m	F	B	S		Tenn	July		Croup	10 days
28	Albert Galyon	4	M				Tenn	Nov		Quinsy	8 months
29	Alvira E. Magill	4	F				Tenn	March		Fever	6 days
30	Emily E. Willis	2	F				Tenn	July		Fever	4 days
31	Jos. Cassaday	22	M				N.C.	June		Flux	2 days
32	George R. Hudson	1	M				Tenn	July		Fits	1 month
33	Abijah E. Cassaday	1	M				Tenn	July		Flux	2 days
34	Eliza J. Cox	4	F				Tenn	June		Fever	3 months
35	Nancy Hensley	33	F				Va	July		Cholic	7 days

COUNTY OF ROBERTSON, STATE OF TENNESSEE.

PAGE NO. 619 PERSONS WHO DIED DURING THE YEAR ENDING 1st JUNE, 1850.

Civil Districts No. 10 & 5, 8 & 6 & 9
Clinton Green

No. of Visit	Name	Age	Sex	Color	Free or Slave	Married/Widowed	Place of Birth	Month Died	Occupation	Disease or Cause of Death	No. Days Ill
1	Woodard's, George	30	M	B	S		Tenn	March		Consumption	200 days
2	Pitt's, George	9	M	B	S		Tenn	March		Lightening	1 day
3	Byrn's, Artemissa	1m	F	B	S		Tenn	June		Hives	2 days
4	Gunn's, Infant	1m	M	B	S		Tenn	Feb		Spasms	2 days
5	Well's, Charity	2m	F	M	S		Tenn	Nov		Choked	12 days
6	Willson Watts	37	M			M	Tenn	May	Shoemaker	Cholic	8 days
7	Mary Standback	5m	F				Tenn	Sept		Inflamation of bowels	10 days
8	Sterling Warren	74	M			M	Va	Dec	Farmer	Gravel	8 days
9	Jas. L. Fiser	28	M			M	Tenn	Oct	Farmer	T. fever	60 days
10	Lethe Mathews	1	F				Texas	Sept		Inflamation of bowels	60 days
11	Elizabeth Glissen	35	F			M	N.C.	April		Child bed	1 day
12	Benjamin E. Batts	1	M				Tenn	Dec		Bronchitis	21 days
13	Batt's, John	10	M	B	S		Tenn	May		T. fever	25 days
14	Ellis', Sarah	4m	F	B	S		Tenn	Dec		Croup	14 days
15	Robert H. Cobb	1	M				Tenn	June		Fever	30 days
16	Jas. H. Gooch	9m	M				Tenn	Jan		Dropsy	11 days
17	Woodard's, Joe	28	M	B	S		Tenn	Feb		Apoplexy	1 day
18	Martha W. Holloway	3	F				Tenn	Nov		Croup	6 days
19	Johnson's slave	1	M	B	S		Tenn	Dec		Inflamation of lungs	30 days
20	Hugh F. Bell	93	M			W	Va	April		Old age	
21	Bell's infant slave	2m	M	M	S		Tenn	Jan		unknown	3 days
22	Fort's, Lydia	6m	F	B	S		Tenn	Aug		T. fever	14 days
23	Fort's, Infant slave	1m	M	B	S		Tenn	March		Croup	1 day
24	Charlotte Hannison	70	F			M	Penn	Jan		Inflamation of bowels	14 days
25	William Burgess	40	M			M	Va	Dec	Sch-teacher	T. fever	25 days
26	William D. Burgess	17	M				Tenn	Dec	Farmer	T. fever	25 days
27	Bell's, Bedia	25	F	B	S		Tenn	April		Inflamation of bowels	105 days
28	James Johnson	93	M			W	Penn	April	none	Old age	
29	Nancy Gunn	52	F			M	Tenn	Aug		Cholic	1 day
30	Chamber's, Martha	6	F	M	S		Tenn	Sept		Congestive chill	3 days
31	Polk's, Harris	3m	M	B	S		Tenn	Aug		Inflamation of bowels	15 days
32	Whited's, Lucy	1	F	B	S		Tenn	Feb		Croup	7 days
33	Gardner's, Curtis	5	M	B	S		Tenn	Feb		Inflamation of brain	40 days
34	Gardner's, Jackson	1	M	B	S		Tenn	Feb		Inflamation of brain	40 days
35	James Byrns	64	M			M	S.C.	Feb	Farmer	Inflamation of bowels	6 days

COUNTY OF ROBERTSON, STATE OF TENNESSEE.

PAGE NO. 622 PERSONS WHO DIED DURING THE YEAR ENDING 1st JUNE, 1850.

Civil District No. 1, 11 & 10
Clinton Green

No. of Visit	Name	Age	Sex	Color	Free or Slave	Married/Widowed	Place of Birth	Month Died	Occupation	Disease or Cause of Death	No. Days Ill
1	Byram's, Lotty	37	F	B	S		Tenn	Aug		Dropsy	365 days
2	Byram's, Infant	1m	F	B	S		Tenn	July		unknown	30 days
3	Duvall's, Isham	43	M	B	S		Va	Oct		Pul. Consumption	730 days
4	Elizabeth Graves	1m	F				Tenn	Jan		Thrash	10 days
5	Thomas W. Stringer	1	M				Tenn	May		Cholera Inf.	14 days
6	Mary Arnold	17	F				Tenn	Jan		Consumption	134 days
7	Mary Payne	20	F			M	Tenn	May		Consumption	42 days
8	Payne's, Malvina	16	F	M	S		Tenn	April		Plague	8 days
9	Payne's, Infant	2m	F	B	S		Tenn	Dec		unknown	14 days
10	Jesse George	46	M			M	Tenn	Oct	Millwright	Consumption	365 days
11	Jone's, Infant	2m	F	B	S		Tenn	Sept		Suffocation	
12	Jas. W. Briggs	2	M				Tenn	Oct		Cholera Inf.	180 days
13	Jane Shreve	51	F			M	Va	July		Consumption	60 days
14	Turner's, William	3	M	B	S		Tenn	July		Whooping cough	21 days
15	Mary Birney	80	F			W	N.C.	Sept		Palsy	1095 days
16	Birney's, Alvira	1	F	B	S		Tenn	Sept		Whooping cough	30 days
17	Cole's, Infant	1m	F	B	S		Tenn	Feb		Croup	6 days
18	George Underwood	60	M			M	N.C.	Feb	Farmer	Consumption	15 days
19	Elizabeth Jones	65	F			M	Kentucky	Jan		Burnt	1 day
20	William T. Shannon	21	M				Tenn	Sept	Farmer	Fever	33 days
21	Bushe's, Infant	1m	M	S			Tenn	June		unknown	30 days
22	William T. Channing	8m	M				Tenn	July		Cholera Inf.	3 days
23	Anna Choat	29	F			M	Tenn	July		Consumption	365 days
24	Wallace's, Henry	25	M	B	S		Tenn	Dec		Burnt	
25	Wallace's, Jordan	20	M	B	S		Tenn	Nov		Consumption	400 days
26	Wallace's, Jane	10m	F	M	S		Tenn	June		Whooping cough	120 days
27	Wallace's, Cordelia	9	F	B	S		Tenn	June		Whooping cough	120 days
28	McMurry's, Anthony	22	M	B	S		Tenn	June		Consumption	14 days
29	Sarah Payne	13	F				Tenn	Dec		Consumption	270 days
30	James Johnson	70	M				Va	March	none	Inflamation of stomach	240 days
31	Harriet England	4	F				Tenn	Aug		Whooping cough	5 days
32	R. B. Dorris	7m	M				Tenn	Aug		Whooping cough	8 days
33	Lydia Clark	50	F			W	Tenn	May		Congestive fever	13 days
34	Sally H. Baird	5	F				Tenn	Jan		Croup	3 days
35	Martha Farmer	10	F				Tenn	April		T. fever	120 days

COUNTY OF ROBERTSON, STATE OF TENNESSEE.

PAGE NO. 623 PERSONS WHO DIED DURING THE YEAR ENDING 1st JUNE, 1850.

Civil District No. 3, 2 & 1

Clinton Green

No. of Visit	Name	Age	Sex	Color	Free or Slave	Married/Widowed	Place of Birth	Month Died	Occupation	Disease or Cause of Death	No. Days Ill
1	William J. Barbee	7	M				Tenn	Oct		Polypus	90 days
2	Michael Keller	33	M			M	Kentucky	July	Farmer	Cholera	1 day
3	Mary Hampton	72	F			W	Va	Nov		Accidental	1 day
4	Moore's, Lavina	29	F	B	S		N.C.	April		Inflamation of brain	10 days
5	William Rust	11m	M				Tenn	Aug		Inflamation of brain	4 days
6	Baird's, Miles	7	M	B	S		Tenn	Aug		Burnt	30 days
7	Nancy Pope	22	F			M	Tenn	Aug		T. fever	16 days
8	Alexander Petty	37	M			M	N.C.	March	Farmer	Consumption	90 days
9	Dosse's, Jack	61	M	B	S		N.C.	Sept		Hemorrhage of lungs	90 days
10	Dosse's, Jerry	19	M	B	S		Tenn	May		Consumption	240 days
11	John Yates	70	M			M	Va	April	Farmer	Gravel	60 days
12	Mary M. Link	86	F				Va	Sept		Old age	
13	Patterson's, Infant	1m		B	S		Tenn	Dec		Cholera Inf.	2 days
14	Mary Brewer	2m	F				Tenn	Dec		Cholera Morbus	10 days
15	Martha Brewer	1m	F				Tenn	Nov		Suffocation	
16	William Turner	7m	M				Tenn	June		Cholera Inf.	1 day
17	House's, Archer	1m	M	B	S		Tenn	Aug		Croup	5 days
18	Brewer's, Sidney	4m	M	B	S		Tenn	Nov		Suffocation	
19	Mary Rose	24	F			M	Tenn	July		Consumption	365 days
20	Nancy Johns	24	F			M	Tenn	Aug		Child bed	4 days
21	Fisher's, Isabella	8m	F	B	S		Tenn	Jan		unknown	
22	Fisher's, Infant	1m	F	B	S		Tenn	Jan		Suffocation	
23	Missouri Randolph	1m	F				Tenn	Nov		Croup	7 days
24	Ephraim Krisle	50	M			M	Tenn	Aug	Farmer	Consumption	180 days
25	Brook's, Henry	2	M	B	S		Tenn	Jan		Cholera Inf.	15 days
26	Martin's, Frank	1m	M	B	S		Tenn	Aug		Hives	2 days
27	Mary J. Kelly	20	F				Tenn	Oct		T. fever	15 days
28	Emedatha Wright	20	F				N.C.	May		Consumption	56 days
29	Infant Wright	1m	M				Tenn	July		unknown	3 days
30	Infant of Webb	1m	F				Tenn	Oct		Spasms	4 days
31	Aaron Cordle	9m	M				Tenn	April		Quinsy	7 days
32	Thomas Summers	72	M			M	Va	March	Farmer	Dropsy	50 days
33	Jas. C. Eubanks	5m	M				Tenn	Aug		Cholera Inf.	90 days
34	George Stovall	4	M				Tenn	Oct		Croup	4 days
35	Colly's, Rachael	55	F	B	S		Kentucky	Sept		Dropsy	120 days

COUNTY OF ROBERTSON, STATE OF TENNESSEE.

PAGE NO. 626 PERSONS WHO DIED DURING THE YEAR ENDING 1st JUNE, 1850.

Civil District No. 9, 4 & 3
Clinton Green

No. of Visit	Name	Age	Sex	Color	Free or Slave	Married/Widowed	Place of Birth	Month Died	Occupation	Disease or Cause of Death	No. Days Ill
1	Margaret Langford	5	F				Tenn	Aug		Congestive chill	1 day
2	Cheatham's, Green	20	M	B	S		Tenn	Oct		Consumption	121 days
3	George C. Conrad	50	M			M	Tenn	Nov	Marchant	Bronchitis	90 days
4	Conrad's, Lemon Ann	2	F	B	S		Tenn	Jan		Fever	15 days
5	Jno. W. Gorham's, Infant	1m	M				Tenn	Aug		Inflamation of bowels	10 days
6	Robert M. Orndorff	8m	M				Tenn	June		Cholera Inf.	14 days
7	N. H. Ryan	46	M			M	N.C.	Sept	none	Fever	14 days
8	Thomas Ryan	17	M				Tenn	July	Student	Fever	1 day
9	John T. Dale	3m	M				Tenn	March		Cholera Inf.	21 days
10	Jno. Edward's, Stewart	3m	M	B	S		Tenn	Jan		Suffocation	sudden
11	Infant of W. H. Johnson	1m	F				Tenn	Jan			sudden
12	Infant of W. H. Johnson	5m	F				Tenn	April		unknown	30 days
13	Benton's, Martha	15	F	B	S		Tenn	Sept		T. fever	18 days
14	Drucilla Cohea	15	F				Tenn	Oct		T. fever	20 days
15	Bridge's, Jim	13	M	B	S		Tenn	May		Scrofula	210 days
16	Green's, Louisa	35	F	B	S		Kentucky	Oct		Scrofula	60 days
17	Mary Mantle	38	F			M	Tenn	April		Apoplexy	2 days
18	Infant Mantle	1m	M				Tenn	Feb		unknown	3 days
19	Matilda Highsmith	37	F			M	Kentucky	Sept		Inflamation of stomach	11 days
20	Elizabeth Eddings	39	F			M	Tenn	May		Fever	50 days
21	Joseph Eddings	2m	M				Tenn	July		Diarrhea	4 days
22	Robert Perry	2	M				Tenn	July		Cholera	1 day
23	McIntosh's, Isham	1m	M	B	S		Tenn	May		Whooping cough	16 days
24	Mark's, Amy	73	F	B	S		S.C.	Dec		Apoplexy	sudden
25	Ellen Holland	39	F			M	Maryland	Jan		Consumption	150 days
26	Mary Long	1	F				Tenn	June		Cholera Inf.	3 days
27	McIntosh's, Infant	3m	M	B	S		Tenn	April		Chicken pox	60 days
28	Johnson's, William	72	M	B	S		Africa	April			sudden
29	Dony Ann Taylor	1	F				Tenn	Nov		Whooping cough	30 days
30	Tabitha Pearson	7m	F				Tenn	July		Cholera Inf.	2 days
31	Clarissa Rose	36	F			M	Tenn	June		Fever	24 days
32	Nancy S. Pitt	40	F			M	Tenn	March		Apoplexy	sudden
33	Cordelia Benson	10	F				Tenn	Oct		T. fever	40 days
34	Malissa A. Barbee	2	F				Tenn	Sept		Croup	3 days
35	Green;s, Infant	2m	F	B	S		Tenn	Oct		Fever	21 days

COUNTY OF ROBERTSON, STATE OF TENNESSEE.

PAGE NO. 627 PERSONS WHO DIED DURING THE YEAR ENDING 1st JUNE, 1850.

Civil District No. 13 & 12
Clinton Green

No. of Visit	Name	Age	Sex	Color	Free or Slave	Married/Widowed	Place of Birth	Month Died	Occupation	Disease or Cause of Death	No. Days Ill
1	Bryan's, Infant	2m	M	B	S		Tenn	July		unknown	14 days
2	Joakinn J. Green	5	M				Tenn	Nov		Croup	7 days
3	Thomas B. Fountain	71	M			M	Va	April	Farmer	Palsy	7 days
4	William H. Cobbs	26	M			M	Tenn	Feb		Inflamation of liver	15 days
5	Jas. S. Justice	54	M			M	N.C.	Nov	Farmer	T. fever	50 days
6	Marshal Morris	5	M				Tenn	April		T. fever	14 days
7	Tempy Clark	42	F			M	Tenn	July		Disease of womb	5 days
8	Rachael A. Millican	4	F				Tenn	July		Croup	14 days
9	Priscilla Chambless	30	F				Tenn	June		Consumption	120 days
10	Jesse Green	84	M				N.C.	March	Wagonmaker	Consumption	90 days
11	Martha C. Martin	20	F				Tenn	June		Consumption	90 days
12	Knight's, Infant	3m	M				Tenn	April		unknown	sudden
13	Nancy Pike	49	F				Tenn	Nov		Apoplexy	sudden
14	Josiah Ely	67	M			M	Va	April	Carpenter	T. fever	13 days
15	M. H. Barns	1	M				Tenn	Nov		Croup	7 days
16	Jas. B. Culbertson	74	M			W	N.C.	Nov	Farmer	Dropsy	30 days
17	Frances Robertson	17	F			M	Tenn	Aug		T. fever	30 days
18	Winneford Adcock	40	F				Va	May		unknown	210 days
19	Indiana Williams	2	F				Tenn	May		Fever	10 days
20	Sarah C. Morris	2	F				Tenn	April		Scrofula	210 days
21	Rosanna Wines	25	F			M	Tenn	March		Consumption	210 days

COUNTY OF ROBERTSON, STATE OF TENNESSEE.

PAGE NO. 630 PERSONS WHO DIED DURING THE YEAR ENDING 1st JUNE, 1850.

Civil District No. 7 & 15
Clinton Green

No. of Visit	Name	Age	Sex	Color	Free or Slave	Married/Widowed	Place of Birth	Month Died	Occupation	Disease or Cause of Death	No. Days Ill
	7th District										
1	M & G Washington's, Rosetta	21	F	B	S		Robertson Co	March		Consumption	42 days
2	Mallory's, Henry	1	M	B	S		Tenn	Oct		Croup	2 days
3	Newsom Holland	11m	M				Tenn	Oct		Croup	6 days
4	Pennington's, Albert	1	M	B	S		Tenn	July		Croup	7 days
5	Darden's, George	40	M	B	S		Tenn	Feb		Froze	
6	Darden's, Elizabeth	5	F	B	S		Tenn	Feb		Inflamation of bowels	14 days
7	Hughe's, Elizabeth	15	F	M	S		Tenn	Sept		Lock jaw	2 days
8	Hughe's, Harriet	16	F	B	S		Tenn	Nov		Pulmonary	180 days
9	Connel's, George	6m	M	M	S		Tenn	March		Inft. Consumption	90 days
10	Connel's, Jo	60	M	B	S		S.C.	June		Old age	
11	Elliott's, Harriet	22	F	B	S		Tenn	March		Scrofula	500 days
12	Elliott's, Anderson	8	M	B	S		Tenn	March		unknown	200 days
13	Elliott's, Mason	2	M	B	S		Tenn	July		Cholera Inf.	14 days
14	Darden's, Emily	3m	F	B	S		Tenn	Aug		Cholera Inf.	6 days
	15th District										
15	Anderson Hunt	20	M			M	Tenn	Oct	Farmer	Cholic	14 days
16	Sanders' Infant	1m	F				Tenn	March		Croup	1 day
17	Hugen's, Darcus	55	F	B	S		Georgia	May		Cough	365 days
18	Lewis', Infant	1m	M				Tenn	Aug		unknown	14 days
19	Anderson Stewart	71	M			M	Va	Jan	Farmer	Consumption	60 days
20	Walker's, Jim	1	M	B	S		Tenn	April		unknown	14 days
21	Felix Harris	1m	M				Tenn	Aug		unknown	10 days
22	Martha Durham	45	F			M	N.C.	Aug		unknown	10 days
23	Bridgete Sullivan	3	F				Ireland	May		Fever	200 days
24	Foster's, Rose	84	F	B	S		Va	June		Disease of heart	1 day
25	Jno. T. Nichols	1	M				Tenn	Sept		Inflamation of brain	10 days
26	William Thompson	92	M			M	Ireland	April		Old age	
27	Thompson's, Mary	30	F	B	S		Va	May		unknown	14 days

COUNTY OF ROBERTSON, STATE OF TENNESSEE.

PAGE NO. 630 PERSONS WHO DIED DURING THE YEAR ENDING 1st JUNE, 1850.

Civil District No. 7 & 15

No. of Visit	Name	Age	Sex	Color	Free or Slave	Married/Widowed	Place of Birth	Month Died	Occupation	Disease or Cause of Death	No. Days Ill
28	White's, Adaline	6m	F	B	S		Tenn	Oct		unknown	26 days
29	A. J. Hunt	20	M				Tenn	Oct	Farmer	Bil. cholic	14 days
30	Carter's Infant	1m	M				Tenn	May		Hives	2 days
31	Hunt's, Fanny	1	F	B	S		Tenn	Sept		unknown	180 days
32	Pace's, infant	1m	M				Tenn	Jan		Croup	1 day
33	Thomas G. Morris	21	M				Tenn	March	Farmer	T. fever	8 days
34	George W. Stewart	37	M			M	Tenn	April	Saddler	Ulcerated bowels	90 days
35	Mary Stewart	4	F				Tenn	Sept		Croup	1 day

COUNTY OF RUTHERFORD, STATE OF TENNESSEE.

PAGE NO. 631 PERSONS WHO DIED DURING THE YEAR ENDING 1st JUNE, 1850.

McCrackin's District

E. D. Hancock

No. of Visit	Name	Age	Sex	Color	Free or Slave	Married/Widowed	Place of Birth	Month Died	Occupation	Disease or Cause of Death	No. Days Ill
1	William Wood	70	M				Va	Sept	none	Flux	180 days
2	Margaret Walkup	2m	F				Tenn	Sept		Flux	8 days
3	Joshua L. Sullivan	7m	M				Tenn	March		unknown	13 days
4	Saybella Tennison	78	F			W	Penn	Dec		unknown	40 days
5	Christopher Beaty	50	M			M	Va	April	Farmer	Fever	28 days
6	Martha Beaty	2m	F	B	S		Tenn	March		unknown	1 day
7	Thomas H. Hall	5m	M				Tenn	Feb		unknown	90 days
8	Leah Lines	29	F	B	S		Tenn	Jan		unknown	300 days
9	John W. Gilliam	4	M				Tenn	Nov		Sc. fever	11 days
10	James S. Jamison	7	M				Tenn	July		Flux	13 days
11	Alfred Jamison	10m	M	B	S		Tenn	July		Flux	15 days
12	Jackson Cometzer	17	M				Tenn	July	none	unknown	15 days
13	Robert Harris	18	M				Tenn	May	none	unknown	120 days
14	Martha H. Coch	22	F				Tenn	Aug		Fever	21 days
15	Jack Coch	18	M	B	S		Alabama	Sept		Fever	40 days
16	Amanda Coch	13	F	B	S		Tenn	Aug		Fever	15 days

COUNTY OF RUTHERFORD, STATE OF TENNESSEE.

PAGE NO. 633 PERSONS WHO DIED DURING THE YEAR ENDING 1st JUNE, 1850.

Trimble's District
E. D. Hancock

No. of Visit	Name	Age	Sex	Color	Free or Slave	Married/Widowed	Place of Birth	Month Died	Occupation	Disease or Cause of Death	No. Days Ill
1	John J. Miller	1m	M				Tenn	March		Croup	1 day
2	Frank Miller	5m	M	B	S		Tenn	April		unknown	150 days
3	Sarah Miller	1m	F	B	S		Tenn	Jan		unknown	1 day
4	Jack Miller	7	M	B	S		Tenn	April		sudden	sudden
5	Elizabeth Miller	6	F	B	S		Tenn	July		unknown	1 day
6	John P. Davis	15	M				Tenn	Jan	Farmer	Tetanus	118 days
7	John Davis	1m	M	B	S		Tenn	May		Marasmus	15 days
8	Jane Barkley	86	F			M	N.C.	Jan		Crippled	5 years
9	John Barkley	84	M			M	N.C.	July	Farmer	Cholera	3 days
10	Martha Barkley	1	F	B	S		Tenn	April		Whooping cough	20 days
11	Isreal Barkley	33	M	B	S		Tenn	June		Drowned	
12	Tom Barkley	17	M	B	S		Tenn	June		Drowned	
13	Jack Barkley	6m	M	B	S		Tenn	Jan		Whooping cough	7 days
14	Amy Barkley	2	F	B	S		Tenn	April		unknown	240 days
15	Rebecca Beaty	35	F				Kentucky	May		Bil. Cholic	5 days
16	Jane Palmer	39	F				Va	April		unknown	50 days
17	Mary McKee	63	F				N.C.	June		unknown	180 days
18	James T. McKnight	2m	M				Tenn	Oct		Croup	2 days

COUNTY OF RUTHERFORD, STATE OF TENNESSEE.

PAGE NO. 635 PERSONS WHO DIED DURING THE YEAR ENDING 1st JUNE, 1850.

Milton District
E. D. Hancock

No. of Visit	Name	Age	Sex	Color	Free or Slave	Married/Widowed	Place of Birth	Month Died	Occupation	Disease or Cause of Death	No. Days Ill
1	Cela Taley	18	F	B	S		Va	May		unknown	60 days
2	William Alexander	27	M				Tenn	Oct	Merchant	Bil. Cholic	8 days
3	James Knott	28	M	B	S		Va	Sept		T. fever	40 days
4	Nancy Loutes	17	F				Tenn	Aug		T. fever	20 days
5	Wilson	22	M	B	S		Tenn	July		unknown	20 days
6	Frances Woods	90	F				Va	March		Palsy	9 days
7	Henry Dillen	1	M	B	S		Tenn	Aug		unknown	60 days
8	Sally Raynels	30	F				Va	July		Flux	40 days
9	John Raynels	2m	M				Tenn	Sept		Inflamation of brain	14 days
10	David T. Parker	5	M				Tenn	Aug		Measles	17 days
11	Nathan N. Parker	1	M				Tenn	Aug		Measles	7 days
12	William S. Parker	3m	M				Tenn	Jan		Hives	4 days
13	Mary J. Overall	25	F				Tenn	March		T. fever	50 days
14	Jane Adams	38	F				Tenn	Aug		T. fever	9 days
15	Mary Adams	3m	F				Tenn	Nov		unknown	80 days
16	Sarah Dill	24	F	B	S		Tenn	Aug		unknown	20 days
17	Sally Cartright	105	F	B	S		unknown	March		Old age	10 days

COUNTY OF RUTHERFORD, STATE OF TENNESSEE.

PAGE NO. 637 PERSONS WHO DIED DURING THE YEAR ENDING 1st JUNE, 1850.

Brown's Mill District
E. D. Hancock

No. of Visit	Name	Age	Sex	Color	Free or Slave	Married/Widowed	Place of Birth	Month Died	Occupation	Disease or Cause of Death	No. Days Ill
1	Philip Jetter	60	F?	B	S		unknown	Jan		Dropsy	60 days
2	Lany Brown	60	M	B	S		Va	March		Pneumonia	14 days
3	John Smith	2m	M	B	S		Tenn	Feb		unknown	sudden
4	Philip J. Brown	32	F?				Va	July	Farmer	Consumption	360 days
5	Phillis Crouse	30	F	B	S		Tenn	June		unknown	60 days
6	Caroline Butler	17	F	B	S		Tenn	July		Consumption	130 days
7	Isham Overall	20	M	B	S		Tenn	June		Drowned	
8	Anna Overall	1	F	B	S		Tenn	March		Scrofula	300 days
9	Sarah L. Overall	7m	F				Tenn	Aug		unknown	3 days
10	Samuel Huchinson	7m	M	B	S		Tenn	Feb		unknown	5 days
11	Milly Huchinson	1	F	B	S		Tenn	April		unknown	7 days
12	Elihugh Staton	76	M				Va	March	Farmer	unknown	14 days
13	Joel P. Lorence	14	M				Tenn	June		Cholera	2 days

COUNTY OF RUTHERFORD, STATE OF TENNESSEE.

PAGE NO. 639 PERSONS WHO DIED DURING THE YEAR ENDING 1st JUNE, 1850.

Fleming's District
E. D. Hancock

No. of Visit	Name	Age	Sex	Color	Free or Slave	Married/Widowed	Place of Birth	Month Died	Occupation	Disease or Cause of Death	No. Days Ill
1	Sarah A. Breshere	1	F				Tenn	May		Consumption	90 days
2	John Breshere	1m	M	B	S		Tenn	Feb		unknown	7 days
3	Susan Breshere	1m	F	B	S		Tenn	Feb		unknown	7 days
4	Amy Hartwell	3	F	B	S		Tenn	March		unknown	90 days
5	Robert Sharp	76	M			M	Penn	June	Farmer	Apoplexy	sudden
6	Rachael Sharp	3	F	B	S		Tenn	Dec		Burned	sudden
7	Mary Anderson	4m	F	B	S		Tenn	Jan		unknown	7 days
8	Logan Wasson	32	M			M	Tenn	Dec	Farmer	Dyspepsia	sudden
9	Mary Kerlough	70	F				Tenn	March		Palpitation of heart	30 days
10	Jane Johnson	3	F	B	S		Tenn	July		unknown	20 days
11	Jane Flemming	22	F				Tenn	Jan		Consumption	10 days
12	Milly Flemming	6m	F	B	S		Tenn	Jan		unknown	1 day
13	Sally Rucker	40	F	B	S		Tenn	Aug		Cholera	10 days
14	Madison Qualls	2	M	B	S		Tenn	July		Whooping cough	10 days
15	Mary Qualls	1	F	B	S		Tenn	June		Whooping cough	30 days
16	Tennessee Mitchel	1	F	B	S		Tenn	Oct		Cold	15 days
17	Martha Lawrence	16	F			M	Tenn	Jan		Child birth	8 days
18	Zack T. Picket	2	M				Tenn	Dec		Sc. fever	8 days
19	James T. Picket	2	M				Tenn	Sept		Sc. fever	330 days
20	Joseph Harrison	69	M			M	Maryland	Feb	Farmer	Fistula	7 days
21	George Watkins	5m	M	B	S		Tenn	Aug		Croup	1 day

COUNTY OF RUTHERFORD, STATE OF TENNESSEE.

PAGE NO. 641 PERSONS WHO DIED DURING THE YEAR ENDING 1st JUNE, 1850.

Valley District
E. D. Hancock

No. of Visit	Name	Age	Sex	Color	Free or Slave	Married/Widowed	Place of Birth	Month Died	Occupation	Disease or Cause of Death	No. Days Ill
1	Essex Mathes	37	M	B	S		N.C.	Aug		Cholera	1 day
2	Lucy Mathes	20	F	B	S		Tenn	July		Cholera	1 day
3	Tom Mathes	1	M	B	S		Tenn	May		unknown	30 days
4	Isabella Mathers	1	F				Tenn	May		Inflamation of brain	20 days
5	Madora Norvel	1	F				Tenn	Aug		unknown	70 days
6	Athelia Brown	40	F				N.C.	April		unknown	30 days
7	Lester Robinson	70	M	B	S		Va	April		unknown	30 days
8	Eliza Farris	2	F	B	S		Tenn	April		Teething	2 days
9	John Johns	6m	M	B	S		Tenn	Oct		unknown	3 days

COUNTY OF RUTHERFORD, STATE OF TENNESSEE.

PAGE NO. 643 PERSONS WHO DIED DURING THE YEAR ENDING 1st JUNE, 1850.

Yourie District
E. D. Hancock

No. of Visit	Name	Age	Sex	Color	Free or Slave	Married/Widowed	Place of Birth	Month Died	Occupation	Disease or Cause of Death	No. Days Ill
1	Jane Hooper	1m	F				Tenn	Oct		unknown	3 days
2	David C. Beavers	24	M				Tenn	Sept	Cabinet-mkr	Pleurisy	5 days
3	Eliza J. Harney	20	F				Tenn	March		T. fever	7 days
4	William N. Garner	22	M				Tenn	Sept	Farmer	T. fever	35 days
5	Anna Herald	21	F			M	Tenn	Nov		unknown	7 days
6	James A. Bowen	11m	M				Tenn	Oct		unknown	75 days
7	William Loving	42	M				unknown	Nov	Farmer	T. fever	15 days
8	Nancy Lyons	5m	F				Tenn	July		Summer disease	28 days
9	Mary Lyons	6m	F	B	S		Tenn	June		Inflamation of brain	14 days
10	Jesse Lyons	6	M	B	S		Tenn	Oct		Inflamation of brain	60 days
11	Emma Lyons	23	F	B	S		Tenn	Oct		T. fever	50 days
12	Adam McElroy	1m	M	B	S		Tenn	Sept		Hives	2 days

COUNTY OF RUTHERFORD, STATE OF TENNESSEE.

PAGE NO. 645 PERSONS WHO DIED DURING THE YEAR ENDING 1st JUNE, 1850.

Big Spring District
E. D. Hancock

No. of Visit	Name	Age	Sex	Color	Free or Slave	Married/Widowed	Place of Birth	Month Died	Occupation	Disease or Cause of Death	No. Days Ill
1	Mary M. Markins	8m	F				Tenn	Dec		unknown	11 days
2	Thomas Yardly	73	M			W	N.C.	Dec	none	Palsy	270 days
3	Jane Lowe	35	F			M	Va	Jan		Palsy	11 days
4	Anna Newman	60	F			M	unknown	Aug		unknown	60 days
5	B. F. Ship	33	M				Va	Feb	Grocery	Consumption	120 days
6	John Zumbro	62	M			M	Va	May	Farmer	Dropsy	380 days
7	Daniel Ellison	69	M			M	N.C.	March	Farmer	Gravel	10 days
8	John Sirat	1m	F?				Tenn	March		unknown	9 days
9	Maranda Stephenson	40	F			M	Tenn	May		Consumption	60 days
10	Jesse M. Lee	1	M				Tenn	April		Inflamation of brain	4 days

COUNTY OF RUTHERFORD, STATE OF TENNESSEE.

PAGE NO. 647 PERSONS WHO DIED DURING THE YEAR ENDING 1st JUNE, 1850.

Millersburg District
E. D. Hancock

No. of Visit	Name	Age	Sex	Color	Free or Slave	Married/Widowed	Place of Birth	Month Died	Occupation	Disease or Cause of Death	No. Days Ill
1	Sarah Webb	21	F			M	Tenn	Dec		Consumption	250 days
2	A. G. Goodlett	69	M			M	Va	April	Physician	Angina Pectoris	14 days
3	Steffer Grear	50	M	B	S		Va	May		unknown	365 days
4	John Grear	1	M	B	S		Tenn	May		unknown	7 days
5	Sam Grear	1m	M	B	S		N.C.	May		unknown	7 days
6	Ben Williams	60	M	B	S		Tenn	June		Diarrhea	14 days
7	Thomas Richardson	7m	M				Tenn	Jan		Inflamation of brain	15 days
8	Nancy Adkinson	1m	F	B	S		Tenn	June		unknown	sudden
9	John McGill	5	M	B	S		Tenn	June		unknown	sudden
10	Pitts Nelson	12	M				Tenn	Sept		T. fever	5 days
11	Joseph Newman	90	M			W	Va	Nov	none	unknown	sudden
12	Mary Miller	3	F	B	S		Tenn	Feb		Burned	3 days
13	Hal White	25	M	B	S		Tenn	Sept		Consumption	150 days
14	Edmond White	6	M	B	S		Tenn	Dec		Consumption	300 days
15	Martha White	1m	F	B	S		Tenn	May		Croup	1 day
16	Reuben White	4	M	B	S		Tenn	May		Worms	310 days
17	George W. Kelton	3	M				Tenn	Dec		unknown	12 days
18	Mary Pruit	20	F				Tenn	June		Consumption	180 days
19	Sarah Pruit	7	F				Tenn	April		Consumption	100 days
20	Cela Sisk	40	F			M	N.C.	March		Diarrhea	14 days

COUNTY OF RUTHERFORD, STATE OF TENNESSEE.

PAGE NO. 649 PERSONS WHO DIED DURING THE YEAR ENDING 1st JUNE, 1850.

Fosterville District
E. D. Hancock

No. of Visit	Name	Age	Sex	Color	Free or Slave	Married/Widowed	Place of Birth	Month Died	Occupation	Disease or Cause of Death	No. Days Ill
1	Jane Gather	1m	F				Tenn	March		unknown	14 days
2	Susan Brothers	1m	F				Tenn	June		Croup	1 day
3	William M. Clark	8	M				Tenn	Sept		Scrofula	40 days
4	John Kelton	1m	M				Tenn	Jan		unknown	10 days
5	Susan McCulloch	1m	F				Tenn	March		unknown	7 days
6	John Johnson	1m	M				Tenn	Sept		unknown	14 days
7	William H. Smith	1m	M				Tenn	Aug		unknown	3 days
8	Mary Nichols	45	F	B	S		Va	Dec		Consumption	50 days
9	Susan Majors	60	F	B	S		Va	Feb		Apoplexy	sudden
10	Jacob Batton	4m	M	B	S		Tenn	Sept		unknown	3 days
11	William W. Jordon	1m	M				Tenn	May		Inflamation of brain	10 days
12	Mariah Marshel	35	F			M	Tenn	Feb		Dropsy of heart	90 days
13	Michael Malony	45	M				Ireland	Oct	Laborer	unknown	sudden
14	Elizabeth Norman	60	F			M	S.C.	Feb		unknown	365 days

COUNTY OF RUTHERFORD, STATE OF TENNESSEE.

PAGE NO. 651   PERSONS WHO DIED DURING THE YEAR ENDING 1st JUNE, 1850.

Forecamp District
E. D. Hancock

No. of Visit	Name	Age	Sex	Color	Free or Slave	Married/Widowed	Place of Birth	Month Died	Occupation	Disease or Cause of Death	No. Days Ill
1	Robert Philips	1	M	B	S		Tenn	Jan		Pneumonia	7 days
2	Aaron Kirk	1m	M	B	S		Tenn	Jan		unknown	7 days
3	Edgar Wilson	5m	M				Tenn	April		Erysipelas	20 days
4	Narcissa Carney	2	F	B	S		Tenn	Dec		unknown	30 days
5	Robert Hughs	21	M				Tenn	Dec	Farmer	Liver complaint	4 days
6	John Kirlough	5m	M	B	S		Tenn	April		Bronchitis	30 days
7	James Lawrence	1	M	B	S		Tenn	Aug		unknown	20 days
8	Margaret Jones	44	F			W	N.C.	Oct		Dropsy	360 days
9	Sarah Childress	34	F			M	Tenn	March		Consumption	150 days
10	Anna Childress	19	F	B	S		Tenn	Jan		T. fever	60 days

COUNTY OF RUTHERFORD, STATE OF TENNESSEE.

PAGE NO. 653   PERSONS WHO DIED DURING THE YEAR ENDING 1st JUNE, 1850.

The Town of Murfreesboro
E. D. Hancock

No. of Visit	Name	Age	Sex	Color	Free or Slave	Married/Widowed	Place of Birth	Month Died	Occupation	Disease or Cause of Death	No. Days Ill
1	May E. Gannaway	1	F				Penn	June		Cholera	5 days
2	Martha Good	1	F	B	S		Tenn	Aug		Bronchitis	30 days
3	Dick Leiper	1	M	B	S		Tenn	Oct		Worms	2 days
4	Caroline Lemmon	40	F	B	S		N.C.	April		Insanity	300 days
5	Virginia Nelson	3m	F				Tenn	July		Inflamation of brain	7 days
6	James Hancock	1m	M	B	S		Tenn	May		unknown	sudden
7	Lucinda M. Carington	33	F			M	Tenn	Dec		Erysipelas	10 days
8	John Spence	9	M				Tenn	June		Cholera	1 day
9	Henry Spence	5	M				Tenn	June		Cholera	4 days
10	Harriet Spence	18	F	B	S		Tenn	June		Cholera	3 days
11	Bess	1	F	B	S		Tenn	June		Cholera	3 days
12	John Wendel	1m	M	B	S		Tenn	Aug		Tetanus	4 days
13	Elizabeth Rothes	26	F			M	Tenn	July		Cold	7 days
14	Martha Dill	5	F				Tenn	Dec		Burned	15 days
15	John Fletcher	74	M			M	N.C.	Aug	Farmer	unknown	1 day
16	Rachal Ready	23	F	B	S		Tenn	Dec		Dropsy	300 days
17	Westly Avent	8	M	B	S		Tenn	May		_____	sudden
18	W. B. Huchenson	11	M				Tenn	June		unknown	120 days
19	Charles Rothes	15	M	B	S		Tenn	May		T. fever	20 days
20	Amos Henry	5	M	B	S		Tenn	April		Scrofula	40 days
21	Lonetta W. Haynes	7	F				Tenn	Jan		Dropsy of brain	30 days
22	Simeon C. Randle	6m	M				Tenn	May		Consumption	13 days
23	Nancy Prichard	70	F	B	S		Va	June		unknown	100 days
24	Virgil	35	M	B	S		Tenn	June		T. fever	sudden
25	Isaac Anderson	18	M				Tenn	Feb	none	Consumption	14 days
26	Jackson Williams	28	M	B	S		Tenn	Dec		Scrofula	14 days
27	Elisha Williams	4m	M	B	S		Tenn	May		unknown	90 days
28	Martha Galloway	30	F			M	Tenn	March		Diarrhea	7 days
29	Jerry Lytle	45	M	B	S		Tenn	Aug		Rheumatism	360 days
30	James Lytle	48	M	B	S		N.C.	Aug		Cholera	1/8 day
31	Minerva Lytle	35	F	B	S		Tenn	Aug		Cholera	3½ days
32	Jane Lytle	3	F	M	S		Tenn	Sept		Worms	7 days
33	Edward Lytle	1	M	B	S		Tenn	Sept		Worms	2 days

Remarks: The eastern part of Rutherford County is broken and healthy. Abounding in a variety of growths among which are: elm, ash, dogwood, hickory, white, red and post ash, wild cherry, buckeye, sugar maple, poplar, beech, mulberry, walnut, honey locust, paw paw, sassafras, persimmons, _____, sycamore, box-elder, hackberry, and an immence quantity of cedar with some sweet-gum. The rock is entirely limestone and the water also. No minerals of any kind. Never was a battle fought in the County so far as this Census taker has been able to learn.

COUNTY OF RUTHERFORD, STATE OF TENNESSEE.

PAGE NO. 655 PERSONS WHO DIED DURING THE YEAR ENDING 1st JUNE, 1850.

Middleton & Versailles District
Wm. M. Mason

No. of Visit	Name	Age	Sex	Color	Free or Slave	Married/Widowed	Place of Birth	Month Died	Occupation	Disease or Cause of Death	No. Days Ill
1	Isaac N. Patterson	21	M			M	Tenn	Aug	Farmer	Fever	35 days
2	Peggy D. Harrison	39	F			M	Va	Oct		Dropsy	C
3	Jas. H. Waddle	2	M				Tenn	Nov		Croup	15 days
4	Amanda C. Fowler	5m	F				Tenn	July		Dropsy	42 days
5	Crecy	81	F	B	S		Va	March		Old age	21 days
6	Tabitha Ellis	58	F			M	Va	March		Fits	sudden
7	Martha E. McClure	18	F			M	Tenn	Dec		Congestion of brain	7 days
8	W. R. Alexander	25	M				Tenn	Oct	Merchant	T. fever	7 days
9	Henry	1m	M	B	S		Tenn	Nov		Overlaid	sudden
10	Caroline Wadley	19	F			M	Tenn	Nov		Fever	35 days
11	Frances Underwood	22	F				Tenn	Dec		Congestive brain	4 days
12	John F. Grimes	2	M				Tenn	Dec		Croup	2 days
13	William Smotherman	67	M			W	N.C.	June	Farmer	Pleurisy	5 days
14	Charles	1m		B	S		Tenn	June		unknown	sudden
15	M. M. Taylor	34	F			M	unknown	Dec		Child bed	2 days
16	Casander Halstead	26	F			M	Tenn	Nov		Child bed	1 day
17	Wardwill Donald	4	M				Tenn	Nov		Croup	5 days
18	Caroline	2m	F	M	S		Tenn	Nov		unknown	7 days

Remarks: I certify that the foregoing schedule of No. 3 contains 1 page, given under my hand on November 30, 1850. W. N. Mason, Asst. Marshal.

COUNTY OF RUTHERFORD, STATE OF TENNESSEE.

PAGE NO. 658 PERSONS WHO DIED DURING THE YEAR ENDING 1st JUNE, 1850.

2nd Division
R. H. Mason

No. of Visit	Name	Age	Sex	Color	Free or Slave	Married/Widowed	Place of Birth	Month Died	Occupation	Disease or Cause of Death	No. Days Ill
1	Coleman	4	M	B	S		Tenn	Feb		T. fever	9 days
2	Charles	1	M	B	S		Tenn	July		T. fever	5 days
3	Houston	4m	M	B	S		Tenn	July		Whooping cough	7 days
4	James	4m	M	B	S		Tenn	July		Whooping cough	30 days
5	Van Buren Traylor	15	M				Tenn	Sept		Consumption	C
6	Elizabeth Phelps	63	F				N.C.	Jan		Dropsy	C
7	Robert N. Gunns	1	M				Tenn	May		Sc. fever	28 days
8	J. B.-Rachel	83	F	B	S		Va	May		Old age	60 days
9	Ebenezer McGowen	84	M			M	London, Eng.	April		Old age	21 days
10	Elizabeth Wrather	23	F				Tenn	July		T. fever	9 days
11	Virginia Sawyers	74	F			W	Va	Aug		Consumption	20 days
12	Caroline Watkins	37	F			M	Tenn	Nov		Cold	2 days
13	Marilla	6m	F	B	S		Tenn	Jan		Whooping cough	12 days
14	Walter Wade	55	M			M	Maryland	Aug	Farmer	Inflamation of stomach	28 days
15	J. M. T.- Benjamin	55	F?	B	S		Va	April		Pneumonia	14 days
16	J. H. - Franky	90	F	B	S		Va	March		unknown	C
17	B. S. - Isaac	15	M	B	S		Tenn	Aug		T. fever	15 days
18	Jeffrey Peak	77	M			M	Va	Feb	Farmer	Consumption	C
19	V. D. C. - Hannah	26	F	B	S		Tenn	July		T. fever	35 days
20	Lafayette Collier	15	M				Tenn	April		T. fever	21 days
21	Margaret	6m	F	B	S		Tenn	July		Congestive chills	1 day
22	B. M. - Harrison	24	M	B	S		Tenn	July		T. fever	14 days
23	W. W. - Amanda	2	F	B	S		Tenn	June		Bowel complaint	C
24	J. W. - Jane	5	F	B	S		Tenn	Aug		unknown	C
25	J. S. - Peter	22	M	M	S		Kentucky	Dec		Murdered	30 days
26	J. Etter - Infant	1m	F	B	S		Tenn	Dec		Cold	2 days
27	Jno. Clinton Ralston	23	M				Tenn	Aug	Farmer	T. fever	21 days
28	Charles L. Muse	15	M				Tenn	Aug		T. fever	40 days

COUNTY OF RUTHERFORD, STATE OF TENNESSEE.

PAGE NO. 658 PERSONS WHO DIED DURING THE YEAR ENDING 1st JUNE, 1850.

2nd Division
R. H. Mason

No. of Visit	Name	Age	Sex	Color	Free or Slave	Married/Widowed	Place of Birth	Month Died	Occupation	Disease or Cause of Death	No. Days Ill
29	L. Muse - Dick	31	M	B	S		Va	Aug		T. fever	40 days
30	T. C. W. - Isaac	40	M	B	S		Tenn	Jan		Hemorrhage of lungs	3 days
31	George	1m	M	B	S		Tenn	May		unknown	C
32	Charles	3	M	B	S		Tenn	July		Dropsy	C
33	Robert	1	M	B	S		Tenn	Aug		Cholera Morbus	4 days
34	A. B. W. - Malissa	5m	F	B	S		Tenn	July		Cold	7 days
35	G. T. - Randall	35	M	B	S		Va	April		unknown	sudden

COUNTY OF RUTHERFORD, STATE OF TENNESSEE.

PAGE NO. 659 PERSONS WHO DIED DURING THE YEAR ENDING 1st JUNE, 1850.

2nd Division
R. H. Mason

No. of Visit	Name	Age	Sex	Color	Free or Slave	Married/Widowed	Place of Birth	Month Died	Occupation	Disease or Cause of Death	No. Days Ill
1	A. B. Wreathers - Infant	100d	F	B	S		Tenn	May		unknown	3 days
2	J. J. - Frank	18	M	B	S		Tenn	Aug		Drowned	sudden
3	Jack	22	M	B	S		Tenn	Sept		Consumption	C
4	Frank	2	M	B	S		Tenn	Aug		T. fever	60 days
5	B. S. R. - Laura	10m	F	B	S		Tenn	Dec		unknown	11 days
6	M. R. - Rachel	3	F	B	S		Tenn	March		T. fever	14 days
7	M. G. A. - Thomas	1	M	B	S		Tenn	Feb		Worms & Bowel disease	7 days
8	E. Ridley - Mary	26	F	B	S		Tenn	July		unknown	sudden
9	Lewis Y. Walden	25	M				Tenn	June	Sch-teacher	Consumption	C
10	William D. McNeal's-Infant	1m	M	B	S		Tenn	Aug		unknown	3 days
11	J. C. K. - Jane	2	F	B	S		Tenn	Nov		Fits	sudden
12	Allazera Kirkpatrick	1m	F				Tenn	Nov		Sc. fever	30 days
13	M. J. - Rhoda	46	F	B	S		Va	Feb		Diarrhea	14 days
14	J. B. B. - Cooper	18	M	B	S		Tenn	Aug		T. fever	20 days
15	J. H. - Mary A.	2m	F	B	S		Tenn	June		Diarrhea	C
16	Frances Kimbro	18	F				Tenn	March		Consumption	C
17	J. K. - Daniel	75	M	B	S		N.C.	March		Old age	C
18	Orlander Haynes	1m	M				Tenn	Sept		Inflamation of brain	sudden
19	Benjamin F. Gambell	1	M				Tenn	Sept		unknown	30 days
20	Robert Caldwell	77	M			M	S.C.	Feb	Farmer	Old age & Palsy	C
21	J. C. B. - Mary Ann	9	F	B	S		Tenn			Sc. fever	3 days
22	Joseph May	75	M			W	N.C.		Farmer	Cancer	C
23	Mary F. Martin	3	F				Tenn	Dec		Burnt	sudden
24	Eliza Mullins	28	F			M	Tenn	Feb		unknown	C
25	C. A. D. - Allen	1	M	B	S		Tenn	Sept		Diarrhea	C
26	Infant slave	3m	M	B	S		Tenn	Oct		unknown	3 days
27	Maria	3m	F	B	S		Tenn	Sept		Diarrhea	14 days
28	T. R. - Lewis	2	M	B	S		Tenn	Oct		Diarrhea	C
29	Infant Beaty	1m	F				Tenn	April		unknown	sudden
30	A. B. - Peter	50	M	B	S		Va	Jan		Asthma	28 days
31	W. V. - Jacob	70	M	B	S		N.C.	May		Murdered	sudden
32	Infant	1m	F	B	S		Tenn	Feb		Smothered	sudden
33	W. V. - Infant	1m	M	B	S		Tenn	Nov		Lock jaw	7 days
34	Sarah	1	F	B	S		Tenn	Jan		Smothered	sudden
35	Martha M. Smith	30	F			M	Tenn	Dec		Erysipelas	7 days

COUNTY OF RUTHERFORD, STATE OF TENNESSEE.

PAGE NO. 661 PERSONS WHO DIED DURING THE YEAR ENDING 1st JUNE, 1850.

2nd Division
R. H. Mason

No. of Visit	Name	Age	Sex	Color	Free or Slave	Married/Widowed	Place of Birth	Month Died	Occupation	Disease or Cause of Death	No. Days Ill
1	Sarah	1	F	B	S		Tenn	Aug		Cholera	3 days
2	Robert	100	M	B	S		Va	March		Cancer	C
3	Viney	3	F	B	S		Tenn	Sept		unknown	1 day
4	Mary J. Smithey	11m	F				Tenn	Oct		Inflamation of brain	35 days
5	Jacob	5m	M	B	S		Tenn	June		unknown	4 days
6	Martha	4m	F	B	S		Tenn	May		Bold Hives	1 day
7	Louiza J. Vaughan	7	F				Tenn	March		Sc. fever	30 days
8	Martha J. Hickman	6	F				Tenn	Jan		Sc. fever	12 days
9	Charles S. Hickman	3	M				Tenn	Jan		Sc. fever	4 days
10	Adaline A. Boyd	24	F				Tenn	March		T. fever	60 days
11	Charlotte	60	F	B	S		Va	March		Old age	C
12	Frances E. Gates	1m	F				Tenn	July		Bold hives	7 days
13	Martha A. E. Vaughan	27	F			M	Tenn	Jan		Child bed	1 day
14	Martha A. E. Vaughan	1m	F				Tenn	Feb		unknown	28 days
15	Peter	60	M	B	S		N.C.	Oct		Striction of Urine	C
16	Nancy	1	F	B	S		Tenn	Feb		Croup	1 day
17	Zip	8m	M	B	S		Tenn	Feb		Croup	1 day
18	Hardy T. Snell	49	M			M	N.C.	Feb	Farmer	Consumption	C
19	Margaret Bowman	80	F			W	Atlantic Ocean	June		Old age	C
20	Julia	7	F	B	S		Tenn	Sept		Sorethroat	7 days
21	Minerva	6	F	B	S		Tenn	Oct		Sorethroat	7 days
22	Jordan	3	M	B	S		Tenn	Oct		Sorethroat	7 days
23	Nancy	5m	F	B	S		Tenn	June		Croup	1 day
24	Jno. Ransom	57	M			M	N.C.	Sept	Farmer	unknown	14 days
25	Caroline H. McFadden	35	F			M	Alabama	Dec		Child bed	7 days
26	Elizabeth Wood	58	F			M	Va	April		Dropsy	C
27	Joseph	25	M	B	S		Va	Jan		Old age	sudden
28	George L. Ransom	1	M				Tenn	Aug		Croup	7 days
29	Jas. T. Sudberry	1	M				Tenn	Nov		unknown	3 days
30	William C. Snell	1	M				Tenn	March		Disease of lungs	C
31	David Trail	15	M				Tenn	July		Fever	11 days
32	Thomas L. May	4	M				Tenn	Oct		Croup	7 days
33	Infant May	1m	M				Tenn	March		St. Anthony's fire	7 days
34	John Lyle	83	M			W	Va	Sept		Old age	C
35	Infant	2m	M	M	S		Tenn	Dec		Overlaid	sudden

COUNTY OF RUTHERFORD, STATE OF TENNESSEE.

PAGE NO. 664 PERSONS WHO DIED DURING THE YEAR ENDING 1st JUNE, 1850.

2nd Division
R. H. Mason

No. of Visit	Name	Age	Sex	Color	Free or Slave	Married/Widowed	Place of Birth	Month Died	Occupation	Disease or Cause of Death	No. Days Ill
1	Elizabeth Shelton	1	F				Tenn	April		Inflamation of brain	17 days
2	Mary A. Touns	27	F			M	Tenn	March	none	Dropsy	C
3	Joseph W. Bell	1	M				Tenn	Oct		Thrash	C
4	Lewis	24	M	B	S		Tenn	May		Consumption	20 days
5	Permelia Ridges	30	F			M	Tenn	March		T. fever	21 days
6	Kitty	5	F	B	S		Tenn	Feb		Sc. fever	3 days
7	Eliza	6	F	B	S		Tenn	March		Sc. fever	4 days
8	Walter	6	M	B	S		Tenn	Sept		Congestion	4 days
9	Infant	1m	F	B	S		Tenn	April		unknown	sudden
10	Ann	10m	F	B	S		Tenn	Jan		Inflamation	
11	Infant	1m	F	B	S		Tenn	Feb		unknown	
12	Elizabeth	20	F	B	S		Tenn	March		Consumption	C
13	Solomon	5m	M	B	S		Tenn	March		Overlaid	sudden
14	Infant Lanton	7m	F	M			Tenn	Oct		unknown	sudden
15	Mary Lanton	35	F	M		M	Tenn	Sept		Whites	C
16	William	5m	M	B	S		Tenn	April		Croup	sudden
17	Joseph Flowers	38	M			M	Tenn	July	Farmer	Drowned	sudden
18	Catharine	4m	F	B	S		Tenn	Dec		Smothered	sudden
19	Calvin Summers	18	M				N.C.	Sept	Farmer	Cholera	1 day
20	Hannah	50	F	B	S		Va	April		Cancer	C
21	Robert	4m	M	B	S		Tenn	Jan		unknown	1 day
22	Gentry	1	M	B	S		Tenn	March		Croup	sudden
23	Mary M. Thomas	50	F			W	N.C.	Oct		T. fever	30 days
24	Isabella McGregor	35	F			M	Tenn	Aug		Consumption	C
25	Sarah Alexander	3	F				Tenn	March		Inflamation of lungs	12 days
26	Sicily	21	F	B	S		Tenn	Dec		Inflamation	3 days
27	Agnes	8m	F	B	S		Tenn	Sept		Whooping cough	
28	Robert T. Rowlett	1	M				Tenn	Sept		Erysipelas	8 days
29	Infant, of Mrs. Malone	1m	M	B	S		Tenn	July		Inflamation of bowels	10 days
30	Peyton R. Wrather	23	M				Tenn	Aug	Farmer	T. fever	8 days
31	Edmond Drake	4m	M				Tenn	July		Inflamation of head, birth	
32	Susan	11m	F	B	S		Tenn	Oct		Whooping cough	4 days
33	Olley	4m	F	B	S		Tenn	Oct		Whooping cough	5 days
34	Isaac Pearce	1m	M				Tenn	Aug		-- illegible --	3 days
35	Lucy Blake	28	F				Tenn	June		Consumption	C

COUNTY OF RUTHERFORD, STATE OF TENNESSEE.

PAGE NO. 665 PERSONS WHO DIED DURING THE YEAR ENDING 1st JUNE, 1850.

2nd Division
R. H. Mason

No. of Visit	Name	Age	Sex	Color	Free or Slave	Married/Widowed	Place of Birth	Month Died	Occupation	Disease or Cause of Death	No. Days Ill
1	Infant	1m	F	B	S		Tenn	Oct		Lock jaw	7 days
2	Jas. Hollo_dell	32	M			M	N.C.	Dec	Farmer	Pneumonia	25 days
3	L. B. - George	19	M	B	S		Va	May		Consumption	C
4	A. H. - Anna	18	F	B	S		Tenn	May		Scrofula	C
5	J. B. - Issabella	12	F	B	S		Tenn	April		Apoplexy	sudden
6	Benjamin F. Pope	23	M				Tenn	Aug	Clerk	Congestive chills	7 days
7	Lucinda	21	F	B	S		Tenn	July		T. fever	8 days
8	Susan	70	F	B	S		Va	Aug		unknown	7 days
9	Wilson Revil	27	M			M	Tenn	Dec	Hse-joiner	Consumption	6 days
10	Elizabeth	6m	F	B	S		Tenn	Feb		Overlaid	sudden
11	Meacha Haynes	39	F			M	Tenn	April		Cancer	C
12	Richard Vaughan	72	M			M	Va	April	Farmer	Rheumatism	C
13	Edward Hays	41	M			M	Va	Dec	Farmer	Consumption	C
14	Lewis Johnson	78	M			W	Va	Sept	Farmer	Old age & Turmor	C
15	S. T. - Lucy	85	F	B	S		unknown	May		Old age	14 days
16	Sampson	3m	M	B	S		Tenn	Nov		Overlaid	sudden
17	Allice	3m	F	B	S		Tenn	April		Overlaid	sudden
18	Nancy P. Ross	28	F			M	Tenn	Oct		Consumption	C
19	Wilson V. Ross	23	M				Tenn	Dec	Farmer	Consumption	C
20	Jas. H. Floyd	27	M			M	Tenn	Sept	Farmer	T. fever	28 days
21	T. N. - Albert	6m	M	B	S		Tenn	March		unknown	sudden
22	William	80	M	B	S		Va	Feb		Old age	21 days
23	Mary	2	F	B	S		Tenn	April		Croup	
24	John Jobe	4m	M				Tenn	July		Diarrhea	28 days
25	T. V. - Benjamin	21	M	B	S		Tenn	July		Atrophy	C
26	Tabitha M. Beaty	30	F			M	Tenn	May		Cholera	2 days
27	Anne	20	F	B	S		Tenn	March		T. fever	C
28	Isabella	25	F	B	S		Tenn	Aug		unknown	sudden
29	Lucretia	31	F	B	S		Tenn	March		Dropsy	C
30	W. B. B. - Liza	12	F	B	S		Va	Aug		Pneumonia	6 days

COUNTY OF RUTHERFORD, STATE OF TENNESSEE.

PAGE NO. 667 PERSONS WHO DIED DURING THE YEAR ENDING 1st JUNE, 1850.

2nd Division
R. H. Mason

No. of Visit	Name	Age	Sex	Color	Free or Slave	Married/Widowed	Place of Birth	Month Died	Occupation	Disease or Cause of Death	No. Days Ill
1	Edmund	6m	M	B	S		Tenn	May		Sorethroat	sudden
2	Allen	7m	M	B	S		Tenn	Nov		Choked	sudden
3	Infant	1m	M	B	S		Tenn	Jan		Spasms	7 days
4	Jemima A. Cannon	66	F			W	N.C.	Aug		unknown	7 days

Remarks: It will be seen from the foregoing that Typhoid Fever and a few cases of Scarlet Fever have been most fatal of all the diseases and several deaths occured by smothering and being overlain by the carelessness of slave mothers, but for so large a population, the fatality is comperatively small being but 213 in all.   R. H. Mason.

COUNTY OF RUTHERFORD, STATE OF TENNESSEE.

PAGE NO. 670 PERSONS WHO DIED DURING THE YEAR ENDING 1st JUNE, 1850.

2nd Division
R. H. Mason

No. of Visit	Name	Age	Sex	Color	Free or Slave	Married/Widowed	Place of Birth	Month Died	Occupation	Disease or Cause of Death	No. Days Ill
1	Delaney	6	F	B	S		Tenn	March		Croup	3 days
2	Jno. M. Burns	28	M				Tenn	May	Farmer	Consumption	C
3	J. D. Anderson	4d	M	B	S		Tenn	Feb		unknown	sudden
4	Elizabeth F. Brashears	9m	F				Tenn	Sept		unknown	14 days
5	Nancy	80	F	B	S		Va	March		Old age	4 days
6	Ephraim	19	M	B	S		Tenn	May		Dropsy of heart	14 days
7	James	11	M	B	S			Oct		Scrofula	C
8	Sarah	12	F	B	S		Tenn	Oct		T. fever	8 days
9	Samuel	68	M	B	S		Va	Feb		Pneumonia	21 days
10	Harrison	23	M	B	S		Tenn	May		Congestion of brain	7 days
11	Sarah J. Todd	1	F				Tenn	Oct		Croup	1 day
12	Sarah J. Hubbar	4	F				Tenn	Nov		T. fever	35 days
13	Peggy	38	F	B	S		Maryland	June		Dropsy	C
14	Madison	22	M	B	S		Tenn	May		T. fever	9 days
15	Fanny	9m	F	B	S		Tenn	July		Lock jaw	5 days
16	Jane	16	F	B	S		Tenn	July		T. fever	17 days
17	William A. McCullock	17	M				Tenn	Sept	Farmer	T. fever	17 days
18	Jane	13	F	B	S		Tenn	Sept		T. fever	10 days
19	Jane McCoy	83	F				Va	April		unknown	7 days
20	Thomas Welsh	50	M				N.C.	Sept	none	Palsy	C
21	Judy	45	F	B	S		Tenn	Jan		T. fever	15 days
22	Andrew	35	M	B	S		Tenn	July		T. fever	10 days
23	Spencer	35	M	B	S		N.C.	Dec		Scrofula	C
24	Ella Ledbetter	1	F				Tenn	July		T. fever	14 days
25	Isabella	6m	F	B	S		Tenn	March		Croup	3 days
26	Infant	6m	F	B	S		Tenn	March		Croup	1 day
27	Infant	1m	M	B	S		Tenn	Oct		Lock jaw	3 days
28	David S. Thompson	33	M			M	Tenn	May	Farmer	Consumption	C
29	Nancy	8	F	B	S		Tenn	Sept		unknown	3 days
30	Henry	22	M	B	S		Va	May		Cholera	1 day
31	James	3m	M	B	S		Alabama	March		Convulsions	21 days
32	Martha Beasley	5	F				Tenn	Aug		Croup	1 day
33	Robert Smith	9m	M				Tenn	Oct		Sorethroat	2 days
34	Moses	6	M	B	S		Tenn	Oct		Sorethroat	3 days
35	Alvira	6	F	B	S		Tenn	Oct		T. fever	14 days

COUNTY OF SCOTT, STATE OF TENNESSEE.

PAGE NO. 671 PERSONS WHO DIED DURING THE YEAR ENDING 1st JUNE, 1850.

Civil District No. 18
Allen McDonald

No. of Visit	Name	Age	Sex	Color	Free or Slave	Married/Widowed	Place of Birth	Month Died	Occupation	Disease or Cause of Death	No. Days Ill
1	Thany Loyd	65	F			M	Va	July		unknown	180 days
2	Laky McDonald	42	F			M	Tenn	Dec		Chronic	83 days
3	John Nettles	54	M			M	Va	Jan	Farmer	Chronic	60 days
4	Amos Wilson	74	M			M	N.C.	March	Farmer	Chronic	100 days
5	Rachel Angel	7	F				Tenn	March		Burn	9 days

Remarks: This County, for health, is not surpassed in the United States.
Allen McDonald.

COUNTY OF SEVIER, STATE OF TENNESSEE.

PAGE NO. 675 PERSONS WHO DIED DURING THE YEAR ENDING 1st JUNE, 1850.

12th Subdivision, E. District
L. Duggan

No. of Visit	Name	Age	Sex	Color	Free or Slave	Married/Widowed	Place of Birth	Month Died	Occupation	Disease or Cause of Death	No. Days Ill
1	Joseph Yarborough	3m	M				Tenn	Jan		unknown	3 weeks
2	Catharine Lanedy	6	F				Tenn	Oct		Croup	7 days
3	James Fox	1	M				Tenn	July		unknown	14 days
4	Sarah Bird	49	F			M	Tenn	Oct		Dropsy	90 days
5	Atemiah Breeden	13	F				Tenn	Dec		Dropsy	C
6	Margaret Zolkinge	82	F			M	Penn	June		unknown	C
7	Martha Ogle	43	F			M	N.C.	Feb		Fever	21 days
8	Isaac Ogle	5m	M				Tenn	May		Croup	2 days
9	Mark Reagan	4	M				Tenn	Nov		unknown	21 days
10	Benjamin Roberts	83	M			M	Penn	Feb		Killed by falling timber	sudden
11	George Brock	53	M			M	S.C.	Sept		Fever	11 days
12	Martha McFall	8	F				Tenn	Jan		unknown	42 days
13	John Robertson	11	M				Tenn	March		Burned in building	sudden
14	James Robertson	3	M				Tenn	March		Burned in building	sudden
15	Ailsy B. Murphy	33	F			W	Tenn	March		Consumption	C
16	Elizabeth Maples	57	F			M	Tenn	Nov		Dropsy	C
17	Elizabeth Cates	6m	F				Tenn	Feb		Croup	2 days
18	Lucinda Robertson	21	F				Tenn	Dec		unknown	11 days
19	Deborah Snapp	9m	F				Tenn	Sept		unknown	28 days
20	Horatio Butler	52	M			M	Va	Dec		Dyspepsia	C
21	Mary Hester	21	F				Tenn	Sept		unknown	35 days
22	Malvine Anderson	2m	F				Tenn	Aug		Croup	3 days
23	Sarah Cary	11	F				Tenn	May		Fits	21 days
24	William Spurgen	9	M				Tenn	Dec		unknown	21 days
25	Mary Clabough	1	F				Tenn	Sept		unknown	14 days
26	Louisa Fox	10m	F				Tenn	Nov		unknown	28 days
27	Artencey Anderson	6	F				Tenn	Sept		Fever	14 days
28	John Richards	10	M				Tenn	Sept		Fever	C
29	Randle Hill	55	M			W	Tenn	Sept	Farmer	Fever	8 days
30	Joseph Atchley	55	M			M	Tenn	Aug	Farmer	Fever	8 days
31	Daniel Atchley	6	M				Tenn	Jan		Croup	7 days
32	Esther Plumley	83	F			W	N.C.	June		Palsy	C
33	Thomas Jones	43	M			M	Tenn	Aug	Farmer	Fever	3 days
34	Henry Jenkins	43	M			M	Tenn	Nov	Farmer	unknown	6 days
35	Drucilla Jarnagin	42	F			M	N.C.	May		unknown	42 days

Remarks: There has no particular malady been prevalent in the County. The County is well supplied with bold springs of pure and limped limestone and freestone water. Much limestone abounds here.

COUNTY OF SEVIER, STATE OF TENNESSEE.

PAGE NO. 678 PERSONS WHO DIED DURING THE YEAR ENDING 1st JUNE, 1850.

12th Subdivision, E. District
Lemuel Duggan

No. of Visit	Name	Age	Sex	Color	Free or Slave	Married/Widowed	Place of Birth	Month Died	Occupation	Disease or Cause of Death	No. Days Ill
1	Mary Walker	74	F			W	S.C.	Dec		Breast complaint	C
2	Jerusa Burnett	4m	F				Tenn	June		Inflamation of liver	14 days
3	Mary Evans	85	F			W	N.C.	July		Old age	sudden
4	Mary McCrosky	2m	F				Tenn	Feb		Whooping cough	21 days
5	Elender Lawson	25	F				Tenn	Dec		Consumption	60 days
6	Anne McCrosky	2	F	B			Tenn	Dec		Flux	90 days
7	Sarah Rose	49	F			M	Va	Sept		unknown	7 days
8	Jacob Frazier	8m	F?				Tenn	Nov		Croup	1 day
9	Elizabeth Thomas	9	F				Tenn	Oct		Fever	10 days
10	John A. Wayland	8	M				Tenn	Oct		unknown	2 days
11	Sincler Cagle	10m	M				Tenn	Dec		Croup	31 days
12	J. Boling	2m	M				Tenn	Jan		unknown	42 days
13	Martha Chandler	5	F				Tenn	Nov		Sorethroat	7 days
14	____ Stockton	4m					Tenn	Jan		unknown	60 days
15	John Herington	1	M				Tenn	May		Bowel complaint	60 days
16	Sarah Cates	1m	F				Tenn	Oct		unknown	2 days
17	Susan Cates	3m	F				Tenn	Dec		unknown	3 days
18	Mary Atchly	10	F				Tenn	Sept		Fever	42 days
19	John Brown	83	M			M	N.C.	Jan	Farmer	Cancer	21 days
20	Nancy Ellis	73	F			W	unknown	Sept		unknown	6 days
21	George Hudson	85	M			M	Va	Jan	none	Old age	21 days

COUNTY OF SHELBY, STATE OF TENNESSEE.

PAGE NO. 679 PERSONS WHO DIED DURING THE YEAR ENDING 1st JUNE, 1850.

2nd Ward, Memphis
H. T. Guion

No. of Visit	Name	Age	Sex	Color	Free or Slave	Married/Widowed	Place of Birth	Month Died	Occupation	Disease or Cause of Death	No. Days Ill
1	Miss Echols	1	F				Tenn	Sept		Cholera	1 month
2	Alley Newman	59	F			M	Ireland	July		Bil. fever	1 week
3	Cath. King	14	F				Georgia	July		Cholera	12 hours
4	Sarah Yeats	18	F			M	Tenn	March		Hemorrhage	1 month
5	William Yeats	2m	M				Tenn	April		Infant	1 week
6	Dick Yeats	30	M	B	S		____	April		Cholera	4 days
7	George Yeats	30	M	B	S		____	April		Cholera	2 days
8	Haden Yeats	17	M	B	S		____	April		Drowned	sudden
9	Elisa Yeats	50	F	B	S		____	April		Cholera	3 days
10	Katy Yeats	25	F	B	S		____	April		Cholera	8 days
11	Billy Yeats	60	M	B	S		____	April		Cholera	1 week
12	N. B. Holt's, slave	50	M	B	S		____	Dec		Cholera	20 hours
13	Mary Kennedy	35	F			M	Ireland	July		Consumption	1 year
14	David (Allison)	26	M	B	S		____	July		Cholera	8 hours
15	Polly (Rose)	50	F	B	S		____	July		Cholera	1 week
16	Jo. Morse	21	M				Penn	Aug	Printer	Cholera	2 days
17	George Jerry	49	M			M	Va	June	Carpenter	Cholera	6 hours
18	Eli Jerry	20	M				S.C.	June	Laborer	Cholera	8 days
19	Hardiman Jerry	17	M				Alabama	Sept	Laborer	Chills	5 days
20	Francis Jerry	10	M				Alabama	Nov		Dropsy	2 months
21	Robert Jerry	2m	M				Tenn	Nov		Chills	4 weeks
22	Lucy Prunells	40	F			W	Va	June		Cholera	1 week
23	Harriet Prunells	9	F				Va	June		Cholera	10 hours
24	Jo. Place	8	M				Tenn	June		Cholera	8 hours
25	Jacob Hadacre	63	M			M	Switz.	Aug	Calico Printer	Fever	6 days
26	Martha Combs	18	F			M	Tenn	Feb		Consumption	1 year
27	Infant Combs	1m	M				Tenn	March		Fits	3 days
28	Jas. Wright	25	M				Indiana	June	Trader	Cholera	2 days
29	Frances Williams	11m	F				Miss	July		Cholera Inf.	Chronic

COUNTY OF SHELBY, STATE OF TENNESSEE.

PAGE NO. 679 PERSONS WHO DIED DURING THE YEAR ENDING 1st JUNE, 1850.

2nd Ward, Memphis
H. T. Guion

No. of Visit	Name	Age	Sex	Color	Free or Slave	Married/Widowed	Place of Birth	Month Died	Occupation	Disease or Cause of Death	No. Days Ill
30	W. McIntire	40	M				unknown	Dec	Trader	Consumption	Chronic
31	Henry (Chism)	5	M	M	S			April		Cholera	1 day
32	Eliz. Barnett	12	F				Miss	July		Cholera	2 days
33	Hannah (Cooper)	35	F	B	S			Feb		Small pox	10 days
34	Elijah (Cooper)	35	M	B	S					Apoplexy	2 days
35	Betsey (Powell)	32	F	B	S			June		Cholera	1 month

COUNTY OF SHELBY, STATE OF TENNESSEE.

PAGE NO. 682 PERSONS WHO DIED DURING THE YEAR ENDING 1st JUNE, 1850.

10th Ward, Memphis
H. L. Guion

No. of Visit	Name	Age	Sex	Color	Free or Slave	Married/Widowed	Place of Birth	Month Died	Occupation	Disease or Cause of Death	No. Days Ill
1	William Maddox	14	M				Tenn	Dec		Small pox	17 days
2	Prys (Cross)	35	M	B	S			Aug	Laborer	Chronic Diarrhea	
3	M. McMillan	26	F				Ireland	July		Cholera	10 hours
4	Jane Long	20	F				Ireland	July		Cholera	2 days
5	Thomas Garvin	22	M				Ireland	July	Laborer	Cholera	1 day
6	Jane McMillan	6m	F				Tenn	Aug		Chronic Diarrhea	
7	John McGuire	4	M				Ireland	Aug		Chronic Diarrhea	5 weeks
8	Jas. McGuire	2m	M				Tenn	Aug		Chronic Diarrhea	2 weeks
9	Eliz. Dooley	3m	F				Tenn	June		Cholera Inf.	1 month
10	Ann Willis	2	F				Tenn	Aug		Fever	1 week
11	William Monay	1	M				Illinois	Oct		Diarrhea	4 months
12	Epper Strahl	55	F			M	Germany	June		Cholera	2 days
13	Eliz. Fister	28	F				Germany	July		Cholera	10 days
14	Mary Garvin	1	F				Tenn	Jan		Small pox	15 days
15	Michl. Burk	40	M			M	Ireland	June	Laborer	Cholera	6 hours
16	And. Malone	14	M				Ireland	Jan		Drowned	sudden
17	William Maher	57	M			M	Ireland	Feb	Laborer	Consumption	4 days
18	W. Brown	18	M				unknown	unknown	Laborer	unknown	
19	W. Cleveland	45	M				unknown	Dec	Laborer	unknown	
20	Robert Richards	13	M				Kentucky	June		Cholera	10 hours
21	John Cunningham	70	M			M	Ireland	June	Hatter	Diarrhea	2 weeks
22	Eliza Pickerill	1	F				Tenn	Sept		Diarrhea	4 months
23	Esther (Christian)	21	F	B	S		Va	June		Cholera	6 days
24	Jack (Morgan)	1	M	B	S		Tenn	April		Overlaid	sudden
25	Ellen Wilkins	2	F				Tenn	June		Cholera	20 hours
26	Nancy McCreary	43	F			M	N.C.	June		Small pox	8 months
27	Martin Reardon	1	M				Ohio	July		Teething	3 months
28	Matilda Thompson	50	F	B	S			June		Small pox	2 days
29	Emma Henderson	3	F				Miss	Aug		Cholera Inf.	5 days
30	Jas. Dillon	22	M				Ireland	Nov	Laborer	Fit	sudden
31	Slave	38	M	B	S			Dec	Laborer	Cholera	sudden
32	W. Willis	20	M			W	unknown	June	Laborer	Cholera	1 week
33	David Etheridge	35	M			M	Tenn	July	Carpenter	Cholera	1 week
34	John Echols	20	M			M	Germany	Sept	Gunsmith	Cholera	1 week
35	Mary Echols	23	F			W	Germany	Sept		Cholera	2 weeks

Remarks: The First Ward ends at No. 21. The Second commences at No. 22 on this page.

COUNTY OF SHELBY **, STATE OF TENNESSEE.**

PAGE NO. 683 **PERSONS WHO DIED DURING THE YEAR ENDING 1st JUNE, 1850.**

3rd Ward, Memphis
W. L. Guion

No. of Visit	Name	Age	Sex	Color	Free or Slave	Married/Widowed	Place of Birth	Month Died	Occupation	Disease or Cause of Death	No. Days Ill
1	Mary Birdsong	5m	F				Tenn	Sept		Diarrhea	3 weeks
2	Maria (Hancock)	10	F	B	S			Jan		Lungs	5 months
3	Katsy (Kirk)	50	F	B	S			April		Consumption	C
4	Maria (Kirk)	40	F	B	S			Feb		Fever	1 month
5	Jim (Kirk)	12	M	B	S			March		Fever	2 months
6	Willie Kirk	6m	F				Tenn	Dec		Pneumonia	3 weeks
7	Nannie B. Penn	18	F			M	Tenn	Dec		Consumption	1 year
8	Ellen (Manning)	37	F	B	S			June		Cholera	6 hours
9	Isabella (Manning)	90	F	B	S			June		Cholera	2 days
10	Jacob (Manning)	2	M	B	S			May		Fits	5 days
11	Mrs. Peal	35	F			M	England	July		Consumption	C
12	James J. Clarkson	42	M				Maryland	Aug	Cath-Clergy	Inflamation of brain	1 week
13	Samuel Miller	9m	M					Dec		unknown	6 hours
14	Andy (Huston)	55	M	B	S			Aug		Apoplexy	1 week
15	Solomon Armour	16	M				Tenn	April	Student	Casualty	sudden
16	Mary A. Gibson	29	F			M	Tenn	April		Abortion	8 days
17	Thomas Bradshaw	21	M				Kentucky	April	Boatsman	Congestion of brain	3 weeks
18	Franklin Goff	1	M				Tenn	Sept		Thrash	5 months
19	Ralph Harris	1	M				Tenn	July		Pneumonia	2 months
20	Jas. Stanwood	30	M				unknown	Nov	Lawyer	Congestive chill	1 month
21	Patsey Temple	26	F	B	S			June		Cholera	6 hours
22	Lydia R. Quinn	30	F				Rhode Island	June		Cholera	8 hours
23	George W. Terry	33	M				N.C.	May	Barkeeper	Stricture	10 days
24	Vina (Lamphier)	30	F	B	S			Dec		Cholera	12 hours
25	Slave (L. Penn)	1	M	B	S			March		Scrofula	2 months
26	Rutha Nicholson	62	F			W	N.C.	Sept		Consumption	C
27	Rhody (Robinson)	15	M?	B	S			Dec		Dropsy	6 months
28	Emanuel (Robinson)	4	M	B	S			July		Worms	1 month
29	John (Robinson)	2	M	B	S			July		Chill	3 days
30	George (Robinson)	1	M	B	S			July		Worms	1 month
31	Reuben (Cheek)	22	M	B	S			Sept		Diarrhea	6 months
32	Milly (Cheek)	40	F	B	S			March		Diarrhea	6 months
33	Horace (Cheek)	2	M	B	S			Sept		Diarrhea	2 months
34	Infant (Cheek)	1m	M	B	S			Aug		unknown	sudden
35	Lydia Guion	10	F				Tenn	Nov		Fever	5 days

COUNTY OF SHELBY, STATE OF TENNESSEE.

PAGE NO. 686 PERSONS WHO DIED DURING THE YEAR ENDING 1st JUNE, 1850.

2nd Ward, Memphis
W. L. Guion

No. of Visit	Name	Age	Sex	Color	Free or Slave	Married/Widowed	Place of Birth	Month Died	Occupation	Disease or Cause of Death	No. Days Ill
1	Infant (Powel)	4m	F	B	S		Tenn	June		Cholera	1 day
2	Lewis Hoyle	1	F?				Tenn	July		unknown	3 months
3	John Maguire	63	M			M	Maryland	Dec	Teacher	Dyspepsia	1 year
4	William Tinsley	8m	M				Tenn	June		unknown	12 days
5	Mary Leach	17	F			M	Tenn	June		Chronic Diarrhea	____
6	Bob Cheek	50	M	B	S			Sept		Inflamation of brain	2 weeks
7	Silas Simpson	30	M				N.C.	Jan	Cap Watch	Small pox	2 weeks
8	Henry (Bostick)	1	M	B	S		unknown	July		Cholera	sudden
9	M. Whitley	35	M			M	unknown	Feb	Carriage mkr	Cholera	1 week
10	Henry Stratton	61	M			M	Va	Sept	Merchant	Congestive fever	4 days
11	Betty (Stratton)	50	F	B	S			Feb		Apoplexy	5 hours
12	Mary Trader	26	F			M	Va	June		Consumption	10 days
13	Ellick (Trader)	35	M	B	S			July		Cholera	2 hours
14	Phil (Shanks)	65	M	B	S			April		Rheumatic disease of heart	C
15	Sarah Winfield	3	F				Michigan	Aug		Consumption	1 year
16	David Warson	20	M				Tenn	April	Laborer	unknown	sudden
17	James Province	18	M				Miss	Oct	Laborer	unknown	4 days
18	William White	21	M				Indiana	June	Saddler	Cholera	3 hours
19	Henry C. Winn	28	M				Kentucky	Dec	Carpenter	Consumption	C
20	Emily (Leath)	1	F	B	S			March		Dropsy	C
21	Lucy (Shaller)	40	F	B	S			June		Cholera	2 days
22	Beverly (Hill)	18	M	B	S			Dec		Drowned	____
23	Slave (Hill)	28	F	B	S			Jan		Breast complaint	3 months
24	Chill (Hill)	2m	M	M	S			Jan		unknown	____
25	Boy (Hill)	5	M	B	S			Feb		Diarrhea	____
26	Pamelia Fowlkes	15	F				Va	June		Cholera	5 days
27	Randol (Fowlkes)	25	M	B	S			July		Diarrhea	10 days
28	Liah (Fowlkes)	40	M	B	S			Feb		Pleurisy	5 days
29	Horrace (Rhodes)	17	M	M	S			June		Brain fever	5 days
30	Betty (Rhodes)	22	F	M	S			Sept		Fever	12 days
31	Moses Meeker	1	M				Tenn	Aug		Teething	3 months
32	George Rumer	1	M				Tenn	June		Cholera Inf.	13 weeks
33	G. Frierson	47	F	B	S			June		Consumption	C
34	Slave	40	F	B	S			July		Cholera	2 days
35	Perry Birdsong	26	M			M	Kentucky	April	Blk-smith	Cold	1 month

Remarks: The Second Ward ends at No. 14. The Third Ward commences at No. 15 on this page.

COUNTY OF SHELBY, STATE OF TENNESSEE.

PAGE NO. 687 PERSONS WHO DIED DURING THE YEAR ENDING 1st JUNE, 1850.

5th Ward, Memphis

H. L. Guion

No. of Visit	Name	Age	Sex	Color	Free or Slave	Married/Widowed	Place of Birth	Month Died	Occupation	Disease or Cause of Death	No. Days Ill
1	John Henry	8m	M				Tenn	Dec		unknown	C
2	Candice (Newby)	10	F	B	S			Sept		Consumption	3 months
3	Eliza Giles	20	F				Tenn	June		Cholera	12 hours
4	Delpha (Giles)	35	F	B	S			July		Cholera	2 hours
5	Fanny (Giles)	38	F	B	S			July		Diarrhea	C
6	Jim (Giles)	12	M	B	S			July		Diarrhea	C
7	John	30	M				Germany	June	Carpenter	Diarrhea	4 days
8	Anna (Hunt)	55	F	B	S			Sept		Disease of womb	C
9	Alfred (Porter)	25	M	M	S			April		Consumption	C
10	Sarah Meek	49	F			M	N.C.	Feb		Cholera	3 days
11	Jas. Holaway	29	M				N.C.	Aug		Cholera	2 days
12	William Holaway	7m	M				Tenn	Aug		Cholera	3 hours
13	George Holaway	10	M				N.C.	Aug		Cholera	2 days
14	Charles Holaway	3	M				Tenn	Aug		Cholera	1 day
15	Jacob Craft	25	M				Tenn	Nov		S. B. Explosion	sudden
16	A. M. Alsop	27	M				Indiana	April	Cabinet-mkr	Cholera	5 days
17	unknown	1	M				France	July		Cholera	3 months
18	Harriet (East)	21	F	B	S			May		Small pox	2 weeks
19	Patsey (Temple)	22	F	B	S			July		Cholera	7 hours
20	George Leach	42	M				England	Feb	Grocery	Fever	9 weeks
21	Samuel (Moore)	4	M	B	S			March		unknown	C
22	Mary Ryan	2	F				Tenn	June		unknown	6 days
23	Pat Ryan	33	M				Ireland	July	Laborer	Casuality	4 days
24	John Ford	11m	M				Tenn	June		Inflamation of brain	3 days
25	Nancy (Latham)	35	F	B	S		Tenn	July		Cholera	1 week
26	Eliza Penny	1	F	B	S		Tenn	July		Teething	2 days
27	Isabella English	10	F				Alabama	July		Fever	3 weeks
28	Infant Barker	40?	F				Tenn	June		Inflamation of navel	1 day
29	Thomas (Coe)	2	M	M	S			Dec		Croup	1 day
30	Elizabeth Nicholson	39	F				S.C.	July		Fever	12 days
31	Frances Nicholson	2	F				Miss	Aug		Fever	4 days
32	Lucy (Duncan)	20	F	B	S			March		Inflamation of brain	1 day
33	Davidson (Duncan)	1	M	B	S			June		Cholera	1 day
34	Elmira McGinnis	27	F				Tenn	June		Cholera	4 days
35	Henry McGinnis	5	M				Tenn	June		Cholera	10 hours

Remarks: The 5th Ward ends at No. 28. The 6th begins at No. 29 on this page. Several deaths of transient persons, who have been landed from Steam Boats, have occured in this Ward, at the landings, of whom I can get no reliable report, some say 15 or 20, probably more.

COUNTY OF SHELBY **, STATE OF TENNESSEE.**

PAGE NO. 690 **PERSONS WHO DIED DURING THE YEAR ENDING 1st JUNE, 1850.**

4th Ward, Memphis

H. L. Guion

No. of Visit	Name	Age	Sex	Color	Free or Slave	Married/Widowed	Place of Birth	Month Died	Occupation	Disease or Cause of Death	No. Days Ill
1	Rhina (Winchester)	75	F	B	S		Africa	April		Old age	sudden
2	Nixon Winchester	3m	M				Tenn	June		Convulsions	C
3	Eliza D. Tannehill	3	F				Tenn	Sept		Brain fever	10 days
4	Infant Cornwell	10	F				Tenn	May		Inflamation	1 day
5	Henry Witter	42	M			M	Germany	Oct	Boarding Hse	Consumption	2 weeks
6	George Leffel	26	M				Germany	July	Shoemaker	Casuality	sudden
7	Orville Earle	35	M				N.C.	March	Bar Keeper	Suicide	sudden
8	Chany (Newton)	35	F	B	S		___	Aug		Consumption	C
9	Ellen (Taylor)	18	F	B	S		___	May		Consumption	C
10	Billy (Watkins)	55	M	B	S		___	June		Cholera	10 hours
11	Aug Bringent	25	M				France	Aug	Wagon-maker	unknown	1 day
12	Lucy (Jackson)	3	F	B	S		___	May		Diarrhea	2 months
13	Caroline Thompson	18	F				Alabama	March		Consumption	6 months
14	Jack (Emerson)	20	M	B	S		___	April		Small pox	4 weeks
15	Mary E. Emerson	57	F				N.C.	April		Small pox	3 weeks
16	Eliza (Emerson)	1	F	B	S		___	April		Small pox	2 weeks
17	Charles H. Burnett	1m	M				Tenn	Sept		Disease of spine	C
18	Anna Henderson	1	F				Tenn	July		Convulsions	4 days
19	John (Locke)	35	M	B	S		Tenn	Sept		Cholera	3 days
20	Infant (Frayser)	1	M	B	S		Tenn	July		Cholera Inf.	2 weeks
21	Infant (Robinson)	2m	F	B	S		Tenn	Feb		unknown	2 weeks
22	Mr. Reid	35	M				Kentucky	Jan	Farmer	Cholera	2 days
23	Mary Lamberson	4m	F				Ohio	Oct		Croup	2 days
24	Mr. Aldridge	38	M				Maine	April	Merchant	Cholera	8 hours
25	Mr. Prispont	37	M				Maine	April	unknown	Cholera	12 hours
26	William Oldham	54	M				N.C.	May	Farmer	Congestive chills	6 days
27	William Fowler	3	M				Tenn	March		Bronchitis	3 days
28	Hercules (Fowler)	16	M	B	S		___	Oct		T. fever	2 months
29	Peter (Fowler)	20	M	B	S		___	July		Cholera	1 day
30	Ennis (Fowler)	15	M	B	S		___	June		Cholera	6 hours
31	Jas. Tate	5m	M				Tenn	June		Whooping cough	1 month
32	Elizabeth Patillo	19	F				Va	Aug		Bronchitis	C
33	Billy (Pritchett)	2m	M	B	S		___	May		Inflamation of bowels	1 week
34	Gray (Patillo)	16	M	B	S		___	April		Consumption	C
35	Infant (Patillo)	6m	M	B	S		___	April		Casuality	sudden

Remarks: The 4th Ward ends at No. 20. The 5th begins at No. 21 on this page.

COUNTY OF SHELBY, STATE OF TENNESSEE.

PAGE NO. 691 PERSONS WHO DIED DURING THE YEAR ENDING 1st JUNE, 1850.

6th Ward, Memphis
H. L. Guion

No. of Visit	Name	Age	Sex	Color	Free or Slave	Married/Widowed	Place of Birth	Month Died	Occupation	Disease or Cause of Death	No. Days Ill
1	Katy Walker	60	F	B	F	M	unknown	Aug		Cholera	2 days
2	Paskel Williams	2	M	M	F			June		Diarrhea	1 week
3	Amanda Stovall	10m	F	M	F			July		Diarrhea	2 weeks
4	Mary Chew	1	F	B	F		Tenn	July		Cholera	5 days
5	Patrick (Woods)	33	M	B	S			July		Cholera	8 hours
6	Richard (P. Hopton)	10m	M				Tenn	June		Cholera Inf.	9 days
7	John Ware	52	M			M	Va	Jan	Farmer	Cholera	1 day
8	Janet Ware	16	F				Va	Jan		Cholera	12 hours
9	Georgianna Gray	11m	F				Tenn	July		Cholera Inf.	C
10	Jane Gibson	61	F			W	Va	Oct		Congestion	C
11	Gatta (Ferguson)	39	F	B	S			June		Cholera	1 day
12	Susan Ann Causey	23	F			M	Alabama	March		Dyspepsia	6 months
13	Josephine Wedgewood	10m	F				Tenn	Sept		Consumption	6 weeks
14	Julia Fermisco	30	F			M	Ireland	July		Cholera	1 hour
15	Thomas McCraith	70	M			M	Ireland	Sept	Laborer	Diarrhea	3 months
16	Richard Hennessee	30	M			W	Ireland	Sept		Drowned	sudden
17	Joel Hume	20	M				Indiana	Dec	Millwright	Bowels	Chronic
18	John Rodgers	46	M			M	Penn	June		unknown	
19	Peter (Rawlings)	65	M	B	S			June		Cholera	3 days
20	Phil (Rawlings)	50	M	B	S			June		Cholera	2 months
21	Ann (Rawlings)	1	F	B	S			Jan		Whooping cough	3 weeks
22	Sally Herndon	52	F			M	N.C.	Feb		Bronchitis	C
23	M. S. Wright	1m	M				Tenn	June		Inflamation	5 days
24	Harrison Mordica	6	F?				Alabama	Jan		Burnt	1 day
25	Francis Fleshardt	19	M				Alabama	Feb	Clerk	Casuality	sudden
26	Bean Wallace	10m	M				Tenn	June		Inflamation of brain	10 days
27	Francis Jenkins	3	M				Tenn	Aug		unknown	6 weeks
28	Edward Jenkins	2d	M				Tenn	March		unknown	1 day
29	Mary Pillow	26	F			M	Va	Feb		Consumption	C
30	Willis (Pillow)	30	M	B	S			March		Pneumonia	3 days
31	Sally (Hill)	8m	F	M	S			July		unknown	C
32	Robert Hester	61	M			M	N.C.	June	Carpenter	Cholera	8 hours
33	Caroline Hester	46	F				N.C.	June		Cholera	8 hours
34	Martha Hester	18	F			W	N.C.	June		Cholera	3 days
35	William Hester	23	M				N.C.	June	Carpenter	Cholera	8 hours
	Mary Everson	18	F				N.C.	June		Cholera	5 hours
	Eliza Moore	1	F				Tenn	June		Inflamation of brain	30 days
	Ernest Greenlaw	6m	M				Tenn	Jan		Inflamation of brain	14 days
	Mary (Driver)	6	F	M	S		Tenn	Dec		Inflamation of brain	1 day

Remarks: I, H. L. Guion, do hereby certify that the whole number of pages in this returns is ten (10) whole numbers of deaths reported. Three hundred and fifty four (354) and that they were made according to the tenor of my official oath. Memphis, December 20, 1850
H. L. Guion.

COUNTY OF SHELBY, STATE OF TENNESSEE.

PAGE NO. 694 — PERSONS WHO DIED DURING THE YEAR ENDING 1st JUNE, 1850.

6th Ward, Memphis
H. L. Guion

No. of Visit	Name	Age	Sex	Color	Free or Slave	Married/Widowed	Place of Birth	Month Died	Occupation	Disease or Cause of Death	No. Days Ill
1	Susan (McGinnis)	4	F	B	S			June		Cholera	12 hours
2	Mary (Pascall)	2	F	B	S		Tenn	June		Cholera	3 days
3	Lucy Jones	2m	F				Tenn	Aug		unknown	2 weeks
4	Hannah (Murphy)	14	F	B	S			Oct		Consumption	C
5	John (Banks)	25	M	B	S			March		Small pox	2 months
6	Mary Pope	11m	F				Tenn	Sept		Diarrhea	C
7	Brunson Crubbin	8m	M				Tenn	July		Croup	2 days
8	Mary (Chester)	33	F	B	S			April		Diarrhea	C
9	James (Chester)	5	M	M	S			April		Pleurisy	1 month
10	Thomas Polk	2	M				Missouri	May		Cholera	1 week
11	Abram (Howard)	24	M	B	S			Dec		Cholera	2 days
12	John H. Carr	29	M				Va	July	Farmer	Inflamation of stomach	8 days
13	Infant Williams	3d	F				Tenn	April		Premature	
14	Infant Williams	1d	F				Tenn	April		Premature	
15	Cath. Green	28	F				Ireland	June		Cholera	1 day
16	Cath. Ann Green	1	F				Tenn	June		Cholera	1 day
17	Mrs. Allen	20	F				unknown	March		Cholera	8 days
18	unknown		M				unknown	July	unknown	Bil. fever	5 days
19	Ellen (Allen)	25	F	B	S			June		Cholera	36 days
20	Sarah (Allen)	5	F	B	S			June		Cholera	36 days
21	George (Allen)	3	M	M	S			June		Cholera	36 days
22	Jas. McGee	11m	M				Tenn	July		Teething	6 weeks
23	Daniel Suiter	38	M				Germany	Aug	Teacher	Cholera	3 days
24	William Watkins	37	M				Maryland	Oct	Brickmason	Casuality	sudden
25	Nelson (Southall)	28	M	B	S			Jan		Breast	3 days
26	John (Southall)	25	M	M	S			Dec		Cholera	4 days
27	Henry (Southall)	35	M	B	S			Dec		Fever	1 week
28	Mutt (Southall)	101	M	B	S			June		Cholera	1 day
29	Lewis Brewer	58	M	B	F		N.C.	Jan	Laborer	Fever	1 week
30	Daniel Bogart	2m	M				Tenn	Jan		Heart	C
31	John Townsend	1	M				Tenn	June		Cholera	2 days
32	Preston (Bradford)	30	M	B	S			June		Cholera	12 hours
33	Mary Bradford	6m	F				Tenn	Aug		unknown	1 month
34	William R. James	49	M				Kentucky	June	Merchant	Cholera	5 days
35	Becky Walker	45	F	B	S		unknown	Aug		Cholera	1 week

COUNTY OF SHELBY, STATE OF TENNESSEE.

PAGE NO. 695 PERSONS WHO DIED DURING THE YEAR ENDING 1st JUNE, 1850.

1st Ward, Memphis
H. L. Guion

No. of Visit	Name	Age	Sex	Color	Free or Slave	Married/Widowed	Place of Birth	Month Died	Occupation	Disease or Cause of Death	No. Days Ill
1	Mary Pains	4	F				Miss	Aug		Inflamation of bowels	7 days
2	James Grace	53	M			M	Kentucky	Aug	Plaster	Cholera	6 months
3	S. M. Champ	55	M			M	Kentucky	Nov	Capt. Police	Steamboat explosion	————
4	Bridget Flanegan	2	F				Ireland	Jan		Worms	————
5	Molly Fox	3	F				Tenn	July		Cholera	2 hours
6	Ed. Wade	37	M			M	Ireland	Oct	Boatmaker	Inflamation of brain	3 months
7	Mary Fitzgivins	8	F				unknown	March		Burnt	sudden
8	Jas. Rigney	55	M			M	Ireland	July	Laborer	Consumption	6 weeks
9	July Carney	12	F				Kentucky	Aug		Congestive chill	1 day
10	John Carney	3	M				Tenn	Aug		Cholera	1 day
11	Jer. Ragan	40	M				Ireland	Aug	Laborer	Cholera	1 day
12	Thomas Brattleburg	35	M				Ireland	Sept	Laborer	unknown	4 days
13	O. Daniel	33	M				Ireland	May	Laborer	Cholera	11 hours
14	Mr. Schrokman	45	M				Scotland	March	Laborer	Cholera	6 hours
15	Thomas Hennessee	35	M				Ireland	March	Laborer	Cold	2 weeks
16	Cornielia (Tarlton)	1	F	B	S		Tenn	July		Brain fever	1 day
17	Rachael (Tarlton)	1m	F	B	S		Tenn	Jan		Fits	sudden
18	Harmon Biers	46	M			M	New York	Jan	Carpenter	Fever	2 years
19	John Fox	10m	M				Arkansas	April		Fever	4 days
20	Eppy Strahl	49	F			M	Germany	July		Cholera	12 hours
21	Infant Worth	1m	M				Tenn	May		Premature birth	————
22	Nancy Brock	44	F			W	Alabama	Dec		Cholera	10 hours
23	Alphis Peplow	6m	F				Tenn	June		Diarrhea	1 month
24	Moses (Redford)	6m	M	M	S		Tenn	May		Cholera	sudden
25	Pat. Gillorn	1	M				Ireland	June		Teething	9 days
26	Bridget Mary	25	F				Ireland	Aug		Fever	8 days
27	Owen Brannon	35	M			M	Ireland	Dec	Merchant	Casuality	sudden
28	John Doyle	19	M				Ireland	Jan	Laborer	Fever	2 weeks
29	Daniel Daley	56	M			W	Ireland	Sept	Laborer	--illegible--	sudden
30	Bridget Daley	40	F			M	Ireland	July		unknown	Chronic
31	Michl. Marvoney	1	M				Tenn	Jan		Dropsy	Chronic
32	Thomas Marvoney	1	M				Tenn	Jan		Dropsy	Chronic
33	H. L. Ingram	1	M				Tenn	June		Cholera Inf.	Chronic
34	Bristo (Barray)	50	M	B	S		————	July		Apoplexy	sudden
35	Eliza (Barray)	15	F	B	S		————	Aug		Sup. Mens.	6 months

Remarks: In this part of the City, there are many very poor people, many of them are foreigners. Some are almost destitute of the necessities of life which together with the want of comfortable quarters when sick, will account for the number of deaths in this part of the City.

COUNTY OF SHELBY **, STATE OF TENNESSEE.**

PAGE NO. 698 **PERSONS WHO DIED DURING THE YEAR ENDING 1st JUNE, 1850.**

1st Ward, Memphis
H. L. Guion

No. of Visit	Name	Age	Sex	Color	Free or Slave	Married/Widowed	Place of Birth	Month Died	Occupation	Disease or Cause of Death	No. Days Ill
1	Mary Ann Cobb	29	F			M	Kentucky	June		Fever	10 days
2	Robert D. Cobb	11m	M				Tenn	July		Fever	20 days
3	George (Cobb)	16	M	B	S			May		Drowned	sudden
4	unknown	40	M				unknown	June	unknown	Congestion	sudden
5	J. R. Chilcut	40	M			W	Tenn	June	Clerk	Drunkness	5 days
6	Cintha E. Barns	10m	F				Kentucky	June		Teething	2 weeks
7	Claibourn	33	M	B	S			June		Cholera	sudden
8	J. F. Wilks	5	M				Alabama	Aug		Hemorrhage	sudden
9	Sarah Early	24	F				S.C.	Oct		Cholera	10 hours
10	William Burks	45	M			M	Tenn	June	Laborer	Cholera	6 weeks
11	Sarah J. Early	8	F				Illinois	May		Inflamation of brain	5 weeks
12	Cornelia McMahon	3	F				Miss	Feb		Inflamation of brain	2 weeks
13	C. C. Branson	25	M				Alabama	Jan	Farmer	Congestive chill	6 weeks
14	Robert Barnett	3	M				Tenn	Jan		Inflamation of brain	3 years
15	Infant Houston	1m	M				Tenn	Aug		Spasms	1 day
16	Hez. Nevel	55	M			W	unknown	Feb	Grocer	Cholera	2 weeks
17	Jerome Nevel	21	M				unknown	Feb	Laborer	Cholera	2 weeks
18	Robert Bane	30	M			M	unknown	Jan	Laborer	Fever	8 months
19	Martha Bane	19	F				unknown	Jan		Fever	2 weeks
20	Infant Bane	2	F				unknown	Jan		Inflamation of brain	Chronic
21	Frances Dacus	7	F				Tenn	April		Inflamation of brain	2 days
22	Daniel Winchester	41	M			M	unknown	Nov	Farmer	Congestive chill	2 days
23	Mrs. Shellan	35	F				Germany	July		Cholera	1 week
24	Augusta Shellan	8m	M				Germany	July		Cholera	3 days
25	Mr. Canfield	32	M			M	unknown	Oct	Laborer	Drunkness	3 months
26	J. W. Blamit	12	M				Indiana	April		Inflamation of brain	6 days
27	Elijah (Wright)	23	M	M	S			Nov		Cholera	10 days
28	S. Hill	12	M				Tenn	June		Congestive chills	4 days
29	Thomas Seary	22	M				Ireland	Nov	Laborer	Drowned	sudden
30	Pat. Diller	35	M				Ireland	Aug		Fever	5 days
31	Jr. Becholdt	3	M				Tenn	July		Cholera	10 days
32	Cath. Kanile	14	F				Germany	July		Cholera	8 hours
33	Cor. Higgins	14	F				Miss	Oct		Fever	2 weeks
34	Jefferson Higgins	12	M				Miss	Oct		Fever	1 week
35	Stephen Duke	65	M	M	F	M	Va	June	Banker	Cholera	1 week

Remarks: Cholera was epidemic in Memphis in June and July 1849 and in January and February 1850. Small pox during the winter and spring of 1850. The water from wells is rotten limestone. Cisterns are being introduced generally throughout the City. The water from cisterns is thought to be much healthier than that from wells.

COUNTY OF SHELBY, STATE OF TENNESSEE.

PAGE NO. 699 PERSONS WHO DIED DURING THE YEAR ENDING 1st JUNE, 1850.

The Hospital
H. L. Guion

No. of Visit	Name	Age	Sex	Color	Free or Slave	Married/Widowed	Place of Birth	Month Died	Occupation	Disease or Cause of Death	No. Days Ill
1	Francis Maguire	—	M					Jan		Mania -- illegible --	2 days
2	Allen (Negro)	—	M	B	S			Jan		Small pox	12 days
3	Tom (Negro)	—	M	B	S			Jan		Cholera	2 days
4	John Black	—	M					Feb		Diarrhea	C
5	Pat. Mullens	—	M					Jan		Cholera	6 days
6	Andrew Podestra	—	M					Jan		Pneumonia	8 days
7	Thomas McGraw	—	M					Jan		Cholera	5 days
8	John McGraw	—	M					Jan		Cholera	2 days
9	William McGraw	—	M					Jan		Cholera	2 days
10	Edward Bird	—	M					Jan	) (	Scalded by explosion of	5 days
11	Victor Wilt	—	M					Jan	) ------ (	Stmr. Josephus	2 days
12	Thomas Lurry	—	M					Jan	) (	" "	5 days
13	Job Chalfant	—	M					Jan	) (	" "	12 days
14	Mrs. Darcus	—	F					Jan		Cholera	1 day
15	Jerry Sullivan	—	M					Feb		T. fever	2 days
16	Albert (Negro)	—	M	B	S			Feb		Small pox	2 days
17	B. G. Huffner	—	M					March		Suicide & Mania pat.	25 days
18	Allen (Negro)	—	M	B	S			March		Small pox	36 days
19	Pat. Foay	—	M					March		Diarrhea	7 days
20	Jacob Walker	—	M					March		Diarrhea	C
21	Phillis (Negro)	—	F	B	S			March		Small pox	8 days
22	James Dennis	—	M					March		Effects of liquor	6 days
23	Robert Gilberry	—	M					March		Cholera	2 days
24	Flem (Negro)	—	M	B	S			April		Small pox	13 days
25	Henry Spencer	—	M					March		Consumption	12 days
26	Reuben Gillock	—	M					April		Cholera	2 days
27	Lewis (Cooper)	—	M	B	S			April		Small pox	9 days
28	Mrs. Clark	—	F					April		Small pox	4 days
29	John Burk	—	M					April		Diarrhea	4 days
30	Elisha Curry	—	M					April		Small pox	7 days
31	A. L. Matt	—	M					May		T. fever	13 days
32	John Gray	—	M					May		Cholera	8 Days
33	Robert (Brown)	—	M	B	S			May		Small pox	22 days
34	Ann Clark	—	F					May		Small pox	7 days
35	Charles Penrose	—	M					May		Diarrhea	8 days
36	John Hennessee	—	M					May		Congestive fever	2 days

Remarks: The above has been carefully copied from the "Hospital Book" kept by the Hospital Physicians. No ages, places of birth or occupation are given therein.
I, H. L. Guion, do hereby certify that the whole number of pages in this report is twenty two (22) one of which the 18 is blank.
The whole number of deaths reported in Memphis is 354
 "   "   "   "   "   " the County and out of Memphis 469
 "   "   "   "   "   " the Hospital 71
Total in Shelby County, Tennessee 894
and that the same has been made according to the tenor of my official oath. Memphis, December 20, 1850,
H. L. Guion, Asst. Marshal.

COUNTY OF SHELBY, STATE OF TENNESSEE.

PAGE NO. 702   PERSONS WHO DIED DURING THE YEAR ENDING 1st JUNE, 1850.

The Hospital
H. L. Guion

No. of Visit	Name	Age	Sex	Color	Free or Slave	Married/Widowed	Place of Birth	Month Died	Occupation	Disease or Cause of Death	No. Days Ill
1	Charles Grave	—	M			—		June		Cholera	1 day
2	Santo Pernando	—	M			—		June		Mania pat.	2 days
3	William W. Gruver	—	M			—		July		Insanity & Diarrhea	28 days
4	Alfred Bray	—	M			—		June		Cholera	3 days
5	Martha Bray	—	F			—		June		Cholera	5 days
6	Eby Bray	—	F			—		June		Cholera	7 days
7	Indian Agy	—	F	Indian		—		June		Cholera	1 day
8	William Noble	—	M			—		July		unknown	3 days
9	Jacob Lefieldt	—	M			—		July		Concussion brain	5 days
10	William D. Mitchell	—	M			—		Aug		Congestive fever	2 days
11	Pat. Phalon	—	M			—		Sept		Diarrhea	32 days
12	Joseph Bowers	—	M			—		Aug		Diarrhea	4 days
13	James Mulchaly	—	M			—		Aug		Sub.Acute Infl. of stomach	1 day
14	John Garrison	—	M			—		Sept		Phrenitis	12 days
15	John Maccacey	—	M			—		Dec		Dropsy	C
16	Ferrel Murray	—	M			—		Oct		Diarrhea	20 days
17	Mrs. Graham	—	F			—		Aug		Consumption	C
18	Frances Jerry	—	F			—		Oct		Dropsy	C
19	Robert Jerry	—	M			—		Nov		Intermit. fever	30 days
20	William Jerry	—	M			—		Nov		Intermit. fever	31 days
21	Walter Farrel	—	M			—		Oct		Intermit. fever	3 days
22	William Ridley	—	M			—		Oct		Perf. Hemorhage	7 days
23	John Smith	—	M			—		Nov		unknown	2 days
24	John P. Parsons	—	M			—		Dec		Scalded & Mania Prot.	4 days
25	Lawrence Long	—	M			—		Dec		T. fever	2 days
26	William Trimble	—	M			—		Dec		Cholera	4 days
27	James Nicholson	—	M			—		Dec		Cholera	2 days
28	Albert C. Dubois	—	M			—		Feb		Dropsy	C
29	Thomas O'Shanghnessy	—	M			—		Dec		T. fever	4 days
30	Bartley Ward	—	M			—		Dec		Mania P.	2 days
31	James Rush	—	M			—		Dec		Diarrhea	2 days
32	James Carr	—	M			—		Jan		T. fever	10 days
33	John McLackey	—	M			—		Dec		Dropsy	C
34	Hiram Lewis	—	M			—		March		Sore foot	75 days
35	George (Negro)	—	M	B	S	—				Small pox	10 days

Remarks: The Memphis Hospital has an annual appropriation from the State of about $5,000. The City of Memphis defrays the expenses of all paupers sent them by the City authorities.

COUNTY OF SHELBY, STATE OF TENNESSEE.

PAGE NO. 703 PERSONS WHO DIED DURING THE YEAR ENDING 1st JUNE, 1850.

5th Civil District
H. L. Guion

No. of Visit	Name	Age	Sex	Color	Free or Slave	Married/Widowed	Place of Birth	Month Died	Occupation	Disease or Cause of Death	No. Days Ill
1	Maurice (Trigg)	30	M	B	S			July		Cholera	1 day
2	William (Trigg)	4	M	B	S			Oct		Dropsy	C
3	Infant (Trigg)	1m	F	B	S			March		unknown	2 days
4	Charles Branson	26	M				Alabama	Jan	Farmer	Cholera	2 hours
5	Martin Barnett	2	M				Tenn	Jan		Cholera	
6	Cherry (Barnett)	18	F	B	S			Feb		Labor	12 hours
7	Infant (Barnett)		F	B	S			Feb		Still born	0
8	William (Keele)	20	M	M	S			March		Inflamation of brain	3 weeks
9	Ruth Dewhurst	7	F				Indiana	Aug		Cholera	9 hours
10	Mich. Farrell	34	M				Ireland	July	Laborer	Cholera	2 days
11	Stephen Arrington	3m	M				Tenn	March		Inflamation of brain	1 week
12	Terrance McMahon	58	M			W	Ireland	June	Laborer	Chills & Fever	1 week
13	Emaline Carmichael	7m	F				Illinois	July		Cholera	12 hours
14	Infant (Coe)	1	F	B	S			Aug		Chills	C
15	Jas. Osborn	39	F?			W	Tenn	Aug	Farmer	Fever	6 weeks
16	Henry Winn	27	M			W	Kentucky	Dec	Carpenter	Consumption	C
17	Narcissa Newsom	35	F			M	Va	March		Diarrhea	C
18	Georgetta Newsom	14	F				Va	March		Diarrhea	3 weeks
19	Samuel L. Bagley	2m	M				Tenn	Feb		Inflamation of brain	6 days
20	Green D. Harralson	22	M				Alabama	March	none	Bil. Cholic	2 days
21	Theodore Trezecant	2	M				Tenn	Dec		Bowels	3 months
22	York Rembest	45	M	B	S			June		Cholera	10 days
23	Matilda (Rembest)	43	F	B	S			June		Cholera	1 day

Remarks: Country quite level. Soil _____ and quite fertile. Timber white, black and post oak, cypress, poplar and gum all plenty. Water rotten limestone. One well slightly impregnated with sulphur. No rock. Soil well adapted for Indian corn, grapes, turnips and potatoes and produces the largest watermellons..

COUNTY OF SHELBY, STATE OF TENNESSEE.

PAGE NO. 706 PERSONS WHO DIED DURING THE YEAR ENDING 1st JUNE, 1850.

5th Civil District
H. L. Guion

No. of Visit	Name	Age	Sex	Color	Free or Slave	Married/Widowed	Place of Birth	Month Died	Occupation	Disease or Cause of Death	No. Days Ill
1	Littleton (Rembest)	1	M	B	S		Tenn	Aug		Inflamation of bowels	1 week
2	Maria (Peyton)	45	F	B	S			June		White swelling	C
3	Charles A. Leath	29	M				Tenn	Aug	Farmer	Scrofula	C
4	Infant (Leath)	2m	F	M	S			May		Cholera Inf.	2 weeks
5	Cath. S. Cook	45	F			W	S.C.	Dec		Inflamation of stomach	5 days
6	Mary S. Wheatley	29	F			M	Tenn	Dec		Inflamation of stomach	14 days
7	Jack (Caldwell)	55	M	B	S			Jan		Diarrhea	C
8	Sarah Trapp	24	F			W	S.C.	Jan		Fever	2 weeks
9	Fanny (Allen)	90	F	B	S			July		Old age	C
10	Carroline Thompson	5	F				Miss	Sept		Worms	7 days
11	Infant Thompson	1m	M				Tenn	Sept		Croup	3 days
12	Maranda (Yerger)	28	F	B	S			Oct		unknown	4 weeks
13	Infant Mosley	3d	M	B	S			Aug		unknown	
14	Valentine Mosley	5	M	B	S			July		Congestive chills	3 days
15	Infant Bettis	7m	F	B	S			April		unknown	3 days

COUNTY OF SHELBY **, STATE OF TENNESSEE.**

PAGE NO. 707 **PERSONS WHO DIED DURING THE YEAR ENDING 1st JUNE, 1850.**

6th Civil District
H. L. Guion

No. of Visit	Name	Age	Sex	Color	Free or Slave	Married/Widowed	Place of Birth	Month Died	Occupation	Disease or Cause of Death	No. Days Ill
1	Isam (Westbrooks)	5	M	B	S		____	Jan		Chill	sudden
2	Infant Westbrooks	1d	M				____	Dec		Infant	
3	Infant Snead	3m	F				Tenn	June		Inflamation of brain	C
4	Mary Henry	30	F				N.C.	May		Inflamation of brain	2 days
5	Danl. Allen	12	M				N.C.	Oct		Casuality	sudden
6	Mary (Anderson)	8m	F	B	S		____	March		Casuality	sudden
7	Infant Lovell	3m	F				Tenn	April		Hives	7 days
8	Simeon Marsh	67	M			W	N.C.	April	Farmer	Mortification	56 days
9	Jane (Marsh)	16	F	B	S		____	Oct		Scrofula	C
10	Margaret Chafus	38	F	B	F		N.C.	Dec		Quinsy	4 days
11	Alfred Hart	1	M	B	S		____	Sept		Diarrhea	20 days
12	Henry (Hart)	1	M	B	S		____	Oct		Diarrhea	30 days
13	McChristy Sanderlin	44	M			M	N.C.	Feb	Farmer	Small pox	21 days
14	John A. Jones	11	M				Georgia	March		Small pox	14 days
15	Warren (Jones)	50	M	B	S		____	March		Small pox	14 days
16	Rose (Jones)	38	F	B	S		____	March		Small pox	19 days
17	Infant (Jones)	1d	F	B	S		____	March		Small pox	1 day
18	Joseph L. Smith	33	M			M	N.C.	Nov	Farmer	Cholera	
19	Benjamin West	76	M			M	N.C.	March	Farmer	Asthma	12 days
20	E. C. Garrett	9	F				S.C.	March		Burnt	20 days
21	Joseph McPherson	84	M				Penn	May	Pauper	Pneumonia	2 months
22	Reuben (Rutland)	11m	M	B	S		____	July		unknown	

COUNTY OF SHELBY, STATE OF TENNESSEE.

PAGE NO. 710 PERSONS WHO DIED DURING THE YEAR ENDING 1st JUNE, 1850.

6th Civil District
H. L. Guion

No. of Visit	Name	Age	Sex	Color	Free or Slave	Married/Widowed	Place of Birth	Month Died	Occupation	Disease or Cause of Death	No. Days Ill
1	Theodrick (Harrell)	1	M	B	S		——	Jan		Inflamation of brain	3 days
2	Josephine (Harrell)	1	F	B	S		——	Jan		Worms	5 days
3	Ellen (Braswell)	7m	F	B	S		——	Oct		unknown	C
4	Jas. Huffman	1m	M				Tenn	Jan		Croup	1 day
5	Julius Henderson	21	M	B	S		——	April		Cachexia	C
6	Craft (Locke)	4m	M	B	S		——	Dec		Inflamation of brain	1 day
7	Benjamin Hawkins	50	M			M	Tenn	Feb	Physician	Bronchitis	C
8	Patty (Hawkins)	3	F	B	S		——	Jan		Dropsy	C
9	Sarah Alsabrooks	25	F			M	N.C.	Jan		Consumption	C
10	John Alsabrooks	3m	M				Tenn	March		unknown	
11	Sidney McCollum	5m	M	B	S		——	May		Disease of lungs	7 days
12	Alexander (Dickens)	2	M	B	S		——	July		Fever	7 days
13	James (Dickens)	4	M	B	S		——	July		Fever	3 days
14	Infant (Dickens)	1m	F	B	S		——	unknown		unknown	
15	Lilly (Dickens)	6	F	B	S		——	May		Burnt	7 days
16	Reuben (Bryant)	11m	M	B	S		——	July		Diarrhea	14 days
17	George Hocott	2	M				Tenn	June		Cholera	1 day
18	Rhoda Davis	48	F			W	N.C.	July		Cholera	1 day
19	Robert Davis	3	M				Miss	July		Cholera	7 days
20	Roena Pryor	9m	F	B	S		——	March		Teething	6 days
21	Bailey Anderson	54	M			M	S.C.	Feb	Farmer	Murdered	sudden
22	Banjamin (Anderson)	45	M	B	S		——	March		Rheumatism	C
23	Elizabeth Hamrick	11	F				Tenn	Sept		Congestion	3 days
24	William Ferguson	35	M			M	Indiana	Aug	Farmer	Consumption	C
25	John Petworth	9m	M				Tenn	Aug		Dropsy	C
26	John Lewis	3	M				Tenn	July		Congestion	5 days
27	Henry L. Taylor	26	M				Alabama	March	Farmer	Gastritis	C
28	William (Bolton)	2	M	B	S			March		Teething	30 days
29	Allen Ceveley	22	M				Tenn	March	Laborer	Pleurisy	30 days
30	Virginia Kimbro	24	F			M	N.C.	Oct		Pneumonia	21 days
31	Infant (Pope)	3m	F	B	S		——	April		Scrofula	C
32	Infant (Pope)	4m	F	B	S		——	April		Pneumonia	7 days
33	Infant (Pope)	5m	M	B	S		——	May		Pneumonia	6 days
34	Conjo. (Holmes)	60	M	B	S			May		Lungs	C
35	John D. White	55	M			M	Georgia	Sept	Farmer	Enlarhement prostate	C

Remarks: I find that the people will not report many many diseases correctly, for instance: "Hernia", "Gonorrhea", "Mania Paten" and other secret diseases. They are disposed to evade by giving other names rather that the correct ones!

COUNTY OF SHELBY, STATE OF TENNESSEE.

PAGE NO. 711 PERSONS WHO DIED DURING THE YEAR ENDING 1st JUNE, 1850.

8th Civil District
H. L. Guion

No. of Visit	Name	Age	Sex	Color	Free or Slave	Married/Widowed	Place of Birth	Month Died	Occupation	Disease or Cause of Death	No. Days Ill
1	John Rives	81	M			W	Va	May		Diarrhea	15 days
2	Susannah Horne	76	F			W	N.C.	June		Palsy	10 days
3	Rietta Horne	2	F				Tenn	Aug		Whooping cough	14 days
4	Infant (Hays)	1m	F	B	S			Jan		unknown	
5	Monday (Hays)	4	M	B	S			Jan		Whooping cough	
6	Peter (Hays)	1	M	B	S			Aug		Whooping cough	
7	Jacob (Hays)	3	M	B	S			Aug		Whooping cough	
8	Amy (Hays)	2	F	B	S			Sept		Whooping cough	
9	Infant (Hays)	1d	F	B	S			Sept		unknown	
10	Alfred (Hays)	1	M	B	S			Oct		Whooping cough	
11	Stephen (Hays)	1m	M	B	S			Oct		Whooping cough	
12	Adaline (Hays)	4	F	B	S			Oct		Whooping cough	
13	Atney (Hays)	2	M	B	S			Nov		Whooping cough	
14	Rachel Briggs	35	F			W	Tenn	May		Consumption	C
15	Infant (Griffin)	1m	M	B	S			May		Inflamation of bowels	4 days
16	Andy (Griffin)	2	M	B	S			Oct		Diarrhea	7 days
17	Sarah Williams	4m	F				Tenn	June		Inflamation of brain	8 days
18	Edward Woodson	41	M			W	Va	July	Farmer	Measles	49 days
19	Parrot (Royster)	50	M	B	S			July		Pneumonia	4 days
20	Edy (Gillespie)	7	F	B	S			May		Fever	20 days
21	Infant (Donaldson)	1m	M	B	S			May		unknown	
22	Esther (Donaldson)	80	F	B	S			Dec		Old age	C
23	William Cherry	1	M				Tenn	Sept		Phthisic	C
24	Sarah Neal	5	F				Tenn	Nov		Scalded	6 days
25	Thomas (Tourman)	4	M	B	S			Oct		Rheumatism	8 days
26	Mahaly (Tourman)	6	F	B	S			April		Bil. fever	60 days
27	Tessa Wherry	28	F	B	S			Nov		T. fever	20 days
28	Emma Starr	11	F				Tenn	Sept		Congestive fever	3 days
29	Albert (Leak)	1	M	B	S			Jan		Dropsy	C
30	George H. Peoples	1m	M				Tenn	June		unknown	
31	Charles J. Pleasants	32	M				Va	Aug	Physician	Apoplexy	sudden
32	Infant (Wash)	1m	F	B	S			July		unknown	

Remarks: Surface quite rolling. Soil generally thin. White oak, gum and black oak plenty.

H. L. Guion, Asst. Marshal.

COUNTY OF SHELBY **, STATE OF TENNESSEE.**

PAGE NO. 714 **PERSONS WHO DIED DURING THE YEAR ENDING 1st JUNE, 1850.**

7th Civil District

H. L. Guion

No. of Visit	Name	Age	Sex	Color	Free or Slave	Married/Widowed	Place of Birth	Month Died	Occupation	Disease or Cause of Death	No. Days Ill
1	Joseph Howard	4m	M				Va	Dec		Croup	7 days
2	Joshua (Sanders)	8m	M	B	S		Tenn	June		Inflamation of brain	5 days
3	Nancy Pittman	26	F			M	N.C.	Jan		Palsy	C
4	John Sparkman	50	M			M	N.C.	April	Farmer	Dropsy	C
5	Willoby (Daniel)	14	M	M	S			Jan		Burnt	14 days
6	Frank (Daniel)	60	M	B	S			Jan		Dropsy	C
7	Mary McGowen	2	F				Tenn	unknown		Cholera Inf.	7 days
8	Ransom Buck	20	M				N.C.	Oct	Farmer	Consumption	C
9	Sarah (Robins)	6m	F	B	S			June		Inflamation of brain	7 days
10	Martha (Robins)	5m	F	B	S			June		Inflamation of brain	7 days
11	Jane Jones	12	F	B	S			March		Burnt	4 days
12	Eliza (Cole)	30	F	B	S			Jan		unknown	C
13	Sally Willet	5	F	B	S			Aug		Consumption	C
14	Martha Abernathy	1m	F					Aug		unknown	36 days
15	Martha (Anderson)	2m	F	B	S			Oct		Burnt	13 days
16	Eliza (Massey)	1	F	B	S			March		Cold	7 days
17	William (Pulliam)	1	M	B	S			March		unknown	C
18	Infant Pulliam	9m	F					Jan		Cold	10 days
19	Thomas Wood	50	M				Va	Aug	Carpenter	Dropsy	C
20	John (Bond)	16	M	B	S			Oct		Consumption	C
21	Jack (Bond)	25	M	B	S			March		Bronchitis	C
22	Isabella (Bond)	1	F	B	S			March		Diarrhea	C
23	Infant (Bond)	11m	F	B	S			Oct		Croup	sudden
24	Jane (Walsey)	2	F	B	S			July		unknown	C
25	Suckey Ward	40	F	B	S			Feb		Pleurisy	14 days
26	Infant Ward	3m	M	B	S			Nov		unknown	
27	Infant (Bond)	1m	F	B	S			May		unknown	
28	Infant (Harwell)	7m	M	B	S			May		unknown	
29	Infant (Harwell)	7m	F	B	S			unknown		unknown	
30	Thomas H. Bland	11m	M				Tenn	Aug		Consumption	C
31	Infant (Bland)	1m	M	B	S			July		Hives	3 days

Remarks: White oak, black oak and post oak. Surface gently undulated.

COUNTY OF SHELBY, STATE OF TENNESSEE.

PAGE NO. 715 PERSONS WHO DIED DURING THE YEAR ENDING 1st JUNE, 1850.

10th Civil District
H. L. Guion

No. of Visit	Name	Age	Sex	Color	Free or Slave	Married/Widowed	Place of Birth	Month Died	Occupation	Disease or Cause of Death	No. Days Ill
1	Tennessee Yeates	17	F				Tenn	July		Congestion of brain	9 days
2	Amy F. Yeates	2m	F				Tenn	July		Diarrhea	17 days
3	William D. Briley	1m	M				Tenn	Nov		unknown	
4	Infant McDonald	1	F				Tenn	July		Inflamation of brain	40 days
5	Cynthia Hunter	41	F			M	N.C.	July		Cholera Mor.	7 days
6	Elizabeth Hunter	15	F				N.C.	July		Cholera Mor.	7 days
7	Elizabeth Turner	16	F			M	Tenn	May		Erysipelas	10 days
8	Andrew J. Whitehead	15	M				N.C.	Sept	Farmer	T. fever	7 days
9	Alfred (Edmondson)	17	M	B	S		N.C.	Dec		T. fever	8 days
10	Hordy (Edmondson)	1	M	B	S			July		Consumption	C
11	Ann Sullivan	20	F	B	S			March		Fever	14 days
12	Infant Downs	2m	F				Tenn	July		Inflamation of bowels	4 days
13	Esther (Hammond)	33	F	B	S			March		Cold	40 days
14	Jim (Dean)	25	M	B	S			Dec		Pneumonia	10 days
15	Susan (Warner)	2m	F	B	S			May		Lock jaw	1 day
16	Eli (Warner)	20	M	B	S			Jan		Burnt	14 days
17	Infant (Warner)	1m	F	B	S			May		unknown	
18	Martha (Best)	2m	F	B	S			Nov		Scrofula	C
19	Infant Jarmon	1m	M				Tenn	Sept		unknown	
20	Betsey (Gilliland)	11	F	B	S			June		T. fever	20 days
21	Infant (Applewhite)	1	F	B	S			Jan		Whooping cough	60 days
22	Infant (Applewhite)	1	F	B	S			March		Whooping cough	C
23	Infant (Applewhite)	1	M	B	S			Sept		Whooping cough	90 days
24	Sofa (Taylor)	40	F	B	S			Aug		Chronic Dysentery	
25	Harriet (Taylor)	2	F	B	S			March		Worms	2 days
26	Stephen (Taylor)	2	M	B	S			March		Diarrhea	7 days
27	Infant (Taylor)	4m	M	B	S			April		Diarrhea	
28	Infant (Coopwood)	4m	M	B	S			May		Casuality	sudden
29	Infant (McKinney)	1m	M	B	S			Dec		Spasms	C
30	Bob (Polk)	11m	M	B	S			Jan		Cold	10 days
31	Infant Abington	1m	F	B	S			March		Thrash	7 days
32	Stith (Smith)	18	M	B	S			Feb		T. fever	28 days
33	William Smith	4	M				Tenn	Feb		T. fever	21 days
34	David Harvey	1m	M				Tenn	Oct		Spasms	C
35	Dinah (Trezivant)	25	F	B	S			April		unknown	C
36	Carroline (Smith)	4	F	B	S			March		T. fever	20 days
37	Gilbert Miller	60	M	B	S			May		Congestive chills	14 days
38	Sarah B. Webb	67	F				Va	April		T. fever	5 days

Remarks: Surface level. Soil fertile and well adapted to cotton. Timber plenty on the creeks, on the uplands scarce, owing to most of them being in cultivation.

H. L. Guion, Asst. Marshal.

COUNTY OF SHELBY, STATE OF TENNESSEE.

PAGE NO. 718 PERSONS WHO DIED DURING THE YEAR ENDING 1st JUNE, 1850.

9th Civil District
H. L. Guion

No. of Visit	Name	Age	Sex	Color	Free or Slave	Married/Widowed	Place of Birth	Month Died	Occupation	Disease or Cause of Death	No. Days Ill
1	Robert L. Williams	1	M				Tenn	July		unknown	35 days
2	Henry (Crenshaw)	8	M	B	S			Sept		Disease of heart	C
3	John (Crenshaw)	27	M	B	S			Aug		Sun stroke	sudden
4	Infant (Crenshaw)	1m	F	B	S			unknown		unknown	
5	Infant (Crenshaw)	1m	M	B	S			Nov		Croup	1 day
6	Ann (Allen)	1	F	B	S			March		Pneumonia	7 days
7	Eraminta Tulley	8	F				Tenn	Dec		T. fever	15 days
8	Martha (Williams)	7m	F	B	S			unknown		Hives	14 days
9	Lucy (Ecklin)	5	F	B	S			June		Burnt	60 days
10	Elizabeth Knox	54	F				N.C.	May		Consumption	C
11	Jim (Ecklin)	6m	M	B	S			Sept		unknown	7 days
12	Zeek (Ecklin)	50	M	B	S			Dec		Dropsy	C
13	Wallace (Crenshaw)	13	M	B	S			Feb		Cholic	sudden
14	Mary Allen	11	F				Va	July		Congestion	4 days
15	Infant (Sanderlin)	1m	F	B	S			Nov		Croup	1 day
16	John Rutledge	2m	M				Tenn	Dec		Hives	1 day
17	Robert (Reid)	17	M	B	S			July		T. fever	8 days
18	Sally (Reid)	7m	F	B	S			Nov		unknown	C
19	Infant Cathey	1m	F					Sept		unknown	
20	Harvey Compton	27	M				Alabama	July	Physician	Consumption	C
21	Aron Compton	66	M			M	S.C.	Oct	Farmer	Consumption	C
22	William Wesson	30	M				Va	Nov	Farmer	Consumption	C
23	William A. Strong	16	M				Tenn	July	Farmer	T. fever	21 days
24	Martha Strong	11	F				Tenn	March		T. fever	35 days
25	Ann (Hamner)	5	F	B	S			May		unknown	7 days
26	Joel Rutledge	22	M				Tenn	June	none	Enlarged head	C
27	Ann (Rogers)	20	F	B	S			Feb		Pneumonia	7 days
28	Elisha (Patrick)	6m	M	B	S			Jan		Fit	sudden
29	Infant (Abington)	1m	F	B	S			March		Thrush	7 days

Remarks: Part of this District is level and the soil good. Part of this District is rolling and the soil thin. This District is level low and wet. White oak, gum and black oak, plenty.   H. L. Guion, Asst. Marshal.

COUNTY OF SHELBY, STATE OF TENNESSEE.

PAGE NO. 719 PERSONS WHO DIED DURING THE YEAR ENDING 1st JUNE, 1850.

11th Civil District
H. L. Guion

No. of Visit	Name	Age	Sex	Color	Free or Slave	Married/Widowed	Place of Birth	Month Died	Occupation	Disease or Cause of Death	No. Days Ill
1	William Fellows	1m	M				Tenn	July		Spasms	18 days
2	Maria Tyus	40	F	B	S			Feb		unknown	14 days
3	Elijah (Man)	90	M	B	S			Dec		Dropsy	C
4	Harvey (Daugherty)	26	M	B	S			Jan		Cholera	8 days

Remarks: Fine water-power may be obtained in this District on the Wolf River. It is a fine stream of never failing water. In the dryest seasons, there is plenty of water passing down this stream to turn any amount of machinery. enough rock may be obtained near it for foundations.

COUNTY OF SHELBY, STATE OF TENNESSEE.

PAGE NO. 722 PERSONS WHO DIED DURING THE YEAR ENDING 1st JUNE, 1850.

11th Civil District
H. L. Guion

No. of Visit	Name	Age	Sex	Color	Free or Slave	Married/Widowed	Place of Birth	Month Died	Occupation	Disease or Cause of Death	No. Days Ill
1	Simeon L. Echles	1	M				Tenn	Aug		Cholera	2 days
2	Jane (Echles)	2m	F	B	S			Sept		Casuality	7 days
3	Henry E. Massey	4	M				Tenn	Oct		Croup	6 days
4	Martha (Williams)	15	F	B	S			June		Congestion	4 days
5	Nancy (Small)	8	F	B	S			Dec		Casuality	sudden
6	Henry (Stephenson)	3m	F	B	S			Jan		Casuality	sudden
7	Sofa (Stephenson)	47	F	B	S			March		Gravel & Pneumonia	C
8	Josephine (Rutland)	1	F	B	S			Nov		unknown	C
9	Preston (Rutland)	3	M	B	S			Sept		Diarrhea	17 days
10	Robin (Rutland)	3	M	B	S			Nov		Croup	4 days
11	Harriet (Rutland)	1	F	B	S			Jan		Sc. fever	20 days
12	Ann Odom	35	F			W	Va	March		Cancer	C
13	Emeline Odom	5	F				Arkansas	April		Paralysis	C
14	Mary Ann Gray	24	F			M	Alabama	April		T. fever	13 days
15	Benjamin Simmons	51	M			M	Va	July	Carpenter	unknown	C
16	Alexander S. Rhodes	31	M				Kentucky	Oct	Grocery	Casuality	
17	Tilman Goodrich	2	M				Tenn	July		Diarrhea	C
18	Infant (Goodrich)	1m	M	B	S			March		unknown	
19	Infant (Goodrich)	1m	F	B	S			April			
20	Luckey (Walker)	30	F	B	S			May		Consumption	C
21	Rosetta (Mosby)	16	F	B	S			Aug		T. fever	28 days
22	John Fellow	2	M				Tenn	Aug		Diarrhea	9 days
23	William Bishop	3	M				Tenn	Jan		Cholera Inf.	6 days
24	Infant Rhodes	1m	M				Tenn	Sept		unknown	
25	Abner Rhodes	61	M				N.C.	Nov	Millwright	Consumption	C
26	Levi C. Hodges	8m	M				Tenn	June		Cholera Inf.	5 days
27	Fred Frick	1m	M				Tenn	May		unknown	3 days
28	Infant Eldridge	6m	F				Tenn	Nov		Inflamation of brain	1 day
29	Pleasant Harrison	47	M	B	S			June		Congestive brain	3 days
30	Robert Williamson	3m	M				Tenn	Sept		Congestive chills	1 day
31	Mary Williamson	3	F				Tenn	Sept		Congestive chills	3 days
32	Laura (Quemichett)	7m	F	B	S			unknown		Fits	C
33	Watson (Quemichett)	3m	M	B	S			unknown		unknown	2 days
34	Infant (Quemichett)	1m	M	B	S			unknown		unknown	sudden
35	Chany (Harrison)	57	F	B	S			Sept		unknown	sudden

Remarks: Same remarks as on "No. 10", will apply to this.

COUNTY OF SHELBY, STATE OF TENNESSEE.

PAGE NO. 723 PERSONS WHO DIED DURING THE YEAR ENDING 1st JUNE, 1850.

12th Civil District

H. L. Guion

No. of Visit	Name	Age	Sex	Color	Free or Slave	Married/Widowed	Place of Birth	Month Died	Occupation	Disease or Cause of Death	No. Days Ill
1	Martha (Mathews)	8	F	B	S			March		Casuality	1 day
2	Jack (Watson)	5m	M	B	S			April		Fits	C
3	Lucy J. Wilbourn)	1	F				Tenn	Nov		Cancer	C
4	Infant (Wilbourn)	2m	F	B	S			July		Casuality	sudden
5	David Vance	45	M			M	Va	Jan	Farmer	Heart & Lungs	28 days
6	Infant (Holmes)	7m	F	B	S			Dec		Worms	3 days
7	Isaac Vanhook	2	M				Tenn	Aug		Teething	42 days
8	Tinsly Davis	62	M			W	Va	Jan	Farmer	Pleurisy	8 days
9	Dolly (Davis)	50	F	B	S			Nov		Liver	C
10	Fanny (Davis)	4m	F	B	S			Dec		Cold	1 day
11	Maria (Davis)	1	F	B	S			Aug		Croup	14 days
12	Will (Templeton)	60	M	B	S			June		Cholera	4 days
13	Emma (Plunket)	22	F	B	S			March		Sc. fever	21 days
14	Infant Pool	5m	F					Feb		unknown	C
15	Infant (Smith)	1	F					May		unknown	C
16	Sarah (Baker)	40	F	B	S			March		unknown	C
17	Jos. (Baker)	6	M	B	S			March		Measles	C
18	Lewis (Baker)	25	M	B	S			Aug		Lightening	sudden
19	Hannah (Lewis)	3	F	B	S			Dec		Croup	1 day
20	Willie (Dunn)	10m	M	B	S			unknown		unknown	30 days

COUNTY OF SHELBY, STATE OF TENNESSEE.

PAGE NO. 726 PERSONS WHO DIED DURING THE YEAR ENDING 1st JUNE, 1850.

12th Civil District

H. L. Guion

No. of Visit	Name	Age	Sex	Color	Free or Slave	Married/Widowed	Place of Birth	Month Died	Occupation	Disease or Cause of Death	No. Days Ill
1	Shelah (Roseborough)	80	F	B	S			Dec		Old age	3 weeks
2	Betty (Roseborough)	5	F	B	S			Jan		Cold	2 weeks
3	Malinda (Roseborough)	23	F	B	S			March		Pneumonia	1 month
4	Infant (Owen)	1m	M	B	S			Jan		Tetanus	3 days
5	Infant (Owen)	1m	M	B	S			Feb		Tetanus	3 days
6	Osbern (Nelson)	34	M	B	S			April		Consumption	C
7	Jane Reynolds	50	F			W	N.C.	Dec		Pneumonia	8 days
8	Infant (Howard)	2m	F	B	S			May		Worms	7 days
9	Wash (Trezevant)	30	M	B	S			Sept		Congestive chills	4 days
10	Bil (Jones)	25	M	B	S			May		Casuality	sudden
11	Kate (White)	38	F	B	S			April		T. fever	35 days
12	Infant (Williams)	2m	F	B	S			Jan		Casuality	sudden
13	Error here in original copy.										
14	Nancy (Norris)	60	F	B	S			Jan		Pneumonia	3 days
15	Bil (Norris)	12	M	B	S			Jan		Worms	2 days
16	Mary Key	32	F			M	Va	Nov		T. fever	C
17	Floyd (Herron)	5m	M	B	S			May		Congestive brain	4 days
18	Infant (Herron)	1m	M	B	S			March		Casuality	sudden
19	Infant (Herron)	3m	F	B	S			April		Casuality	sudden
20	Infant (Herron)	7m	F	B	S			April		Diarrhea	3 days
21	Susan S. Bradley	25	F			M	Va	July		Inflamation of bowels	9 days
22	William (Bradley)	3	M	B	S			June		Worms	7 days
23	Infant (Bradley)	1m	M	B	S			Sept		unknown	
24	Henry (Walker)	3	M	B	S			May		T. fever	14 days
25	Pinkney (Dawson)	20	M	B	S			April		Pneumonia	10 days
26	Washington (Ragland)	3	M	B	S			March		Worms	7 days
27	Maria (Ragland)	38	F	B	S			May		unknown	C
28	Justin Smith	77	M				Conn	May	Druggist	Disease of lungs	C
29	David Greer	6m	M	B	S			May		Fever	21 days
30	Adelia Beck	10m	F				Tenn	July		Teething	60 days

COUNTY OF SHELBY, STATE OF TENNESSEE.

PAGE NO. 726 PERSONS WHO DIED DURING THE YEAR ENDING 1st JUNE, 1850.

12th Civil District
H. L. Guion

No. of Visit	Name	Age	Sex	Color	Free or Slave	Married/Widowed	Place of Birth	Month Died	Occupation	Disease or Cause of Death	No. Days Ill
31	Ned (Hamlin)	23	M	B	S		—	May		Pneumonia	7 days
32	Infant (Douglass)	3m	F	B	S		—	March		Cold	40 days
33	Lucy (Sims)	41	F	B	S		—	Sept		Diarrhea	C
34	Isaac Mathews	62	M			M	S.C.	Sept	Farmer	Congestive lungs	10 days
35	Anna (Mathews)	27	F	B	S		—	June		Labor	9 days

Remarks: White, black oak and post oak plenty. Surface level or gently undulating. Water, freestone. Soil fertile and well adapted to the growth of cotton.

COUNTY OF SHELBY, STATE OF TENNESSEE.

PAGE NO. 727 PERSONS WHO DIED DURING THE YEAR ENDING 1st JUNE, 1850.

13th Civil District
H. L. Guion

No. of Visit	Name	Age	Sex	Color	Free or Slave	Married/Widowed	Place of Birth	Month Died	Occupation	Disease or Cause of Death	No. Days Ill
1	William (Mitchell)	1	M	B	S		—	May		unknown	3 months
2	Hixey (Mitchell)	1	F	B	S		—	April		Inflamation of brain	1 day
3	Alfred (Penson)	5	M	B	S		—	March		Burnt	15 days
4	Aron (Lundy)	27	M	B	S		—	Nov		T. fever	21 days
5	Shad (Lundy)	50	M	M	S		—	March		Consumption	C
6	Jacob (Eldridge)	75	M	B	S		—	Jan		Pneumonia	14 days
7	Lewis Stinson	9m	M				Tenn	Sept		Chills	30 days
8	Phoeby (Wheatley)	55	F	B	S			May		Flow memstoris	C
9	Jim (Wheatley)	22	M	B	S		—	June		unknown	sudden
10	Infant Peoples	2m	F				Tenn	May		Casuality	sudden
11	Vina (Johnson)	37	F	B	S		—	March		Consumption	C
12	Eliza (Johnson)	5	F	B	S		—	April		Consumption	C
13	Alex (Johnson)	4	M	B	S		—	April		Scrofula	C
14	Jessee (Mays)	18	M	B	S		—	May		Liver complaint	40 days
15	Infant (Persons)	5m	M	B	S		—	July		Pneumonia	2 days
16	Infant (Persons)	7m	M	B	S		—	Sept		Congestive chills	3 days
17	Sally (Persons)	2	F	B	S		—	Sept		Congestive chills	3 days
18	Annis (Rodgers)	16	F	B	S		—	July		Sub. menses	3 days

Remarks: In this District, a Mr. Williams, his wife, two or three children and two or three of his negroes, died. I could find no one to report them correctly. Was told they died of typhoid fever.
Soil alluvial and fertile. Well adapted to cotton, corn and grapes. Timber abundant and large, white oak, poplar, gum, cypress, hickory, ash, and cottonwood. Water plenty generally good. This District is on the Mississippi River, below Memphis, about falf river bottom, the larger portion of which is subject to inundation.

COUNTY OF SHELBY, STATE OF TENNESSEE.

PAGE NO. 729 PERSONS WHO DIED DURING THE YEAR ENDING 1st JUNE, 1850.

14th Civil District
H. L. Guion

No. of Visit	Name	Age	Sex	Color	Free or Slave	Married/Widowed	Place of Birth	Month Died	Occupation	Disease or Cause of Death	No. Days Ill
1	John (Gilbert)	60	M	B	S			Feb		Small pox	35 days
2	Henry (Gilbert)	40	M	B	S			April		Fever	C
3	William Newberry	48	M				U.S.	Sept	unknown	Murdered	sudden
4	Infant (Lowrance)	1m	M	B	S			Aug		unknown	
5	Daniel Ferguson	19	M				Alabama	April	Laborer	Consumption	C
6	Charles Cosner	3	M				La	Aug		Inflamation of brain	30 days
7	Morris (Triggs)	45	M	B	S			Aug		Consumption	C

Remarks: This District includes the surburbs, south east of Memphis. A great quanitity of timber has been cut in this District, in the last few years, consequently much decayed timber, stumps, etc., are left on the ground. The land is high and dry and apparently there is no local cause for disease.

COUNTY OF SHELBY, STATE OF TENNESSEE.

PAGE NO. 732 PERSONS WHO DIED DURING THE YEAR ENDING 1st JUNE, 1850.

14th Civil District
H. L. Guion

No. of Visit	Name	Age	Sex	Color	Free or Slave	Married/Widowed	Place of Birth	Month Died	Occupation	Disease or Cause of Death	No. Days Ill
1	Benjamin Wester	23	M			M	Va	June	Coach	Cholera	9 hours
2	Elvira (Botts)	16	F	B	S			June		Cholera	18 hours
3	Hannah (Botts)	2	F	B	S			Feb		Sc. fever	4 days
4	Infant (Botts)	4m	F	B	S			Feb		Sc. fever	1 day
5	Martha B. Botts	1	F				Tenn	Feb		Sc. fever	1 day
6	Infant (Stewart)	6m	M	B	S			Dec		unknown	10 days
7	Sarah Delanney	29	F			M	Georgia	Jan		T. fever	10 days
8	Sarah Grooms	3	F				Missouri	Oct		Croup	C
9	Pat. Ahern	35	M			M	Ireland	Aug	Coffeehouse	Congestive chills	1 day
10	Susan Anderson	4	F				Arkansas	Jan		Dropsy	4 weeks
11	Rutha Anderson	1m	F				Arkansas	Jan		Sc. fever	3 days
12	John Hamrick	9	M				Alabama	May		T. fever	9 days
13	Isabel Wayman	1	F				Tenn	July		Cholera	3 weeks
14	Mary (Frazser)	4	F	B	S			March		Worms	3 months
15	Benjamin (Carr)	40	M	B	S			June		Cholera	3 days
16	Henry A. Belost	41	M			M	Tenn	April	Farmer	Consumption	C
17	Sofa (Belost)	42	F	B	S			Feb		Consumption	1 year
18	Emery Carlton	37	M			M	Va	May	Brickmason	Cholera	9 days
19	Frank Madden	41	M			M	Tenn	June	Carpenter	Cholera	1 day
20	Eliza Madden	4	F				Tenn	July		Congestive chills	9 hours
21	George (Madden)	26	M	B	S			Jan		Small pox	9 days
22	Tom (Lewis)	1	M	B	S			June		Worms	2 weeks
23	Mathew (Lewis)	11	M	B	S			July		Scrofula	C
24	Peter (Lewis)	10m	M	B	S			July		Casuality	2 weeks
25	John Pool	1	M				Miss. River	May		Hives	10 hours
26	Fredonia Carawell	27	F			M	Tenn	June		Consumption	C
27	Wash. Belost	33	M	B	S			April		Small pox	15 days
28	Evaline Brown	24	F	B	S			July		Cholera	8 hours
29	Susan McCabe	32	F	B	S			Dec		Cholera	3 hours
30	Infant (McCabe)	1m	F	B	S			Aug		Jaundice	4 days
31	Salina (Connell)	35	F	B	S			Oct		Liver	C
32	Allen (Parton)	26	M	B	S			Dec		Small pox	14 days
33	Robert (Parton)	1m	M	B	S			Dec		unknown	
34	Francis W. Goff	1w	M					April		unknown	
35	Zach (Gilbert)	55	M	B	S			Jan		Small pox	21 days

COUNTY OF SHELBY, STATE OF TENNESSEE.

PAGE NO. 733 PERSONS WHO DIED DURING THE YEAR ENDING 1st JUNE, 1850.

3rd Civil District
H. L. Guion

No. of Visit	Name	Age	Sex	Color	Free or Slave	Married/Widowed	Place of Birth	Month Died	Occupation	Disease or Cause of Death	No. Days Ill
1	Lucy (Harrell)	1	F	B	S		———	Aug		Croup	2 hours
2	Martin Hays	19	M				Tenn	March	Farmer	Congestive chills	2 days
3	Mary McMahan	11m	F				Tenn	June		Croup	60 days
4	Rutha (Person)	25	F	B	S		———	March		Congestive chill	sudden
5	Ned (Moore)	50	M	B	S		———	April		Abscess of lungs	6 days
6	Sarah Bass	11m	F				Tenn	May		--illegible--	60 days
7	Joel Crenshaw	75	M			M	Va	Dec	Farmer	Old age	C
8	Job (Ralston)	9	M	B	S		———	Sept		unknown	C
9	Margaret (King)	2	F	B	S		———	Oct		Worms	C
10	Garnet (Golasby)	22	M	B	S		———	Aug		T. fever	14 days
11	Susan (Golasby)	13	F	B	S		———	Aug		T. fever	8 days
12	Adaline (Golasby)	12	F	B	S		———	Aug		T. fever	8 days
13	John (Golasby)	13	M	B	S		———	Aug		T. fever	42 days
14	Mary (Golasby)	11	F	B	S		———	Aug		T. fever	28 days
15	Infant (Golasby)	9m	M	B	S		———	Sept		T. fever	30 days
16	Infant (Golasby)	8m	F	B	S		———	Sept		T. fever	30 days
17	Emily Crenshaw	16	F				Tenn	Feb		T. fever	28 days
18	Mathew Dubose	15	M	B	S		———	Nov		T. fever	42 days
19	Eugenia (Dubose)	3	F	B	S		———	Nov		Bronchitis	14 days
20	Martha Simmons	2	F				Tenn	Aug		Bil. fever	9 days
21	Susan (Ward)	32	F	B	S		———	Jan		Pneumonia	10 days

Remarks: Surface level. Soil good. White oak and poplar plenty, some cypress. No rocks. Considerable portion low wet land. Good water power.

COUNTY OF SHELBY, STATE OF TENNESSEE.

PAGE NO. 736 PERSONS WHO DIED DURING THE YEAR ENDING 1st JUNE, 1850.

4th Civil District
H. L. Guion

No. of Visit	Name	Age	Sex	Color	Free or Slave	Married/Widowed	Place of Birth	Month Died	Occupation	Disease or Cause of Death	No. Days Ill
1	Lydia Laws	18	F				N.C.			Cholera	1 day
2	James Fry	32	M				Tenn	Oct	Farmer	Quinsy	3 days
3	Ann Henderson	2m	F				Miss	Aug		Inflamation of brain	3 days
4	Isaac Ball	2	M				Tenn	June		Inflamation of brain	1 day
5	Thomas Osbern	34	M			M	Alabama	Jan	Farmer	Casuality	sudden
6	William T. Bateman	1	M				Tenn	Sept		Worms	1 day
7	Infant Ruffin	0	F				Tenn	April		Infant	0 day
8	Fanny McCoy	40	F			M	N.C.	April		Chills	C
9	Goffy Ann Whitworth	7	F				Tenn	Sept		Casuality	4 days
10	Mary Whitworth	4	F				Tenn	Dec		unknown	C
11	Jo (Harrell)	40	M	B	S		———	Dec		Apoplexy	sudden
12	Ellen (Ware)	21	F	B	S		———	May		unknown	25 days
13	Quash (Whitfield)	48	M	B	S		———	unknown		Pneumonia	10 days
14	Infant (Whitfield)	6m	F	B	S		———	unknown		Casuality	14 days

Remarks: This District lies immediately above Memphis on the Mississippi River. About half of it is subject to overflow. Surface either level or very broken. White oak, cypress, red gum, ash, cottonwood and yellow poplar in abundance. Soil where above overflow and not too broken. Very fertile land. Cheap, say from $1.00 to $10.00 per acre.

COUNTY OF SHELBY, STATE OF TENNESSEE.

PAGE NO. 737 PERSONS WHO DIED DURING THE YEAR ENDING 1st JUNE, 1850.

2nd Civil District
H. L. Guion

No. of Visit	Name	Age	Sex	Color	Free or Slave	Married/Widowed	Place of Birth	Month Died	Occupation	Disease or Cause of Death	No. Days Ill
1	Hugh B. Smith	18	M				Tenn	Sept	Farmer	Inflamation of bowels	11 days
2	Joseph T. Johnson	4	M				Tenn	Aug		Fever	5 days
3	Frances Johnson	1m	F				Tenn	Feb		unknown	10 days
4	Infant Sloan	1d	M				Tenn	June		unknown	1 day
5	Simeon (Dubose)	21	M	B	S		____	April		Casuality	2 days
6	Infant (Corbit)	4d	F	B	S		____	April		unknown	
7	Cesar A. Jones	37	M				Va	Dec	Physician	T. fever	14 days
8	Dianah (Jones)	27	F	B	S		____	Jan		Labor	3 days
9	Prince (Jones)	95	M	B	S		____	Sept		Old age	C
10	Infant (Bolton)	1m	F	B	S		____	April		unknown	sudden
11	Susan (Bolton)	1	F	B	S		____	June		Teething	3 days
12	Infant (Dickens)	1	M	B	S		____	Jan		unknown	
13	Infant (Dickens)	3m	F	M	S		____	Feb		unknown	
14	Infant (Dickens)	1m	M	M	S		____	Feb		unknown	
15	John May	51	M				N.C.	Dec	none	Consumption	C
16	Infant (Geers)	3m	F	B	S		____	Feb		Casuality	sudden

Remarks: Surface level. Soil very good. White oak, black oak and yellow poplar plenty.

COUNTY OF SHELBY, STATE OF TENNESSEE.

PAGE NO. 740 PERSONS WHO DIED DURING THE YEAR ENDING 1st JUNE, 1850.

1st Civil District
H. L. Guion

No. of Visit	Name	Age	Sex	Color	Free or Slave	Married/Widowed	Place of Birth	Month Died	Occupation	Disease or Cause of Death	No. Days Ill
1	Robert Dallas	35	M			M	Tenn	Sept	Farmer	Consumption	C
2	Leonard Goss	11m	M				Tenn	Dec		Teething	40 days
3	Jeremiah McBride	3	M				Tenn	May		T. fever	21 days
4	John Miller	8	M	B	S		____	Oct		Casuality	sudden
5	Mary Lane	1m	F				Tenn	Feb		Hives	20 days
6	Infant Ruddle	1m	M				Tenn	Dec		Croup	2 days
7	Mariah Battle	130	F	B	S		Africa	June		Old age	C
8	Infant Kelly	1d	M				Tenn	June		unknown	
9	Kissiah (Faulk)	2	F	B	S		____	Oct		unknown	4 days
10	Jas. Ballard	1m	M				Tenn	July		unknown	35 days
11	William Branch	1	M				Tenn	Sept		Burnt	24 days
12	Elvira L. Dickerson	22	F			M	Tenn	Jan		Congestion	3 days
13	John Maloney	1	M				Tenn	Sept		Diarrhea	14 days
14	Margaret (Starks)	26	F	B	S		____	Oct		Consumption	C
15	Frances Seward	41	F			M	Va	Oct		Cancer	C
16	Infant (Sanderlin)	2d	M	B	S		____	Oct		unknown	
17	Infant (Sanderlin)	2d	M	B	S		____	Oct		unknown	
18	Matilda Hill	28	F			M	N.C.	April		Labor	3 hours
19	Polly Bledsoe	64	F	B	S		____	Oct		Intermit. fever	10 days
20	Infant (Bolton)	1w	F	B	S		____	Jan		unknown	
21	Edy (Bolton)	30	F	B	S		____	Jan		Labor	1 day
22	Jake (Bolton)	8m	M	B	S		____	Jan		Diarrhea	1 day
23	Infant (Bolton)	2w	F	B	S		____	Jan		unknown	
24	Infant Parker	3m	F				Tenn	March		Diarrhea	20 days
25	Infant Parker	3m	F				Tenn	March		Diarrhea	28 days
26	James Ward	3m	M				Tenn	June		Diarrhea	7 days
27	Nancy Hays	78	F			W	Va	Dec		Old age	sudden

Remarks: Soil generally good. Surface level or gently undulating. Water through this Country is generally freestone, except near Memphis. It is rotten limestone. The very best of white oak abounds in this District.

COUNTY OF SMITH, STATE OF TENNESSEE.

PAGE NO. 741 PERSONS WHO DIED DURING THE YEAR ENDING 1st JUNE, 1850.

South Division
Jefferson Jones

No. of Visit	Name	Age	Sex	Color	Free or Slave	Married/Widowed	Place of Birth	Month Died	Occupation	Disease or Cause of Death	No. Days Ill
1	Joseph Bridges	75	M			M	N.C.	July	Laborer	Cholera	3 days
2	Judah Sawers	40	F	B	S		Va	Aug		Chronic	60 days
3	Garland McAllister	65	M			M	N.C.	May	Laborer	Palsy	3 days
4	Federick Barksdale	35	M	B	S		Tenn	April		Accident	sudden
5	David Chambers	1m	M				Tenn	July		Chronic	10 days
6	Sarah Barksdale	75	F	B	S		Va	Aug		Chronic	10 days
7	Milly Barksdale	50	F	B	S		N.C.	Sept		Chronic	30 days
8	William	2	M				Tenn	June		Dysentery	20 days
9	Ruth Hicks	2	F				Tenn	July		unknown	18 days
10	Cyntha Burton	23	F			M	Tenn	Aug		unknown	15 days
11	Mich'd Douglass	36	F?				Va	Aug		Flux	17 days
12	Benjamin	2	M	B	S		Tenn	March		Chronic	31 days
13	Reuben Page	23	M	B	S		Tenn	May		Cholera	2 days
14	Carrol	19	M	B	S		Tenn	Feb		Chronic	6 days
15	Martha Stone	20	F			M	Tenn	July		Flux	9 days
16	Ann	31	F	B	S		Tenn	Sept		Consumption	100 days
17	Burton	1	M	B	S		Tenn	Dec		Scrofula	60 days
18	Ann	3	F	B	S		Tenn	Dec		Cholera	1 day
19	Margriet Norris	27	F			M	Tenn	Aug		Inflamation of stomach	11 days
20	Shearard Rucks	79	M	M	S		N.C.	May		Old age	90 days
21	Franklin	40	M	B	S		Kentucky	May		Accident	3 days
22	Lydia	25	F	M	S		Tenn	July		Cholera	1 day
23	Isaac	15	M	B	S		Tenn	Nov		Fever	10 days
24	Catherine Moore	34	F			M	Tenn	June		Consumption	30 days
25	Armstead Moore	7	M				Tenn	June		Flux	11 days
26	John Gaddy	7	M				Tenn	June		Flux	40 days
27	Lazzett	4	F	B	S		Tenn	Jan		Chronic	30 days
28	James	6m	M	M	S		Tenn	Feb		Smothered	sudden
29	John	3m	M	B	S		Tenn	Dec		Croup	sudden
30	Tabitha Flippin	35	F			M	Tenn	Oct		Fever	2 days
31	Malina	21	F	B	S		Tenn	Dec		Chronic	40 days
32	Susan Hazzard	55	F			W	Va	Aug		Palsy	2 days
33	Martin McCall	22	M			M	Tenn	Feb	Doctor	Fever	20 days
34	Harris	9	M	B	S		Tenn	March		Drowned	sudden
35	Edward F. Dillard	1	F?				Tenn	Dec		Chronic	30 days

Remarks: The small-pox, an unusual disease in my District prevailed during the months March, April and May, in a fearful form. The supposed cause of its inception, the neighborhood where it raged, is attributed to the discharging of a green matter, being and rabed on the barrel and lock by a Physician clandestinely individual who fired off the gum was attacked of soil disease on the 9th day afterward. There were 152 cases and 28 deaths.

COUNTY OF SMITH, STATE OF TENNESSEE.

PAGE NO. 743 PERSONS WHO DIED DURING THE YEAR ENDING 1st JUNE, 1850.

South Division
Jefferson Jones

No. of Visit	Name	Age	Sex	Color	Free or Slave	Married/Widowed	Place of Birth	Month Died	Occupation	Disease or Cause of Death	No. Days Ill
1	Ann Pane	18	F	M	S		Tenn	Jan		Consumption	100 days
2	Edith	38	F	B	S		Tenn	May		Fever	8 days
3	Pheba	19	F	M	S		Tenn	Dec		Consumption	100 days
4	Peter	8m	M	M	S		Tenn	July		Inflamation of brain	10 days
5	Phillip Pope	86	M			M	N.C.	May	Laborer	Fever	9 days
6	Levi	50	M	B	S		Tenn	June		Cholera	15 days
7	David	19	M	B	S		Tenn	June		Flux	15 days
8	Lucinda	5	F	M	S		Tenn	June		Cholera	2 days
9	Amy	7	F	B	S		Tenn	Feb		Fever	10 days
10	Tatton Hughes	80	M			M	Va	April		Chronic	90 days
11	William Voilett	9m	M				Tenn	June		Diarrhea	15 days
12	Ann Enochs	67	F				N.C.	Nov		Cholera	3 days
13	Ewing Bell	42	M			M	Tenn	Sept	Laborer	Fever	15 days
14	Bryant Warde	12	M				Tenn	Feb		Fever	30 days
15	Martha Warde	41	F			M	N.C.	April		Fever	35 days
16	Susan	32	F	B	S		Tenn	April		Fever	10 days
17	Harriet	12	F	B	S		Tenn	March		Fever	10 days
18	Susan	13	F	B	S		Tenn	Nov		Fever	15 days
19	Nancy D. Wilson	23	F				Tenn	Nov		Fever	15 days
20	James Green	54	M				Va	Oct	Laborer	unknown	12 days
21	Mary	6	F	B	S		Tenn	March		Fever	20 days
22	Elizabeth Morran	1	F				Tenn	Jan		Flux	5 days
23	Martha Bray	47	F				Va	Sept		Chronic	sudden
24	Zerelda Pascal	21	F				Tenn	April		Small pox	6 days
25	Louisa Pascal	2	F				Tenn	March		Small pox	6 days
26	Elizabeth Bradford	35	F			M	Tenn	Oct		Fever	30 days
27	James Bradford	7	M				Tenn	Oct		Fever	65 days
28	Sarah Bradford	9	M?				Tenn	Aug		Fever	22 days
29	Robert Bradford	1	M				Tenn	Aug		Fever	20 days
30	Lucy	18	F	B	S		Tenn	Oct		Fever	25 days
31	Alexander Dickerson	16	M				Tenn	Jan	Laborer	Fever	3 days
32	Leroy Dickerson	7	M				Tenn	Jan		Fever	10 days
33	Martha Dickerson	2	F				Tenn	June		Fever	5 days
34	John	6m	M	B	S		Tenn	March		sudden	
35	Nathan	10m	M	B	S		Tenn	Sept		Fever	3 days

Remarks: The character of the water, limestone, is the most common, there are few freestone springs and also a few sulphur springs. The soil is generally black however in some portions of my District, the soil is oa a Molatto colour. Rock, limestone, black and gray fine rock and stone and flint rock.

COUNTY OF SMITH, STATE OF TENNESSEE.

PAGE NO. 745 PERSONS WHO DIED DURING THE YEAR ENDING 1st JUNE, 1850.

South Division
Jefferson Jones

No. of Visit	Name	Age	Sex	Color	Free or Slave	Married/Widowed	Place of Birth	Month Died	Occupation	Disease or Cause of Death	No. Days Ill
1	Charles	1m	M	B	S		Tenn	July		sudden	
2	John Deney	29	M				Tenn	Aug	Laborer	Cholera	4 days
3	Agness House	1	F	B	S		Tenn	Aug		unknown	50 days
4	William C. Hubbard	38	M			M	Tenn	March	Laborer	Consumption	78 days
5	John Federick	70	M			M	Va	Aug	Blk-smith	Gravel	4 years
6	James Smith	55	M			M	N.C.	Feb		Palsy	sudden
7	Elias House	20	M				Tenn	April	Laborer	Fever	10 days
8	Harriet Paschal	40	F			M	Va	June		Henorrhage	1 day
9	Ester Averett	70	F				N.C.	Oct		Chronic	15 days
10	Willis Averett	1m	M	B	S		Tenn	Oct		Cold	3 days
11	Willis Whitley	44	M			M	N.C.	Feb	Laborer	Consumption	60 days
12	Sarah Andrews	36	F			M	Va	Dec		Chronic	100 days
13	Jessey Andrews	6m	M				Va	July		Fever	20 days
14	Stephen Sampson	69	M			W	Va	June	Laborer	Chronic	sudden
15	William Jackson	1m	M				Tenn	Aug		Croup	1 day
16	Ammon Borum	10m	M				Tenn	Sept		Bowels	10 days
17	Darthula Borum	24	F			M	Tenn	Jan		Fever	21 days
18	Daniel Allen	9	M				Tenn	Dec		sudden	
19	Ann E. Whitley	29	F			M	Va	June		Chronic	50 days
20	Elizabeth Parrot	31	F			M	Tenn	May		Cold	15 days
21	Hardy Boze	90	M			W	Va	July	Carpenter	Chronic	60 days
22	Mary Parrot	4	F				Tenn	Aug		Cholera	2 days
23	Cornelia	6m	F	B	S		Tenn	Aug		unknown	5 days
24	Rachael	15	F	B	S		Tenn	Oct		Consumption	100 days
25	Arrena Porter	1	F				Tenn	April		Chronic	30 days
26	Margaret	27	F	B	S		Tenn	Jan		Pleurisy	10 days
27	John F. Winfry	46	M			M	Va	June	Laborer	Consumption	150 days
28	Margaret	80	F	B	S		N.C.	Oct		Old age	00
29	Christopher Manners	19	M				Tenn	Nov	Laborer	Dropsy	30 days
30	Mary Manners	1	F				Tenn	Sept		Teething	20 days
31	Mathew C. Cowen	10m	M				Tenn	July		Croup	1 day
32	George	1	M	B	S		Tenn	Feb		Fever	10 days
33	James Manners	22	M			M	Tenn	Aug	Laborer	Consumption	100 days
34	Elizabeth Andrews	4	F				Tenn	June		Croup	3 days
35	Delila Bush	10	F				Tenn	Dec		Dropsy	100 days

Remarks: The natural growth of timber: beech, poplar, white, black, red and chenquepin oak, white and black walnut, sygartree, elm, white and black ash, cedar, hickory, chestnut, sweetgum, dogwood, paw paw, mulberry and a few cherry trees comprise the natural growth of timber in my division. Considerable quantity of lime is made. No mines, or ore in the division.

COUNTY OF SMITH, STATE OF TENNESSEE.

PAGE NO. 747 PERSONS WHO DIED DURING THE YEAR ENDING 1st JUNE, 1850.

South Division
Jefferson Jones

No. of Visit	Name	Age	Sex	Color	Free or Slave	Married/Widowed	Place of Birth	Month Died	Occupation	Disease or Cause of Death	No. Days Ill
1	Martha Canton	12	F				Tenn	June		Fever	5 days
2	James Wilson	1	M				Tenn	July		Dropsy	20 days
3	John Bailiff	2	M				Tenn	June		Bronchitis	4 days
4	James Parker	30	M				Tenn	April	Laborer	Consumption	100 days
5	Joel Grindstaff	1	M				Tenn	Dec		Chronic	15 days
6	Mariah Terry	45	F			M	Va	March		Fever	12 days
7	Thomas Terry	19	M				Tenn	Oct	Laborer	Fever	40 days
8	Ann Turner	51	F				Va	March		Small pox	15 days
9	Harriet Turner	36	F				Va	June		Fever	5 days
10	Washington Woodson	40	M			M	Tenn	Feb	Laborer	unknown	2 days
11	Ann Rutland	2	F				Tenn	Dec		Fever	15 days
12	Robert Dawell	23	M			M	Va	March	Laborer	Small pox	4 days
13	Rachael	60	F	B	S		Va	May		Chronic	100 days
14	William Newbell	75	M			M	Va	May	Laborer	Gravel	6 days
15	Wilson D. Turner	46	M			M	Va	March	Laborer	Small pox	14 days
16	Malinda Turner	2	F				Tenn	April		Small pox	15 days
17	Ellen Patterson	11m	F				Tenn	April		Chronic	30 days
18	Elizabeth Dawell	76	F				Va	April		Small pox	10 days
19	Nancy Waller	54	F			W	N.C.	April		sudden	00
20	Willis Dawell	45	M			M	Va	March	Laborer	Small pox	13 days
21	Thomas Dawell	1	M				Tenn	March		Small pox	10 days
22	Arch	35	M	M	S		Tenn	April		Small pox	13 days
23	Sarah James	2m	F				Tenn	Feb		Hives	4 days
24	Reuben Bearde	48	M			M	N.C.	Aug	Laborer	Flux	21 days
25	Samuel Jones	3	M				Tenn	Aug		Flux	6 days
26	Nancy Walker	27	F	M	F	M	Tenn	Feb		Consumption	125 days
27	George Twidwell	30	M				Tenn	March	Laborer	Chronic	50 days
28	Nancy Johnson	22	F			M	Tenn	Aug		Fever	11 days
29	Harry Givens	9	M				Tenn	May		Flux	10 days
30	Elizabeth Atwood	9	F				Tenn	April		Small pox	10 days
31	Robert Phillips	10	M				Tenn	April		Small pox	6 days
32	Martha Phillips	3	F				Tenn	April		Small pox	6 days
33	Ross Davis	69	M			W	N.C.	March	Laborer	Small pox	12 days
34	Christian Davis	45	F				Kentucky	March		Small pox	12 days
35	Elizabeth Turner	35	F			M	Tenn	March		Small pox	8 days

Remarks: The Devil'd Garden on the Caney Fork River surrounded by a range of high hills containing about nine acres. Sometime in the summer of 1849, about two acres sled from the hill, making a chasm of about fifteen feet and about 12 feet deep. It is supposed from the indications, that there is a bed of coal beneath the avalanche and is accessable only by river. Some 2 or 3 families are the Lords of the retreat.

COUNTY OF SMITH, STATE OF TENNESSEE.

PAGE NO. 749   PERSONS WHO DIED DURING THE YEAR ENDING 1st JUNE, 1850.

South Division

Jefferson Jones

No. of Visit	Name	Age	Sex	Color	Free or Slave	Married/Widowed	Place of Birth	Month Died	Occupation	Disease or Cause of Death	No. Days Ill
1	Robert Turner	3	M				Tenn	March		Small pox	8 days
2	Francis Turner	1m	M				Tenn	March		Small pox	1 day
3	Lucinda Rogers	17	F				Tenn	May		Small pox	30 days
4	Ross Fuller	52	M				S.C.	April	Laborer	Chronic	60 days
5	James Walker	8	M				Tenn	Oct		Inflamation of lungs	20 days
6	William Barnet	60	M			M	N.C.	May	Laborer	Dropsy	1 year
7	Patience	19	F	B	S		Tenn	Aug		Consumption	100 days
8	Willis	1	M	B	S		Tenn	Aug		Worms	5 days
9	Amanda	5m	F	B	S		Tenn	Sept		unknown	30 days
10	John H. Bradford	3	M				Tenn	July		Inflamation of brain	20 days
11	James T. Bradford	1	M				Tenn	July		Inflamation of brain	20 days
12	Willis Jones	42	M			M	Tenn	Dec	Laborer	Consumption	100 days
13	Elizabeth Tolia	16	F				Tenn	April		Fever	25 days

COUNTY OF SMITH, STATE OF TENNESSEE.

PAGE NO. 751   PERSONS WHO DIED DURING THE YEAR ENDING 1st JUNE, 1850.

North of Cumberland & East of Caney Fork River.

A. S. Watkins

No. of Visit	Name	Age	Sex	Color	Free or Slave	Married/Widowed	Place of Birth	Month Died	Occupation	Disease or Cause of Death	No. Days Ill
1	Lucy Goud	1	F				Tenn	April		Diarrhea	7 days
2	Booker Pate	47	M			M	Tenn	April	Farmer	Consumption	C
3	Infant of John Carver	0	F				Tenn	Aug		Premature birth	0
4	Ellis Knight	7m	M				Tenn	July		Hives	1 day
5	Minerva Huddleston	20	F				Tenn	Nov		Congestive fever	6 weeks
6	Infant of Jas. S. Lane	0	M				Tenn	July		Premature birth	0
7	Elenn Russell	58	F			M	Va	Sept	Farmer	Cholera	3 days
8	Infant of Edward Russell	0	F				Tenn	Aug		Premature birth	0
9	Infant of Edward Russell	0	M				Tenn	Aug		Premature birth	0
10	Benjamin Goud	1d	M				Tenn	May		Hives	1 day
11	Infant of Christian Austin	0	M				Tenn	Aug		unknown	0
12	Infant of George Cook	0	M				Tenn	April		unknown	0
13	George Nash	49	M			M	N.C.	April	Farmer	Whiskey gout	3 months
14	Effa Dielihay	46	F			M	N.C.	Dec		Consumption	1 year
15	Infant of Brice M. Taylor	0	M				Tenn	Jan		unknown	0
16	Alfred H. Richardson	24	M			M	Tenn	Sept	Farmer	T. fever	4 weeks
17	Infant of James P. Garret	0	M				Tenn	Aug		unknown (born dead)	0
18	Martha Beasley	25	F			M	Tenn	Sept		Cholera	5 days
19	Napoleon Beasley	2	M				Tenn	Sept		Cholera	5 days
20	Infant of Henry Piper	0	M				Tenn	Dec		Premature birth(born dead)	0
21	Tabitha Taylor	54	F			W	Va	Nov		Congestive chill	1 day
22	Sarah Hannah	1	F		S		Tenn	Aug		Teething	2 weeks
23	Sarah Carmon	55	F			M	N.C.	June		Apoplexy	17 days
24	William Smith	31	M			M	N.C.	June	Farmer	Dead Palsy	13 months
25	Malinda Anderson	6m	F				Tenn	Jan		Bold Hives	3 weeks
26	James Jenkins	2w	M				Tenn	March		unknown	1 day
27	Infant of Moses Burns	3d	F				Tenn	June		unknown	1 day
28	Infant of James Kirby	4m	M				Tenn	July		Chills & Fever	2 weeks
29	Pamelia J.	7w	F		S		Tenn	Dec		unknown	sudden
30	Harriet	1	F		S		Tenn	Aug		Teething	3 days
31	Infant of H. S. Crain	0	F				Tenn	Nov		Born dead	0
32	Frances Black	7m	F				Tenn	March		Inflamation of brain	3 weeks
33	Infant of Chas.W.Murry	0	M				Tenn	Nov		Born dead	0
34	Hannah Hart	80	F	B			Va	June		Old age	2 weeks
35	Charles Black	27	M			W	Tenn	June	Farmer	River fever	4 days

COUNTY OF SMITH, STATE OF TENNESSEE.

PAGE NO. 754 PERSONS WHO DIED DURING THE YEAR ENDING 1st JUNE, 1850.

(continued)

No. of Visit	Name	Age	Sex	Color	Free or Slave	Married/Widowed	Place of Birth	Month Died	Occupation	Disease or Cause of Death	No. Days Ill
1	Samuel D. McMurry	53	M			M	Tenn	April	M.D.	Dyspepsia	4 weeks
2	Patsey	18	F	B	S		unknown	June		Erysipelas	C
3	Infant, slave	1d	M	B	S		Tenn	Oct		unknown	1 day
4	Infant of Turman Leath	1w	F				Tenn	May		Hives	1 week
5	Nancy Brevard	0	F				Tenn	Feb		unknown	0
6	Harvey Carter	50	M	B	S		Tenn	Sept		T. fever	5 weeks
7	Ben Carter	24	M	B	S		Tenn	March		T. fever	8 days
8	Malinda Carter	14	F	B	S		Tenn	May		T. fever	25 days
9	Joseph Woodmore	4	M				Tenn	Oct		Dropsy	8 months
10	Infant of Thos. Woodmore	3w	M				Tenn	Oct		Thrash	3 weeks
11	Charity	26	F	B	S		Tenn	Aug		Phthisic	5 months
12	John	9m	M	B	S		Tenn	Sept		Fits	6 months
13	Mary	40	F	B			Va	Aug		unknown	6 months
14	Catharine	22	F	B	S		Tenn	Oct		T. fever	1 week
15	James Glassgow	76	M			W	N.C.	Sept	Farmer	Cholera	2 weeks
16	Hampshire	6m	M	B	S		Tenn	Dec		Smothered	sudden
17	John Kirby	56	M			M	Va	Aug	Farmer	Nervous eff.	3 years
18	Elinder Dickens	33	F			M	Va	Oct		unknown	8 days
19	Lamisa	1	F	M	S		Tenn	Jan		unknown	sudden
20	William Carmon	1	M				Tenn	July		Worms	5 days
21	Nancy Grisham	68	F			W	N.C.	Feb		Liver complaint	5 months
22	Martha J. Adcock	7m	F				Tenn	July		Teething	4 days
23	Branch Nunly	78	M			M	Va	June	Farmer	Old age	5 days
24	Elizabeth	17	F	B	S		Tenn	April		Cold	2 months
25	Infant of Wm. A. Nynly	0	M				Tenn	Feb		Still born	0
26	Nancy A. Culbreath	19	F				Va	Dec		T. fever	30 days
27	Edmund Culbreath	12	M				Tenn	Feb		Dropsy in chest	18 days
28	Susan S. Culbreath	22	F			M	Tenn	Aug		T. fever	8 days
29	Malinda Parker	25	F			M	Tenn	Aug		Congestive fever	5 days
30	Richard R. Bransford	54	M			M	Va	April	Farmer	Breast complaint	3 months
31	John	6m	M	B	S		Tenn	Oct		Worms	3 days
32	James	10	M	B	S		Tenn	July		Negro consumption	4 months
33	Infant slave, no name	5d	M	B	S		Tenn	Jan		unknown	5 days

COUNTY OF SMITH, STATE OF TENNESSEE.

PAGE NO. 755 PERSONS WHO DIED DURING THE YEAR ENDING 1st JUNE, 1850.

North of Cumberland &
East of Caney Fork River
A. S. Watkins

No. of Visit	Name	Age	Sex	Color	Free or Slave	Married/Widowed	Place of Birth	Month Died	Occupation	Disease or Cause of Death	No. Days Ill
1	Campbell Burke Pickett	2	M				Tenn	Sept		Hydrocephalus	28 days
2	Mariah	40	F	M	S		unknown	Feb		Consumption	C
3	Pompey	3m	M	B	S		Tenn	Aug		Thrash	12 days
4	Samuel High	44	M			M	N.C.	Jan	Farmer	Cholera	1 day
5	George A. High	3m	M				Tenn	Sept		Bowel complaint	C
6	Martin	21	M	B	S		Tenn	Oct	Laborer	Consumption	C
7	Josiah	4m	M	M	S		Tenn	Feb		Hydrocephalus	
8	Sarah	1m	F	B	S		Tenn	Oct		unknown	20 days
9	Sarah	1	F	M	S		Tenn	Aug		Disease of lungs	C
10	Sam	1	M	B	S		Tenn	Feb		Disease of lungs	C
11	York	30	M	B	S		Tenn	Sept		Consumption	C
12	Anthony	60	M	B	S		Va	May		Consumption	20 days
13	John	1w	M	B	S		Tenn	Sept		Croup	6 days
14	Anthony	1w	M	B	S		Tenn	July		Croup	6 days
15	Gabriel	48	M	B	S		Va	March		Consumption	C
16	Francis Shoemake	45	F			M	Va	Nov		T. fever	40 days
17	Allick	10m	M	B	S		Tenn	June		Croup	60 days
18	Mary E. Williams	2	F				Tenn	March		Sc. fever	12 days
19	William Smith	3w	M				Tenn	July		Hives	3 days
20	Mary J. Smith	6m	F				Tenn	March		Dropsy	C
21	Isabella Brown	49	F			M	Tenn	Feb		Consumption	C
22	Martin Shoemake	40	M			M	unknown	Jan	Farmer	Cholera	sudden
23	William Vaden	83	M			W	N.C.	Aug	Farmer	Old age	C
24	William Sloane	73	M				N.C.	April	Farmer	unknown	2 days
25	Sypison	2m	M	B	S		Tenn	April		unknown	sudden
26	Infant of D. Harris	0	F				Tenn	Aug		Asphyxia	0
27	Infant of Jno. H. Mann	0	F				Tenn	Jan		unknown	0
28	Lilly A. Stewart	23	F	M			Tenn	April		Consumption	12 months
29	Richard Vaughn	83	M			W	Va	Nov	none	Old age	
30	Morgan	18	M	B	S		Tenn	March		Poisoned	12 months
31	Abergale L. Lee	2	F				Kentucky	Nov		Sc. fever	1 month
32	Hester C. Coggins	2	F				Tenn	Dec		Sc. fever	13 days
33	Sanford Smith	16	M				Tenn	Oct	Laborer	Sc. fever	12 days
34	Thomas Garner	28	M			M	Tenn	Sept	Farmer	T. fever	22 days
35	William Braswell	25	M				Tenn	Jan	Farmer	Consumption	12 months

Remarks: The water in this region is entirely limestone, and limestone rocks is very abundant. Timber: oak, hickory, black walnut, sugartree, beech. Remittent fever, the prevailing disease in the fall. The past season, we had a great deal of diarrhea but no cholera, in winter numerous plursey is common.

COUNTY OF SMITH, STATE OF TENNESSEE.

PAGE NO. 758 PERSONS WHO DIED DURING THE YEAR ENDING 1st JUNE, 1850.

North of Cumberland &
East of Caney Fork River
A. S. Watkins

No. of Visit	Name	Age	Sex	Color	Free or Slave	Married/Widowed	Place of Birth	Month Died	Occupation	Disease or Cause of Death	No. Days Ill
1	Elizabeth Ponder	31	F			M	Tenn	March		Consumption	12 months
2	Tyree G. Crowder	20	M				Va	Aug	Farmer	T. fever	15 days
3	Robert Braswell	55	M			M	N.C.	Nov	Farmer	Palsy	3 months
4	Infant of Wm. McCall	5d	M				Tenn	March		unknown	
5	Albert H. Petty	3	M				Tenn	Oct		Sc. fever	3 weeks
6	William Haynes	66	M			M	N.C.	Jan	Farmer	Piles	5 weeks
7	Mary J. Huddleston	2	F				Tenn	Oct		Sc. fever	6 days
8	Matilda Bullard	4	F				Tenn	Sept		Sc. fever	5 days
9	Billy	2	M	B	S		Tenn	Aug		Sc. fever	15 days
10	Archibald Scruggs	66	M			M	Va	March	Farmer	Dropsy	5 years
11	Sarah J. Rex	1	F				Tenn	Oct		Sc. fever	1 week
12	Lavina High	2	F				Tenn	Oct		Sc. fever	4 days
13	Patsey Darnold	26	F				Tenn	Dec		Fits	sudden
14	William H. Nichol	2	M				Tenn	July		Sc. fever	8 days
15	Sarah C. Gill	1	F				Tenn	Sept		Sc. fever	3 weeks
16	Cornelia Cullom	6	F				Tenn	Nov		Brain fever	3 weeks
17	Warren Perry	25	M				Tenn	April	Farmer	unknown	sudden
18	William C. Kemp	6	M				Tenn	Jan		Croup	5 days
19	Louisa A. Kemp	9m	F				Tenn	July		Fever	8 weeks
20	William T. Bennett	52	M			M	Va	Nov	Farmer	Cholera, in Memphis	sudden
21	William Thomas	61	M			M	Va	Dec	Farmer	unknown	4 days
22	Louisa	2	F	B	S		Tenn	Sept		Drowned	
23	Jesse J. Gregory	7m	M				Tenn	July		Diarrhea	2 weeks
24	Sarah Climer	35	F			M	Tenn	Nov		Consumption	3 months
25	Elizabeth King	9m	F				Tenn	July		Diarrhea	_ week
26	Josiah McClellan	9d	M				Tenn	Aug		Hives	9 days
27	Sarah Pankey	65	F			W	Va	April		Paralysis	6 days
28	Andrew McClellan	1d	M				Tenn	Oct		Hives	1 day
29	Infant slave of M. Duke	0	M				Tenn	Nov		unknown	0
30	James Martin	23	M				Tenn	May	Farmer	Diarrhea	3 days
31	Logan Reece	1	M				Tenn	Aug		unknown	4 days
32	Charles	24	M	B	S		N.C.	March		Consumption	6 months
33	Fanny Searcy	4d	F				Tenn	May		unknown	4 days
34	Thomas Marmon	70	M			M	N.C.	Aug		Cancer in mouth	12 months
35	Infant of Jef. Dean	0	M				Tenn	March		unknown	0

COUNTY OF STEWART, STATE OF TENNESSEE.

PAGE NO. 759 PERSONS WHO DIED DURING THE YEAR ENDING 1st JUNE, 1850.

William Ellis

No. of Visit	Name	Age	Sex	Color	Free or Slave	Married/Widowed	Place of Birth	Month Died	Occupation	Disease or Cause of Death	No. Days Ill
1	Jane Reynolds	1	F				Tenn	May		Liver condition	30 days
2	George Roper	1	M				Tenn	March		Whooping cough	7 weeks
3	Infant		F				Tenn	Oct		sudden	
4	Sarah Lewis	2	F				Tenn	June		Cholera	9 days
5	Dinah	16	F		S		Tenn	June		unknown	4 months
6	Emulous Hargroves	11	M				Tenn	Oct		Cold	5 days
7	John Cobb	5	M				Tenn	June		Fever	4 months
8	Lewis Lesenby	25	M				Tenn	Jan	Sch-teacher	Cholera	7 hours
9	William	3	M		S		Tenn	Oct		Scrofula	6 months
10	Desey Langford	2	F				Kentucky	April		unknown	2 years
11	Thomas Cunningham	14	M				Tenn	Sept		Inflamation of bowels	2 months
12	Mary Carr	11	F				Kentucky	Oct		Fever	21 days
13	James Ellis	1	M				Tenn	Oct		Diarrhea	6 months
14	Marion	18	M	B	S		Tenn	Oct		Cold	2 days
15	John Terrill	78	M				S.C.	Oct	Farmer	Old age	2 months
16	Cretia	55	F	B	S		N.C.	June		unknown	3 months
17	William	2	M	B	S		Tenn	April		Worms	30 days
18	James Stinson	30	M				Va	Feb	Physician	Pleurisy	4 days
19	Sarah Rogers	2	F				Tenn	July		unknown	2 days
20	George Wells	1m	M				Tenn	July		Croup	14 days
21	Levina Brandon	6m	F				Tenn	April		Whooping cough	2 months
22	Eli Maning	13	M				Tenn	Feb		Dropsy	30 days
23	Jane	2m	F	B	S			Sept		unknown	sudden
24	Malinda Kelly	13	F					Feb		Drowned	
25	Lucy Roulet	64	F				N.C.	Feb		Palsy	4 days
26	Lawrence Maning	40	M				Tenn	July	Farmer	Fever	6 days
27	Westly Houston	1	M				Tenn	Sept		Bowel complaint	6 days
28	Aaron Parker	48	M				unknown	Nov		Chills	3 days
29	Marcella	4	F	B	S		Tenn	unknown		Fever	1 year
30	Esthy Langford	9m	F				Tenn	Dec		Cold	9 days
31	Martha Morris	3m	F				Tenn	April		Hives	2 days
32	Sarah Wynns	19	F			M	Tenn	Nov		Consumption	4 months
33	Infant not named		F		S			March			6 hours
34	William Askew	7	M					Sept		Hives	14 days
35	Francis	6	F					Oct		Dropsy	sudden

Remarks: As in other parts of the County, I have no unusual or natural phenomenon to record that is of interest to the general public.

COUNTY OF STEWART, STATE OF TENNESSEE.

PAGE NO. 762   PERSONS WHO DIED DURING THE YEAR ENDING 1st JUNE, 1850.

William Ellis

No. of Visit	Name	Age	Sex	Color	Free or Slave	Married/Widowed	Place of Birth	Month Died	Occupation	Disease or Cause of Death	No. Days Ill
1	Martha Mixon	18	F	B	S		Tenn	Sept		Scrofula	3 years
2	Bob	1	M	B	S		Kentucky	Dec		Croup	7 days
3	Fany Alsbrooks	9	F				Tenn	Sept		Cholera	1 day
4	Martha Alsbrooks	14	F				Tenn	Sept		Cholera	1 day
5	James Nichols	1	M				Kentucky	Sept		Faver	9 weeks
6	Susan Slaughter	18	F				Tenn	Aug		Cholera	8 days
7	Mary Slaughter	14	F				Tenn	Aug		Cholera	7 days
8	Corbon Tansile	4m	M				Tenn	Sept		Cholera	7 days
9	Elisha Langford	4m	M				Tenn	March		Croup	4 days
10	Fanny Alsbrooks	9	F				Tenn	July		Cholera	10 hours
11	Martha Lancaster, Infant		F				Tenn	April		Croup	21 days
12	Gustavus Robbs, Infant		M				Tenn	Aug		Hives	1 day
13	Mary Wyatt	38	F				Tenn	Sept		Fit	1 day
14	John Barnes, Infant		M				Tenn	Feb		unknown	10 days
15	Samuel Norris	30	M			M	unknown	May		Cholera	7 hours
16	Mary Chambers	2	F				unknown	March		Worms	3 months
17	Elizabeth Elam	60	F				Va	Nov		unknown	30 days
18	Relen Smith	42	M				N.C.	March	Farmer	Rheumatism	2 months
19	David Griffey	3m	M		S		Tenn	Jan		sudden	
20	Elizabeth Longmire	1m	F				Tenn	March		unknown	2 hours
21	Adaline	12	F		S		Tenn	May		Bronchitis	2 months
22	Danfy	15	F		S			Sept		Scrofula	2 years
23	James	16	M		S			Nov		Fever	21 days
24	Anna	14	F		S			Jan		unknown	11 days
25	Infant	1m	M					Jan		unknown	6 days
26	William Moore	22	M			M		April	Batonic Dr.	Liver complaint	18 months
27	Sarah	95	F		S		S.C.	March		Old age	4 months
28	Infant not named	1m	M				Tenn	Aug		Bowel complaint	21 days
29	Winny Brewer	20	F				Tenn	Nov		unknown	3 days
30	Jane Brewer	50	F				N.C.	Aug		Chills	15 days
31	Elenora McGee	5m	F				Tenn	June		unknown	14 days
32	Eudora McGee	5m	F				Tenn	June		unknown	14 days
33	Infant not named	5m	M				Tenn	Sept		Bold hives	7 days
34	Ann Reynolds	1m	M?					July		unknown	15 days
35	Martha Reynolds	8	F					May		Disease of heart	2 years

Remarks: Very broken with numerous quarries, good limestone and abounds with abundance of iron ore. Is well timbered such as; oak, poplar, beech, hickory, walnut and various other kinds of timber which grows naturally in fine. I would state that my County abounds with numerous fine springs of the purest and best water with the exception of the northern part of it, adjoining Ky., which is not so well watered.

COUNTY OF STEWART, STATE OF TENNESSEE.

PAGE NO. 763 PERSONS WHO DIED DURING THE YEAR ENDING 1st JUNE, 1850.

William Ellis

No. of Visit	Name	Age	Sex	Color	Free or Slave	Married/Widowed	Place of Birth	Month Died	Occupation	Disease or Cause of Death	No. Days Ill
1	Mary Meadow	50	F				Georgia	March		Cold	21 days
2	Charles Brigham	7m	M				Tenn	April		unknown	28 days
3	Assallie	19	F	B	S		Tenn	Jan		Disease of -------	8 months
4	Robert Wyatt	70	M				N.C.	April	Farmer	Cold	21 days
5	David Weaver	8m	M				Tenn	July		Cholera	4 days
6	Ellen Petty	2	F				Tenn	July		Cholera	9 days
7	James Weaver	60	M				N.C.	July	Farmer	Diarrhea	28 days
8	Jacob	4	M		S		Tenn	Jan		Inflamation of brain	6 days
9	Mary Gillam	5	F				Tenn	Jan		unknown	sudden
10	Duncan Ellis	41	M				Tenn	Jan	Manager	Pneumonia	12 days
11	Stephen Morgan	34	M	B	S		Tenn	Dec		Killed by falling	
12	Nancy	52	F	B	S		Tenn	Dec		Consumption	3 months
13	Bill	14	M	B	S		Tenn	Dec		Tetanus	15 days
14	William Gold	28	M			M	Va	Feb 1850	Clerk	Chronic diarrhea	2 years
15	Ellick	27	M	B	S		Tenn	Jan		--illegible--	1 year
16	Bob	27	M	B	S		Tenn	Jan		Consumption	1 year
17	Jake	43	M	B	S		_____	Sept		Bil. cholic	2 days
18	Larkin	31	M	B	S		_____	May		Cholera	2 days
19	Henry	31	M	B	S		_____	Jan		From a fall	
20	Edith	40	F	B	S		_____	April		Dropsy	30 days
21	Charley	9	M	B	S		_____	Jan		Drowned	
22	Jerry	26	M	B	S		_____	March		Fever	8 days
23	Moses	34	M	B	S		_____	Dec		Fever	8 days
24	Moses	26	M	B	S		_____	Feb		Pneumonia	10 days
25	George	30	M	B	S		_____	Nov		Pneumonia	10 days

Remarks: 130 deaths in the County. I certify and affirm that I have compared with the original and find that they agree in number and that the same was done according to my oath and instructions to the best of my knowledge and belief.

William Ellis, Asst. Marshal.

COUNTY OF STEWART, STATE OF TENNESSEE.

PAGE NO. 766 PERSONS WHO DIED DURING THE YEAR ENDING 1st JUNE, 1850.

William Ellis

No. of Visit	Name	Age	Sex	Color	Free or Slave	Married/Widowed	Place of Birth	Month Died	Occupation	Disease or Cause of Death	No. Days Ill
1	George Stackier	10	F?	B	S		Tenn	May		Fever	21 days
2	John Milam	5d	F?				Tenn	March		unknown	7 days
3	William Anderson	1	F?				Tenn	Oct		Croup	1 day
4	Henry Self	10	M				Tenn	Jan		unknown	8 days
5	Emulius Knash	1	M				Tenn	July		unknown	2 days
6	Peter Gray	1	M		S		Tenn	June		unknown	20 days
7	____ Gray	6m	F		S		Tenn	Oct		Croup	3 days
8	Mariah George	16	F				Kentucky	April		Cold	40 days
9	Rachel Wyatt	21	F				Tenn	April		Consumption	17 months
10	Elizabeth Andrews	40	F				Tenn	May		Dropsy	9 years
11	Penny	100	F		S		N.C.	July		Old age	7 years
12	Ann	5m	F		S		Tenn	April		Whooping cough	20 days
13	Charley	1	M		S		Tenn	Dec		Cholic	3 days
14	Reuben Hendon	20	M				Tenn	March	Farmer	Cholera	4 days
15	Ephram Galtin	9m	M				Tenn	Feb		Chills	10 days
16	Mary McClain	20	F				Kentucky	Sept		unknown	2 days
17	Charles McClain	2	M				Tenn	May		Whooping cough	15 days
18	Martha Reed	29	F				Tenn	March		Cholera Mor.	5 days
19	Robert McDougle	45	M			W	N.C.	Sept	Farmer	Chronic	90 days
20	Thomas Brigham	75	M			M	Tenn	Sept		Dropsy	3 years
21	Jemimah Phillips	60	F				N.C.	Aug		Dropsy	3 years
22	Jackson Bosswell	11m	M				N.C.	Jan		Hives	1 day
23	Lewis	47	M		S		N.C.	Jan		Fever	5 days
24	Willis	30	M		S			Jan		Chills	4 days
25	Pinkney	10m	M		S			Jan		Fever	10 days
26	Lucy	70	F		S		Va	March		unknown	6 days
27	William Barnet	40	M			M	N.C.	Aug	Farmer	Fever	15 days
28	William Canada	1m	M				Tenn	May		unknown	30 days
29	Thomas Barbee	12	M				N.C.	March		unknown	4 years
30	Calvin Robinson	2	M				Tenn	Sept		unknown	3 months
31	Luct Batton	2	F				Tenn	Jan		Cold	21 days
32	Lewis	1	M		S		Tenn	Dec		Croup	14 days
33	Preston	34	M		S		Tenn	June		Cholera	8 days
34	John	1m	M		S			April		unknown	sudden
35	Nathan	17	M		S			Feb		unknown	12 days

Remarks: In my remarks, I would first state to you that there has been no particular malady or disease in my District in the year ending June the 1st 1850, neither any local causes exist in my District for producing disease but such as one comes now to all mankind. I would further state that the character of the water in my District is generally limestone and the soil of my County, the farming part, is lively and productive but in the main......

COUNTY OF SULLIVAN, STATE OF TENNESSEE.

PAGE NO. 768   PERSONS WHO DIED DURING THE YEAR ENDING 1st JUNE, 1850.

1st Division
L. D. Gaines

No. of Visit	Name	Age	Sex	Color	Free or Slave	Married/Widowed	Place of Birth	Month Died	Occupation	Disease or Cause of Death	No. Days Ill
1	Agness Snapp	6m	F	B	S		Tenn	Nov		unknown	30 days
2	Jas. M. Teathers	1	M				Tenn	May		Croup	14 days
3	Lucy Evans	10	F				Tenn	Aug		Disease of tonsils	5 days
4	Almeda Davis	4	F				Tenn	July		Quinsy	21 days
5	David Steel	66	M			M	Va	Dec	Farmer	Dyspepsia	6 days
6	Henry Turner	30	M			M	Ireland	March		Pleurisy	11 days
7	Martha Rhea	74	F			W	Tenn	Oct		Dropsy	20 days
8	Nancy M. Anderson	36	F			M	Va	Jan		Bronchitis	C
9	Agness Garner	58	F	B		M	Tenn	March		Dropsy	C
10	Polly Livingston	4	F	B			Tenn	May		Scrofula	C
11	Simon Harr	2	M				Kentucky	May		Fever	14 days
12	Elizabeth Blackamore	67	F			W	Va	Jan		Inflamation of heart	C
13	Rebecca Harr	57	F			W	Tenn	Nov		Dropsy	C
14	Adaline Birdleman	6	F	B	S		Tenn	May		Consumption	35 days
15	Eliza	4	F	B	S		Tenn	May		Consumption	30 days
16	Mary Stopher	6m	F				Tenn	May		unknown	C
17	Amanda Vance	26	F	B	S		Tenn	June		Consumption	C
18	Mary Friend	1	F				Tenn	Oct		Diarrhea	14 days
19	Elizabeth Lindamon	10	F				Tenn	Jan		Bil. fever	20 days
20	Mary Mais	2	F				Va	Aug		Cholera Mor.	60 days
21	Rachel Jones	60	F			M	Tenn	July		Palsy	C
22	William Berry	13	M				Tenn	Dec		--illegible--	12 days
23	Robert Porterfield	35	M			M	Tenn	June	Farmer	Pneumonia	8 days
24	Adline Jones	38	F			M	Tenn	April		Child birth	10 days
25	Magdalene Davault	70	F			M	Penn	Nov		Dropsy	C
26	not named	1m	M				Tenn	Jan		Liver Disease	3 days
27	Benjamin F. Malone	1	M				Tenn	Sept		Croup	2 days
28	David Alinroad	21	M			M	Tenn	April	Farmer	Bil. fever	30 days
29	Ceaser Rhea	60	M	B	S		Africa	Sept	Farmer	Dropsy	C
30	Levi Gardner	39	M	M	S		Tenn	Nov	Blk-smith	Consumption	C
31	Lucinda Carver	35	F			M	Tenn	Nov		Ulcer	C
32	Jno. Smith	20	M				Tenn	Oct	Brk-mason	unknown	C
33	Jno. Tentry (Gentry)	1m	M				Tenn	Sept		unknown	7 days
34	Jesse Hughes	31	M				Tenn	Aug	Farmer	Bil. fever	21 days
35	Elizabeth Morrell	58	F				Tenn	Sept		unknown	C

Remarks: The most prevailent diseases of the County are intermittant and remittent fevers. Causes: The malaria of the Holston River and the low grounds contigous thereto. There has been one epidemic of scarlet fever, one of measles, one of eupipelas and two of typhoid fever within the last ten years. The Autumn of 1846 was the most unhealthy ....(continued)

COUNTY OF SULLIVAN, STATE OF TENNESSEE.

PAGE NO. 769 PERSONS WHO DIED DURING THE YEAR ENDING 1st JUNE, 1850.

1st Division
L. D. Gaines

No. of Visit	Name	Age	Sex	Color	Free or Slave	Married/Widowed	Place of Birth	Month Died	Occupation	Disease or Cause of Death	No. Days Ill
1	Susan Davault	6m	F				Tenn	June		Diarrhea	C
2	Jno. Woods	1	M				Tenn	Oct		Croup	3 days
3	Jas. Wilder	96	M			M	N.C.	Aug	Farmer	Old age	C
4	Robert C. Scott	18	M				Tenn	June	Farmer	Cholera Mor.	7 days
5	Martha J. Beard	1	F				Tenn	Oct		Cold	C
6	Joseph Torbett	77	M			M	Va	Sept	Farmer	Palsy	C
7	Eliza Arants	50	F			M	Tenn	July		Bil. fever	20 days
8	Ireson L. Arants	19	M				Tenn	July	Farmer	Bil. fever	20 days
9	Elizabeth Arants	18	F				Tenn	Oct		T. fever	20 days
10	Fanny Rhea	86	F			W	Ireland	April		Old age	C
11	Patsy Anderson	27	F	B	S		Tenn	May		Consumption	C
12	Thomas	7m	M	B			Tenn	Dec		unknown	sudden
13	Elizabeth Millard	68	F			M	Penn	May		Bil. fever	20 days
14	Thomas Titsworth	46	M			M	Tenn	April	Farmer	C. Cholic	12 days
15	Rachel Hickman	60	F			M	Tenn	Jan		Disease of glands	16 days
16	Louisa Rhea	9m	F	B	S		Tenn	Dec		Hives	sudden
17	Mary J. Dixon	4m	F				Tenn	Feb		Inflamation of bowels	3 days
18	not named	1m	F	M	S		Tenn	Dec		unknown	10 days
19	Lucinda Johnson	39	F				Tenn	Jan		Consumption	C
20	Elizabeth Johnson	76	F			M	Va	Nov		Dropsy	C
21	Barbary Minga	75	F			M	Penn	Nov		Dropsy	C
22	Nancy Smith	71	F			W	Maryland	April		Dropsy	C
23	Mary Combs	1	F				Tenn	July		Inflamation of brain	7 days
24	Rebecca Rivers	1m	F				Tenn	Aug		unknown	20 days
25	Milly Rhea	21	F	B			Tenn	Dec		Drowned	
26	Rhoda	16	F	B			Tenn	Sept		Scrofula	C
27	Margaret Malone	60	F			W	Tenn	Jan		unknown	C
28	George Short	13	M				Tenn	Dec		Inflamation of brain	7 days
29	Nancy Hood	43	F			M	Tenn	June		Fever	21 days
30	William Hood	1m	M				Tenn	July		unknown	C
31	R. Light	90	M			W	Tenn	May	Revolution	Old age	C
32	Sarah Light	90	F			W	Va	Feb		Old age	C
33	Jas. Bray	19	M				Tenn	May	Farmer	T. fever	11 days
34	Jackson McCarrol	3m	M				Tenn	Aug		Croup	5 days
35	Elizabeth Roberts	1	F				Tenn	Oct		Diarrhea	14 days

Remarks: season we have had for 10 years. Intermittent and remittent fever of a malignant grade then prevailed to a great extent along the river and larger creeks. It is worthy of remark that an epidemic _____ fever followed immediately after the erysyselas disappeared. Our climate is remarkably unequal, seldom manifesting extreme degrees of heat and cold.

COUNTY OF SULLIVAN, STATE OF TENNESSEE.

PAGE NO. 772   PERSONS WHO DIED DURING THE YEAR ENDING 1st JUNE, 1850.

1st Division
L. D. Gaines

No. of Visit	Name	Age	Sex	Color	Free or Slave	Married/Widowed	Place of Birth	Month Died	Occupation	Disease or Cause of Death	No. Days Ill
1	Gabriel Morgan	78	M			M	Penn	July	Farmer	Paralysis	49 days
2	Joseph McCaleb	4	M				Tenn	March		unknown	2 days
3	George Pickens	1	M				Tenn	Sept		Croup	3 days
4	Hugh Niece	2m	M				Tenn	April		Inflamation of brain	16 days
5	Jno. Grimsby	32	M			M	Tenn	Oct	Farmer	Stabbed	14 days
6	Nancy Allen	6	F				Tenn	June		Worms	4 days
7	Ellen Vincent	88	F			W	Va	Dec		Old age	C
8	David Pickens	29	M			M	Tenn	March	Farmer	Disease of lungs	C
9	Nancy Chase	30	F			M	Tenn	April		Disease of lungs	C
10	R. P. Chase	8	M				Tenn	Jan		Falling tree	sudden
11	Mary Depew	40	F			M	Tenn	Sept		Dyspepsia	C
12	William Hiter	3	M				Tenn	July		Worms	5 days
13	Nelson Roler	34	M	B		M	Tenn	Aug		Bil. fever	8 days
14	Dennis Roller	26	M	B			Tenn	Jan		Inflamation of bowels	8 days
15	Adam Cline	2	M				Tenn	Nov		Croup	2 days
16	Nancy A. Poe	2	F				Tenn	May		Drowned	
17	Ann Sherfey	80	F			W	Va	May		Old age	C
18	Jno. Beard	81	M				Va	March	Farmer	Disease of lungs	7 days
19	Ruth Beard	75	F				Va	March		Disease of lungs	6 days
20	Jacob Loudermilk	71	M	M			Va	May	Farmer	C. Cholic	2 days
21	Elizabeth Bowery	7m	F				Tenn	Sept		Fall	sudden
22	Eliza Vandewinter	1	F				Tenn	Aug		Diarrhea	21 days
23	Wallace Willoughby	76	M			W	Penn	March	Farmer	Bronchitis	C
24	Samuel Roberts	62	M			M	Va	Oct	Farmer	Dysentery	Accute
25	Thomas Henderson	36	M			M	Tenn	Aug	Saddler	Bil. fever	10 days
26	Christinah Myers	85	F			W	Va	April		Old age	C
27	Rosanah Peters	23	F				Tenn	March		unknown	C
28	Rachel Peters	12	F				Tenn	Sept		unknown	C
29	Jno. Davidson	56	M				Va	July	Carpenter	Disease of lungs	C
30	Henry C. Keyes	35	M	B	S		N.C.	Sept	Collier		sudden
31	Mariah Keyes	2	F	B	S		Tenn	March		Inflamation of lungs	7 days
32	Jas. Godsey	1	M				Tenn	Dec		unknown	28 days
33	Jno. Underwood	80	M			M	Tenn	May	Farmer	Old age	sudden
34	Nancy Smith	28	F			M	Tenn	Oct		Nervous disease	C
35	David F. Obrum	1m	M				Tenn	Dec		unknown	3 days

Remarks: The thermometer during the winter months rarely showing more than 5 to 10 degrees below the freezing point, which in summer months it so rarely shows a higher temperature than 50 degrees above the freezing point. In consequence of this mildness and eveness of temperature, consumption and other diseases of the lungs are very rare. One of our Physicians remarked .....(continued)....

COUNTY OF SULLIVAN, STATE OF TENNESSEE.

PAGE NO. 773 PERSONS WHO DIED DURING THE YEAR ENDING 1st JUNE, 1850.

1st Division
L. D. Gaines

No. of Visit	Name	Age	Sex	Color	Free or Slave	Married/Widowed	Place of Birth	Month Died	Occupation	Disease or Cause of Death	No. Days Ill
1	Moses Price	73	M			W	Conn	Dec	none	Consumption	C
2	Hartsell Wetherford	40	M			M	Va	Oct	Farmer	Kicked by horse	sudden
3	Catharine Lynn	2	F				Tenn	March		Inflamation of lungs	C
4	Jas. G. Cox	28	M			M	Tenn	Dec	Shoemaker	Consumption	C
5	Martha Cox	11m	F				Tenn	Nov		unknown	3 days
6	David C. Coats	6m	M				Tenn	March		unknown	4 days
7	Amy Parker	6	F				Tenn	Feb		Fever	4 days
8	Eliza Cloud	25	F	B	S		Tenn	April		Snake bitten	C
9	Infant child	1m	M	—			Tenn	Jan		Inflamation of bowels	20 days
10	Malinda	17	F	—			Tenn	Oct		Female disease	C
11	G. W. Caroll	6m	M				Tenn	Feb		Inflamation of brain	10 days
12	Elizabeth Olick	12	F				Tenn	Dec		Fits	C
13	Eliza Johnson	70	F			M	Va	May		Dropsy	C
14	William H. Browder	13	M				Tenn	Nov		Jaundice	C
15	William Jones	46	M			M	Va	May	Blk-smith	Disease of lungs	C
16	Jas. Faringsworth	38	M			M	Va	March	Farmer	T. fever	21 days
17	Fanny Bachman	51	F			W	Tenn	June		Pneumonia	4 weeks
18	Frances R. Bachman	20	F				Tenn	Sept		Consumption	C

Remarks: that he has not met with a single case of tubercular consumption in the last 20 years. The water is pure limped limestone and in great abundance. Limestone rocks are abundant in the beds and along the banks of every stream. Timber: white, red and black oak, dogwood, hickory, sugar maple, etc. The face of the County is .... (continued)....

I certify that the foregoing is a true return of the deaths in the 1st division, Sullivan County, Tennessee, for 12 months ending 1st June 1850, so far as information could be had. Given under my hand this 13th day of December 1850. L. D. Gaines, Asst. Marshal.

Remarks: uneven and in many parts hilly and broken. The soil thin but very productive compared with other soil of similar apparent fertility. Marl is found in abundance on some of the creeks. Iron ore is sufficiently abundant for the production of iron and castings to an almost indefinate amount. The country abounds in water power to an unlimited extent and thus offering every facility for manufactoring.

COUNTY OF SUMNER, STATE OF TENNESSEE.

PAGE NO. 776 PERSONS WHO DIED DURING THE YEAR ENDING 1st JUNE, 1850.

District No. 1
James L. McKain

No. of Visit	Name	Age	Sex	Color	Free or Slave	Married/Widowed	Place of Birth	Month Died	Occupation	Disease or Cause of Death	No. Days Ill
1	James Winn	52	F?	W	F	W	Va	Jan		Consumption	300 days
2	Jane Winn	1m	F	W	F		Tenn	July		Accident	1 day
3	Dolly	90	F	B	S		Va	May		Old age	20 days
4	Lewis	2	M	B	S		Tenn	June		Croup	10 days
5	Sarah Crenshaw	15	F	B	F		Tenn	Sept		Consumption	60 days
6	Holly	50	F	B	F		N.C.	July		Cholera	3 days
7	George	23	M	B	F		Tenn	July		Cholera	5 days
8	Booker Dalton	60	M	W	F	M	Va	Aug	Farmer	Congestive fever	9 days
9	Joseph Holt	24	M	W	F		Tenn	July	Teacher	T. fever	10 days
10	Sarah Mohorn	60	F	W	F	W	Va	April		Inflamation of brain	18 days
11	Elizabeth	11	F	B	S		Tenn	April		Drowned	
12	Sylva	5	F	B	S		Tenn	July		Drowned	
13	Washington	22	M	B	S		Tenn	July	Farmhand	Cholera	
14	Lucy	28	F	B	S		Tenn	Feb		Congestive fever	20 days
15	Susan	3m	F	B	S		Tenn	Feb		Hives	1 day
16	Winney	30	F	B	S		N.C.	Sept	Farmhand	Consumption	21 days
17	Stephen	55	M	B	F		Tenn	July		Cholera	1 day
18	Bennetta Mills	3m	F	W	F		Tenn	Aug		Brain fever	8 days
19	Louiza Mills	1	F	W	F		Tenn	March		Fever	12 days
20	Mary	10m	F	B	S		Tenn	Aug		Cholera	9 days
21	Fanny	6m	F	B	S		Tenn	Aug		Cholera	4 days
22	Jane	1m	F	B	S		Tenn	Aug		Cholera	5 days
23	Mary	1	F	B	S		Tenn	Sept		Cholera	2 days
24	Charles	50	M	B	S		Tenn	July	Farmhand	Cholera	2 days
25	Molly	40	F	B	S		Tenn	Aug	Cook	Cholera	1 day
26	Frank	75	M	B	S		N.C.	June		Cholera	2 days
27	Milly	30	F	B	S		Tenn	Sept		Consumption	50 days
28	Nancy Brigendine	38	F	W	F	M	Maryland	June		Cholera	5 days
29	Jane Wheellock	22	F	W	F		Kentucky	June		Cholera	10 days
30	Joseph	21	M	B	S		Tenn	Aug	Farmhand	Fever	16 days
31	Sarah	6	F	B	S		Tenn	Sept		Fever	10 days
32	Jackson	14	M	B	S		Tenn	Oct		Fever	20 days
33	Letty	30	F	B	S		Tenn	Dec		Consumption	50 days
34	Robert	60	M	B	S		Va	Aug	Farmhand	Cholera	5 days
35	Mary Hamilton	18	F	W	F	M	Tenn	July		Cholera	2 days

Remarks: The cholera prevailed here in June, July and August, and was very fatal.

COUNTY OF SUMNER, STATE OF TENNESSEE.

PAGE NO. 777 PERSONS WHO DIED DURING THE YEAR ENDING 1st JUNE, 1850.

District No. 2
James L. McKain

No. of Visit	Name	Age	Sex	Color	Free or Slave	Married/Widowed	Place of Birth	Month Died	Occupation	Disease or Cause of Death	No. Days Ill
1	Nancy	20	F	B	S		Tenn	June		Cholera	2 days
2	Thomas	6m	M	B	S		Tenn	Sept		Diarrhea	3 days
3	Tabitha	20	F	B	S		Tenn	June		Cholera	2 days
4	Thomas	50	M	B	S		Va	July	Farmhand	Hemorrhage of lungs	10 days
5	Adeline	18	F	B	S		Tenn	June		Cholera	2 days
6	Ann	1	F	B	S		Tenn	Aug		Worms	18 days
7	Marcus Parker	18	M	W	F		Tenn	Sept	Farmer	T. fever	20 days
8	Simon	27	M	B	S		Va	July	Farmer	T. fever	19 days
9	Milly	17	F	B	S		Va	Aug		T. fever	17 days
10	Gabriel	22	M	B	S		Va	May	Farmer	Consumption	90 days
11	Stephen	50	M	B	S		N.C.	Jan	Farmer	Consumption	120 days
12	Agnes E. Jackson	27	F	W	F	S	Tenn	Aug		Consumption	90 days
13	Sarah	40	F	B	S		Tenn	June		Cholera	2 days
14	Robert	75	M	B	S		Va	June		Cholera	6 days
15	Jacob	72	M	B	S		Va	May		Pneumonia	10 days
16	Joseph Exom	30	M	W	F	S	Tenn	Feb	Farmer	T. fever	8 days
17	Sarah A. Caloway	20	F	W	F		Tenn	Aug		Bilious	10 days
18	John Proctor	1	M	W	F		Tenn	July		Sc. fever	12 days
19	John W. Thompson	6m	M	W	F		Tenn	Aug		Brain fever	12 days
20	Jane Bonds	14	F	W	F		Tenn	June		Cholera	1 day
21	Priscilla Hale	81	F	W	F	W	N.C.	Sept		Old age	300 days
22	John W. Thompson	8m	M	W	F		Tenn	Aug		T. fever	7 days
23	Harriet Fleetwood	41	F	W	F		Va	Feb		T. fever	40 days
24	James Dickerson	71	M	W	F		Va	Aug	Farmer	Diarrhea	4 days
25	Infant	1d	F	B	S		Tenn	Aug		Born dead	
26	Dolly	70	F	B	S		Va	Aug		Flux	10 days
27	Infant		M	W	F		Tenn	July		Born dead	
28	Richard	1	M	B	S		Tenn	Aug		Bowel Complsint	30 days
29	Louiza	34	F	B	S		Tenn	June		Cholera	1 day
30	Lavinia	29	F	B	S		Tenn	June		Cholera	3 days
31	Infant		F	B	S		Tenn	June		Born dead	
32	Levi	45	M	B	S		Tenn	Aug		T. fever	10 days
33	John	7m	M	B	S		Tenn	Nov		Croup	4 days
34	James	7m	M	B	S		Tenn	Aug		Dropsy	7 days
35	Richard	9m	M	B	S		Tenn	June		Cholera	1 day

COUNTY OF SUMNER, STATE OF TENNESSEE.

PAGE NO. 780 PERSONS WHO DIED DURING THE YEAR ENDING 1st JUNE, 1850.

District No. 3 & 4
J. L. McKain

No. of Visit	Name	Age	Sex	Color	Free or Slave	Married/Widowed	Place of Birth	Month Died	Occupation	Disease or Cause of Death	No. Days Ill
1	Edy	4	F	M	S		Tenn	Oct		Burnt	1 day
2	William Lanesdale	48	M	W	F	M	Va	Aug	Miller	Ground in mill	20 days
3	Josiah Bowman	1	M	W	F		Tenn	Aug		Bil. fever	10 days
4	Jackson	15	M	B	S		Tenn	July	Farmhand	Drowned	
5	Andrew Brown	3	M	W	F		Tenn	Sept		Dropsy	90 days
6	Catharine Johnson	65	F	W	F	W	Va	Aug		Congestive chills	5 days
7	Jessee McElwrath	23	M	W	F	M	Tenn	Sept	Carpenter	Consumption	30 days
8	Susan O. McElwrath	1	F	W	F		Tenn	Aug		Consumption	always
9	Nathaniel McGee	48	M	W	F		Kentucky	Sept	Farmer	T. fever	15 days
10	Martha	50	F	B	S		Tenn	Aug	Cook	Cholera	1 day
11	Robert Carter	67	M	W	F	W	Va	May	Farmer	Liver complaint	90 days
12	Thomas Saunders	40	M	W	F	M	Va	Oct	Wagon-maker	Bil. fever	30 days
13	Elizabeth Mitchener	60	F	W	F	M	N.C.	Sept		Pleurisy	C
14	Jane J. Shelton	15	F	W	F		Tenn	Sept		d. unknown	4 days
15	William A. Shelton	45	M	W	F		Tenn	Jan	Farmer	Cold	6 days
16	Duncan Livingston	52	M	W	F	M	Va	Aug	Hatter	H. lungs	1 day
17	Sinah	55	F	B	S		Tenn	April		Dropsy	60 days
18	Sarah C. Patton	28	F	W	F	M	Tenn	June		Child birth	12 days
19	Milly	7m	F	M	S		Tenn	Nov		D. unknown	
20	Eliza Patton	29	F	W	F		Tenn	Oct		Drowned	
21	Malvina M. Walsh	33	F	W	F	M	Tenn	Sept		T. fever	12 days
22	William Weatherford	28	M	W	F	M	Kentucky	June	Farmer	Cholera	5 days
23	Richard Parker	47	M	W	F	M	Tenn	July	Farmer	Cholera	2 days
24	Lucinda Davenport	17	F	W	F	S	Tenn	Aug		Drowned	
25	James P. Miller	50	M	W	F	M	Kentucky	June	Farmer	Intemperance	5 days
26	Samuel	6	M	B	S		Tenn	Oct		T. fever	9 days
27	Anna E. King	20	F	B	F		Tenn	June		Fever	10 days
28	Thomas	15	M	B	S		Tenn	Sept		Fever	15 days
29	Acy	14	M	B	F		Tenn	Aug		Fever	10 days
30	Martha	12	F	B	F		Tenn	Aug		Cholera	3 days
31	Hanna	3	F	B	F		Tenn	July		Cholera	1 day
32	Jane	1	F	B	F		Tenn	Sept		Cholera	3 days
33	Charlotte	40	F	B	F		Tenn	July		Cholera	1 day
34	Reuben	37	M	B	F		Tenn	July		Cholera	1 day
35	Sidney	26	F	B	F		Tenn	July		Cholera	1 day

COUNTY OF SUMNER, STATE OF TENNESSEE.

PAGE NO. 781 PERSONS WHO DIED DURING THE YEAR ENDING 1st JUNE, 1850.

District No. 5
James L. McKain

No. of Visit	Name	Age	Sex	Color	Free or Slave	Married/Widowed	Place of Birth	Month Died	Occupation	Disease or Cause of Death	No. Days Ill
1	Elizabeth Adams	41	F	W	F	M	N.C.	Nov		Consumption	90 days
2	Margaret Williamson	13	F	W	F		Tenn	Aug		Cholera	1 day
3	Mary L. Williamson	1m	F	W	F		Tenn	March		Croup	5 days
4	Charles	6m	M	M	S		Tenn	Aug		Cholera	1 day
5	John	3	M	B	S		Tenn	Aug		Cholera	3 days
6	Julia	1	F	B	S		Tenn	Aug		Worms	4 days
7	Christopher Crutcher	22	M	W	F		Tenn	Feb		Fever	15 days
8	Benjamin Nokes	9m	M	W	F		Tenn	May		Whooping cough	20 days
9	Tabby	80	F	B	S		N.C.	Aug		Cholera	1 day
10	Edy	50	F	B	S		Tenn	Aug		Dyspepsia	30 days
11	Ellen Johnson	24	F	W	F	M	Va	June		Cholera	2 days
12	James E. Johnson	3	M	W	F		Tenn	June		Brain fever	9 days
13	John	3m	M	B	S		Tenn	July		Whooping cough	8 days
14	Tony	33	M	B	S		Kentucky	Aug		Cholera	1 day
15	Samuel	32	M	B	S		Kentucky	Aug		Cholera	1 day
16	Mary Draphus	35	F	W	F	M	Va	Aug		Cholera	7 days
17	Susan	19	F	B	S		Kentucky	July		T. fever	30 days
18	Walt	75	M	B	S		Va	Aug		Cholera	1 day
19	Phillis	60	F	B	S		N.C.	July		Dropsy	10 days
20	James Essex	20	M	W	F		Tenn	July	Clerk	Cholera	2 days
21	Cato Moss	5	M	W	F		Tenn	July		Cholera	2 days
22	Infant	1m	F	W	F		Tenn	July		Cholera	1 day
23	Mary M. Clark	9	F	W	F		Conn	Aug		T. fever	8 days
24	Harry	38	M	B	S		Tenn	Aug		Cholera	1 day
25	Starling	50	M	B	S		Tenn	Aug		Cholera	1 day
26	Emily	30	F	B	S		Kentucky	Aug		Cholera	1 day
27	Infant	4m	M	B	S		Tenn	Aug		Cholera	1 day
28	Moses	50	M	B	S		Tenn	Aug		Cholera	1 day
29	Julia Blackington	14	F	W	F		Tenn	Aug		Congestive chills	1 day
30	Susan Warner	11	F	W	F		Tenn	Aug		Cholera	2 days
31	Robert	50	M	B	S		Tenn	Aug		Cancer	50 days
32	Sarah McCrary	28	F	W	F	M	Tenn	Aug		Cholera	1 day
33	Jane McCrary	10	F	W	F		Tenn	Aug		Cholera	1 day
34	Polly	45	F	B	S		Tenn	Aug		Cholera	1 day
35	Joseph Rice	25	M	W	F		Tenn	Aug	Tailor	Cholera	1 day

COUNTY OF SUMNER, STATE OF TENNESSEE.

PAGE NO. 784 PERSONS WHO DIED DURING THE YEAR ENDING 1st JUNE, 1850.

District No. 5

James L. McKain

No. of Visit	Name	Age	Sex	Color	Free or Slave	Married/Widowed	Place of Birth	Month Died	Occupation	Disease or Cause of Death	No. Days Ill
1	Nancy	60	F	B	S		Va	Aug	Cook	Cholera	1 day
2	Kate Baltzell	14	F	W	F		Tenn	Aug		Cholera	1 day
3	Jane Warner	12	F	W	F		Tenn	Aug		Cholera	1 day
4	Frances Solomon	9	F	W	F		Tenn	Aug		Cholera	1 day
5	Jack	20	M	B	S		Tenn	Aug		Cholera	1 day
6	Charlotte	50	F	B	S		Va	Aug		Cholera	2 days
7	Mary Stanfield	4	F	M	F		Tenn	Aug		Cholera	1 day
8	Milly	40	F	M	F		Tenn	Aug		Cholera	1 day
9	Nancy Harrell	50	F	M	S		N.C.	Aug		Cholera	1 day
10	William F. Edwards	35	M	W	F	W	Tenn	Aug		Cholera	1 day
11	Mary Sylver	24	F	W	F	M	Tenn	Aug		Cholera	1 day
12	Edward Bartram	4	M	W	F		Tenn	Aug		Cholera	1 day
13	James Bartram	22	M	W	F		Tenn	Aug	Clerk	Cholera	1 day
14	David Richardson	55	M	W	F		N.C.	Aug		Cholera	2 days
15	Ned	45	M	B	F	M	Tenn	Aug		Cholera	2 days
16	Nancy Scales	60	F	W	F	M	Tenn	Aug		Consumption	90 days
17	Mary Rice	45	F	W	F	W	N.C.	Aug		Cholera	2 days
18	James Enlow	2	M	W	F		Tenn	Aug		Cholera	1 day
19	William Exom	75	M	W	F	M	N.C.	Aug		Cholera	1 day
20	Nancy Exom	72	F	W	F	M	N.C.	Aug		Cholera	1 day
21	William Warner	5	M	W	F		Tenn	Aug		Cholera	1 day
22	Jane Floyd	81	F	W	F		Ireland	Aug		Cholera	4 days
23	Nancy Bugg	60	F	B	F		Tenn	Sept		Cholera	8 days
24	Smith Munday	20	M	W	F		Va	Sept	Clerk	Cholera	8 days
25	Mary E. Weaver	35	F	W	F		Tenn	Sept		Cholera	8 days
26	Thomas	1	M	B	S		Tenn	Sept		Cholera	1 day
27	William Woodmore	35	M	W	F	M	Va	Sept	Farmer	Cholera	9 days
28	George	40	M	B	S		Va	Sept		Cholera	1 day
29	Lucinda Woodmore	30	F	W	F	M	Tenn	June		Cholera	1 day
30	Eveline Hadly	35	F	W	F	W	Va	June		Cholera	1 day
31	Simus	70	M	B	S		Tenn	June		Cholera	1 day
32	Milly	33	F	B	S		Tenn	June		Cholera	2 days
33	Fanny Duke	30	F	M	F		Tenn	June		Cholera	3 days
34	Maria	3	F	M	F		Tenn	June		Cholera	7 days
35	Harriett	21	F	B	F		Tenn	June		Cholera	1 day

COUNTY OF SUMNER, STATE OF TENNESSEE.

PAGE NO. 785 PERSONS WHO DIED DURING THE YEAR ENDING 1st JUNE, 1850.

District No. 5
James L. McKain

No. of Visit	Name	Age	Sex	Color	Free or Slave	Married/Widowed	Place of Birth	Month Died	Occupation	Disease or Cause of Death	No. Days Ill
1	Infant	4m	F	W	F		Tenn	June		Consumption	20 days
2	Matilda Howell	28	F	W	F		Kentucky	June		Cholera	1 day
3	Infant	6m	M	M	F		Tenn	June		Cholera	1 day
4	Jane Goode	3	F	M	F		Tenn	June		Cholera	6 days
5	Infant	2m	F	B	S		Tenn	June		Cholera	1 day
6	Lea	55	F	B	S		Tenn	June		Cholera	1 day
7	Phillip	77	M	B	S		Va	June		Cholera	1 day
8	Catharine Douglass	26	F	W	F	S	Tenn	June		Cholera	1 day
9	Cynthia Douglass	19	F	W	F	S	Tenn	June		Cholera	1 day
10	Micajah Howard	20	M	W	F	S	N.C.	June		Cancer	120 days
11	Julia Richardson	40	F	W	F	M	Tenn	June		Cholera	1 day
12	John Steward	80	M	W	F	W	Va	July	Carpenter	Cholera	3 days
13	Jane Alexander	24	F	W	F	M	Tenn	July		Cholera	1 day
14	Nancy Walsh	50	F	W	F	M	Va	July		Consumption	30 days
15	Sylva	25	F	B	S		Va	July		Cholera	1 day
16	John	1	M	B	S		Tenn	July		Cholera	1 day
17	J. W. Judd	1	M	W	F		Tenn	July		Worms	1 day
18	Mary Dale	30	F	W	F	M	Tenn	July		Cholera	1 day
19	Nancy Lawrence	50	F	W	F		Tenn	July		Cholera	1 day
20	Jane George	32	F	W	F	M	N.C.	Aug		Entern.	5 days
21	Claibourne	60	M	B	S		Tenn			T. fever	10 days
22	Eva Wilson	50	F	W	F		Tenn	Jan		Cholera	2 days
23	Leella Baldridge	3m	F	W	F		Tenn	May		Fever	23 days
24	Ned	50	M	M	S		Louisiana	Aug		Bowel complaint	1 day
25	Jane	1	F	M	S		Va	July		Cholera	5 days
26	John	10	M	M	S		Tenn	Aug		Teething	1 day
27	Louiza	6	F	M	S		Tenn	Aug		Cholera	2 days
28	Mary	4	F	B	S		Tenn	Sept		Cholera	6 days
29	Maria	35	F	M	S		Tenn	Aug		Worms	1 day
30	Priscilla	9	F	B	S		Va	Aug		Cholera	25 days
31	Jo	20	M	B	S		Tenn	Feb		Cons.	7 days
32	Louiza	8	F	B	S		Tenn	Feb		Fever	4 days
33	John	1m	M	M	S		Tenn	Jan		Fever	
34	William	1	M	B	S		Tenn	March		Lock jaw	3 days
35	Infant	6m	M	B	S		Tenn	June		Cholera	5 days

COUNTY OF SUMNER, STATE OF TENNESSEE.

PAGE NO. 788 PERSONS WHO DIED DURING THE YEAR ENDING 1st JUNE, 1850.

District No. 5
James L. McKain

No. of Visit	Name	Age	Sex	Color	Free or Slave	Married/Widowed	Place of Birth	Month Died	Occupation	Disease or Cause of Death	No. Days Ill
1	Dolly	48	F	B	S		Tenn	March		Dropsy	90 days
2	Emily	17	F	B	S		Tenn	Aug		T. fever	12 days
3	James	1m	M	M	S		Tenn	Aug		T. fever	6 days
4	Elizabeth Miller	12	F	W	F		Kentucky	May		White swelling	60 days
5	Peggy	50	F	B	S		Kentucky	July		Dropsy	70 days
6	Ellen	1	F	B	S		Tenn	June		Bowel complaint	10 days
7	Lee	6m	M	B	S		Tenn	Jan		Brain disease	5 days
8	Matilda	8m	F	B	S		Tenn	July		Brain disease	8 days
9	Joseph Jenkins	27	M	W	F	M	N.C.	Dec	Tailor	Consumption	90 days
10	Ellen Jenkins	6m	F	W	F		Tenn	Feb		Consumption	60 days
11	William C. May	54	M	W	F	M	N.C.	Aug	Farmer	T. fever	15 days
12	Luke	20	M	B	S		Va	April		Dropsy	30 days
13	William Crump	71	M	W	F	M	Va	Aug	Wheelwright	Cholera	1 day
14	Leandor Crump	69	F	W	F	M	Va	Aug		Cholera	2 days
15	Hannah Crump	20	F	W	F	M	Va	Aug		Cholera	2 days
16	Samuel Crump	18	M	W	F		Va	Aug	Stonecutter	Thrown from horse	
17	Lewis W. Crump	52	M	W	F	M	Va	Aug	Stonecutter	Cholera	1 day
18	Bennett Wallace	2	M	W	F		Tenn	Aug		Worms	15 days
19	George	27	M	B	S		Tenn	Aug		Cholera	1 day
20	Mary J. Dill	2	F	W	F		Tenn	Dec		Worms	6 days
21	Mildred Harris	67	F	W	F	W	Va	March		Consumption	80 days
22	Martha Edwards	57	F	W	F	M	N.C.	Aug		Consumption	20 days
23	Thankfull Harper	17	F	W	F	S	Tenn	Aug		T. fever	4 days
24	Edmund	35	M	B	S		Tenn	Feb		Consumption	45 days
25	Elizabeth Blakemore	1	F	W	F		Tenn	Dec		Worms	4 days
26	Stephen Wilson	61	M	W	F	M	Tenn	Aug		Cholera	1 day
27	Katy	66	F	B	S		Maryland	Sept		Sore head	25 days
28	Sandy	1	M	B	S		Tenn	Nov		King's Evil	20 days
29	Infant		M	B	S		Tenn	Aug		Born dead	
30	Thomas Lloyd	45	M	W	F	M	Tenn	Nov		Consumption	60 days
31	David Dannel	65	M	W	F	M	N.C.	Oct		Consumption	50 days
32	Christopher Dannel	24	M	W	F	M	N.C.	June		Accident	4 days
33	Infant		F	B	S		Tenn	June		Born dead	
34	John Carter	1m	M	W	F		Tenn	May		Born dead	
35	Susan	2	F	B	S		Tenn	Sept		Drowned	

COUNTY OF SUMNER, STATE OF TENNESSEE.

PAGE NO. 789 PERSONS WHO DIED DURING THE YEAR ENDING 1st JUNE, 1850.

District No. 13, 14, & 15
James L. McKain

No. of Visit	Name	Age	Sex	Color	Free or Slave	Married/Widowed	Place of Birth	Month Died	Occupation	Disease or Cause of Death	No. Days Ill
1	Mildred Yourie	22	F	W	F	M	Tenn	May		Cramp cholic	1 day
2	Elizabeth Henry	15	F	W	F		Tenn	Oct		Cholera	3 days
3	Richard	2	M	B	S		Tenn	Dec		Teething	4 days
4	Samuel	10m	M	B	S		Tenn	Dec		Fever	9 days
5	Susan	6m	F	B	S		Tenn	Sept		Worms	5 days
6	Alice	4	F	B	S		Tenn	June		Croup	1 day
7	Martha Nance	76	F	W	F	W	Va	Sept		Old age	10 days
8	Samuel H. Bradley	1	M	W	F		Tenn	Sept		Teething	5 days
9	Martha Lauderdale	1	F	W	F		Tenn	Sept		Scald head	120 days
10	James D. Ballery	9m	M	W	F		Tenn	June		Croup	2 days
11	Reuben D. Brown	74	M	W	F	M	Va	July	Farmer	Cholera	1 day
12	James Dickerson	18	M	W	F	M	Tenn	July	Farmer	Cholera	1 day
13	Jane	1	F	B	S		Tenn	Sept		Brain fever	3 days
14	Thomas Lyttleton	14	M	W	F		Tenn	Oct		T. fever	6 days
15	Martha	12	F	B	S		Tenn	Aug		Cholera	3 days
16	Herman	3	M	B	S		Tenn	July		Cholera	1 day
17	William A. Elkins	1	M	W	F		Tenn	July		Chills	30 days
18	John W. Lauderdale	52	M	W	F		Tenn	Sept	Farmer	Murdered	
19	Thomas Gilmore	70	M	W	F		Va	March	Farmer	Consumption	90 days
20	Frances H. Gilliam	20	F	W	F		Tenn	June		T. fever	9 days
21	Rebecca Maburry	26	F	W	F		Tenn	May		Consumption	40 days
22	Martha Caldwell	28	F	W	F		Tenn	July		Child birth	1 day
23	Samuel	5	M	B	S		Tenn	May		Worms	8 days
24	Ned	6	M	B	S		Tenn	June		Worms	8 days
25	Samuel Stewart	4	M	B	F		Tenn	April		Consumption	28 days
26	Eliza Stewart	2	F	B	F		Tenn	March		Consumption	20 days
27	Elijah Stewart	36	M	B	F		Tenn	June	Farmer	Milk posion	40 days
28	Martha	16	F	B	S		Tenn	Aug		Drowned	
29	Samuel	7	M	B	S		Kentucky	Dec		Worms	7 days
30	Thomas	2	M	B	S		Tenn	July		Teething	8 days
31	Mary Cruize	19	F	W	F		Tenn	Aug		Cholera	1 day
32	John	9	M	B	S		Tenn	July		Drowned	
33	John Merritt	21	M	W	F		Tenn	Jan	Farmer	Pleurisy	9 days
34	Harvey Maize	2	M	W	F		Tenn	May		Burnt	
35	James Miers	1	M	W	F		Tenn	June		Croup	5 days

COUNTY OF SUMNER, STATE OF TENNESSEE.

PAGE NO. 791 PERSONS WHO DIED DURING THE YEAR ENDING 1st JUNE, 1850.

District No. 6
Thos. S. Watson

No. of Visit	Name	Age	Sex	Color	Free or Slave	Married/Widowed	Place of Birth	Month Died	Occupation	Disease or Cause of Death	No. Days Ill
1	Alfred W. Douglass	28	M				Tenn	Aug	Min.E.P.M.	Cholera	
2	Thomas Hunt	73	M			W	N.C.	Aug	Farmer	Cholera	
3	Sion Hunt	40	M			M	Tenn	Aug	Farmer	Cholera	
4	Martha A. Guthrie	20	F				Tenn	Aug		Cholera	
5	Ann	14	F	B	S		Tenn	Aug		Cholera	
6	Michel	17	M	B	S		Tenn	March		Fever	1 week
7	Augustus	30	M	B	S			Feb		Liver	1 week
8	William W. Stratton	24	M					April		Cholera	
9	Simon	38	M	B	S			April		Cholera	
10	Rachel	18	F	B	S			Aug		Cholera	
11	Jacob Thompson	83	M				Va	Aug		Dropsy	1 year
12	George Elliot	52	M				N.C.	Aug		Cholera	
13	Dave	45	M	B	S		Tenn	July		Cholera	
14	Robert	30	M	B	S			July		Cholera	
15	James	39	M	B	S			July		Cholera	
16	Mary	25	F	B	S			Sept		Cholera	
17	Martha	27	F	B	S			July		Consumption	1 year
18	Hiram	16	M	B	S		Kentucky	June		Fever	1 week
19	Isaac	40	M	B	S		Tenn	Aug		Cholera	
20	Jane	12	F	B	S			Aug		Cholera	
21	Maria	50	F	B	S		Tenn	July		Cancer	1 year
22	John	62	M	B	S			July		Consumption	2 years
23	John Wallace	62	M			M		July		Cholera	2 days
24	William	13	M	B	S			March		T. fever	2 weeks
25	Samuel Wilson	52	M			M	Tenn	Aug	Farmer	Cholera	4 days
26	Sarah Morgan	23	F			M		Dec		Fever	2 weeks
27	Mary	11	F	B	S			Sept		Fever	4 weeks
28	John	20	M	B	S			April		Fever	5 weeks
29	George	1	M	B	S			Feb		Cold	2 weeks
30	Martin	55	M	B	S			July		Cholera	1 day
31	Richard	20	M					April		Pleurisy	2 weeks
32	Julia	2	F	B	S			Oct		Fever	1 week
33	Mary	52	F	B	S			Oct		C	3 weeks
34	Thomas	2	M	B	S			Aug		Fever	2 weeks
35	Lavina	22	F	B	S			Oct		Fever	3 weeks
36	Lucy	2	F	B	S		Tenn	Nov		T. fever	1 week
37	Jane	6	F	B	S		Tenn	June		C	4 weeks
38	Betsy	3	F	B	S		Tenn	Nov		C	7 weeks
39	William	34	M	B	S		Tenn	Oct		T. fever	2 weeks
40	Ann	18	F	B	S			July		Cholera	2 days
41	Rachel	13	F	B	S			Sept		Fever	3 weeks
42	Delia	12	F	B	S			Sept		Fever	2 weeks
43	Milly	1	F	B	S			Dec		Dropsy	6 weeks
44	Enoch Simp	89	M					June		Dropsy	8 weeks
45	Thomas Baird	69	M					July		C	3 weeks

COUNTY OF SUMNER, STATE OF TENNESSEE.

PAGE NO. 793   PERSONS WHO DIED DURING THE YEAR ENDING 1st JUNE, 1850.

District No. 16, 18 & 19

Thos. S. Watson

No. of Visit	Name	Age	Sex	Color	Free or Slave	Married/Widowed	Place of Birth	Month Died	Occupation	Disease or Cause of Death	No. Days Ill
1	Colin Campbell	89	M				N.C.	May	none	Dropsy	3 months
2	Nancy Campbell	84	F				N.C.	Aug		unknown	1 month
3	Sarah Staggs	44	F				Tenn	Aug		Consumption	4 months
4	Mary Dismukes	44	F				Tenn	Sept		Fever	5 days
5	Tom	4m	M	B	S			Sept		Croup	1 day
6	Bob	60	M	B	S		Tenn	July		Cholera	1 day
7	William Green	33	M				Tenn	Aug		C	1 year
8	Elizabeth Harrel	63	F				Tenn	Aug		Cholera	2 days
9	Jacob	90	M	B	S		Tenn	March		Dropsy	5 months
10	Martha	50	F	B	S			March		Dropsy	3 weeks
11	Benjamin Sutton	45	M				N.C.	Sept		Const.	1 year
12	George	14	M	B	S			Dec		Fever	3 weeks
13	Calvin	4	M	B	S		Tenn	Jan		Fever	9 days
14	Charles	35	M	B	S			April		C	6 months
15	Richard	35	M	B	S			June		Cholera	2 days
16	Mary	20	F	B	S			Aug		Cholera	3 days
17	David Strother	21	M					Aug		Cholera	3 days
18	Susan Strother	7	F				Tenn	Nov		unknown	15 days
19	Joseph Cotton	41	M			M		Aug		Fever	7 days
20	Sam	19	M	B	S		Tenn	Dec		C	7 days
21	Ransom	5	M	B	S			Feb		Cons.	2 months
22	Judah	22	M	B	S			April		Cons.	2 months
23	Chloe	8	F	B	S			July		Pleurisy	20 days
24	Polly	14	F	B	S			Feb		Cholera	
25	Reuben	10	M	B	S			Feb		Fever	6 days
26	Jane	1	F	B	S			Aug		B. Complaint	7 days
27	Harry	30	M	B	S			Oct		T. fever	30 days
28	Docia	40	F	B	S			Aug		Dropsy	6 months
29	Patsey	56	F	B	S			Nov		C	40 days
30	Nancy	21	F	B	S			Aug		unknown	30 days
31	Lucy	3	F	B	S			April		Sc. fever	10 days
32	Peter	1	M	B	S			April		Sc. fever	10 days
33	Martha Douglass	1	F				Tenn	Feb		Croup	
34	John Latimore	1	M				Tenn	March		Croup	

COUNTY OF SUMNER, STATE OF TENNESSEE.

PAGE NO. 795   PERSONS WHO DIED DURING THE YEAR ENDING 1st JUNE, 1850.

District No. 16, 18 & 19

Thos. S. Watson

No. of Visit	Name	Age	Sex	Color	Free or Slave	Married/Widowed	Place of Birth	Month Died	Occupation	Disease or Cause of Death	No. Days Ill
1	Jane Osburn	9m	F				Tenn	June		unknown	20 days
2	Ruth Meador	25	F			M	Tenn	July	none	Con.	4 months
3	Rachel Owen	2	F				Tenn	June	none	C	1 day
4	Sarah	40	F	B	S		Tenn	Sept	none	Dropsy	4 months
5	Mary House	42	F			M	Tenn	June	none	Palsy	1 year
6	Jane	24	F	B	S			June		Scrofula	3 months
7	Suckey	21	F	B	S		Tenn	Oct		Burnt	sudden
8	Dilsey	2	F	B	S			Sept		Worms	2 months
9	Jesse Bradley	4	M				Tenn	June		C	10 days
10	Noah Somers	1	M					Aug		Bowel complaint	14 days
11	Margaret	66	F	B	S			Oct		C	1 year
12	Mary	1	F					July		Inflamation of brain	20 days
13	Jane Kelly	45	F				Tenn	Feb		Consumption	6 months
14	Sarah Kirby	65	F			W	Tenn	Aug		Cancer	2 years
15	Aaron Thompson	41	M					Aug		Fever	2 weeks
16	Kuran Thompson	35	F			M		June		Fever	3 weeks
17	Jane	20	F	B	S			Aug		unknown	3 months
18	Dick	2	M	B	S			Dec		unknown	2 months
19	Julia	8m	F	B	S			Feb		unknown	11 days
20	William H. Briggs	2	M					Oct		Cholera Inf.	12 days
21	Maria Duffer	15	F					Oct		C	6 weeks
22	Elizabeth Dowel	28	F				Tenn	May		C	4 months
23	Edmond Hill	45	M				Tenn	Sept		Fever	27 days
24	Jane Turner	4m	F					Aug		Hives	6 days
25	Sarah Bracken	62	F					Feb		Fever	9 days
26	Jane	52	F	B	S			March		Consumption	1 year
27	Jeremiah	29	M	B	S			May		C	2 months
28	Phebe	22	F	B	S			Jan		Const.	3 months
29	John Hobdy	1	M					Oct		Croup	5 days
30	William Perkins	83	M					March		Pleurisy	15 days
31	Sarah Caldwell	60	F					June		C	3 months
32	Maria	1	F	B	S			Oct		Croup	3 days
33	Emily Denning	22	F					Oct		Fever	3 months
34	Solomon Brown	77	M					May		Old age	
35	Ann Hodges	10m	F					Aug		Worms	21 days

COUNTY OF SUMNER, STATE OF TENNESSEE.

PAGE NO. 797 PERSONS WHO DIED DURING THE YEAR ENDING 1st JUNE, 1850.

District No. 6 & 7
Thos. S. Watson

No. of Visit	Name	Age	Sex	Color	Free or Slave	Married/Widowed	Place of Birth	Month Died	Occupation	Disease or Cause of Death	No. Days Ill
1	Catharine Garrettson	80	F			W	Va	June		Old age	
2	Nancy	1	F	B	S		Tenn	Aug		Whooping cough	4 weeks
3	George	80	M	B	S			Feb		Old age	
4	Francis	6m	M	M	S		Tenn	July		Whooping cough	3 weeks
5	Thomas Sanderson	18	M				Tenn	Sept	Farmer	Lock jaw	4 days
6	Hannah	60	F	B	S		Tenn	Oct		Consumption	6 months
7	Daniel	1	M	B	S		Tenn	May		Whooping cough	4 weeks
8	Lemuel	1	M	B	S		Tenn	April		Whooping cough	5 weeks
9	Isom	1	M	B	S			May		Teething	3 weeks
10	James Wise	1	M				Tenn	Sept		Teething	2 weeks
11	Harriet	28	F	B	S		Tenn	Jan		C	
12	Chaney	2	F	B	S		Tenn	Feb		Worms	14 days
13	Elizabeth Starks	6m	F				Tenn	Aug		Hives	2 days
14	Charles	5m	M	B	S			Aug		Hives	2 days
15	William Talley	8	M				Tenn	June		Fever	20 days
16	Alfred Pryor	22	M				Tenn	May	Blk-smith	T. fever	30 days
17	Cecelia Bradford	18	F				Tenn	Aug		Accident	sudden
18	William Henry	22	M				Va	Jan		C	6 months
19	Mary Cantrell	74	F			W	E. Tenn	Jan		C	40 days
20	John	6m	M	B	S		Tenn	Jan		Hives	2 days
21	James	6m	M	B	S		Tenn	June		Hives	2 days
22	Henry	6m	M	B	S		Tenn	June		Teething	10 days
23	Robert B. Allen	28	M				Tenn	April	Farmer	Drowned	sudden
24	Sarah	6	F	B	S			Sept		Worms	4 days
25	Isaac	69	M	B	S			April		T. fever	20 days
26	Hugh	6m	M	B	S		Tenn	Oct		Croup	
27	William	12	M	B	S		Tenn	April		Consumption	5 months
28	Bob	3	M	B	S			Feb		Worms	1 week
29	Mary Fulks	1	F					Feb		unknown	
30	James	9	M	M	S			Dec		unknown	5 weeks
31	David Nye	89	M				Mass	March		Old age	
32	Jane Ketring	53	F				Kentucky	Sept		C	4 weeks
33	Sarah Montgomery	55	F				N.C.	Jan		unknown	3 weeks
34	Joab Dorris	13	M				Tenn	Sept		Fever	4 weeks
35	Margaret Frazer	36	F				Tenn	Feb		Fever	1 week

COUNTY OF TIPTON, STATE OF TENNESSEE.

PAGE NO. 799   PERSONS WHO DIED DURING THE YEAR ENDING 1st JUNE, 1850.

R. S. Barret

No. of Visit	Name	Age	Sex	Color	Free or Slave	Married/Widowed	Place of Birth	Month Died	Occupation	Disease or Cause of Death	No. Days Ill
1	Nancy	4m	F	B			Tenn	Feb		Pneumonia	3 weeks
2	Caroline	3m	F	B	S		Tenn	July		Cholera	2 weeks
3	Charles	6m	M	B	S		Tenn	July		Cholera	4 days
4	James Clark	80	M	B	S		N.C.	Sept		Chronic	5 months
5	Fanny	6m	F	B	S		Tenn	April		Chronic	
6	Stephen	50	M	B	S		N.C.	April		Chronic	8 years
7	————	1	F	B	S		Tenn	Aug		Worms	sudden
8	Margaret	20	F	B	S		Tenn	Dec		Consumption	8 months
9	Barthenia	10m	F	B	S		Tenn	Aug		Croup	3 weeks
10	Venus	19	F	B	S		Tenn	June		Consumption	6 months
11	Samuel	10	M	B	S		Tenn	June		Hemorrhage of lungs	5 months
12	Infant	2m	F	B	S		Tenn	June		Inf. fever	3 days
13	Lucy Pilkington	7	F				Tenn	Oct		Croup	4 days
14	Malinda A. Fortner	3	F				Tenn	Nov		Croup	2 days
15	Logan	6	M	B	S		Tenn	April		sudden	
16	Erasmus Rose	1m	M				Tenn	April		Croup	2 weeks
17	Otway	60	M	B	S		Va	May		Dropsy	3 months
18	Eliza	18	F	B	S		Va	Dec		Womb	1 year
19	Polly	1	F	B	S		Tenn	Aug		unknown	1 year
20	William	1	M	B	S		Tenn	Sept		sudden	
21	Sally	8	F	B	S		Tenn	Feb		Chronic	5 years
22	Granville	8m	M	B	S		Tenn	March		Fever	5 weeks
23	Taylor	1	M	B	S		Tenn	July		Inflamation of brain	2 weeks
24	John	45	M	B	S		Tenn	————		Cholera	
25	Willis	6m	M	B	S		Tenn	May		Cholera Inf.	12 days
26	Willis	30	M	B	S		Tenn	Oct		Bil. cholic	1 day
27	David	14	M	B	S		Tenn	April		Consumption	3 months
28	————	1m	F	B	S		Tenn	Jan		Suddenly	
29	George J. Clement	17	M				Va	May	Student	sudden	
30	Betsy	1	F	B	S		Tenn	Oct		Chronic	3 months
31	Sarah	23	F	B	S		Tenn	July		Inflamation of brain	10 days
32	Nancy	50	F	B	S		Tenn	April		Chronic	3 months
33	Milly	54	F	B	S		N.C.	Nov		Dropsy	1 year
34	J. A. Somerville	1	F				Tenn	Aug		Cholera Inf.	3 months
35	Rose	8m	F	B	S		Tenn	Aug		Inflamation of brain	3 days

Remarks: State of Tennessee, Tipton County. I, Richard S. Barret, Assistant Marshal for said County and State, do certify that the foregoing four pages of persons who died in said County was well and truly made according to the tenor of my oath of office to the best of my knowledge and belief. Sworn to and subscribed before me this 18 December 1850.   R. S. Barret, Asst. Marshal.

COUNTY OF TIPTON, STATE OF TENNESSEE.

PAGE NO. 801 PERSONS WHO DIED DURING THE YEAR ENDING 1st JUNE, 1850.

R. S. Barret

No. of Visit	Name	Age	Sex	Color	Free or Slave	Married/Widowed	Place of Birth	Month Died	Occupation	Disease or Cause of Death	No. Days Ill
1	Elizabeth Farmer	24	F			M	Tenn	Jan		unknown	4 months
2	John Williams	4m	M				Tenn	Nov		Hives	1 day
3	James L. Holland	5m	M				Arkansas	Dec		unknown	2 months
4	John R. Davenport	1m	M				Tenn	Feb		unknown	3 days
5	Isaac Reed	17	M				Ohio	May		Shot	sudden
6	John Abbott	60	M				New York	May		unknown	3 weeks
7	O. Rose	14	F				Tenn	April		Inflamation of brain	2 weeks
8	Nancy Rose	55	F					Aug		Cholera	5 days
9	James	16	M	B	S		Tenn	Jan		Cholera	1 day
10	James W. Cross	1m	M				Tenn	April		Hives	1 day
11	Abram	50	M	B	S		____	July		Cholera	1 day
12	Benjamin	45	M	B	S		____	July		Cholera	1 day
13	Aaron	22	M	B	S		____	July		Cholera	1 day
14	Jacob	15	M	B	S		____	July		Cholera	1 day
15	Bill	21	M	B	S		____	July		Cholera	1 day
16	Robert	38	M	B	S		____	July		Cholera	____
17	Ann	70	F	B	S		____	July		Cholera	____
18	Leah	12	F	B	S		____	July		Cholera	____
19	Emily	14	F	B	S		____	July		Cholera	____
20	Abram	14	M	B	S		____	July		Cholera	____
21	Peter	22	M	B	S		____	July		Cholera	____
22	Nelson	18	M	B	S		____	July		Cholera	____
23	Mary	17	F	B	S		____	July		Cholera	____
24	Alice Boyd	1	F				Tenn	Oct		Croup	4 days
25	Alvira Elam	9m	F				Tenn	Sept		Hives	1 day
26	W. W. Bright	25	M				N.C.	April	Farmer	Consumption	12 months
27	Eliza T. Boothe	2m	F				Tenn	Aug		Inflamation	2 weeks
28	John Lemmons	85	M				N.C.	Dec	Farmer	Dropsy	18 years
29	Henry A. Crow	5	M				Tenn	Aug		Fever	2 days
30	Robert Robinson	75	M				Va	Aug	Farmer	Chronic	8 months
31	James Clark	8m	M				Missouri	Aug		Chronic	1 month
32	Bartlett	35	M	B	S			Dec		Chronic	2 months
33	Alexander	45	M	B	S		____	July		sudden	sudden
34	Kit	60	M	B	S		____	Sept		Fever	1 month

COUNTY OF TIPTON, STATE OF TENNESSEE.

PAGE NO. 804   PERSONS WHO DIED DURING THE YEAR ENDING 1st JUNE, 1850.

R. S. Barret

No. of Visit	Name	Age	Sex	Color	Free or Slave	Married/Widowed	Place of Birth	Month Died	Occupation	Disease or Cause of Death	No. Days Ill
1	Benjamin	14	M	M	S		N.C.	Feb		Accident	sudden
2	Irene Matthews	3	F				Tenn	Aug		Fever	14 days
3	William	10m	M	M	S		Tenn	May		Croup	30 days
4	Iva Wiseman	7m	F				Tenn	Dec		Croup	14 days
5	Sarah Holmes	29	F			M	Va	Feb		T. fever	10 days
6	Julia	23	F	B	S		Tenn	June		Fever	3 months
7	Iva Ann Vincent	3	F				Tenn	June		Worms	6 hours
8	Lewis C. Winford	6m	M				Tenn	July		Fever	3 months
9	Mary A. Freeman	10m	F				Tenn	Oct		Thrash	3 weeks
10	Elizabeth M. Holmes	4	F				Tenn	Sept		Pneumonia	18 days
11	Rowena Lauderdale	23	F			M	N.C.	April		Consumption	3 months
12	Rowena Lauderdale	1m	F				Tenn	May		unknown	sudden
13	Allen	6	M	B	S		Tenn	Sept		Fever	6 days
14	_____(blank)	1m	M				Tenn	March		unknown	sudden
15	Dick	1	M	B	S		Tenn	March		unknown	sudden
16	Marsilla	17	F	B	S		Tenn	June		Consumption	4 months
17	Creesey	23	F	B	S		Va	April		Consumption	4 months
18	Samuel	10m	M	B	S		Tenn	Nov		Inflamation of brain	6 days
19	Mary C. Holmes	1	F				Tenn	April		Worms	6 days
20	Lucinda	27	F	B	S		Va	March		Consumption	6 days
21	Caroline	1	F	B	S		Tenn	Aug		Pneumonia	6 days
22	Joseph Witherington	24	M				Tenn	March	Farmer	Consumption	2 years
23	Benjamin F. Myers	10m	M				Tenn	July		Inflamation of brain	7 days
24	Mary Billings	9m	F				Tenn	April		Inflamation of brain	2 weeks
25	Robert Myers	33	M				Kentucky	Nov	Farmer	Pneumonia	2 weeks
26	Mary H. Alston	31	F				N.C.	Jan		T. fever	10 days
27	A. S. J. Alston	8	M				Miss	Jan		T. fever	1 day
28	Caroline	30	F	B	S		N.C.	Jan		T. fever	4 days
29	G. Smith	67	F				N.C.	Oct		Spinal affect	6 months
30	Catharine C. Brown	15	F				Tenn	July		Fever	11 days
31	Sarah E. Brown	19	F				Alabama	Aug		Fever	11 days
32	John S. Brown	19	M				Tenn	Sept		Fever	4 weeks
33	Nancy Starnes	40	F				N.C.	Jan		Consumption	7 months
34	Stephen Herring	65	M				N.C.	Jan	Farmer	Consumption	4 months
35	Anderson Ralph	55	M				N.C.	March	Farmer	sudden	sudden

COUNTY OF TIPTON, STATE OF TENNESSEE.

PAGE NO. 806   PERSONS WHO DIED DURING THE YEAR ENDING 1st JUNE, 1850.

R. S. Barret

No. of Visit	Name	Age	Sex	Color	Free or Slave	Married/Widowed	Place of Birth	Month Died	Occupation	Disease or Cause of Death	No. Days Ill
1	Thomas Butler	100	M	B	S		Va	Jan		Old age	
2	Lucy Wynn	35	F				Tenn	Sept		Chronic	2 years
3	Martha Wynn	9m	F				Tenn	Dec		Chronic	9 months
4	Louisa	14	F	B	S		Tenn	Feb		Congestion	4 days
5	Gilbert	95	M	B	S		N.C.	April		Inflamation, fever	20 days
6	Margaret J. Adkins	49	F				Va	Dec		T. fever	21 days
7	George McBride	39	M				Tenn	Aug		Bil. fever	3 days
8	Julia F. Elmore	2	F				Tenn	Aug		Diarrhea	6 weeks
9	Martha Dickson	62	F				S.C.	Sept		Consumption	2 years
10	Abram	1m	M	B	S		Tenn	April		unknown	1 week
11	Sarah Smith	5	F				Tenn	Aug		Fever	4 weeks
12	Minerva	2	F	B	S		Tenn	Oct		Fever	2 weeks
13	Juda	2m	F	B	S		Tenn	Sept		Croup	2 months
14	Mary Little	23	F				Kentucky	Oct		Consumption	5 months
15	Lavina	50	F	B	S		N.C.	Aug		Pleurisy	3 months
16	Lavina	2m	F	B	S		Tenn	Aug		unknown	1 month
17	Richard	1m	M	B	S		Tenn	Feb		Cold	2 days
18	Margaret	1	F	B	S		Tenn	June		unknown	8 days
19	John Hoffer	89	M				Va	April	Farmer	Old age	2 months
20	Lauretta Strong	24	F				Tenn	March		Consumption	2 years
21	Elias	9	M	B	S		Tenn	April		sudden	sudden
22	Sarah	15	F	B	S		Tenn	Oct		T. fever	15 days
23	Judy	85	F	M	S		Maryland	May		Old age	15 days
24	Elizabeth McMinn	37	F				S.C.	Dec		Consumption	1 year
25	Jubiter	10m	M	B	S		Tenn	Feb		Inflamation	10 days
26	William Wright	21	M				S.C.	Feb	Farmer	Consumption	18 months
27	Hannibal	65	F	B	S		Va	July		Consumption	2 years
28	Lucy	60	F	B	S		Tenn	Feb		sudden	sudden
29	Charles	12	M	B	S		Tenn	Jan		Inflamation	8 months
30	W. D. Taylor	21	M				Va	March		Chronic	20 days
31	Mary A. Fallen	24	F				Tenn	Nov		Child birth	5 days
32	Arrena	1m	F	B	S		Tenn	Feb		sudden	
33	Amy	20	F	B	S		N.C.	July		Chronic	5 months
34	Ann	2	F	B	S		Tenn	Oct		Diarrhea	2 months
35	Charles	2	M	B	S		Tenn	Jan		Chronic	6 months

COUNTY OF VAN BUREN, STATE OF TENNESSEE.

PAGE NO. 810 PERSONS WHO DIED DURING THE YEAR ENDING 1st JUNE, 1850.

All the Districts
John Gillentine

No. of Visit	Name	Age	Sex	Color	Free or Slave	Married/Widowed	Place of Birth	Month Died	Occupation	Disease or Cause of Death	No. Days Ill
1	Mary Douglass	3m	F	B	S		Tenn	Feb		Accident	sudden
2	Infant of John T. Lane	1m	M				Tenn	Nov		Croup	4 days
3	Infant of John Sparkman	2m	F				Tenn	March		unknown	12 days
4	Infant of William Moore	1m	M				Tenn	Feb		unknown	instantly
5	Infant of William Moore	1m	M				Tenn	Feb		unknown	instantly
6	Infant of William Moore	1m	M				Tenn	May		unknown	instantly
7	William L. Bryant	11	M				Tenn	May		Mortified	14 days
8	Stacy Baker	26	F			M	Tenn	Jan	House-kpr	Child bearing	11 days
9	Joseph Duney	1m	M				Tenn	March		unknown	1 day
10	Martha Moore	4	F				Tenn	Jan		unknown	instantly
11	Rebecca Moore	1	F				Tenn	March		Croup	35 days
12	July Moore	10	F	B	S		Tenn	Dec		Fall of tree	3 days
13	James Mitchell	22	M			M	Tenn	Nov	Farmer	Consumption	2 years
14	Clayton McCormack	1m	M				Tenn	Dec		of weakness	17 days
15	Mary Tolley (Talley)	63	F			M	Va	April	Spinster	Dropsy	8 months
16	David Keener	50	M			M	Va	Oct	Farmer	Fever	32 days
17	Washington Groves	1m	M				Tenn	Dec		Weakness	instantly
18	Jackson Groves	1m	M				Tenn	April		Weakness	instantly
19	1 child, Huddleston	1m	M	B	S		Tenn	Feb		Weakness	1 day
20	William Bruster	1	M				Tenn	Dec		Inflamation	30 days
21	Clemmontine Malloy	33	F			M	Tenn	March	House-kpr	Child bearing	12 days
22	Burshely Jane Tash	8	F				Tenn	April		Fever	3 months
23	George M. Owins	1	M				Tenn	Dec		Croup	3 days
24	Scott Hall	3	M				Tenn	Aug		Croup	2 days
25	Benjamin Hall	1	M				Tenn	Aug		Croup	1 day
26	Mary Philips	44	F			M	Tenn	July	House-kpr	A. T. Fits	instantly
27	Francis York	66	F			M	Va	March	House-kpr	Consumption	90 days

Remarks: There was but twenty seven deaths in the year ending 1st June 1850, as appears above, there is several children not named, as you will see, having died without being named by their parents and mothers. John Gillentine, Asst. Marshal.

COUNTY OF WARREN, STATE OF TENNESSEE.

PAGE NO. 811 PERSONS WHO DIED DURING THE YEAR ENDING 1st JUNE, 1850.

A. C. Rodgers

No. of Visit	Name	Age	Sex	Color	Free or Slave	Married/Widowed	Place of Birth	Month Died	Occupation	Disease or Cause of Death	No. Days Ill
1	Thomas C. Davis	77	M			M	Va	Oct	Shoemaker	Dropsy	6 months
2	Perry J. Brackens	23	M				Alabama	Oct	Farmer	unknown	7 days
3	Sarah J. Guthry	21	F				Tenn	Nov		Scarletina	5 days
4	Sarah Gibbs	27	F				Va	May		Chronic	7 weeks
5	Harrison	18	M	B	S		Tenn	Aug		Accident	
6	Nelly	12	F	B	S		Tenn	Nov		Pneumonia	3 months
7	Henry Swader	59	M			M?	Va	Feb		Small pox	12 days
8	Richard Parker	75	M			M	Va	Feb	Farmer	Cancer	4 months
9	Martha J. Stroud	2	F				Tenn	Jan		Croup	14 days
10	Hannah Stroud	66	F			M	Va	Sept		Chronic	20 days
11	Lucy J. Perkins	10	F				Tenn	Dec		unknown	9 days
12	Archibald Stewart	83	M				Ireland	Feb	Hatter	unknown	4 days
13	Thomas Mitchell	30	M			M	Tenn	May	Farmer	Suicide	
14	Louisa Stubblefield	21	F				Tenn	Jan		Chronic	7 months
15	Wilmuth Stubblefield	67	F			M	Va	Jan		Chronic	6 months
16	Carrol Fults	20	M				Tenn	Nov	Farmer	Chronic	4 days
17	William S. Milton	1	M				Tenn	March		Croup	28 days
18	John H. Fletcher	43	M			M	N.C.	Jan	Farmer	Small pox	4 days
19	Telithia J. Allison	18	F				Tenn	Aug		unknown	7 months
20	Moses Moyers	30	M				Tenn	March	Farmer	Apoplexy	

Remarks: I, Archibald C. Rodgers, Assistant Marshal for the County of Warren, State of Tennessee, do certify upon oath that the above returns were made as near as surrounding circumstances would admit according to my oath and instructions to the best of my knowledge and belief. January 11th, 1851.
A. C. Rodgers.

COUNTY OF WARREN, STATE OF TENNESSEE.

PAGE NO. 814   PERSONS WHO DIED DURING THE YEAR ENDING 1st JUNE, 1850.

A. C. Rodgers

No. of Visit	Name	Age	Sex	Color	Free or Slave	Married/Widowed	Place of Birth	Month Died	Occupation	Disease or Cause of Death	No. Days Ill
1	Infant		F				Tenn	March		unknown	sudden
2	not named	1m	M	B	S		Tenn	April		Smothered	
3	Rhody Morell	21	F				Tenn	March		unknown	13 days
4	Levi Rogers	70	M			W	N.C.	June	Farmer	unknown	6 months
5	Elisha Whitman	20	M				Tenn	May	Laborer	Fits	14 days
6	John McColm	83	M			W	N.C.	May	Laborer	Old age	20 days
7	Nancy Moffett	19	F				Tenn	June		Palsy	4 weeks
8	Benjamin Derosset	5	M				Tenn	Dec		Influenza	3 weeks
9	Margaret A. Derosset	1m	F				Tenn	Dec			sudden
10	Mary Cantrell	4m	F				Tenn	Feb		Abscess	4 months
11	James Settles	5	M				Tenn	Feb		unknown	4 weeks
12	John P. Caton	33	M				N.C.	May	Farmer	Chronic	7 months
13	Infant		F				Tenn	July			sudden
14	Rebecca E. Davis	7	F				Tenn	March		unknown	1 day
15	Elwood Perry	12	M				N.C.	May		Fits	Chronic
16	not named	13d	F	B	S		Tenn	Nov		unknown	
17	Nicholas Edington	56	M			M	Tenn	Dec	Teacher	Fits	
18	Richard Webb	15	M				Tenn	Aug	Laborer	Cholera Mor.	21 days
19	Lavina Webb	1	F				Tenn	Oct		Croup	4 days
20	Olive	1	F	M	S		Tenn	Sept		Chronic	
21	Sarah McSpadden	70	F			M	Va	Aug		Cholera	2 days
22	Elizabeth Ferrell	30	F			M	Tenn	Aug		Cholera	2 days
23	John M. Hibden	1	M				Tenn	Aug		Cholera	9 days
24	James McCagg	10m	M				Tenn	Jan		unknown	2 months
25	Mildred Ware	6	F				Tenn	Nov		Phrenitis	2 days
26	Isaac Anderson	19	M				Tenn	Feb	Student	Fever	7 days
27	James Davenport	10m	M				Tenn	May		unknown	3 months
28	Molly M. Prater	78	F			M	N.C.	Aug		unknown	6 months
29	Andrew Orrick	25	M			M	Tenn	Jan	Farm-labor	unknown	10 days
30	Elizabeth Orrick	23	F				Tenn	March		Fever	24 days
31	Faddy L. Robinson	41	F			M	N.C.	July	Farmer	Chronic	6 months
32	John N. Hammers	4	M				Tenn	Jan		Fever	21 days
33	Thomas Brown	105	M			W	N.C.	Sept	Farmer	Old age	3 years
34	Martha Giles	63	F			M	N.C.	Sept		Cough	4 weeks
35	Mary A. Fennell	20	F				N.C.	Jan		Fever	5 weeks

COUNTY OF WARREN, STATE OF TENNESSEE.

PAGE NO. 818   PERSONS WHO DIED DURING THE YEAR ENDING 1st JUNE, 1850.

A. C. Rodgers

No. of Visit	Name	Age	Sex	Color	Free or Slave	Married/Widowed	Place of Birth	Month Died	Occupation	Disease or Cause of Death	No. Days Ill
1	Susan E. Mitchell	1	F				Tenn	July		Phrenitis	35 days
2	Alexander Thompson	3	M				Tenn	Nov		Scarletina	4 days
3	Barbara Boren	6m	F				Tenn	Sept		Croup	2 months
4	Moses Perkins	88	M			W	Va	Sept	Farmer	Old age	
5	Infant Perkins	1m	F				Tenn	Feb		Croup	4 days
6	Nelly Hays	1	F				Tenn	Oct		Croup	7 days
7	David J. Parris	22	M			W	Tenn	Nov	Farmer	Pleurisy	7 days
8	Elizabeth Evans	53	F				N.C.	Feb		Asthma	9 months
9	Jacob Helms	47	M			M	unknown	March	Farmer	Fall from horse	2 days
10	Elbert Mayfield	30	M				Tenn	Sept	Farmer	Fits	sudden
11	Infant Mayfield	1m	F				Tenn	July		unknown	sudden
12	Vasti A. Henshaw	21	F				Tenn	Aug		Fever	8 days
13	Nathan Rawlings	2	M				Tenn	June		Flux	14 days
14	Infant Rawlings	1m	F				Tenn	May		unknown	21 days
15	Anderson Jaco	3m	M				Tenn	July		Erysipelas	6 days
16	Martha E. McElvany	2m	F				Tenn	Nov		Croup	3 days
17	Thomas Gribble	73	M			M	N.C.	Aug	Farmer	Consumption	90 days
18	Robert Bishop	17	M				Tenn	July	Farmer	sudden	
19	Infant Bishop, unnamed	1	M				Tenn	June		unknown	2 days
20	Charles	5	M	B	S		Tenn	March		Small pox	9 days
21	Louisa Crum	3	F				Tenn	Oct		Sc. fever	4 months
22	Jacob	30	M	B	S		Tenn	Aug		Gastritis	7 days
23	Betsy	27	F	B	S		Tenn	Oct		unknown	3 months
24	James Walker	35	M				Tenn	Dec	Farmer	Killed in fight	
25	Elizabeth Jennings	74	F				Va	May		Chronic	6 months
26	Henry Chrisian	24	M				Tenn	May	Laborer	Drowned	
27	not named	3m	M	M	S		Tenn	May		sudden	
28	William J. Dodson	11m	M				Tenn	June		Worms	14 days
29	James H. Safley	12	M				Tenn	March		Rheumatism	4 months
30	Rhody	10m	F	B	S		Tenn	Aug		unknown	10 months
31	Salena Martin	28	F				Tenn	Oct		Consumption	11 months
32	Jane E. Martin	16	F				Tenn	April		Fever	8 weeks
33	Isabella Bolin	2	F				Tenn	April		Worms	10 days
34	Sylva Bolin	25	F				Tenn	March		Fever	14 days
35	Jacob Woodlie	61	M			M	Va	Feb	Farmer	unknown	17 days

COUNTY OF WASHINGTON, STATE OF TENNESSEE.

PAGE NO. 820 PERSONS WHO DIED DURING THE YEAR ENDING 1st JUNE, 1850.

4th Subdivision, E. District
Jos. S. Rhea

No. of Visit	Name	Age	Sex	Color	Free or Slave	Married/Widowed	Place of Birth	Month Died	Occupation	Disease or Cause of Death	No. Days Ill
1	Polly Ballinger	63	F			W	Tenn	Feb	Farmer		C
2	Susannah Campbell	65	F			W	Tenn	Oct	Farmer		C
3	Sarah J. Carson	5	F				Tenn	Aug		Inflamation of bowels	2 days
4	Edmond Eavens	1m	M	B	F		Tenn	Aug		unknown	
5	Joan Kinnic	10	F				Tenn	Aug		Fever	17 days
6	Polly Sherfy	28	F			M	Tenn	July		Fever	90 days
7	Catherine Hammer	83	F			W	Va	Feb			C
8	James Fletcher	86	M			W	Va	April	Blk-smith		C
9	John Carts	73	M			W	Maryland	April	Blk-smith	Dropsy	90 days
10	David S. Wiley	9m	M				Tenn	April		Dropsy	80 days
11	John Pruit	52	M			M	Va	Oct	Farmer		C
12	Margaret Matthews	80	F			W	Maryland	Aug	Farmer		C
13	Jane E. Duncan	40	F			M	Va	Jan	Farmer	Inflamation of liver	8 days
14	Infant of Jacob Bowman	3d	M				Tenn	April		unknown	
15	Mariah J. Bowman	21	F				Tenn	March		Consumption	60 days
16	Mary A. Bayless	1	F				Tenn	March		Inflamation of bowels	20 days
17	Keziah Falic	104	F	B	F		Maryland	Aug		Old age	
18	John E. Waldres	1	M				Tenn	Aug		Diarrhea	60 days
19	Elizabeth Cloyd	2	F				Tenn	Jan		Fever	30 days
20	Thomas Cloyd	28	M				Tenn	Nov	Wagon-maker	Fever	8 days
21	John Jurdon	60	M				Tenn	March	Farmer	Pal. of heart	C
22	Infant of E. S. Mathes	14d	F				Tenn	Nov		Croup	3 days
23	George Watterford	1	M	M			Tenn	March		Fever	12 days
24	Joshua Babb	49	M			M	Tenn	Jan	Farmer	Fever	20 days
25	Family of Heaz. Taylor	63	M	B	S		Tenn	Feb		Consumption	60 days
26	Elizabeth Lane	65	F				N.C.	May		Polypus	6 months
27	Nancy Walker	41	F				N.C.	Aug		Fits	sudden
28	Infant of W. Shepherd	5d	F				Tenn	Jan			sudden
29	John Hunter	57	M			M	N.C.	April	Farmer	Palsy	90 days
30	Susan Pearson	1	F				Tenn	Aug		Worms	60 days
31	Permelia Good	29	F			M	Tenn	Feb		Child birth	1 day
32	William Patterson	73	M			M	Va	Nov	Farmer	Palsy	6 months
33	David S. Britt	4d	M				Tenn	March		Fits	1 day
34	Jeremiah Woodruff	40	M			M	N.C.	May	Shoemaker	Consumption	90 days
35	Henry Stragh	38	M			M	Tenn	Sept	Blk-smith	Fever	12 days

Remarks: No malady has prevailed within the limits of this County the last year and as usual the citizens have comparetively enjoyed good health. The soil is rich upon the whole, and well adapted. The raising of cattle, horses, mules, sheep and hogs, as well as farming. Portions of the County are hilly but even these are productive while the land on the water courses are remarkably productive.

COUNTY OF WASHINGTON, STATE OF TENNESSEE.

PAGE NO. 829 PERSONS WHO DIED DURING THE YEAR ENDING 1st JUNE, 1850.

4th Subdivision, E. District
Jos. S. Rhea

No. of Visit	Name	Age	Sex	Color	Free or Slave	Married/Widowed	Place of Birth	Month Died	Occupation	Disease or Cause of Death	No. Days Ill
1	Family of Chas. Wickeek	1	M	B	S		Tenn			unknown	
2	James G. Casson	1	M				Tenn	May		Croup	1 day
3	Family of L. C. Hoss	14	F	B	S		Tenn	Feb		Hemorrhage of lungs	20 days
4	Family of A. E. Jackson	1	F	B	S		Tenn	July		Cholera Mor.	3 days
5	Amanda V. Hornbarger	3	F				Tenn	July		Fever	3 days
6	Family of Samuel Greer	1	F	M	S		Tenn	July		Whooping cough	60 days
7	Elizabeth Willet	72	F			W	Va	July		Old age	
8	Caroline W. Brown	3	F				Tenn	June		Fever	10 days
9	Ann E. Nelson	33	F			M	Tenn	May		Fever	52 days
10	Thomas T. L. Drain	8	M				Tenn	July		Scrofula	8 months
11	Thomas Matthews	19	M				Tenn	March	Blk-smith	Fever	
12	Family of Susan F. Watkins	5	M	B	S		Tenn	unknown		Spasms	
13	Elbert G. Hale	37	M			W	Tenn	Feb	Farmer	Consumption	C
14	Family of Mack Hale	25	M	M	S		Tenn	Feb		Killed	sudden
15	Allen Oliver	25	M			M	Tenn	March	Farmer	Fever	16 days
16	Family of Archibald Hale	5	M	B	S		Tenn	July		unknown	8 days
17	Family of Peter Miller	3m	M	B	S		Tenn	March		Croup	1 day
18	Jesse Moore	1	M				Tenn	Aug		Neuralgia	56 days
19	Frances Hoss	62	F			M	Maryland	Nov		Consumption	14 days
20	Henry Swadley	13d	M				Tenn	Feb		Diarrhea	13 days
21	William H. Manning	6m	M				Tenn	July		Cholera Mor.	3 days
22	Elizabeth Boring	25	F				Tenn	June		Fever	40 days
23	Jane Gibson	27	F			M	Tenn	Feb		Fever	90 days
24	Peter Range	Cd	M				Tenn	Aug		Inflamation of brain	3 days
25	John Sailor	25	M			M	Tenn	Oct	Miller	Fever	10 days
26	Hendric Crouch	19	M				Tenn	Nov	Tanner	Fever	49 days
27	Rebecca King	73	F			M	Tenn	June		Pleurisy	42 days
28	Blewford Branch	2m	F				Tenn	Feb		Croup	6 days
29	Michael Krause	6m	M				Tenn	July		Cholera Inf.	2 days
30	Thomas H. Kelsey	3	M				Tenn	June		Inflamation	7 days
31	Abraham H. Beard	1	M				Tenn	Aug		Diarrhea	90 days
32	Ira S. Strasbury	15	M				Tenn	Feb		Inflamation of bowels	4 days
33	Isaac M. Hale	11m	M				Tenn	Aug		Cholera Mor.	2 days
34	Levi Hartman	69	F?			W	Va	June	Farmer	Dropsy	4 days
35	Jane H. Horton	6d	F				Tenn	Feb		Croup	4 days

Remarks: The agriculture of the County is as well conducted as that of any County in the Eastern Division of the State. Wheat and corn are the chief staples. The four is of excellent quality and together with bacon and other provisions is largely exported. Iron ore is very abundant in the County. A valuable lead mine has been recently discovered in the southern part of the County. It has been worked futher than .....

COUNTY OF WASHINGTON, STATE OF TENNESSEE.

PAGE NO. 823 — PERSONS WHO DIED DURING THE YEAR ENDING 1st JUNE, 1850.

4th Subdivision, E. District
Jos. S. Rhea

No. of Visit	Name	Age	Sex	Color	Free or Slave	Married/Widowed	Place of Birth	Month Died	Occupation	Disease or Cause of Death	No. Days Ill
1	Maranda Cassady	1	F				Tenn	Nov		Croup	2 days
2	Abram Andes	5	M				Tenn	April		Killed	sudden
3	Mary Andes	55	F			M	Kentucky	April		Fits	sudden
4	Lucinda Stafford	10	F				Tenn	Feb		Fever	7 days
5	Andrew J. Hampton	18	M				Tenn	Sept	Tanner	Consumption	30 days
6	Amos Perkins	23	M				Tenn	April	Collier	Fever	11 days
7	Family of Thomas J. Cox	1	F	B	S		Tenn	July		Croup	3 days
8	Infant of W. R. Huffman	2w	F				Tenn	Nov		unknown	7 days
9	Daniel M. White	28	M			M	Tenn	March	Blk-smith	Fever	16 days
10	Elizabeth Smith	37	F			M	Tenn	Oct		unknown	1 year
11	Hannah Harris	1	F				Tenn	Jan		unknown	3 days
12	Mary A. Tillson	15	F				Tenn	Aug		unknown	7 days
13	Martha Tillson	8m	F				Tenn	Oct		Whooping cough	60 days
14	Rhoda Masters	21	F			M	Tenn	Aug		Fever	48 days
15	Sarah Banner	1	F				Tenn	Feb		Fever	15 days
16	Thomas Edwards	17	M				Tenn	Sept	Farmer	Fever	8 days
17	Martha A. Brown	1	F				Tenn	Sept		unknown	200 days
18	Charles Loveless	14	M				Tenn	April		unknown	60 days
19	John Parks	31	M				Tenn	Feb	Blk-smith	Fever	19 days
20	James Osburn	11	M				Tenn	April		Fever	4 days
21	Samuel Templing	14	M	B	S		Tenn	Aug		Fever	40 days
22	Thomas L. Gallion	1	M				Tenn	July		Fever	35 days
23	Eleanor Brazele	79	F			W	Va	Sept		———	C
24	Eleanor Brazele	5	F				Tenn	July		Pneumonia	35 days
25	Margaret Waddle	5m	F				Tenn	April		Whooping cough	35 days
26	Ruth C. Brown	20	F				Tenn	June		Fits	4 days
27	Richard Greenway	64	M			M	Tenn	June	Farmer	unknown	120 days
28	Sherwood Vaughn	79	M			W	Tenn	Dec	Farmer	unknown	sudden
29	William H. Helbert	6	M				Tenn	Nov		unknown	90 days
30	Delia Bacon	69	F			M	Tenn	June		———	C
31	Margaret Kirk	39	F			M	Tenn	Dec		Consumption	200 days
32	Mary H. Beals	1	F				Tenn	March		unknown	14 days
33	Mahala Davidson	18	F				Tenn	Oct		Whooping cough	21 days
34	Rosannah Hodge	23	F				Tenn	Jan		Bronchitis	30 days
35	Mary Carr	78	F			W	Va	Aug		———	C

Remarks: making (or running out) at one time of about one thousand pound of pure lead, supposed to be equal in quality to any in the Union. There are larger quantities of limestone, the amount of which is unexhaustable. There also exsists in parts of the County marl to a considerable extent. The water is principally limestone and of an excellent quality. There are in the County some mineral springs of chalybeate property, supposed to be equal in virture for the restoration of health to any in any County.

COUNTY OF WASHINGTON, STATE OF TENNESSEE.

PAGE NO. 825 PERSONS WHO DIED DURING THE YEAR ENDING 1st JUNE, 1850.

4th Subdivision, E. District
Jos. S. Rhea

No. of Visit	Name	Age	Sex	Color	Free or Slave	Married/Widowed	Place of Birth	Month Died	Occupation	Disease or Cause of Death	No. Days Ill
1	Eliza Swaner	47	F			M	Tenn	Oct		unknown	1 year
2	Margaret Pritchet	1	F				Tenn	June		Whooping cough	35 days
3	William Mitchell	79	M			W	Tenn	Jan	Farmer	Gravel	28 days
4	Susannah Gallaway	37	F			M	Tenn	March		unknown	60 days
5	John Pruit	62	M			M	Va	Aug		Ulcer	30 days
6	Matthew J. Whitlock	5m	M				Tenn	Jan		Inflamation of lungs	7 days
7	Rebecca Charlton	3	F				Tenn	April		Whooping cough	7 days
8	Mary R. McCrery	3	F				Tenn	Jan		Croup	3 days
9	John Whitlock	54	M			M	Tenn	Nov	Gunsmith	Dropsy	1 year
10	Ann Mulkey	40	F			M	Tenn	Dec		Dropsy	30 days
11	John Brown	60	M			M	Tenn	Oct		Killed	sudden
12	Mary Miller	52	F			M	Va	Jan		Ulcer	50 days
13	Adam Eutsler	9	M				Tenn	March		Fever	5 days
14	William Melson	100	M			W	Tenn	March		Old age	
15	Robert Bacon	3m	M				Tenn	Feb		unknown	sudden
16	Samuel R. Haws	22	M				Tenn	April	Farmer	Consumption	200 days
17	Edward Deakons	20	M	B			Tenn	Feb		Fever	14 days
18	Catherine White	28	F				Tenn	Aug		Fever	21 days

Remarks: The principal growth of timber consists of black, red and white oak, poplar, sugar trees, black walnut, cherry, black and red gum, sycamore, linn, hemlock, chestnut, white, red and yellow pine, cedar, hickory and locust. The water being fair. The air pure. Consequently with the blessing of a kind Providence, no malady has prevailed in our County.

COUNTY OF WAYNE, STATE OF TENNESSEE.

PAGE NO. 827 PERSONS WHO DIED DURING THE YEAR ENDING 1st JUNE, 1850.

Civil District No. 1, 2, 3, 14, 6, 11, 12, 5, 7, & 8

A. K. Hardin

No. of Visit	Name	Age	Sex	Color	Free or Slave	Married/Widowed	Place of Birth	Month Died	Occupation	Disease or Cause of Death	No. Days Ill
1	Mary Young	50	F			M	unknown	Feb		Chronic	12 months
2	Nancy McAdoo	38	F			M	Tenn	Sept		Chronic	21 months
3	Nancy Robinson	38	F			M	Tenn	Feb		sudden	
4	Nancy G. Rink	24	F			M	Tenn	Aug		Fever	8 days
5	M. J. Lafferty	46	F			M	Georgia	June		Pleurisy	7 days
6	_____	35	F	B	S		_____	May		Fever	10 days
7	_____	16	M	B	S		_____	May		sudden	
8	Rhody Dicus	77	F			M	N.C.	July		Dropsy	6 months
9	_____	50	M	M	S		_____	Oct		Cancer	9 months
10	James Scott	3	M				Tenn	June		sudden	
11	Mary Warfield	20	F				Missouri	April		T.F.F.	7 weeks
12	T. B. Melton	37	M			M	Tenn	Nov	Farmer	Fever	6 days
13	William Daniel	62	M			M	N.C.	Nov	Farmer	Fever	7 weeks
14	Irwin Daniel	11	M				Tenn	Aug		Fever	10 days
15	Thomas Fisher	6m	M				Tenn	Sept		Fever	10 days
16	Elizabeth Brewer	24	F				Kentucky	Oct		Fever	16 days
17	Mary Hollis	2	F				Tenn	Oct			
18	Elizabeth Taylor	2m	F				Tenn	Nov		B. hives	2 days
19	Marthy E. Frison	4	F				Tenn	March		Dropsy	9 days
20	Lucindy Blackshear	26	F				Tenn	Sept		Apoplexy	
21	Elizabeth Gofourth	11m	F				Tenn	Nov		Fever	7 days
22	Elizabeth Honey	1	F				Tenn	June		Croup	4 days
23	Mary Grimes	36	F			M	Tenn	March		Consumption	6 months
24	William E. Arnold	8	M				Tenn	June		Dropsy	3 months
25	Martha F. Hawe	24	F				Tenn	Nov		sudden	
26	Samuel Cypert	19	M				Tenn	Jan	Farmer	Fever	18 days
27	Leander Cypert	4m	M				Tenn	Nov		sudden	
28	William Loson	32	M			M	Tenn	Sept	Farmer	T. fever	15 days
29	Mary Sutherland	3	F				Tenn	Dec		Fever	2 days
30	Rachel Horton	29	F			M	Tenn	Nov		sudden	
31	Mathew Atkerson	4m	M				Tenn	Oct		Fever	11 days
32	William D. McAnally	27	M			M	Tenn	Oct	Farmer	Chronic	6 months
33	Mary White	60	F				S.C.	Aug		Fever	9 days
34	William H. Anderson	8	M				Tenn	July		Fever	3 weeks

COUNTY OF WAYNE, STATE OF TENNESSEE.

PAGE NO. 830 PERSONS WHO DIED DURING THE YEAR ENDING 1st JUNE, 1850.

Civil District No. 9, 10, 4 & 13

A. K. Hardin

No. of Visit	Name	Age	Sex	Color	Free or Slave	Married/Widowed	Place of Birth	Month Died	Occupation	Disease or Cause of Death	No. Days Ill
1	L. E. Curtis	3	F				Tenn	Aug		Diarrhea	4 weeks
2	Nancy E. Gillis	8	F				Tenn	April		sudden	
3	Lucinda Balantine	29	F			M	Alabama	Dec		sudden	
4	Anna Alen	45	F			M	Tenn	Sept		Fever	7 days
5	Sarah Thornton	87	F				N.C.	Oct		Old age	
6	John Nale	9m	M				Tenn	Dec		Croup	7 days
7	William L. Darby	22	M				Tenn	May	Farmer	T. fever	15 days
8	_____	65	M	B	S		Tenn	Nov		B. fever	7 days
9	Nancy Jones	28	F			M	Tenn	Feb		unknown	7 days
10	_____	10	M	B	S		Tenn	March		Fever	9 days
11	Lyda Casteel	8	F				Tenn	Feb		Worms	2 days
12	John N. Shields	44	M			M	Georgia	July	Farmer	T. fever	7 days
13	_____	9m	M	B	S		Tenn	Feb		Strangled	
14	_____	1	M	B	S		Tenn	Feb		Consumption	90 days
15	_____	45	F	B	S		Tenn	March		Terminal disease	3 months
16	Eliza T. P. Ramsey	2	F				unknown	June		Consumption	9 months
17	_____	15	F	B	S		Tenn	June		Consumption	92 days
18	_____	18	M	B	S		Missouri	Feb		T. fever	19 days
19	_____	1	F	B	S		Va	April		Cold	10 days

COUNTY OF WEAKLEY, STATE OF TENNESSEE.

PAGE NO. 831 PERSONS WHO DIED DURING THE YEAR ENDING 1st JUNE, 1850.

Civil Districts

J. M. Drewry

No. of Visit	Name	Age	Sex	Color	Free or Slave	Married/Widowed	Place of Birth	Month Died	Occupation	Disease or Cause of Death	No. Days Ill
1	Sarah	12	F	B	S		Tenn	Sept			C
2	S. Priest	21	M				Tenn	June	Farmer	Pleurisy	5 days
3	W. Dempsy	2	M				Tenn	Feb		Croup	3 days
4	W. M. Lardner	8m	M				Tenn	Nov		Croup	6 days
5	S. McClane	7	F				Tenn	Feb		Accident	sudden
6	S. Alen	1	F				Tenn	March		Croup	5 days
7	Edmond	26	M	B	S		Tenn	April		Accident	sudden
8	J. Hornbeak	67	M			M	Tenn	June	Farmer	Pneumonia	19 days
9	P. Mosley	40	F			W	Tenn	March			C
10	J. Pierce	56	M			W	N.C.	Feb	Farmer	Consumption	2 years
11	M. E. T. Orald	5	F				Va	April		Accident	sudden
12	J. W. Jenkins	2	M				Tenn	June		unknown	2 weeks
13	N. C. Herin	11m	F				Tenn	Dec		Hives	1 week
14	F. T. Scates	45	M			M	Va	June	Farmer	Intemperance	2 days
15	N. Cachem	11	F				Tenn	July		Consumption	2 years
16	J. T. Pate	3	M				Tenn	April			C
17	M. C. Hopper	26	F				Tenn	Sept		unknown	1 day
18	S. Perry	1	F				Tenn	Sept			C
19	R. Dollahite	2	M				Tenn	Oct			C
20	W. McLane	49	M				N.C.	July	Farmer	Consumption	3 years
21	M. L. Drury	51	F			M	N.C.	Sept		Diabetes	1 week
22	S. L. Drury	28	M			M	Tenn	June	Farmer	Consumption	3 years
23	L. C. Drury	6m	F				Tenn	Sept		Consumption	2 weeks
24	N. Wilkes	13	F				Tenn	April			C
25	J. Lillum	18	F				Tenn	Feb		Pneumonia	4 weeks
26	E. Butler	19	F				Tenn	May		Consumption	2 years
27	W. B. Partin	9	M				Tenn	Sept		T. fever	5 days
28	L. Billingsby	50	F				Kentucky	June		Consumption	1 year
29	W. Billingsby	10	M				Tenn	July			C
30	S. J. Burns	70	M			M	Tenn	March	Carpenter		11 days
31	E. P. Adams	58	M			M	N.C.	April	Farmer	Pneumonia	11 days

COUNTY OF WEAKLEY, STATE OF TENNESSEE.

PAGE NO. 831 PERSONS WHO DIED DURING THE YEAR ENDING 1st JUNE, 1850.

Civil Districts: J. M. Drewry

No. of Visit	Name	Age	Sex	Color	Free or Slave	Married/Widowed	Place of Birth	Month Died	Occupation	Disease or Cause of Death	No. Days Ill
32	L. Porter	24	M				Tenn	Dec	Farmer	Accident	Drowned
33	D. L. Bradshaw	2	M				Tenn	March		Bil. fever	10 days
34	L. Cravens	30	F			M	Illinois	Sept			C
35	E. Williams	4	F				Tenn	Jan		Accident	Burned

COUNTY OF WEAKLEY, STATE OF TENNESSEE.

PAGE NO. 834 PERSONS WHO DIED DURING THE YEAR ENDING 1st JUNE, 1850.

Civil Districts: J. M. Drewry

No. of Visit	Name	Age	Sex	Color	Free or Slave	Married/Widowed	Place of Birth	Month Died	Occupation	Disease or Cause of Death	No. Days Ill
1	John Fuller	15	M				Tenn	Sept	Farmer	T. fever	5 days
2	J. C. Thompson	24	M				N.C.	March	Farmer	Consumption	1 year
3	H. Thompson	6m	M				Tenn	Dec		Croup	2 weeks
4	F. Dodson	2	M				Tenn	Sept		Diarrhea	21 days
5	D. Williams	2	F				Tenn	Aug		Diarrhea	15 days
6	T. R. West	3	M				Tenn	July		Accident	7 days
7	Hariet	12	F	B	S		Kentucky	May		T. fever	14 days
8	J. H. Hope	23	M				Louisiana	March	Trader	T. fever	21 days
9	C. Bright	10	F				Kentucky	Aug		T. fever	10 days
10	J. C. Johnson	4	M				Tenn	April		Accident	sudden
11	F. Johnson	1	F				Tenn	Dec		Bil. fever	12 days
12	J. W. Wheeler	1	M				Tenn	Oct		T. fever	8 days
13	J. L. Young	30	M			M	Tenn	June	Farmer	Pneumonia	10 days
14	T. J. Spear	1	M				Tenn	Feb		Inflamation of brain	24 days
15	M. F. Simpson	10	F				Kentucky	April		--illegible--	3 days
16	B. H. Farmer	8	M				Tenn	Dec		Croup	10 days
17	M. Winstead	2	F				Tenn	March		Whooping cough	6 weeks
18	A. Sison	3	M				Kentucky	April		Croup	6 days
19	W. Hedspeth	1	M				Tenn	April		Sc. fever	7 days
20	W. B. Boaz	24	M				Va	Jan	Farmer	Dropsy	5 months
21	S. Spence	1	F				Tenn	Dec		unknown	1 days
22	B. G. Temple	30	M			M	N.C.	Dec	Farmer	Pneumonia	6 days
23	James	36	M	B	S		N.C.	Feb		Accident	1 day
24	V. Hayberg	3	M				Tenn	Jan			C
25	George	18	M	B	S		Va	Dec		Pneumonia	10 days
26	Henry	8m	M	B	S		Tenn	June			C
27	S. E. Simpson	4	F				Tenn	Dec			C
28	L. G. Beckum	29	F			M	Tenn	April		Pneumonia	3 days
29	W. Castle	26	M				Tenn	March	Farmer	Accident	2 weeks
30	P. Jeffreys	8m	F				Tenn	April		Croup	5 days
31	S. M. Gardner	20	F			M	Kentucky	March		unknown	4 weeks
32	J. Gardner	66	M			M	Va	July	Farmer	Dropsy	14 days
33	Adam	26	M	M	S		N.C.	Dec		Cholera	3 days
34	J. Cook	2	M				Tenn	Feb		Croup	3 days
35	H. P. Freeman	1	M				Tenn	April		Accident	Burned

COUNTY OF WEAKLEY, STATE OF TENNESSEE.

PAGE NO. 835 PERSONS WHO DIED DURING THE YEAR ENDING 1st JUNE, 1850.

Civil Districts

No. of Visit	Name	Age	Sex	Color	Free or Slave	Married/Widowed	Place of Birth	Month Died	Occupation	Disease or Cause of Death	No. Days Ill
1	Stephen	23	M	B	S		Tenn	June			C
2	Lethe	7	F	B	S		Tenn	Feb		Worms	7 days
3	J. Julin	45	M			M	Tenn	Nov	Farmer	Pneumonia	8 days
4	Taylor	5m	M	B	S		Tenn	March		Hives	4 days
5	J. Thomas	12	F				Tenn	April		T. fever	6 weeks
6	Anna	2	F	M	S		Tenn	July			C
7	J. A. Mathews	6m	M				Tenn	April		Fits	15 days
8	Larry	54	M	B	S		N.C.	March		Pneumonia	10 days
9	M. E. House	9m	F				Tenn	Oct			C
10	Scott	22	M	B	S		N.C.	April		Pneumonia	9 days
11	J. Morgan	6	M				N.C.	Nov		Pneumonia	9 days
12	Jane	50	F	B	S		N.C.	Dec		Apoplexy	5 hours
13	J. T. Horton	3	M				N.C.	Dec			C
14	J. T. Hendrick	2	M				Tenn	July			C
15	W. Vaughn	50	M			M	N.C.	June	Farmer	White swelling	2 months
16	W. J. Hawks	21	M				N.C.	Dec	Farmer	Pneumonia	7 days
17	F. Lowry	48	F			M	Kentucky	April		unknown	6 days
18	J. H. Mangrum	59	M			M	N.C.	March	Farmer	Bil. fever	14 days
19	Elizabeth	60	F	B	S		Va	Jan			C
20	W. R. Todd	2	M				Tenn	June		Flux	16 days
21	W. H. Todd	1	M				Tenn	March		Worms	10 days
22	Samuel	55	M	B	S		Va	March		unknown	5 days
23	C. McWherter	21	F			M	Tenn	July			C
24	M. Lay	30	F			M	Tenn	March			C
25	D. Bias	55	M			M	N.C.	April	Farmer	Cholera	1 day
26	J. Bias	21?	M				Tenn	Feb			C
27	S. C. Ridgway	19	M				Tenn	March	Farmer	Pneumonia	12 days
28	L. M. Lafawn	9m	F				Tenn	Oct		Croup	5 days
29	A. Canida	44	F			M	N.C.	June		Consumption	4 months
30	W. Canida	1	M				Tenn	Sept			C
31	C. Cilabrew	2m	M				Tenn	Jan		Worms	2 weeks
32	J. Hart	5m	M				Tenn	Oct		Fits	4 days
33	L. Roberds	7	M				Tenn	Feb		Pneumonia	12 days
34	J. R. Coley	4	M				Tenn	Oct		Hives	2 days
35	C. Adams	40	F				Va	March		unknown	sudden

COUNTY OF WEAKLEY, STATE OF TENNESSEE.

PAGE NO. 838 PERSONS WHO DIED DURING THE YEAR ENDING 1st JUNE, 1850.

Civil Districts: J. M. Drewry

No. of Visit	Name	Age	Sex	Color	Free or Slave	Married/Widowed	Place of Birth	Month Died	Occupation	Disease or Cause of Death	No. Days Ill
1	Clara	21	F	B	S		Tenn	Sept		unknown	4 days
2	Nancy	40	F	B	S		Va	July		Diabetes	3 months
3	Susan	2	F	B	S		Tenn	Feb		Worms	3 days
4	W. R. Brooks	1m	M				Tenn	June		Sc. fever	6 days
5	James	35	M	B	S		N.C.	March		unknown	8 days
6	Thomas	14	M	B	S		N.C.	March		unknown	7 days
7	Milla	27	F	M	S		unknown	June		sudden	1 day
8	F. A. E. Todd	8m	F				Tenn	June		unknown	14 days
9	E. Cook	6	F				N.C.	Aug		Worms	3 days
10	T. B. Duke	11m	F				Tenn	Sept		Teething	14 days
11	Charles	22	M	B	S		N.C.	Sept		unknown	15 days
12	J. Love	1m	M				Tenn	April		unknown	14 days
13	H. Sears	70	M			M	N.C.	Sept	Farmer	Consumption	3 years
14	M. B. Fowler	27	F			M	N.C.	Nov			C
15	A. A. Wing	7	F				Tenn	Aug		Sc. fever	6 weeks
16	M. E. Jorden	1	F				Tenn	Aug		Worms	7 days
17	Edward	22	M	B	S		Va	Nov		Accident	3 months
18	H. E. Sneed	18	F				Tenn	April		unknown	5 weeks
19	Evaline	8	F	B	S		Tenn	Nov		unknown	3 months
20	Alfred	6m	M	B	S		Tenn	July		unknown	10 days
21	T. M. Span	4	M				Tenn	June		Pneumonia	9 days
22	J. Span	45	M			M	Kentucky	Feb	Farmer	Pneumonia	9 days
23	Andrew	21	M	B	S		Tenn	May		Cholera	4 days
24	A. Bradshaw	1	F				Tenn	May		Inflamation of brain	3 days
25	J. A. Crawford	1	M				Tenn	July		Worms	10 days
26	M. Ralston	1	F				Tenn	Jan		Whooping cough	20 days
27	Samuel	38	M	B	S		Tenn	April		Cold	3 months

COUNTY OF WHITE, STATE OF TENNESSEE.

PAGE NO. 839 PERSONS WHO DIED DURING THE YEAR ENDING 1st JUNE, 1850.

Civil District No. 1, 2, 3 & 4

W. W. Moore

No. of Visit	Name	Age	Sex	Color	Free or Slave	Married/Widowed	Place of Birth	Month Died	Occupation	Disease or Cause of Death	No. Days Ill
1	Temperance	19	F	B	S		Tenn	June		Dropsy	60 days
2	Winefred Clark	89	F			W	Va	March		Old age	90 days
3	Ann Clark	3	F				Tenn	Oct		Croup	1 day
4	Charles J. Manning	51	M			W	New York	Feb	Speculator	Poisoned	6 days
5	Matilda Jones	26	F				Tenn	April		Dropsy	35 days
6	Sarah Mitchell	48	F			M	Kentucky	July		Dropsy	4 years
7	Michael Corbet	55	M			M	Ireland	April	Tailor	Intemperance	sudden
8	Lucy Claybrooks	80	F				Va	May		Old age	3 months
9	John W. Medley	1	M				Tenn	June		Inflamation	12 days
10	Sarah Newman	6m	F				Tenn	Sept		Diarrhea	3 weeks
11	Infant of D. Smith	1m	F				Tenn	March		Croup	1 day
12	Vance Jones	6m	M				Tenn	Sept		Croup	1 day
13	Barbara	70	F	B	S		Va	July		unknown	6 days
14	Susan Fancher	33	F			M	Tenn	May		Fever	10 days
15	Ann	17	F	B	S		Tenn	Aug		Fever	9 days
16	Smith	3m	M	M	S		Tenn	Dec		Dropsy	15 days
17	Frances White	89	F			W	Va	Oct		unknown	2 months
18	James G. McCoy	17	M				Tenn	Nov	Farmer	Fever	12 days
19	Narcissa Davis	5m	F				Tenn	May		Dropsy	1 month
20	James L. Kerby	12	M				Tenn	Jan		Dropsy	1 year
21	Julia	85	F		S		Va	April		Old age	3 months
22	Drury McBride	4m	M				Tenn	Dec		Fits	sudden
23	Sarah Underwood	78	F				Tenn	June		Consumption	1 year
24	Infant of C. Denny	2d	M				Tenn	July		Croup	1 day
25	Rachael	4d	F	B	S		Tenn	Jan		Inflamation	1 day
26	Allen Kerby	13	M				Tenn	March		Cold	2 days
27	Sarah Warren	67	F			W	N.C.	March		Fever	12 days
28	Jabry Dodson	38	F			M	Tenn	May		unknown	2 days
29	Henderson Dodson	21	M				Tenn	March	Farmer	Winter fever	12 days
30	Mary E. Fraser	14	F				Tenn	March		Inflamation of brain	6 days
31	Green W. George	2	M				Tenn	Jan		Croup	1 day
32	Sarah Sweet	7	F				S.C.	May		Dropsy	3 months
33	James Walling	69	M			M	Va	Oct	Farmer	Fall from horse	7 days
34	Sarah P. Underwood	2m	F	M			Tenn	June		unknown	2 days
35	Margaret Adair	60	F			M	Tenn	March		unknown	3 weeks

COUNTY OF WHITE, STATE OF TENNESSEE.

PAGE NO. 841 PERSONS WHO DIED DURING THE YEAR ENDING 1st JUNE, 1850.

Civil District No. 5, 6 & 8

No. of Visit	Name	Age	Sex	Color	Free or Slave	Married/Widowed	Place of Birth	Month Died	Occupation	Disease or Cause of Death	No. Days Ill
1	Mary A. Carrell	6	F				Tenn	Sept		Fever	9 days
2	John Kerr	77	M			W	Va	Oct	Farmer	Dropsy	6 months
3	Infant of N. Rickman	7d	F	M			Tenn	Dec		unknown	7 days
4	Infant of John Phifer	1d	F				Tenn	Nov		unknown	9 days
5	William Watson	6m	M				Tenn	May		Bold hives	1 day
6	Edward Freeman	65	M			M	Va	May	Blk-smith	Cramps ---	5 days
7	Infant of N. Rickman	9d	F	M			Tenn	Dec		unknown	9 days
8	James Harrison	6m	M				Tenn	April		unknown	6 months
9	Thomas M. Bosson	65	M			W	Mass	May	Physician	Consumption	8 years
10	Mahala Marlow	46	F			M	N.C.	Oct		Dyspepsia	3 years
11	Richard C. Jones	10	M				Tenn	Dec		Fever	6 weeks
12	Nancy Denton	8	F				Tenn	July		unknown	3 days
13	John Rickman	7	M	M			Tenn	July		Intemperance	1 day
14	Elizabeth Swindle	70	F			W	N.C.	Feb		Cholic	2 days
15	Melvina Greenfield	1	F				Tenn	Sept		Diarrhea	4 days
16	Joseph Washington	12	M				Tenn	April		unknown	1 year
17	Obadiah M. Hodge	2	M				Tenn	Aug		Hives	3 days
18	John Short	6	M				Tenn	Sept		Diarrhea	20 days
19	Nathaniel Marcum	59	M			M	Georgia	Nov	Fanner	Fell off bluff	sudden
20	Jane Glenn	85	F			W	N.C.	Dec		Old age	8 weeks
21	Edward Helton	90	M			W	Va	Aug	Farmer	Old age	10 days
22	Logan Glenn	23	M				Tenn	Nov		unknown	2 weeks
23	Louisa Smith	19	F				Tenn	Oct		Fever	12 days
24	Nancy Robbens	32	F			M	Tenn	May		Liver complaint	2 months
25	Infant of A. Flemming	9d	M				Tenn	July		unknown	9 days
26	Lucinda	20	F	B	S		Tenn	Sept		Consumption	1 year
27	William Irwin	70	M			W	N.C.	March	Carpenter	unknown	8 days
28	Bird McDole	1	M				Tenn	July		Sc. fever	20 days
29	Creasy		F	B	S		Tenn	Aug		Consumption	2 months
30	Jane Irwin	74	F			M	Va	March		Chronic	4 months
31	Sarah Stewart	26	F			W	Tenn	March		———	6 days
32	Infant of J. W. Short	1d	M				Tenn	March		unknown	1 day
33	Mary Bennet	84	F			W	Va	Oct		Old age	2 months
34	Margaret England	2	F				Tenn	Oct		Diarrhea	2 days
35	Eliza J. Walker	28	F			M	Tenn	Oct		Inflamation	23 days

COUNTY OF WHITE, STATE OF TENNESSEE.

PAGE NO. 844 PERSONS WHO DIED DURING THE YEAR ENDING 1st JUNE, 1850.

Civil District No. 9 & 12

William W. Moore

No. of Visit	Name	Age	Sex	Color	Free or Slave	Married/Widowed	Place of Birth	Month Died	Occupation	Disease or Cause of Death	No. Days Ill
1	Tennessee Dearing	2m	F				Tenn	July		Cholera	8 days
2	Lewis Harris	74	M			M	Kentucky	May	Farmer	Dyspepsia	3 months
3	Peter	75	M	B	S		Tenn	April		Inflamation of stomach	3 months
4	Mary Frye	37	F			M	Tenn	April		Consumption	1 year
5	John S. Clouse	1	M			M?	Tenn	Sept		Flux	18 days
6	Infant of C. Sliger	2d	M				Tenn	Aug		Inflamation of brain	2 days
7	James H. Pass	53	M			W	N.C.	Feb	Farmer	Dyspepsia	1 year
8	Mary Pass	53	F			W	Va	Aug		unknown	1 day
9	Infant of J. R. Glenn	3m	M				Tenn	Sept		Croup	3 days
10	Randolph Ramsey	60	M			M	N.C.	Dec	Farmer	Inflamation of brain	5 days
11	Charlton J. McBride	31	M			M	Tenn	Oct	Farmer	Consumption	1 year
12	Bertha Davis	43	F				Tenn	May		_____	1 day
13	Charley Pearson	1	M				Tenn	Feb		Croup	3 days
14	Sarah McGuire	72	F			M	Tenn	April		Consumption	6 months
15	Sarah A. Spurr	4m	F				Tenn	July		Hives	1 day
16	Thomas	99	M	B	S		Va	June		Old age	6 days
17	Nancy A. Lefevers	3	F				Tenn	Nov		Choked	9 days
18	Mary Ditty	83	F			W	Penn	Nov		Old age	21 days
19	Christopher C. Tilly	2	M				Tenn	Jan		Sc. fever	7 days
20	George W. Tilly	2	M				Tenn	Jan		Sc. fever	4 days
21	E. W. Kilgrove	47	M			M	N.C.	Oct	Waggoner	unknown	sudden
22	Martha E. Martin	1	F				Tenn	March		Sc. fever	21 days
23	Emaline E. Howell	8	F				Tenn	Aug		unknown	1 day
24	Elijah Elmore	90	M			W	N.C.	Nov	Farmer	Gravel	15 days
25	John Johnson	1m	M				Tenn	July		Croup	6 days
26	Andrew J. Simms	2m	M				Tenn	Aug		Croup	1 day
27	John H. Brown	1m	M				Tenn	April		Croup	2 weeks
28	Richard	12	M	B	S		Tenn	Aug		Fever	7 days
29	Jefferson	10	M	B	S		Tenn	Aug		Fever	14 days
30	Nancy Boham	57	F			M	Tenn	May		unknown	10 weeks
31	Luther Miller	23	M				Tenn	April	Farmer	Fever	9 days
32	Leah Graham	85	F				N.C.	July		unknown	sudden
33	Isaac Conley	65	M			M	N.C.	Feb		unknown	sudden
34	John Potts	65	M			M	S.C.	Jan		unknown	sudden
35	John E. Simpson	2m	M				Tenn	Sept		Croup	2 weeks

COUNTY OF WHITE, STATE OF TENNESSEE.

PAGE NO. 846 PERSONS WHO DIED DURING THE YEAR ENDING 1st JUNE, 1850.

Civil District No. 12, 13, 14, 10 & 15

W. M. Moore

No. of Visit	Name	Age	Sex	Color	Free or Slave	Married/Widowed	Place of Birth	Month Died	Occupation	Disease or Cause of Death	No. Days Ill
1	Mary Potts	83	F			M	N.C.	July		Dropsy	3 months
2	Frances J. Finley	2	F				Tenn	Aug		Croup	2 days
3	Zachariah T. Anderson	3	M				Tenn	Oct		Croup	1 day
4	John Delavine	74	M			M	New York	Aug	Farmer	Dyspepsia	13 months
5	Benjamin Mars	81	M			M	S.C.	Feb		Gravel	8 days
6	Jesse Adkin	6m	M				Tenn	July		unknown	4 months
7	Dibrell Bartlett	2	M				Tenn	March		unknown	1 day
8	Henry Robinson	1m	M				Tenn	April		unknown	sudden
9	Mary Brown	53	F			M	N.C.	May		unknown	6 months
10	Rhoda	53	F	B	S		N.C.	May		Cold	4 months
11	Lucinda A. Cyder	17	F				Tenn	Sept		Cold	1 month
12	Ann Whitaker	80	F			W	N.C.	Oct		Old age	5 months
13	Elizabeth J. Henisee	17	F				Kentucky	Nov		Fever	1 month
14	George Maidwell	7m	M				Tenn	Jan		Croup	sudden
15	Watson Harp	47	M			M	Tenn	Jan	Farmer	Fever	4 weeks
16	Rhoda A. Harp	13	F				Tenn	June		Fever	2 weeks
17	Mary E. Glover	6m	F				Tenn	Feb		Inflamation of brain	7 days

COUNTY OF WILLIAMSON, STATE OF TENNESSEE.

PAGE NO. 847 PERSONS WHO DIED DURING THE YEAR ENDING 1st JUNE, 1850.

Civil District No. 7

William McCrary

No. of Visit	Name	Age	Sex	Color	Free or Slave	Married/Widowed	Place of Birth	Month Died	Occupation	Disease or Cause of Death	No. Days Ill
1	William J. Wiggins	24	M				Tenn	May	Farmer	Shot	sudden
2	Marshall Frayzier	1m	M				Tenn	Sept		Fits	1 day
3	Jacob Manley	8	M	B	S		Tenn	Feb		Fever	7 days
4	Thomas Smith	5m	M	B	S		Tenn	May		Croup	4 days
5	William Peare	24	M				Tenn	Nov	Farmer	Fever	14 days

Remarks: I made out the Social Statistics of the Civil Districts separate but could not procure the blanks therefore I put the Districts on one schedule of my division. This District is a rich and level District with fine water embedded with limestone rocks. Forest growth, oak, ash, poplar. sugartree, cherry, walnut, hickory, boxelder, lynn, and a variety of kinds of growth. There is no establishment of products of industry that amounts to 500 dollars annually in this district to return. I will here state that schedule No. 2, as they are double columns. I understand them as such and so counted them.

COUNTY OF WILLIAMSON, STATE OF TENNESSEE.

PAGE NO. 849   PERSONS WHO DIED DURING THE YEAR ENDING 1st JUNE, 1850.

Civil District No. 5

William McCrary

No. of Visit	Name	Age	Sex	Color	Free or Slave	Married/Widowed	Place of Birth	Month Died	Occupation	Disease or Cause of Death	No. Days Ill
1	Anderson Maury	22	M	M	S		Tenn	Aug		Fever	10 days
2	Joseph Campbell	85	M	B	S		New Jersey	May		Old age	14 days
3	Milly Hamilton	8m	F	M	S		Tenn	Jan		Cold	4 days
4	Nancy J. Jones	2	F				Tenn	July		Chronic	360 days
5	Katharine Kale	16	F	B	S		Tenn	May		Chronic	90 days
6	Green Marshall	25	M	B	S		Tenn	May		Dropsy	63 days
7	Penelope Ragsdale	60	F			W	Va	April		Chronic	1 day
8	Jane Scrugs	17	F	B	S		Tenn	April		Fever	10 days
9	Caroline Scrugs	14	F	B	S		Tenn	April		Fever	10 days
10	Martha Scrugs	21	F	B	S		Tenn	March		Fever	4 days
11	Dotia Scrugs	21	F	B	S		Tenn	May		Fever	10 days
12	Drury Scrugs	21	M				Tenn	April	Farmer	Fever	20 days
13	Green Buford	10m	M	B	S		Tenn	Aug		Bowel complaint	7 days
14	Margarett Buford	3m	F	B	S		Tenn	Dec		unknown	sudden
15	Infant Neely	1m	M				Tenn	Jan		Disease of heart	2 days
16	Daniel Neely	22	M	B	S		Tenn	Sept		Fever	7 days
17	Margarett Thompson	2	F	B	S		Tenn	Sept		Chronic	60 days
18	Thomas Thompson	2	M	B	S		Tenn	July		unknown	21 days
19	James Swanson	67	M			M	Tenn	March	Farmer	Inflamation of brain	5 days
20	Albert Swanson	6m	M	B	S		Tenn	Aug		Chronic	180 days
21	Sarah Swanson	4m	F	B	S		Tenn	April		Burnt	7 days
22	Thomas M. Scrugs	2	M				Tenn	Aug		Fever	14 days

Remarks: The face of this District, level and rich, with some marshy branches. The growth: poplar, oak, ash, elm, hornbean, dogwood, with some chestnut. Embedded with Limestone and sand rocks. Finely watered. I will here state schedule No. 2, as they are double columns, I understand them as such and so counted them.

COUNTY OF WILLIAMSON, STATE OF TENNESSEE.

PAGE NO. 851   PERSONS WHO DIED DURING THE YEAR ENDING 1st JUNE, 1850.

Civil District No. 4

William McCrary

No. of Visit	Name	Age	Sex	Color	Free or Slave	Married/Widowed	Place of Birth	Month Died	Occupation	Disease or Cause of Death	No. Days Ill
1	Loderick Beech	59	M			W	Va	Feb	Farmer	Chronic	180 days
2	Ann B. Stringfellow	88	F			W	Va	Sept		Old age	180 days
3	Lucinda P. Thomas	6m	F				Tenn	Feb		Inflamation of bowels	9 days
4	Henry Helm	2m	M	B	S		Tenn	Dec		Accident	sudden
5	Rose Puryear	22	F	B	S		Tenn	Feb		Fever	20 days
6	Moses Puryear	9	M	B	S		Tenn	March		Fever	28 days
7	Louis Watson	21	M	B	S		Tenn	May		Fever	15 days
8	Hannah Watson	12	F	B	S		Tenn	May		Fever	15 days
9	Jacob Watson	45	M	B	S		Va	April		Killed	sudden
10	Louisa A. Perkins	13	F				Tenn	Feb		Fever	40 days
11	Jane Perkins	15	F	B	S		Tenn	Feb		Burnt	2 days
12	Joseph Burnett	50	M			M	Va	July	Farmer	Fever	13 days
13	Joseph Witt	11	M				Tenn	Sept		unknown	3 days
14	Albert Fleming	8m	M	B	S		Tenn	Nov		Croup	1 day
15	Adaline Coitez	9	F	B	S		Tenn	May		Chronic	180 days
16	Elizabeth Dodson	43	F			M	Va	Jan		Chronic	30 days

Remarks: This District is rich soil, finely timbered with oak, ash, poplar, sugartree, elm, hornbean, and a variety of other growth. Limestone rocks. Finely watered and a popular Sulphur Spring near the center of the District and I will here state schedule No. 2 as they are double columns, I understand them as such and so counted them.

COUNTY OF WILLIAMSON, STATE OF TENNESSEE.

PAGE NO. 583 PERSONS WHO DIED DURING THE YEAR ENDING 1st JUNE, 1850.

Civil District No. 3
William McCrary

No. of Visit	Name	Age	Sex	Color	Free or Slave	Married/Widowed	Place of Birth	Month Died	Occupation	Disease or Cause of Death	No. Days Ill
1	Mary Short	7	F	B	S		Tenn	March		White swelling	365 days
2	Richard Bond	11	M	B	S		Tenn	Jan		Chronic	90 days
3	Harvey Bond	13	M	B	S		Tenn	Dec		Chronic	365 days
4	Benjamin Bond	1	M	B	S		Tenn	Jan		Cold	60 days
5	Mary Bond	1	F	B	S		Tenn	March		Cold	180 days
6	Phillis Hunter	70	F	B	S		Va	May		Fever	21 days
7	James Stroud	4m	M	M	S		Tenn	April		unknown	7 days
8	Elizabeth Meacheam	43	F			M	Tenn	July		Chronic	270 days
9	Louis M. Ragsdale	23	M				Tenn	May	Blk-smith	Fever	56 days
10	Martha Bingham	19	F				Tenn	March		Chronic	50 days
11	Frederick Maberry	1	M	B	S		Tenn	March		unknown	60 days
12	Mary R. Rodgers	25	F			M	Tenn	Jan		unknown	sudden

Remarks: This District, the eastern part, is very productive and level. The western part, hilly, finely watered, embedded with limestone rock. Growth of timber oak, ash, poplar, sugartree, and nearly all kinds that grow in western country. I will here state schedule No. 2 as they are double columns, I understand them as such and so counted them.

COUNTY OF WILLIAMSON, STATE OF TENNESSEE.

PAGE NO. 855 PERSONS WHO DIED DURING THE YEAR ENDING 1st JUNE, 1850.

Civil District No. 2
William McCrary

No. of Visit	Name	Age	Sex	Color	Free or Slave	Married/Widowed	Place of Birth	Month Died	Occupation	Disease or Cause of Death	No. Days Ill
1	Celia Potts	75	F			W	S.C.	April		unknown	10 days
2	Nancy Hargrove	41	F			M	Tenn	March		Chronic	100 days
3	Rachel Shannon	45	F			M	Tenn	March		Chronic	60 days
4	Joseph T. Robertson	1	M				Tenn	Sept		Fever	9 days

Remarks: This District hilly with gravelly soil. Well watered, embedded with limestone rock. Forest growth oak, chestnut, sugartree, poplar, ash and elm. I will here state schedule No. 2 as they are double columns. I understand them as such and so counted them.

COUNTY OF WILLIAMSON, STATE OF TENNESSEE.

PAGE NO. 857 PERSONS WHO DIED DURING THE YEAR ENDING 1st JUNE, 1850.

Civil District No. 1
William McCrary

No. of Visit	Name	Age	Sex	Color	Free or Slave	Married/Widowed	Place of Birth	Month Died	Occupation	Disease or Cause of Death	No. Days Ill
1	Lucinda E. Baird	20	F				Tenn	Feb		unknown	14 days
2	Mary E. Pruitt	1	F				Tenn	June		St. Anthony's fire	7 days

Remarks: The eastern part of this District hilly with gravelly soil. The western part level. Timbered barrens one of the best watered Districts in the country with a popular Sulphur Spring near the center of the District with limestone and yellow rock. Forest growth oak, chestnut, sugartree, gum, poplar, and a variety of other kinds of growth. I will here state that schedule No. 2 as they are double columns. I understand them as such and so counted them.

COUNTY OF WILLIAMSON, STATE OF TENNESSEE.

PAGE NO. 859 PERSONS WHO DIED DURING THE YEAR ENDING 1st JUNE, 1850.

Civil District No. 6
William McCrary

No. of Visit	Name	Age	Sex	Color	Free or Slave	Married/Widowed	Place of Birth	Month Died	Occupation	Disease or Cause of Death	No. Days Ill
1	Cary Motherald	12	M	B	S		Tenn	March		Disease of spine	400 days
2	Neoma Mitchell	50	F				Va	Sept		Chronic	150 days
3	Infant Sawyer	1m	M				Tenn	Dec		Hives	14 days
4	Matthew Teneson	73	M				N.C.	April	Farmer	unknown	127 days
5	Cane Bradley	110	M	B	S		Va	April		Old age	90 days
6	Martha Bradley	5	F	B	S		Tenn	Nov		Chronic	180 days
7	Fanny King	57	F				N.C.	Sept		unknown	5 days
8	Jane Baker	91	F				N.C.	June		Chronic	180 days
9	Mary E. Hughes	1	F				Tenn	Sept		Bowel complaint	90 days
10	Wilmoth Barclay	4m	M				Tenn	Aug		unknown	120 days
11	Mary Bateman	36	F	B	S		Tenn	Jan		Apoplexy	sudden
12	Mary E. B. Marr	1m	F				Tenn	July		unknown	1 day

Remarks: This District is very rich and productive. Growth of timber: oak, poplar, ash, hickory, elm, sugartree, chestnut, and beech. Embedded with limestone rock. Finely watered. I will here state schedule No 2 as they are double columns, I understand as such and so counted them.

COUNTY OF WILLIAMSON, STATE OF TENNESSEE.

PAGE NO. 861 PERSONS WHO DIED DURING THE YEAR ENDING 1st JUNE, 1850.

Civil District No. 8

William McCrary

No. of Visit	Name	Age	Sex	Color	Free or Slave	Married/Widowed	Place of Birth	Month Died	Occupation	Disease or Cause of Death	No. Days Ill
1	Ned Perkins	75	M	B	S		Tenn	May		Old age	180 days
2	Adam McGavock	75	M	B	S		Va	Aug		Old age	28 days
3	Mary Johnson	18	F	B	S		Tenn	Feb		Chronic	90 days
4	Ann Johnson	11	F	B	S		Tenn	March		Fever	9 days
5	Jane Buford	1m	F	B	S		Tenn	Jan		unknown	sudden
6	James Buchanan	1	M				Tenn	July		Brain fever	14 days
7	Fanny Porter	73	F			W	N.C.	April		Chronic	90 days
8	Frederick McKey	25	M	B	S		Tenn	July		Cholera	3 days
9	Sarah B. Richardson	5m	F				Tenn	July		Inflamation of bowels	6 days
10	Sarah Caruthers	1m	F	B	S		Tenn	April		Croup	1 day
11	Patsey Sweeny	70	F	B	S		N.C.	Aug		Chronic	20 days
12	Mary Perkins	3	F	B	S		Tenn	March		Fever	7 days
13	Infant Perkins	1m	F	B	S		Tenn	March		Disease of navel	8 days
14	Orbille Maney	13	M	B	S		Tenn	May		Fever	49 days
15	Chloe Maney	80	F	B	S		N.C.	Oct		Old age	365 days
16	Ellis Hodge	34	M	M	S		Tenn	May		Fever	21 days
17	Eliza Hodge	25	F	M	S		Tenn	May		Fever	35 days
18	Clarissa Hodge	18	F	B	S		Tenn	April		Fever	8 days
19	Nicy Brooks	38	F			M	Tenn	Aug		Chronic	8 days
20	Thornton Jordan	11m	M	B	S		Tenn	Feb		Disease of lungs	1 day

Remarks: The northern part of this District broken and hilly. The southern part level and very productive. Well watered and embedded with limestone rock. The common forest growth of the District is poplar, oak, ash, walnut, sugartree, elm, beech, cherry and a variety of other timber. I will here state that schedule No. 2 as they are double columns, I understand them as such and so counted them.

COUNTY OF WILLIAMSON, STATE OF TENNESSEE.

PAGE NO. 863 PERSONS WHO DIED DURING THE YEAR ENDING 1st JUNE, 1850.

Civil District No. 17, 18, 19, 20, 21, 22, 23, & 24

J. C. Irvin

No. of Visit	Name	Age	Sex	Color	Free or Slave	Married/Widowed	Place of Birth	Month Died	Occupation	Disease or Cause of Death	No. Days Ill
1	James Warler	52	M			M	Va	March	Farmer	C	C
2	Rachel	75	F	B	S		Va	May		C	C
3	Tessy Bethel	4	M				Tenn	Feb		unknown	90 days
4	Lucy	17	F	B	S		Tenn	July		Inflamation	7 days
5	S. Peoples	3	F				Tenn	June		Inflamation of bowels	20 days
6	Green	5m	M	B	S		Tenn	June		Croup	12 days
7	Manuel	3m	M	B	S		Tenn	June		Croup	12 days
8	Sarah Williamson	33	F			M	Tenn	Aug		Liver complaint	90 days
9	Sibby	30	F	B	S		Tenn	Feb		Child bed	6 days
10	John Bostick	56	M			M	N.C.	Feb	Farmer	C	C
11	William	23	M	M	S		Tenn	Sept		Consumption	100 days
12	Caroline	7	F	B	S		Tenn	March		Consumption	90 days
13	Green	5	M	B	S		Tenn	Jan		Consumption	190 days
14	Syrous	2	M	B	S		Tenn	Feb		Consumption	140 days
15	Nancy Moore	76	F			W	Va	June		Diarrhea	5 days
16	N. McClary	35	F			M	Va	Aug		Apoplexy	1 day
17	S. King	67	F			M	Va	Sept		Palsy	7 days
18	Susan	14	F	B	S		Tenn	June		Consumption	50 days
19	Fanny	60	F	B	S		N.C.	Feb		Consumption	5 days
20	Favorette	8m	F	B	S		Tenn	March		unknown	4 days
21	Tompson Woods	66	M			M	Va	June	Farmer	Liver complaint	11 days
22	J. H. Hughes	24	M			M	Tenn	March	Farmer	Consumption	14 days

COUNTY OF WILLIAMSON, STATE OF TENNESSEE.

PAGE NO. 863 PERSONS WHO DIED DURING THE YEAR ENDING 1st JUNE, 1850.

Civil District No. 17, 18, 19, 20, 21, 22, 23, & 24

J. C. Irvin

No. of Visit	Name	Age	Sex	Color	Free or Slave	Married/Widowed	Place of Birth	Month Died	Occupation	Disease or Cause of Death	No. Days Ill
23	M. Revis	66	F				Va	Jan		Consumption	16 days
24	J. Marable	40	M				Va	May	Farmer	T. fever	14 days
25	S. Marable	27	M			M	Va	April		T. fever	30 days
26	S. C. Jourdan	26	F				Tenn	Aug		Bowel complaint	10 days
27	Billy	16	M	B	S		Va	June		T. fever	24 days
28	Joshuaway	3m	M	M	S		Tenn	April		Hives	1 day
29	J. Page	30	M			M	Tenn	Aug		T. fever	50 days
30	Jim	6	M	B	S		Tenn	June		Bowel complaint	5 days
31	Joanah	23	F	M	S		Tenn	Aug		Hemorrhage	21 days
32	Margaret	7	F	B	S		Tenn	June		Sc. fever	2 days
33	Louisa	4	F	B	S		Tenn	June		Sc. fever	3 days
34	Susan	2m	F	B	S		Tenn	Sept		Croup	2 days
35	Rubin	2	M	B	S		Tenn	Aug		Dropsy	12 days

COUNTY OF WILLIAMSON, STATE OF TENNESSEE.

PAGE NO. 866 PERSONS WHO DIED DURING THE YEAR ENDING 1st JUNE, 1850.

Civil District No. 17, 18, 19, 20, 21, 22, 23, & 24

J. C. Irvin

No. of Visit	Name	Age	Sex	Color	Free or Slave	Married/Widowed	Place of Birth	Month Died	Occupation	Disease or Cause of Death	No. Days Ill
1	Malinda	35	F	B	S		Tenn	March		Child bed	1 day
2	Daniel	1	M	B	S		Tenn	June		Bowel complaint	4 days
3	Litha	22	F	B	S		Maryland	May		Dropsy	90 days
4	Sarah	12	F	B	S		Tenn	Aug		Sore throat	6 days
5	George Tea	93				W	N.C.	May	Shoemaker	Old age	30 days
6	Rachael	2m	F	B	S		Tenn	July		Croup	3 days
7	Mary Robison	23	F			M	Tenn	April		Dyspepsia	10 days
8	Ann	12	F	B	S		Tenn	April		T. fever	10 days
9	Mary Hamlet	22	F				Tenn	March		Consumption	60 days
10	Siley Kellow	82	F			W	Maryland	Dec		C	
11	Mary Tullons	59	F			W	Georgia	Nov		C	
12	Sarah Tullons	19	F				Tenn	Sept		Inflamation of brain	150 days
13	Tabbitha	6	F	B	S		Tenn	Dec		C	
14	John Warren	15	M				Tenn	May	Farmer	Killed by horse	
15	James Jamison	16	M	B			Tenn	May		T. fever	20 days
16	Sam	47	M	B	S		N.C.	Jan		Pleurisy	35 days
17	Sela	30	F	M	S		Tenn	Jan		Dropsy	44 days
18	Julia	58	F	M	S		Tenn	Sept		Dropsy	84 days
19	James W. Morton	23	M				Tenn	Aug	Farmer	T. fever	8 days
20	Frank	18	M	B	S		Tenn	Aug		T. fever	8 days
21	Martha Taynor (Taylor)	19	F				Tenn	June		Dropsy	180 days
22	Swan	9m	M	B	S		Tenn	Feb		sudden	
23	Lewis	20	M	B	S		Tenn	May		T. fever	5 days
24	Catherine	96	F	B	S		Va	Dec		Old age	100 days
25	Betty	80	F	B	S		Va	Dec		Old age	20 days
26	James W. Waggoner	6	M				Tenn	Aug		--illegible--	30 days
27	Lunda	6m	M	B	S		Tenn	May		Whooping cough	10 days
28	Jim	6m	M	B	S		Tenn	April		sudden	
29	Tildy	2m	F	B	S		Tenn	April		Fever	10 days
30	Nancy Murry	82	F				N.C.	Aug		Old age	10 days
31	George Shegog?	11m	M				Tenn	May		Whooping cough	12 days
32	John	1	M	B	S		Tenn	Oct		sudden	
33	Nancy S. Whitsel	26	F			M	Tenn	Aug		T. fever	28 days
34	Margaret Morton	21	F			M	Tenn	Aug		T. fever	23 days
35	Margaret Morton	2	F				Tenn	July		Inflamation of brain	2 days

COUNTY OF WILLIAMSON, STATE OF TENNESSEE.

PAGE NO. 867 PERSONS WHO DIED DURING THE YEAR ENDING 1st JUNE, 1850.

Civil District No. 17, 18, 19, 20, 21, 22, 23, & 24

J. C. Irvin

No. of Visit	Name	Age	Sex	Color	Free or Slave	Married/Widowed	Place of Birth	Month Died	Occupation	Disease or Cause of Death	No. Days Ill
1	George	5	M	B	S		Tenn	April		sudden	
2	Malinda	11m	F	B	S		Tenn	Nov		Teething	12 days
3	Mary	1	F	B	S		Tenn	July		Whooping cough	25 days
4	Cathrine Sanford	33	F				Tenn	April		C	
5	P. R. Sanford	8m	M				Tenn	June		T. fever	30 days
6	Susan	15	F	B	S		Tenn	April		T. fever	30 days
7	P. C. McCord	5	M				Tenn	March		T. fever	30 days
8	Willice	9m	M	B	S		Tenn	May		Inflamation of brain	2 days
9	Marthy Hughes	53	F			M	N.C.	June		C	
10	Lucy	9	F	B	S		Tenn	June		T. fever	20 days
11	Granville	25	M	B	S		Tenn	July		T. fever	21 days
12	Feraby	45	F	B	S		Va	Aug		T. fever	15 days
13	Mariah	14	F	B	S		Tenn	Aug		T. fever	20 days
14	Andy	1	M	B	S		Tenn	Aug		Cholera	6 days
15	Harvy Traylor	24	M				N.C.	April	Farmer	T. fever	18 days
16	P. R. Cherry	35	M			M	Va	July	Blk-smith	Consumption	90 days
17	John Floyd	7	M				Tenn	Sept		T. fever	30 days
18	Lewis	40	M	B	S		Tenn	July		Cancer	300 days
19	P. Stokes	28	F			M	Tenn	April		Bronchitis	90 days
20	A. M. Stokes	5m	F				Tenn	July		Croup	12 days
21	Abram	6m	M	B	S		Tenn	July		Bowel	6 days
22	Henry	3m	M	B	S		Tenn	Aug		Hives	2 days
23	John	3m	M	B	S		Tenn	Aug		Croup	4 days
24	Sam	19	M	B	S		Tenn	Nov		T. fever	28 days
25	Alphy	70	F	B	S		N.C.	Feb		unknown	37 days
26	Kiziah	46	F	B	S		Tenn	Nov		Consumption	120 days
27	B. T. Dennen	4	F				Tenn	April		Croup	1 day
28	Cathrine	18	F	B	S		Tenn	April		Pneumonia	15 days
29	Jeff	8	M	B	S		Tenn	July		T. fever	20 days
30	Charles A. Stephens	3m	M				Tenn	Aug		Fever	21 days
31	Benjamin	8m	M	B	S		Tenn	Jan		unknown	6 days
32	Sam	6m	M	B	S		Tenn	Feb		Croup	3 days

Remarks: I have traveled through a portion of several States, I have never during all the course of my travels, seen such a heaven favored country or the portion of Williamson therein which I have traveled. They have a great many academies and fine schools and churches and halls, all of which it seems should make man happy if there be any thing on earth could do that thing thereon. Lands must in a few years inhance double their present value.

Personally appeared before me, E. W. Pollard, an acting Justice of the Peace, in and for the County of Williamson and State of Tennessee. J. C. Irvin, Assistant Marshal, who made oath that the foregoing return was made by him according to this oath and instructions to the best of his knowledge and belief. Sworn to before me this 12 Nov 1850.

J. C. Irvin, Asst. Marshal.

The County through which I have traveled is rich and fertile. If there be a heaven favored land, it must be the east portion of Williamson through which I traveled. The general growth of the timber is poplar, walnut, sugartree, boxelder, beech and Popular Springs numerous and water good, and beautiful places to build near them. There are no people on earth more kind and hospitable. They have every thing to make them happy and content.

COUNTY OF WILLIAMSON, STATE OF TENNESSEE.

PAGE NO. 871 PERSONS WHO DIED DURING THE YEAR ENDING 1st JUNE, 1850.

Civil District No. 16
D. Cameron

No. of Visit	Name	Age	Sex	Color	Free or Slave	Married/Widowed	Place of Birth	Month Died	Occupation	Disease or Cause of Death	No. Days Ill
1	Wallace Crosby	48	M				Tenn	Feb	Farmer	Consumption	90 days
2	Leah Bell	1	F	B	S		Tenn	Nov		unknown	120 days
3	Crecy Herbert	25	F	B	S		Tenn	Dec		unknown	150 days
4	Barbara H. Edmondson	16	F				Tenn	July		unknown	90 days
5	Louisa Davis	23	F				Tenn	Oct		Fever	21 days

Remarks: I certify that these are nine pages of schedules, No. 3, of persons who died during the year ending June 1st 1850, as enumerated by me, and that the returns are in accordance with the law and instructions of the Secretary of the Interior.
Sworn to and subscribed on the 9th day of January, 1851. John G. Boyd, J.P.

COUNTY OF WILLIAMSON, STATE OF TENNESSEE.

PAGE NO. 873 PERSONS WHO DIED DURING THE YEAR ENDING 1st JUNE, 1850.

Civil District No. 15
D. Cameron

No. of Visit	Name	Age	Sex	Color	Free or Slave	Married/Widowed	Place of Birth	Month Died	Occupation	Disease or Cause of Death	No. Days Ill
1	Mary Pate	22	F				Tenn	June		Cholera	1 day
2	Nelson Crockett	3m	M				Tenn	June		Smothered	
3	Alexander C. Ewing	22	M				Tenn	Aug	none	Consumption	40 days
4	Susan Cartwright	85	F			W	N.C.	Oct		Old age	21 days
5	Martha Johnson	63	F			W	Va	Sept		unknown	40 days
6	Jerea Johnson	48	F	B	S	W	N.C.	May		Dropsy	365 days
7	Harriett Johnson	9	F	B	S		Tenn	Aug		Sc. fever	15 days
8	Louisa Johnson	10	F	B	S		Tenn	Aug		Sc. fever	15 days
9	James Bond	93	M			M	Maryland	July	none	Old age	
10	Samuel H. Read	11	M				Tenn	Oct		Accident	
11	Elizabeth Nickens	8	F				Tenn	May		Fever	14 days
12	Mary Hadley	40	F	B	S	M	Tenn	March		unknown	30 days
13	Sam Crockett	29	M	B	S		Tenn	May		T. fever	30 days
14	Sam Crockett	2	M	B	S		Tenn	Aug		Bowels	15 days
15	Joseph Shaw	9	M				Tenn	Feb		Fever	17 days

COUNTY OF WILLIAMSON, STATE OF TENNESSEE.

PAGE NO. 875 PERSONS WHO DIED DURING THE YEAR ENDING 1st JUNE, 1850.

Civil District No. 14

D. Cameron

No. of Visit	Name	Age	Sex	Color	Free or Slave	Married/Widowed	Place of Birth	Month Died	Occupation	Disease or Cause of Death	No. Days Ill
1	Amelia Starnes	2	F	B	S		Tenn	May		Measles	12 days
2	George Mosely	2	M	B	S		Tenn	June		Croup	1 day
3	Fielding Pratt	67	M				Va	June	Farmer	Drowned	
4	Jane Lumpkin	1	F	B	S		Tenn	Aug		Teething	42 days
5	Jullan Lumpkin	1	F	B	S		Tenn	Aug		Teething	3 days
6	Jane Nolen	1	F	B	S		Tenn	July		unknown	180 days
7	Berry Nolen	73	M			W	Va	March		Apoplexy	1 day
8	Richard Stevens	4	M	B	S		Tenn	Nov		Fever	21 days
9	Elizabeth Wright	20	F				Va	Oct		Fever	20 days
10	Martha Wright	13	F				Tenn	Oct		Fever	30 days
11	William Wright	7	M				Tenn	Nov		Fever	30 days
12	Howell Wright	5	M				Tenn	Nov		Fever	22 days
13	Dafrey McCutchen	56	F	B	S	M	Va	June		unknown	5 days
14	Francis Cunningham	1m	M				Tenn	Feb		unknown	20 days

COUNTY OF WILLIAMSON, STATE OF TENNESSEE.

PAGE NO. 877 PERSONS WHO DIED DURING THE YEAR ENDING 1st JUNE, 1850.

Civil District No. 13

D. Cameron

No. of Visit	Name	Age	Sex	Color	Free or Slave	Married/Widowed	Place of Birth	Month Died	Occupation	Disease or Cause of Death	No. Days Ill
1	Patrick Gibson	40	M			M	Tenn	March	Farmer	Consumption	60 days
2	Dick Harris	50	M	B	S		Va	Feb		unknown	30 days
3	Alley Kinnard	22	F	B	S		Tenn	Nov		Consumption	150 days
4	Elizabeth Hatcher	4	F	B	S		Tenn	May		Lock jaw	7 days
5	Mary J. Pennington	1	F				Tenn	July		unknown	30 days
6	Nancy Pennington	17	F				Tenn	March		Consumption	730 days
7	Polly Smithson	74	F				Va	May		Dropsy	365 days
8	James Andrews	69	M			M	N.C.	July	Farmer	Fever	65 days
9	Fanny Patton	32	F	B	S		Tenn	Nov		unknown	180 days
10	Mary McGuire	26	F				Tenn	Aug		T. fever	56 days
11	William J. West	3m	M				Tenn	July		Cold	17 days
12	John S. Worf	18	M				Va	April	Farmer	T. fever	16 days
13	Josephine Farmer	3m	F				Tenn			unknown	7 days

COUNTY OF WILLIAMSON, STATE OF TENNESSEE.

PAGE NO. 879 PERSONS WHO DIED DURING THE YEAR ENDING 1st JUNE, 1850.

Civil District No. 12
D. Cameron

No. of Visit	Name	Age	Sex	Color	Free or Slave	Married/Widowed	Place of Birth	Month Died	Occupation	Disease or Cause of Death	No. Days Ill
1	Caroline Cruther	20	F	B	S		Tenn	July		Lock jaw	9 days
2	Elizabeth Sweet	49	F				Kentucky	April		unknown	750 days
3	Cynthia McCall	40	F				Tenn	Sept		unknown	10 days
4	Alexander Giles	23	F?	B	S		Tenn	Aug		Consumption	100 days
5	Fanny Giles	1	F	B	S		Tenn	April		unknown	4 days
6	Mary Waddy	16	F	B	S		Tenn	Dec		Consumption	60 days
7	Sarah Lavender	40	F	B	S		Tenn	Jan		unknown	3 days
8	John A. Smithson	2	M				Tenn	March		Cold	40 days
9	Mark L. Andrews	3	M				Tenn	Nov		Croup	6 days
10	Benjamin C. Helm	40	M				Va	Oct	Farmer	T. fever	35 days

COUNTY OF WILLIAMSON, STATE OF TENNESSEE.

PAGE NO. 881 PERSONS WHO DIED DURING THE YEAR ENDING 1st JUNE, 1850.

Civil District No. 11
D. Cameron

No. of Visit	Name	Age	Sex	Color	Free or Slave	Married/Widowed	Place of Birth	Month Died	Occupation	Disease or Cause of Death	No. Days Ill
1	James D. Horton	21	M				Tenn	Oct	Teacher	T. fever	30 days
2	unnamed Shannon	1m	F				Tenn	Sept		unknown	5 days
3	unnamed Williams	—	F	B	S		Tenn	April		Birth	1 day

COUNTY OF WILLIAMSON, STATE OF TENNESSEE.

PAGE NO. 884 PERSONS WHO DIED DURING THE YEAR ENDING 1st JUNE, 1850.

Civil District No. 11
D. Cameron

No. of Visit	Name	Age	Sex	Color	Free or Slave	Married/Widowed	Place of Birth	Month Died	Occupation	Disease or Cause of Death	No. Days Ill
1	Peter King	55	M	B	S		N.C.	July		Dropsy	120 days
2	Isabella Davis	60	F	B	S		Va	Aug		Old age	70 days
3	Nicholas Davis	3	M	B	S		Tenn	Aug		Brain fever	21 days
4	James Dortch	7	M	B	S		Tenn	July		Worms	2 days
5	Humprey Buford	60	M	B	S		Tenn	Jan		Scrofula	100 days
6	Thomas Buford	4m	M	B	S		Tenn	Feb		unknown	3 days
7	unnamed Buford	1m	M	B	S		Tenn	May		unknown	3 days
8	Washington Womack	4m	M	B	S		Tenn	Oct		Inflamation of bowels	5 days
9	Bethenia McLemore	2m	F	B	S		Tenn	May		unknown	4 days
10	James M. Banks	23	M				Tenn	July	Physician	Consumption	180 days
11	Moses Crutcher	1	M	B	S		Tenn	April		unknown	3 days
12	Letty McCarroll	23	F	B	S		Tenn	June		Fever	20 days
13	Mrs. Harriet Beech	21	F			M	Tenn	June		Inflamation of bowels	8 days
14	Jenny Pointer	62	F	B	S		Va	Feb		Dyspepsia	730 days
15	Grace Pointer	30	F	B	S		Tenn	Feb		Bil. cholic	2 days
16	Sally Pointer	18	F	B	S		Tenn	May		Pneumonia	35 days
17	Sam Pointer	40	M	B	S		Tenn	Jan	Farmer	Dropsy	365 days
18	Grace Pointer	2m	F	B	S		Tenn	March		unknown	30 days
19	Mary E. Stephenson	16	F				Tenn	Aug		T. fever	13 days
20	Amanda C. Hampton	18	F				Tenn	Jan		Pneumonia	7 days
21	Martha Spratt	17	F	B	S		Tenn	July		--illegible--	8 days
22	John D. Spratt	8m	M	B	S		Tenn	July		Whooping cough	15 days
23	Nathan Petway	2	M	B	S		Tenn	July		Fever	7 days
24	James McCord	57	M				Georgia	Nov	Farmer	Dyspepsia	15 days
25	William Bissell	2	M				Tenn	Oct		Inflamation of brain	4 days
26	Sarah McLaughlin	9	F	B	S		Tenn	Feb		Scrofula	18 days
27	Ben Oden	1	M	B	S		Tenn	March		unknown	5 days
28	Sam Oden	1	M	B	S		Tenn	April		Fever	8 days
29	Samp. Oden	2	M	B	S		Tenn	Feb		Sorethroat	4 days
30	Jack Early	73	M	B	S		Va	July	Farmer	Cold	70 days
31	Leanna Yarbrough	77	F				Va	June		Dropsy	12 days
32	Mary Sharp	3m	F				Tenn	March		unknown	30 days
33	Simon Fleming	28	M	B	S		Va	May		Measles	90 days
34	Amanda Thompson	1	F	B	S		Tenn	March		Burn	1 day
35	Henry H. Blythe	8m	M				Tenn	March		Complicated	35 days

COUNTY OF WILLIAMSON, STATE OF TENNESSEE.

PAGE NO. 885 PERSONS WHO DIED DURING THE YEAR ENDING 1st JUNE, 1850.

Civil District No. 10
D. Cameron

No. of Visit	Name	Age	Sex	Color	Free or Slave	Married/Widowed	Place of Birth	Month Died	Occupation	Disease or Cause of Death	No. Days Ill
1	Nancy Smith	4	F	B	S		Tenn	April		Worms	20 days
2	Abby M. Smith	8m	F	B	S		Tenn	May		Worms	16 days
3	Rachel Smith	25	F	B	S		Tenn	Feb		Consumption	70 days
4	unnamed Black	8m	M	B	S		Tenn	Oct		Lung fever	2 days
5	Eliza Murphree	17	F	B	S		Tenn	Jan		unknown	
6	Nancy Henning	60	F	B	S		Va	June		Old age	60 days
7	Child of T. A. Graham	1	F	B	S		Tenn	Feb		Worms	10 days
8	Alexander Walton	18	M				Tenn	March	Farmer	T. fever	19 days
9	Diana Rice	1m	F	B	S		Tenn	Dec		Croup	1 day
10	Elizabeth Daniel	16	F				Tenn	Aug		T. fever	9 days
11	Charles Ratcliffe	14	M	B	S		Tenn	Feb		Scrofula	
12	Ann Tomlin	22	F				Tenn	March		Bil. fever	15 days
13	Eliza Halfacre	25	F	B	S		Tenn	May		Complicated	365 days
14	John Parks	67	M				N.C.	Feb	Farmer	Accident	
15	Eliza Neely	12	F	B	S		Tenn	May		Cold	35 days
16	Nancy J. Halfacre	5	F				Tenn	July		Cholera	2 days
17	Jacob Halfacre	83	M				Germany	Oct	Farmer	Old age	
18	John Hughes	4	M	B	S		Tenn	Aug		Scrofula	25 days
19	Samuel Winstead	3m	M	B	S		Tenn	May		unknown	4 days
20	James D. Graffenreid	8	M	B	S		Tenn	Feb		unknown	15 days
21	Thomas D. Graffenreid	6	M	B	S		Tenn	March		Worms	7 days

COUNTY OF WILLIAMSON, STATE OF TENNESSEE.

PAGE NO. 887 PERSONS WHO DIED DURING THE YEAR ENDING 1st JUNE, 1850.

Civil District No. 9
D. Cameron

No. of Visit	Name	Age	Sex	Color	Free or Slave	Married/Widowed	Place of Birth	Month Died	Occupation	Disease or Cause of Death	No. Days Ill
1	E. J. Hall	18	F				Franklin, Tenn	April		T. fever	19 days
2	Anderson Campbell	7	M	B	F		Franklin, "	May		T. fever	14 days
3	George W. White	26	M				Franklin, "	March	none	Consumption	240 days
4	Mary Susan Hollins	18	F				Franklin, "	May		Pneumonia	16 days
5	Charles Boyd	13	M	B	S		Tenn	June		T. fever	28 days
6	Nancy Cloid	2	F	B	S		Tenn	Feb		Worms	6 days
7	Fanny Parker	12	F				Tenn	April		Consumption	60 days
8	Green Marshall	24	M	B	S	M	Tenn	May	Blk-smith	Dropsy	90 days
9	unnamed child	4m	F	B	S		Tenn	Nov		unknown	1 day
10	Thomas L. Robinson	72	M			M	Maryland	Nov	none	Dropsy	3 days
11	Eliza	27	F	B	S		Tenn	Dec		unknown	sudden
12	unnamed child	8m	F	B	S		Tenn	Jan		Worms	
13	John G. Elsbeck	23	M				Tenn	Feb	Coachtrimmer	Murdered	
14	Asa Smith	17	M				Ohio	Feb	none	T. fever	23 days
15	Natt Whitfield	25	M	B	S	M	Tenn	April	Farmer	Consumption	240 days
16	William P. Barham	27	M			W	Tenn	Feb	Tailor	Murdered	
17	Richard Reid	30	M				Penn	May	Saddler	Small pox	10 days
18	Mrs. Elizabeth West	65	F			M	Va	July		Inflamation	21 days
19	Elizabeth Cunningham	26	F			M	Tenn	May		P.S. Throat	8 days
20	Eva C. Cunningham	6	F				Tenn	May		P.S. Throat	8 days
21	James Jones Baugh	1	M				Tenn	July		Inflamation	60 days
22	Nancy Perkins		F	B	S		Tenn	Feb		T. fever	10 days
23	Henrietta Park	10m	F				Tenn	June		Whooping cough	90 days
24	unnamed Park	1m	M				Tenn	April		Still born	1 day
25	Thomas Karr	10	M				Tenn	Nov		T. fever	9 days
26	Andrew Johnston	86	M			M	Ireland	March	Farmer	Consumption	150 days
27	Eliza Criddle	1	F	B	S		Tenn	June		Lung fever	56 days
28	Sylva Criddle	50	F	B	S		Tenn	Nov		Consumption	108 days
29	Mary Susan Hart		F				Tenn	Sept		Birth	1 day

COUNTY OF WILLIAMSON, STATE OF TENNESSEE.

PAGE NO. 887   PERSONS WHO DIED DURING THE YEAR ENDING 1st JUNE, 1850.

Civil District No. 9
D. Cameron

No. of Visit	Name	Age	Sex	Color	Free or Slave	Married/Widowed	Place of Birth	Month Died	Occupation	Disease or Cause of Death	No. Days Ill
30	Turner Hines	3	M	B	S		Tenn	May		Worms	20 days
31	Rachel Harris	35	F	B	S		Tenn	March		unknown	30 days
32	Nancy H. Crutcher	22	F			M	Tenn	April		Consumption	20 days
33	Ann Perkins	26	F	M	S		Tenn	May		Pneumonia	60 days
34	Rachel E. M. Caldwell	26	F			W	Tenn	Feb		T. fever	25 days
35	Mary C. B. Lewis	50	F				Va	April		Consumption	12 years

COUNTY OF WILSON, STATE OF TENNESSEE.

PAGE NO. 889   PERSONS WHO DIED DURING THE YEAR ENDING 1st JUNE, 1850.

Civil District No. 25
Shadrack Jarmon

No. of Visit	Name	Age	Sex	Color	Free or Slave	Married/Widowed	Place of Birth	Month Died	Occupation	Disease or Cause of Death	No. Days Ill
1	Martha C. Crudeys (?)	2m	F				Tenn	Sept			6 days
2	Lavenia Wright	4m	F				Tenn	Nov		Croup	1 day
3	Melissa J. Medlin	1	F				Tenn	July		Mesentric	6 days
4	Isabella Rice	21	F				Tenn	June		Consumption	5 days
5	James Steel	45	M			M	Tenn	Sept		unknown	10 days
6	Rossalany Wilis	16	F				Tenn	Sept		Consumption	2 years
7	Barnett Guill's, Joe	30	M	B	S		N.C.	Sept		Chronic	2 years
8	Susan Ligon	16	F				Tenn	Dec		Chronic	130 days
9	John E. Baker's, James	22	M	B	S		Tenn	Nov		Bleeding	5 days
10	Martha McDearmore	18	F				Tenn	July		Consumption	6 months
11	Joseph Wright's, Mary	9m	F	B	S		Tenn	Dec		Fever	6 days
12	James Basham's, Tom	18	M	B	S		Tenn	Feb		unknown	8 days
13	Rebecca Martin	71	F			W	N.C.	May		Consumption	150 days
14	Sophia Lain	4	F				Tenn	Aug		Dropsy	2 days
15	Tillman Milberry	1	F?	B	S		Tenn	July		Teething	35 days
16	Virginia T. Hardy	8m	F				Tenn	July		Fever	6 days
17	Jordan Roberson	47	M			M	N.C.	Dec		Cholera	4 days
18	Martha E. Baird	1	F				Tenn	Aug		Fever	12 days
19	Rachel Jolly	21	F			M	Tenn	July		Fever	14 days
20	Margaret Jolly	8m	F				Tenn	Aug		Pleurisy	10 days
21	Ray Jack	25	M	B	S		Tenn	June		Pleurisy	12 days
22	Thomas Rice	54	M			M	N.C.	March		Cancer	112 days
23	Green Myars	2	M				Tenn	Oct		Chronic	6 days
24	Josaphine Gwynn	1m	F				Tenn	May		Fits	5 days
25	Elizabeth Sommers	21	F				Tenn	March		Consumption	90 days
26	George L. Sommers	41	M			M	N.C.	April		Consumption	5 days
27	Martha Stroud	5	F				Tenn	Nov		Fever	14 days
28	Thomas Partton	52	M			M	S.C.	Sept		Chronic	90 days
29	Angelina Kirkpatrick	50	F			M	Tenn	Sept		Consumption	180 days
30	Tate Orsbourn	60	M	B	S		N.C.	Feb		Fever	10 days
31	Jesse Jackson	57	M			M	Va	May		Chronic	60 days
32	Bill's, Tom	35	M	B	S		Tenn	Feb		Pleurisy	30 days
33	Nancy Garret	1m	F				Tenn	June		unknown	1 day
34	Bond's, Ann	1	F	B	S		Tenn	July		Consumption	60 days
35	Bond's, Martha	1	F	B	S		Tenn	Sept		Consumption	240 days

COUNTY OF WILSON, STATE OF TENNESSEE.

PAGE NO. 891 PERSONS WHO DIED DURING THE YEAR ENDING 1st JUNE, 1850.

Civil District No. 18
Shadrack Jarmon

No. of Visit	Name	Age	Sex	Color	Free or Slave	Married/Widowed	Place of Birth	Month Died	Occupation	Disease or Cause of Death	No. Days Ill
1	Gilliam's, Sally	3	F	B	S		Tenn	May		Worms	3 days
2	Gilliam's, Mary	1	F	B	S		Tenn	May		Teething	
3	Nancy Hudson	4	F				Tenn	Dec		Fever	42 days
4	Ann Gilliam	71	F			W	N.C.	Dec		Palsy	90 days
5	Gilliam's, Robb	27	M	B	S		Tenn	Oct		Chronic	150 days
6	Gilliam's, Elizabeth	1m	F	B	S		Tenn	July		unknown	14 days
7	Gilliam's, Patience	20	F	B	S		Tenn	Aug		Scrofula	270 days
8	Word's, Lewis	7	M	B	S		Tenn	July		unknown	90 days
9	Jeremiah Temple	50	M			M	N.C.	Dec		Fever	56 days
10	Martha Carpenter	1	F				Tenn	July		Diarrhea	35 days
11	Numon Treble	2	M				Tenn	June		Measles	
12	Martha Patterson	2m	F				Tenn	March		Chills	42 days
13	Jarmon's, Virginia	3m	F	B	S		Tenn	March		Croup	1 day
14	Allen's, Virginia	4m	F	B	S		Tenn	Feb		unknown	1 day
15	Martin's, Judith	12	F	B	S		Tenn	Jan		Fever	16 days
16	John Jewell	9m	M				Tenn	April		Croup	4 days
17	Hiram Jewell	9m	M				Tenn	April		Croup	4 days
18	Emeline Jennings	7	F				Tenn	Oct		Fever	15 days
19	Jenning's, Rhoda	17	F	B	S		Tenn	Oct		Fever	14 days
20	Martha Young	2	F				Tenn	Aug		Cholera	42 days
21	William Word	63	M			M	Va	July		Chills	4 days
22	Word's, Willis	1	M				Tenn	Dec		Croup	1 day
23	Joseph Rion	19	M				Va	Aug		unknown	4 days
24	Henry Williams	14	M				Tenn	Oct		Dropsy	30 days
25	Nimrod Williams	2	M				Tenn	Nov		unknown	6 days
26	James Griffin	22	M				Tenn	June	Saddler	Cholera	2 days
27	Cartwright's, Easter	2m	F	B	S		Tenn	Aug		Chronic	30 days
28	George Lash	37	M			W	N.C.	Aug		Cholera	2 days
29	Richard Jones	25	M				Tenn	Feb		Consumption	90 days
30	Womack's, Luke	45	M	B	S		Tenn	Dec		Hurt	365 days
31	Cornelia Clark	11	F				Tenn	March		Fever	3 days
32	Emma Ellis	2	F				Tenn	July		Flux	28 days
33	William Winchester	1	M				Tenn	Aug		Hives	7 days
34	Burton Williams	25	M			M	Tenn	Aug		Rising	20 days
35	Philips', Anthony	6m	M	B	S		Tenn	Oct		unknown	1 day

COUNTY OF WILSON, STATE OF TENNESSEE.

PAGE NO. 894 PERSONS WHO DIED DURING THE YEAR ENDING 1st JUNE, 1850.

Civil District No. 15

Shadrack Jarmon

No. of Visit	Name	Age	Sex	Color	Free or Slave	Married/Widowed	Place of Birth	Month Died	Occupation	Disease or Cause of Death	No. Days Ill
1	Eliza Raker	11	F				Tenn	Aug		unknown	120 days
2	Jenning's, Cely	8m	F	M	S		Tenn	Jan		unknown	
3	James', Rosanna	6	F	B	S		Tenn	June		Scrofula	20 days
4	James', Margaret	7m	F	B	S		Tenn	Feb		Fits	1 day
5	Victory James	1m	F				Tenn	Dec		Croup	1 day
6	Munroe Tally	8	M				Tenn	Jan		Spinal effection	60 days
7	Missouri Bryant	2	F				Tenn	March		Hives	1 day
8	William Tolbert	9	M				Tenn	April		Killed by cart	1 day
9	James W. Lester	2	M				Tenn	April		Scrofula	21 days
10	Susan McCoffrey	1m	F				Tenn	July		unknown	1 day
11	Sarah Gatlon	2m	F				Tenn	Sept		Chronic	30 days
12	Isaiah Jones	46	M				Va	April		Consumption	42 days
13	Marshall's, Jack	28	M	M	S		Tenn	Dec		Fever	21 days
14	Jane Sadder	80	F			W	N.C.	Nov		Fever	48 days
15	Mary Coats	87	F				N.C.	March		Dropsy	60 days
16	Samuel L. Thomas	8m	M				Tenn	May		Croup	5 days
17	James Thomas	57	M				N.C.	Jan		unknown	14 days

COUNTY OF WILSON, STATE OF TENNESSEE.

PAGE NO. 895 PERSONS WHO DIED DURING THE YEAR ENDING 1st JUNE, 1850.

Civil District No. 22

Shadrack Jarmon

No. of Visit	Name	Age	Sex	Color	Free or Slave	Married/Widowed	Place of Birth	Month Died	Occupation	Disease or Cause of Death	No. Days Ill
1	Elizabeth F. Rodgers	19	F			M	Tenn	Jan		Fever	10 days
2	Thomas Gates	30	M			M	Tenn	April		Consumption	25 days
3	Herralson's, Louisa	1m	F	B	S		Tenn	Sept		unknown	30 days
4	Sarah T. Clemmons	42	F			M	Tenn	April		Consumption	270 days
5	CLemmon's, Rebecca	68	F	B	S		N.C.	Nov		Phthisic	12 days
6	Clemmon's, George	11m	M	B	S		Tenn	Aug		Diarrhea	30 days
7	Patience Clemmons	36	F				Tenn	Nov		Chronic	120 days
8	Blacknel's, Rebecca	19	F	B	S		Tenn	June		Cold	42 days
9	Blacknel's, Prisciller	15	F	B	S		Tenn	Sept		Cold	150 days
10	Blacknel's, Charlot	1	F	B	S		Tenn	Nov		unknown	
11	William T. Holland	24	M				Tenn	March		Fever	21 days
12	Shannon's, Nancy	6m	F	B	S		Tenn	Oct		Chronic	18 days
13	Martha Sherrell	25	F			M	Tenn	May		Consumption	90 days
14	Nancy Clemmons	32	F			M	Tenn	March		Consumption	30 days
15	Hancock's, Alfred	6	M	B	S		Tenn	Jan		Cold	2 days
16	John M. Holloway	10	M				Tenn	Jan		Cramp	1 day
17	Ferdiman Camper	5	M				Tenn	Nov		Burn	2 days
18	Hancock's, Mary	12	F	M	S		Tenn	April		Consumption	
19	George Willborn	1m	M				Tenn	Aug		unknown	12 days
20	John W. Seat	29	M				Tenn	July		Cholera	4 days
21	Mary Fields	40	F			M	Tenn	Oct		Cold	16 days
22	William Read	49	M			M	Tenn	Aug		Cholera	5 days
23	Hancock's, John	2	M	B	S		Tenn	March		Worms	3 days
24	John Skean	68	M			M	N.C.	May		Gravel	42 days
25	Fite's, Tennessee	1m	F	B	S		Tenn	May		Croup	1 day
26	Celany Bevins	40	F			M	N.C.	June		Flux	11 days
27	Bevin's, Caroline	18	F	B	S		Tenn	July		Chronic	150 days
28	Harris', Wincey	22	F	B	S		N.C.	April		Chronic	3 days
29	Mark Brinkley	49	M			M	N.C.	July		Cholera	1 day
30	Richard Terrell	47	M			M	Va	Dec		Dropsy	15 days
31	-- blank --										
32	Nancy Merritt	101	F			W	Va	April		Cold	6 days
33	Francis Balentine	2	F				Tenn	May		Croup	1 day

COUNTY OF WILSON, STATE OF TENNESSEE.

PAGE NO. 895 PERSONS WHO DIED DURING THE YEAR ENDING 1st JUNE, 1850.

Civil District No. 22
Shadrack Jarmon

No. of Visit	Name	Age	Sex	Color	Free or Slave	Married/Widowed	Place of Birth	Month Died	Occupation	Disease or Cause of Death	No. Days Ill
34	Thomas J. Huddleston	1	M				Tenn	Aug		Teething	7 days
35	Mack Roberts	73	M			M	Va	Feb		Cancer	270 days

COUNTY OF WILSON, STATE OF TENNESSEE.

PAGE NO. 898 PERSONS WHO DIED DURING THE YEAR ENDING 1st JUNE, 1850.

Civil District No. 20
Shadrack Jarmon

No. of Visit	Name	Age	Sex	Color	Free or Slave	Married/Widowed	Place of Birth	Month Died	Occupation	Disease or Cause of Death	No. Days Ill
1	Dement's, Mariah	13	F	B	S		Tenn	Oct		Cold	60 days
2	Harris H. Simmons	30	M			M	N.C.	Aug		Cholera	3 days
3	Martha Preston	50	F			M	Va	March		Palsy	90 days
4	Neal's, Brook	24	M	B	S		N.C.	Jan		Cold	18 days
5	Matilday Floriday	14	F				Tenn	July		Flux	14 days
6	James Rows	11	M	M	S		Tenn	July		Worms	13 days
7	Hiram Rows	30	M	M	S		Tenn	March		Pleurisy	20 days
8	Jincy Rows	32	F	M	S		Tenn	Sept		Sore leg	28 days
9	Zachariah Rucker	8m	M				Tenn	July		Fever	6 days
10	Nancy L. Oneal	25	F			M	Tenn	March		Consumption	90 days
11	James Bennett	33	M			M	Tenn	Sept		Fever	12 days
12	Martha Edwards	13	F				Tenn	Oct		Fever	4 days
13	Foster's, Ransford	11	M	M	S		Tenn	Feb		Scrofula	60 days
14	Lucy Dobbs	1	F				Tenn	July		unknown	60 days
15	Alexander Main	74	M			M	Va	Feb		Broken leg	60 days
16	Franky Jones	17	F				Tenn	Feb		Fever	4 days
17	Miles Williams	19	M				Tenn	March		Fever	3 days
18	Anny Donald	63	F			W	N.C.	April		Rising	3 days
19	McKey's, Andrew	9m	M	B	S		Tenn	Jan		Cold	30 days
20	Margaret L. Wynn	31	F			M	Tenn	April		Dropsy	50 days
21	Mary Bland	8m	F				Tenn	Feb		Hives	1 day
22	Howell Williams	69	M			M	Va	Jan		Dropsy	270 days
23	William's, Angeline	4	F	B	S		Tenn	May		Croup	3 days
24	Catherine Ward	7	F				Tenn	Sept		Fever	21 days
25	Lewis Patterson	22	M				Tenn	March		Dropsy	3 days
26	John A. Jennings	55	M			M	Kentucky	Oct		Dropsy	14 days
27	Narcissa Warren	6	F				Tenn	Dec		Fever	28 days
28	Thomas Warren	1	M				Tenn	July		Cold	21 days
29	George Robertson	5	M				Va	Feb		Croup	3 days
30	Mary C. Williams	1	F				Tenn	Aug		Fever	14 days
31	Thompson's, Winney	42	F	B	S		Va	July		Pleurisy	14 days
32	Jane Thompson	2	F				Tenn	July		Pleurisy	3 days
33	Mary J. Alexander	1	F				Tenn	July		unknown	10 days

COUNTY OF WILSON, STATE OF TENNESSEE.

PAGE NO. 899 PERSONS WHO DIED DURING THE YEAR ENDING 1st JUNE, 1850.

Civil District No. 6
R. Hallum

No. of Visit	Name	Age	Sex	Color	Free or Slave	Married/Widowed	Place of Birth	Month Died	Occupation	Disease or Cause of Death	No. Days Ill
1	Squire	1	M	B	S		Tenn	May		Worms	1 month
2	William A. Tomlinson	8	M				Tenn	Dec		Sore throat	3 weeks
3	John A. Tomlinson	8m	M				Tenn	Jan		Sore throat	3 weeks
4	Charlotte	10m	F	B	S		Tenn	Feb		Chronic	4 weeks
5	George	3m	M	B	S		Tenn	June		Accident	sudden
6	Mary B. Calhoun	66	F			M	N.C.	March		Wounded	3 months
7	Finis	7	M	B	S		Tenn	May		Fever	8 days
8	Phillip	51	M	B	S		Tenn	Feb		Gravel	3 months
9	James	7	M	B	S		Tenn	July		Fever	10 days
10	Elizabeth	15	F	B	S		Tenn	April		Fever	2 weeks
11	Milton	2	M	B	S		Tenn	Oct		Cholera Inf.	2 weeks
12	Andrew	7m	M	B	S		Tenn	May		Smothered	sudden
13	Darcus	80	F	B	S		Va	Dec		Old age	
14	James W. Dodd	4	M				Tenn	Jan		unknown	1 week
15	Martha Motley	48	F			W	N.C.	June		Flux	14 days
16	John D. Motley	31	M				Tenn	Dec		Chronic	4 weeks
17	Zachariah Williams	8m	M				Tenn	Sept		Chronic	2 months
18	John	7m	M	B	S		Tenn	June		Chronic	1 month
19	Mary Weiz	28	F				Tenn	June		Consumption	1 year
20	Celia	23	F	B	S		Tenn	July		Fever	1 month
21	John	2	M	B	S		Tenn	July		Chronic	1 year
22	Samuel	12	M	B	S		Tenn	Aug		Consumption	3 months
23	Eliza	13	F	B	S		Tenn	Aug		Cholera	sudden
24	Josephine Bell	1	F				Tenn	Sept		Fever	18 days
25	George	3	M	B	S		Tenn	June		Fever	10 days
26	Reuben	17	M	B	S		Tenn	June		Diarrhea	8 days
27	William Wheeler	10	M				Tenn	Aug		Diarrhea	3 weeks
28	William Tilford	30	M			M	Tenn	July		Cholera	sudden
29	Mary Tilford	25	F			M	Tenn	July		Cholera	sudden
30	Sarah Tilford	62	F			M	Va	Oct		Consumption	1 year
31	Knotley C. Drain	9m	M				Tenn	Jan		Hives	8 days
32	Infant	1m	M	B	S		Tenn	Oct			sudden
33	Tempy	30	F	B	S		Tenn	July		Flux	1 week
34	Sally	30	F	B	S		Tenn	July		Flux	1 week
35	Infant	2	M	B	S		Tenn	July		Flux	1 week

COUNTY OF WILSON **, STATE OF TENNESSEE.**

PAGE NO. 902 **PERSONS WHO DIED DURING THE YEAR ENDING 1st JUNE, 1850.**

Civil District No. 7
R. Hallum

No. of Visit	Name	Age	Sex	Color	Free or Slave	Married/Widowed	Place of Birth	Month Died	Occupation	Disease or Cause of Death	No. Days Ill
1	David	22	M	B	S		Tenn	Jan		Fever	11 days
2	Louis	48	M	B	S		Tenn	April		Fever	2 weeks
3	Martha Calhoun	20	F				Tenn	May		Chronic	1 year
4	James A. Corley	2	M				Tenn	Nov		Fever	1 week
5	Infant	1m	F	B	S		Tenn	Dec		_____	sudden
6	Vina	28	F	B	S		Tenn	Oct		Chronic	9 months
7	Parker Pemberton	47	F?			M	Va	Oct		Cancer	1 year
8	Rebecca	87	F	B	S		Va	March		Old age	_____
9	Julia A. Bobo	21	F			M	Tenn	June		Chronic	1 year
10	Preston	1	M	B	S		Tenn	June		Chronic	1 year
11	Henry	1	M	B	S		Tenn	June		Chronic	1 year
12	Harriet	25	F	B	S		Tenn	June		Chronic	1 year
13	Elizabeth	2	F	B	S		Tenn	June		Chronic	1 year
14	Rhina	2	F	B	S		Tenn	June		Chronic	1 year
15	Infant	1m	M	B	S		Tenn	Feb		Chronic	sudden
16	Christine Swann	60	F			M	Va	Aug		Chronic	18 months
17	Tabitha J. Small	3	F				Tenn	Feb		Fever	1 week
18	Manuel	43	M	B	S		Tenn	April		Fits	sudden
19	Alfred	5m	M	B	S		Tenn	April		_____	sudden
20	Jane	70	F	B	S		Va	April		_____	sudden
21	Anderson	18	M	B	S		Tenn	April		Scrofula	1 year
22	Mary Andrews	42	F			M	Tenn	Oct		Dropsy	1 month
23	James F. Cartwright	1	M				Tenn	Oct		Teething	1 week
24	Infant	1m	M	B	S		Tenn	Jan		_____	sudden
25	Thornton	8m	M	B	S		Tenn	Aug		_____	sudden
26	Wilson B. H---	4m	M				Tenn	Nov		_____	_____
27	Foster	60	M	B	S		Va	April		Pleurisy	15 days
28	Saraphine	1m	F	B	S		Tenn	April		_____	sudden
29	Bethelly D. Williams	4	M				Tenn	March		Fever	5 days
30	Ben	1	M	B	S		Tenn	April		Fever	7 months
31	Lucy	11	F	B	S		Tenn	April		_____	sudden
32	Alexander	5	M	B	S		Tenn	Feb		Fever	2 months
33	Sophia	18	F	B	S		Tenn	Dec		Fever	10 days
34	Mary Barbee	74	F			M	Va	July		Chronic	4 months
35	Infant	1m	M				Tenn	July		_____	sudden

COUNTY OF WILSON, STATE OF TENNESSEE.

PAGE NO. 903 PERSONS WHO DIED DURING THE YEAR ENDING 1st JUNE, 1850.

Civil District No. 4
R. Hallum

No. of Visit	Name	Age	Sex	Color	Free or Slave	Married/Widowed	Place of Birth	Month Died	Occupation	Disease or Cause of Death	No. Days Ill
1	Margaret	4m	F	B	S		Tenn	July		Inflamation	2 weeks
2	Isaac Wright	73	M				N.C.	Nov	Meth. Mins.		sudden
3	Mary	3m	F	B	S		Tenn	Dec		Croup	sudden
4	Winfield S. Faker	1	M				Tenn	July		Cholera Inf.	4 days
5	Tenah	70	F	B	S		Va	Feb		Old age	
6	Meredith	1	M	B	S		Tenn	Oct		Worms	4 days
7	Lydia	24	F	B	S		Tenn	March		Inflamation	14 days
8	Millner Walker	47	M				Va	Sept	Farmer	Fever	1 week
9	Samuel Walker	35	M				Tenn	Sept	Farmer	Fever	2 weeks
10	Rogers	51	M	B	S		Va	July		Cholera	sudden
11	William P. Harriss	50	M				N.C.	Oct	Meth. Mins.	Consumption	3 months
12	Mary S. Morriss	13	F				Tenn	Sept		Fever	18 days
13	Charles Conyers	24	M				Tenn	Aug	Blk-smith	Cholera	sudden
14	Richard H. Mack	39	M				Va	Aug	Farmer	Fever	4 weeks
15	Burton	2	M	B	S		Tenn	April		Scrofula	6 months
16	Edmund	13	M	B	S		Tenn	Feb			sudden
17	James Chambless	12	M				Tenn	Jan			2 days
18	John Chambless	23	M				Tenn	Aug	Farmer	Cholera	sudden
19	Elizabeth Nolen	29	F				N.C.	Nov		Chronic	6 months
20	Piety	28	F	B	S		Tenn	Dec		Fever	2 years
21	William Owen	3	M				Tenn	June		Fever	6 weeks
22	John Rutledge	32	M				Tenn	Aug	Farmer	Cholera	sudden
23	George	6	M	B	S		Tenn	Sept		Chronic	2 years
24	Hanah	40	F	B	S		Tenn	May		Fever	10 days
25	Jim	28	M	B	S		Tenn	April		Inflamation	2 months
26	Jenny	50	F	B	S		Tenn	Aug		Cholera	sudden
27	Armsted	34	M	B	S		Tenn	Aug		Cholera	sudden
28	David	60	M	B	S		Tenn	Aug		Cholera	sudden
29	Rebecca	55	F	B	S		Tenn	Aug		Cholera	sudden
30	William	55	M	B	S		Tenn	Aug		Cholera	sudden
31	Aletha	14	F	B	S		Tenn	Aug		Cholera	sudden
32	Emily	8	F	B	S		Tenn	Aug		Cholera	sudden
33	Watson	3	M	B	S		Tenn	Aug		Cholera	sudden
34	Mariah	2	F	B	S		Tenn	Aug		Cholera	sudden
35	Parthe Harrington	1m	F				Tenn	Aug		Cholera	sudden

COUNTY OF WILSON **, STATE OF TENNESSEE.**

PAGE NO. 906   **PERSONS WHO DIED DURING THE YEAR ENDING 1st JUNE, 1850.**

Civil District No. 10
R. Hallum

No. of Visit	Name	Age	Sex	Color	Free or Slave	Married/Widowed	Place of Birth	Month Died	Occupation	Disease or Cause of Death	No. Days Ill
1	George Graves	23	M				Ohio	Aug		Cholera	sudden
2	Frances Brown	21	F				Tenn	Aug		Cholera	sudden
3	Sephronia Brown	14	F				Tenn	July		Cholera	sudden
4	David	17	M	B	S		Tenn	July		Cholera	sudden
5	Ailsy	16	F	B	S		Tenn	Dec		Dropsy	3 months
6	Moses	7	M	B	S		Tenn	Aug		Cholera	sudden
7	John Weaver	33	M				Penn	July	Plasterer	Cholera	sudden
8	Harriss	26	M	B	S		Tenn	July		Cholera	sudden
9	Benjamin Owen	37	M				Tenn	July	Physician	Cholera	sudden
10	Robert W. Bonner	11	M				Tenn	Aug		Cholera	sudden
11	James M. Getund	32	M				Tenn	Aug	Physician	Cholera	sudden
12	Elizabeth D. Getund	25	F				Tenn	Aug		Cholera	sudden
13	Emily Hancock	10	F				Tenn	Aug		Cholera	sudden
14	James P. Hancock	1	M				Tenn	Aug		Cholera	sudden
15	Martha W. Castleman	18	F				Tenn	May		Fever	5 weeks
16	James Haynes	4	M				Tenn	Aug		Cholera	sudden
17	Richard Haynes	6m	M				Tenn	Aug		Cholera	sudden
18	Ann	3	F	B	S		Tenn	Aug		Cholera	sudden
19	Martha M. Smith	1	F				Tenn	Aug		Cholera	sudden
20	Emma Drifoos	6	F				Tenn	Aug		Cholera	sudden
21	Julia Drifoos	2	F				Tenn	Aug		Cholera	sudden
22	Dolly	40	F	B	S		Tenn	Aug		Cholera	sudden
23	Eliza	15	F	B	S		Tenn	Aug		Cholera	sudden
24	Willis	19	M	B	S		Tenn	Aug		Cholera	sudden
25	Edwin S. Stuart	5	M				Tenn	Sept		Fever	1 month
26	Jefferson	31	M	B	S		Tenn	Aug		Cholera	sudden
27	Phillis	70	F	B	S		Tenn	Dec		Phthisic	4 weeks
28	Jenny	74	F	B	S		Tenn	Aug			sudden
29	Mary Sypress	50	F			M	Tenn	June		Cholera	3 weeks
30	Tabitha Morris	2	F				N.C.	Aug		Cholera	sudden
31	Francis B. Drake	28	M				Tenn	Aug	Marchant	Cholera	sudden
32	Martha Drake	25	F				Tenn	Aug		Cholera	sudden
33	John Payton	6	M				Tenn	Aug		Cholera	sudden
34	Henry	13	M	B	S		Tenn	Aug		Cholera	sudden
35	Rebecca	17	F	B	S		Tenn	Aug		Cholera	sudden

COUNTY OF WILSON, STATE OF TENNESSEE.

PAGE NO. 907 PERSONS WHO DIED DURING THE YEAR ENDING 1st JUNE, 1850.

Civil District No. 12
R. Hallum

No. of Visit	Name	Age	Sex	Color	Free or Slave	Married/Widowed	Place of Birth	Month Died	Occupation	Disease or Cause of Death	No. Days Ill
1	Catharine Markes	59	F				Va	July		Chronic	3 months
2	Thomas J. Spring	22	M				Tenn	March		Fever	10 days
3	Samuel Patterson	50	M			M	Tenn	July		Flux	3 weeks
4	James A. Patterson	23	M				Tenn	July		Flux	6 days
5	Mary A. Tracy	3	F				Tenn	Aug		Flux	10 days
6	Elizabeth George	51	F			M	Va	Sept		Cancer	6 weeks
7	Jacob Vantrice	77	M			M	Tenn	June		Cholera	sudden
8	Jube	4	F	B	S		Tenn	Oct		Chronic	4 months
9	Polly	1m	F	B	S		Tenn	Oct			sudden
10	Nancy Harrington	18	F			M	Tenn	May		Fever	2 weeks
11	Mary Felton	90	F				Va	Sept		Old age	
12	Infant Williamson	1m	M				Tenn	May			sudden
13	Elizabeth Robinson	3	F				Tenn	Dec		Croup	sudden
14	Sarah Young	92	F			W	N.C.	Oct		Dropsy	12 months
15	Edward Jacobs	79	M			M	Maryland	Aug	Shoemaker	Cholera	sudden
16	Bedrix Jacobs	77	F			M	N.C.	Aug		Dropsy	5 years

COUNTY OF WILSON, STATE OF TENNESSEE.

PAGE NO. 909 PERSONS WHO DIED DURING THE YEAR ENDING 1st JUNE, 1850.

Civil District No. 1
R. Hallum

No. of Visit	Name	Age	Sex	Color	Free or Slave	Married/Widowed	Place of Birth	Month Died	Occupation	Disease or Cause of Death	No. Days Ill
1	Ellen	6m	F	B	S		Tenn	Jan		Accident	
2	Lucy	12	M	B	S		Tenn	March		Fever	2 weeks
3	Malvina	45	F	B	S		N.C.	April		Fever	1 week
4	Abram	5	M	B	S		Tenn	Oct		Croup	2 weeks
5	Masouria Sharp	14	F				Tenn	Nov		T. fever	2 weeks
6	Sarah Briant	33	F			M	Tenn	Dec		T. fever	1 week
7	William Murry	88	M			W	Va	Aug	Meth. Mins.	Chronic	50 days
8	Caroline Hooper	16	F				Tenn	June		Consumption	6 months
9	Martha E. Anderson	1	F				Arkansas	April		Chronic	4 weeks
10	Dick	2	M	B	S		Tenn	Oct		Chronic	3 weeks
11	John	1	M	B	S		Tenn	Sept		unknown	5 days
12	Elizabeth Tate	1m	F				Tenn	July			sudden
13	Marshy Daniel	9	F				Tenn	Aug		Spine	4 weeks
14	Infant child		M				Tenn	Oct			sudden
15	Caroline	10	F	B	S		Tenn	Oct		Fever	6 weeks
16	Elizabeth A. Grimes	1	F	M	S		Tenn	June		Whooping cough	1 month
17	Hillyard	6m	M	B	S		Tenn	Jan		Whooping cough	6 weeks
18	Wily	20	M	B	S		Tenn	March		Fever	2 weeks
19	Isabella	70	F	B	S		Va	Nov		Old age	2 years
20	William	40	M	B	S		Va	Feb		Fits	sudden
21	Alexander	2m	M	B	S		Tenn	Feb		Croup	sudden
22	Mary J. Bradshaw	20	F				Tenn	July		Consumption	3 months
23	Joseph Bradshaw	21	M				Tenn	Jan	Farmer	Fever	4 weeks
24	Joseph Price	30	M				Tenn	Jan		Small pox	3 weeks
25	Margaret Price	4	F				Tenn	Jan		Small pox	3 weeks
26	Winny Eatherly	16	F				Tenn	Jan		Consumption	3 months
27	Abijah Jones	40	F			W	Tenn	July		Cholera	sudden
28	Martha	2m	F	B	S		Tenn	April			sudden
29	Eugene Cook	1m	F				Tenn	Jan		Inflamation	30 days
30	Benjamin N. Kimbrell	44	M				N.C.	July	Blk-smith	Cholera	sudden
31	Henry	18	M	B	S		Tenn	Sept		Liver	3 weeks
32	Elizabeth	22	F	B	S		Tenn	Sept		Fever	3 weeks
33	John Griffin	31	M				Tenn	Oct	Farmer	Fever	4 weeks
34	Mary Taylor	30	F				N.C.	Jan		Consumption	5 weeks
35	Isaac H. Dennis	38	M			M	Va	July		Cholera	sudden

COUNTY OF WILSON **, STATE OF TENNESSEE.**

PAGE NO. 912 **PERSONS WHO DIED DURING THE YEAR ENDING 1st JUNE, 1850.**

Civil District No. 2
R. Hallum

No. of Visit	Name	Age	Sex	Color	Free or Slave	Married/Widowed	Place of Birth	Month Died	Occupation	Disease or Cause of Death	No. Days Ill
1	Mary Wright	37	F			M	Tenn	April		Inflamation	10 days
2	Jonathan Pence	1	M				Tenn	Feb		Fits	1 month
3	David	1m	M	B	S		Tenn	June			sudden
4	Elvina A. Estes	4	F					June		Fits	sudden
5	Alexander	3m	M	B	S		Tenn	April			sudden
6	Child	1m	F	B	S		Tenn	March			sudden
7	Boss	15	M	B	S		Tenn	Oct		Pneumonia	8 days
8	Martha	1	F	B	S		Tenn	Aug		Pneumonia	1 week
9	Martha Hamilton	1	F				Tenn	July		Cholera	3 weeks
10	Willis	1	M	B	S		Tenn	Nov		Diseased head	1 week
11	Infant	1	F	B	S		Tenn	Nov			sudden
12	Ruy Bettis	2	F				Tenn	June		Worms	sudden
13	Charlotte S. Syprett	19	F				Tenn	March		Chronic	2 years
14	Cresia	70	F	B	S		N.C.	June		Old age	
15	Mary	1	F	B	S		Tenn	July		Fever	3 weeks
16	Elizabeth A. Porter	25	F			M	Tenn	June		Consumption	6 months
17	Mary Allen	3	F				Tenn	Dec		Burnt	2 weeks
18	John	2	M	B	S		Tenn	Sept		Scrofula	2 years
19	Andrew Donnell	19	M				Tenn	June		Consumption	3 months
20	Sophia J. Cook	7m	F				Tenn	Jan			3 days
21	Sophia Cartwell	17	F				Tenn	Aug		Consumption	3 months
22	Louiza	2	F	B	S		Tenn	Aug		Worms	1 week
23	John H. Jarrell	3m	M				Tenn	June		Cholera Inf.	10 days
24	James	6m	M	B	S		Tenn	July		Erysipelas	10 days
25	Harry	1	M	B	S		Tenn	Aug		Croup	sudden
26	Jane	1	F	B	S		Tenn	Nov			sudden
27	Susan	6m	F				Tenn	May			sudden
28	Jacen	3m	M	B	S		Tenn	July			sudden
29	Jim	2m	M	B	S		Tenn	Aug			sudden
30	Edward H. Bandy	23	M				Tenn	April		Consumption	4 weeks
31	John	1	M	B	S		Tenn	Jan		Thrash	3 days
32	Mary	4	F	B	S		Tenn	May		Chronic	4 months
33	Nelson	58	M	B	S		Tenn	Aug		Cholera	sudden
34	Caroline	4	F	B	S		Tenn	Aug		Congestion	sudden
35	Cella	2	F	B	S		Tenn	Aug		Dropsy	4 days

COUNTY OF WILSON, STATE OF TENNESSEE.

PAGE NO. 913 PERSONS WHO DIED DURING THE YEAR ENDING 1st JUNE, 1850.

Civil District No. 10
R. Hallum

No. of Visit	Name	Age	Sex	Color	Free or Slave	Married/Widowed	Place of Birth	Month Died	Occupation	Disease or Cause of Death	No. Days Ill
1	John Winford	12	M				Tenn	Aug		Cholera	sudden
2	William H. Reece	32	M				Tenn	Aug	Carpenter	Fever	6 weeks
3	Joseph A. Hughy	9	M				Tenn	Aug		Cholera	sudden
4	William Waggoner	26	M				Tenn	Aug	Blk-smith	Cholera	sudden
5	Mary Waggoner	1	F				Tenn	Aug		Diarrhea	3 weeks
6	James Jones	6	M				Tenn	Aug		Cholera	sudden
7	Nancy Ward	3	F				Tenn	Aug		Cholera	sudden
8	Sarah Matherel	86	F			W	N.C.	May		Old age	2 months
9	Ann	24	F	B	S		Tenn	July		Hemorrhage	4 months
10	Minos	50	M	B	S		N.C.	Aug		Cholera	sudden
11	Alfred	21	M	B	S		Tenn	Jan		Fever	3 weeks
12	Eustes	18	M	B	S		Tenn	Aug		Cholera	sudden
13	Hugh L. White	1	M				Tenn	Aug		Cholera	sudden
14	Nancy Jarrell	17	F				Tenn	Aug		Cholera	sudden
15	Eve Dill	70	F			W	Va	Feb		Chronic	10 days
16	Washington Baily	49	M			W	Va	July	Baptist Min.	Cholera	sudden
17	Elizabeth W. L. Donnell	11m	F				Tenn	Aug		Sore throat	3 weeks
18	Jesse J. Ragland	3m	M				Tenn	Aug		Croup	6 weeks
19	Samuel Mosely	41	M			W	Va	July		Cholera	sudden
20	_____ Baker	10	M				Tenn	July		Cholera	sudden
21	Cisly	55	F	B	S		Va	July		Cholera	sudden
22	Frances Davis	21	F			W	Tenn	Aug		Cholera	sudden
23	Emma Ireland	2	F				Tenn	July		Cholera	sudden
24	Nancy Harriss	16	F				N.C.	Aug		Erysipelas	11 weeks
25	Mary J. Parish	20	F			M	Tenn	July		Cholera	sudden
26	Mary J. Parish	1m	F				Tenn	Aug		Cholera	sudden
27	Rachel A. Anderson	38	F			M	Tenn	Dec		Consumption	6 months
28	Rebecca	23	F	B	S		Tenn	March		Dropsy	2 months
29	Bennett White	2	M				Tenn	Sept		Fever	1 week
30	Bob	32	M	B	S		Tenn	Aug		Cholera	sudden
31	Sarah T. Lester	4	F				Tenn	July		Cholera	sudden
32	Matilda	24	F	B	S		Tenn	Aug		Cholera	sudden
33	Obedience Guthery	90	F			W	N.C.	Feb		Old age	
34	Thomas H. Guthery	25	M				Tenn	April		Consumption	1 month
35	Infant	1	M	B	S		Tenn	Jan		Croup	4 days

COUNTY OF WILSON, STATE OF TENNESSEE.

PAGE NO. 916 PERSONS WHO DIED DURING THE YEAR ENDING 1st JUNE, 1850.

Civil District No. 10
R. Hallum

No. of Visit	Name	Age	Sex	Color	Free or Slave	Married/Widowed	Place of Birth	Month Died	Occupation	Disease or Cause of Death	No. Days Ill
1	Alphia	2	F	B	S		Tenn	Jan		Fever	3 days
2	John P. Williams	35	M			M	Tenn	March	Silversmith	Consumption	1 year
3	Henry	17	M	B	S		Tenn	March		Chronic	8 months
4	Spencer Vaughan	28	M				Va	July	Wheelwright	Cholera	sudden
5	Thomas Dawson	3m	M				Tenn	July		Cholera	sudden
6	William Prindle	84	M			W	Va	March		Old age	
7	Higden Harrington	65	M			W	N.C.	Aug		Cholera	sudden
8	Mary E. Johnson	52	F			W	S.C.	Aug		Cholera	sudden
9	Sarah	44	F	B	S		Tenn	Dec		Dropsy	1 year
10	Jefferson Estes	24	M				Va	July		Chronic	4 months
11	Thomas B. Dew	21	M				Tenn	Oct	Painter	Chronic	5 months
12	Tyree	54	M	B	S		Tenn	Aug		Cholera	sudden
13	Rose	45	F	B	S		Tenn	Aug		Cholera	sudden
14	Rachel	55	F	B	S		Tenn	Aug		Cholera	sudden
15	Henry Rye	52	M			M	N.C.	Aug	Farmer	Cholera	sudden
16	Giles	1	M	B	S		Tenn	May		Inflamation	2 days
17	William Eason	45	M				Va	Sept		Fever	sudden
18	Phebe J. Eason	3	F				Va	May		Cholera	sudden
19	Elizabeth Asten	51	F				Tenn	April		Chronic	10 days
20	David	70	M	B	S		Tenn	March		Old age	
21	Elizabeth A. -----	1	F				Tenn	Nov		Croup	sudden
22	Elizabeth	44	F	B	S		Tenn	March		Chronic	6 months
23	Jefferson Berdine	45	M			M	Tenn	May	Farmer	Chronic	5 months
24	Laura T. Vaughan	11m	F				Tenn	Nov		Croup	sudden
25	Tena	26	F	B	S		Tenn	Oct		Chronic	4 months
26	Mary Mahone	1	F				Tenn	Jan		Hives	1 month
27	Martha	12	F	B	S		Tenn	April		Chronic	3 weeks
28	Daniel	3	M	B	S		Tenn	Feb		Chronic	sudden
29	Eliza	2m	F	B	S		Tenn	Oct		Chronic	sudden
30	Joel Underwood	42	M				N.C.	Sept	Farmer	Fever	3 weeks
31	William Miles	27	M				Tenn	Aug		Shot	sudden
32	Mary Chambers	30	F				Tenn	May		Consumption	6 months
33	Charles	2	M	B	S		Tenn	June		Worms	8 days
34	Harriet	1	F	B	S		Tenn	May		Croup	sudden

INDEX

ABBOTT
John, 801
ABERNATHY
Adison A., 562
James, 276
John Y., 255
Martha, 714
Mary J., 273
Sarah E., 273
ABNEY
Francis, 568
ACUFF
Elizabeth, 281
Emily T., 441
Nicholas, 281
ADAIR
Margaret, 839
ADAMS
Archibald, 23
Avrilla, 482
Bolivar, 482
C., 835
Charles, 302
E. J., 64
E. P., 831
Elijah, 492
Elizabeth, 781
Hezekiah, 614
James, 512
Jane, 633
John, 489
Mariah, 157
Martha J., 187
Mary, 511
May, 635
Prudence, 492
William, 487
William L., 43
ADCOCK
J. T., 129
Lot, 179
Martha I., 754
Winneford, 627
ADKINS
Chesley, 45
Harriett, 281
Jesse, 846
Margaret I., 806
Martha A., 273
Minerva, 45
Ransome, 45
ADKINSON
Anna, 531
Charles, 398
Elijah G., 551
Ellen, 489
Florence, 604
Katherine, 587
Levi, 604
ALFORD
Elizabeth J., 604
AGEE
Ann E., 48
AHERN
Pat., 732
AIKEN
____, 37
AIKMAN
Thomas, 37
AIRES
Elizabeth, 437
AIRHART
A. C., 136
AKIN
Darcas, 550
AKINS
Malinda J., 332
ALBERSON
Sarah, 598
ALBRIGHT
L. Lee, 755
ALDERMAN
Armsted, 402
Josiah, 383
ALEXANDER
Adley, 64
Ezekiel, 327
Francis, 43
Jane, 785
Joseph, 399
Mary J., 898
Nancy, 562
Nancy P., 182
Sarah, 562, 664
Seanah, 327
W. R., 655
William, 635
ALFRED
Enoch C., 558
Lucinda, 558
ALINROAD
David, 768
ALLEN
Amanda J., 546
Anna, 830
Betsey, 562
Catherine E., 333
Daniel, 707, 745
Drury, 579
Henry, 383
John, 217
Josephine, 161
Mary, 589, 718, 912
Mathew, 363
Nancy, 161, 333, 772
Robert B., 797
S., 831
Samuel H., 179
Thomas, 217
William, 179
William H., 448
ALLBROOK
Fanny, 762
ALLCORN
Martha, 409
ALLISON
Jasper, 39
Louisa A., 598
Polly, 615
Teletha J., 811
William, 114
ALLMAN
Catherine, 156
ALLRED
Ann, 595
Polly, 595
ALRED
Rebecca, 229
ALSABROOKS
John, 710
Sarah, 710
ALSBROOKS
Fany, 762
Martha, 762
ALSOP
A. M., 687
ALSTON
A. S. J., 804
Mary H., 804
ALSUP
Jefferson C., 31
ALTMAN
James F., 245
Nancy E., 245
ALVES
Charles, 492
AMENT
Henry, 153
AMOS
Samuel, 178
ANDERSON
Alexander T., 675
Artencey, 675
Bailey, 710
Calvin C., 325
Drucilla J., 433
Edward, 409
G., 499
Isaac, 653, 814
James, 9
Jane T., 321
Joseph, 96
Joseph D., 433
Lucinda, 412
Malinda, 751
Malyine, 675
Martha Ann, 482
Martha E., 909
Mary, 383
Mary A., 604
Mary C., 190
May, 521
Nancy Ann, 254
Nancy M., 768
Rachel, 913
Rhoda, 129
Rose E., 433
Rutha, 732
Sarah, 615
Susan, 732
William, 766
William H., 827
Zachariah, 846
ANDES
Abram, 823
Mary, 823
ANDREW
Dorchus, 244
Elizabeth, 745
ANDREWS
Amanda, 493
Anna, 493
Azubra, 327
Elizabeth, 766
James, 877
Jessey, 745
Mark L., 879
ANDREWS
Mary, 902
Sarah, 745
ANGEL
Rachel, 671
ANGLIN
Josanna, 333
Rosanna, 333
ANTHONY
Jasper N., 5
John, 99
Mary, 444
Robert, 221
Susan M., 5
APPLE
George, 174
APPLEBY
Samuel, 366
APPLETON
Cathrine, 220
ARANTS
Eliza, 769
Elizabeth, 769
Ireson L., 769
ARCHER
David Albert, 390
ARLSHIL
Joseph L., 286
ARMER
John, 415
ARMFIELD
Harman, 484
ARMOUR
Solomon, 683
ARMSTRONG
James T., 432
Mahala, 604
Nancy, 42
Nathaniel, 332
Polly P., 437
ARNELL
James, 543
ARNN
Sarah, 383
ARNOLD
____, 433
Charlot, 474
James, 452
John, 5, 551
Margaritte, 395
Mary, 551, 622
William, 358
William E., 827
William J., 49
ARNY
Willie, 335
ARRINGTON
Stephen, 703
ARTERBURN
Isaac, 338
ARVINE
Martha, 281
ARY
Sarah A., 604
ASEWOOD
Louisa, 163
ASH
Elizabeth, 281
ASHLEY
Almsted, 605

ASHLOCK
    Clark, 1
ASHMORE
    John W., 452
    Lavira, 452
    Mary, 452
ASHWORTH
    Serena E., 550
ASTEN
    Elizabeth, 916
ASTIEN
    Francis, 759
    William, 759
ATCHBY
    Mary, 678
ATCHLEY
    Daniel, 675
    Joseph, 675
ATKERSON
    Mathew, 827
ATKINS
    Mary, 571
    Milbery, 391
    Sarah Matilda, 390
    W. H., 193
ATKINSON
    Elizabeth, 29
    Mary E., 9
ATTAWAY
    Nicy, 355
ATWOOD
    Elizabeth, 747
AULSTON
    Elizabeth, 31
AULTUM
    Matilda, 4
AUSTIL
    Sarah C., 103
AUSTIN
    Manon, 503
    Salina, 448
    Susan C., 448
    William, 421
AUSTON
    Sarah, 592, 503, 592
AVANT
    Mildred M., 316
AVERETT
    Ester, 745
AVERY
    Caroline, 245
AXLEY
    Nancy, 475
AYDLOTT
    Priscilla, 402
AYRES
    Rhoda L., 453

BABB
    Joshua, 820
BABO
    Julin, 902
BACHMAN
    Fanny, 772
    Frances R., 772
BACON
    Delila, 823
    Robert, 825
BAGLEY
    Samuel L., 703
BAGGET
    Francis, 193

BAGLEY
    Henry C., 511
    John B., 470
BAGWELL
    Jonathan, 618
BAIBIAM
    Louisa, 592
BAILEY
    Elizabeth O., 221
    J. C., 570
    John, 254
    M. J., 196
    Mary, 137
    Thomas J., 221
    William A., 221
BAILIFF
    John, 747
BAILY
    Milly J., 366
    Washington, 913
BAIN
    Mary, 327
BAIRD
    James T. P., 217
    Martha E., 182, 889
    Martha M., 448
    Sally H., 622
    Thomas, 791
BAKER
    Amanda P., 224
    Caroline, 233
    Cassy, 421
    Charles, 329
    Cumfret, 48
    Dorcas, 399
    George W., 37
    James, 103, 136, 335
    Jane, 604
    John S. C., 614
    Mary, 132
    Nathan J., 146
    Samuel, 412, 913
    Stacy, 810
BALANTINE
    Lucinda, 830
BALDRIDGE
    Liella, 785
BALDWIN
    Alcester, 224
BALENTINE
    Francis, 895
BALINGER
    Jacob, 479
    Merideth, 479
BALL
    Isaac, 736
    Nancy, 615
    Sarah, 335
BALLARD
    James, 740
    Matilda, 758
BALLENGER
    Polly, 820
BALLERY
    James D., 789
BALLEW
    Henry H., 286
    William, 478
BALTZELL
    Kate, 784
BANDY
    Cora, 493

BANDY
    Edward H., 912
    Jesse W., 609
    William, 559
BANE
    Martha, 698
    Robert, 698
BANET
    William, 766
BANKS
    Alexander, 52
    Martha A., 106
BANKSTON
    Elizabeth, 170
BANNER
    Sarah, 823
BANNON
    Owen, 695
BANZOR
    George, 171
BARBEE
    Chaney, 574
    Edith, 571
    Malissa A., 626
    Mary, 902
    Thomas, 766
    William J., 623
BARCLEY
    Wilmoth, 859
BARGER
    Alexander, 42
    James, 363
    William R., 36
BARKER
    John, 493
    Marshall, 493
BARKLEY
    John (2), 633
BARKLY
    John, 237
    William, 286
BARKSDALE
    William, 741
BARN
    William Asa, 394
BARNARD
    William, 305
BARNES
    Cintha E., 698
    James T., 241
    John, 441, 466, 762
    Sarah, 102
    William C., 550
BARNET
    Robert F., 36
    Samuel, 570
    William, 749, 766
BARNETT
    Elizabeth, 679
    Jane, 49
    Katherine, 268
    Martin, 703
    Pamelia L., 332
    Robert, 698
BARNHILL
    James, 395
BARNS
    John M., 670
    M. H., 627
BARNWELL
    Susan, 437
BARR
    _____, 179

BARRET
    Cornelia, 338
BARREN
    William, 277
BARROW
    Andrew, 393
BARTON
    Azariah, 277
    David, 277
    Elijah, 277
    Jackson, 383
    Judy, 571
    Mary D., 132
    S. A. N., 99
BARTRAM
    Edward, 784
    James, 784
BARTWELL
    James, 482
BASKETT
    Wilson, 614
BASS
    Ephraim W., 254
    Sarah, 733
BASEHAM
    William T., 445
BASYNE
    Joseph F., 333
BATEMAN
    Henry, 114
    William T., 736
BATES
    Horace, 55, 102
    Leon M. C., 470
    William A., 240
BATSON
    Joan, 578
BATTLE
    William M., 143
BATTON
    Lucy, 766
BATTS
    Benjamin E., 619
BATY
    Anna, 229
BAUCOM
    William, 224
BAXTER
    Robert, 578
BAYLERS
    Sarah, 37
BAYLISS
    Mary A., 820
BEALS
    Mary H., 823
BEAN
    Robert, 302
    Wallace, 691
    William, 609
BEAR
    Lucy, 335
BEARD
    Abm. H., 822
    Counsel, 317
    Elizabeth M., 470
    John, 772
    Lanton, 96
    Martha J., 769
    Robert, 251
    Ruth, 772
BEARDE
    Reuben, 747

BEARDEN
    Hortense, 276
BEARDIN
    William, 463
BEASLEY
    Freedona, 408
    Martha, 670
BEASLY
    Martha, 751
    Napoleon, 751
BEATY
    Christopher, 631
    Elizabeth, 36
    John, 463
    Rebecca, 633
    Tabitha M., 665
BEAVER
    David C., 643
    Dewit C., 178
BEAVERS
    Spencer, 260
BECHOLDT
    Jo., 698
BECK
    Edward, 574
    Henry, Sr., 466
BECKUM
    L. G., 834
BEDFORD
    James T., 749
    John H., 749
BEDWELL
    Mary, 608
BEECH
    Loderick, 851
BEEK
    Adelia, 726
BEEL
    Hugh F., 619
    Joseph W., 664
BEENY
    Thomas, 484
BELAMY
    William J., 85
BELCHER
    James M., 338
    John, 478
BELL
    Caroline, 114
    Ewing, 743
    G. W., 248
    Jacob D., 286
    John, 190
    Josephine, 899
    Laura, 277
    Louisa, 482
    Mary, 108, 437
    Thomas D., 190
BELOAT
    Henry A., 732
BENGE
    Mary, 614
BENICA
    Oleon, 587
BENNET
    Mary, 841
    Mary E., 340
BENNETT
    James, 898
    Jonathan, 412
    William F., 758
BENNITT
    Thomas S., 182

BENSON
    Cordelia, 626
    Frances, 297
    Polly Ann, 482
BERDINE
    Jefferson, 916
BERDIT
    Alvira, 559
BERKS
    Francis, 23
BERRIER
    Sarah, 474
BERRY
    Amanda A., 61
    Franklin, 89
    John T., 467
    Sarah F., 467
    William, 768
BETTIS
    Ruy, 912
BEVERLY
    Driscal, 470
BEVIN
    Celany, 895
BEWLY
    John G., 424
BIAS
    D., 835
    J., 835
BIBB
    Daniel M., 57
    Jacob, 290
    Neely T., 57
BICKERS
    Sarah, 502
BIERS
    Harmon, 695
BIGGERS
    Elizabeth, 519
BIGHAM
    _____, 507
BILBO
    William E., 156
BILBREY
    John C., 595
    Malicy E., 595
BILL
    Fielding, 493
    Franklin, 589
BILLINGS
    Mary, 804
BILLINGSLEY
    L., 831
    W., 831
BILLS
    Lillus, 509
    William W., 245
BINY
    Peter, 618
BIRCH
    Thomas, 475
BIRD
    Edward, 699
    Martha, 366
    Sarah, 383, 675
    William, 402
BIRDSONG
    Mary, 683
    Perry, 686
BIRNEY
    Mary, 622
BISHOP
    Robert, 818

BISHOP
    William, 722
    William D., 320
BIVENS
    Leonard, 408
BLACK
    _____, 268
    Alexander, 254
    Carolus, 751
    Frances, 751
    Jacob, 575
    John, 699
    Katharine, 4
    Thompson, 290
BLACKAMORE
    Elizabeth, 768
BLACKBURN
    Sophiah, 437
BLACKINGTON
    Julia, 781
BLACKNEL
    Thomas, 463, 511
BLACKSHEAR
    Lucindy, 827
BLACKWELL
    Fletcher, 529
    James, 23
    John, 605
BLAIR
    Alexander M., 297
    Nancy E., 379
    William, 559
BLAKE
    Lucy, 661
    Martha E., 167
    Mary, 167
    Nancy, 521
    William D., 463
BLAKELEY
    Sarah, 551
BLAKEMORE
    Francis, 386
    Margaret E., 8
    Thomas F. A., 8
BLAMIT
    J. W., 698
BLAND
    Joseph A., 142
    Mary, 898
    Sarah Ann, 390
    Thomas H., 714
BLANE
    Elizabeth, 117
BLANKENSHIP
    John H., 354
    Susan, 470
    W. D., 17
    William, 42
BLANTON
    John, 55
    Thomas, 99
BLASER
    Christopher, 93
    James H., 97
BLEDSOE
    James, 171
    James, Jr., 171
BLEVINS
    John H., 355
BLIZZARD
    Penelope, 39
BLOW
    Mary L., 64

BLUCHER
    Fanny, 462
BLUE
    Margaret B., 462
BOATMAN
    Henry, 277
BOATRIGHT
    Annanias, 366
    James T., 333
    William, 255
BOAZ
    W. B., 834
BODEN
    Rebecca, 383
BODENHEIMER
    James M., 260
BOGART
    Daniel, 694
    Mary, 615
BOGEL
    Hiriam, 53
BOGUS
    John, 317
BOHAM
    Nancy, 844
BOLES
    Elizabeth, 598
BOLIN
    Isabella, 818
    John, 309
    Sylvia, 818
BOLING
    J., 678
BOMAN
    Daniel, 175
    Lucinda, 175
BOND
    Elizabeth, 604, 608
    Emily C., 53
    Rebecca, 345
    Sarah S., 503
    William, 202
BONDS
    Jane, 777
BONNER
    Robert W., 906
BONVILLE
    Harriett, 170
BOOKER
    Franklin F., 538
    John, 539
    John F., 531
BOON
    John D., 495
    Benjamin, 245
BOOTH
    James C., 344
BOOTHE
    Eliza J., 801
BORAN
    Barbara, 818
BORING
    Elizabeth, 822
BORUM
    Ammon, 745
    Darthula, 745
BOSSON
    Thomas M., 841
BOSSWELL
    Jackson, 766
BOSWELL
    G. W. F., 64
    Samuel, 595

BOTTS
    Martha B., 732
BOUTIN
    Virginia, 33
BOWDEN
    James M., 507
BOWDERS
    Elias, 390
BOWEN
    James A., 643
    John M., 432
    Manerva E., 106
    Martha T., 125
    Mary M. A., 52
    Samuel, 61
    William, 257
    William V., 49
BOWERS
    Abner F., 579
    Eliza A., 125
    James, 241
    John, Sr., 288
    Joseph, 702
    Lawson, 290
    Sarah, 579
    Thomas, 241
BOWERY
    Elizabeth, 772
BOWMAN
    Josiah, 780
    Margaret, 661
    Mariah J., 820
    William, 89
BOWNIER
    Elvira Ann, 587
BOWS
    William, 187
BOX
    Malvina, 175
    Sarah, 589
BOYCE
    Meshack, 276
BOYD
    Adaline A., 661
    Alice, 801
    Edmund H., 77
    Franklin, 36
    George, 153
    Jane, 409
    Nancy M., 61
    Robert, 110, 174
BOYDSTON
    _____, 441
BOYER
    John, 478
BOZE
    Hardy, 745
BRACKEN
    Sarah, 795
BRACKINS
    Perry J., 810
BRADBERY
    Nancy Ann, 579
BRADEN
    Angeline, 444
    Elijah, 48
    Felix, 482
    James, 4
BRADFORD
    Cecelia, 797
    Elisha, 466
    Elizabeth, 743

BRADFORD
    James, 743
    Levi, 245
    Mary, 694
    Robert, 57, 743
    Sarah, 743
BRADLEY
    Jessee, 795
    Mary J., 280
    Ructna, 309
    Samuel H., 789
    Susan S., 726
BRADSHAW
    A., 838
    D. L., 831
    Joseph, 909
    Mary, 909
    Thomas, 683
BRADWELL
    Samuel, 43
BRADY
    John C., 64
    Nancy, 444
BRAKFIELD
    Darcus, 233
BRANCH
    Bleuford, 822
    Richard E., 225
    William, 740
BRANDON
    Francis, 52
    George C., 52
    Julian, 231
    Levina, 759
    Nancy, 493
    Ruth B., 52
BRANNON
    Ruth, 286
    William, 558
BRANSON
    C. C., 698
    Charles, 703
    Solomon, 440
BRANTFORD
    Richard R., 754
BRANTLEY
    John, 39
BRANTLY
    Martha, 23
    Mary, 313
BRANUM
    Nancy, 43
    Sarah, 43
    William, 558
BRASHEARS
    Elizabeth F., 670
    Elizabeth J., 458
BRASWELL
    Robert, 758
    William, 755
BRATTLEBURY
    Thomas, 695
BRATTON
    Granville, 257
    Margaret, 498
BRAY
    Alfred, 702
    Eby, 702
    Hannah, 359
    James, 769
    Martha, 702, 743
    Mary, 1

BRAY
    Melinda, 535
    Rewlen, 535
BRAZELE
    Eleanor (2), 823
BREANT
    William L., 33
BREAZEALE
    Hosanah, 615
BREEDING
    Henry L., 598
    Letta, 598
BRENTS
    Arena S. M. A., 511
BRESHERE
    Sarah A., 639
BRETT
    Nancy, 175
BREWARD
    Nancy, 754
BREWER
    Barthena, 305
    Benjamin, 55
    Elizabeth, 827
    Jane, 762
    Jessee, 55
    Martha, 623
    Mary, 623
    Sneed, 305
    Winny, 762
BRIANT
    David, 248
    Sarah, 909
BRICE
    Mary, 338
BRIDGES
    Elizabeth, 48
    Joseph, 741
    Morris, 48
    Rachael, 31
    Sarah, 506
BRIDGEWATER
    William E., 203
BRIEN
    Sarah, 440
BRIGENDINE
    Nancy, 776
BRIGGS
    James W., 622
    Rachel, 711
    William A., 795
BRIGHAM
    Charles, 763
    Thomas, 266
BRIGHT
    C., 834
    John, 559
    W. W., 801
BRILEY
    _____, 148
    William D., 715
BRIMER
    Barbary, 421
BRINGENT
    Aug., 690
BRINKLEY
    David M., 157
    Mark, 895
    Susan, 408
BRINN
    Mary, 551
    R. W., 551

BRISON
    John, 228
BRITT
    Ann, 75
    David S., 820
    James T., 345
    Rhoda, 77
    Solomon G., 115
BRITTAIN
    Wiley P. M., 273
BROADMAN
    William C., 96
BROCDEN
    Elizabeth, 391
BROCK
    Cristian, 48
    George, 675
    Juda, 89
    Lucinda M., 4
    Mary C., 458
    Nancy, 695
BROCKWELL
    John M., 592
    Maston, 592
BRODY
    William, 408
BROGANS
    Milly, 89
BROOKS
    Aaron M., 52
    George A., 503
    John T., 132
    M. B., 167
    Mary, 85, 503
    Moses, 229
    Nealy, 898
    Samuel, 399
    W. R., 838
BROOKSHER
    William, 11
BROOMFIELD
    Mary, 39
BROTHERS
    Susan, 649
BROTHERTON
    William, 286
BROWDER
    Joseph E., 598
    William H., 773
BROWN
    Abigail, 273
    Abner, 359
    Alfred, 187
    Allen, 424
    Andrew, 780
    Anna M., 409
    Athelia, 641
    Benjamin, 409
    Caroline W., 822
    Caroll, 409
    Catherine C., 804
    Edward, 163
    Elizabeth, 174
    Ellen, 174
    Frances, 906
    Henry H., 178
    Isabella, 755
    J. B. W., 174
    James, 57, 335, 421
    James S., 228
    John, 413, 437, 558,
        678, 825

BROWN
    John H., 844
    John S., 804
    Joseph, 409
    Joshua, 190
    Martha, 190
    Martha A., 823
    Martha J., 429
    Mary A., 470
    Milley M., 409
    Nelson, 571
    Philip J., 637
    Reuben D., 789
    Ruth C., 823
    Sarah, 827, 608
    Sarah E., 313, 804
    Sephronia, 906
    Solomon, 795
    Susan, 506
    Susanah H., 562
    Tennessee, 571
    Thomas, 814
    W., 682
    William, 190(2), 470, 593
    Wyatt A., 52
BROWNIN
    John, 350
BROWNING
    Elizabeth, 412
BROYLES
    George M.D., 293
BRUCE
    Thomas, 89
BRUDEN
    Atemiah, 675
BRUSTER
    William, 810
BRYAN
    James J. L., 106
    Sarah, 106
BRYANT
    Caroline, 320
    H. G., 170
    James, 291
    Jasper, 412
    John, 291
    Matilda, 412
    Missouri, 894
    Rosannah J., 64
    William L., 810
BRYSON
    James M., 538
    Mary F., 538
BUCHANAN
    Ethelinda J., 448
    Nancy E., 466
    Sarah E., 260
BUCK
    Margaret J., 77
    Mary E., 163
    Ransom, 714
BUCKHANNAN
    Sarah, 417
BUCKLE
    Mary, 65
BUDD
    Joseph, 254
BUENT
    Henry V., 587
    Sarah A., 587
BULL
    Lucindy, 281

BULLEN
    Dicy, 281
    Jaily, 281
BULLOCK
    John, 452
BULMAN
    Rachel D., 93
BUMPASS
    John, 390
    Lucy A., 452
BURDWELL
    James, 420
BURFORD
    Hiram, 344
BURG
    Johannah C., 106
BURGESS
    Ann H., 273
    John, 529
    William, 619
    William D., 619
BURK
    Isaac, 618
    John, 699
    Joseph M., 303
    Michael, 682
    Sarah, 305
    William, 383
BURKS
    James J., 178
    John F., 102
    William, 698
BURNET
    Winefred, 479
BURNETT
    Catharine, 503
    H., 690
    Jerusa, 678
    Louiza, 217
    Martha, 542
    Susan, 503
BURNS
    Anna, 427
    S. J., 831
BURR
    Daniel, 174
BURRELL
    Virginia, 299
BURRIS
    Anna, 420
BURROUGH
    John J., 106
BURROW
    Malinda F. L., 210
BURRUSS
    Joseph, 106
BURRY
    Thomas, 484
BURT
    William C., 206
BURTEN
    Cynthia, 741
BURTON
    Elizabeth, 340
    Frances J., 409
    Zizizy, 182
BUSETON
    Robert, 587
    Willis, 587
BUSH
    Armstrong A., 412
    Delila, 745

BUSSELL
    Bird, 85
BUTLER
    Benjamin F., 273
    E., 831
    Emily, 102
    Horatio, 675
    Jacob M., 558
    James, 313
    John W., 102
    Mary J., 614
    William O., 459
    William R., 1
BUTS
    Daniel, 1
BYERS
    Mary, 503
BYFORD
    Thomas, 49
BYRD
    Eddy E., 327
    George, 329
BYRN
    Rychard, 61
BYRNE
    Elizabeth, 171
BYRNS
    James, 619
CACHEM
    N., 831
CACKS
    Moses, 437
CADERAGE
    Eliza, 417
CAGLE
    Sincler, 678
CAIN
    John, 605
CALAHAN
    Philip, 171
CALDWELL
    Alfred, 609
    Cyndrillia, 421
    Martha, 789
    Robert, 659
    Sarah, 795
CALHOUN
    Abegail, 589
    Mary B., 899
    Mathew, 902
CALLAWAY
    Richard, Col., 237
CALOWAY
    Sarah A., 777
CAMATZER
    Jackson, 49
CAMMELL
    Jane, 467
CAMP
    Armistead, 143
CAMPBELL
    Anna, 49
    Brison, 49
    Colin, 793
    Columbus, 338
    Colvin, 161
    Elizabeth, 89
    Jane, 601
    Jane E., 499
    John, 615
    Margarette, 615
    Mary, 338

CAMPBELL
    Matthew, 280
    Nancy, 793
    Samuel, 589
    Sarah, 302
    Sarah E., 333
    Susannah, 820
    Thomas, 81
    V. M., 478
    Washington D., 119
    William J., 52
CAMREN
    John, 302
CANADA
    William, 766
CANADY
    L., 193
CANATSWER
    Abraham, 595
    Easter, 595
CANE
    John, 571
CANFIELD
    M., 698
CANIDA
    A., 835
    W., 835
CANIN
    M., 157
CANNON
    Andrew, 595
    Anthony, 190
    Frances A., 61
    James, 48
    Jemima, 667
    Katy, 595
    Samuel, 479
CANTON
    Martha, 747
CANTRELL
    _____, 186
    Elias, 183
    Gabriel, 479
    Jonathan, 81
    Mary, 797, 814
    Mary L., 179
CAPPS
    John B., 183
CARAWELL
    Fredonia, 732
CARD
    Susann, 132
CARIGER
    Catherine, 467
    Christine, 467
    Finetta, 467
    Margaret, 467
    Mary A., 467
CARINGTON
    Lucinda M., 653
CARLISLE
    Burnetta, 417
    Elizabeth, 417
    Esther, 102
    Nancy, 102
    Sally, 417
    Sarah (2), 417
CARLTON
    Emery, 732
    Mary E., 64
CARLS
    Sarah J., 293

CARMACK
  James G., 595
  S. W., 466
CARMAN
  Elizabeth, 146
  Martha A., 421
  Pagitte, 146
CARMICHAEL
  Emaline, 703
  Henry F., 93
  Susan, 93
CARMON
  Sarah, 751
  William, 754
CARNALL
  John J., 444
CARNEY
  John, 695
  Julia, 695
CAROLL
  G. W., 773
CARPENTER
  Joseph, 167
  Martha, 891
  Spicey, 257
CARR
  James, 702
  John H., 694
  John R., 211
  Mary, 759, 823
CARRELL
  Mary A., 841
CARRIN
  Henry J., 313
CARROL
  Margarette M., 618
  Henry, 77
CARROLL
  J. B., 129
  Martha, 52
  Rufus, 589
CARROLTON
  Jackson, 409
  Sarah E., 409
CARSON
  John, 425
  Samuel, 425
  Sarah J., 820
CARTER
  Alford M., 73
  Ambrose, 220
  Angeline, 492
  Cynthia, 463
  Easter, 605
  Fanny, 605
  Frances, 448
  James, 412, 605
  Janie, 436
  Jessee, 478
  John, 788
  Joshua, 351
  Mariah, 492
  Martha, 367
  Martha Ann, 387
  Robert, 780
CARTNELL
  Sophia, 912
CARTRIGHT
  Jane, 33
CARTS
  John, 820
CARTWRIGHT
  James, 902

CARTWRIGHT
  John, 170
  Samuel, 559
CARVER
  James, 64
  James A., 57
  Lucinda, 768
CARY
  Sarah, 675
CASEY
  Francis C., 248
  L. B., 241
  Mary E., 241
CASH
  Henry, 103
  Thomas, 598
CASSADAY
  Abijah E., 618
  Joseph, 618
  Maranda, 823
CASSION
  Moses, 589
CASTEEL
  Elizabeth (2), 8
  Jemima, 286
  Lyda, 830
CASTELAW
  Joseph, 345
CASTELLO
  Mary, 93
CASTHELL
  Joseph M., 241
CASTLE
  W., 834
CASTLEMAN
  John, 8
  Martha W., 906
CATE
  Andrew R., 555
  Charles, 39
  James, 39
CATES
  Charles, 115, 535
  Elizabeth, 675
  Sarah, 395, 678
  Susan, 678
  William, 42
CATHEY
  Mary E., 517
  William A., 466
CATHRAN
  William A., 210
CATON
  John P., 814
  Rebecca A., 436
CATTREY
  Elizabeth, 521
CAUDER
  William Penn, 507
CAUGHRAN
  Sarah, 550
CAUSEY
  Sarah, 386
  Susan Ann, 691
CAVELL
  George, 555
CAVENDER
  Susan, 303
CAVER
  Jane, 412
CAVINESS
  Isaah, 320

CAVERPER
  Ferdinan, 895
CECIL
  John W., 455
CHADWELL
  David M., 85
CHAINY
  Nancy, 598
CHALFANT
  Job, 699
CHAMBER
  Henry, 421
CHAMBERLAIN
  William, 489
CHAMBERS
  David, 741
  Mary, 762, 916
CHAMBLESS
  Priscilla, 627
CHAMBLISS
  Sarah, 273
CHAMLESS
  James (2), 903
CHAMP
  S. M., 695
CHANDER
  Sophia, 244
CHANDLER
  Elvira, 424
  James D., 424
  Martha, 678
CHANNING
  William T., 622
CHANY
  Thomas, 160
CHAPIN
  John H., 598
CHAPMAN
  Harriet, 618
  Jasper, 260
  Letty, 286
CHAPPEL
  Mahulda, 395
CHARLES
  John, 103
  Mahala, 106
  Martha C., 106
  Mary B., 106
  Rachael J., 106
  Richard J., 103
CHARLTON
  Rebecca, 825
CHASE
  B. P., 772
  Nancy, 772
  William, 280
CHAUSTEEN
  Mary L., 231
  Wilson, 231
CHEEVERS
  Cicely, 236
CHENNAULT
  ___. 445
CHERRY
  Elizabeth, 599
  Nancy, 136
  Sarah S., 329
  William, 711
  William D., 231
CHILCUT
  J. R., 698
  Letta, 42

CHILDRES
  James, 440
CHILDRESS
  Eliza, 387
  Marvail C., 440
  Mary, 589
  Sarah, 651
CHILES
  Rowlin, 1
CHILTON
  Alice, 417
  Margaret, 570
  Sarah, 112
  William Carrol, 383
CHISENHALL
  James, 152
CHISMHALL
  Milly, 571
CHISOLM
  Mary, 137
CHOAT
  Anna, 622
  Betsy, 229
CHRISIAN
  Henry, 818
CHRISTIAN
  Leah, 344
  Mariah, 452
  Thomas J., 338
  William, 618
CHRISTIE
  William, 244
CILABREW
  C., 835
CIMBROD
  William, 405
CIVELS
  Mary, 475
CLABAUGH
  Mary, 670
CLAPP
  Mary J., 281
CLAPPS
  George, 507
  James, 507
  Mary, 224
CLARK
  Abner, 228
  Ann, 699, 839
  Benjamin, 615
  Benjamin D., 93
  Cornelia, 891
  Elizabeth, 281
  Henderson, 363
  James, 97, 801
  Jane, 97
  John, 383
  Lydia, 622
  Nancy, 503
  Neley, 391
  Mary M., 781
  Sarah, 517
  Tempy, 627
  Thomas, 61
  William M., 649
  Winefred, 839
CLARKE
  John, 132
  Margaret J., 332
  Martha J., 507
CLARKSON
  James I., 683

CLAYBROOKS
  Lucy, 839
CLAYTON
  John W., 321
CLEMENT
  George J., 799
CLEMENTS
  Mary, 415
  Matilda A., 245
CLEVELAND
  Eli, 297
  Martin, 281
  N. B., 156
  R. J., 156
  W., 682
CLICK
  Phebe, 96
CLIFTON
  Joseph, 36
  Susan, 484
  William James, 445
CLIMER
  Sarah, 758
CLIMMONS
  Nancy, 895
  Patience, 895
  Sarah T., 895
CLINARD
  Mary, 161
CLINE
  Adam, 772
CLINING
  Thomas, 506
CLINTON
  Martha, 409
CLOUD
  Jane, 85
  Joseph M., 507
CLOUSE
  John S., 844
CLOYD
  Elizabeth, 820
  Thomas, 820
CLYMER
  Andrew, 399
  Dudley, 399
  George, 402
COAKER
  Elizabeth, 236
COATS
  David C., 772
  Mary, 894
COBB
  John, 759
  John L., 345
  Mary Ann, 698
  Robert D., 698
  Robert H., 619
  Rispy, 479
  Susan, 487
COBBS
  Martha, 112
  William, 112
  William H., 627
  Willie, 112
COBBLE
  Anna, 290
COCH
  Martha H., 631
COCHRAN
  James, 37
COCKE
  John, 575

COCKRUM
  Melissa, 542
CODY
  Anthony H., 96
  Pierce, 277
COFER
  Cyrus, 254
COFFEE
  John, 379
COFFER
  James, 558
COFFEY
  Elvira, 13
  Jefferson, 538
COFFMAN
  Ellen, 599
  Mary, 433
  Simeon, 281
COGGINS
  Hester C., 755
COGHILL
  Ann, 475
COHEA
  Drucilla, 626
COKER
  Jessee, 492
COLBAUGH
  Mary, 555
COLE
  Hanna S., 61
  John, 429
COLEMAN
  Alexander, 217
  Isaac N., 484
  Joel D., 240
  Margaret E., 217
  Myra A., 33
COLIER
  Abner, 8
COLLET
  Mary, 281
COLLIER
  Lafayette, 658
COLLINS
  Esquire, 281
  Fanny W., 499
  Thomas A., 255
  Richard, 280
  William, 542
  William W., 351
COLLY
  J. R., 835
COLMAN
  George, 142
COLQUITT
  Martha, 598
COLWELL
  Elizabeth, 503
  Robert A., 57
  Susan E., 57
COMBS
  _____, 679
  Christiana, 313
  Martha, 679
  Mary, 186, 769
  Narcissa, 31
COMER
  Elizabeth, 415
COMETZER
  Jackson, 631
COMMINGS
  Franklin, 320
COMMONS
  Louiza, 466

COMPEN
  Cristeane, 601
COMPTON
  Aron, 718
  Harvey, 718
  Mary, 255
  Richard, 466
  Uriah, 272
CONDOR
  Samuel, 178
CONDRA
  Benjamin, 506
CONELY
  Rebecca, 49
CONLEY
  Isaac, 844
CONN
  William, 161
  William J., 161
CONNELL
  Emily, 231
  William, 175
CONRAD
  George, 574
  George C., 626
CONWAY
  Beattus J., 221
CONYARS
  Amanda B., 383
CONYERS
  Charles, 903
COOK
  Catherine S., 706
  E., 838
  Eugene, 909
  George, 614
  Henry, 248
  James H., 146
  John A., 609
  Josiah, 399
  Martin, 478, 558
  Mary, 587
  Michael, 618
  N.C., 27
  Sophia I., 912
  W. H.H., 27
  Washington L., 479
COOKE
  Margaret, 409
COOLEY
  Rebecca, 405
  Sebourne, 405
  Viley, 405
COOPER
  Andrew, 49
  Anna, 49
  Elie, 1
  Eliza J., 71
  Elizabeth, 49
  Frances, 391
  Geraldine, 387
  Hester, 244
  Nancy A., 424
  Robert, 97
  Thomas, 229
  William B., 390
COPELAND
  Andrew, 437
  John W., 479
  James J., 247
  Martha, 598
  Mary, 598
COPLEY
  John, 9

CORBET
  Michael, 839
CORBETT
  Nancy, 163
CORBIT
  Sarah, 112
CORBITT
  Foster, 129
  W. P., 129
CORDLE
  Aaron, 623
CORLEY
  James A., 902
CORN
  Pamilia, 236
CORNWELL
  _____, 690
CORRETHERS
  Mary, 53
CORTNER
  Sarah, 23
COSBEY
  Framcis M., 264
COSNER
  Charles, 729
COSSON
  James G., 822
COTRELL
  Vina, 436
COTTINGHAM
  Sarah, 31
COTTON
  James, 129
  John, 129
  Joseph, 793
  Martha, 129
COUGHRAN
  John, 251
COULTER
  Jane, 53
COURTNEY
  Mary, 479
COVINGTON
  Ravenia S., 555
COWAN
  James M., 555
COWDEN
  John, 605
COWEN
  Elizabeth, 313
  Joel W., 421
  Mathew C., 745
COX
  Davidson, 297
  Eliza J., 618
  Febee, 48
  James G., 773
  Josiah, 277
  Martha, 773
  Poline, 171
CRABTREE
  Daniel, 295
  John, 466
  Louiza, 466
  Susan, 466
  Susan C., 233
  William A., 231
CRADDOCK
  A., 163
  John, 244
CRAFT
  Jacob, 687
CRAFTON
  John, 405

CRAGG
    Jesse, 604
    Richard, 601
CRAIG
    John T., 511
    Mary J. W., 773
    Richard J., 268
    Susan A., 268
    William G., 383
CRAIN
    _____, 535
CRANDELL
    Charles, 129
    Ellen, 129
CRANE
    Charles P., 55
    William T., 187
CRANN
    John, 288
CRAVENS
    L., 831
CRAWFORD
    Diana J., 293
    Elizabeth, 466
    J. A., 838
    James Y., 338
    Rachael, 531
    Simes A., 429
    Thomas, 33
    William J., 281
CREECH
    Ellen, 146
CREECK
    Benjamin, 142
CRENSHAW
    Emily, 733
    Joel, 733
    William Y., 276
CRE-O-
    _____, 458
CREWS
    James, 324
    Mary, 387
    Mary A. V., 445
    Robert H., 429
CRIDER
    Catharine, 425
CRIGLER
    Hanibald, 338
CRIPPEN
    James M., 433
    Raphael, 437
CRISP
    Mansel, 313
CRITTENDEN
    George W., 608
CROCKER
    Samuel, 112
CROCKETT
    John, 405
    John W., 403
CROLL
    A., 171
    N., 171
CROMAN
    James, 178
CROOK
    James, 182
CROSLIN
    Eliza, 102
CROSS
    James W., 801

CROUCH
    Hendric, 822
CROW
    Henry A., 801
    James R., 67
    Jane, 609
CROWDER
    Fyree G., 758
    James B., 390
    John W., 559
    Margaret, 390
CROWELL
    Mary, 495
CROWLEY
    Jackson, 391
CRUISE
    James, 327
CRUIZE
    Mary, 789
CRUM
    Lavisa, 818
CRUMLESS
    Hugh F., 614
CRUMP
    Hannah, 788
    Leander, 788
    Lewis W., 788
    Samuel, 788
    William, 788
CRUMPLER
    Rachael, 190
CRUNK
    Edward, 463
CRUTCHER
    Christopher, 781
CRUTCHFIELD
    Thomas, 302, 478
CUBBIN
    Brunson, 694
CUDE
    Mary J., 601
CULBERTSON
    James B., 627
CULBREATH
    Edmund, 754
    Nancy A., 754
    Susan S., 754
CULLENDER
    George D., 299
CULLOM
    Cornelia, 758
CULLUM
    Thomas J., 202
CULLY
    Eliza, 25
CUMMINGS
    Thomas J., 529
    Wesley N., 529
CUNNINGHAM
    D. H., 269
    H. E.(R.E.), 160
    J. K., 106
    John, 391, 682
    Matilda, 386
    Milton T., 448
    Sarah, 190
    Thomas, 103, 759
CUP
    James W., 801
CUPP
    James, 425
CURLEY
    Allen, 710

CURLEY
    George, 170
    Lucy, 170
CURRIER
    James A., 436
CURRY
    Elisha, 699
    Margaret C., 115
CURTIS
    _____, 265
    Catharine, 179
    Easter J., 52
    Jesse, 179
    L. E., 830
    Minor, 405
    Thomas, 193
    William, 193
CURTISS
    Moses, 511
CUSTER
    Margarett, 106
CUTLER
    John H., 179
CYDER
    Lucinda A., 846
CYPERT
    Leander, 827
    Samuel, 827

DACUS
    Francis, 698
DAILEY
    Elijah, 601
DAIM
    John, 506
    Manervy, 506
DALE
    John T., 626
    Mary, 785
    Mary Ann, 1
DALEY
    Bridget, 695
    Daniel, 695
DALLAS
    Robert, 740
DALTON
    Booker, 776
    Delphia, 280
    James M., 492
    Louisa, 280
    Mary J., 280
    Riley, 280
DAMEWOOD
    Leroy, 281
DANIEL
    Charles, 231
    Horace, 386
    Irwin, 827
    Jane, 325
    John, 578, 788
    Lucinda, 474
    Marshy, 909
    Nancy M. L. C., 329
    O., 695
    Rebecca, 432
    Wesley, 601
    William, 827
    William E., 248
DANNEL
    Christopher, 788
    John, 788
DARBY
    William S., 830

DARIE
    Henry, 424
DARNOLD
    Patsey, 758
DARDAN
    William, 31
DARRIS
    Mary Ann, 31
DAVAULT
    Hagdalene, 768
    Susan, 769
DAVENPORT
    James, 814
    John R., 801
    Lucinda, 780
    Nicy, 53
DAVID
    L. Moore, 375
DAVIDSON
    James M., 244
    John, 772
    Judith, 589
    Kiziah, 31
    Mahala, 823
    Nancy, 31
    Nancy J., 117
    Silas, 347
DAVIS
    Ally, 459, 466
    Almeda, 768
    Amos, 293
    Arnon C., 42
    Bertha, 844
    Charles, 420
    Christian, 747
    Dicey, 427
    Eliza A., 547
    Francis, 913
    George, 45
    George W., 386
    H. C., 129
    Ivin, 303
    J. C., 129
    James, 478, 517, 519
    Jane, 363
    John, 466
    John M., 614
    John P., 633
    Joseph, 297
    Joshua, 85
    Lucinda, 599
    Mary, 325
    Mary A., 248
    Nancy, 96, 592
    Narcissa, 839
    Rachael, 231
    Rebecca F., 814
    Rhoda, 710
    Robert, 710
    Ross, 747
    Sarah, 31
    Susan, 513
    Tennessee, 42
    Thomas C., 811
    Tinsley, 723
    William, 93, 485
    William, Sr., 93
    William M., 466
    Wilson P., 507
DAVISON
    Margaret, 229
DAVON
    Lucy F., 440

DAWSON
    Compton J. P., 286
    Isom T., 578
    John, 110
    Thomas, 916
DAY
    Archibald, 479
    Rhoda, 475, 555
    Thomas, 562
DEAN
    ____, 758
    Charlotte, 542
    Nancy, 27
    Sarah, 542
DEARING
    Tennessee, 844
DEARMAN
    N. L., 186
DEARMON
    J. B., 193
DEASON
    Warner, 17
DEAVENPORT
    Martha J., 444
    Rachel H., 265
    William, 268
DEBERRY
    Mat., 502
DECKER
    Daniel, 493
DEDRICK
    James D., 424
DEER
    John, 374
DEFOE
    Elizabeth, 445
De FORD
    William, 293
DELAUNEY
    Sarah, 732
DELAVINE
    John, 846
DELOZIN
    Perina, 618
DEMPSY
    W., 831
DENE
    Thomas B., 916
DENEY
    John, 745
DENNEN
    B. T., 867
DENNING
    Jane D., 391
DENNINS
    Emily, 795
DENNIS
    Aaron, 281
    Coleman, 475
    Crigton, 475
    Isaac H., 909
    James, 699
    John P., 108
    Nancy P., 475
    Parasine, 281
    Ruthy, 478
    Sarah, 93
DENTON
    Infant, 432
    Nancy, 841
DENUM
    Sousanah, 305

DEPEW
    Mary, 772
DEPRIEST
    Malinda J., 398
DERLING
    ____, 182
DEROSSET
    Benjamin, 814
    Margaret A., 814
DETON (DENTON)
    Priscilla, 432
DEVERS
    Martha Ann, 459
DEWHURST
    Ruth, 703
DEWS
    Thomas B., 170, 916
DIBRELL
    A. F., 248
    Lithia L., 248
DICE
    Sarah, 174
DICKENS
    Elender, 754
DICKENSON
    James, 777
DICKERSON
    Alexander, 743
    Elvira L., 740
    James, 789
    Leroy, 743
    Lucinda, 293
    Martha, 743
DICKEY
    John, 425
DICKSON
    Amanda L., 445
    Margaret A., 458
    Martha, 806
    William, 515
DICKY
    Martha, 440
DICUS
    Rhody, 827
DIELIHAY
    Effa, 751
DIGGS
    Nancy, 391
DILL
    Eve, 913
    Martha, 653
    Mary J., 788
DILLARD
    Edward F., 741
DILLEN
    Henry, 599
DILLER
    Pat., 698
DILLON
    James, 682
DINSMORE
    Mary A., 288
DINWIDDIE
    Judida A.(C.), 391
    M. L., 391
DISMUKE
    Mary, 793
DITTY
    Mary, 844
DIXON
    ____, 264
    James, 114
    Mary J., 769
    N. D., 531

DOAK
    Oliver, 562
DOBBS
    Lucy, 898
DOBKINS
    Levi, 89
DOCKERY
    William, 608
DODD
    ____, 182
    Margaret E. C., 382
    Martha, 899
    Thomas, 582
DODSON
    Elisha, 272
    F., 834
    Henderson, 839
    Jabry, 839
    Marvel, 281
    Mary, 281
    William G., 316
    William J., 818
DOEHERTY
    William, 153
DOHERTY
    Robert, 559
DOLLAHITE
    R., 831
DOLASON
    M. D., 241
DOLTON
    Charlotte, 379
DONALD
    Anny, 898
    Wardwill, 655
DONALDSON
    Laura, 571
DONEGAN
    Nelson, 156
DONLAE
    H. O., 405
DONNEL
    Karian, 174
    Sarah, 467
DONNELL
    Andrew, 912
    Elizabeth, 913
DONNELSON
    John, 592
DONSMORE
    Mary A., 288
DOOLEY
    Elizabeth, 682
    Sarilda C. M. J., 546
DOOLY
    McKinney, 85
DORHARITY
    Nicholas, 303
DORRIS
    Joab, 797
    R. B., 622
    Rebecca, 160
DOSIER
    Priscilla H., 186
    William H., 186
DOSS
    George W., 503
DOSSON
    Burr, 183
DOUGHERTY
    ____, 250
DOUGLAS
    William, 515

DOUGLASS
    Alfred W., 791
    Catharine, 785
    Cynthia, 785
    Elizabeth (2), 595
    Henry C., 595
    James, 45
    John P., 595
    Martha, 793
    Micha, 741
    Samuel, 45
    Thomas, 562
    William, 106
DOWDY
    Joseph N., 333
    Mary, 517, 519
DOWEL
    Elizabeth, 795
DOWELL
    Elizabeth, 747
    Robert, 747
    Thomas, 747
    Willis, 747
DOYLE
    John, 695
DRAIN
    Knotley C., 899
    Thomas T. L., 822
DRAKE
    Edmond, 664
    Frances B., 906
    Martha, 906
DRAPER
    Robert, 335
DRAPHUS
    Mary, 781
DREWRY
    John A., 489
    L. C., 831
    M. L., 831
    S. L., 831
DRIFOOS
    Julia, 906
    Martha, 906
DRIVER
    Amanda, 179
    Matilda, 179
DRUMMONS
    Tabitha, 89
DUBOIS
    Albert C., 702
DUDLY
    John, 432
DUFF
    Roena A., 427
    W. W., 166
    William, 427
DUFFEE
    Marie, 795
DUFFER
    John M., 558
DUGGER
    German, 187
    Lucinda, 293
    Mary, 535
DUGGIN
    James, 53
DUKE
    Elizabeth, 390, 455
    Fanny, 784
    James M., 220
    Maria, 784
    Mary, 412

336

DUKE
    T. B., 838
    W. H., 193
DUNAWAY
    S. W., 499
DUNCAN
    _____, 507
    Henry, 255
    Jane E., 820
    Polly A., 413
DUNEY
    Joseph, 810
DUNKIN
    Elizabeth, 99
    George W., 75
DUNLAP
    Margaret, 390
    Samuel, 408
    William, 186
DUNLASS
    William H., 399
DUNN
    Nancy, 485
    William, 320
DUNWOODY
    Adam, 290
    John, 424
DUPREE
    Rebecca, 211
DUPRIEST
    Emma H., 383
DURHAM
    Etheldred N., 179
    Martha, 630
    Samuel E., 458
DUVALL
    Martha, 280
DWIGGINS
    Agnes, 8
DYER
    Mary, 280
    Milly, 281
DYKE
    Ellen, 293

EAKIN
    Moses, 170
    William, 174
    John, Esq., 19
EARLE
    Orville, 690
EARLICK
    Andrew J., 467
EARLY
    Sarah, 698
    Sarah J., 698
EARNHART
    George, 25
    Susanah, 27
EASELY
    Sarah Ann, 329
EASHIRLEY
    Winny, 909
EASLEY
    Bird, 402
    Emily, 402
EASON
    M. L., 196
    Phebe I., 916
    Sarah E., 146
    Treacy, 60
    William, 916

EASTER
    Alexander, 89
    Elizabeth, 43
EASTERLY
    George, 288
EASTLAND
    Sally, 466
EASTRIDGE
    Jeremiah, 89
EASTUS
    Elizabeth, 21
EATON
    Henry, 448
ECHOLS
    John, 682
    Mary, 682
ECKLES
    Simeon L., 722
EDDINGS
    Elizabeth, 626
    Joseph, 626
EDENS
    Angeline, 599
    Eve, 71
EDES
    Mildred, 341
EDGIN
    Infant, 539
EDINGTON
    Nicholas, 814
    Rhoda S., 558
EDMONDS
    James, 579
EDMONSON
    Gracy, 551
EDMUNDS
    Sarah Jane, 383
EDONS
    Manela, 305
EDWARDS
    Eliza J., 499
    Martha, 788, 898
    Mary A., 163
    Mary Jane, 383
    Mary J., 615
    Moses, 592
    Sarah M., 244
    T. J., 244
    Thomas, 823
    William F., 784
ELAM
    Alvira, 801
    Elizabeth, 762
ELDER
    John, 555
    Narcissa A., 221
ELDREDGE
    Jane, 599
ELDRIDGE
    Hannah, 42
    Mary J., 42
    Nancy, 598
ELKINS
    William A., 789
    Rebecca J., 615
ELLEDGE
    Joseph, 433
ELLET
    John, 409
    Mary, 409
ELLIGE
    William F., 55

ELLIOT
    George, 791
ELLIOTT
    Anna, 424
    Elizabeth, 233
    Harriet, 1
    Lawson, 233
    Nancy, 117
ELLIS
    Abner, 440
    Duncan, 762
    Emma, 891
    James, 759
    John, 478
    John H., 137
    Martha, 408
    Mary, 538
    Nancy, 678
    Sarah A., 93
    Tabitha, 655
    William, 186
ELLISON
    Daniel, 645
    Eliza J., 609
    Mary A. E. C., 609
ELMOORE
    Mary E., 321
ELMORE
    Elijah, 844
    Elizabeth, 421
    Julia F., 806
    William, 531
ELROD
    Sarah, 305
ELSBECK
    John G., 595
ELY
    Calvin B., 595
    Celina, 595
    Josiah, 627
EMERSON
    Francisco, 102
    Mary, 690
EMERY
    Josiah, 386
    Nancy, 236
EMISON
    William, 160
EMORY
    Jessie, 191
ENGLAND
    Harriet, 622
    Martha, 228
    Mary N., 841
ENGLISH
    Isabella, 687
    Margaret H., 255
ENLOW
    James, 784
ENNIS
    Elizabeth, 459
ENOCHS
    Ann, 743
ENSLEY
    Joseph W., 112
    Thomas J., 153
EPPENSON
    R. P., 608
EPPERSON
    Robert, 521
EPPS
    Mary, 85

ERVIN
    John, 254
ERWIN
    John W., 250
    Sarah J., 409
    William, 179
ESSEX
    James, 781
ESTES
    _____, 182
    Elvina A., 912
    Jefferson, 916
    Martha, 539
    Thomas H., 132
ESTHAM
    Amanda, 183
ETHEREDGE
    David, 682
ETHERIDGE
    Sarah J., 191
ETHRIDGE
    James, 115
EUBANKS
    James C., 623
EULESS
    Ely S., 5
EUTSLER
    Adam, 825
EVANS
    Elijah, 284
    Elizabeth, 818
    J. A., 21
    James, 325
    Lucy, 768
    Mary, 182, 601, 608, 678
    Nancy, 8
    Stephen M., 1
    Thomas, 254
    Walter, 412
    William, 445
    William H., 509
EVARD
    Philip, 288
EVERETT
    George W., 157
    William F., 157
EVERSON
    Mary, 691
EVINS
    Martha J., 81
EVITT
    Charles M., 303
EWERS
    Caroline, 171
    May, 171
    William, 171
EWING
    Margaret W., 160
EXOM
    Joseph, 777
    William (2), 784
EXUM
    John, 211
EZELL
    Benjamin, 437
    Sarah, 615

FAGAN
    Phillip, 462
FAGG
    Katharine, 420

FAINE
　　Richard, 36
FAKES
　　Winfield T., 903
FALKNER
　　Martha, 57
FALLEN
　　Mary A., 806
FALWELL
　　Virginia A., 221
FANCHER
　　Susan, 839
FANE
　　John E., 424
FANN
　　Wiley, 409
FANNING
　　John W., 288
FARINGSWORTH
　　James, 772
FARIS
　　Frances, 228
FARMER
　　B. H., 834
　　Elizabeth, 801
　　Frederick, 506
　　Harriet, 489
　　Martha, 622
FARNELL
　　Elizabeth, 171
　　Patrick, 174
FARRAR
　　James C., 558
　　Jane, 458
　　Polly Ann, 558
FARREL
　　Michael, 703
　　Walter, 702
FARRINGTON
　　Joshua, 340
FARRIS
　　Barthana, 233
　　Julia, 558
　　Sarah E., 233
　　William, 233
FARRISS
　　Charles, 156
FAUBIAN
　　Polly, 97
FAUGHT
　　Nancy, 260
FAULKENBERRY
　　Loucinda C., 52
FAULKNER
　　Margaret B., 495
FEASEL
　　Mary Ann, 290
FEATHERS
　　James, 768
FEDERICK
　　John, 745
FELKINS
　　Joycy, 599
FELLERS
　　Adolphus, 288
　　Barbara, 288
　　John, 288
　　Mary, 288
FELLOW
　　John, 722
FELLOWS
　　William, 719

FELTON
　　Crissy, 196
　　Mary (2), 907
FENNELL
　　Mary A., 814
FERGUSON
　　Abram, 551
　　Daniel, 729
　　John, 161
　　Mary, 436
　　R. W., 551
　　William, 710
FERMISCO
　　Julia, 691
　　Richard, 691
FERNFRO
　　Elizabeth, 558
FERRELL
　　Charity, 193
　　Dent, 193
　　Lucy A., 575
　　William, 186
　　Willis, 193
FERRIL
　　Elizabeth, 814
FINCH
　　Eveline, 390
　　James, 117
FINCHEM
　　James, 96
　　Matilda, 96
FINCHER
　　Christian, 293
　　Priscilla M., 286
FINDLY
　　George, 178
　　Lucindy, 615
FINLEY
　　Archbald, 49
　　Frances J., 846
　　Isaac H., 52
　　Lewis Whitnell, 383
FINLY
　　Harriet, 528
　　Margaret A., 528
　　Thomas P., 528
FINNEY
　　Amos, 96
　　Patrick, 161
FINNINGS
　　Melissa, 474
FISER
　　James L., 619
FISHER
　　Elizabeth, 682
　　George, 244
　　James R., 542
　　Jane, 521
　　M. R., 178
　　Nancy, 178
　　Thankful, 332
　　Thomas, 827
FISTER
　　Eliza, 682
FITZGERALD
　　William, 303
FITZGIVINS
　　Mary, 695
FITZHUGH
　　Amanda, 108, 146
FLANEGAN
　　Bridget, 695

FLANNAGAN
　　Orpha, 427
FLATFORD
　　John, 48
FLATT
　　William S., 332
FLEETWOOD
　　Harriet, 777
FLEMING
　　E., 156
　　George, 479
　　Jane, 639
　　John, 156
　　Thomas, 156
　　William D., 333
FLESHARDT
　　Francis, 691
FLETCHER
　　A. D., 245
　　James, 820
　　John, 653
　　John H., 811
FLIN
　　Martha A., 417
FLEPPIN
　　Tabitha, 741
FLOID
　　John, 280
　　Lemuel, 280
FLORIDAY
　　Matilday, 898
FLOWERS
　　Joseph, 664
　　Matilda, 458
FLOYD
　　Elizabeth, 102
　　James H., 665
　　Jane, 784
　　John H., 5
　　Mary, 162
　　Sarah F., 162
FLY
　　J. S., 554
　　William, 132
FOAY
　　Pat., 699
FOGLEMAN
　　George W., 21
　　Samuel, 21
FORD
　　Hannah, 467
　　John, 687
　　Mary, 250
　　Moses G., 493
　　Robert M., 89
　　Samuel, 170
FOREST
　　Lydia, 57
FORMALT
　　Rebecca, 463
FORMAN
　　Sarah A., 23
FORREST
　　Elizabeth, 387
FORSHEE
　　_____ (2), 538
FORTNER
　　Avarilla, 340
　　George, 286
　　James, 408
　　Malinda A., 799
FORTRELL
　　Mary A., 166

FOSSETT
　　Mary K., 156
FOSTER
　　Agusta, 171
　　Benjamin, 143
　　C. H., 3rd., 157
　　Hartwell J., 9
　　Henry H., 9
　　James G., 143
　　Manerva J., 106
　　Margarete, 286
　　Nancy, 474
　　V., 193
　　William W., 9
FOUNTAIN
　　Thomas B., 627
FOUTE
　　G. W., Jr., 286
FOWLER
　　Amanda E., 655
　　Ambrose F., 507
　　Ann E., 440
　　Catharine, 179
　　John F., 604
　　Josiah, 433
　　M. B., 838
　　Parmelia C., 433
　　Sarah N., 529
　　William, 690
FOWBERT
　　Cymbert, 160
FOWLKES
　　Pamilia, 686
FOX
　　James, 675
　　John, 695
　　Louisa, 670
　　Martha E., 39
　　Molly, 695
FOY
　　William P., 4
FRAEZER
　　Margaret, 797
FRALEY
　　E. N., 174
FRANCIS
　　Elizabeth, 53
　　Robert, 240
FRANKLIN
　　Bird, 233
　　P. G., 531
FRANKS
　　Martha, 484
　　Sarah Ann, 329
　　Sarah E., 329
FRASER
　　Mary E., 839
FRASIER
　　Sophronia, 574
FRAZIER
　　Jacob, 678
　　Joshua, 65
　　Mary, 272
　　Nicholas G., 609
FREASON
　　E. J., 21
FREDERICK
　　John, 420
FREDRIX
　　Jane, 506
FREELAND
　　Margaret, 542
　　Samuel J., 386

FREELS
   Sarah, 4
FREEMAN
   Ann H., 604
   Edward, 839
   H. P., 834
   James, 608
   Mary, 559
   Mary A., 804
   Samuel, 489
FREMAN
   James, 605
FREMONT
   Mary Angeline, 463
FRENSLEY
   Thomas, 112
FRICK
   Fred, 722
FRIE
   Philip W., 327
FRIEND
   Mary, 768
FRIERSON
   Robert A., 546
FRILDS
   Mary, 895
FRISON
   Marthy E., 827
FROST
   Sarah K., 4
   William, 5
FRY
   _____, 255
   James, 736
   John, 615
FRYE
   Mary, 844
FULK
   Mary, 797
FULLER
   J. M., 834
   James H., (2), 445
   Jane, 21
   Ross, 749
FULLERTON
   Robert, 466
FULRACK
   Infant, 149
FUQUA
   Aron, 489
FURGERSON
   G., 320
FURIS
   Martha, 254
FUTH
   Carrol, 811
FUTTS
   Mahaly, 297
   Napoleon, 48

GAD
   Elken, 42
GADDY
   John, 741
GAGE
   Joseph, 484
GAINES
   Cynthia A., 492
   Louisa L., 575
GALBRAITH
   Eliza L., 36
   Sarenus, 370

GALE
   Ann M., 110
GALLION
   Thomas L., 823
GALLOWAY
   Martha, 653
   Susannah, 825
GALVAN
   Martha J., 618
GALYON
   Albert, 618
GAMBELL
   Benjamin F., 659
GAMBLE
   Nancy A., 555
   Samuel, 273
   Sarah, 4
GAMBLIN
   John W., 543
GANNAWAY
   May E., 653
GANT
   John T., 170
   Robert, 525
GANTT
   George, 554
GARDENHIER
   Elizabeth, 598
GARDER
   Thomas, 755
GARDNER
   E., 499
   Lucinda, 386
   Mary L., 575
GARGUES
   Cenith, 538
GARLAND
   Isaac, 65
GARNER
   _____, 137
   David, 233
   Eliza, 240
   William N., 643
GARRETT
   E. C., 707
   Elizabeth, 273
   Louisa, 482
   Martha, 250
   Sarah, 187
GARRETSON
   John, 277
   Sarah, 277
GARRETTSON
   Catharine, 797
GARRISON
   Elizabeth, 529
   John, 702
   Nancy, 609
GARROT
   Nancy, 889
GARVIN
   Mary, 682
   Thomas, 682
GASSETT
   Eliza, 482
GATES
   A. J., 542
   Andrew, 215
   Frances E., 661
   Thomas, 895
GATHER
   Jane, 649
GATLIN
   Ephram, 766

GATLIN
   Sivena, 251
GATLOH
   Sarah, 894
GAWT
   Littltia, 421
GELLAM
   John T., 367
GENTREY
   Ruben, 417
GENTRY
   Bartlet, 598
   James E., 436
   Jesse, 417
   Nancy, 36(2), 593
   Samuel A., 33
   Sarah S., 436
   Theodocia, 517
GEORGE
   Elizabeth (2), 907
   Green W., 839
   James M., 55, 474
   Jane, 785
   Jesse, 622
   Lucinda A., 220
   Mariah, 766
   Mary E., 55
   Vanburen, 402
GETUND
   Elizabeth D., 906
   James M., 906
GETURN
   Mary A., 152
GIBBS
   _____ (2), 281
   John H., 437
   John R., 492
   Martha J., 498
   Sarah, 811
GIBSON
   Elizabeth A., 143
   Jane, 822
   Malcomb B., 268
   Mary A., 683
   Sarah A., 453
   William, 244
   William C., 244
GILBERRY
   Robert, 699
GILBERT
   Nancy, 305
   Orphey, 305
   Samuel, 1
   William, 102
GILBREATH
   Elizabeth R., 479
GILES
   Eliza, 687
   John, 687
   Martha, 814
   Mary C., 64
GILL
   Sarah C., 758
GILLAM
   Mary, 763
GILLIAM
   Ann, 891
   Frances H., 789
   John W., 163, 631
GILLILAND
   Mary, 595
GILLIS
   Nancy E., 830

GILLOCK
   Reuben, 699
GILLORN
   Pat., 695
GILLUM
   Sarah H., 257
GILLY
   Elizabeth, 55
GILMORE
   Ann, 452
   Anna, 255
   John Silvester, 255
   Thomas, 789
GINES
   General Allen, 257
   John, 462
GIPSON
   Charlotta, 305
   Elizabeth, 562
   Mary Jane, 305
   Robert, 305
GISDNER
   Eve E., 286
GITTINGS
   Martha, 420
GIVENS
   Harry, 747
GIVINS
   _____ (2), 305
   Celia, 178
GLASCOCK
   Peter, 241
GLASS
   Samuel D., 187
GLASSGOW
   James, 754
GLENN
   Jane, 841
   Joshua, 503
   Logan, 841
   Mary, 224
GLIDEWELL
   Bird, 467
GLINN
   James M., 153
GLISSEN
   Elizabeth, 619
GLISSON
   A., 248
GODSEY
   Hyram, 33
GODSY
   Jas., 772
GODWIN
   Stephen T., 280
GOFF
   Francis W., 732
   Franklin, 683
GOFOURTH
   Elizabeth, 827
GOIN
   Harvy L., 89
GIONS
   Elizabeth, 39
   Sarah E., 39
GOLD
   Seratha, 39
   Seratha L., 42
   William, 763
GOLDRICH
   H. M., 156
GOLDSBY
   Jane, 599

GOLLADAY
  Mary, 582
GOOCH
  David M.D.L., 260
  James H., 619
GOOD
  Permelia, 820
  Sarah E., 462
GOODLETT
  A. G., 647
GOODLEE
  Adaline, 546
GOODLOW
  John, 196
GOODMAN
  Alexander, 604
  Ruth, 37
  Solomon, 186
GOODNIGHT
  John K. D., 178
GOODRICH
  Ann, 137
  Mary A., 137
  Mary I., 146
  Tilman, 722
GOODWIN
  Michael, 458
  S. E., 153
  Sarah, 190
  William W., 160
GORD
  Cintha, 506
GORDON
  Elizabeth, 214, 345
  James, 608
  Thomas C., 547
GORGDON
  Bartly, 25
GORHAM
  Infant, 626
GORNEY
  Darca, 229
  Jane, 229
  Polk, 229
GOSS
  James, 605
  James H., 425
  Leonard, 740
  Mary Ann, 174
  Nancy E., 186
  Sarah, 286
GOSSETT
  Drewry, 395
  Octave B., 182
GOUD
  Benjamin, 751
  Lucy, 751
GOULINGHAM
  M., 163
GOWER
  E. W., 452
GRACE
  James, 695
GRADY
  Emeline, 137
GRAHAM
  Jane, 506
  Leah, 844
  Richard M., 395
  Sarah, 178, 589(2)
GRANADA
  William C., 391

GRANT
  John, 362
  Thomas, 459
GRANTHAM
  Elizabeth, 313
  Martha E., 313
GRATH
  Sarah, 562
GRAVES
  Ellen, 519
  George, 906
  James R., Jr., 152
  Miles J., 386
  Thomas J., 433
GRAY
  Calvin B., 186
  Elizabeth, 108, 187
  Georgianna, 691
  James, 96
  John, 699
  Louransey, 506
  Margaret, 547
  Mary, 48
  Mary Ann, 722
  Rachal, 463
  William, 595
GREEN
  Cath., 694
  Cath. Ann, 694
  Eliza, 96
  Frederick, 558
  Hannah, 110
  Isabella, 429
  James, 743
  Jesse, 627
  Joakinn J., 627
  Josiah, 132
  Martha A., 341
  Martha L., 604
  Mary, 558, 587, 604
  Milly, 351
  Milly A., 604
  Sarah, 604
  Sarah J., 211
  William, 599, 793
  William A., 179
  William C., 448
  Zachary T., 558
GREENE
  Dalilah, 611
  Joseph, 157
GREENFIELD
  Melvina, 841
GREENLAW
  Ernest, 691
GREENWAY
  David, 37
  Richard, 823
GREER
  Celia, 329
  David, 8
  Dianah, 8
  Thomas D., 199
  Mary E., 33
  William F., 383
GREGORY
  Fenton, 474
  Jerome, 493
  Jesse J., 758
  Lucretia E., 19
GRESHAM
  Martha E., 412

GRIBBLE
  Thomas, 818
GRIER
  Jacob, 241
  James, 241
GRIFFIN
  Elizabeth, 395
  John, 421, 909
  Mary G., 264
  Patience, 547
  Robert, 61
GRIFFITH
  Byron, 609
  Charles P., 506
  Jehew, 506
GRIFFON
  James, 891
GRIFFY
  Benjamin, 36
GRIFF
  _____, 535
GRIGSBY
  Elizabeth, 558
GRILLS
  Martha H., 479
GRIMES
  John F., 655
  Julian, 399
  Mary, 527(or 327)
GRIMSBY
  Jno., 772
GRINDSTAFF
  Joel, 754
GRISHAM
  Nancy, 754
GRISHOLM
  Robert, 332
GRISSAM
  Elizabeth, 475
GRIZZARD
  Robert M., 57
GROOMS
  Cordelia, 170
  Darca, 229
  Sarah, 732
  William, 604
GROVE
  Charles, 702
GROVES
  Elizabeth, 622
  Jackson, 810
  Washington, 810
GRUBBS
  Thomas, 166
  Thomas W., 273
  William, 166
GRUCY
  Mary A., 907
GRUNNETT
  Seborn, 402
GRUVER
  William W., 702
GUEST
  Moses, 29
GUILLIAMS
  Polly, 97
  Thomas J., 97
GUILLIN
  Clorina, 57
GUINN
  B. W., 210
  John, 286
  Nancy, 619

GUION
  Lydia, 683
GULLETT
  Malvina, 347
GUNNS
  Robert N., 658
GUNTER
  Daniel, 42
  William A., 146
GUTHERIE
  Martha A., 791
GUTHERY
  Obedience, 913
  Thomas, 913
GUTHRY
  Sarah J., 811
GWINN
  Jacob, 1
  S. R., 608
  Tyler O., 175
GWYNN
  Josephine, 889
HACKNEY
  Mary, 37
HADACRE
  Jacob, 679
HADLY
  Eveline, 784
HAGGARD
  Jane, 429
HAGGS
  Infant, 436
HAGY
  Margaret A., 156
HAIL
  Elizabeth, 420
  Gideon, 417
  J., 574
  William O., 33
HAILE
  John, 255
HAILY
  Edward, 398
HAINES
  Benjamin, 492
  Lusanna, 492
HAINS
  Elizabeth H., 39
HAISE
  Almira G., 313
HALE
  Benjamin, 810
  Catharine, 236
  Elbert G., 822
  Isaac M., 822
  James, 290
  Jane, 478
  John, 290
  Linton, 186
  Mabry T., 409
  Nancy L., 478
  Priscilla, 777
  Samuel W., 175
  Sarah, 409
HALEY
  Henry, 129
  Martha, 129
  William, 112
HALEYBARTON
  _____, 441
HALFACRE
  Eliza, 885

HALFACRE
  Jacob, 885
  Nancy J., 885
HALL
  Abel, 244
  Angeline, 167
  Elender, 562
  Elizabeth A., 96
  Garrett, 190
  John F., 531
  John R., 61
  Lucy M., 237
  Martha H., 495
  Mary, 36
  Mikeal C. A., 595
  Sallay, 417
  Sarah, 587
  Thomas B., 631
  William, 39, 146
HALLEY
  Phebe A., 293
HAM
  Jasper, 482
  Sarah, 316
HAMBRIGHT
  Benjamin F., 479
  James M., 479
HAMILTON
  A. J., 236
  Catharine, 33
  E. P., 196
  Grant, 236
  Joseph, 85
  Martha, 531, 912
  Mary, 775
  Nancy, 236
  Sarah, 85
  Sylva, 335
  W. E., 196
  William L., 236
HAMLET
  Mary, 866
HAMLIN
  Kenneth, 21
  Mary Jane, 21
HAMMER
  A. M., 531
  Catherine, 820
  John A., 814
HAMMOCK
  Cymantha, 492
HAMMOND
  Jane, 421
HAMMONDS
  Sarah, 507
HAMPTON
  Agnes, 93
  Andrew J., 823
  Mary, 623
  William P., 57
HAMRICK
  Elizabeth, 710
  John, 732
HANABLE
  George, 161
HANCOCK
  Emily, 906
  James P., 906
  Martha, 248
  William, 268
HANCOK
  Mary, 895

HANDCOCK
  James, 417
HANEY
  Elizabeth, 827
HANILL
  Lawson, 244
HANK
  F. W., 157
HANKS
  Sarah, 167
HANN
  Nancy J., 421
HANNAH
  ___ (2), 608
  James, 255
  John W., 61
HANNER
  Hugh, 42
HANNON
  Alexander, 170
HANNISON
  Charlotte, 619
HANNLY
  Thomas, 284
HAN-BY
  J. T., 313
HARALSON
  William H., Jr., 340
HARBEN
  Samuel, 277
HARBISON
  Eliza J., 547
  Racheal, 550
  Robert, 125
HARBOARD
  David, 412
HARBON
  Lurinda, 474
HARDAGE
  Sarah, 498
HARDER
  Josiah P., 398
HARDIN
  Alexander M., 329
  Elizabeth, 327
HARDING
  Moses, 470
HARDISON
  Laura V., 245
HARDISTER
  Eliza T., 452
HARDY
  John L., 214
  Martha, 479
  Virginia T., 889
HAREWOOD
  Henry, 39
HARGES
  Thomas, 503
HARGROVES
  Emulous, 759
HARGUS
  Nabednargo, 562
HARMON
  Adam Alex., 383
  Alexander, 170
  Elisha, 383
  Henry, 440
  Mary J., 383
  Thomas, 383
HARNEY
  Eliza J., 643

HARP
  James, 595
  Sarah, 599
HARPER
  Thankfull, 788
HARPOLE
  C. A., 245
  Rachael, 106
HARPOOL
  Henry, 409
  Mary, 412
HARR
  Rebecca, 768
  Simon, 768
HARRAHAN
  Green D., 703
HARREL
  Elizabeth, 793
  Stephen, 178
HARRELL
  Benjamin, 64
  Buckner, 207
  E. J., 196
  Thomas, 64
HARRES
  Polly, 595
HARRINGTON
  Nancy, 399, 907(2)
  Parthe, 903
  William, 399
HARRIS
  B. F., Jr., 244
  Beersheba, 479
  Claiborn, 487
  Eliza, 52
  Erasmus, 387, 394
  Felix, 630
  Hannah, 823
  J. E., 551
  James, 103
  John, 608
  John H., 167
  Lewis, 509, 844
  Mary E., 444
  Mildred, 788
  Nancy, 143, 913
  R. E., 547
  Ralph, 683
  Rebecca, 207
  Robert, 631
  Thomas, 525
  William L., 286
  William P., 903
HARRISON
  B., 163
  Hannah, 615
  James, 841
  Joseph, 639
  Mordica, 691
  Martha, 599
  Martha Jane, 290
  Mary, 539
  Matilda, 93
  Nancy, 29
  Peggy D., 655
  Robert, 248
HARRISS
  Charles, 156
HART
  Alston, 99
  Ann E., 495
  Elijah, 221
  F. E., Jr., 167

HART
  Francis, 582
  George G., 559
  Isaac F., 167
  J., 835
  Joseph T., 344
  Susan, 108
HARTLEY
  ___, 437
HARTMAN
  Elizabeth, 171
  Emily, 171
  H., 171
  Levi, 293, 822
  May, 171
HARVELL
  Buckner, 207
HARVEY
  David, 715
  Elizabeth J., 643
  John, 64
  John B., 578
HARWELL
  Franklin, 251
  John M., 250
  Samuel, 265
  Sarah, 273
  Sarah A., 273
  Susan E., 265
HASKINS
  Catharine, 440
  Sarah, 110
  Tennessee, 110
HASS
  ___, 182
  James P., 182
HASTING
  Jane, 8
HASTINGS
  Martha, 355
HATCHEN
  John, 568
HATCHET
  Isaac, 492
HATHAWAY
  Ann, 167
  Jane, 179
HATTISHILL
  A. E., 474
HAUN
  Elias, 745
HAUSE
  Jane, 592
HAWKINS
  B. D., Jr., 170
  Benjamin, 710
  Gideon, 441
HAWKS
  W. J., 835
HAWL
  Martha F., 827
HAWS
  Samuel R., 825
HAYBERG
  V., 834
HAYES
  Mary, 521
HAYNES
  Elizaneth, 479
  James, 906
  Lorretia W., 653
  Meacha, 665
  Orlander, 659

HAYNES
    Richard, 906
    Thomas, 424
    William, 758
HAYS
    Edward, 665
    Elizabeth, 92
    James, 478
    Margaret, 49
    Martin, 733
    Mary, 186
    Nancy, 740
    Nelly, 818
    Nimrod, 478
    Rebecca, 49
    William, 478
HAYSE
    Henderson, 55
HAYSTING
    Cynthia, 8
    Samuel, 8
HAYWOOD
    Eliza,
HAZLEWOOD
    James K., 206
HAZZARD
    Susan, 741
HEADRICK
    James, 335
    Mary, 335
HEARD
    George, 599
    Rebecca, 36
HEARN
    Stephen, 351
    William B., 902
HEATHERBY
    Parlena, 48
    William, 115
HEATON
    Sarah, 478
HEDGEFRETH
    Rebecca, 459
HEDSPETH
    W., 834
HELLEN
    Patterson, 747
HELMS
    Benjamin C., 879
    Jacob, 818
    John R., 484
HELSEY
    E., 156
HELTON
    John, 75
HENARICH
    James, 163
HENDERSON
    Ann, 736
    Anna, 690
    Bennett H., 206
    Emma, 682
    James, 482, 559
    James F., Jr., 448
    James F., Sr., 448
    Mahala, 280
    Silvetta A. B., 206
    Thomas, 772
    William, 421
    William E., 424
    William F., 482
HENDON
    Reuben, 766

HENDREX
    ____, 405
HENDRICK
    J. P., 835
HENDRICKS
    Eli, 193
    Elizabeth, 382
    Mary, 347, 362
HENDRIX
    Cicero H., 482
    Editha, 69
HENDRIXSON
    Alfred, 186
HENISEE
    Elizabeth J., 846
HENNINSEE
    John, 699
    Thomas, 695
HENNING
    George B. G., 441
    Sarah A., 441
HENRY
    E. A., 156
    Elizabeth, 789
    Francis A., 441
    John, 687
    Martha, 156
    Mary, 707
    Nancy (2), 156
    Olivia, 502
    Susan A., 156
    William, 797
HENSHAW
    Vasti A., 818
HENSLEY
    Henderson, 559
    Nancy, 618
HENSON
    Elizabeth, 559
    John R., 175
    P., 196
HERALD
    Anna, 643
    Edwin, 338
HERD
    Catharine, 309
    Margaret M., 335
HERIGUS
    B. A., 167
    Elizabeth, 167
HERIN
    N. C., 831
HERINGTON
    John, 678
    Mary, 571
    Sarah J., 4
HERNDEN
    John, 568
    Sarah, 568
HERNDON
    Sally, 691
HERREL
    Eli, 484
HERRIFORD
    Jediah C., 598
HERRIMAN
    Sarah J., 325
HERRING
    Stephen, 804
HERRON
    John, 48
    Samuel, 210

HESTER
    Mary, 675
    Mary E., 8
HEYES
    Susan C., 170
HIBDEN
    John M., 814
HICKEY
    Fergus, 161
    Sarah, 96
HICKMAN
    Charles S., 661
    Manerva, 335
    Martha J., 661
    Polly, 538
    Rachel, 769
    Zachariah, 538
HICKS
    Celina B., 417
    Henry, 37, 183
    John, 559
    Josiah, 17
    Mary, 39
    Ruth, 741
    William R., 17
HIGGINS
    Cor., 698
    Jefferson, 698
    Philamel, 459
    George A., 755
HIGH
    John W., 575
    Lavina, 758
    Samuel, 755
HIGHSMITH
    Matilda, 626
HIGHTOWER
    George, 485
HILBERT
    William H., 823
HILDA
    Hila, 81
HILL
    Albert, 429
    Anna M., 244
    Barnette, 611
    Benjamin F., 42, 272
    C. P., 433
    Chambles, 432
    Edmond, 795
    George Washington, 390
    Gustavus B., 344
    Huldah, 521
    James K., 509
    John, 543
    Joyce, 546
    Matilda, 49, 740
    Obediance, 452
    Randle, 675
    Rebecca, 289, 344
    Sarah J., 482
    Su., 698
    Virginia, 110
    Washington, 110
HILLHOUSE
    Elizabeth, 265
HILLIARD
    William D., 207
HILTON
    Edward, 841
    Mary, 521
HINSON
    John, 382

HIRST
    Arthur H., 570
HISAW
    Martha, 33
HISTER
    Caroline, 691
    Martha, 691
    Robert, 691
    William, 691
HITE
    Franklin W., 167
    Richard A., 167
HITEN
    Lagrand, 568
HITER
    William, 772
HIX
    Isaac N., 8
    James H., 8
HIXSON
    James, 36
HOAGE
    Katharine, 587
HOBBS
    Ezekiel, 299
    Sarah, 408
HOBDY
    John, 795
HOCOTT
    George, 710
HODGE
    Lavina, 277
    Obadiah, 841
    Philip, 425
    Rosannah, 823
HODGES
    Ann, 795
    Elizabeth, 85
    Flemming, 85
    Levi C., 722
    Olly, 85
    Sarah, 85
HOFFLER
    John, 806
HOGAN
    Babe, 264
    Eliza, 424
    Synthia, 593
    Tilman, 589
HOGDEN
    Thomas J., 329
HOGG
    Susanna, 383
HOIL
    Nancy, 479
    Sarah, 479
HOLADAY
    L. B., 57
HOLAWAY
    Francis M., 33
HOLBROOK
    Laura F., 507
HOLCOMB
    James M., 445
    Susan, 551
HOLDER
    John, 241, 440
    Ruth J., 272
HOLE
    Scott, 810
HOLIDAY
    Elizabeth, 390

342

HOLLAND
  A., 193
  Ellen, 626
  James, 19
  James H., 542
  James L., 801
  John B., 103
  John C., 511
  Juliana, 383
  Nancy, 281
  Newsom, 630
  Sabra E., 493
  William, 895
HOLLAWAY
  Rebecca, 587
HOLLEY
  Malinda, 371
HOLLIDAY
  John, 320
HOLLINSWORTH
  John, 55
HOLLIS
  Easter, 52
  Elizabeth, 49
  Emily I., 117
  Mary, 827
HOLLOCDELL
  James, 665
HOLLOWAY
  Elizabeth, 587
  John M., 895
  Martha W., 619
HOLMES
  Augustus P., 61
  David L., 61
  Sarah, 804
  Elizabeth M., 804
  Mary C., 804
  Sarah A., 458
HOLOWAY
  Charles, 687
  Gen., 687
  James, 687
  Martha, 433
  William, 687
HOLSTEAD
  Casander, 655
HOLT
  Henry, 281
  John S., 115
  Joseph, 776
  Thomas, 467
HOLTON
  M., 320
HOLYFIELD
  Pleasant, 484
HOMEWOOD
  Henry,
HONEYCUT
  Margaret, 578
HOOD
  Julia A., 129
  Nancy, 769
  William, 769
HOOKER
  Lorenzo, 19
HOOKS
  Polly, 598
  Tennessee C., 332
HOOPER
  Caroline, 909
  Jane, 643
  Joseph, 405
  Moses, 37

HOOSIER
  Harriet, 5
HOOVER
  Mary, 15
  Sarah Ann, 17
HOP
  J. H., 834
HOPKINS
  Elihugh, 9
  Joshua, 317
  N. W., 241
HOPPER
  Alexander L., 92
  M. C., 831
  Nancy, 233
HOPTON
  Richard, 691
HOPWOOD
  Presley, 507
HORDON
  William G., 440
HORN
  Frederick, 174
  Margaret, 114
  Peter, 114
  R., 160
HORNBARGER
  Amanda V., 822
HORNBEAK
  J., 831
HORNE
  Margaret, 445
  Rietta, 711
  Susannah, 711
HORNSBY
  Kimbro, 313
HORTON
  Adelia, 495
  George W., 402
  J. T., 835
  Jane H., 822
  Rachel, 827
HOSDON
  William G., 440
HOSKINS
  George, 4
HOSS
  Frances, 822
HOTTOM
  M., 320
HOUCHINS
  Francis, 146
  Nancy, 146
HOUSE
  M. E., 835
  Mary, 795
HOUSEWRIGHT
  Delila, 338
HOUSTON
  Eliza, 175
  Eliza S., 69
  Henry, 33
  Jonathan, 237
  Margaret, 507
  Margaret C., 511
  Westly, 759
HOWARD
  Alexander, 21
  Anderson, 587
  Calaway D., 102
  Elizabeth J., 57
  Harriet L., 550
  Hiram, 598

HOWARD
  Isaac T., 427
  John S., 103
  Joseph, 714
  Martha, 398
  Micajah, 785
  Stephen, 444
  William B., 427
  William L., 550
HOWEL
  Charlott, 425
HOWELL
  Elijah, 436
  Emaline E., 844
  Jane O., 277
  Jethro, 554
  Matilda, 785
  William, 898
HOWERTON
  Mary E., 152
HOYLE
  Lewis, 686
HUBBER
  Sarah J., 670
HUBBARD
  William C., 745
HUCABY
  William, 459
HUCHENSON
  W. B., 653
HUDD
  James, 8
HUDDLESTON
  David, 92
  Field, 598
  Mary I., 758
  Minerva, 751
  Sarah E., 409
  Thomas I., 895
  William J., 598
HUDLESTON
  David, 45
HUDSON
  Baker, 199
  Catherine, 347
  Elizabeth, 405
  George, 678
  George R., 618
  Jane, 405
  Mary A., 224
  Nancy, 891
HUDSPETH
  James G., 547
HUFF
  Oliver, 45
  Uriah S., 558
HUFFMAN
  ___, 614
  Jas., 710
  R. A. F., 61
  Thomas (2), 153
HUFFNER
  B. G., 699
HUFMAN
  George, 5
HUGGINS
  Phillip, 579
  Sarah J., 482
HUGHES
  Charles, 211
  Elizabeth, 589
  Jessee, 768
  Margaret A., 210

HUGHES
  Sarah, 420
  Tattan, 743
HUGHS
  Alley, 251
  Elizabeth, 302
  Marena, 409
  Mary, 302
  Robert, 651
  Samuel, 302
HUGHY
  Joseph A., 913
HUKMAN
  John, 281
HUMBLE
  John L., 395
HUME
  Joel, 691
HUMONTREE
  Hannah, 37
HUMPHRES
  David A., 39
HUMPHREY
  David, 43
HUMPHREYS
  Alexander, 37
  America, 390
  John, 37
  Priscilla, 571
  Robert, 37
HUMPHRIES
  Elizabeth, 77
  John, 152
  Joseph S., 69
HUNDLY
  George R., 156
HUNT
  A. J., 630
  Anderson, 630
  F. W., 157
  Jane, 391
  Jessee, 598
  M. W., 210
  Sarah, 237
  Sion, 791
  Thomas, 791
HUNTER
  Anderson, 303
  Cynthia, 715
  Elizabeth, 502, 715
  Ephraim, 36
  John, 820
  Patience, 190
  Thomas, 555
  Virginia C., 551
HURLEY
  Elizabeth, 327
  Raechael, 327
  Zachariah, 291
HURST
  Emily, 85
HURT
  David, 61
HUSKISON
  Clemant, 39
HUTCHINSON
  Katharine, 1
HUTCHISON
  L. C., 248
HUTSON
  Mary, 48
HUTTON
  Henry H., 190

HYDE
    Jane, 121
    Tennessee, 121
IDEL
    Vestina, 281
INGLE
    Margaret, 487
INGRAM
    B. Nancy A., 81
    Drury, 241
    H. L., 695
    Jacob, 437
    James G., 445
    John, 433
    Mary, 498
    Thomas, 81
INMAN
    Henry, 103
    Prudence, 482
INNMAN
    John W., 260
IRBY
    Fanny, 571
IRELAND
    Emma, 913
IRONS
    Amelia, 316
IRVINE
    James D., 551
    Sarah E., 618
IRWIN
    Jane, 641
    William, 161, 841
ISHAM
    Elijah, 614
ISOM
    George W., 458
IVINES
    William T., 252
IVY
    Richard, 8

JACK
    Elizabeth, 506
JACKSON
    Agnes E., 777
    Andrew, 452, 503
    Anna E., 142
    Barrenton, 251
    Catharine, 305
    Charlotte I., 163
    Corbin, 280
    David W., 61
    Delia, 432, 614
    Elizabeth F., 321
    Isaac, 408
    Jesse, 889
    K., 321
    Louisa, 578
    Lucinda, 73
    May E., 288
    Nancy Ann, 73
    William, 462, 745
    William H., 166
JACO
    Anderson, 818
JACOBS
    Bendit(2), 907
    Edward(3), 907
    Hardin, 114
    John D., 166

JAGGERS
    Martha A., 546
JAMES
    Orville, 160
    Sarah, 747
    Thomas, 604
    William R., 694
JAMISON
    James S., 631
    Siddy, 578
JAMMESON
    Lucy D., 210
JANSON
    Patsey, 297
JARMON
    Eli, 48
JARNIGIN
    Drucilla, 675
JARREL
    Nancy, 913
JARELL
    Alexander, 146
    John H., 912
JEFFREYS
    P., 834
JEMISON
    Sarah Jane, 254
JENKINS
    Ellen, 788
    Fanny E., 440
    Henry, 675
    Hiram, 605
    J. W., 831
    James, 751
    Joseph, 788
    Louisa Ann, 291
    Martha, 570
    Mary, 291
    Thomas, 67
JENNETT
    _____, 110
JENNINGS
    Elizabeth, 546, 818
    Emeline, 891
    John E., 898
    Ruth M., 288
JENTRY
    Jno., 768
JERRALD
    Richard, 408
JERRY
    Eli, 679
    Frances, 702
    Francis, 679
    George, 679
    Hardiman, 679
    Robert, 679, 702
    William, 702
JEWELL
    Hiram, 891
    John, 891
JOBE
    John, 665
JOHNS
    Nancy, 623
JOHNSON
    _____, 626
    A., 499
    Alex., 499
    Amy, 175
    Andrew, 39
    Andrew R., 555
    Aquilla, 36

JOHNSON
    Catharine, 780
    Catharine W., 571
    Edwin M., 568
    Eliza, 773
    Elizabeth, 599, 769
    Ellen, 781
    F., 834
    Frances, 737
    J. C., 834
    J. S., 547
    James, 179, 183, 619, 622
    James O., 781
    John, 332, 649, 844
    John B., 224
    Joseph T., 737
    Julius, 574
    Levi, 186
    Lewis, 665
    Lewis J., 427
    Lucinda, 769
    Luther, 102
    Maddison B., 555
    Martha, 445
    Martha J., 4
    Mary, 543
    Mary A., 157, 543
    Mary E., 916
    Mitchell, 320
    Nancy, 747
    Nancy E., 117
    Parilla, 599
    Parthenia, 136
    Rebecca, 341
    Robert G., 582
    Sally, 272
    Samuel E., 288
    Sarah, 136, 156
    Sarah J., 329
    Sinai H., 276
    Sterling, 359
    Susan, 186
    Susan A., 542
    Susannah, 618
    Thomas, 599
    Unas F., 445
    Virginia, 167
    W. F. M., 547
    William, 92
    William T., 166
JOHNSTON
    Ann, 608
    Elizabeth, 265
    Hester, 43
JOINER
    Thomas, 317
JOLLY
    Margaret, 889
    Rachel, 889
JONES
    _____, 182, 515
    Aarch, 112
    Abijah, 909
    Adeline, 280
    Adline, 768
    Amanda, 99
    Catherine, 487
    Cesar A., 737
    Cleopatra, 507
    D., 495
    Delilah, 37
    Edward, 592

JONES
    Elisa A., 190
    Elisha, 390
    Elizabeth, 436, 487, 492, 622
    Franky, 898
    Harriet, 574
    Harriet J., 551
    Helen(2), 495
    Isaiah, 894
    James, 913
    James D., 52
    James H., 425
    James W., 515
    John, 102
    John A., 707
    Joseph, 264
    Lavinia, 37
    Louisa, 546
    Louiza, 89
    Lucresa, 52
    Lucy, 694
    Madison M., 562
    Marcus M., 161
    Margaret, 280, 651
    Margaret A., 53
    Mary, 344
    Mary B., 61
    Mary E., 146
    Mary L., 241
    Matilda, 839
    Melissa A., 398
    Moses, 29
    Nancy, 830
    Nancy A., 52
    Nancy H., 390
    Nelly C., 52
    Rachel, 768
    Reuben, 114
    Richard, 891
    Richard C., 841
    Samuel, 747
    Samuella, 161
    Sarah, 4, 17
    Sevina, 421
    Thomas, 675
    Vance, 839
    William, 250, 345, 773
    William B., 175
    William P., 425
    Willis, 749
    Zachariah, 305
JONSON
    John, 470
    Luther R., 25
    Martha J., 470
    Phillip, 506
JORDAN
    Jangaline, 57
    John, 820
    William W., 649
    Zachariah, 367
JORDEN
    M. E., 838
    William, 568
JOSCELIN
    William B., 117
JOYCE
    Elizabeth, 398
JUDD
    J. W., 785
JUDKINS
    Edmund, 179

JULIAN
  Delila, 81
JULIN
  J., 835
JUSTICE
  Becky D., 598
  James A., 49
  James S., 627

KANIER
  Isabella, 513
KANILE
  Cath., 698
KARD
  Elizabeth I., 233
KARNS
  Ellen, 190
  Nancy D., 327
KEAF
  William T., 182
KEAFF
  James, 153
KEE
  William L. S., 224
KEELING
  James A., 458
  Joseph M., 458
KEELY
  Robert B., 383
KEEN
  Mary, 599
KEENER
  David, 810
KEENY
  Michael, 4
KEER
  Annie, 251
KEETH
  Martha P., 415
KEETON
  John, 33
KEEZEE
  Charles, 543
KEGLEY
  Jacob, 37
  Katharine, 37
KELLER
  Joseph, 467
  Michael, 623
  Milly, 45
  Nancy E., 25
KELLEY
  William, 506
KELLOW
  Siley, 866
KELLY
  James W., 64, 115
  Jane, 795
  Malinda, 759
  Martin, 93
  Mary J., 623
  Nancy, 93
KELSEY
  Thomas H., 822
KELTON
  George W., 647
  John, 649
KEMP
  Louisa A., 758
  Nathan, 485
  William C., 758
KENADAY
  James, 161

KENADAY
  Patrick, 161
KENNADY
  Elizabeth S., 378
KENNEDY
  Mary, 679
KENNON
  Isabella, 459
KEOFF
  James, 153
KERBY
  Allen, 839
  Lewis, 166
  James L., 839
  Margaret, 166
  Martha, 313
  P. Irvin, 166
  Pleasant H., 4
  Pleasant W., 186
  Rachel, 166
  Sarah, 562
  William, 166
KERLOUGH
  Mary, 639
KERLY
  Elmira J., 492
KERR
  John, 841
  Maria R., 133
  Nancy, 608
KESTERSON
  Daniel J., 291
KETNER
  William, 506
KETRINS
  Jane, 792
KEY
  Emma C., 355
  Mary, 726
KEYHILL
  Mary Ann, 436
KIBEN
  George, 432
KIDD
  Thomas, 427
KIDWELL
  Elizabeth, 272
KILBORN
  Artemus, 445
  John M., 445
KILE
  James, 562
KILGORE
  E. W., 844
KIMBLE
  John, 604
KIMBRILL
  Benjamin, 909
KIMBRO
  Frances, 659
  Virginia, 710
KIMBROUGH
  Duke, 421
  Jane, 608
KING
  _____, 615
  Albert, 73
  Alcy, 367
  Allen, 458
  Cath., 679
  Eliza, 559
  Elizabeth, 758
  Erasmus, 408

KING
  Fanny, 859
  James P., 9
  James V., 458
  John A., 458
  Joseph, 436
  Maret J., 55
  Margaret, 432
  Rebecca, 822
  S., 863
  Solomon, 161
  William, 179, 513
  William H., 484
KINGCADE
  _____, 618
KINCAIDE
  Joseph L., 264
KINCANNON
  Elizabeth C., 327
KINCHUM
  John, 160
KINGRY
  Warren, 8
KINKTON
  Elenor, 229
KINNEY
  Elizabeth, 293
  John, 153
KINNIE
  Joan, 820
KIRBY
  John, 754
  Sarah, 795
KIRK
  Margaret, 823
  Willie, 683
  Young, 458
KIRKAM
  Esther, 436
KIRKLAND
  Sarah, 405
  William, 408
KIRKLIN
  Bissy, 467
KIRKMAN
  E., 157
  John F., 157
  Martin, 484
KIRKPATRICK
  Allazera, 659
  Michael, 437
  William, 421
KIRKS
  Martha, 542
KIRLEY
  Martha J., 313
KISSER
  John, 290
KITE
  James W., 71
KIZER
  James, 379
KNAPP
  Julia, 115
KNASH
  Emulius, 766
KNIGHT
  Addison, 236
  Allen, 25
  B. B., 263
  Ellie, 751
KNON
  Elizabeth, 718

KNOX
  John W., 433
  Josephine, 433
KRISLE
  Ephraim, 623
KROUSE
  Michael, 822
KULE
  Nancy, 99
KYLE
  Catherine, 575, 578

LACEFIELD
  John, 484
LACEVILLE
  Mary, 108
  Rosana, 108
LACK
  Moses, 179
LACKEY
  Mary Ann, 333
  Samuel, 421
LACY
  L. F., 199
LADD
  Constintine, 503
  Milly, 236
LAFAYETTE
  Elizabeth, 390
LAFAWN
  L. M., 835
LAFARTY
  M. J., 827
LAFOLLET
  Mary, 290
LAFORCE
  Martha, 92
LAIN
  Sophia, 889
LAKE
  Justice, 317
LAMANDY
  Angus, 427
LAMAR
  Mary, 92
LAMASTER
  Martha, 762
LAMB
  Matilda, 371
LAMBERTSON
  Mary, 690
  Thomas L., 601
LAMFILEY
  Mary, 187
LANCASTER
  Parmelon, 175
  William A., 398
LANDRITH
  Henry, 221
LANDROM
  Mary E., 582
LANE
  Charity, 89
  Cleopatra, 106
  Elizabeth, 820
  Hulet, 489
  Louisa, 244
  Malinda, 601
  Mary, 740
  Nathan, 143
  Rufus, 290
LANEDY
  Catherine, 675

345

LANGFORD
  Desey, 759
  Elisha, 762
  Esthy, 759
  Margaret, 626
LANGLEY
  Ann H., 214
  Sarah, 455
LANGLY
  John, 444
LANIER
  Benjamin, 515
LANON
  Jane, 332
LANSDALE
  William, 780
LANTON
  Mary, 264
LARAMORE
  Mary, 265
LARDNER
  J., 834
  S. M., 834
  W. M., 831
LARENCE
  Joel P., 637
LARKINS
  Martha, 405
LARMON
  Catherine M., 579
LASATER
  Nicholas L., 179
LASH
  George, 891
LASKINS
  Virginia, 110
LATIMORE
  John, 793
LATTIMORE
  Amanda, 153
LAUDERDALE
  Elizabeth, 452
  John W., 789
  Martha, 789
  Rowena(2), 804
  Willis, 452
LAUGHLIN
  Eliza, 484
LAUGHNER
  Catherine, 290
LAVENDER
  Frances, 554
LAWSON
  Ellender, 678
LAWRANCE
  Andrew, 507
LAWRENCE
  Charles, 248
  Jennings, 152
  Jeremiah, 99
  Joshua, 503
  Martha, 639
  Nancy, 785
  William, 395
LAWS
  ____, 190
  Lydia, 736
LAY
  Anna, 48
  Jessee, 45
  M., 835
LAYTON
  Amanda, 487

LEA
  Catharine, 475
LEACH
  George, 687
  James E., 284
  Mary, 686
LEAKE
  G. T., 160
LEARY
  Thomas, 698
LEATH
  Charles A., 706
LEATHERWOOD
  Sarah, 462
LEDBETTER
  Ella, 670
  John W., 276
LEDFORD
  Martha J., 313
LEE
  Edwin, 539
  Francis, 320
  Jessee M., 645
  Mary, 595
  Mary Ann, 485
  Nancy, 485
  Nancy Ann, 99
LEECH
  Joseph D., 61
LEET
  Julia H., 444
LEFEVERS
  Nancy A., 844
LEFFEL
  George, 690
LEFIELFT
  Jacob, 702
LEGGET
  Eveline, 521
  Jackson, 521
LEMMONS
  Clementine, 390
  John, 801
LEMORTON
  Gilbreath F., 452
LENTZ
  Jacob, 153
LEONARD
  Jacob, 474
  Mary, 474
LESENBY
  Hezekiah, 582
  Lewis, 759
  Matilda, 440
LESTER
  James, 894
  Judy, 534
  Sarah, 531
  Sarah S., 913
LETSINGER
  July A., 452
LETTON
  Martha, 593
LEVINS
  Mary Ann, 103
LEWIS
  Aaron R., 424
  Hiram, 702
  John, 710
  Mary, 293
  Nancy, 96
  Rachel, 295
  Samuel E., 427

LEWIS
  Sarah, 759
LEWNA
  Letha, 183
  Mary A. L., 183
LIGHT
  John H., 196
  R., 769
  Samuel, 335
  Sarah, 769
LIGHTNER
  Agnes, 31
LIGON
  John P., 568
  Susan, 889
LIKE
  Adam, 429
  John, 429
LILLARD
  Lavina, 93
LILLUM
  J., 831
LINCH
  George, 421
LINCOLN
  Margaret, 509
LINDAMOND
  Elizabeth, 768
LINDSEY
  William, 31
LINDSLEY
  Elijah, 115
LINEBARGER
  Moses, 93
LINK
  Mary M., 623
LINVILLE
  Nancy, 493
LINZY
  Ann, 421
LIONS
  Tabeth, 467
LITTLE
  Mary, 555, 806
LITTLETON
  Mary A., 102
LITREL
  Jacob, 290
LITSINGER
  July A., 452
LIVINGSTON
  Duncan, 780
LLOYD
  Thomas, 788
LOCK
  G. A., 248
  George, 303
  James, 260
LOCKE
  Franklin, 609
  Nancy C., 255
LOCKHART
  Martha, 550
LOCKMAN
  Susan, 484
LOCKRIDGE
  Harriet, 531
  Samuel, 534
LODY
  Oliver M., 291
LOFTES
  Catharine, 42

LOGAN
  Benjamin, 589
  Robert, 115
LOGMIRE
  Elizabeth, 762
LOHORN
  Nancy, 599
LONAS
  John, 433
LONDON
  ____, 608
  Amos, 269
  Elizabeth H., 509
LONG
  George, 479
  Hugh W., 175
  Jane, 682
  Joseph, 609
  Lavina, 335
  Lawrence, 702
  Margaret A., 202
  Mary, 626
  Matilda, 175
  Nicholas L., 535
  Robert, 614
  Sarah, 420
LONGMIRE
  G. M., 499
LOOKEY
  Malinda M., 228
LOONEY
  Sarah E., 543
LORD
  Lorenzo, 255
LOSON
  William, 827
LOTSPEICH
  Barbary, 96
LOUDY
  William R., 1
LOUIS
  Elizabeth, 578
LOUTES
  Nancy, 635
LOVE
  J., 838
  James, 424
  Mathew, 448
  Robert, 433
  Samantha, 387
  Samuel, 436
  Stephen, 436
LOVEL
  Leannah, 48
  Thomas, 255
LOVELACE
  Sarah P., 402
LOVELADY
  Artemace, 420
LOVELESS
  Charles, 823
LOVELL
  ____, 137, 707
LOVING
  Cornelius W., 220
  William, 643
LOVRING
  Mary E., 196
LOW
  John H., 333
LOWE
  Jane, 645
  Lorenza D., 290
  Louisa S., 277

LOWRING
  Francis, 210
LOWRY
  F., 835
  James, 478
  Margaret, 290
  William F., 609
LOWWELL
  Mary, 27
LOYD
  Elizabeth, 333
  J. R., 21
  Theny, 671
LUCH
  Abner, 53
  Infant, 53
  William B., 437
LUDD
  Welford C., 277
LUMA
  John W., 441
LUMMS
  Sarah, 517
LUND
  John M., 511
LUNY
  Jackson, 485
LURRY
  Thomas, 699
LUSH
  Mary J., 49
LUSTER
  Margaret, 335
LUTEN
  Philip, 403
LUTHRELL
  Baker, 467
LUTRELL
  Elizabeth, 436
LUTTRELL
  George, 302
LYFORD
  Ananias, 89
LYLE
  John, 661
  Thomas, 77, 570
LYNCH
  David, 575
  James, 254
  John, 499
  Lewis M., 85
  Mary F., 15
  Nancy Thomas, 15
  Robert, 163
  Susan, 15
  Susanah, 15
  William, 231
LYNES
  Presley, 574
LYNN
  Andrew, 106
  Catharine, 773
  Thomas, 106
LYONS
  Martha F., 132
  Nancy, 643
LYTTLETON
  Thomas, 789

MABERRY
  Clarenda, 417
MABURRY
  Rebecca, 789

MACCACEY
  John, 702
MACK
  Nathan, 539
  Richard H., 903
  Sarah, 539
  Virginia E., 542
MACKEY
  Ann E., 378
MACKLIN
  Francis, 273
  James, 273
MACOFFRAY
  Susan, 894
MACON
  A. J., 317
  Martha J., 317
MADDEN
  Ann, 409
  Rolan, 409
MADDIN
  Eliza, 732
  Frank, 732
MADDOX
  William, 682
MADDY
  Elizabeth, 562
MADEN
  John, 85
MAFAS
  James, 589
MAGGET
  Gainum, 436
  Samuel, 436
  Thomas, 436
MAGILL
  Alvira E., 618
  Elizabeth J., 611
MAGUFFEY
  Jane, 671
  Shelby, 571
MAGUIRE
  Francis, 699
  John, 686
MAHAN
  James, 178
MAHER
  William, 682
MAIDWELL
  George, 846
MAIN
  Alex., 898
MAIS
  Mary, 768
MAIZE
  Harvey M., 789
MAJOR
  John, 437
  Nicholas, 437
MALCOM
  Mary, 37
MALER
  James, 445
MALICOAT
  Henry, 48
MALLORY
  Martha,
MALONE
  And., 682
  Benjamin F., 768
  George W., 245
  Joseph, 550
  Margaret, 769

MALONEY
  John, 740
MALONY
  Michael, 649
MALORY
  Infant, 268
MALUGEN
  Willie, 399
MANARD
  Robert, 420
  Sally, 417
MANEAR
  John, 517
MANERS
  James, 217
MANESS
  Lucinda, 485
MANGRUM
  Catherine, 317
  J. H., 835
MANHAL
  John I., 166
  L. J., 166
MANICE
  Jacob, 39
MANING
  Elei, 759
  Lawrence, 759
MANN
  Sarah J., 161
MANNERS
  Christopher, 745
  James, 745
  Mary, 745
MANNING
  Charles J., 839
  William H., 822
MANON
  _____, 186
MANSEL
  Jake, 412
MANSON
  Rachel H., 277
MANTLE
  Mary, 626
MANTOOTH
  Sarah, 97
MANUNERD
  Sarah A. M., 153
MANVILL
  Nancy, 506
MAPLES
  Elizabeth, 675
MARABLE
  J., 863
  James, 115
  Mary S., 578
  S., 863
MARBERRY
  John, 391
MARCUM
  Ellen, 136
  Lucy, 136
  Nathaniel, 841
MARDICA
  Harrison, 691
MARKES
  Catherine(2), 907
MARKIN
  Adolphus, 174
  Mary M., 645
MARKS
  William, 160

MARLIN
  A. S., 160
  Henry, 114
MARLOW
  Mahala, 841
MARLY
  Patsy, 615
MARMON
  Thomas, 758
MARR
  Mary E., 859
MARRS
  James, 601
MARS
  Benjamin, 846
MARSH
  Jonah, 288
  Louisa, 499
  Simeon, 707
MARSHALL
  David, 64
  Jordan, 288
  Joseph J., 115
  Laura, 123
  Mary A., 344
MARSHEL
  Mariah, 649
MARSTON
  Jack, 163
MARTIN
  Edward H., 236
  G. H., 248
  Hillery, 420
  Infant, 268
  Jacob, 57
  James, 199, 758
  James G., 136
  Jane E., 818
  Jasper, 574
  John, 175
  Lucretia, 395
  Martha C., 627
  Martha E., 844
  Mary, 475
  Mary F., 659
  Obedience, 506
  Rebecca, 889
  Salena, 818
  Sarah, 609
  Sarah Quincy, 11
  William A., 324
  William M., 248
  William N., 183
  Zachariah, 420
MARTON
  James W., 866
  Margaret(2), 866
MARVONEY
  Michael, 695
  Thomas, 695
MASON
  Bennet, 466
  John M. A., 452
  Martha, 166
  Sarah J. C., 448
MASONER
  Anna, 290
MASSEY
  _____, 466
  Henry L., 722
  Leonard K., 170
  Mary Jane, 441
  Nancy, 31

MASSEY
  Pheraby, 302
MASTERS
  Rhoda, 823
MASTRESS
  Elizabeth, 420
  Margara, 420
  William, 420
MATHEREL
  Sarah, 913
MATHERS
  Isabella, 641
MATHEW
  George, 441
MATHEWS
  E. J., 502
  Harriet, 53
  Isaac, 726
  J. A., 835
  John, 405
  Litha, 619
  Silas, 453
  William F., 217
MATHIS
  George, 592
  Susan J., 33
  Walker, 441
MATLOCK
  James, 171
  Maria F., 142
MATT
  A. L., 699
MATTHEWS
  Agnes, 599
  Emeline, 534
  Irene, 804
  Margaret, 820
  Thomas, 822
MAULDEN
  July, 528
MAZWELL
  Manervy, 436
  Mary, 599
  Mary C., 329
  Rachel, 484
  Sarah, 599
MAY
  John, 737
  Joseph, 659
  Thomas S., 661
  William C., 788
  William H., 191
MAYERS
  Moses, 811
MAYFIELD
  Elbert, 818
  Manervy, 320
  William, 405
MAYO
  Laura M., 225
  Sally E. M. D., 225
MAYS
  Susan, 85
MAYORS
  Isabel, 163
  Margaret, 163

McADOO
  Benjamin, 395
  E. R., 498
  Frances E., 64
  Josephine, 55
  Malissa, 55
  Nancy, 827

McAFEE
  Nancy, 482
McALISTER
  Samuella, 114
McALLEN
  Andrew J., 558
  Mary A., 558
McALLISTER
  Garland, 741
McAMISH
  Jacob F., 295
  Margarete, 286
McANALLY
  Harriette, 281
  Jemima, 277
  Thomas P., 281
  William D., 827
McANULTY
  John G., 324
McBRIAN
  Jeremiah, 740
McBRIDE
  Charlton J., 844
  Drury, 839
  George, 806
  L. B., 196
  Lettitia, 424
McCAGG
  James, 814
McCALEB
  James K., 245
  Joseph, 772
McCALL
  Cynthia, 879
  John M., 37
McCALLIN
  John, 127
McCALLISTER
  Robert D., 248
McCALLUM
  Felix M., 269
McCALPIN
  Thomas, 484
McCALUP
  Sarah K., 409
McCAMPBELL
  Sarah, 394
McCANN
  Amanda, 482
McCARES
  Hugh, 327
McCARKLE
  J. M., 193
McCARLEY
  Laura, 320
McCAROLL
  Jackson, 769
McCARTER
  Abel, 421
McCARVER
  Cynthia, 420
McCASLIN
  Samuel, 37
McCAUGHAN
  William, 420
McCAUL
  Malvina, 521
McCAULEY
  America F., 578
  George, 578
McCLAIN
  Charles, 766
  Mary, 766

McCLANE
  Martha E., 655
  S., 831
  W., 831
McCLANNAHAN
  Johenry, 402
  Susan, 402
McCLARIE
  Eve, 313
McCLARY
  N., 863
McCLELEN
  Jesse, 413
McCLELLAN
  James C., 436
  Mariah J., 438
McCLELLAND
  John, 153
McCREARY
  Nancy, 682
McCRERY
  Mary R., 825
McCRORY
  Frances C., 495
  Jane, 781
  Mary A., 495
  Sarah, 781
McCROSKY
  Mary, 648
McCULLOCH
  A., 193
  Susan, 649
  William A., 670
McCULLOUGH
  Martha, 604
McCULLY
  Jones, 598
  Sarah(2), 598
McCUTCHEON
  Cintha P., 19
McDANIEL
  Harriet, 421
  Martha J., 286
  Randle, 485
  Selina, 412
  Sarah, 503
  William, 255
McDEARMORE
  ____, 889
  Martha, 889
McDOLE
  Bird, 841
McDONALD
  Laky, 671
  Sarah M., 272
  Titus, 462
  Tomazine, 273
McDOUGALD
  Allen M., 241
  Lewis, 241
McDOUGLE
  Robert, 766
McDUFFIE
  John, 558
McELROY
  Sarah, 593   William J., 49
McELVANY
  Martha E., 818
McELWRATH
  Jessee, 780
  Susan A., 780
McFADDEN
  Caroline H., 661

McFADDEN
  Jane, 143
McFALL
  ____, 535
  Henry, 378
  Martha, 675
McFARLAN
  Frances, 163
McFARLAND
  Mary, 605
McFARLIN
  Charles J., 444
McGAHEY
  Margaret, 525
McGEE
  Charles, 171
  E. N., 21
  Ebenezer N., 13
  Elenora, 762
  Ellen, 171
  Eudora, 762
  Jas., 293, 694
  Panthaniel, 780
  Robert, 293
  Sarah, 589
  W. H., 324
McGHEE
  Elvia, 37
  John, 433
McGINIS
  Susan, 281
McGINNIS
  E., 170
  Elmira, 687
  Henry, 687
  Mary E., 186
McGOUDER
  James, 601
McGOWEN
  Ebenezer, 658
  Mary, 714
McGRAW
  John, 699
  Thomas, 699
  William, 699
McGREGOR
  Isabella, 664
McGUIRE
  Jas., 682
  John, 682
  Mary, 877
  Sarah, 844
McHENRY
  George, 85
McINRAE
  Michael, 408
McINTIRE
  W., 679
McINTOSH
  Sarah M., 157
McKEE
  John, 506
  Mary, 633
McKENSON
  Catharine, 39
McKENZIE
  Margaret, 463
  Robert, 248
  William, 463
McKEY
  Mary J., 543
  Rebecca, 543

McKIMMY
  Tamsey, 438
McKINDLEY
  Allis, 412
McKINLEY
  Frances, 551
  Peggy C., 433
McKINNEY
  John V., 463
  Martha, 484
McKINSAY
  Mary J., 374
McKINZIE
  Kenneth, 485
  P. A., 248
  Reuben L. M., 555
McKNIGHT
  James T., 633
  Moses, 53
  William H., 452
McKOY
  James, 1
McLACKEY
  John, 702
McLANE
  Henry, 463
  _. W., 831
McLANHAN
  Sarah, 96
McLAUGHLIN
  Nancy, 293
  Porter, 485
McLEAN
  Hugh, 320
  Samuel, Sr., 445
McLEARY
  Elizabeth, 521
  Ewing, 521
McLEMORE
  Sterling, 114
  Young T., 61
McLIMORE
  Sarah, 429
McLUSKY
  Catharine, 599
McMAHAN
  David, 85
  Mary, 733
  Terrance, 703
McMAHON
  Cornelia, 698
  James, 502
McMACKIN
  Leander, 293
  Nancy, 293
McMILLAN
  Chansey, 297
  Jane, 682
  M., 682
McMILLEN
  Archibald, 466
  Mary, 290
McMILLION
  James, 272
McMINN
  Elizabeth, 806
  Isabella, 395
  James W., 395
McMURPHY
  Robert, 433
McMURRAY
  Samuel D., 754

McMURTRY
  Thomas, 408
  William, 408
McNABB
  Didannia, 97
McNAIRY
  Albert, 482
  John S., 115
McNate
  Nancy, 370
McNIELL
  Nancy J., 236
McNOTT
  James, 467
  John, 498
McNUTT
  _____, 429
McPHERSON
  Joseph, 706
  Susan, 618
McQUEEN
  _____, 427
McQUEST
  Andrew, 506
McREYNOLDS
  Robert, 614
McSEMORE
  Rebecca, 102
McSPADDEN
  Robert, 421
  Sarah, 814
McSPOON
  Joseph H., 479
McVEY
  George, 482
McWHIRTER
  C., 835
  Franklin, 589
  Rubin, 589
McWHORTER
  H. Z. B., 244
McWILLIAMS
  James, 498
McYATES
  Joseph, 390

MEACHEAM
  Elizabeth, 853
MEAD
  Martha, 152
  Nancy E., 615
MEADOR
  Ruth, 795
MEADOW
  Ira, 492
  Lucinda, 489
  Mary, 763
MEADOWS
  Jonas, 589
  William, 129
MEDLEN
  Melissa, 889
MEDLEY
  George, 409
  John W., 839
MEDLIN
  G. B., 502
MEEK
  Elenor E., 448
  Lydia Ann, 562
  Mary M., 448
  Sarah, 687
  William, 332

MEHANAY
  Edward E., 417
MEIRATH
  Polly, 420
MELSER
  Frederick S., 290
MELTON
  Joanna, 210
  Margaret, 479
  Marion, 210
  Priscilla, 485
  T. B., 827
  William, 210
MENARY
  Jos., 97
MERCHANT
  Joseph W., 161
  Mary, 161
MEREDITH
  Susan, 196
  William, 453
MERIT
  David, 281
MERITT
  Barbary, 506
  Easter, 55
MERRITT
  John, 789
  Nancy, 895
MERONEY
  E., 502
MESSIC
  Catharine, 99
  Lucy Ann, 99
MESSMORE
  Mariah, 615
METZELL
  Joseph, 171
MICALL
  Martin, 741
MICCOLS
  John W., 102
MICKIE
  Caledonia, 487
MICKLE
  Mary A., 190
MIKEL
  Samuel, 474
MILAM
  John, 766
  Mahala I., 329
  Polly Ann, 329
MILES
  Emeline, 280
  Mary, 425
  Nancy, 453
  William, 898, 916
MILLARD
  Elizabeth, 769
MILLER
  _____, 499
  Adam, 81
  Agnes L., 228
  Aster, 615
  Calvin, 598
  Elizabeth, 236, 788
  Garland, 237
  Jacob, 288
  James P., 780
  Jane, 196
  John, 237, 405
  John J., 633
  John Z., 233

MILLER
  Joseph D., 160
  Lucy, 48
  Luther, 844
  Margarette J., 615
  Mary, 825
  Samuel, 683
  Sarah, 81
  William, 65
  William J., 13
MILLICAN
  Moses S., 614
  Rachael A., 627
MILLIGAN
  Mary B., 53
MILLS
  _____, 535
  Ally, 309
  Benjamin, 492
  Bennetta, 776
  Elijah, 487
  Holland, 309
  Louise, 776
  M. J., 196
  Mary, 163
  Simon, 309
MILTON
  Joseph, 571
  Mary, 448
  William S., 811
MIMS
  Elisha, 347
MINGA
  Barbary, 769
MINOR
  Minerva, 395
  Sophronia C., 202
MINTON
  Elvin, 433
  Thursey, 305
MINTOR
  Franklin, 317
MIRSE
  James,
MISE
  Lucy N.,
MISER
  A-ah, 506
  Benjamin, 506
MITCHAEL
  Elias, 250
  Susan E., 818
  Thomas, 811
MITCHEL
  Benjamin, 277
  Fliphem, 592
  George, 302
  India, 280
  John W., 452
  Mary, 452
MITCHELL
  Elizabeth, 485
  James, 810
  John H., 317
  George W., 225
  Neoma, 859
  Samuel D., 515
  Sarah, 839
  William, 825
  William D., 702
MITCHENER
  Elizabeth, 780

MIXON
    Sarah J. C., 448
MIZELL
    Elizabeth, 31
MOBLEY
    Collin G., 244
MOFFETT
    Nancy, 814
MOHORN
    Nancy, 916
    Sarah, 776
MOLLOY
    Clemmontine, 810
MONAY
    William, 682
MONK
    William H., 191
MONOHAN
    Michael, 161
MONROE
    Abijal, 211
    James, 163
    Josiah, 390
    Orlence, 284
MONTGOMERY
    John W., 171, 332
    Nancy, 498
    Sally, 797
    William, 5
MOODY
    Jeremiah, 387
MOON
    Nathan, 391
    Thomas, 391
MOONEY
    Josiah, 335
MOOR
    Armstead, 741
    Catherine, 741
    Daniel R., 459
    Julia A., 425
    William M., 445
MOORE
    Aiden, 313
    Delila A. E., 386
    Eliza, 691
    Eliza J., 33
    Elizabeth, 160, 604
    Elmira, 167
    Frances, 335
    Francis J., 445
    George M., 470
    Isaac, 555
    J. T., 196
    James, 89
    Jessie, 822
    John, 462
    John W., 555
    Margaret, 160
    Martha, 810
    Mrs., 495
    Nancy, 61
    Nathaniel, 316
    Ransom M., 1
    Rebecca, 810
    Sarah, 97, 614
    Susan, 316
    William, 325
MOORHEAD
    John,
    Sarah,
MOORELAND
    Nicholas, 427

MOORLAND
    Landan, 83
MORE
    Anna, 43
    Tennessee, 303
MORELAND
    Malinda, 374
MORELL
    Rhody, 814
MORELOCK
    Martha M., 277
MORGAN
    Amanda, 412
    Angeline, 398
    Gabriel, 772
    J., 835
    James B., 33
    Richard, 791
    Robert, 615
    Sarah, 791
    William D., 571
MORMAN
    William E., 125
MORRAN
    Elizabeth, 743
MORRELL
    Elizabeth, 768
MORRIS
    _____, 440
    Elizabeth, 478
    Enoch E., 114
    Henrietta C., 452
    James E., 332
    John, 240
    Leroy, 609
    Marshal, 627
    Martha, 759
    Mary A., 371
    Mary S., 903
    Rebecca, 425
    Rebecca A., 332
    Rhoda, 507
    Sarah C., 627
    Solomon, 492
    Tabitha, 906
    Thomas G., 630
MORRISON
    Byram, 55
    John, 115
    Lydia, 601
    Samuel A., 575
    William M., 139
MORROW
    Esaw, 286
MORSE
    Jo., 679
MORTON
    C. D., 21
    Jacob, 383
    John, 554
MOSELY
    Samuel, 913
MOSER
    Sarah, 425
MOSKINS
    May M., 645
MOSLEY
    P., 831
MOSS
    A., 174
    Cato, 781
    F., Mrs., 142
    Felix, 142

    J. B., 196
MOTHERELL
    William, 248
MOTLEY
    John D., 899
    Martha, 899
MOTON
    Nicholas E., 399
MOULTRIE
    Moses, 593
MOUNGER
    Peter S., 4
MOWREY
    William S., 437
MULCHALY
    James, 702
MULKEY
    Ann, 825
MULLENS
    Pat., 699
    Sarah, 599
MULLIGAN
    Everline, 313
    Z., 313
MULLINS
    Eliza, 659
    Emeline, 85
    Mary F., 297
MULWIE
    _____, 427
MUNCHER
    John, 288
MUNDAY
    Smith, 784
MUNDY
    Elizabeth A., 327
    Mary E., 327
MUNROE
    James, 57
    Sally(2), 894
MURDER
    Susan E., 196
MURPHEY
    Margaret, 595
MURPHY
    Ailey B., 675
    Green, 229
    Margaret E., 440
    Zachariah, 42
MURRAY
    Ferrel, 702
    Louisa, 589
    Pleasant, 601
    Sarah, 153
MURREY
    William, 909
MURRY
    Nancy, 866
    Susanna, 417
MUSE
    Charles L., 658
    John, 231
    Thomas, 485
MUSGROVES
    Richard, 27
MUSINGO
    John H., 48
MYARS
    Green, 889
MYER
    John, 43

MYERS
    Benjamin F., 804
    Christenah, 722
    Robert, 804
    Sarah, 448
    William G., 288
MYRES
    Charles W., 432
    James P., 33
MYRICK
    Eliza E., 313
    H. A., 387
    William, 387
NALE
    John, 830
NANCE
    Clara, 383
    Lean, 244
    Martha, 789
NARY
    Bridget, 695
NASH
    George, 751
NAVE
    Nathaniel, 436
NEAL
    Ann L., 217
    Benjamin A., 217
    Jesse, 425
    Jane, 182
    John O., 340
    Sarah, 711
    Wiley, 273
    William, 341
NEALEY
    Elizabeth, 42
    Jane R., 228
NEEDHAM
    Anna, 281
    Sarah, 320
NEELY
    Jane, 462
NEESE
    Martin, Jr., 386
    Martin, Sr., 386
NEIGHBOURS
    Joseph, 320
NEIL
    George, 521
    James(2), 521
    Sarah, 555
NEILD(NEELD)
    Frances, 463
NELMS
    William, 593
NELSON
    Able, 13
    Ann E., 822
    J. O., 459
    Josephine O., 459
    Pitts, 647
    Robert M., 290
    Susan, 48
    Virginia, 653
    William, 825
NETTLES
    John, 671
NEVIL
    Her, 698
    Jerome, 698
NEWBELL
    William, 747

NEWBERN
    Mary, 114
    Thomas, 112
NEWBERRY
    William, 729
NEWBY
    Narsisa M., 55
NEWMAN
    Alley, 679
    Anna, 645
    Arthur, 478
    Joseph, 647
    Sarah, 839
    William F., 474
    William L., 170
NEWSOM
    _____, 110
    Georgetta, 703
    Lorinda, 503
    Narcissa, 703
NEWSON
    Margaret, 8
    William B., 15
NEWTON
    Henry, 559
NICCOLE
    John W., 102
NICELER
    Albert, 31
NICHOL
    Elenor R., 174
    Drusilla, 539
    Haywood, 604
    William H., 758
NICHOLAS
    B. F., 27
NICHOLS
    Ashberry, 115
    Caroline, 97
    Eli, 49
    George W., 327
    James, 762
    John, 97
    John T., 630
    Robert, 458
    William W., 513
NICHOLSON
    Elizabeth, 687
    Frances, 687
    James, 702
    Mariah, 618
    Rutha, 783
    William, 539
NICKERS
    Elizabeth, 873
NIECE
    Hugh, 772
NIEL
    James C., 85
NIKLY
    George, 281
NIPPER
    Sarah C., 615
NISBETT
    Zylpha, 333
NIX
    Florida, 399
    Simeon, 467
    Susan, 589
    Warren, 601
NIXON
    Mary E., 340

NOBLE
    William, 702
NOBLET
    Finders, 264
NOKES
    Benjamin, 781
NOLEN
    Berry, 875
    Robert, 190
NORMAN
    Elizabeth, 649
    F. B., 8
NORRIS
    Joel, 467
    Liddy, 595
    Margaret, 229, 741
    Mary, 229
    Rose, 229
    Serena, 191
NORTH
    Marion, 93
NORTON
    Henry, 498
    James W., 92
    Nathaniel M., 19
    Thomas, 386
    William, 4
NORVELL
    Elizabeth, 137
NORWOOD
    Thomas I., 332
NOWEL
    Madora, 641
NOWELL
    Catharine, 31
NOWLEN
    Frances J., 455
    Houston, 303
    Lethe W., 455
    Mary A., 455
NUDERY
    Francis, 592
NULL
    Infant, 529
    William J., 529
NUNLEY
    Branch, 754
NYE
    David, 797
    Martha, 108

OAKLEY
    Elizabeth, 547
    George, 182
    Jeremiah, 547
OAKLY
    Asa D., 237
    Samuel, 182
OATS
    John T., 211
OATWELL
    John, 31
O'BARR
    C., 405
OBEDIENCE
    Frances, 149
OBRUM
    David F., 772
O'DANIEL
    William, 248
ODEL
    John, 288
    Thomas C., 288

O'DELL
    Mary, 96
ODOM
    Absolom, 578
    Ann, 722
    Emeline, 722
    Sarah J., 53
    William, 409
ODUM
    Mary, 485
OEALD
    M. E. T., 831
OGLE
    Isaac, 675
    Martha, 675
OLDHAM
    William, 690
OLER
    Martha J., 288
OLICK
    Elizabeth, 773
OLIPHANT
    James A., 286
    James K. P., 547
OLIVER
    Allen, 822
    Charles Y., 437
    John W., 317
OLLIVER
    Winna E., 427
OLONIGER
    Phebe, 608
ONEAL
    Nancy, 898
O'NEAL
    Sarah, 350
ONLY
    Andrew, 503
ORALDY
    M. E. T., 831
O'REAR
    Easther J., 236
O'RILEY
    James C., 546
ORNDORFF
    Robert M., 626
ORR
    Charles, 9
    Nelson, 425
ORREL
    William, 27
ORRICK
    Andrew, 814
    Elizabeth, 814
ORSBROOKS
    David, 190
ORTON
    Mary E., 163
OSBERN
    Thomas, 161, 736
OSBORN
    Isaac, 427
    Malinda A., 615
    Sarah, 427
OSBORNE
    _____, 509
    Martha F., 244
OSBURN
    James, 703, 823
    Jane, 795
O'SHAUGHNESSY
    Thomas, 702

OSWALL
    Mary J., 635
    Sarah L., 637
OTHERTON
    Margarett, 293
OTTERLY
    John, 475
OTTINGER
    Jacob, 93
OUTLAN
    Sarah, 592
OVERALL
    Mary H., 179
OVERSTREET
    Narcissa, 538
OWEN
    Abner, 493
    Benjamin, 906
    Emily, 52
    Mary, 108
    Rachel, 795
    William, 903
OWENS
    Artemicia, 102
    Barret, 458
    F. P., 484
    James, 137, 167, 546
    James A., 143
    James W., 403
    John, 475
    Ruben T., 215
    Sarah, 260
    William, 167
OWINS
    George M., 810
OWSLEY
    John, 89
OXSHER
    Mary, 36
OYENS
    Stephen, 503
OZIER
    John, 199

PACE
    Amanda P., 571
PACK
    Malvina, 42
PACKS
    John, 823
PADGET
    John, 93
PADGETT
    Ruben, 598
PAGE
    Adaline, 186
    Jacob(2), 186
    Jane, 186
    Zachary T., 254
PAIN
    Ariminta, 568
    Lucinda, 405
PAINE
    Greenwood, 152
    Mary, 695
PAINTER
    Nancy, 288
PALMER
    Baily, 93
    Jane, 633
    Joseph F., 329
PALMOUR
    John N., 228

PAMPLIN
    Delinda, 470
    Henry H., 470
PANKEY
    Sarah, 758
PANNY
    John, 604
PARCHMAN
    Friona, 354
    Hollensbury, 354
PARHAM
    Andrew J., 452
PARISH
    Eliza Priscilla, 394
    Elizabeth, 492
    Mary J.(2), 913
    Mathew, 199
    Rowan, 394
PARK
    Henrietta, 887
PARKER
    ____, 179
    A., 317
    Adam, 759
    Alexander, 255
    Alice D., 499
    Amy, 773
    David T., 635
    Delila, 437
    Hosea, 244
    James, 747
    Jane, 52
    John W., 64
    Lydia, 399
    Malinda, 754
    Marcus, 777
    Mathew, 182
    Nathan N., 635
    Richard, 780, 811
    Sarah, 57
    Thomas, 571
    W. H., 499
    William D., 182
    William S., 635
PARKS
    Eliza Ann, 562
    James, 228
    John, 885
    Susannah, 484
    Thomas J., 251
    Willy, 199
PARMENTER
    James, 341
    John K., 341
PAROTTE
    Mary E., 190
PARRIS
    David J., 818
    Susanna, 608
PARRISH
    James A., 394
    Susannona, 420
    Thomas H., 170
PARROT
    Elizabeth, 745
    Mary, 745
PARSLEY
    Hannah, 424
    Mary, 186
PARSONS
    George, 42
    John P., 702
    Samuel, 542

PARTEE
    Haywood, 547
PARTTON
    Thomas, 889
PASCAL
    Louisa, 743
    Mary, 335
    Zeralda, 743
PASCALL
    Mary, 694
PASCHALL
    Hariet, 745
PASS
    James H., 844
    Mary, 844
PASSMOORE
    Elias, 543
PATE
    Booker, 751
    J. T., 831
PATER
    Julia, 228
PATERSON
    Margaret E., 299
    Nancy J., 299
PATILLO
    ____, 690
PATRICK
    William, 237
PATTERSON
    A., 244
    Andrew, 132
    Caroline, 367
    Cave, 187
    Effy, 452
    Ellen, 747
    James, 187
    James A., 907
    Jean C. N., 655
    Lewis, 898
    Margaret, 129
    Martha, 891
    Robert, 178
    Samuel(2), 907
    Susan W., 187
    William, 820
PATTIE
    Anna Jane, 299
PATTON
    Eliza, 780
    Daniel, 137
    Jasper N., 49
    Nancy, 417
    Salina, 299
    Sarah C., 780
    Zadok, 191
PATY
    Winy, 229
PAY
    Joseph, 106
PAYNE
    Jedaziah, 103
    John A., 286
    H. J. G., 157
    Laura G., 152
    Lindsey, 445
    Mary, 622
    Martha Jane, 329
    Penelope, 229
    Sarah, 622
    Thomas P., 329
PAYTON
    John, 906

PEABODY
    John, 153
PEAK
    Jeffrey, 658
    Mary J., 598
PEARCE
    Elizabeth, 254
    Isaac, 664
    James H., 405
    Thomas, 244
PEARE
    William, 847
PEARSON
    Charly, 844
    Mary E., 503
    Nellie, 440
    Nelly, 440
    Susan, 820
    Tabitha, 626
    William, 5
    William B., 8
PEATERS
    Mary A., 598
PECAR
    Albert, 166
    Louisa, 166
PECK
    Joseph H., 425
PEDIGA
    Jonathan J. H., 332
PEEBLES
    Emma V., 340
    Mary, 276
PEETE
    Edwin H., 340
PEMBERTSON
    Parker, 902
PENCE
    Jonathan, 912
PENDLETON
    James A., 55
PENINGTON
    B. F., 27
PENN
    Nannie B., 683
PENNINGTON
    Mary J., 877
    Nancy, 877
    R. L., 245
    Rebecca F., 452
PENNUAL
    Mary H., 132
    Mary J., 132
PENNY
    Lavinia, 568
PENNYWELL
    William, 510
PENROSE
    Charles, 699
PEOPLES
    Elizabeth, 57
    George H., 711
    S., 863
PEPKINS
    H., 317
PEPLOW
    Alphis, 695
PERKINS
    Amos, 823
    Caroline, 487
    Harriet, 254
    Jane, 112
    Lucy J., 811

PERKINS
    Louisa A., 851
    Moses, 818
    Susannah, 327
    William, 795
PERKYPILE
    Elizabeth, 277
PERNANDO
    Santo, 702
PERRY
    Elwood, 814
    Harris, 237
    James A., 248
    John, 417
    John A., 52
    Martha J., 474
    Mary Ann, 55
    O. H., 535
    Robert, 626
    S., 831
    Warren, 758
    William, 539
PETERS
    Rachel, 772
    Rosannah, 772
    Sarah E., 440
PETERSON
    William, 609
PETIT
    Mary, 555
    William H. T., 167
    William J., 555
PETTIT
    Martha, 475
PETTY
    Albert H., 758
    Alexander, 623
    Ellen, 763
    George W., 156
    J. M., 156
    James D., 156
    Julia Ann, 257
    Tennessee, 156
    Unity, 156
PETWORTH
    John, 710
PEW
    James, 171
    Joseph, 170
PEWETT
    Frances A., 344
PEYTON
    William, 55
PHALAN
    Pat., 702
PHARRIS
    Elizabeth, 517
PHELPS
    Elizabeth, 42, 658
PHILIPS
    Andrew, 137
    Eliza, 106
    Eliza A., 293
    Maletha, 366
    Mary, 810
    William, 57, 295
PHILLIPS
    Frances, 48
    Jane, 592
    John, 390
    Lemimah, 766
    Martha, 747
    Mary A. B., 495

PHILLIPS
   Nancy, 412
   Robert, 747
   William W., 8
PHIPPS
   Sarah Ann, 290
PHIPS
   John, 297
PICKERILL
   Eliza, 682
PICKETT
   Campbell Burke, 755
   Charles, 487
   James T., 639
   Zack, 639
PICKINS
   David, 772
   George, 772
PIERCE
   A., 193
   J., 831
   Orpha Jane, 65
   Valentine, 196
PIKE
   Nancy, 485, 627
PILBURN
   William, 302
PILES
   Coonrod, 229
PILKINGTON
   Lucy, 799
PINCKNAY
   John, 433
PINEY
   John, 589
PINKERTON
   Ruth, 567
PINKEY
   Jacob, 614
PINSON
   Iverson, 64
   Thomas, 64
PIPER
   Mary A., 432
PIPKINS
   H., 317
PIPPEN
   Red, 412
PIPPIN
   Simon C., 452
PITT
   Nancy S., 626
PITTMAN
   Nancy, 714
PITTS
   Orpha, 291
PLACE
   Jo., 679
PLEASANTS
   Charles J., 711
PLOT
   Sarah A., 272
PLUMBEY
   Esther, 675
PLUMMER
   Eliza D., 217
PLUNCKET
   Holden W., 178
PLUNK
   Catherine, 485
   John, 485
POAR
   Huldah W. P., 178

PODESTRA
   Andrew, 699
POE
   John, 231
   Nancy A., 772
POINTER
   Elizabeth, 758
POKE
   John, 470
POKES
   Benjamin, 781
POLK
   J. B., 543
   James K., 157
   John H., 452
   Thomas, 694
POLLOCK
   Louis M., 5
POOL
   John, 732
   John O., 327
POPE
   Benjamin F., 665
   Mary, 694
   Nancy, 623
   Philip, 743
PORTER
   Arrena, 745
   Elizabeth A., 912
   Frances W., 550
   Infant, 436
   L., 831
   Maria L., 390
   Sarah E., 329
   Susan, 546
   W. B., 831
   William, 341
PORTERFIELD
   Robert, 768
POSTON
   M. E., 570
POTTER
   Louisa, 484
   Sarah H., 265
POTTS
   Celia, 855
   John, 844
   Mary, 846
POUNDS
   James M., 248
POWELL
   John, 315
   Newton, 521
POWERS
   Amanda, 142
   Betsy, 575
   Delpha, 102
   Dorcas, 374
   Henry, 114
   Jackson, 374
   Nancy, 345
POYNTER
   William, 391
PRAISEWATER
   George, 97
PRATER
   Molly M., 814
PRATHER
   Rachel, 482
PRATT
   Elizabeth, 338, 429
   Fielding, 875
   Jane, 338

PRATT
   Mary, 338
   Mary E., 857
PRESLEY
   Green, 598
   John F., 217
   Richard, 559
PRESSON
   Drucilla, 31
PRESTON
   Martha, 898
   Rebecca, 55
PREWET
   William(2), 558
PRICE
   Dolly, 103
   Elizabeth, 444
   J., 229
   John, 97
   Joseph, 909
   Margaret, 909
   Moses, 773
   Pleasant, 555
   Susan, 297
PRIER
   Henry, 245
PRIEST
   S., 831
PRIMM
   Rebecca C., 402
PRINCE
   Rebecca, 402
PRINDLE
   William, 916
PRISPONT
   Mr., 690
PRITCHET
   Margaret, 825
PROCK
   Andrew, 492
PROCTOR
   James, 422
   John, 777
PROFIT
   Rhoda, 89
PROPES
   Martha Jane, 429
PROVINCE
   James, 586
PROWELL
   Honour, 550
PRUIT
   Mary E., 857
   May, 647
PRUITS
   John, 820, 825
PRUNELLS
   Harriett, 679
   Lucy, 679
PRYON
   Alfred, 797
PUCKETT
   Jane, 302
PUGH
   ____, 137
   Abner, 437
   Catharine, 437
   Richard, 317
   Martha, 437
   William, 37
PULLEY
   John, 320

PULUM
   David, 43
PURCELL
   Eliza, 420
   Nancy, 420
PURKEY
   Sarah E., 305
PUTNAM
   John, 61
PUTNEY
   Elizabeth, 228
PUTNUM
   Simeon, 231

QUARLES
   Elizabeth, 417
QUEENER
   Daniel, 48
   Elizabeth, 4
   Henry, 48
QUINN
   Lydia R., 683
   Margaret, 146

RABBADIEU
   Margaret, 115
RABURN
   Adam, 99
RACHAT
   Elizabeth, 436
RACKLEY
   Louisa, 53
   Mary, 255
RAGAN
   Anna, 229
   Jer, 695
   Lewis, 592
   Susan E., 245
RAGSDALE
   John, 344
   Joseph, 563
   Lewis M., 853
   Penelope, 849
   Sarah Ann, 102
RAIBRAM
   Louisa, 592
RAIGIN
   William B., 317
RAINBOLT
   Elizabeth, 427
RAINES
   Eliza J., 244
   Margaret, 240
RAINEY
   Richard, 525
RAINS
   Amanda, 142
   Maria, 142
   Matilda, 302
   Phillips, 302
   William S., 157
RAKER
   Eliza, 894
RALPH
   Anderson, 804
RALSTON
   John Clinton, 658
   M., 838
RAMA
   Ira, 485
RAMBO
   William H., 288

RAMER
    Azilla, 123
    Malinda, 484
RAMEY
    Allen, 578
    James A., 578
RAMSAY
    Jesse, 608
RAMSEY
    Alexander, 39
    Eliza F., 830
    Randolph, 844
RANDLE
    Euin, 64
    Simeon C., 653
RANDOLPH
    E., 462
    Francis W., 333
    James P., 42
    Josephine, 229
    Laviny, 485
    Missouri, 623
    Sarah, 153
RANGE
    Emaline, 71
    Peter, 822
RANKHAM
    Joseph, 183
RANKIN
    Lucinda, 244
    Martha, 503
RANSOM
    George B., 661
    Jane, 462
    John, 661
RAULINS
    John H., 236
    T. E., 236
RAWLINGS
    Nathan, 818
RAWLS
    Nancy Elizabeth, 390
RAY
    H. J., 170
    Isaac, 408
    W. C., 9
RAYBORN
    D., 466
RAYLANE
    Jesse I., 913
RAYNELS
    John, 635
    Sally, 635
REA
    Robert, 255
READ
    Grissy, 236
    James, 115
    Jane, 203
    John, 236
    Mary E., 502
    Olivia, 125
    Samuel H., 873
    William, 895
REAGAN
    Mark, 675
REARDON
    Martin, 682
REASE
    Mary L., 470
REASONS
    George, 313

REAVES
    Lydia, 313
RECORD
    Margaret, 507
RECTOR
    Cumberland, 609
    Sarah J., 478
REDD
    Paninah, 110
REDDEN
    Barbara A., 332
REDEN
    Julia A., 57
REECE
    Isaac, 587
    Logan, 758
    William H., 913
REED
    Adaline, 167
    Clara, 157
    Elbert, 592
    Henry, 193
    John, 48, 482, 492
    John F., 409
    Joseph S., 436
    Mary P., 49
    Mathew, 766
    Prudence
    Samuel, 53, 146
    Sarah, 521
    Thomas, 157
    William G., 402
REELING
    William, 43
REESE
    Daniel, 427
REEVES
    Albert P., 167
    Caroline, 593
    John, 592
    Jonathan, 395
    Linsey, 592
    Mary, 599
    Moses, 286
    William, 408
REID
    Elizabeth, 153
    Isaac, 801
    Margaret, 114
    Richard, 887
RENION
    John B., 424
RENEGAR
    William, 470
RENOW
    Hezekiah, 302
RENTFROO
    John, 618
REVIL
    Wilson, 665
REVIS
    Eliza, 542
REX
    Sarah I., 758
REYNOLDS
    Ann, 762
    Elizabeth, 444
    Jane, 726, 759
    John, 429
    Martha, 762
    Salina, 479
RHEA
    Delany, 1

RHEA
    Fany, 769
    Martha, 768
    Thomas, 260
RHODES
    Abner, 485, 722
    Alexander S., 722
    Elisha, 110
    Mary, 108
RICE
    Asenath, 277
    Isabella, 889
    Martha, 478
    Mary, 784
    Joseph, 781
    Thomas, 889
RICHARD
    Henderson, 593
    Jemima, 415
RICHARDS
    Emily, 399
    John, 675
    Robert, 682
    Susan, 402
RICHARDSON
    Alfred, 751
    Amos, 254
    David, 784
    Elizabeth, 325
    John, 48
    Joseph W., 245
    Sarah B., 861
    William, 103, 245
    William B., 324
RICHERSON
    James W., 220
    Thomas, 647
RICKER
    S. M., 286
RICKETTS
    Sarah E., 546
RICKMAN
    Jane, 589
    John, 841
    Lavina, 589
    Sarah, 589
RIDDLE
    Justina, 475
    Quintinena, 558
RIDENS
    Joel, 405
RIDER
    Nancy A., 190
RIDGE
    Alfred, 599
    Hall, 506
RIDGES
    Permelia, 664
RIDGWAY
    S. C., 835
RIDLEY
    William, 702
RIGGINS
    James, 233
RIGHT
    Ellis, 45
    Richard, 4
    William, 4, 417
RIGNEY
    Jas., 695
RIGSBY
    Matilda, 117

RINK
    Nancy G., 827
RINKLE
    Nancy, 42
RION
    Joseph, 891
RISDON
    Robert, 1
RIVERS
    Rebecca, 769
RIVES
    John, 711
    Nancy, 459
ROACH
    Calvin C., 178
    Mary J., 99, 280
    Nancy, 64
ROANE
    Franklin, 167
    Solomon, 333
ROARK
    Hugh, 493
ROBARDS
    A. J., 498
ROBBINS
    Nancy, 841
    Rice, 237
ROBBS
    Gustavus, 762
ROBERDS
    L., 835
ROBERSON
    Jordan, 889
    Mary, 321
ROBERT
    James, 387
ROBERTS
    A., 160
    Abigail, 347
    Benjamin, 675
    Eliza, 509
    Elizabeth, 402, 769
    Harriet, 265
    Hugh, 420
    Isaac, 297
    Jefferson P., 420
    Jesse, 303
    John, 39, 402
    Mack, 895
    Margaret, 297
    Morton, 521
    Nancy, 269, 614
    Philip, 297
    Richard, 272
    Samuel, 178, 772
ROBERTSON
    Amanda, 211
    Charlott, 11
    Elizabeth E., 332
    Frances, 627
    George, 898
    James, 675
    John, 675
    Joseph I., 855
    Lucinda, 675
    Rachel, 166
    Rutha A., 277
    Sarah, 332
    William N., 293
ROBESON
    H., 196
ROBINSON
    _____, 137

354

ROBINSON
  Albert, 37
  Calvin, 766
  Elizabeth(2), 907
  Francis R., 614
  Henry, 846
  James, 237
  James N., 614
  Mary, 228
  Mary A., 137
  Nancy, 827
  Reuben, 341
  Robert, 801
  Sarah A., 614
  Waddy L., 814
ROBISON
  Mary, 866
ROCHAT
  Elizabeth, 436
ROCHAELS
  John W., 210
  William M., 210
RODDEN
  Infant, 608
RODDY
  Samuel, 559
RODES
  Ohella, 394
RODEY
  William V., 93
RODGERS
  Elizabeth, 895
  John, 691
  Levi, 814
  Mary R., 853
  Rachell, 320
  Willis, 8
ROGER
  Seth, 425
ROGERS
  Easter, 53
  James K., 386
  Lucinda, 42, 749
  Mary, 403
  Rebecca, 440
  Richard H., 9
  Sarah, 759
  Thomas, 427
ROLIN
  May, 19
ROMINES
  Catharine(2), 558
ROMION
  William, 96
RONE
  John, 521
RONTSITT
  Thomas L., 182
ROOK
  Eaton T., 313
ROPER
  Elizabeth, 386
ROSE
  Clarissa, 626
  Edward, 618
  Erasmus, 799
  John, 96
  Mary, 39, 623
  Nancy, 801
  O., 801
  Sarah, 678
  William, 618
  William C., 233

ROSER
  Emily, 609
ROSS
  E. W., 313
  F., 405
  Hezekiah, 402
  Hugh, 355
  Nancy P., 665
  Reuben, 485
  Wilson V., 665
ROSSER
  Eliza J., 224
  George, 759
ROSWELL
  Jeremiah, 31
ROTHES
  Elizabeth, 653
ROULET
  Mary, 759
ROUTEN
  Tennessee, 390
ROWE
  John, 521
  Martha, 77
  Mary, 539
  Rutha, 470
ROWLETT
  Robert T., 664
ROY
  S. A., 244
ROYLSTON
  Moses, 440
RUBLE
  Rachael, 39
RUCKER
  James D., 52
  Mary, 29
RUDDLE
  Isabella G., 317
RUINS
  Thomas, 42
RUMER
  George, 686
RUNELS
  Elizabeth, 467
RUNION
  William, 96
RUNNELLS
  Hamilton, 103
  Henry, 103
  Jesse, 103
  Lucinda, 103
  Nailinda, 102
  Nancy, 103
RUNNELS
  Elizabeth, 286
RUSH
  James, 702
RUSHING
  Isabel, 405
  Levin, 31
RUSKER
  Zachariah, 898
RUSOR
  Felix G., 493
RUSSEL
  Jane, 8
RUSSELL
  Alexander, 327
  Clara, 570
  David, 408
  Elam, 290
  Elenn, 751

RUSSELL
  Emily, 190
  Emily B., 551
  Francis, 290
  Frederick, 290
  Harvey, 290
  Infant (2), 751
  Jefferson, 605
  John, 327, 444
  Margaret A., 547
  Mary, 241
  Mary A., 245
  Oliver H. P., 386
  Robert, 327
  Sarah, 290
  Thomas H., 290
  William, 605
RUST
  William, 623
RUTH
  Adam, 485
RUTHERFORD
  Absolem, 437
  James, 475
  Mary, 479
  Thomas, 132
RUTLAND
  Ann, 747
RUTLEDGE
  Joel, 718
  John, 718, 903
  S., 191
RUTTIGER
  Martha J., 248
RYAN
  B. R., 448
  Mary, 626--James, 609
  N. H., 626
  Pat., 687
  Thomas, 626
  Thomas S., 166
RYE
  Henry, 170, 916
  Serona V., 574

SACK
  Elizabeth, 297
SADLER
  Jane, 894
  John D., 399
  Zurelda, 417
SAFELEY
  Joseph, 49
SAFFELL
  Samuel, 37
SAFLEY
  James H., 818
SAILOR
  John, 822
SAIN
  Daniel, 297
  Tennessee L., 52
SALE
  George W., 244
  William, 244
  William H., 244
SALEM
  Elizabeth, 903
SAMPSON
  Margaret, 332
  Martha E., 555
  Stephen, 745

SAMUELS
  Richard, 153
SANDERLIN
  McChristy, 707
SANDERS
  _____, 445
  Eliza B., 125
  Lemuel, 484
  Victoria M., 340
SANDERSON
  Thomas, 797
SANDFORD
  Cathrine, 867
  Mary, 531
SANGER
  Elizabeth, 409
SARGANT
  Angelina, 233
SATTERLEE
  B., 571
SAUNDERS
  George, 408
  Parlee, 31
  Riley, 31
  Thomas, 780
SAVAGE
  Elizabeth, 303
  James, 153
  Pernina, 399
  William, 89
SAWYER
  W. F., 193
SAWYERS
  John, 421
  Virginia, 658
SCALES
  Joseph H., 108
  Nancy, 784
SCATES
  F. T., 831
SCISCO
  Mahala, 420
  Malenda, 420
SCOBY
  J., 193
SCOT
  Maria, 474
SCOTT
  _____, 257
  David, 106
  Henry C., 97
  James, 827
  James F., 538
  Robert T., 378
  M., 313
  Robert A., 440
  Robert B., 769
  Silas, 429
  Thomas N., 466
  William, 220
  William H., 57
  William J., 179
  William M., 257
  Winfield, 183
SCRAGS
  James A., 433
SCRUGGS
  Archibald, 758
  George, 559
  James, 424
SCRUGS
  Drury, 849

SCRUGS
    Thomas M., 849
SEABURG
    William, 174
SEAGLE
    John W., 39
SEARCH
    Margaret, 475
SEARCY
    Fanny, 758
SEARLES
    Matilda, 142
SEARS
    H., 838
SEARY
    Thomas, 698
SEAT
    John W., 895
    Martha, 137
    Permala, 142
SEATON
    Ryan, 507
    William, 332
SEBBY
    Gemima, 33
SEHROKMAN
    Mr., 695
SELF
    Henry, 766
    Lucy, 293
    Samuel, 405
SELLARS
    Elizabeth, 452
SELLERS
    Joseph, 320
SELVAGE
    George, 562
    Mary, 615
SENSING
    Caroline, 190
SERCA
    Barbry, 412
SERCY
    Margaret, 412
SETTLER
    James, 814
SEVIER
    John E., 611
    William, 340
SEWARD
    Frances, 740
SEWELL
    John, 485
    Richard, 895
SEXTON
    Rhuben D., 39
    Tabitha, 284
SEYMORE
    John W., 347
SHACKLEFORD
    William W., 316
SHADON
    Robert, 412
SHADRIC
    Martha, 302
SHAFER
    William F., 153
SHAHAN
    Julia, 618
SHANKS
    Jane, 37
SHANNON
    Rachel, 855
    William T., 622

SHARBER
    James P., 550
SHARP
    Henry, 89
    Joel, 459
    Joseph, 320
    Mary, 884
    Lucrecy, 89
    Missouri, 909
    Patterson, 427
    Peny, 89
    Robert, 639
    Sarah, 48
    Turner, 478
SHAVER
    Jacob, 89
SHAW
    Elizabeth C., 207
    Joseph, 873
    Josephine, 531
    Martha G., 458
SHEARMAN
    Charley, 383
    Mary, 475
SHEARN
    Mary J., 316
SHEARRON
    Thomas W., 574
SHEBERLY
    _____, 429
SHEFFIELD
    Talton, 818
SHEGOG
    George, 866
SHELL
    A. E., 329
SHELLAN
    Augusta, 698
SHELTON
    Elizabeth, 459, 506, 664
    George, 506
    Jane G., 780
    Leander, 437
    Louisa, 485
    Polly Ann, 579
    Robert F., 265
    Susan, 152
    W. W., 196
    William, 39
    William A., 780
SHENICK
    Hannah (2), 142
    Jeremiah, 142
    Jerry, 142
SHEPARD
    Charles E., 167
    James, 470
    Jasper, 604
    Mary A., 167
SHEPHARD
    Thomas, 424
SHEPHERD
    Charlotte, 534
    Dolly A., 93
SHEPPARD
    Jane, 114
SHERBERLY
    George, 429
SHERFEY
    Ann, 772
SHEROD
    Lemuel, 547

SHERWOOD
    James H. B., 429
SHIELDS
    _____, 264
    Jane, 280
    John, 250
    John N., 830
    Mary, 324
    Mary A., 280
    Sarah M., 264
    Susan A., 157
SHILCUTT
    Thomas, 146
SHIP
    B. F., 645
SHIPLEY
    John, 338
    Josiah, 277
SHIRES
    Margaret, 513
    William, 521
SHIRFY
    Polly, 820
SHOAT
    Nancy, 338
SHOEMAKER
    Sarah, 186
SHOES
    Josiah, 320
SHOFNER
    Amelia, 13
SHOFTNER
    Armand J., 5
SHOMAKE
    Washington, 598
SHOOK
    Jacob, 478
SHORE
    Paulina, 593
SHORES
    George, 160
    Lewis, 160
SHORT
    George, 769
    John, 841
SHOWELL
    Martha, 895
SHREVE
    Jane, 622
SHUFFLE
    Jodan, 61
SHUMAKE
    Francis, 755
    Martin, 755
SIBERT
    John, 479
SIKES
    Sarah, 17
SIMMONS
    Benjamin, 722
    Erastus, 408
    George, 386
    Harris H., 898
    Henry, 408
    Martha, 733
    Martha A., 297
    Mary, 402
    Nancy, 245
    Pitman, 408
    S., 193
SIMMS
    A., 174
    Andrew J., 844

SIMP
    Enoch, 791
SIMPSON
    Jesse, 436
    John E., 844
    M. F., 834
    Mary, 320, 484
    Peter, Sr., 52
    Rosana, 302
    S. E., 834
    Silas, 686
SIMS
    Carroll D., 409
    Elizabeth, 85
    Mary A., 587
    Nancy, 409
    Rebecca, 21
SINGLETON
    David, 589
    Valentine, 305
SIRAT
    John, 645
SISK
    Ann J., 42
    Cela, 647
SISON
    A., 834
SIVELY
    Robert T., 470
SIVLEY
    Elizabeth, 302
    Rebecca, 302
SIZEMORE
    Esther I., 417
SKANE
    Margaret, 425
SKEAN
    John, 895
SKEKAG
    George, 866
SKELTON
    _____, 608
    Anna, 398
    Druinda, 398
    Isaac, 398
    Jane, 338
SKILES
    David, 33
SKIPWORTH
    Sempson, 415
SLAUGHTER
    Elvena, 412
    Mary, 762
    Susan, 762
SLAYDEN
    Edney, 187
SLOAN
    James A., 492
SLOUNE
    William, 755
SLUDER
    James M., 604
SMALL
    Tabitha J., 902
SMALLY
    John H., 618
SMITH
    _____, 608
    Abner, 427
    Andrew E., 170
    Andy, 448
    Ann, 542
    Annirva, 429

SMITH
  Asa, 887
  Cyntha, 466
  David, 36
  Eda, 284
  Eleanor, 276
  Eliza, 293, 462
  Elizabeth, 335, 440,
    823
  Euricus, 48
  F. C., 196
  Finley, 81
  G., 804
  G. F., 615
  George, 71, 229
  Harriet, 542
  Harriet A., 571
  Helen, 762
  Hugh, 265
  Hugh B., 737
  Isabella, 178, 190
  Jacob, 81
  Jackson, 81, 595
  James, 48, 81, 745
  James D., 412
  James H., 604
  James S., 415, 420
  Jane, 417
  Joel, 408, 604
  John, 153, 408,
    702, 768
  John W., 61
  Joseph H., 297
  Joseph L., 707
  Josephine, 161, 190
  Julia Ann, 437
  Justin, 726
  Larkin, 36
  Lewis C., 61
  Louisa, 841
  Lucy, 53, 114
  Martha, 48
  Martha M., 569, 906
  Mary, 286
  Mary A., 344
  Mary Ann, 383
  Mary J., 467
  Mary L., 355
  Mary T., 467
  Mordica, 599
  Nancy, 413, 769,
    772
  Nancy A., 255
  Olivia, 220
  P., 152
  Pheba, 475
  Phebe S., 437
  Rancelor, 293
  Rebecca, 506
  Robert, 670
  Rolen, 762
  Samuel, 178
  Samuel T., 415
  Sanford, 755
  Sarah, 470, 485,
    806
  Sarah A., 609
  Sarah C., 574
  Sarah J., 136
  Virginia, 99
  Virginia A., 53
  William, 31, 153,
    715, 751, 755

SMITH
  William H., 433, 649
  William M., 170
  William P., 437
  William S., 73
  Young B.,
  Zachariah, 49
SMITHEY
  Mary J., 661
SMITHSON
  Emily C., 55
  John A., 879
  Nathaniel, 550
  Polly, 877
SMOTHERMAN
  Susanah, 519
  William, 655
SMOTHERS
  Ellen, 341
  Sarah, 492
SNAPP
  Deborah, 675
SNEED
  H. E., 838
SNELL
  Hardy T., 661
  John F., 163
  William C., 661
SNIDER
  Abraham, 290
  Francis, 290
  Frederic, 421
  Jacob, 81
  Mahala, 555
  Margaret S., 81
  Michael, 81
  Samuel, 277
SNODERLY
  Penny, 1
SNODGRASS
  _____,
SNOW
  Martha T., 452
SNOWDEN
  John B., 157
SOLOMON
  Frances, 784
  Gooden, 280
SOMERS
  Mary, 795
  Noah, 795
SOMERVILLE
  J. A., 799
SOMMERS
  Elizabeth, 889
  George S., 889
SOUTHERN
  Berton, 85
  Robert, 92
SOWARD
  James, 614
SOWELL
  Argentine A., 551
SPAIN
  William, 153
SPAN
  J., 836
  T. M., 838
SPANN
  Elizabeth, 408
SPARKMAN
  Frances, 106
  John, 714

SPAULDING
  _____, 265
SPEAR
  T. J., 834
SPECK
  Elizabeth, 474
SPENCE
  Henry, 653
  John, 653
  S., 834
SPENCER
  Elizabeth, 448
  Henry, 699
  John, 186
  Margaret, 332
  Mary, 528
  Mary A., 528
SPIRES
  Mary, 335
SPOON
  Barbary, 277
SPRADLEY
  Jane, 614
SPRAY
  Nancy, 462
SPRING
  Florence, 907
  Thomas I., 907
SPRINGER
  Thomas, 57
SPRINKLES
  _____, 538
  Moses, 538
SPROUCE
  Mary, 9
SPURGEN
  William, 675
SPURLOCK
  Elies, 413
SPURR
  Sarah A., 844
SQUIRES
  William, 156
STAFFORD
  Daniel, 225
  Jesse, 225
  Joseph, 417
  Lucinda, 823
  Martha, 225
  Mary, 225, 417
  Nancy, 417
  Sarah (2), 417
STAGG
  Sarah, 793
STAGH
  Henry, 820
STALY
  John, 280
STANBURY
  Ira S., 822
STANDBACK
  Mary, 619
STANFIELD
  Robert, 475
  Thomas, 142
STANLEY
  Ann E., 206
STANSBURY
  Susanah, 277
STANTON
  Charles, 595
  Julius, 595
  Nancy, 595

STANTON
  Polly A., 595
STANWOOD
  Jas., 683
STARKS
  Elizabeth, 797
STARNES
  Benjamin, 462
  Joseph B., 462
  Nancy, 804
STARR
  Emma, 711
STATON
  Eliza W., 64
  Elizabeth, 637
STEARNES
  Mary F., 163
STED
  Ninian A., 329
STEEL
  Ann G., 562
  David, 768
  Elizabeth, 503
  James, 889
  Robert, 42
STEELY
  Robert R., 383
STENNER
  John, 587
STEP
  Mary L., 478
STEPHEN
  Charles A., 867
  Edward P., 507
  Elizabeth, 102
  John, 587
  Matilda, 587
  Sarah, 507
  Shadrack, Jr., 587
STEPHENSON
  James C., 534
  Maranda, 645
  Mary E., 884
  Pressly W., 273
  Susan, 487
STERLING
  Margaret J., 429
STEVENS
  Catharine, 412
STEVENSON
  Elizabeth C., 157
  James C., 160
  Solomon, 589
STEWARD
  _____, 255
  James, 129
  John, 785
  Rachael, 132
  Sarah, 506
STEWART
  Andrew, 630
  Archibald, 811
  Edwin S., 186
  Elizabeth, 286
  George W., 630
  Hannah, 5
  Harriet, 570
  James, 379
  Joseph, 117
  John, 61, 229
  Marianna, 390
  Mary, 630
  Mildred, 599

STEWART
    Sarah, 355, 841
    Sarah J., 199
STILL
    John, 115
STILLWELL
    Rebecca, 525
STINNETT
    Jane, 508
STINSON
    James, 759
    Lewis, 727
    Susanah, 493
STIPLING
    Elizabeth, 421
STITH
    Missouria, 415
STIVERS
    Catharine, 276
STOCKARD
    _____ (2), 535
STOCKERD
    Richard, 546
STOCTON
    Nancy A., 595
STOKELY
    James N., 562
    Stephen, 97
STOKES
    A. M., 867
    Elizabeth, 555
    Henry F., 467
    Louisa, 555
    P., 867
    William, 463
    William H., 467
STONE
    Abigail, 503
    Elizabeth A., 276
    George W., 5
    Keziah, 578
    Martha, 741
    Mary, 99
    Nancy, 421
STOPHER
    Mary, 768
STORY
    Atlas, 429
    Rebecca, 21
STOUBLEFIELD
    Robert, 45
STOUT
    John R., 413
STOVALL
    A., 484
    Aley An, 484
    Ann, 237
    Caleb, 142
    George, 623
STOVER
    Mary R., 478
STRAHL
    Epper, 682
    Eppy, 695
STRAIN
    William, 444
STRATTON
    Henry, 686
    Levi, 475
    William W., 791
STREET
    Mary, 521

STRICKLAND
    John, 333
STRICKLIN
    John G. D., 175
STRINGER
    Thomas W., 622
STRINGFELLOW
    Ann B., 851
STROGHN
    Mark A., 228
STRONG
    Jane, 432
    Lauretta, 806
    Martha, 718
    William A., 718
STROTHER
    David, 793
    Susan, 793
    Winford D., 233
STROUD
    Hannah, 811
    Martha, 889
    Martha J., 811
    Selus, 593
STUART
    Edwin, 906
    James, 452
    R. E., 452
STUBBLEFIELD
    Louisa, 811
    Wilmuth, 811
STUDDART
    Samuel J., 395
STUKSBURY
    Parly, 1
STULL
    Mariah, 170
STURDEVANT
    John, 136
SUDBERRY
    James T., 661
SUFORD
    Jane, 8
SUITER
    Benjamin, 484
    Daniel, 694
SULIVAN
    Mary, 186
SULLENBARGER
    Sarah, 335
SULLIVAN
    Bridget, 630
    Elizabeth, 187
    Jerry, 699
    John, 305
    Joshua L., 631
    Nancy, 52
    Rebecca, 604
    W. W., 161
SULLIVANT
    Thomas, 166
    Thomas E., 166
SUMMERS
    Calvin, 664
    Edith, 459
    Thomas, 466, 623 John W., 280
SUMNER
    Malinda, 280
SUNDERLAND
    Abraham, 424
SURGENES
    Thomas, 338

SUTHERLAND
    Alfred, 33
    Mary, 827
    Samuel, 299
SUTTON
    Benjamin, 793
    Daniel, 229
    E., 493
    Eliza, 229
    Elizabeth, 484
    James, 229
    Mary, 273
    Polly, 229
    Sarah, 521
    Wilkinson, 492
SWADER
    Henry, 811
SWADLEY
    Henry, 822
SWAFFORD
    Nancy, 36
    Sarah, 33
    Teresa A., 36
SWAN
    Anderson D., 233
    Jane S., 42
    Moses M., Jr., 433
    Seabury, 233
    Thomas McC., 432
    William, 233
SWANER
    Eliza, 825
SWANN
    Christina, 902
SWANSON
    C., 157
    James, 849
SWATSELL
    Mary, 290
SWATZELL
    Alfred C., 286
SWEENY
    Harriet, 129
    Mary, 129
    Caroline, 879
    Sarah, 839
SWIFT
    James, 578
    Stephen L., 225
    Thomas, 250
SWIMM
    Marshall, 302
SWINDLE
    Elizabeth, 841
SWINK
    Peter, 499
SWINNEY
    Wyat F., 276
SWOFERD
    Calvin L., 506
SYLER
    Eliza, 237
    Martha Ann, 237
    Maria Jane, 237
SYLVER
    Mary, 784
SYPES
    Eli, 484
    Eliza, 485
SYPNETT
    Mary, 906
SYPRETT
    Charlotte, 912

TABERS
    Francis, 506
TACKET
    Mary J., 413
TAILOR
    William (2), 559
TALENT
    Paraln, 335
TALLEY
    William, 797
TALOR
    Andrew J., 474
    John, 467
    Thomas, 467
TANNEHILL
    Eliza D., 690
TANNER
    John, 102
    Mary, 102
TANSILE
    Corbon, 762
TARDIFF
    Mary, 114
TARE
    John, 39
TARKINGTON
    Jefferson O., 448
TARRANT
    Benjamin W., 458
    Silla, 293
TARRENT
    B., 193
TARTAR
    Nancy, 338
TARVER
    John, 171
TASH
    Burshely Jane, 810
TATE
    _____, 446
    Elizabeth, 909
    James, 690
TATUM
    George W., 441
    Jesse R., 399
TAUNT
    Cynthia, 146
TAYLOR
    Alexander, 186
    Arden, 363
    Delila, 538
    Dorry Ann, 626
    Elim, 37
    Elizabeth, 827
    Emily J., 1
    George, 601
    Harriet J., 277
    Henry L., 710
    Jessie W., 183
    Joseph, 129
    Josiah, 363
    M. M., 655
    Margaret A., 71
    Mary, 909
    Morgan, 236
    Novilla L., 71
    Sarah A., 1
    Starling, 350
    Susan, 142, 599
    Tabitha, 751
    Virginia, 102
    W. D., 806
    William G., 236

TAYLOR
    Z., 231, 237
    Zachary, 498
TAYNOR
    Martha, 866
TAYSE
    William F., 448
TEA
    George, 866
TEAL
    Amanda, 102
TEATHER
    Jas. M., 768
TEDDER
    Ann E., 614
TEMPLE
    B. S., 834
    Jeremiah, 891
    Pleasant J., 429
TEMPLETON
    Mary, 462
TENESON
    Matthew, 859
TENNISON
    Mary, 137
    Saybella, 631
TENPENNY
    John, 55
TERAN
    William, 592
TERRASS
    James, 114
TERRILL
    John, 759
TERRY
    Caroline L., 409
    Celestia, 206
    Elizabeth, 409
    Emily, 479
    George W., 747
    Moriah, 747
    Thomas, 747
    William, 409
TESDEL
    Daniel E., 412
TESTAMENT
    William, 305
TETTON
    Crisby, 196
THEYSE
    Susan C., 170
THOM
    Paulina, 593
THOMAS
    Alonzo, 485
    Drusy M., 53
    E., 193
    Elizabeth, 678
    Ezekiel, 64
    J., 835
    James, 894
    Joseph, 187
    Lucinda P., 851
    Margaret A., 421
    Margaret N., 543
    Mary, 489
    Mary M., 664
    Phineas, 345
    Samuel L., 894
    William, 9, 67, 758
THOMASON
    Arnold, 57

THOMPSON
    _____, 479
    Aaron, 795
    Alexander, 818
    Caroline, 690
    Carroline, 706
    David S., 670
    Ellender, 485
    Francis M., 170
    George W., 103
    H., 834
    Harriet P., 23
    J. C., 834
    Jacob, 791
    James H., 8
    James W., 85
    Jane W., 609
    Jesse F., 321
    John, 601
    John W. (2), 777
    Kuran, 795
    Marion, 470
    Nancy, 293
    Priscilla, 609
    Robert, 604
    Sarah L., 502
    Susan L., 49
    William, 383, 630
THOMSON
    Roda D., 123
THORN
    John, 187
    Presley, 27
THORNBURG
    Samuel, 559
THORNBURY
    Malinda, 39
THORNHILL
    Susan J., 170
THORNTON
    George L., 112
    Martha, 305
    Sarah, 830
THREADGILL
    Anna, 359
THREAT
    Nancy, 17
THURMAN
    Elizabeth, 535
    C. L., 193
THURMIN
    William, 506
THRUSTON
    Elizabeth, 52
TILFORD
    Mary, 899
    Sarah, 899
    William, 899
TILLERY
    Rebecca, 433
TILLOM
    Mary (2), 691
TILLSON
    Martha, 823
    Mary A., 823
TILLY
    Christopher, 844
    George W., 844
TILMAN
    Stephen, 317
TINSLEY
    William, 686

TIPTON
    James A., 73
    Joseph, 592
TITSWORTH
    Thomas, 769
TODD
    F. A. E., 838
    Sarah J., 670
    W. H., 835
    W. R., 835
TOLBERT
    William, 894
TOLIA
    Elizabeth, 749
TOLLEY
    Mary, 810
    Lilly, 466
TOMBLIN
    Columbus, 228
TOMBLINSON
    George, 507
TOMKINS
    Edward, 691
    Francis, 691
TOMLIN
    Ann, 885
    Perry, 228
TOMLINSON
    John A., 899
    Virginia, 534
    William A., 899
TOMPSON
    Sam, 898
TORBET
    John, 609
TORBETT
    Helen, 503
    Joseph, 769
TOSH
    Benjamin F., 57
TOWNS
    Mary A., 664
TOWNSEND
    John, 694
TRACY
    Emily, 445
    Mary A., 907
TRADER
    Mary, 686
TRAIL
    David, 661
    Perlina, 309
TRAMEL
    Jacob T., 186
    William, 182
TRAPP
    Sarah, 706
TRACE
    Phebe M. J., 277
TRAVIS
    Jackson, 168
    Margaret C., 53
TRAYLOR
    Harvey, 867
    Hiram B., 405
    Van Buren, 658
TRAYWICK
    Mary, 57
    Mary A., 57
TREBLE
    Numon, 891
TREZEVANT
    Theodore, 703

TRICE
    Randolph A., 582
    William, 379
TRIGG
    Mary, 4
TRIMBLE
    George M., 340
    William, 702
TRIP
    Jonathan, 474
TROBAUGH
    Lucinda A., 448
TROOPER
    Matilda, 248
TROTTER
    Ruth W., 206
TRUETT
    Elijah, 182
TRUSTY
    Lawson H., 186
TUCKER
    Emeline, 4
    George, 309
    James, 562
    M., 193
    Nancy E., 260
    Rebecca, 562
TUGWELL
    James S., 240
TULLEY
    Araminta, 718
TULLOCK
    Elbert S., 293
TULLONS
    Mary, 866
    Sarah, 866
TUNE
    Mary, 182
TURBEVILLE
    Ansill, 112
TURMAN
    Wiley, 302
TURNAGE
    L. V., 196
TURNBOW
    Samuel, 604
TURNER
    Ann, 747
    Dicy M., 48
    Elizabeth, 715, 747
    Francis, 749
    George, 43
    Harriet, 747
    Harriet A., 444
    Henry, 768
    J. T., 405
    Jane, 795
    John N., 175
    John W., 441, 444
    Lucy, 236
    Malina, 747
    Margaret, 193
    Prior L., 437
    Richard A., 136
    Robert, 749
    Susan, 240
    William, 115, 623
    Wilson D., 747
TURNEY
    William, 240
TURPIN
    Lucindy E., 614

TUTER
  George C., 615
TUTOR
  Thomas A. J., 575
TWEED
  Samuel, 459
TWIDWELL
  George, 747
TWITTY
  Dick, slave, 459
TYLER
  John T., 542
TYNOR
  William, 139
TYSON
  Lany, 499
  Uriah, 574

UNDERWOOD
  Frances, 655
  George, 622
  James T., 4
  Joel, 916
  John E., 4
  Sarah, 839
  Sarah P., 839
UPTON
  Edmond F., 240
URSERY
  Caledonia, 487
  Clarinda, 269

VADEN
  William, 755
VALIENT
  Jane, 484
VANADA
  Hugh, 175
VANCE
  John, 492
VANCLEER
  Lucy Taylor, 390
VANDEGRIFF
  Nancy, 302
VANDEVENTER
  Eliza, 772
VANDYKE
  Rachel, 478
VANER
  David, 723
VANN
  Phebe, 562
VANNIBOK
  Isaac, 723
VANNOY
  William, 305
VANSSETT
  Isabella, 220
VANTRESSE
  Mary A., 502
VANTRIECE
  Jacob (2), 907
VANZANT
  Isaac, 237
VARMER
  John, 52
VARNER
  Mary Jane, 436
VAUGHAN
  James, 102
  Laura S., 916
  Louiza J., 661
  Martha A. E. (2), 661

VAUGHAN
  Mary A., 492
  Richard, 665
VAUGHN
  ____, 445
  Johnson, 110
  Mary E., 578
  Richard, 755
  Robert, 338
  Sherwood, 823
  Thomas, 445
  W., 835
VAUGN
  Lafayette, 143
  Jane, 137
VEACH
  John M., 175
VENABLE
  Campbell A., 92
VICK
  James L., 272
VICKERS
  John, 115
VICKORY
  Mary A., 388
VICTORY
  James, 894
VINCENT
  Albert, 395
  Ellen, 772
  Iva Ann, 804
  John C. M., 558
VINSON
  Jesse, 415
  Martha, 415
  Tomesia, 55
VINYANT
  Houston, 559
VIOLETT
  William, 743
VITITO
  Louisa, 281
  Rebecca B., 281

WADDLE
  James H., 655
  Margaret, 823
WADE
  Edw., 695
  Lucinda, 412
  Martin M., 269
  Thomas R., 555
  Walter, 658
  William R., 241
  William S., 9
WADLEY
  Caroline, 655
WADLINGTON
  Nancy, 437
WAFORD
  Tobias, 115
WAGGONER
  James W., 866
  Mary I., 913
  William, 913
WAGNER
  Henry, 114
  Nancy C., 427
WAGONER
  Rasmas, 31
WAGSTER
  Charles T., 19

WAITES
  Alexander, 110
WAITMAN
  Robert, 338
WALDEN
  Lewis Y., 659
  Louisa, 114
  Uriah, 93
WALDREN
  John E., 820
WALDROUP
  John Willis, 390
WALDRUM
  Angeline, 175
WALE
  Martin B., 55
WALKER
  ____, 452
  Allen, 592
  Bersana, 402
  Buckner, 615
  Daniel, 592
  Edward, 417
  Eliza J., 841
  Harriet, 386
  Jacob, 699
  James, 749, 818
  James F., 559
  Mahala E., 615
  Margaret, 202
  Mary, 102, 678
  Mary F., 264
  Matthew, 272
  Millner, 903
  Nancy, 820
  Nancy E., 290
  Nelly, 395
  Samuel, 903
  William, 487
  William S., 241
WALKUP
  Margaret, 631
WALLACE
  Ann, 542
  Benjamin, 114
  Bennett, 788
  Frances, 186
  Jefferson, 493
  John, 791
  Mary S., 462
WALLEN
  Freelan, 152
  Isaac, 478
  Mary, 152
  Ransom, 152
WALLENBARGER
  David, 293
WALLER
  John B., 221
  Eliza Jane, 260
  Lewis, 747
  Nancy, 747
WALLING
  James, 839
WALPOLE
  Lydia, 444
WALSH
  James T., 498
  Malvina M., 780
  Nancy, 785
WALTER
  James, 479

WALTON
  Alexander, 885
  Sarah, 444
WARD
  ____, 137
  Bartley, 702
  Catharine, 898
  Charity, 478
  James, 740
  Littleton, 592
  Minerva, 604
  Nancy, 913
  William, 891
WARDE
  Bryant, 743
  Martha, 743
WARDLOW
  Mary, 21
  Salina, 482
WARE
  Janet, 691
  John, 691
  John H., 244
  Mansfield, 340
  Mildred, 814
WARF
  John S., 877
WARFIELD
  Mary, 827
WARLER
  James, 863
WARMOTH
  James, 142
  John, 142
WARNER
  Jane, 784
  Susan, 781
  William, 784
WARREN
  Elmira, 531
  John, 866
  Mary, 114, 550
  Milton, 8
  Nancy C., 329
  Narcissey, 898
  Rosella, 589
  Sarah, 839
  Sterling, 619
  Thomas, 898
  Thomas J., 305
WARRICK
  William, 1
WARSON
  David, 686
WARWICK
  Velena, 437
WASHAM
  Carrol, 592
  Franky B., 1
WASHBOURN
  H. H., 408
WASHBURN
  Elizabeth, 608
  Martha, 608
WASHINGTON
  Joseph, 841
WASSON
  Logan, 639
WATERS
  Henry, 571
  John P., 332
  Margaret, 174
  Samuel C., 424

WATHINGTON
    Ann, 568
WATKINS
    America S., 27
    Caroline, 658
    E., 547
    John, 421
    L. H., 547
    Luke, 276
    M. A., 547
    Mary J., 153
    Spence, 425
    Tabitha, 4
    William, 694
WATSON
    Adolphus F., 358
    Daniel R., 146
    George W., 153
    Martha E., 495
    Mary C., 175
    Thomas M., 175
    William, 839
    William A., 175
WATTS
    C. A., 405
    Nicy Ann, 405
    Willson, 619
WAYLAND
    John A., 678
WAYMAN
    Isabel, 732
WEAKLEY
    Nathaniel, 571
WEARE
    Jamima, 43
WEATHEHEAD
    William, 780
WEATHERBY
    Allen, 502
WEATHERFORD
    Columbus, 568
    William, 432
WEATHERS
    Jeptha, 350
    Mary J., 57
WEATHERSPOON
    H., 245
WEAVER
    David, 763
    George, 421
    Harriet, 437
    James, 763
    John, 906
    Linsley, 521
    Mary, 608
    Mary C., 784
    Thursy O., 1
    William, 1
WEBB
    _____, 429
    Charles, 503
    Elizabeth P., 255
    George A., 297
    Jacob, 93
    Jane, 598
    Lavina, 814
    Nancy, 85
    Richard, 814
    Sarah, 647
    Sarah B., 715
    Sarah M., 29
    Silas, 119

WEBSTER
    C. W., 546
    Julia, 390
    T. T., 196
WEDGEWOOD
    Josephine, 691
WEDROUP
    Alfred, 390
WEEKES
    Moses, 686
WEEMS
    Daniel Smith, 489
    Serephena, 293
    Solanda J., 489
WEIZ
    Mary, 899
WELCH
    W. J., 178
    William R., 327
WELSH
    Sally A., 579
    Thomas, 670
WELLES
    Jesse, 436
WELLINGS
    Susan A., 320
WELLS
    Elizabeth, 187
    George, 759
    Mary E., 555
    Mary J., 470
    Ruth, 309
    Samuel, 542
WERE
    Edward, 114
WESLEY
    John, 108
WESLING
    H. H., 171
WESSON
    William, 718
WEST
    Benjamin, 707
    Elizabeth, 440, 887
    James, 335
    John, 231
    John L., 609
    Joseph, 333
    Richard, 466
    Sarah, 550
    Sarah A., 139
    Sarah E., 245
    T. R., 834
    William, 335
    William J., 877
WESTER
    Benjamin, 732
    Cornelius S., 448
WESTMORELAND
    Robert, 542
WETHERFORD
    Hartsell, 773
WHALEY
    Lemuel V., 183
WHEATLEY
    Mary S., 703
WHEELER
    Celia, 108
    J. W., 834
    John, 436
    Martha A., 9
    Mary E., 48
    Peter, 436

WHEELER
    Sarah, 429
    William, 899
WHEELOCK
    Jane, 776
WHEELY
    Lavinia, 478
WHITAKER
    Ann, 846
WHITE
    Andrew A., 562
    Benjamin, 73
    Bennett, 913
    Catherine, 825
    Daniel M., 823
    Eason, 341
    Eliza, 316
    Elizabeth, 589
    Frances, 839
    Franklin W., 507
    George W., 887
    Holden, 178
    Hugh, 604
    Hugh L., 913
    James, 4, 374
    Joel A., 604
    John, 42, 595
    John D., 710
    Joseph M., 248
    Lawson H., 83
    Mary, 827
    Mary E., 432
    Mary J., 48
    Narcissa, 408
    Priscilla, 327
    Redick, 327
    Richard, 424
    Tabitha, 316
    Tennessee, 117
    William, 686
    William J., 453
WHITEHEAD
    Andrew J., 715
    Benjamin, 420
WHITESIDE
    William, 593
WHITESIDES
    Elizabeth, 64
WHITFELD
    Fanny, 49
WHITLEY
    Ann E., 745
    Betsy, 484
    Nancy, 484
    Sally, 484
    William, 686
    Willis, 745
WHITLOCK
    Charles, 391
    John, 825
    Nathan J., 825
WHITMAN
    Elisha, 814
    James, 485
WHITSEL
    Nancy J., 866
WHITTENBURG
    Margaret H., 290
WHITTINGTON
    Francisco, 386
WHITWORTH
    Goffy Ann, 736
    Mary, 736

WIGGINS
    Archabald, 210
    William, 335
    William J., 846
WILBOURN
    Lucy J., 723
WILCUM
    Sarah M., 166
WILDER
    James, 769
WILEY
    Alexander J., 462
    David S., 820
    John, 302
    Sarah (2), 302
WILHOIT
    Alsa, 8
WILIS
    Roxsalany(?), 889
WILKERSON
    Allen Y., 257
WILKINS
    Elizabeth, 313
    Ellen, 682
    John A., 547
    N., 831
WILKINSON
    Elizabeth, 231
    Frances Ann, 231
    William, 231
WILKS
    J. F., 698
    Minor, 17
    Richard, 269
    William T., 255
WILLARD
    Henry W., 444
WILLBON
    George, 895
WILLEBY
    Sollomon, 325
    Vincin, 325
WILLET
    Elizabeth, 822
    Polly Ann, 487
    Wilson, 290
WILLEY
    Elizabeth, 190
WILLIAMS
    _____, 179, 608
    Arthur, 217
    Bethelly D., 902
    Burton, 891
    Catharine, 89
    D., 834
    E., 831
    Francis, 679
    Hardin, 402
    Henry, 891
    Indiana, 627
    James G., 248
    James K., 5
    James M., 609
    James T., 559
    John, 485, 608, 801
    John F., 452
    John P., 916
    Joseph, 302, 424
    Leanah A., 440
    Margaret, 444
    Margaret D., 244
    Mary C., 898
    Mary E., 755

WILLIAMS
    Matilda, 182
    Nancy, 97
    Nimrod, 891
    Rack, 578
    Robert J., 39
    Robert S., 718
    Rhoda, 65
    Samuel A., 175
    Sarah, 571, 711
    Thomas Hill, 359
    William, 179, 445
    William W., 341
    Zachariah, 899
WILLIAMSON
    Edgar, 589
    Elizabeth E., 412
    Jane, 498
    Margarett, 781
    Mary, 722
    Mary S., 781
    Robert, 722
    Sarah, 863
    Thomas, 332
WILLIS
    Ann, 682
    Emily E., 618
    Jacob W., 432
    James, 309
    John, 85, 153
    Malinda, 288
    Martha E., 39
    Mary, 478
    W., 682
    Ward, 891
WILLOBY
    Esther, 482
WILLOUGHBY
    Wallace, 772
WILLSON
    Andrew, 503
    Elizabeth, 302
    James, 503
    John, 503
    Locky J., 53
    Mary M., 220
    Samuel K., 202
WILMOTH
    William, 595
WILEFORD
    James, 453
WILSON
    Amos, 671
    Augusta, 1
    Boyd, 276
    David, 43
    Edgar, 651
    Elisha P., 615
    Eva, 785
    James, 747
    James A., 615
    James M., 245
    Julian, 599
    Lelitha, 420
    Lucy M., 293
    Martha, 43
    Matilda C., 363
    Mias, 429
    Moses, 519
    Nancy, 458
    Nancy D., 743
    Peter M., 313
    Philip, 615

WILSON
    Samuel, 791
    Samuella, 156
    Sarah, 175
    Smith, 92
    Stephen, 788
    William, 99
WILT
    Victor, 699
WINCHAM
    John, 229
WINCHESTER
    Daniel, 698
    Nixon, 690
    William, 891
WINES
    Rosanna, 627
WINFIELD
    Sarah, 686
WINFORD
    John, 913
    Lewis C., 804
WINFRY
    John F., 745
WING
    A. A., 838
WINKLER
    James, 231
    Sarah, 309
WINN
    Henry, 703
    Henry C., 686
    James, 776
    James C., 386
    Jane, 776
WINNARD
    Richard, 186
WINNEHAM
    Sarah, 417
WINSTEAD
    M., 834
WINTERS
    Henry, 153
WINTON
    Mary J., 618
WISE
    Henry, 93
    James, 797
WISEMAN
    Iva, 804
WITHERINGTON
    Joseph, 804
WITHERSPOON
    Endora, 502
    Enos S., 53
WITLOCK
    Hetta, 280
WITT
    George, 424
    Joseph, 851
    Russell, 559
    Sarah, 48
WITTENBURG
    Albert H., 97
WITTER
    Henry, 690
WONIGER
    Phebe, 608
WOOD
    Ariadra J., 340
    Delania, 96
    Elizabeth, 241, 661
    George W., 555

WOOD
    John, 329
    Martha, 558
    Martha A., 49
    Martha F., 264
    Mary, 475
    Susan, 475
    Tennessee M., 178
    Thomas, 714
    William P., 240
WOODARD
    Berry L., 467
WOODCOCK
    Lucy, 493
WOODLEY
    Harrison, 506
WOODLIE
    Jacob, 818
WOODMORE
    Joseph, 754
    Lucinda, 784
    William, 784
WOODROUGH
    William, 470
WOODRUFF
    Jeremiah, 820
WOODS
    Archibald, 463
    Clarinda, 224
    E. W., 245
    Frances, 635
    John, 559, 769
    Martha, 291
    Tompson, 863
    William, 631
WOODSON
    Edward, 711
    Sarah, 225
    Thomas, 241
    Washington, 747
WOODWARD
    Elisha, 347
    Linda M., 153
    M. G., 153
    Maxaline J., 224
WOODY
    Joseph, 598
    Sarah A., 547
WOOLDRIDGE
    Jane, 559
WORFORD
    Jordan, 182
WORK
    Samuel, 156
WORKE
    Caroline, 119
    John A., 119
    Samuel, 119
WORKMAN
    A. P., 475
WORLEY
    Mary, 395
WRATHER
    Elizabeth, 658
    Peyton R., 664
WRAY
    Lavina, 57
WREN
    Carroll, 394
WRIGHT
    Burrel L., 413
    Elizabeth, 875
    Emedatha, 623

WRIGHT
    George, 470
    Harriet, 152
    Hollis, 136
    Howell, 875
    Isaac, 903
    Jas., 679
    John, 157, 203
    Lovenia, 889
    M. S., 691
    Margaret, 593
    Martha, 614, 875
    Mary, 912
    Mary E., 196
    Sarah F., 152
    Shaw, 229
    William, 383, 806, 875
    W. B., 459
WYATT
    Judy, 332
    Maria, 112
    Mary, 762
    Rachel, 766
    Robert, 763
WYATTE
    M., 193
WYNN
    Booker, 482
    Lucy, 806
    Margaret, 31, 898
    Martha, 806
    Sarah, 759
WYNNE
    Albert H., 115
YADEN
    Rebecca, 284
YANCY
    Jerome B., 543
YARBOROUGH
    Joseph, 675
YARBROUGH
    M., 325
    Mehulda, 325
YATELY
    Freman, 403
YATES
    Charles, 248
    John, 248, 623
    Joshua, 5
    Laura D., 248
    Lizella, 366
YEARDLY
    Thomas, 645
YEAST
    John, 152
YEATS
    Amy F., 715
    Sarah, 679
    Tennessee, 715
    William, 679
YELTON
    Benjamin E., 595
    Benjamin J. J., 598
    Mary M., 598
YOKELY
    Ellen, 424
YOKLY
    Andrew J., 255
YORK
    Frances, 810
    John W., 276
    Lydia, 276

YORK
    Margaret, 502
YOUNG
    Altamery F., 412
    Elizabeth, 558
    J. L., 834
    Joseph R., 114
    Martha, 891
    Mary, 827
    Nancy, 273
    Parker, 229
    Pleasant, 277
    R. L., 320
    Rebecca, 4
    Robert P., 240
    Sarah (2), 269, 907
    Victoria, 273
    William, 399
YOURIE
    Mildred, 789
YOWELL
    Zilla, 507

ZEGLER
    Mary T., 478
ZEUTZSCHEL
    C., 174
    J. F., 174
    William O., 174
ZOLLINGE
    Margaret, 675
ZUMBRO
    John, 645

www.ingramcontent.com/pod-product-compliance
Lightning Source LLC
Chambersburg PA
CBHW042351070526
44585CB00028B/2891